☑ W9-AZC-274

Teachers Discovering Computers

Integrating Technology and Digital Media in the Classroom

Fifth Edition

Gary B. Shelly
Thomas J. Cashman
Randolph E. Gunter
Glenda A. Gunter

THOMSON
COURSE TECHNOLOGY

THOMSON COURSE TECHNOLOGY
25 THOMSON PLACE
BOSTON MA 02210

SHELLY
CASHMAN
SERIES®

Australia • Canada • Denmark • Japan • Mexico • New Zealand • Philippines • Puerto Rico • Singapore • South Africa
Spain • United Kingdom • United States

THOMSON

COURSE TECHNOLOGY

Teachers Discovering Computers
Integrating Technology and Digital Media in the Classroom
Fifth Edition

Gary B. Shelly
Thomas J. Cashman
Randolph E. Gunter
Glenda A. Gunter

Managing Editor:
Alexandra Arnold

Product Manager:
Heather Hawkins

Senior Marketing Manager:
Tristen Kendall

Director of Production:
Patty Stephan

Associate Product Manager:
Klenda Martinez

Editorial Assistant:
Jon Farnham

Production Editor:
Heather Furrow

Developmental Editor:
Pam Conrad

Proofreader:
Harold Johnson

Indexer:
Elizabeth Cunningham

Manufacturing:
Julio Esperas

Cover and Text Design:
Joel Sadagursky

Composition House:
GEX Publishing Services

ISBN–13: 978-1-4239-1180-7
ISBN–10: 1-4239-1180-6

Integrating Technology and Digital Media in the Classroom
Fifth Edition

CONTENTS

Special Feature

Hardware for Educators   Chapter **4**

Special Feature

Evaluating Educational Technology and Integration Strategies — Chapter 7

Preface

The Shelly Cashman Series® offers the finest textbooks in computer education. We are proud of the fact that our previous *Teachers Discovering Computers* books have been so well received by instructors and students. This latest edition continues with the innovation, quality, and reliability you have come to expect from this series. The previous edition's popularity was due to (1) the integration of the World Wide Web; (2) the currency of the materials; (3) readability; (4) extensive exercises; (5) supplements; and (6) the ancillaries that allow an instructor to teach the way he or she wants to teach.

We are pleased to announce the publication of *Teachers Discovering Computers: Integrating Technology and Digital Media in the Classroom, Fifth Edition*. In addition to the standard technological updates and appropriate content changes, the fifth edition of *Teachers Discovering Computers* includes these enhancements:

- Increased emphasis on technology integration
- New emphasis on teaching and reaching today's digital generation, as well as on digital media
- Complete rewrite of Chapter 1 which now includes information on the new National Technology Standards for Students (NETS-S) and what students need to know
- A new 17-page Special Feature that follows Chapter 3, Creating Web Pages, Blogs, Wikis, and More
- A new 19-page Special Feature that follows Chapter 7, Integrating Web Pages, Blogs, Wikis, and More

The content of the textbook and the companion Web site also have been enhanced to allow for curriculum-specific learning by all K-12 educators. That is, students using the *Teachers Discovering Computers* textbook will be able to learn both how to use, and more importantly, how to integrate technology into their current or future classroom curriculum. In addition, this fifth edition of *Teachers Discovering Computers* has been updated to address the changing learning needs of the digital generation and to provide instructional strategies that will equip students with techniques to address these needs.

Objectives of This Textbook

Teachers Discovering Computers: Integrating Technology and Digital Media in the Classroom, Fifth Edition is intended for use in a one-quarter or one-semester undergraduate or graduate-level introductory computer course for educators. Students will finish the course with a solid understanding of educational technology, including how to use computers, how to access and evaluate information on the World Wide Web, and how to integrate computers and educational technology into classroom curriculum. This book also can be used for in-service training workshops that train teachers, administrators, and counselors how to use and effectively integrate educational technology.

The objectives of this textbook are to:

- Present practical, efficient ways to integrate technology resources and technology-based methods into everyday curriculum-specific practices
- Provide students with an understanding of the concepts and skills outlined in the new National Educational Technology Standards for Students (NETS-S) and the Technology Standards for Teachers (NETS-T)

- Present the fundamentals of computers and educational technology in an easy-to-understand format
- Make use of the World Wide Web as a repository of the latest information and as an educational resource and learning tool for K-12 education
- Provide information about both Macintosh computers and PCs
- Give students an in-depth understanding of why computers are essential components in society, the business world, and K-12 education
- Provide students with the knowledge of how to use educational technology with diverse K–12 student populations
- Offer numerous examples of how to use educational technology in various subject areas and with K–12 students who have special needs
- Provide students with knowledge of responsible, ethical, and legal uses of technology, information, and software resources
- Provide students with knowledge of technology to enhance their personal and professional productivity

Distinguishing Features

Teachers Discovering Computers: Integrating Technology and Digital Media in the Classroom, Fifth Edition includes the following distinguishing features.

The Proven Shelly Cashman Series Pedagogy

More than five million students have learned about computers using the Shelly Cashman Series computer concepts textbooks. With World Wide Web integration and interactivity, streaming audio and animations, extraordinary visual drawings and photographs, unprecedented currency, and the Shelly Cashman Series approach, this book will make your introductory educational technology course for educators exciting and dynamic — an experience your students will remember as a highlight of their educational careers. Students and course instructors will find this to be the finest textbook they have ever used.

World Wide Web

Teachers Discovering Computers continues the Shelly Cashman Series tradition of innovation with its extensive integration of the World Wide Web. The purpose of integrating the World Wide Web into the book is to (1) offer students additional information and currency on topics of importance; (2) make available alternative learning techniques with Web-based curriculum-specific content, learning games, practice tests, and new instructional vidoes; (3) underscore the relevance of the World Wide Web as a basic information tool that can be used in all facets of K-12 education and society; and (4) offer instructors the opportunity to organize and administer their campus-based or distance education-based courses on the Web. The Teachers Discovering Computers Web site (*www.scsite.com/tdc5*) works hand-in-hand with the text in three central ways:

- End-of-chapter assignments and many of the Special Features in the book have Web components. While working on an end-of-chapter assignment, students can go to the Teachers Discovering Computers Web site to look up key terms, explore the vast resources the Web has for education, or get an alternative point of view. The Teachers Discovering Computers Web site provides students with thousands of links to additional sources of information on a chapter-by-chapter basis. These sources have been evaluated for appropriateness and are maintained by a team of educators.

- *Teachers Discovering Computers* Web site provides a rich multimedia learning experience. Students can watch instructional and informational videos to learn about new technologies, reinforce their learning by playing interactive games, and explore new integration concepts like blogs, podcasts, wikis, and screencasts. In addition, a colorful, interactive timeline steps students through the major computer technology developments of the past 70 years, including the most recent advances.

- Throughout the text, marginal annotations titled Web Info provide suggestions on how to obtain additional information via the World Wide Web about an important topic covered on the page. The Teachers Discovering Computers Web site (*www.scsite.com/tdc5*) provides links to these additional sources of information.

This textbook, however, does not depend on Web access to be used successfully. The Web access adds to the already complete treatment of topics within the book.

A Visually Appealing Book that Maintains Student Interest

The latest technology, pictures, drawings, and text have been artfully combined to produce a visually appealing and easy-to-understand book. Many of the figures show a step-by-step pedagogy, which simplifies the more complex computer and educational technology concepts. Pictures and drawings reflect the latest trends in computer and educational technology. In addition, two marginal elements are included: Integration Strategies and FAQs. Integration Strategies boxes contain ideas and suggestions for integrating various end of chapter segments and special features related to topics presented in the text. Frequently asked questions (FAQ) boxes offer common questions and answers about subjects related to the topic at hand. Finally, the text was set in two columns, which research shows is easier for students to read. This combination of pictures, step-by-step drawings, and tested text layout sets a new standard for education textbook design.

Latest Educational Technology and Computer Trends

The terms and examples of educational technology described in this book are the same ones your students will encounter when using computers in the school setting and at home. The latest educational software packages and programs are shown throughout this book.

Macintosh Computers and PCs

Unlike many businesses, both Macintosh computers and PCs are used in the K-12 school environment. This textbook addresses both computer platforms and describes the appropriateness and use of educational software for both Macintosh computers and PCs.

End-of-Chapter Activities

Unlike other books on educational technology fundamentals, a major effort was undertaken in *Teachers Discovering Computers* to offer exciting, rich, and thorough end-of-chapter materials to reinforce the chapter objectives and assist you in making your course the finest ever offered. As indicated earlier, each and every one of the end-of-chapter pages is stored as a Web page on the World Wide Web to provide your students in-depth information and alternative methods of preparing for examinations. Each chapter ends with the following activities:

Key Terms   This list of the key terms with page references will aid students in mastering the chapter material. A complete summary of all key terms in the book, together with their definitions, appears in the index at the end of the book.

Web Info

For more information on how the Web is expanding student learning, visit the Teachers Discovering Computers Web site (*scsite.com/tdc5*), click Chapter 2, click Web Info, and then click Expanding Student Learning.

Integration Strategies

To explore ideas on integrating 21st century communications tools in your curriculum, visit the Teachers Discovering Computers Web site (*scsite.com/tdc5*), click Chapter 2, and then click Digital Media Corner.

FAQ

Are "digital" modems really modems?

According to the definition of a modem (analog to digital conversion and vice versa), the use of the term modem in this context is not correct. However, the industry does refer to DSL and cable modems as digital modems.

Checkpoint Matching and short-answer questions, together with a figure from the chapter that can be labeled, are used to reinforce the material presented within the chapter.

Teaching Today This section is designed to help students gain an appreciation of the value that technology and the World Wide Web have for K-12 education by visiting exciting educational Web pages and completing suggested curriculum integration tasks. The Web pages provide links to challenge students further on a vast array of interesting teacher-related topics.

Education Issues The use of computers and other technologies in education are not without controversy. At the end of each chapter, several scenarios are presented that challenge students to critically examine the use of technology in K-12 education and society in general. Other non-technology related scenarios allow students to explore many current controversial issues in education, such as school violence. The Web pages provide links to challenge students further.

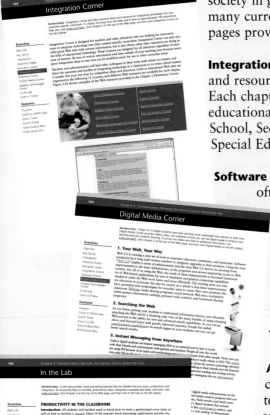

Integration Corner This innovative section provides students with extensive ideas and resources for integrating technology into their classroom-specific curriculum. Each chapter provides information on and links to approximately 100 outstanding educational Web sites organized in 12 Corners: Early Childhood, Elementary, Middle School, Secondary, Reading/Language Arts, Social Studies/History, Math, Science, Special Education, Post Secondary, Administrator, and Research.

Software Corner Today's educators can choose from a variety of high-quality and often inexpensive educational software. Students learn about popular software programs by researching them on the Web and, in many cases, even downloading or ordering a free evaluation copy so they can evaluate a program before buying it.

Digital Media Corner Today's K-12 digital students need their learning to be meaningful and relevant to their lives. Digital Media Corner provides links to videos, ideas, and examples of how students can use digital media to enhance their teaching as well as the learning of their K–12 students. The Web pages provide links to challenge students further.

Assistive Technologies Corner This new section provides information on current hardware, software, and peripherals that will assist students using this text in delivering instruction to their K-12 students with physical, cognitive, or sensory challenges. The Web pages provide extensive additional information and links to dozens of current and emerging assistive technologies.

In the Lab These exercises are divided into two areas: productivity and integration. Students can use the productivity exercises to improve their software-specific skills in using word processing, spreadsheets, database, desktop publishing, curriculum and Web page development, and other productivity software programs. They can use the integration ideas for incorporating these programs into their classroom-specific curriculum. The Web pages provide links to tutorials, productivity ideas, integration examples and ideas, and more.

Learn It Online These exercises allow students to improve their computer and integration skills by learning exciting new skills online. This section includes video clips, practice tests, learning games, and much more.

Special Features

Special Features that follow each chapter in *Teachers Discovering Computers* offer additional information on a multitude of topics: from working with wikis and blogs, to finding the latest online resources, to the latest in new technology.

A World Without Wires   This special feature following Chapter 1 presents an overview of the wireless revolution. It describes the growth of wireless technology and presents the latest in hardware and applications.

Guide to World Wide Web Sites, Searching Techniques, and Search Tools for Education More than 150 popular Web sites are listed and described in a general guide to Web sites that follows Chapter 2. These Web sites are organized into general categories, such as Entertainment, Health and Medicine, Government and Politics, Shopping, and more. This guide also introduces students to searching techniques and provides links to numerous popular education search tools.

Creating Web Pages, Blogs, Wikis, and More   Following Chapter 3, a 17-page special feature provides students with education specific information on Web pages, blogs, wikis, podcasts, and video screencasts. By reviewing videos and completing video-based step-by-step projects, students will acquire many of the basic skills needed to create these digital tools, including learning how to add video and audio to their creations.

Buyer's Guide   A 17-page guide following Chapter 4 introduces students to purchasing a personal computer, desktop computer, notebook computer, Tablet PC, and personal mobile device.

Digital Imaging and Video Technology   This special feature following Chapter 5 introduces students to using a personal computer, digital camera, and video camera to manipulate photographs and video.

Learning Theories and Educational Research   The special feature following Chapter 6 provides information about educational learning theories and research. This feature introduces students to educational terms, learning theories and theorists, educational research, and learning strategies.

Integrating Web Pages, Blogs, Wikis, and More   This special feature that follows Chapter 7 builds upon previous learned skills by providing students with extensive strategies, ideas, and resources for integrating popular tools including curriculum pages, blogs, wikis, podcasts, and screencasts with their digital students.

Guide to Professional, State, and Federal Educational Web Sites   More than 30 popular professional educational organizations are listed and described in the special feature that follows Chapter 8. Also included are resources provided by over 25 federal government agencies and all 50 states and the District of Columbia. The most current URLs for these professional organizations and state and federal educational agencies are located at the textbook Web site.

Shelly Cashman Series Instructor Resources

The Shelly Cashman Series is dedicated to providing you with all of the tools you need to make your class a success. Information about all supplementary materials is available through your Course Technology representative or by calling one of the following telephone numbers: Colleges, Universities, and Continuing Ed departments, 1-800-648-7450; High Schools, 1-800-824-5179; and Career Colleges, Business, Government, Library and Resellers, 1-800-477-3692.

The Instructor Resources CD-ROM for this textbook include both teaching and testing aids. The contents of each item on the Instructor Resources CD-ROM (ISBN 1-4239-1181-4) are described on the following pages.

Instructor's Manual   The Instructor's Manual consists of Microsoft Word files, which include chapter objectives, lecture notes, teaching tips, classroom activities, lab activities, quick quizzes, figures and boxed elements summarized in the chapters, and a glossary page. The new format of the Instructor's Manual will allow you to map through every chapter easily.

Syllabus   Sample syllabi, which can be customized easily to a course, are included. The syllabi cover policies, class and lab assignments and exams, and procedural information.

Figure Files   Illustrations for every figure in the textbook are available in electronic form. Use this ancillary to present a slide show in lecture or to print transparencies for use in lecture with an overhead projector. If you have a personal computer and LCD device, this ancillary can be an effective tool for presenting lectures.

Solutions to Exercises   Solutions for the Checkpoint exercises and In the Lab are available.

Test Bank & Test Engine   In the ExamView test bank, you will find our standard question types (40 multiple-choice, 25 true/false, 20 completion) and new objective-based question types (5 modified multiple-choice, 5 modified true/false and 10 matching). Critical Thinking questions are also included (3 essays and 2 cases with 2 questions each) totaling the test bank to 112 questions for every chapter with page number references, and when appropriate, figure references. A version of the test bank you can print also is included. The test bank comes with a copy of the test engine, ExamView, the ultimate tool for your objective-based testing needs. ExamView is a state-of-the-art test builder that is easy to use. ExamView enables you to create paper-, LAN-, or Web-based tests from test banks designed specifically for your Thomson Course Technology textbook. Utilize the ultra efficient QuickTest Wizard to create tests in less than five minutes by taking advantage of Thomson Course Technology's question banks, or customize your own exams from scratch.

Data Files for Students   All the files that are required by students to complete the exercises are included. You can distribute the files on the Instructor Resources CD-ROM to your students over a network.

PowerPoint Presentations   PowerPoint Presentations is a multimedia lecture presentation system that provides slides for each chapter. Presentations are based on chapter objectives. Use this presentation system to present well-organized lectures that are both interesting and knowledge based. PowerPoint Presentations provides consistent coverage at schools that use multiple lecturers.

Assessment & Training Solutions

SAM 2007

SAM 2007 helps bridge the gap between the classroom and the real world by allowing students to train and test on important computer skills in an active, hands-on environment. SAM 2007's easy-to-use system includes powerful interactive exams, training or projects on critical applications such as Word, Excel, Access, PowerPoint, Outlook, Windows, the Internet, and much more. SAM simulates the application environment, allowing students to demonstrate their knowledge and think through the skills by performing real-world tasks. Designed to be used with the Shelly Cashman series, SAM 2007 includes built-in page references so students can print helpful study guides that match the Shelly Cashman series textbooks used in class. Powerful administrative options allow instructors to schedule exams and assignments, secure tests, and run reports with almost limitless flexibility.

Online Content

Blackboard is the leading distance learning solution provider and class-management platform today. Thomson Course Technology has partnered with Blackboard to bring you premium online content. Instructors: Content may include topic reviews, case projects, review questions, test banks, practice tests, custom syllabi, and more. Thomson Course Technology also has solutions for several other learning management systems. Please visit http://www.course.com today to see what's available for this title.

Blackboard

CourseCasts Learning on the Go.
Always Available...Always Relevant.

Want to keep up with the latest technology trends relevant to you? Visit our site to find a library of podcasts, CourseCasts, featuring a "CourseCast of the Week," and download them to your portable media player at http://coursecasts.course.com. Our fast-paced world is driven by technology. You know because you are an active participant — always on the go, always keeping up with technological trends, and always learning new ways to embrace technology to power your life. Ken Baldauf, a faculty member of the Florida State University (FSU) Computer Science Department, is responsible for teaching technology classes to thousands of FSU students each year. He knows what you know; he knows what you want to learn. He is also an expert in the latest technology and will sort through and aggregate the most pertinent news and information so you can spend your time enjoying technology, rather than trying to figure it out. Visit us at http://coursecasts.course.com to learn on the go!

CourseNotes

Course Technology's CourseNotes are six-panel quick reference cards that reinforce the most important and widely used features of a software application in a visual and user-friendly format. CourseNotes will serve as a great reference tool during and after the student completes the course. CourseNotes for Microsoft Office 2007, Word 2007, Excel 2007, Access 2007, PowerPoint 2007, Windows Vista, and more are available now!

Acknowledgements

For this fifth edition, the authors would like to thank Pam Conrad, Vicki Rath, Robert Kenny, and Maria Garlic for assisting in the development of the end-of-chapter materials and special features.

Gary B. Shelly
Thomas J. Cashman
Randolph E. Gunter
Glenda A. Gunter

Integrating Educational Technology into the Curriculum

Objectives

After completing this chapter, you will be able to do the following:
[ISTE NETS-T Standards I A-B, II A-C, III A-D, V A-B, VI B,E]

- Define curriculum-specific learning

- Explain the difference between computer, information, and integration literacy

- Explain the necessity of moving instructional strategies from traditional to new learning environments

- Describe the evolution of computers and digital media

- Differentiate among the various categories of computers

- Explain why computer technology is important for education

- Describe the National Educational Technology Standards for Teachers (NETS-T) and Students (NETS-S)

- Explain why 21st century skills need to be incorporated in K-12 curriculum

- Describe the characteristics of today's digital students

- Describe six categories of what today's students need to know

- Provide examples of how computers are changing the way people teach and learn

Computer technology and digital media play an essential role in how individuals work, live, play, and, more importantly, learn. Organizations of all sizes — even the smallest schools and businesses — rely on technology to help them operate more efficiently and effectively. At home, work, and school, computers help people work faster, more accurately, and, in some cases, in ways that previously were not possible. People use computers and other technologies at home for education, entertainment, information management, and business purposes. They also use computers as tools to access information and to communicate with others around the world. In the classroom, computers and computer-related technologies are having a profound influence on the way teachers instruct and students learn. Even the activities that are part of your daily routine — typing a report, driving a car, paying for goods and services with a credit card, sending e-mail on your smart phone, or using an ATM — involve the use of computer technology.

Web Info

For more information and ideas about classroom teachers integrating technology, visit the Teachers Discovering Computers Web site (*scsite.com/tdc5*), click Chapter 1, click Web Info, and then click Integration Ideas.

As they have for a number of years, computers and related technologies continue to influence the lives of most individuals. Today, teachers in K-12 schools are educating students who will spend all of their adult lives in a technology-rich society. To help schools better educate students, the federal government, state governments, and school districts are spearheading massive funding efforts to equip classrooms with computers, with connectivity to networks, and with access to the Internet and the World Wide Web. Teachers in these classrooms must be prepared to utilize both current and emerging computer technologies.

The purpose of this book is to provide you with the knowledge you need to use and integrate technology into your specific classroom curriculum. Chapter 1 introduces you to basic computer concepts and digital media as well as to how teachers and administrators integrate computer technology and digital media into K-12 education. As you read, you also will begin to understand the vocabulary used to describe computer technology and digital media and educational technology. Remember that this chapter lays the foundation for you to begin to understand how you can modify your teaching strategies to include the skills that your students will need to be successful and productive citizens.

Curriculum-Specific Learning

As you review the materials and concepts presented in this textbook and the accompanying Web site, continuously ask yourself how you can use and integrate the knowledge you are gaining into your specific curriculum interests. Reflect on three ways you can use your newly acquired knowledge: (1) for your own professional development, (2) using technology as a productivity tool in your classroom, and, most importantly, (3) extensively integrating technology and digital media in your instructional strategies, lessons, student-based projects, and student assessments to improve student learning — in other words, throughout the curriculum. By doing this, you will be involved in **curriculum-specific learning** or **discipline-specific learning**, which is when you are learning how to apply teaching principles, knowledge, and ideas to authentic and practical classroom lessons and projects that can benefit your students.

Traditional 20th educational practices will no longer provide you with the skills you need to teach your students effectively how to become productive citizens in today's high-tech, global workplace. Figure 1-1 lists characteristics representing traditional approaches to learning and corresponding

Establishing New Learning Environments by Incorporating New Strategies

Traditional Learning Environments	→ New Learning Environments
Teacher-centered instruction	Student-centered learning
Single-sense stimulation	Multisensory stimulation
Single-path progression	Multipath progression
Single media	Multimedia
Isolated work	Collaborative work
Information delivery	Information exchange
Passive learning	Active/exploratory/inquiry-based learning
Factual, knowledge-based learning	Critical thinking and informed decision making
Reactive response	Proactive/planned action
Isolated, artificial context	Authentic, real-world context

Source: International Society for Technology in Education (ISTE)

Figure 1-1 This chart shows the characteristics that represent traditional approaches to learning and corresponding strategies often associated with new learning environments for K-12 students.

strategies associated with new learning environments for K-12 students. As you continue to use and integrate educational technology and digital media, you will find yourself transitioning from using traditional teaching and learning strategies to using many new and exciting technology-enriched teaching and learning strategies. Refer to this chart often as you learn how to integrate technology and digital media into your classroom curriculum and practice using these new teaching strategies.

Another important issue is that teachers no longer have the time to create their various lesson plans and other documents from scratch, or in other words, constantly reinvent the wheel. The primary reason for extensively Web-enhancing this textbook is to provide you with hundreds of outstanding curriculum-specific sources of information and integration ideas that you can modify for use in your classroom curriculum. These resources are organized so you can choose the best curriculum-specific content to improve your students' learning. We encourage you to interact with the curriculum-specific content that works for you and then adopt and modify the content and other information, integrating it into your classroom curriculum.

Computer, Information, and Integration Literacy

Today, the vocabulary of computing is all around you. Before the advent of computers, memory was an individual's mental ability

to recall previous experiences; storage was a place for out-of-season clothing; and communication was the act of exchanging opinions and information through writing, speaking, or sign language. In today's world, these words and countless others have taken on new meanings as part of the vocabulary used to describe computers and their uses.

When you hear the word "computer," initially you may think of computers used in schools to perform activities such as creating flyers, memos, and letters; managing student rosters and calculating grades; or tracking library books. In the course of a day or week, however, you encounter many other computers. Your home, for instance, can contain a myriad of electronic devices, such as cordless telephones, VCRs, DVD players, handheld video games, digital cameras, and stereo systems including small computers.

Computers help you with your banking when you use automatic teller machines (ATMs) to deposit or withdraw funds. When you buy groceries, a computer tracks your purchases and calculates the amount of money you owe; it may even generate custom coupons based on your buying patterns. Even your car is equipped with computers that operate the electrical system, control the temperature, and run sophisticated antitheft devices.

Today, most occupations involve the use of computers on a daily basis (Figure 1-2). As the world of computers and computer-related technologies advances, it is essential that you gain some level of **computer literacy;**

Integration Strategies

To access dozens of integration ideas specific to your classroom curriculum, visit the Teachers Discovering Computers Web site (*scsite.com/tdc5*), click Chapter 1, click Integration Corner, and then click your grade-level corner.

Figure 1-2
Computer technology and digital media are present in every aspect of daily living — in the workplace, at home, in the classroom, and for entertainment.

that is, you must have a knowledge and understanding of computers and their uses.

Information literacy means knowing how to find, analyze, use, and communicate information. Information literacy is the ability to gather information from multiple sources, select relevant material, and organize it into a form that will allow the user to make decisions or take specific actions.

Students must learn to make informed decisions based on information obtained in all areas of their lives. For example, suppose you decide to move to a new city and need a place to live. You could find a home by driving around the city looking for a house or apartment within your price range that is close to school or work. As an information literate person, however, you might search for a home using the Internet, which is a global network of computers that contains information on a multitude of subjects. Using Internet resources to locate potential homes before you leave will make your drive through the city more efficient and focused.

How does computer technology relate to information literacy? They relate because, increasingly, information on housing, cars, and other products, as well as information on finances, school systems, travel, and weather, is accessible by computers. For example, with communications equipment, you can use a computer to connect to the Internet to access information on countless topics. After you have accessed the desired information, computers can help you analyze and use that information.

Although computer and information literacy are very important for educators, today's teachers also must use computers as a tool to facilitate learning. Teachers must be able to assess technology resources and plan classroom activities using available technologies. These skills are part of **integration literacy**, which is the ability to use computers and other technologies combined with a variety of teaching and learning strategies to enhance students' learning. Integration literacy means that teachers understand how to match appropriate technology to learning objectives, goals, and outcomes. A solid foundation of computer and information literacy is essential to understanding how to integrate technology into the classroom curriculum successfully.

As an educator, computers will affect your work and your life every day — and will continue to do so in the future. Today, school administrators use computers to access and manage information, and teachers use computers to enhance teaching and learning. The computer industry continually is developing new and different uses for computers and digital media, and making improvements to existing technologies. Learning about computers, digital media, and other technologies will help you function effectively in society and become a better facilitator of learning.

What Is a Computer and What Does It Do?

In basic or traditional terms, a **computer** is an electronic device, operating under the control of instructions stored in its memory, that can accept data, process the data according to specified rules, produce results, and store the results for future use. In other words, a computer is a computational device.

Data is a collection of unorganized facts. Computers manipulate and process data to create information. **Information** is data that is organized, has meaning, and is useful. Examples are reports, newsletters, receipts, pictures, invoices, or checks. As shown in Figure 1-3, for example, computers process several data items to provide a student grade report.

Data entered into a computer is called **input**. The processed results are called **output**. Thus, a computer processes input to create output. A computer can hold data for future use in an area called **storage**. This cycle of input, process, output, and storage is called the **information processing cycle**.

The electronic and mechanical equipment that makes up a computer is called **hardware**. These components are covered in Chapter 4. **Software** is the series of instructions that tell the hardware how to perform tasks. Software is covered in Chapters 3 and 5. Without software, hardware is useless; hardware needs the instructions provided by software to process data into information.

FAQ

Is data singular or plural?

With respect to computers, it is accepted and common practice to use the word data in both singular and plural context.

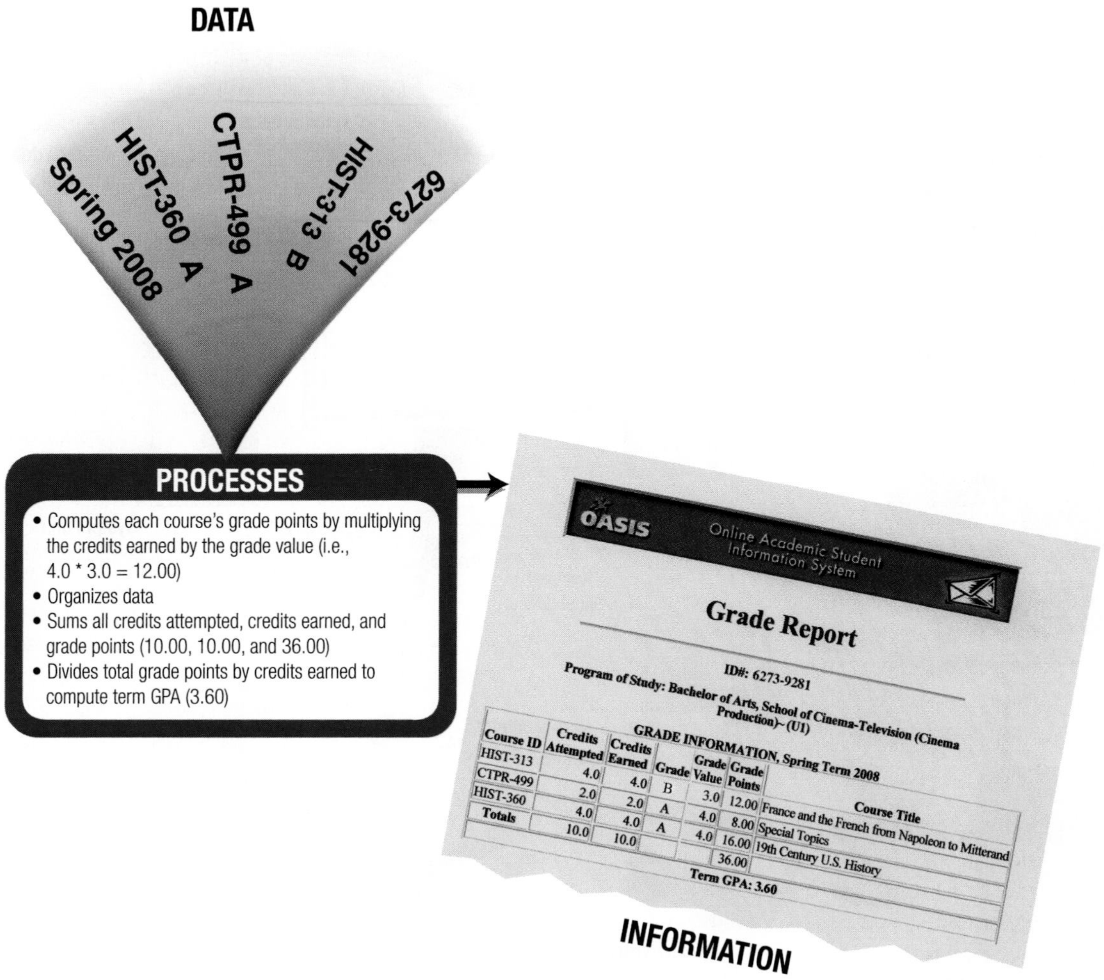

DATA

PROCESSES

- Computes each course's grade points by multiplying the credits earned by the grade value (i.e., 4.0 * 3.0 = 12.00)
- Organizes data
- Sums all credits attempted, credits earned, and grade points (10.00, 10.00, and 36.00)
- Divides total grade points by credits earned to compute term GPA (3.60)

OASIS Online Academic Student Information System

Grade Report

ID#: 6273-9281

Program of Study: Bachelor of Arts, School of Cinema-Television (Cinema Production)- (UI)

GRADE INFORMATION, Spring Term 2008

Course ID	Credits Attempted	Credits Earned	Grade	Grade Value	Grade Points	Course Title
HIST-313	4.0	4.0	B	3.0	12.00	France and the French from Napoleon to Mitterand
CTPR-499	2.0	2.0	A	4.0	8.00	Special Topics
HIST-360	4.0	4.0	A	4.0	16.00	19th Century U.S. History
Totals	10.0	10.0			36.00	

Term GPA: 3.60

INFORMATION

Figure 1-3 A computer processes data into information. In this simplified example, the student identification number, semester, course codes, and course grades all represent data. The computer processes the data to produce the grade report (information).

The Evolution of Computers and Digital Media

The evolution of modern technologies started over 100 years ago, first with the telegraph, then telephones, radios, television, early computers, large and bulky mainframe computers, and, finally, the development of the personal computer in the early 1980s. The enormous popularity of the Internet, in particular the World Wide Web, has resulted in a computer that is more than a simple computational device. In fact, the computer has morphed into a device used for communication, media creation, learning, and so much more.

Recent advancements in personal computers merge the various forms of communications (the telephone, television, and computers) into effective, interactive, digital media systems. Even though the merging of these forms into personal computers is still evolving, the first decade of the 21st century is already being known as the **age of convergence**. This merging of technologies is possible because significantly faster processors and high-speed networks have been able to capitalize on the advancements made in the areas of digital graphics, video, animation, and audio. Today's personal computer architectures take advantage of a computer's individual power, digital media capabilities, and the ability to be interconnected with others in networked environments. As a result, multimedia technology systems have become increasingly more powerful and better able to handle information rich in visual and aural content.

Web Info

For more information on the age of convergence, visit the Teachers Discovering Computers Web site (*scsite.com/tdc5*), click Chapter 1, click Web Info, and then click Age of Convergence.

Figure 1-4 Common computer hardware components associated with a digital media computer.

The goal of multimedia computing and communications is to assist individuals in organizing and managing vast amounts of information in various types of media. Figure 1-4 above shows the components of a typical digital media computer system that allows the average person to use multiple senses when working and communicating. To see just how far personal computer technology has come in a relatively short period of time, compare this figure to the pictures of the original personal computers developed by IBM and Apple in the early 1980s shown on the next page.

WHAT IS DIGITAL MEDIA?

Digital media is defined in a variety of ways; however, for the purposes of this book, **digital media** is defined as those technologies that allow users to create new forms of interaction, expression, communication, and entertainment in a digital format. The term digital media has been coined to reflect the evolution of multimedia computing into multisensory communications. The goal of multimedia and now digital media is to reproduce as closely as possible the reliability and effectiveness found in face-to-face communications and then emulate that in online environments, such as social networking, using computers and other technologies.

In the next few sections, we will briefly review the various categories of computers, including information on mobile computers and mobile devices.

Categories of Computers

Computers can be organized in three general categories: personal computers; mobile computers and mobile devices; and servers, supercomputers, and embedded computers. The next few sections briefly cover these categories; all of these types of computers are discussed in detail in later chapters and special features.

Personal Computers

A **personal computer**, or **PC**, is a computer that performs all of its input, processing, output, and storage activities by itself. A personal computer contains a processor, memory, and one or more input, output, and storage devices.

Many people associate the term personal computer, or PC, with computers that use Microsoft Windows, which is a popular operating system used on many of today's computers. All personal computers, however, do not use Windows. For example, Apple computers use a different operating system, Mac OS, but still are a type of personal computer. Why the confusion?

The first Apple computer, available for personal use, was built in 1976. Subsequent versions, the Apple II and later the Apple IIe, were immediate successes. These Apple com-

puters were quickly adopted by elementary schools, high schools, and colleges.

In 1981, IBM Corporation released its first personal computer, the IBM Personal Computer (Figure 1-5). The IBM Personal Computer was an instant business success and quickly became known by its nickname — the PC. For marketing reasons, IBM allowed other companies to copy its computer design; therefore, many companies started making IBM-compatible computers. These computers were called IBM-compatible because they used software that was the same as or similar to the IBM PC software. All subsequent IBM computers and IBM-compatibles were called PCs.

Three years after the introduction of the first IBM PC, the Apple Computer Company introduced the **Macintosh computer** (Figure 1-6). Macintosh computers could accomplish many of the same tasks as IBM PCs, but they were very different from each other. In addition to the Macintosh computer, Apple also introduced a pointing device called a mouse. Macintosh computers were incompatible with IBM PCs because they used different operating system software than the IBM and IBM-compatible computers. As a result, a distinction developed between the terms Macintosh and PC, even though Macintosh computers are personal computers. This distinction and confusion between the two types of computers continues today. To avoid confusion,

Web Info

For more information about Apple computers, visit the Teachers Discovering Computers Web site (*scsite.com/tdc5*), click Chapter 1, click Web Info, and then click Apple.

Figure 1-5 The original IBM Personal Computer was introduced in 1981.

Figure 1-6 Apple Computer Company produced the Macintosh computer in 1984.

users often refer to these two types of personal computers as Windows environment or Mac environment.

Today, businesses, homes, and K-12 schools use dozens of different models of Apple and IBM-compatible personal computers. To avoid confusion in this textbook, personal computers that use Microsoft Windows are referred to as PCs and all Apple personal computers are referred to as Apple or Macintosh computers (Figure 1-7). When this textbook refers to the terms personal computer, desktop computer, or computer, the subject matter being discussed is applicable to Apple, IBM, and IBM-compatible computers. Most of the concepts and terms covered in this textbook are applicable to all types of personal computers.

Personal computers shown in Figure 1-7 also are called **desktop computers** because they are designed so the system unit, input devices, output devices, and any other devices fit entirely on a desk.

Mobile Computers and Mobile Devices

A **mobile computer** is a personal computer that you can carry from place to place. The most popular type of mobile computer is the notebook computer. A **mobile device** is a computing device small enough to hold in your hand and usually does not have disk drives. Popular mobile devices include handheld computers, PDAs, and smart phones.

MOBILE COMPUTERS

A **notebook computer**, also called a laptop computer, is a portable, personal computer small enough to fit on your lap. Today's notebook computers are thin and lightweight, yet they can be as powerful as the average desktop computer (Figure 1-8). Notebook computers normally are more expensive than desktop computers with equal capabilities.

[a] PC and PC-compatible computers usually use a Windows operating system.

[b] Apple computers, such as the iMac, use the Macintosh operating system.

Figure 1-7 Figure 1-7a shows a typical PC and Figure 1-7b shows a typical Apple computer.

[a]

[b]

Figure 1-8 Notebook computers are available in Windows and Mac environments. Shown in Figure 1-8a is a MacBook; Figure 1-8b shows a typical PC notebook using Windows Vista.

TABLET PC

Resembling a letter-sized slate, the **Tablet PC** is a special type of notebook computer that allows you to write on the screen using a digital pen (Figure 1-9). Users also can use an attached keyboard (not shown). Tablet PCs are covered in later chapters and the special features that follow this chapter and Chapter 4.

MOBILE DEVICES

Many mobile devices are **Internet-enabled**, meaning they can connect to the Internet wirelessly. Mobile devices usually do not have disk drives. Instead, these devices store programs and data permanently in memory chips inside the system unit or in small storage media such as memory cards. Popular mobile devices are handheld computers, PDAs, and smart phones. Some combination mobile devices also are available, for example, a PDA/smart phone.

HANDHELD COMPUTER A **handheld computer** is a computer small enough to fit in one hand while you operate it with the other hand. Because of its reduced size, the screen on a handheld computer is quite small. The primary input device on a handheld computer is either a small keyboard or stylus.

PDA A **personal digital assistant**, or **PDA**, provides personal organizer functions, such as a calendar, appointment book, address book, calculator, and notepad (Figure 1-10). The PDA is one of the more popular lightweight mobile devices in use today. Most PDAs also offer a variety of other application software, such as word processing, spreadsheets, and games. In addition, a large array of educational software is available for use on PDAs, including concept mapping tools, periodic tables, graphic calculators, and much more. Many PDAs are Internet-enabled so users can check e-mail and access the Internet.

SMART PHONES Offering the convenience of one-handed operation, a **smart phone** is an Internet-enabled telephone that usually provides PDA capabilities, too. In addition to basic telephone capabilities, smart phones allow you to send and receive e-mail and

digital pen

Figure 1-9 The Tablet PC combines the features of a traditional notebook computer with the simplicity of pencil and paper.

access the Internet. Most models have color screens, play music, and include built-in cameras so you can share photographs or videos with others as soon as you capture the image; some even allow you to access your online bank account to check your balance, pay bills, transfer money, and more.

As smart phones and PDAs continue to offer more similar functions, it is becoming increasingly difficult to differentiate between the two devices. This trend, known as convergence, has led manufacturers to refer to PDAs and smart phones simply as handhelds. Apple Computers introduced the first

stylus

Figure 1-10 PDAs are widely used in both business and education; many include Internet access and telephone capabilities.

of a new generation of smart phones in the summer of 2007 (Figure 1-11). Smart phones vary greatly in price; some factors that affect a consumer's purchasing decision include the appeal factor, device's size, screen size, and capabilities of available software, as well as the available service provider and monthly access fee.

Figure 1-11 Apple's iPhone offers more features than a cell phone, including many of the features of a PDA, a music player, and a handheld computer.

Servers, Supercomputers, and Embedded Computers

A **server** manages the resources on a network and provides a centralized storage area for software programs and data. You will learn more about servers and how they are used in education in Chapter 2. A **supercomputer** is the fastest, most powerful computer — and the most expensive. The fastest supercomputers are capable of processing more than 135 trillion instructions in a single second. Supercomputers are used for tasks such as analyzing weather patterns, tracking hurricanes, and identifying safety issues regarding the space shuttle. Although schools do not have supercomputers, teachers do use the output from supercomputers in their lessons.

An **embedded computer** is a special-purpose computer that functions as one component in a larger product. Embedded computers are everywhere — at home, in your car, at work, and at school. These computers perform various functions, depending on the requirements of the product in which they reside. Figure 1-12 shows some of the many embedded computers in cars.

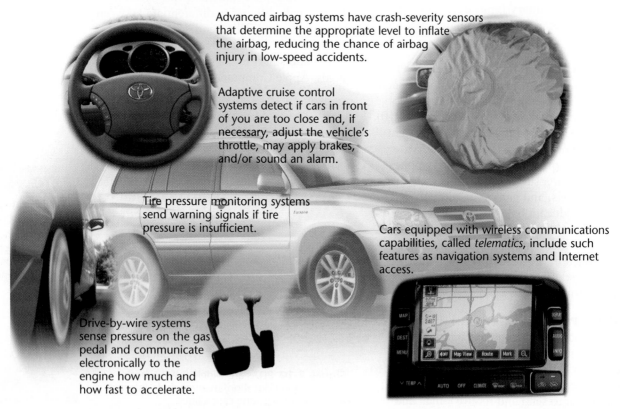

Advanced airbag systems have crash-severity sensors that determine the appropriate level to inflate the airbag, reducing the chance of airbag injury in low-speed accidents.

Adaptive cruise control systems detect if cars in front of you are too close and, if necessary, adjust the vehicle's throttle, may apply brakes, and/or sound an alarm.

Tire pressure monitoring systems send warning signals if tire pressure is insufficient.

Cars equipped with wireless communications capabilities, called *telematics*, include such features as navigation systems and Internet access.

Drive-by-wire systems sense pressure on the gas pedal and communicate electronically to the engine how much and how fast to accelerate.

Figure 1-12 Some of the embedded computers designed to improve safety, security, and performance in today's automobiles.

Why Use Computer Technology in Education?

In any society, educators have the ability to make an enormous positive contribution. Making such a contribution is a challenge, and teachers must willingly embrace new teaching and learning opportunities. Educators are beginning to recognize that they must teach students, the future leaders and citizens of society, using current technologies so that these students will be comfortable using future technologies.

Technology and digital media are everywhere and integrated into every aspect of individuals' lives. Today's educators must provide students with the skills they will need to excel in a technology-rich society. Parents no longer are urging schools to incorporate technology into the classroom; instead, they are insisting on it. When used appropriately, technology has the potential to enhance students' achievement and assist them in meeting learning objectives.

An extensive body of education research is showing that technology can support learning in many ways. Using technology in the classroom, for example, can be motivational. Teachers have found that using computers, digital media, and other computer-related technologies can capture and hold students' attention. Computers also can provide many unique, effective, and powerful opportunities for teaching and learning. These opportunities include skill-building practice, real-world problem solving, interactive learning, discovery learning, and linking learners to a multitude of instructional resources.

Computers also support communications beyond classroom walls, thus enabling schools and communities to provide an environment for cooperative learning, for development of high-order thinking skills, and for solving complex problems. As demonstrated by these examples, technology, when placed in the hands of teachers and students, can provide unique, effective, and powerful opportunities for many different types of instruction and learning.

INTERNATIONAL SOCIETY FOR TECHNOLOGY IN EDUCATION

Several national and international organizations support education and educators in the use of technology. The leading organization is the **International Society for Technology in Education (ISTE)**, which is a nonprofit group that promotes the use of technology to support and improve teaching and learning. ISTE supports all areas of K-12 education, community colleges and universities, administration of K-12 education, and teacher education organizations.

ISTE has been instrumental in developing the National Educational Technology Standards (NETS) for the **National Council for Accreditation for Teacher Education (NCATE)**. NCATE is the official body for accrediting teacher education programs. ISTE has developed standards for K-12 teachers, school administrators, and students.

STANDARDS FOR TEACHERS   As you work through this textbook and its related Web site, you will gain an understanding of the concepts and skills outlined in the **National Educational Technology Standards for Teachers (NETS-T)**, which define the fundamental concepts, knowledge, skills, and attitudes for applying technology in K-12 educational settings (Figure 1-13 on the next page).

STANDARDS FOR SCHOOL ADMINISTRATORS ISTE's standards for school administrators are organized in six broad categories: Leadership and Vision; Learning and Teaching; Productivity and Professional Practice; Support, Management, and Operations; Assessment and Evaluation; and Social, Legal, and Ethical Issues. For information about how to access these standards, see the Web Info on this page.

STANDARDS FOR STUDENTS ISTE also provides National Educational Technology Standards for Students (NETS-S). These standards, refreshed in 2007, are organized into six important categories: Creativity and Innovation; Communication and Collaboration; Research and Information Fluency; Critical Thinking, Problem Solving & Decision Making; Digital Citizenship; and Technology Operations and Concepts.

Web Info

For more information about the International Society for Technology in Education (ISTE), visit the Teachers Discovering Computers Web site (scsite.com/tdc5), click Chapter 1, click Web Info, and then click ISTE.

Web Info

For more information about ISTE's standards for students, teachers, and administrators, visit the Teachers Discovering Computers Web site (scsite.com/tdc5), click Chapter 1, click Web Info, and then click Students, Teachers, or Administrators.

ISTE NATIONAL EDUCATIONAL TECHNOLOGY STANDARDS AND PERFORMANCE INDICATORS FOR TEACHERS

All classroom teachers should be prepared to meet the following standards and performance indicators.

I. TECHNOLOGY OPERATIONS AND CONCEPTS

Teachers demonstrate a sound understanding of technology operations and concepts. Teachers:

A. demonstrate introductory knowledge, skills, and understanding of concepts related to technology (as described in the ISTE *National Educational Technology Standards for Students*).

B. demonstrate continual growth in technology knowledge and skills to stay abreast of current and emerging technologies.

II. PLANNING AND DESIGNING LEARNING ENVIRONMENTS AND EXPERIENCES

Teachers plan and design effective learning environments and experiences supported by technology. Teachers:

A. design developmentally appropriate learning opportunities that apply technology-enhanced instructional strategies to support the diverse needs of learners.

B. apply current research on teaching and learning with technology when planning learning environments and experiences.

C. identify and locate technology resources and evaluate them for accuracy and suitability.

D. plan for the management of technology resources within the context of learning activities.

E. plan strategies to manage student learning in a technology-enhanced environment.

III. TEACHING, LEARNING, AND THE CURRICULUM

Teachers implement curriculum plans that include methods and strategies for applying technology to maximize student learning. Teachers:

A. facilitate technology-enhanced experiences that address content standards and student technology standards.

B. use technology to support learner-centered strategies that address the diverse needs of students.

C. apply technology to develop students' higher-order skills and creativity.

D. manage student learning activities in a technology-enhanced environment.

IV. ASSESSMENT AND EVALUATION

Teachers apply technology to facilitate a variety of effective assessment and evaluation strategies. Teachers:

A. apply technology in assessing student learning of subject matter using a variety of assessment techniques.

B. use technology resources to collect and analyze data, interpret results, and communicate findings to improve instructional practice and maximize student learning.

C. apply multiple methods of evaluation to determine students' appropriate use of technology resources for learning, communication, and productivity.

V. PRODUCTIVITY AND PROFESSIONAL PRACTICE

Teachers use technology to enhance their productivity and professional practice. Teachers:

A. use technology resources to engage in ongoing professional development and lifelong learning.

B. continually evaluate and reflect on professional practice to make informed decisions regarding the use of technology in support of student learning.

C. apply technology to increase productivity.

D. use technology to communicate and collaborate with peers, parents, and the larger community in order to nurture student learning.

VI. SOCIAL, ETHICAL, LEGAL, AND HUMAN ISSUES

Teachers understand the social, ethical, legal, and human issues surrounding the use of technology in PK–12 schools and apply that understanding in practice. Teachers:

A. model and teach legal and ethical practice related to technology use.

B. apply technology resources to enable and empower learners with diverse backgrounds, characteristics, and abilities.

C. identify and use technology resources that affirm diversity.

D. promote safe and healthy use of technology resources.

E. facilitate equitable access to technology resources for all students.

Source: International Society for Technology in Education (ISTE)

Figure 1-13 The ISTE technology standards and performance indicators provide a framework for implementing technology in teaching and learning.

All educators need to understand these standards and, more importantly, strive to make sure that their students meet these standards. This is important as today's students will have to compete in an increasingly flat world. These standards will be covered in greater detail later in this chapter; however, first let's explain what we mean by a flat world.

The World Is Flat

In his book, *The World Is Flat*, Thomas Friedman describes how "lightning-swift changes in technology and communications put people all over the globe in touch with each other as never before — creating an explosion of wealth in India and China, and challenging the rest of us to run faster just to stay in place" (Figure 1-14). In other words, the world has become flat in terms of instant communications and global economics. Friedman and others stress that many young people are not prepared to be successful in a global economy, which in turn is impacting how America competes on the world stage. To see how teachers were inspired after reading Thomas Friedman's book, visit the Flat Classroom Project Web site (see the Web Info on this page). These teachers, one in Georgia and one in Bangladesh, are teaching their students real world skills so they will be able to work effectively in the global economy.

Our high school graduates must be prepared to enter institutions of higher education, and they must strive to become lifelong learners. As you review the remainder of this chapter, start formulating ways that you can incorporate the ideas, concepts, standards, and initiatives presented in this chapter with your students in your curriculum. Working together, we can equip students with the knowledge and skills they will need to be successful. Many states, the federal government, and organizations are trying to help schools and institutions of higher education learn how to provide students with new and emerging skills; skills for the emerging flat world of the 21st century.

Web Info

For more information on the Flat Classroom Project, visit the Teachers Discovering Computers Web site, (*scsite.com/tdc5*), click Chapter 1, click Web Info, and then click Flat Classroom Project.

Figure 1-14 What has emerged in the first decade of the 21st century is a world that is flat as hundreds of millions of workers from dozens of countries interact seamlessly in a global economy.

Web Info

For more information on the Partnership for 21st Century Skills and their P21 Framework, visit the Teachers Discovering Computers Web site (*scsite.com/tdc5*), click Chapter 1, click Web Info, and then click Partnership or P21 Framework.

21st Century Skills

The Partnership for 21st Century Skills is a national organization that focuses on infusing 21st century skills into education — both K-12 and higher education. The partnership's goal is to ensure that students who graduate from our schools have the skills needed to be effective workers, citizens, and leaders in the new global economy. One of the Partnership's initiatives, the *P21 Framework*, details a vision which can be used as a basic framework to improve our education system and prepare students for their future (Figure 1-15). This framework provides information on both student outcomes and necessary support systems.

21st CENTURY STUDENT OUTCOMES

Student outcomes as represented by the rainbow portion of Figure 1-15 include the following: core subjects and 21st century themes; learning and innovation skills; information, media, and technology skills; and life and career skills.

CORE SUBJECTS AND 21st CENTURY THEMES

Core subjects include English, reading, language arts, science, mathematics, foreign languages, civics, government, economics, arts, history, and geography. The Partnership's 21st century themes include global and health awareness along with financial and civic literacy.

LEARNING AND INNOVATION SKILLS The Partnership identifies a number of skills as necessary for students to be able to succeed in the work environment of the increasingly flat world of the 21st century. These skills include the following:

- Creativity and Innovation
- Critical Thinking and Problem Solving
- Communications and Collaboration

INFORMATION, MEDIA, AND TECHNOLOGY SKILLS Students need to be able to use new and emerging technology to learn 21st century skills and knowledge. These skills also are known as ICT literacy or information, communications, and technology literacy.

LIFE AND CAREER SKILLS The Partnership stresses that students need more than content and thinking skills. It includes the following specific life and career skills that

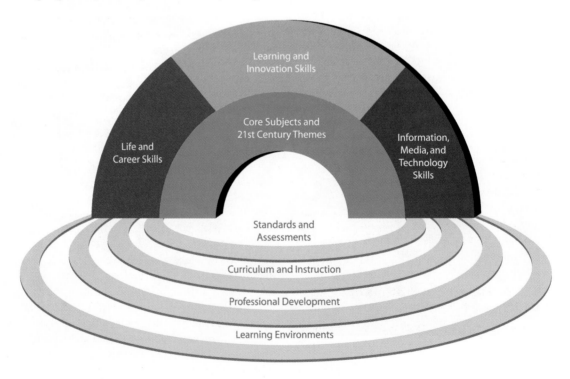

Figure 1-15 This figure shows the vision of the Partnership for 21st Century Skills that can be used to help educators strengthen our education system.

students need to have in order to be able to compete globally:

- Flexibility and Adaptability
- Initiative and Self-Direction
- Social and Cross-Cultural Skills
- Productivity and Accountability
- Leadership and Responsibility

For additional information on the above student outcomes and information on the Partnership's 21st Century Skills Support Systems represented in the lower portion of Figure 1-15, visit The Partnership for 21st Century Skills Web site (see Web Info on previous page).

Technology, if integrated effectively, holds the promise of helping teachers prepare their students with the necessary skills for employment in our changing world — this theme is what this textbook is all about. Next, you will learn about computing in the digital age, how your digital students learn, and what your students need to know to be successful in the workforce of the 21st century.

Computing in the Digital Age

Digital technology allows greater participation in the creative process, turning viewers into producers. Individuals can customize formats, outcomes, and usage of the information presented to them. Today, individuals use digital technology to input, edit, manage, publish, and share all kinds of information that was previously either impossible or too expensive for the average person to create and share. This digital revolution has accomplished in only 50 years that which took hundreds of years to accomplish beginning with the invention of Gutenberg's printing press in the late 16th century — that is, the democratization of information flow, the flow of the production process down to the masses.

DIGITAL STUDENTS: WHO ARE THEY AND HOW DO THEY LEARN?

The digital revolution has resulted in one unintended consequence. Today's youth are much more media-centric than previous generations. In fact, many people believe that the brains of today's youths have actually become rewired to accommodate the thousands of hours they spend in front of computer screens watching and creating video, listening to music, and playing computer games. It also has been said that today's youth actually speak digitally.

Today's students play on electronic playgrounds with a variety of powerful media functioning as their recreational equipment. Watch how they read e-mails, send instant messages and text messages over handheld devices, and speak to one another in short sound bites; also notice how visually oriented these students are. You will soon see that something is different about today's youth. Many have called this new generation the **digital generation**.

The world in which today's students live is significantly different from the past. Today's students use different technologies to communicate and to access information from multiple resources. They use computers, smart phones, pagers, instant messaging, personal digital assistants (PDAs) and other handheld devices, Tablet PCs, and laptops to connect to teachers, friends, family, and others in their community and all over the world. A recent National School Boards Association (NSBA) report stated that 96% of U.S. teens and tweens (students age 8-12) who have Internet access use social-networking to connect with their peers. Digital students now have a virtual world at their fingertips — with all its pitfalls and promises.

Apple Computer defines these **digital students** or **digital kids** as kids who are (1) hypercommunicators who use multiple tools to communicate, (2) multitaskers who do several things at once with ease, and (3) goal oriented as they pursue multiple goals at the same time. Today's digital generation is profoundly different from previous generations and these differences need to be understood by teachers if they are to facilitate effective learning for today's digital students. The stark contrasts and differences between generations become more apparent when they are viewed in graphical form (Figure 1-16).

Today's students are essentially different from previous generations in the way they think, in the way they access, absorb, interpret, process, and apply information and, above all, in the way they view, interact, and communicate in this technology-rich world. Today's digital kids like watching

Integration Strategies

To learn more about integrating video with your students, visit the Teachers Discovering Computers Web site (scsite.com/tdc5), click Chapter 1, and then click Digital Media Corner.

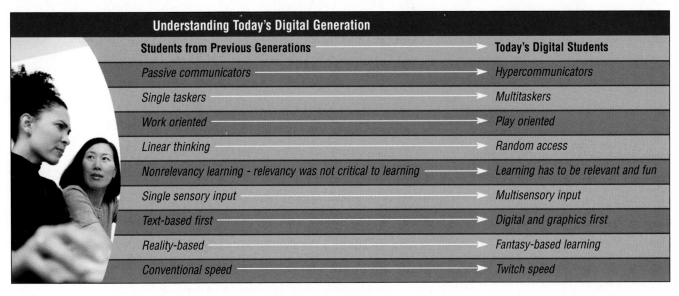

Understanding Today's Digital Generation

Students from Previous Generations	→	Today's Digital Students
Passive communicators	→	Hypercommunicators
Single taskers	→	Multitaskers
Work oriented	→	Play oriented
Linear thinking	→	Random access
Nonrelevancy learning - relevancy was not critical to learning	→	Learning has to be relevant and fun
Single sensory input	→	Multisensory input
Text-based first	→	Digital and graphics first
Reality-based	→	Fantasy-based learning
Conventional speed	→	Twitch speed

Figure 1-16 This table shows some of the characteristics of previous generations of students and today's digital students.

TV, listening to music on their iPods, listening to their favorite shows via podcasts, talking on their cell phones, instant messaging their friends, and blogging. Perhaps the most amazing aspect of this scenario is that they are doing all of these activities while completing their math homework assignment.

Understanding today's digital kids and how they learn has profound implications not only for how teachers teach these digital students, but also, and perhaps more importantly, for how teachers reach them. Educational technology and digital media can be valuable tools when they are integrated into the curriculum appropriately to achieve learning gains, particularly when they are combined with a 21st century curriculum.

Teachers have to decide whether to try to pull digital students away from their native digital world or to motivate digital students by tapping into their digital world and using their natural inclination and inquisitiveness about all that is digital. A quick look at the school system today, which has been so slow to change, makes it easy to see the disconnect between how teachers teach and how students learn.

Most of the schools today were designed for the Industrial Age and yet, the students attending schools today are living in the digital age. The world in which digital students live has changed drastically and it continues to change in a techno fast-paced manner. Unfortunately, many school environments have not kept up with that change. Marc Prensky stated in 2001 that digital kids are the digital natives and teachers are the digital immigrants. Today's students speak digitally; they are all native speakers of the digital language. Review carefully the information shown in Figure 1-17 as it provides insight into the profound differences between how digital kids learn and how digital immigrant teachers teach.

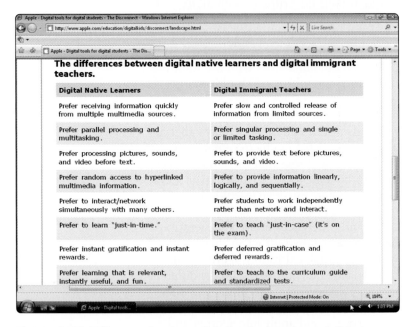

Figure 1-17 Differences between digital native learners and digital immigrant teachers.

DIGITAL STUDENTS: WHAT THEY SHOULD KNOW

Now that you have a better understanding of how today's digital kids learn, let's continue to learn more about what your students need to know. As mentioned earlier, ISTE released the updated National Educational Technology Standards for Students (NETS-S): The Next Generation in June of 2007. These specific technology skills compliment the key elements for 21st century learning that you explored earlier in this chapter. The NETS-S emphasis "what students should know and be able to do to learn effectively and live productively in an increasingly digital world" and are covered in greater detail here.

CREATIVITY AND INNOVATION Figure 1-18 lists the specific NETS-S standards for creativity and innovation. You are teaching a generation of students different from any other. The digital or net generation is one that has grown up in a world that is constantly changing in terms of the use and ubiquity of computers, technology, and digital media; and you need to be aware of this. For this generation of students to be able to learn effectively and productively in a global society, they must have a different set of skills and have the opportunity to create and generate more original ideas. Most generations in the past were willing to work for a lifetime for a large corporation but this digital generation tends to move from job to job, is always thinking of creative ways to develop

their own products, and is predicted to be the most entrepreneurial in history. As teachers, you must find ways to nourish this creative thinking process and have students develop original works through individual and group projects, e-portfolios, and other forms of authentic learning.

Research is showing that these students are independent, possess a thoughtful learning style, and are self-motivated by interactive technology and the ability to use it in innovative ways for personal expression. This might explain why even at a young age, students are successful in using computers, exploring a multitude of online sites, communicating in a variety of ways, and playing video games. Today's students learn differently! Different modes of teaching are required to motivate students and empower them to invest in their own learning.

The good news is there are hundreds of exiting technology tools and education software programs that teachers can use to stimulate student imagination and ingenuity. In addition, there is a whole new generation of educational applications that are emerging — from student-created educational games and simulations to robotics that will empower teachers and students in many positive and far reaching ways.

One way to motivate students to apply existing knowledge in order to generate new ideas or products is to have students create their own video games that demonstrate their understanding of newly acquired information. The creation process should be complex enough that students demonstrate

Integration Strategies

To learn more about integrating innovative educational software programs with your students, visit the Teachers Discovering Computers Web site (*scsite.com/tdc5*), click Chapter 1, and then click Software Corner.

Students demonstrate creative thinking, construct knowledge, and develop innovative products and processes using technology. Students:
a. apply existing knowledge to generate new ideas, products, or processes.
b. create original works as a means of personal or group expression.
c. use models and simulations to explore complex systems and issues.
d. identify trends and forecast possibilities.

Figure 1-18 This table includes the NETS-S standards for creativity and innovation.

Figure 1-19 Gamemaker is an example of a software program that allows students to create video games while fostering opportunities for creativity and innovation.

higher-thinking skills to solve game design problems, yet should still give the students flexibility to modify the characters, scenarios, and settings (Figure 1-19 above). As you continue to explore the thousands of ideas and resources in this textbook and at the textbook Web site, you will find many ways to foster creativity and innovation with your students.

COMMUNICATIONS AND COLLABORATION
Figure 1-20 lists the specific NETS-S standards for communications and collaboration. Since the beginning of time, mankind has always attempted to communicate and collaborate with each other; however, the use of technology has never been as pervasive in society as it is today.

In 1492, people thought the world was flat when Christopher Columbus sailed to prove it was round. Thomas Friedman, in his book describes the world as being flat. Both men saw the world differently, but if the world has become flat due to instant communications and global economics, how do we prepare our students for success in a highly connected society where the power to transform the world has changed from major corporations and giant trade organizations to individuals? Your job as educators is to teach your students not only to get along and communicate with the person sitting next to them but also to teach them to work on team projects and to correspond and cooperate with students in virtual classrooms across the world

Integration Strategies

To learn more about integrating online communications and collaboration tools that your students are using, like blogs, wikis, and podcasts, review the special feature that follows Chapter 7, *Integrating Web Pages, Blogs, Wikis, and More.*

Students use digital media and environments to communicate and work collaboratively, including at a distance, to support individual learning and contribute to the learning of others. Students:

a. interact, collaborate, and publish with peers, experts or others employing a variety of digital environments and media.

b. communicate information and ideas effectively to multiple audiences using a variety of media and formats.

c. develop cultural understanding and global awareness by engaging with learners of other cultures.

d. contribute to project teams to produce original works or solve problems.

Reprinted with permission from *National Educational Technology Standards for Students, Second Edition,* © 2007, ISTE® (International Society for Technology in Education), www.iste.org. All rights reserved.

Figure 1-20 This table includes the NETS-S standards for communications and collaboration.

(Figure 1-21). More importantly, students need to learn how to communicate and work collaboratively in the virtual workplace they will find themselves employed in.

Figure 21 Students learn to interact and collaborate while working together on projects.

In the Special Features following Chapters 3 and 7, there are many project ideas that help address the different ways students and teachers can communicate and collaborate by using wikis, blogs, and podcasts — this is the sharing of ideas through a different medium. Students learn and solve complex problems best within collaborative learning groups and they learn to communicate as they solve problems and make decisions.

RESEARCH AND INFORMATION FLUENCY

Figure 1-22 lists the specific NETS-S standards for research and information fluency. As students learn in this digital world, they have the opportunity to find and conduct various types of research that were not possible before — and the information is right at their finger tips. With a click of the mouse, the Internet provides enormous amounts of research, information, graphics, data, and more directly and instantaneously in front of them. Yet, while you prepare your students with the skills for accessing and searching this information, they must also be taught the skills to evaluate and analyze information. Students must have the capability to gather information, evaluate, and determine if the information they have found is valid and reliable, and then be able to synthesize how they will use the information.

There are many projects designed to help your students practice their research skills and at the same time apply those skills to real world assignments. While your students work on researching topics, you can be teaching them information literacy. Information literacy is an important skill; however, students do not always realize the importance of evaluating the sources of their information. **Information fluency** is when a person has mastered the ability to analyze and evaluate information. They can work confidently using computer, information, and media literacy skills and effectively apply these skills. **Media literacy** is being able to create, develop, and successfully communicate information in all forms. It is the ability to use critical thinking skills to analyze and to question all media — from music videos and Web environments to product placement in films and virtual displays on NASCAR billboards.

A number of organizations are assisting educators with ideas and other resources to help them incorporate information fluency and media literacy into the curriculum. One organization, The State Educational Technology Directors Association (SETDA)

Web Info

For more information on information fluency or media literacy, visit the Teachers Discovering Computers Web site (*scsite.com/tdc5*), click Chapter 1, click Web Info, and then click Information Fluency or Media Literacy.

Students apply digital tools to gather, evaluate, and use information. Students:
a.   plan strategies to guide inquiry.
b.   locate, organize, analyze, evaluate, synthesize, and ethically use information from a variety of sources and media.
c.   evaluate and select information sources and digital tools based on the appropriateness to specific tasks.
d.   process data and report results.

Reprinted with permission from *National Educational Technology Standards for Students, Second Edition*, © 2007, ISTE® (International Society for Technology in Education), www.iste.org. All rights reserved.

Figure 1-22 This table includes the NETS-S standards for research and information fluency.

provides information and an extensive toolkit of resources for educators dealing with media literacy (Figure 1-23).

Figure 1-23 The Web contains an abundance of resources that educators can use to help them ensure that their students are knowledgeable in the areas of media, research, and information fluency.

CRITICAL THINKING, PROBLEM SOLVING, & DECISION MAKING Figure 1-24 lists the specific NETS-S standards for critical thinking, problem solving, and decision making. Traditionally, educators have defined literacy as the ability to read and write; however, 21st century skills include many different types of literacies, as students are learning. Students not only need to investigate data using critical thinking skills, but they must also be able to figure out what the data really means and be able to synthesize, evaluate, and create new

information and knowledge once they have determined its quality.

Today's students prefer to work in collaborative groups to solve complicated problems rather than to problem-solve individually. Activities must be active with authentic learning experiences rather than be passive requiring reading and regurgitation of facts. Researchers learned long ago that retention is low if students are not able to touch and to perform any skill more than once — they actually need to perform a skill many times through real-life learning experiences before they can master the skill. Imagine listening to a radio versus creating a live radio broadcast. There are schools where the students create live radio broadcasts every morning, reporting the events of the day, lunch menus, testing schedules, and current news; students as young as ten years old are creating the actual broadcast. Teachers must look for the most innovative ways to teach their digital students or teachers may lose them. As Clem and Simpson stated in a recent eSchools News article, "In the absence of pedagogical innovation, these students may become instructional casualties of how and what we teach inside the school." Teachers need to change and integrate the technology tools that students adapt so easily to.

In his article, *Information Literacy, Statistical Literacy and Data Literacy*, Milo Schield concludes that information literacy requires both statistical and data literacy. According to Schield, "Students must be information literate: they must be able to think critically about concepts, claims, and arguments: to read, interpret,

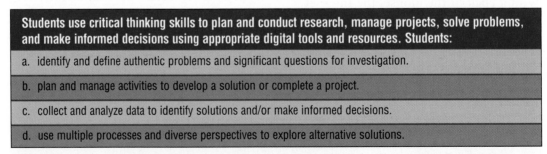

Students use critical thinking skills to plan and conduct research, manage projects, solve problems, and make informed decisions using appropriate digital tools and resources. Students:
a. identify and define authentic problems and significant questions for investigation.
b. plan and manage activities to develop a solution or complete a project.
c. collect and analyze data to identify solutions and/or make informed decisions.
d. use multiple processes and diverse perspectives to explore alternative solutions.

Figure 1-24 This table includes the NETS-S standards for critical thinking, problem solving, and decision making.

Figure 1-25 Using InspireData, students can critically solve problems and interpret data through visualization.

and evaluate information. Statistical literacy is an essential component of information literacy. Students must be statistically literate: they must be able to think critically about basic descriptive statistics. Analyzing, interpreting and evaluating statistics as evidence is a special skill. In addition, students must be data literate."

Data literacy means students need to be able to view, manipulate, analyze, and interpret data. As teachers, we must create instructional strategies that facilitate opportunities for students to become seekers of information in order to develop the ability to interpret and solve complex problems, engage and practice in critical thinking, develop arguments, and then make informed decisions. Teachers need to create activities for students to promote the use of higher order thinking skills that can increase students' critical and problem solving skills while reaching a newer audience — digital kids. An example would be students learning to gather their own data, solve problems through inquiry, and explore solutions with visualization and data plots (Figure 1-25 above).

DIGITAL CITIZENSHIP Figure 1-26 lists the specific NETS-S standards for digital citizenship. Due to the changes in our society, the list of skills needed by students to be productive citizens in a technology-rich society has grown and changed and will continue to evolve in an increasingly flat world.

Integration Strategies

To learn more about digital citizenship and teaching your students about responsibility, visit the Teachers Discovering Computers Web site (*scsite.com/tdc5*), click Chapter 1, and then click Education Issues

Students understand human, cultural, and societal issues related to technology and practice legal and ethical behavior. Students:
a. advocate and practice safe, legal, and responsible use of information and technology.
b. exhibit a positive attitude toward using technology that supports collaboration, learning, and productivity.
c. demonstrate personal responsibility for lifelong learning.
d. exhibit leadership for digital citizenship.

Reprinted with permission from *National Educational Technology Standards for Students, Second Edition*, © 2007, ISTE® (International Society for Technology in Education), www.iste.org. All rights reserved.

Figure 1-26 This table includes the NETS-S standards for digital citizenship.

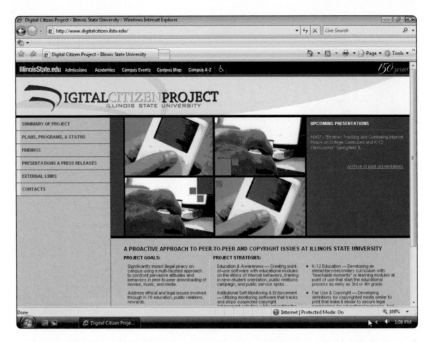

Figure 1-27 The Digital Citizen Project in an example of the many Web sites teachers can use to help them prepare their students to be digital citizens.

Web Info

For more information on the Digital Citizen Project, visit the Teachers Discovering Computers Web site (*scsite.com/tdc5*), click Chapter 1, click Web Info, and then click Digital Citizen Project.

While the technology standards cover concepts of abiding by certain ethical and practical ideals with regard to computer and technology usage, it is still essential that students understand and change their attitudes and corresponding habits. A great way to teach students to be digital citizens is to have a debate activity. For example, the side one often takes in a media copyright debate depends on whether one is a producer or a consumer of videos and music. Students often think that if they found it on the Web then it must be free! Yet, students will understand this debate better as they become producers themselves and the need for them to preserve their individual intellectual property becomes more real. Participating in these kinds of debates, where students are asked to take opposing sides, is a good way for them to begin to value the concepts they are debating and express them in an active way. It is only after thoughtful reflection and critical thinking on creating a personal plan of action that students will begin to organize and prioritize their behaviors and begin to internalize these issues. Debates are great activities for teachers to help students understand land take responsibility for legal and ethical issues.

Being a good digital citizen includes knowledge and commitment for understanding things like etiquette, communication techniques and standards, issues surrounding media and computers, business, commerce, entrepreneurship, privacy rights and responsibilities, ergonomic issues (which are the physical and/or emotional dangers associated with extended computer usage), and information about security and protections from losing data and personal information from computer crashes (backing up for files), asset management, hackers, and other kinds of intruders. You will learn more about security issues and ethics in Chapter 8. In addition, there are many Web sites that can provide you with information on helping students become digital citizens (Figure 1-27 above)

TECHNOLOGY OPERATIONS AND CONCEPTS
Figure 1-28 lists the specific NETS-S standards for technology operations and concepts. As you learned earlier, students must possess computer literacy as a basic skill before they can progress to other skill levels with technology.

Students should have the ability to use computers, technology, and digital media efficiently. They should understand how

Students demonstrate a sound understanding of technology concepts, systems, and operations. Students:
a. understand and use technology systems.
b. select and use applications effectively and productively.
c. troubleshoot systems and applications.
d. transfer current knowledge to learning of new technologies.

Reprinted with permission from *National Educational Technology Standards for Students, Second Edition,* © 2007, ISTE® (International Society for Technology in Education), www.iste.org. All rights reserved.

Figure 1-28 This table includes the NETS-S standards for technology operations and concepts.

computers work, operate, and understand the different hardware, programs, and applications that are associated with them. Most digital students gravitate toward technology very quickly, think they know the technology, and many times jump in without asking any questions; however, many times they do not possess the skills they need. Many business and industry employers report that the students they hire have breadth but not depth of technology skills. Students need a sound foundation of operation and application skills that can be transferred to current new and emerging technologies. Without a sound understanding of technology concepts students cannot compete in a technology rich global society. This knowledge is vital!

Digital media allows teachers to use a combination of technology tools to appeal to an array of learning styles digitally. If integrated properly, digital media also has the capability to stimulate imagination and develop critical thinking skills all while allowing students to take an active role in their own learning. The ARCS Motivational Model, which is discussed next, can help you reflect on ways to modify your teaching techniques and strategies to find innovative ways to motivate today's digital students to learn.

ARCS MOTIVATIONAL MODEL

The **ARCS Motivational Model** was developed by John M. Keller in 1983 and is applicable to learning in the digital age. Keller stressed that even the best designed instructional strategy will fail if students are not motivated to learn. Many students are only performing to pass the test. Without a desire to learn, retention is unlikely. Thus, teachers should strive to create a deeper motivation in learners to learn new skills.

Frustrated that so much of the interest in psychology was concentrated on differences in learner ability, Keller developed a model that would attribute differences in student learning to the amount of effort students were willing to put forth. As a result, he cataloged four specific areas that could account for the differences in student effort. A discussion of these areas follows.

ATTENTION Effective learning techniques seek to capture students' attention to eliminate boredom and arouse natural curiosity. Lessons should increase students' focus by using novel, surprising, out of the ordinary, and uncertain events. Effective techniques should stimulate the sense of wonder and maintain interest. Most students are not only auditory or visual learners, but also multisensory learners. Digital media has the ability to capture the attention of the learner because it addresses a variety of learning styles. Today's students expect to use digital media devices in their daily lives, so these devices, or similar media technology, should be woven seamlessly into their classroom experiences.

RELEVANCE When students feel that learning is relevant or important to their lives, they will become motivated to learn. By using digital media to develop lesson concepts, teachers bring familiar technology into the classroom. Concepts developed with digital media utilize technologies that students value.

Integration Strategies

To learn more about integrating music in your classroom as an effective and novel learning technique, visit the Teachers Discovering Computers Web site (*scsite.com/tdc5*), click Chapter 1, and then click Teaching Today.

Integration Strategies

To learn more about challenging your students by integrating digital media, visit the Teachers Discovering Computers Web site (*scsite.com/tdc5*), click Chapter 1, and then click Digital Media Corner or Learn It Online.

CHALLENGE/CONFIDENCE Students who believe they can achieve often do. Lessons created with digital media allow students to develop confidence by enabling them to succeed. Lessons created with digital media present a degree of challenge that allows for meaningful success through both learning and performance conditions. Lesson content created with digital media can be leveled to challenge multiple skill levels, to generate positive expectations, to provide feedback, and to support internal attributions for success — all of which means students are working at a level at which they can achieve success and gain confidence. Assignments completed using digital media allow students to see just how far their imagination can take them. Using digital media will be natural for some but a struggle for others because not all students will be at the same skill level when it comes to using digital media. It is important to develop lessons that have several achievement levels so students can progress at a pace that meets their needs, that is, that challenges them while building their confidence.

SATISFACTION/SUCCESS Feeling good about one's self is a natural motivator. Digital media provides opportunities for students to use newly acquired knowledge or skills in simulated settings successfully. Lessons developed using digital media can be designed to provide feedback that will sustain the desired behavior. Using digital media, students can showcase their achievements, allowing them to share their successes with others, which increases their desire for positive peer evaluation.

Figure 1-29 summarizes the key concepts of Keller's ARCS Motivational Model. As you continue to explore the concepts and resources provided in this textbook, use the information to help you transition from being a digital immigrant teacher to one that facilitates students' learning in the digital age. Next, you will learn how educators are infusing technology to reach today's digital generation at Ridgedale High School.

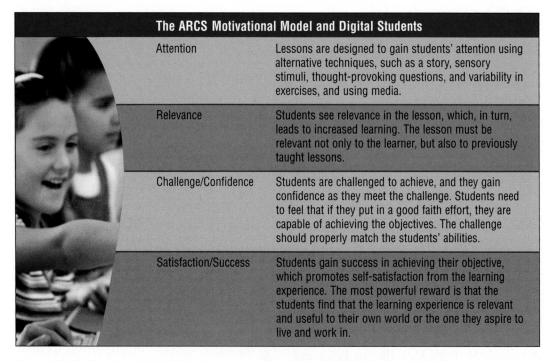

The ARCS Motivational Model and Digital Students	
Attention	Lessons are designed to gain students' attention using alternative techniques, such as a story, sensory stimuli, thought-provoking questions, and variability in exercises, and using media.
Relevance	Students see relevance in the lesson, which, in turn, leads to increased learning. The lesson must be relevant not only to the learner, but also to previously taught lessons.
Challenge/Confidence	Students are challenged to achieve, and they gain confidence as they meet the challenge. Students need to feel that if they put in a good faith effort, they are capable of achieving the objectives. The challenge should properly match the students' abilities.
Satisfaction/Success	Students gain success in achieving their objective, which promotes self-satisfaction from the learning experience. The most powerful reward is that the students find that the learning experience is relevant and useful to their own world or the one they aspire to live and work in.

Figure 1-29 This figure highlights the components of the ARCS Motivational Model.

An Example of How One School Uses Computers

To illustrate how a typical school might use computers and other computer-based technologies, this section takes you on a visual and narrative tour of a typical day at Ridgedale High School, home of the Fighting Tigers. Ridgedale High School is taking advantage of the Federal Communications Commission's **Education Rate**, or **E-Rate**, program, which is a government initiative designed to provide discounts to schools and libraries on all communications services, including network installation and Internet access.

All of the computers at Ridgedale High School are part of a local area network that allows teachers and students to share information with one another and with others around the world. First, Ridgedale networked the computers in all three of its computer labs. Two of these labs contain 30 PCs and the third lab contains 30 Apple computers. The school then installed at least five computers connected with high-speed access to the Internet in each classroom. Ridgedale High School also maintains a Web site to provide up-to-date information for students, teachers, and parents (Figure 1-30).

As the day starts, students are hurrying down the halls toward their classrooms, trying to reach them before the first period bell rings. For these students, the day is just beginning. For the administrators, teachers, and staff of Ridgedale High School, their day started much earlier.

SUPERINTENDENT

Early this morning, Dr. Helen Hartley, superintendent of Washington County Public School District, met with members of the Technology Committee to review the final touches on the district's Three-Year Technology Plan (Figure 1-31). Dr. Hartley is very interested in the progress of the district's Technology Committee, whose members include administrators, teachers, parents, media specialists, technology coordinators, university professors, and business partners from the community.

Although pleased with the work the committee has accomplished thus far, the superintendent has found that, as more technology initiatives are launched, the committee's planning meetings are becoming too long (and are hard to fit into the extremely busy schedules of the members). To help with this problem, Dr. Hartley asked the district Webmaster, Bob Still, to develop an interactive district wiki for the committee to use to communicate as they develop policy and reports. Now, all the committee members can access the wiki with their password and work on policies and other issues.

Web Info

For more information about the FCC's E-Rate Universal Service Program for Schools & Libraries, visit the Teachers Discovering Computers Web site (*scsite.com/tdc5*), click Chapter 1, click Web Info, and then click E-Rate.

Figure 1-30 Ridgedale High School's Web site allows teachers, students, and parents to have direct access to extensive and up-to-date school-related information.

Figure 1-31 Members of the Technology Committee help prepare Dr. Hartley's presentation on the school district's Three-Year Technology Plan. Dr. Hartley will use charts and graphs to present the plan at the next school board meeting.

Web Info

For more information about national Technology Standards for School Administrators (TSSA), visit the Teachers Discovering Computers Web site (*scsite.com/tdc5*), click Chapter 1, click Web Info, and then click TSSA.

Dr. Hartley has several other items to attend to and people to visit before heading to Ridgedale High School for the 3:30 p.m. Teacher/Student Honors Assembly. Dr. Hartley is looking forward to seeing Ridgedale's new multimedia presentation system, which includes a centralized video distribution system, used during the assembly. She plans to arrive early to review the national Technology Standards for School Administrators (TSSA) with the principal of Ridgedale High School.

PRINCIPAL

Mr. Tony Hidalgo, the principal at Ridgedale High School, starts his day by completing several administrative tasks, which he accomplishes by sending various e-mail messages to teachers and staff. He sends an e-mail message to Ms. Jenny Marcus, Ridgedale's technology coordinator, to remind her to test the new presentation system before the Teacher/Student Honors Assembly. Mr. Hidalgo also sends an e-mail message to Dr. Hartley requesting an update on his latest budgeting request for new math and science software and for new software to run the school's grading and attendance system (Figure 1-32).

He also is interested in the new cross-curriculum digital storytelling writing project that some of his teachers have integrated into their curriculum. He has been doing some research on digital storytelling and so far he is intrigued by, but not convinced of, the significance of the project. However, his research does say that if students start writing more and enjoy the learning process, then scores will go up. He decides to find out more about digital storytelling.

Before the students arrive, Mr. Hidalgo sends an e-mail message to all teachers and staff reminding them that the Teacher/Student Honors Assembly begins promptly at 3:30 p.m. He also sends a message to Mrs. Acosta requesting more information about her digital storytelling projects. Mr. Hidalgo finishes his early morning administrative tasks in time to walk the halls and greet students arriving for school.

SCHOOL SECRETARY

When she first started at Ridgedale High School, Ms. Clara Rich, the school secretary, spent much of her day answering and routing incoming telephone calls. Several years ago, however, the school board approved the installation of a computerized telephone system that routes calls directly to the appropriate person. Ms. Rich now starts her day by checking e-mail and voice mail messages to determine if any teachers are going to be late or absent. If necessary, Ms. Rich accesses the school's teacher database to identify potential substitute teachers (Figure 1-33).

Next, Ms. Rich uses her PDA to connect to the school's inventory database. She checks supply quantities and confirms delivery of recent purchases. Ms. Rich reviews the customized certificates she has created for the Honors Assembly. She created the certificates using her desktop publishing program and the school's color printer, and is sure they will impress students, teachers, and parents.

Figure 1-32 Mr. Hidalgo is pondering the wording of his important e-mail message to the superintendent.

Figure 1-33 By using various databases, the school secretary can locate potential substitute teachers and manage equipment purchases, inventory, and supplies easily.

TECHNOLOGY COORDINATOR

Ms. Jenny Marcus, technology coordinator, arrives early to attend to several items and browse the Web to locate information on installing new software and testing the new presentation system. Ms. Marcus has several questions about the presentation system that she is unable to find answers for on the company's Web site. By accessing its technical assistance live chat, she is able to talk directly with a technician. The technician promptly answers most of her questions, but several deal with individual decisions that the principal needs to approve before the installation can be completed. Ms. Marcus calls and leaves a message on Mr. Hidalgo's voice mail asking if they can meet in her office at 10:00 a.m. to resolve these details (Figure 1-34).

Figure 1-34 The technology coordinator leaves a voice message for the principal after she has gathered technical information on the new presentation system from the Web.

TEACHERS

Mrs. Acosta understood from the first day she entered her classroom that she had to start incorporating new strategies for her teaching of history — she knew that her digital students were different and that they learn differently than she had learned in school. She decided to start looking into the principles of **community digital storytelling**, which combines basic educational pedagogy with creative writing, oral history, movies, filmmaking, and digital media. Because it is a community-based project, she plans to involve top local citizens in her classroom as guest speakers. She also hopes her students, as they work on their assignments, will add value to

other community-based projects. Her students will be learning about the art of the **transmedia story** — the art of telling stories using various forms of media.

Mrs. Acosta knows that when students find the assignment fun they also are motivated to learn. She also knows that students become active learners when they use digital media (Figure 1-35). Mrs. Acosta plans to start class by showing a video that Mr. Finley obtained through the state's interlibrary loan program. The video shows how history students across the country are telling stories using various forms of digital media.

Figure 1-35 Students actively engage in their own learning when teachers integrate digital media and other technologies.

Mr. Dourden Boone is in his classroom preparing for his advanced placement biology class. He is having his students work on their class projects in groups of three. The class is using 10 wireless notebook computers that are part of a 10-station wireless mobile lab that the students call the 10 pack. Each wireless notebook computer is connected without wires to the school's network, providing students with instant and wireless access to the Internet and dozens of educational and productivity software programs.

Mr. Boone has found the new wireless mobile lab easy to use and extremely beneficial both for his instruction and for student learning. Before the wireless lab became available, he had to take his students to a traditional computer lab that was located in a different building on the other side of campus. Now, he simply rolls the lab to his students for use in his classroom, saving valuable instructional and on-task time. The students' first assignment is to visit numerous biology Web sites that Mr. Boone has evaluated for

Web Info

For more information and ideas on integrating digital media into your lessons and to learn more about digital storytelling, visit the Teachers Discovering Computer Web site (*scsite.com/tdc5*), click Chapter 1, click Web Info, and then click Digital Storytelling.

appropriateness and instructional value. Then, each group uses the wireless notebook computers to run experiments, log their research findings, type their findings into a report, and create digital presentations for the class (Figure 1-36). Mr. Boone plans to shares his wireless mobile lab experiences with four other science teachers over lunch. He is confident they will benefit from using the lab as well.

Figure 1-36 Students create projects, experiments, research reports, and papers using a wireless notebook computer.

At the other end of the school, two of the physical education instructors, Mrs. Rita Simpson and Mr. Gary Roberts, are installing and testing video equipment so they can video gymnastics routines for personal and class evaluation of performance and techniques. Mr. Roberts, who also is the girls' soccer coach, taped last week's soccer game. He wants to show the soccer team how they can improve for the state finals competition next week.

The school recently received 30 handheld devices and software as the result of a physical education improvement grant (Figure 1-37). A new software program

was purchased with money from the grant, too. The software program helps students evaluate their running techniques, cardiovascular activities, and nutritional needs. The software interfaces with their handheld devices so they can enter data in the handheld device regardless of where they are and what activity they are doing. When students are back at their classroom computer, they connect the handheld device and download all the pertinent data to their password-secure folders on the school's network. This way, they can keep track of and analyze the data.

MEDIA SPECIALIST

Mr. Chris Finley, the media specialist, arrives at school very early because many students need access to media center resources before first period classes begin, for example, some students need resources for their digital storytelling projects. While the students are searching the online catalog for materials, both in their own media center and other centers in the district, Mr. Finley completes his final preparations for Mrs. Acosta's tenth-grade history class.

Mr. Finley and Mrs. Acosta work together to create activities that help students not only learn history and their community, but also sharpen their research skills as they experience learning in a very different way. After confirming that all of the center's computers are up and running, Mr. Finley starts gathering resources for Mrs. Acosta's students, including books, CDs, DVDs, videos, graphics, and other digital media. He also assists students with their research projects. (Figure 1-38).

Integration Strategies

To learn more about integrating technology with your special needs students including physically challenged students, visit the Teachers Discovering Computers Web site (*scsite.com/tdc5*), click Chapter 1, and then click Assistive Technologies Corner.

Figure 1-37 Physical education students are entering personal information, which they will use to monitor and chart their personal fitness, into their handheld devices.

Figure 1-38 After locating electronic resources, textbooks, and other materials in the school media center, the media specialist works with students on their research projects.

STUDENTS

The biggest excitement every morning is the live broadcast of the *Ridgedale News Show* in the TV Production Studio. Students gain experience in TV production and communications as well as learn what it is like to work in front of and behind the camera. Students form the complete production team, from the camera operator to reporters. Crew members rotate on a weekly basis through each of the broadcast production jobs. This project also provides the opportunity for a student to learn how to use video outside the studio and bring it into the classroom in order to share his or her story (Figure 1-39).

Figure 1-39 Prior to doing the live broadcast, students often practice their broadcasting skills using a PC video camera and digital media computer.

Students also are beginning to talk and instant message each other about the new digital storytelling project that Mrs. Acosta is adding to her history curriculum. Many students are not sure how they feel about the new project and what all is involved. Fulton Gaffney, the head of the student government, plans to talk to Mrs. Acosta so he can learn more about what media tools he will need for his project. He has lived in Ridgedale all his life. His grandfather often tells stories about the town. Fulton has gathered pictures, audio clips, and video clips of his grandfather's stories. Fulton is glad he is going to use technology to complete his project. He plans to compile his grandfather's stories on CD, and he knows his grandfather will certainly be surprised when Fulton presents him with the CD.

Addison Kenny is excited to learn more about digital storytelling and oral histories. Her family has only recently moved to Ridgedale and she wants to learn more about her new town. She is going to have to find materials for her video from the media center and, perhaps, the central library, which has an extensive collection of newspaper clippings. Unlike Fulton's story, hers is not going to be a personal history, so she is going to have to find a new angle.

Callie Guthrie has already begun working on her project on her native ancestry. Her ancestors include a line of Native Americans and her story will take on a different perspective, for sure.

PARENT

Using her home computer, Catherine Rosa accesses Ridgedale's Web site to check the time of the Teacher/Student Honors Assembly (Figure 1-40). While she was looking up the time, Catherine notices a new graphic that reads, We Need Your Support! Curious, she clicks the graphic and links to a Web page requesting parent volunteers to chaperone the girls' soccer team on its trip to the state finals. Catherine sends an e-mail message to Mr. Roberts, stating that she gladly will chaperone the trip. Catherine then quickly browses through the state Department of Education Web site to read the latest information released on Ridgedale High School before heading to the school for the assembly. Then, she clicks on the link about the digital storytelling project. Wow, that looks interesting!

Figure 1-40 A parent of a Ridgedale High School student logs on to the school's Web site to find out the start time for a special event.

Integration Strategies

To learn how to create Web pages, blogs, wikis, podcasts, and other online tools that can help with parental involvement, review the special feature that follows Chapter 3, Creating Web Pages, Blogs, Wikis, and More.

COMMUNITY

Kevin Lee, a 72-year-old, retired construction worker, starts his day by reading e-mail messages from 16-year-old Brian Johnson, a student at Ridgedale High School (Figure 1-41). Kevin and Brian communicate online regularly as part of a program called Seniors Online. Seniors Online is a school program designed to match students with special needs with senior citizens, who serve as mentors. Each week Kevin, along with 13 other senior citizens, visits the school to work with a student, one on one.

Figure 1-41 A successful program at Ridgedale High School matches senior citizens with students with special needs. In this photo, a retired construction worker is checking his e-mail for a message from his new friend.

The students teach the senior citizens how to use a computer, send and receive e-mail messages, and browse the Web. Their mentors, in turn, help the students understand the challenges and opportunities they likely are going to experience after they graduate from high school. The interaction between the seniors and students with special needs is a remarkable success story. Brian has decided his digital story will be about Mr. Lee's family history. Brian knows Mr. Lee has lived in the community for 72 years and his family for

150 years. Mr. Lee is thrilled to be able to tell his family's story and so happy to work with Brian!

The students send e-mail messages to their mentors to seek advice or just to share everyday news. For senior citizens, such as Kevin, learning to use a computer is a great experience, but working directly with the students is the most rewarding experience of all. Kevin is looking forward to telling the history of his family as a story. He feels this is a great opportunity to pass on his family's history to the next generation. He also knows it will strengthen his connection with Brian.

Using the Textbook Web Site

Each chapter in this textbook contains 10 end-of-chapter sections, all of which are stored either completely or partially as Web pages on the World Wide Web. In addition, the textbook includes eight special features (one follows each chapter) and one appendix; many of these also are located on the textbook Web site. To enhance your learning experience, be sure to view the end-of-chapter materials and special features on the Web, where you will find curriculum-specific information, integration ideas, interactive exercises, and links to thousands of popular educational sites.

In all eight chapters, annotations in the margins, called Web Info, send you to the textbook Web site, where you will find links to current and additional information about Web Info topics. Also located in the margins are FAQ boxes that consist of frequently asked questions and their answers, as well as Integration Strategies boxes that help you locate integration ideas.

To access the textbook Web site, start your browser and enter the following Web address, *scsite.com/tdc5* (Figure 1-42). To display an end-of-chapter section, click the desired chapter number at the top and then click any of the end-of-chapter sections displayed on the left sidebar; for example, click Chapter 1 and then click Teaching Today (Figure 1-43). The special features located below the end-of-chapter sections may be accessed at anytime. Use the scroll bar to view information on the Web page that is not in the current window (Figure 1-43).

INTERACTING WITH END-OF-CHAPTER MATERIALS

The following sections explain how you can interact in a curriculum-specific way with the resources available in the various end-of-chapter materials. This will help you transition to using the new learning environments described in Figure 1-1 on page 2.

KEY TERMS Click any term to see and hear a term definition. Click the Web link to visit a Web page for supplemental information on the term.

CHECKPOINT Use these interactive questions and answers to check your knowledge level of the chapter and to prepare for quizzes and examinations.

TEACHING TODAY This section provides you with an appreciation of the value that technology and the Web have for K-12 education. Each segment contains one or more links that reinforce the information presented in the segment.

EDUCATION ISSUES Education Issues contains several scenarios that allow you to explore controversial and current issues in education, for example, school violence. Click the links for additional information on the issue.

INTEGRATION CORNER This innovative section provides you with extensive ideas and resources for integrating technology into your classroom-specific curriculum. Each chapter provides information on and links to approximately 100 outstanding educational Web sites organized in the following 12 corners: Early Childhood, Elementary, Middle School, Secondary, Reading/Language Arts, Social Studies/History, Math, Science, Special Education, Post Secondary, Administrator, and Research. Choose your area and explore the resources to learn how to integrate technology into your specific classroom curriculum and how other educators are integrating technology.

chapter links

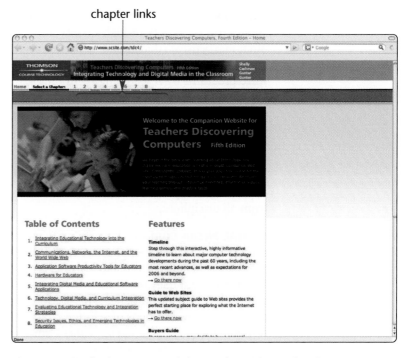

Figure 1-42 The home page of the Teachers Discovering Computers Web site (*scsite.com/tdc5*).

Teaching Today selected   Chapter 1 selected   Teaching Today section displays   click links for current and additional information   scroll bar

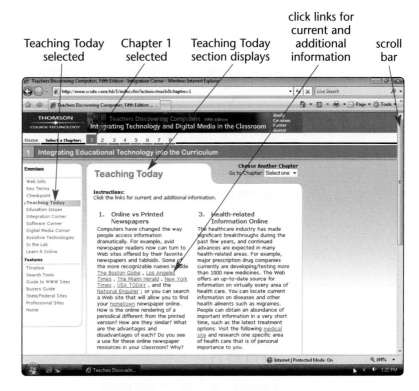

Figure 1-43 Teaching Today end-of-chapter section for Chapter 1 displayed at the textbook Web site. Use the scroll bar to see the additional Teaching Today segments.

SOFTWARE CORNER Today's educators can choose from a variety of high-quality and often inexpensive educational software programs. You can learn about popular software programs by researching them on the Web and in many cases even download or order a free evaluation copy so you can evaluate a program prior to buying it. Software Corner provides you with information on and links to additional information and download instructions for dozens of educational software programs used by teachers from all disciplines.

DIGITAL MEDIA CORNER A recurring theme throughout this book emphasizes that today's teachers need to make learning meaningful and relevant to the lives of today's K-12 digital students. This section provides you with videos of selected chapter topics that can be used to supplement your digital lessons. This section also provides you with ideas and examples of how you can use digital media to enhance your teaching and your students' learning.

ASSISTIVE TECHNOLOGIES CORNER This section provides important information on current hardware, software, and peripherals that will assist you in delivering instruction to students with physical, cognitive, or sensory disabilities. Links and extensive additional information, strategies, ideas, and more are available at the textbook Web site.

IN THE LAB These exercises are divided into two areas: productivity and integration. Use the productivity exercises to improve your software-specific skills in using word processing, spreadsheet, database, desktop publishing, curriculum and Web page development, as well as other productivity software programs. Use the integration ideas for incorporating these programs into your specific classroom curriculum. Click the links for tutorials, productivity ideas, integration examples and ideas, and more.

LEARN IT ONLINE These exercises allow you to improve your computer and integration skills by learning exciting new skills online. This section includes interactive lab exercises, software tutorials, scavenger hunts, practice tests, learning games, and much more.

Timeline — Milestones in Computer History

At the textbook Web site is an interactive, colorful, and highly informative multipage timeline of the history of computers from 1937 to the present. The timeline contains dozens of links to extensive supplemental information, including historical audio segments from National Public Radio, animations, videos, and much more.

To display this interactive special feature, click Timeline on the left sidebar at the textbook Web site (Figure 1-43). All of the graphics and pictures contain links to the Web. Explore the special feature with your mouse; to access the interactive links, click when your mouse pointer changes to a hand.

A World Without Wires

At the end of this chapter is a special feature that introduces you to the revolution in wireless technology and devices that is rapidly changing the way people all over the world interact, work, play, and learn.

Summary of Introduction to Integrating Technology in Education

This chapter presented a broad introduction to concepts and terminology related to computers and computers in education. You now have a basic understanding of what a computer is and how it processes data into information. You were introduced to digital media and how today's digital students learn. You learned about the national technology standards for students and explored what your students should know to become productive citizens in an emerging global economy. You also have seen some examples of how computers are being used in K-12 schools and integrated into classroom settings. You should be starting to formulate your own strategies to teach your digital students. Reading and learning the concepts in this chapter will help you understand these topics as they are presented in more detail in future chapters.

Key Terms

INSTRUCTIONS: Use the Key Terms to help focus your study of the terms used in this chapter. To further enhance your understanding of the Key Terms in this chapter, visit scsite.com/tdc5, click Chapter 1 at the top of the Web page, and then click Key Terms on the left sidebar. Read the definition for each term and then access current and additional information about the term from the Web.

age of convergence [5]
ARCS Motivational Model [23]

community digital storytelling [27]
computer [4]
computer literacy [3]
curriculum-specific learning [2]

data [4]
data literacy [21]
desktop computers [8]
digital generation [15]
digital kids [16]
digital media [6]
digital students [15]
discipline-specific learning [2]

Education Rate (E-Rate) [25]
embedded computer [10]

handheld computer [9]
hardware [4]

information [4]
information fluency [19]
information literacy [4]
information processing cycle [4]
input [4]
install [15]
integration literacy [4]
International Society for Technology in Education (ISTE) [11]
Internet [19]
Internet-enabled [9]

Macintosh computer [7]
media literacy [19]
mobile computer [8]
mobile device [8]

National Council for Accreditation for Teacher Education (NCATE) [11]

National Educational Technology Standards for Teachers (NETS-T) [11]
notebook computer [8]

output [4]

PDA [9]
personal computer (PC) [7]
personal digital assistant (PDA) [9]

server [10]
smart phone [9]
software [4]
storage [4]
supercomputer [10]

Tablet PC [9]
transmedia story [27]

Checkpoint

INSTRUCTIONS: Use the Checkpoint exercises to check your knowledge level of the chapter. To complete the Checkpoint exercises interactively, visit scsite.com/tdc5, click Chapter 1 at the top of the Web page, and then click Checkpoint on the left sidebar.

1. Label the Figure

Instructions: Identify each element of a digital media system by placing the correct label on the numbered lines.

1. _____   2. _____   3. _____   4. _____

5. _____

6. _____

7. _____

8. _____

9. _____

2. Matching

Instructions: Match each term from the column on the left with the best description from the column on the right.

____ 1. media literacy
____ 2. digital students
____ 3. input
____ 4. digital media
____ 5. data literacy

a. able to view, manipulate, analyze, and interpret information
b. data entered into a computer
c. allows users to create new forms of interaction
d. hypercommunicators, multitaskers, and goal oriented
e. able to create, develop, and communicate information

3. Short Answer

Instructions: Write a brief answer to each of the following questions.

1. What is the difference between computer literacy, information literacy, and integration literacy?
2. Define digital students. Why are they different from previous generations of students?
3. Briefly summarize the six National Educational Technology Standards for Students (NETS-S).
4. What is the ARCS Motivational Model? What are the four categories of the ARCS Motivational Model?
5. Briefly summarize why computers should be used in K-12 schools.

Teaching Today

INSTRUCTIONS: Teaching Today provides teachers with integration strategies and ideas for teaching and, more importantly, reaching today's digital generation. Each numbered segment contains one or more links that reinforce the information presented in the segment. To display this page from the Web, visit scsite.com/tdc5, click Chapter 1 at the top of the Web page, and then click Teaching Today on the left sidebar.

1. Online vs. Printed Newspapers

Computers have changed the way people access information dramatically. For example, avid newspaper readers now can turn to Web sites offered by their favorite newspapers. Some of the more recognizable names include *The Boston Globe*, *Los Angeles Times*, *The Miami Herald*, *New York Times*, *USA TODAY*, and *eSchools*; or you can search a Web site that will allow you to find your hometown newspaper online. How is the online rendering of a periodical different from the printed version? How are they similar? What are the advantages and disadvantages of each? Do you see a use for these online newspaper resources in your classroom? Why?

2. Online Bookstores

Just as the automobile led to the end of the horse and buggy, will the growth of the Internet lead to the demise of printed media? Probably not; in fact, booksellers are turning to the Internet to promote their products. Many online bookstores sell books, videos, and games. Some of these are Amazon.com, Barnes & Noble College Bookstores, and Books-A-Million, or you can visit a bookstore directory that links and describes dozens of top bookstore sites and book publishers. Visit a bookstore Web site and compare searching for a book online with finding a book in a traditional bookstore. Try looking for a particular title, a book by a certain author, and books on a specific subject. What are the advantages and disadvantages of shopping for a book online? How likely would you be to buy a book through a bookstore Web site? Why?

3. Health-related Information Online

The healthcare industry has made significant breakthroughs during the past few years, and continued advances are expected in many health-related areas. For example, major prescription drug companies currently are developing/testing more than 1000 new medicines. The Web offers an up-to-date source for information on virtually every area of health care. You can locate current information on diseases and other health ailments such as migraines. People can obtain an abundance of important information in a very short time, such as the latest treatment options. Visit the following medical site and research one specific area of health care that is of personal importance to you.

4. Music in the Classroom?

Why does a classroom have to be quiet? Have you ever heard the phrase "Music can tame your savage soul" or "Music can cheer you up?" Music is very powerful — what memories does music bring back for you? Well consider today's students — because their music is making memories for them. Music can be a powerful learning tool that can be used to engage students and teach everything from Spanish to English to algebra to chemistry. Music is the emotional underscore and highlights the messages of all movies, commercials and presentations. So think what music does in students' daily lives. Can music change student learning — something to think about! What ways could you enhance your instruction using music? Should you use your music or your students' music? Do you think test scores might go up, what about student motivation? How could you make the connection between your content and their music?

Education Issues

INSTRUCTIONS: Education Issues provides several scenarios that allow you to explore controversial and current issues in education. Each numbered segment contains one or more links that reinforce the information presented in the segment. To display this page from the Web, visit scsite.com/tdc5, click Chapter 1 at the top of the Web page, and then click Education Issues on the left sidebar.

1. School Violence

Numerous polls have shown that school safety is now the number-one concern of both parents and teachers. National leaders are calling the increase in school violence a national crisis. What are some of the causes of school violence? Do you agree that school violence should be the main concern of parents? One popular answer to the dramatic increase in the incidences of school violence is to build protective nets around the nation's schools, including fences, metal detectors, high-tech video surveillance, body searches, and armed guards. Do you agree with this solution? Other political and educational leaders stress that turning schools into armed camps is not the solution. Instead, schools and communities must address and attempt to find solutions for the causes of school violence. Do you agree with this solution? What would you suggest to reduce the incidences of school violence?

2. Possible Child Abuse

During your student internship, you notice that 9-year-old Juan Gonzales has bruises all over his arms and legs. He has been one of your more inquisitive students, but lately you have noticed that he has become moody, seems uninterested in class, and his grades are falling. The school nurse casually informs you that she has noticed that Juan has been losing weight the past couple of months. You suspect that Juan may be a victim of child abuse. You ask your supervising teacher what you should do and she says, "Oh! He is the son of a member of the school board; I am sure he is just growing and is at a clumsy age." You really like the school and would like to work there after graduation. Do you tell someone or do you ignore it? If so, whom do you tell? What else could you do?

3. Reality or Fantasy

The space shuttle was first flown in July 1969 and landed on the moon that same year. An ingredient in many popular shampoos has been proven to cause cancer. It is illegal to contact space aliens. None of these statements is true, but each appeared on the Web. In today's society, some people, especially young students, think that anything in print is true, and the Web adds to that because anyone can publish anything on a Web page. Authors with a wide range of expertise, authority, and biases create Web pages. Web pages can be as accurate as the most scholarly journal or no truer than some articles in supermarket tabloids. Ultimately, who is responsible for the accuracy of information on the Web? Why? How can you verify information on the Web? How would you teach your students to make sure information is accurate?

4. Possible Cheating

Today, students come to class with cellular telephones, graphing calculators, pagers, personal digital assistants (PDAs), notebook computers, iPods, and other devices. During a test, you notice that a student is using a cell phone. As you approach the student, you realize that the student is looking at a smart phone with a picture on the screen. The student puts away the phone and apologizes, indicating that he had forgotten to turn off the phone when a call came in. After class, another student informs you that the student you caught with the phone was making calls to another student in the classroom, and they were taking pictures of the equations. This student was almost positive the two students were cheating by sending each other pictures of the answers over their smart phones. How should you handle this situation? Does a way to gather proof exist? What next? Should all handhelds be banned in classrooms? If so, how? What is your role? Explain.

Integration Corner

INSTRUCTIONS: Integration Corner provides extensive ideas and resources for integrating technology into your classroom-specific curriculum. To display this page from the Web and its links to approximately 100 educational Web sites, visit scsite.com/tdc5, click Chapter 1 at the top of the Web page, and then click Integration Corner on the left sidebar.

Exercises

Web Info
Key Terms
Checkpoint
Teaching Today
Education Issues
Integration Corner
Software Corner
Digital Media Corner
Assistive Technologies Corner
In the Lab
Learn It Online

Features

Timeline
Guide to WWW Sites
Search Tools
Buyer's Guide
State/Federal Sites
Professional Sites

Integration Corner is designed for teachers and other educators who are looking for innovative ways to integrate technology into their content-specific curriculum. Integration Corner not only provides great Web sites with current information, but also shows what other educators are doing in the field of educational technology. Integration Corner is designed for all educators regardless of their interests. Expand your resources by reviewing information and sites outside of your teaching area because many great integration ideas in one area can be modified easily for use in other curriculum areas.

Teachers and administrators will find other colleagues in their areas with whom to connect and share the successes and hurdles of integrating technology in a classroom or an entire school system. Consider Integration Corner your one stop for integration ideas and resources. Links to educational Web sites are organized in the following 12 Corners, and different Web resources are available for each chapter. Figure 1-44 shows examples of the Web resources provided in the Chapter 1 Early Childhood Corner.

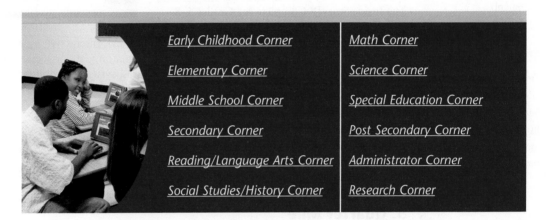

Early Childhood Corner   *Math Corner*

Elementary Corner   *Science Corner*

Middle School Corner   *Special Education Corner*

Secondary Corner   *Post Secondary Corner*

Reading/Language Arts Corner   *Administrator Corner*

Social Studies/History Corner   *Research Corner*

Figure 1-44 Examples of the Web resources provided in the Chapter 1 Early Childhood Corner.

Software Corner

INSTRUCTIONS: Software Corner provides information on popular software programs. Each numbered segment discusses specific software programs and contains a link to additional information about these programs. To display this page from the Web, visit scsite.com/tdc5, click Chapter 1 at the top of the Web page, and then click Software Corner on the left sidebar.

1. A.D.A.M. Interactive Anatomy

For over a decade, A.D.A.M., Inc. has been dedicated to creating new and innovative tools for teaching anatomy and physiology. A.D.A.M. hands-on interactive anatomy, physiology, health, and exercise multimedia software tools help students meet the curriculum goals and objectives while at the same time assist students in understanding the complex terms and systems of the human body. There are several choices in the A.D.A.M. series depending on the age, grade level, and content you are teaching. A.D.A.M.® The Inside Story™ Complete for Grades 5–8 provides the ultimate interactive anatomy and multimedia experience for learning life sciences. A.D.A.M. Interactive Anatomy 4 for secondary students engages students in the learning of the human anatomy and associated topics with detailed full-color illustrations of body parts, organs, structures, systems, and much more.

2. BodyWorks

BodyWorks, from Borderbund, is a visual and textual classroom reference software of the human body. Included with BodyWorks are video lectures, 3-D models, high-resolution images, and thousands of audio pronunciations of medical terms, and a searchable database of more than 400,000 words with useful information on over 1,500 topics for classroom lectures, presentations, and projects. A teacher's guide also is available for this intermediate and secondary science program.

3. Quarter Mile

Quarter Mile is useful in assisting students to learn math skills from basic math facts to difficult skills such as integers, converting percents and fractions, and advanced equations. Quarter Mile is a super remediation program for the exceptional student classroom as well as a great skills practice program for the regular classroom at all educational levels. What makes this program interesting for students is that they race against their own time, allowing them to see their own progress.

4. Timeliner

Timeliner allows teachers and students to create, print, and illustrate timelines using pictures or text with ease for any time period. Timeliner can be used at the elementary level by having students create timelines of their life using personal events to help them gain an understanding of the concept of time and sequence of important events. Elementary teachers can use this program to teach the concept of decade, century, millennium, and more. At the middle and high school levels, Timeliner can be used to show historical progress of specific time periods, chart world-changing occurrences and causes of important events, or even illustrate the different stages of a novel, like *The Red Badge of Courage*.

5. WebBlender

If you are looking for a product that can make it easy for you to create a Web site for your class with a combination of text, graphics, and sound, even a class photo and art gallery, then WebBlender is the perfect tool for you. Its user friendly interface lets you focus on the content and easily share your students' work. If you have been interested in added podcasting to your classroom Web site, look no further because you can share stories, videos, and music in a podcast without knowing how to create RSS feeds — all you do is add the content and WebBlender takes care of the details. You are off and running!

Digital Media Corner

INSTRUCTIONS: Today's K-12 digital students need their learning to be meaningful and relevant to their lives. Digital Media Corner provides videos, ideas, and examples of how you can use digital media to enhance your teaching and your students' learning. To access the videos and links to additional information, visit scsite.com/tdc5, click Chapter 1 at the top of the Web page, and then click Digital Media on the left sidebar.

1. PC or Mac?

Even though there have been almost an infinite number of enhancements over the years, PCs and Apple computers are not yet fully compatible. In the meantime users are being asked to decide between these two platforms. Now that choice is easier than ever. In fact, you do not really have to make a choice. Parallels Desktop for Mac is a product that enables you to run Windows side-by-side with Mac OS X on any Intel-powered Apple computer. With Parallels, you can use Windows and Mac OS X at the same time, providing you the opportunity to utilize either operating system. You can even share files and folders between both operating systems by simply dragging them back and forth. You can even open Windows files with Mac programs and vice versa.

2. Brainplugg

To enhance your classroom content you spend an enormous amount of time looking for great class related videos. Brainplugg.com has created a Web site to help educators stop wasting time and start finding the best educational videos without having to sort through millions of unrelated videos and never-ending search results that yield thousands of hits. Brainplugg is a Web site containing a search engine that organizes and catalogues educational videos uploaded to various user-submitted Web sites like Google Video, YouTube, MetaCafe, and Brightcove, etc. A newly created feature links directly to Wikipedia. All you have to do is click on the wiki button located next to the video to find out more information about the video you are watching. Users can watch, suggest, rate, upload, and bookmark videos to be used in educational settings.

3. Audacity

As educators we are always looking for solutions that are cross platform and cost effective for our students — look no further for software to edit audio files. Audacity is free, open source software for recording and editing all kinds of sounds (including voice and music and ambient sound effects) and is available for Mac OS X, Microsoft Windows, and other operating systems. With Audacity, you can import audio from outside sources such as QuickTime and export your completed project back to them in many different file formats. The program allows you to perform activities, such as equalize (balance), add effects, remove unwanted noise, generate tones, and convert file formats from one format to another to make them playable in the particular media player on your computer.

4. United Streaming

Video can be a key component of digital media. Video, when used appropriately in your lessons, can help students think for themselves. But before video can be viewed, it has to get to students. Until recently, this has been a daunting task for teachers, but not anymore. United Streaming allows teachers and students to access over 50,000 educational video content clips and 5,000 full video titles from The Discovery School easily. United Streaming has a huge server network that soaks up most of the work to download or stream video media. As a result, over 30,000,000 students and teachers from more than 53,000 schools can digitally enhance their lessons, group activities and projects, and much more. Click the United Streaming link to learn more.

Assistive Technologies Corner

INSTRUCTIONS: Assistive Technologies Corner provides information on current hardware, software, and peripherals that will assist you in delivering instruction to students with physical, cognitive, or sensory challenges. To access extensive additional information, visit scsite.com/tdc5, click Chapter 1 at the top of the Web page, and then click Assistive Technologies on the left sidebar.

1. What Is Assistive/Adaptive Technology?

Some people find operating a computer difficult, perhaps impossible because of some physical, cognitive, or sensory disability. Applied to computers, the term assistive/adaptive technology refers to any equipment, modification, or accommodation that can improve a person's capacity to learn, to communicate, to solve a problem, or to complete a task through the use of a computer.

2. Why Learn About Assistive Technologies?

The U.S. Census Bureau reports 7% of boys and 4% of girls ages 5 to 15 have some form of disability. An awareness of assistive/adaptive technology is valuable to each teacher committed to providing new learning environments in the classroom. New technologies designed for specific disabilities benefit those who need them, but anyone, at any time, may be in need of such technology as a result of injury or accident. In addition, as the population ages, more users of any technology will require some specialized accommodations in using that technology.

For a student with special needs, a learning environment without assistive/adaptive technology does not meet the requirements of the Individuals with Disabilities Education Act (IDEA). IDEA is a nondiscrimination law requiring schools to accommodate the needs of children with disabilities to provide them an equal opportunity to participate in and benefit from the general education curriculum. In the area of technology, the law specifies that computers be accessible to students who use them. In K-12 schools, students with disabilities often have an Individualized Educational Program (IEP). The program may specify that some assistive/adaptive technology be used in the student's learning environment. Teachers are often called upon for advice, or to locate, or to make recommendations for purchase of special technology. As you explore each chapter's Assistive Technologies Corner, you will gain extensive knowledge that will allow your students with disabilities to be all they can be and learn all they can.

3. Do Microsoft and Apple Operating Systems Have Built-In Accessibility Features?

In response to the many computer users who need some accommodation to use a computer, Apple and Microsoft provide accessibility features and assistance at their Web sites as well as built-in accessibility features in their operating systems. These features allow users to customize their computers to meet their needs for computer input and output.

In Windows Vista, you use the Ease of Access Center to change settings for accessibility options. To open the Ease of Access Center, click the Start button, click Control Panel, and then click the Ease of Access Center icon. Built-in accessibility features for Windows XP are controlled through the Accessibility Wizard. To access the Accessibility Wizard, click the Start button, point to All Programs, point to Accessories, point to Accessibility, and then click Accessibility Wizard.

Ease of Access Center

The Macintosh OS X System Preferences panel provides the Universal Access feature. To access this feature, click the Apple menu and then click System Preferences. When the System Preferences window displays, click the Universal Access icon. In the Universal Access panel, you will find setup instructions for zooming text, visual alerts, and keyboard and mouse modifications.

Follow the Web instructions at the top of this page to display additional information and this chapter's links on assistive technologies, including alternative input devices and other accessibility features.

In the Lab

INSTRUCTIONS: In the Lab provides word processing exercises that are divided into two areas, productivity and integration. To access the links to tutorials, productivity ideas, integration examples and ideas, and more, visit scsite.com/tdc5, click Chapter 1 at the top of the Web page, and then click In the Lab on the left sidebar.

Exercises

Web Info
Key Terms
Checkpoint
Teaching Today
Education Issues
Integration Corner
Software Corner
Digital Media Corner
Assistive Technologies Corner
In the Lab
Learn It Online

Features

Timeline
Guide to WWW Sites
Search Tools
Buyer's Guide
State/Federal Sites
Professional Sites

PRODUCTIVITY IN THE CLASSROOM

Introduction: Word processing skills are essential for both teachers and students. Improving your word processing skills will save you time and energy! Many powerful word processing software applications are available today. In addition, many of the major word processing applications have online tutorials. These tutorials can provide fast and easy access to learning new skills such as setting page margins, inserting a graphic, and changing the font, font color, and font size. To learn new word processing skills or improve your current skills, click the following links: Microsoft Word, Appleworks, Microsoft Works, and Corel WordPerfect.

1. Creating and Formatting a School Activity Flyer

Problem: As the seventh-grade class trip sponsor, you need to create a flyer to notify parents and students of an upcoming informational meeting. Open your word processing software and create a new flyer as described in the following steps. Use the flyer shown in Figure 1-45 on the next page as an example. (*Hint:* If you do not have the suggested font, use any appropriate font.)

Instructions: Perform the following tasks.

1. Select a class trip destination/title for the project. Display the title in the first heading line centered in 36-point, Comic Sans MS font.
2. Select a school name and display the second heading line centered in 22-point, Arial Narrow, bold font.
3. Choose an appropriate picture, image, or clip-art graphic and insert it centered on the page.
4. Describe the field trip in three lines of text. Display the text in 14-point, Times or Times New Roman font.
5. Create a bulleted list that provides specific information about the meeting. Display the bulleted list with a one-half-inch margin in 12-point, Arial, bold font. Display a portion of each bulleted phrase in orange.
6. Provide contact information at the bottom of the flyer (your name, e-mail address, and current date). Display the information in 14-point, Times or Times New Roman, blue font.
7. Save the document to the location of your choice with a name of your choice. Print the document and then follow your instructor's directions for submitting the assignment.

2. Creating and Formatting a Band Fund-Raiser Flyer

Problem: As the band teacher, you need to create a flyer advertising the fall fund-raiser. Open your word processing software and create a new flyer as described in the following instructions. (*Hint:* If you do not have the suggested font, use any appropriate font.)

Instructions: Display the first heading line in 30-point, Lucinda Sans font. Insert an appropriate picture, image, or clip-art graphic centered on the page. Enter a second heading line below the image in 22-point, Verdana, red font. Next enter four lines of text describing the purpose of the fall fund-raiser in 16-point, Times or Times New Roman font. Create a bulleted list with a one and a half-inch margin in 14-point, Times or Times New Roman font listing the dates, items to be sold, and place of the fund-raising event. Enter a closing phrase following the bulleted list in point, Verdana, blue font. Finally, enter two lines of contact information in 12-point, Times or Times New Roman font that includes the current date, your name, and e-mail address. Display the entire document in bold.

In the Lab

7th Grade Sea Camp Trip
Indian Trails Middle School

The 7th grade class at Indian Trails Middle School has the opportunity to attend Sea Camp April 21 through April 23. This is an exciting educational opportunity! Please join us at the informational meeting to learn more.

- ❖ November 19 **- Join us at 7:00 p.m. in the Media Center**
- ❖ Slide Show **- Watch an informational slide show about Sea Camp**
- ❖ Application Packet **- Packets will be available for distribution**

For more information, please contact:
Mr. Mark Allman
m_allman@ssms.k12.ca.us
November 5, 2009

Figure 1-45

After you have typed and formatted the document, save the document to the location of your choice with a filename of your choice. Print the document and then follow your instructor's directions for submitting the assignment.

3. Creating and Formatting an Announcement Flyer

Problem: You have been asked to create a flyer announcing the upcoming school play.

Instructions: Create a document similar to the flyer illustrated in Figure 1-45. Use appropriate fonts styles, font sizes, font colors, and images. Include the current date, your name, and e-mail address on the bottom of the flyer. After you have typed and formatted the document, save the document to the location of your choice using an appropriate filename. Print the document and then follow your instructor's directions for submitting the assignment.

INTEGRATION IN THE CLASSROOM

1. Your class is studying geometric shapes in architecture. Students will locate pictures of buildings and identify at least three geometric shapes. They will create a flyer that contains the following information: a heading line, an image of the building, a few lines explaining what they found, and a bulleted list with the three different geometric shapes. Create a flyer to use as an example for your students. Include two final lines listing the current date, your name, and your school name.

2. Your students are studying various careers. They conduct research on the Internet and gather information about pay scales, educational requirements, and other benefits of their chosen profession. The students then prepare a flyer to share their information with the class. Create a flyer to present as an example for your students. Use appropriate font styles, font sizes, font colors, and images. Include the current date, your name, and e-mail address on the bottom of the flyer.

3. You are teaching your elementary students about famous painters, including Vincent van Gogh, Pablo Picasso, Henri Matisse, Mary Cassatt, Leonardo da Vinci, Georgia O'Keefe, and Claude Monet. The students work in groups and select their favorite artist. They create a flyer about the life and work of their favorite artist. Create a flyer to present as an example for your students. Use appropriate font styles, sizes, colors, and images. Include the current date, your name, and e-mail address on the bottom of the flyer.

Learn It Online

INSTRUCTIONS: Use the Learn It Online exercises to reinforce your understanding of the chapter concepts and increase your computer, information, and integration literacy. To access dozens of interactive student labs, practice tests, learning games, and more, visit scsite.com/tdc5, click Chapter 1 at the top of the Web page, and then click Learn It Online on the left sidebar.

1. At the Movies

Click the At the Movies link to access thousands of videos that you can match to your curriculum from a very cool site.

2. At the Movies

Click the At the Movies link to watch a video about how the United Nations is part of Second Life.

3. Introduction to Macintosh and PCs

Many software packages provide an introductory tour that offers an overview of the program. These tours usually cover any new features and provide tips on using software; many even use digital media enhancements. To learn more about taking an introductory tour of your personal computer operating system, click the Introduction to Macintosh and PCs link and complete the exercise that follows.

4. Practice Test

Click the Practice Test link. Answer each question. When completed, enter your name and click the Grade Test button to submit the quiz for grading. Make a note of any missed questions. If required, submit your score to your instructor.

5. Who Wants to Be a Computer Genius?

Click the Computer Genius link to find out if you are a computer genius. Directions about how to play the game will be displayed. When you are ready to play, click the Play button. If required, submit your score to your instructor.

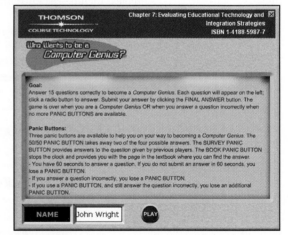

6. Wheel of Terms

Click the Wheel of Terms link to reinforce important terms you learned in this chapter by playing the Shelly Cashman Series version of this popular game. Directions about how to play the game will be displayed. When you are ready to play, click the Play button. If required, submit your score to your instructor.

7. Crossword Puzzle Challenge

Click the Crossword Puzzle link. Complete the puzzle to reinforce skills you learned in this chapter. Directions about how to play the game will be displayed. When you are ready to play, click the Play button. If required, submit the completed puzzle to your instructor.

Special Feature: A World Without Wires

Each time you use your smart phone, tune your television to a soccer game being played on another continent, or listen to satellite radio in your car, you are enjoying the benefits of the world of wireless communications. New wireless devices, including smart phones and pagers, PDAs, Tablet PCs, and notebook computers with high-speed Internet access, simplify and expand your communications abilities. Wireless technology also is changing many other hardware devices that traditionally needed cords to transmit data, such as printers and video projectors.

Wireless communications technology is not new. More than 100 years ago, Guglielmo Marconi sent the first wireless teletype message by using radio waves. Today, Marconi's discoveries allow you to connect peripherals to your desktop computers without using wires and to build a wireless home network. You also can keep in touch with family and associates from anywhere in the world by telephone or e-mail using a variety of wireless products.

Wireless technology has transformed the way people work, communicate, and learn and has won popular acclaim worldwide in a very short period. Even the casual observer notices dramatic changes in the way computers are used in

homes, schools, and businesses, as well as to send e-mail, communicate, access the Internet, share photos, and exchange files. Today's teachers and students are part of this wireless revolution — a revolution that is fundamentally changing the way students and teachers communicate and collaborate with each other.

Although Marconi laid the foundation for wireless technology more than a century ago, today's wireless products and standards represent an evolution of his original discoveries. Each day, the number of wireless devices increases as the price of connectivity decreases. As the world goes wireless, Asia and Western Europe have emerged as world leaders in wireless device use. Experts estimate that over 1 billion wireless devices are in use worldwide and hundreds of millions of wireless devices are sold every year.

This special feature looks at a wide variety of wireless products and illustrates how various segments of society, including K-12 education, use wireless technology. The following section provides a brief overview of wireless networks and some of the terms often associated with wireless technology.

Wireless Networks and Terminology

Several years ago, Nicholas Negroponte, founder and director of MIT's Media Lab, predicted what has come to be known as the Negroponte Flip. Negroponte predicted that communications media that formerly were wireless would become wired, and media that were formerly wired would become wireless. Evidence of the Negroponte Flip can be seen today in the emergence of cable television (wireless TV antennas to wired cables) and the explosion in voice and data services over wireless networks (wired telephones to wireless cell phones).

Wireless networks can be characterized generally by the area they cover. The following sections briefly describe wireless personal area networks, wireless local area networks, and wireless metropolitan and wide area networks.

Wireless Personal Area Networks (WPANs)

A **wireless personal area network (WPAN)** is a short-range wireless network often based on Bluetooth technology. **Bluetooth** technology uses short-range radio waves to transmit data between two Bluetooth devices such as smart phones, headsets, microphones, digital cameras, fax machines, printers, desktop computers, Tablet PCs, notebook computers, and many other wireless devices (Figure 1). Bluetooth-equipped

Figure 1 Bluetooth technology allows users to connect devices wirelessly in a multitude of ways.

devices *discover* each other and form *paired* connections. Examples of paired connections include a cellular telephone and a headset, a keyboard or printer and a PC, or a notebook computer and a PDA. To communicate with each other, Bluetooth devices should be within approximately 10 meters, or 33 feet, of each other; although, some Bluetooth devices will work up to 100 feet or more from each other.

Many devices that traditionally have required wires, such as printers, keyboards, scanners, digital cameras, handheld computers, PDAs, smart phones, microphones, headsets, and notebook computers, are now manufactured with integrated Bluetooth technology. Both Mac OS X and Windows Vista/XP have built-in Bluetooth support that allows users to configure Bluetooth communications easily. For computers and devices not Bluetooth-enabled, you can purchase a Bluetooth wireless port adapter that will convert an existing USB port into a Bluetooth port (Figure 2). Using Bluetooth technology, your notebook or desktop computer can connect wirelessly to a variety of devices. In addition to connecting Bluetooth-enabled devices, you can transfer files easily from a PC to a Macintosh computer and vice versa using Bluetooth technology.

An emerging technology with greater bandwidth capabilities than Bluetooth is **Ultra-Wideband (UWB)**, which provides high-speed, wireless communications to devices throughout a digital home and office. Designed for WPANs, UWB enables wireless connection of multiple devices for transmission of video, audio, and other high-bandwidth data.

Today, most home computer and consumer electronic devices, from digital camcorders and DVD players to high-definition TVs, require wires, turning most home entertainment areas into a wired jungle. UWB and other emerging technologies could eliminate these wires and allow all electronic components for an entire home to be set up and connected to each other without a single wire, a true home without wires.

Wireless Local Area Networks (WLANs)

A **wireless local area network (WLAN)** is a network that uses wireless media, such as radio waves, to connect computers and devices in a

Figure 2 Bluetooth USB adapters, like the one shown, can be purchased for less than $40.

limited space, such as a home, classroom, office building, or school. Wireless LANs are based on the Institute of Electrical and Electronics Engineers (IEEE) 802.11 standard. The term **802.11** refers to a family of specifications developed for wireless local area networks that allows computers and other devices to communicate via radio waves. The nonprofit organization **Wi-Fi Alliance** was established in 1999 and certifies the interoperability of 802.11 products (Figure 3).

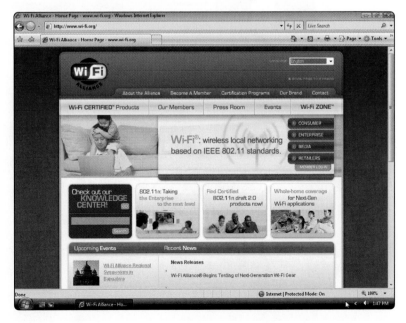

Figure 3 The Wi-Fi Alliance certifies 802.11 products and provides extensive information and resources regarding wireless networks.

Wi-Fi, short for *wireless fidelity*, is a popular term used when referring to any type of 802.11 network. Currently, numerous standards for the 802.11 specification exist. The first and most common is 802.11b; 802.11a, 802.11g, and 802.11n are more recent.

Wi-Fi networking hardware is becoming standard equipment on many notebook computers, PDAs, and other wireless devices. In many public locations, people connect their computers or devices to the Internet wirelessly using Wi-Fi standards through a **public Internet access point.** Users can connect to the Internet if their computers or devices have an appropriate network card and as long as they are in a hot spot. A **hot spot** is an area with the capabilities of wireless Internet connectivity. Two popular hot spot technologies are Wi-Fi and WiMAX. In general, Wi-Fi hot spots have an indoor range of 100 feet and an outdoor range of 300 feet. Wi-Fi hot spots provide wireless network connections to users in public locations such as airports, train stations, hotels, convention centers, ferries, airplanes, cruise ships, schools, campgrounds, marinas, shopping malls, bookstores, libraries, restaurants, and coffee shops (Figure 4). The coverage range for WiMAX hot spots, by contrast, can extend to more than 30 miles and cover entire cities. WiMAX is discussed in more detail in a later section.

Figure 4 Users can access the Web from many locations using Wi-Fi technology.

Some cities are set up as a Wi-Fi mesh network, in which each mesh node routes its data to the next available node until the data reaches its destination, usually an Internet connection. Mesh networking could allow people living in remote areas to connect their networks together for affordable Internet connections.

Some hot spots provide free Internet access, some charge a per-use fee, and others require users to subscribe, to which they pay per access fees, daily fees, or a monthly fee. Per access fees average $3, daily fees range from $5 to $20, and monthly fees range from $20 to $60 for unlimited access, with the higher monthly fee providing greater coverage areas.

Instead of hot spots, some users access the Internet wirelessly through 3G networks. A 3G network uses cellular radio technology to provide users with high-speed wireless Internet connections, as long as they are in the network's range. A 3G network usually includes most major cities and airports. Users access the 3G network through a cellular phone or notebook computer equipped with the appropriate wireless PC Card or Express-Card module. People now have many choices and can use a number of different technologies when accessing the Internet wirelessly (Figure 5).

notebook computer with wireless USB network adapter

notebook computer with wireless PC Card

notebook computer with built-in wireless Centrino technology

Figure 5 Mobile users in this hot spot access the Internet through their notebook computers. One computer uses a wireless USB network adapter, another uses a wireless network PC Card, and another uses Intel's built-in wireless Centrino Duo technology.

Wireless Metropolitan Area Networks (WMAN) and Wireless Wide Area Networks (WWANs)

A **wireless metropolitan area network (WMAN)** is a wireless network designed to cover an urban area. WMANs are being installed in both large and small cities by organizations and for-profit companies dedicated to providing free or for-a-fee wireless access in public spaces.

For example, NYCwireless promotes wireless hot spots in public spaces such as parks, coffee shops, and building lobbies throughout the New York City region (Figure 6). NYCwireless also is working with public and other nonprofit organizations to provide broadband wireless Internet access to underserved communities.

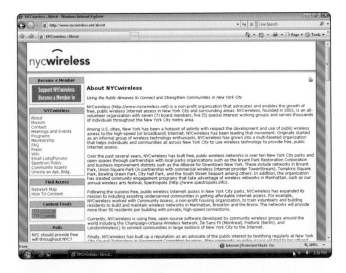

Figure 6 The mission of NYCwireless is to provide free wireless Internet service in public spaces throughout the New York City area.

A **wireless wide area network (WWAN)** is a wireless network that covers a wide geographic area and uses a variety of technologies including radio, satellite, and mobile telephone technologies. A number of major corporations such as Verizon, Sprint, AT&T, MCI, and others are creating wireless wide area networks to provide their customers access to the Internet from any location at any time.

WiMAX, also known as 802.16, is a newer network standard that specifies how wireless devices communicate over the air in a wide area. Using the WiMAX standard, computers or devices with the appropriate WiMAX wireless capability communicate via radio waves with other computers or devices via a WiMAX tower. The WiMAX tower, which can cover up to a 30 mile radius, connects to the Internet or to another WiMAX tower. WiMAX can provide wireless broadband Internet access at a reasonable cost over long distances to business and home users. WiMAX functionality is being incorporated in notebook computers and other wireless devices.

Experts predict that WiMAX service could eventually surpass other broadband Internet access services, such as DSL and cable, because it can reach rural and remote areas easily and inexpensively (Figure 7). The WiMAX standard, similar to the Wi-Fi standard, connects mobile users to the Internet via hot spots. The next generation of video game consoles also plans to support the WiMAX standard.

Figure 7 WiMAX is an emerging technology that one day may replace existing DSL and cable Internet services in homes, schools, and businesses.

Wireless Technology and Society

Messaging is driving the wireless market explosion. Today, over 1 billion people send hundreds of billions of wireless messages monthly. In addition, over 80 percent of teenagers in the United States are sending wireless messages every day. Wireless nodes allow individuals to connect their cellular telephones and notebook computers to wireless Web modems and their handheld computers to school and corporate networks. People can access their e-mail, view photographs, run applications, and more — anytime, any place, and any path.

The following sections describe just a few of the ways that the wireless revolution is impacting society (Figure 8).

Wireless Messaging

Users can send and receive wireless messages to and from smart phones, cellular telephones, or PDAs using text messaging, wireless instant messaging, picture messaging, and video messaging.

TEXT MESSAGING A mobile device with **text messaging** capability allows users to receive short text messages on a smart phone or PDA. Most text messaging services limit messages to a specific number of characters, usually fewer than 300 characters.

WIRELESS INSTANT MESSAGING Wireless **instant messaging** is a real-time Internet communications service that allows wireless mobile devices to exchange messages with one or more mobile devices or online users.

PICTURE MESSAGING Using picture messaging, users can send digital graphics and pictures, as well as text messages, to another smart phone, PDA, or computer. Smart phones and PDAs with picture messaging capability typically have a digital camera built in to the device.

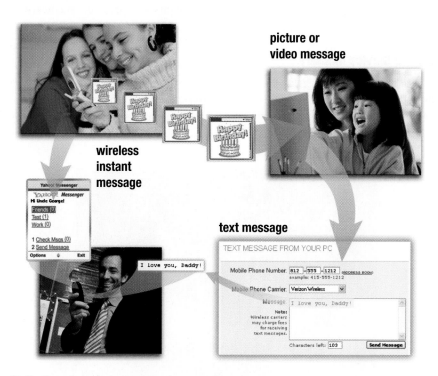

Figure 8 Options for wireless messaging.

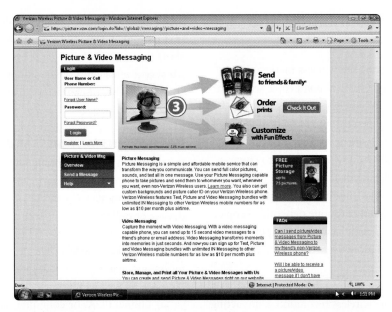

Figure 9 Verizon's wireless video phone allows users to record and send 15-second video clips complete with sound and up to 1000 characters of text to any e-mail address.

VIDEO MESSAGING An emerging technology, **video messaging** allows users to take short video clips (complete with sound and text messaging) with a video phone and send them to another smart phone or computer (Figure 9 above).

Wireless and the Service Industry

Health care professionals, police officers, package couriers, and retail sales personnel are using handheld computers to help them work more efficiently. Ambulance crews use PDAs to collect and transmit patient data while en route to hospitals. Doctors and nurses access patients' records and then record treatments and prescribe medications via handheld computers.

Patrol officers conduct vehicle registration checks (Figure 10) and record crime scene details. Delivery personnel scan bar codes on packages to track pickup and delivery times and record signatures. Retail managers use PDAs to monitor, transfer, and reorder product inventory.

Figure 10 Instant wireless communications and wireless devices have changed the way police officers and other professionals do their jobs.

Wireless and Home Networking

A **wireless home network** connects your home computers and peripherals without the use of wires. Family members simultaneously can collaborate on projects, share digital files, print photos and documents, and access the Internet. Notebook computer users can roam around the house and work from 150 to 1,500 feet from the wireless access point, depending on the type of wireless home network installed. Many home networking products are based on Wi-Fi standards and are becoming more affordable, plentiful, and easy to use; some manufacturers claim a buyer can link two computers together and to the Internet in less than one hour for less than $100. Figure 11 shows the steps to set up a wireless home network.

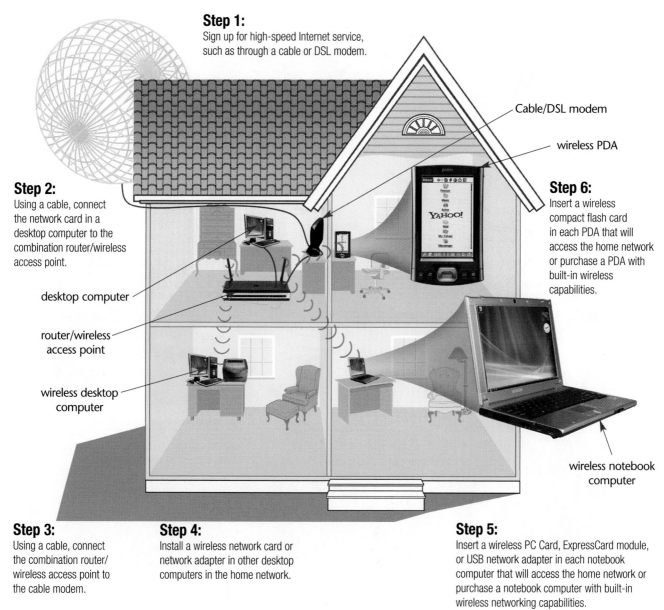

Step 1:
Sign up for high-speed Internet service, such as through a cable or DSL modem.

Step 2:
Using a cable, connect the network card in a desktop computer to the combination router/wireless access point.

desktop computer

router/wireless access point

wireless desktop computer

Cable/DSL modem

wireless PDA

Step 6:
Insert a wireless compact flash card in each PDA that will access the home network or purchase a PDA with built-in wireless capabilities.

wireless notebook computer

Step 3:
Using a cable, connect the combination router/wireless access point to the cable modem.

Step 4:
Install a wireless network card or network adapter in other desktop computers in the home network.

Step 5:
Insert a wireless PC Card, ExpressCard module, or USB network adapter in each notebook computer that will access the home network or purchase a notebook computer with built-in wireless networking capabilities.

Figure 11 This figure shows the steps necessary to set up a wireless home network.

Wireless and Global Positioning

Millions of hikers, boaters, pilots, drivers, and other navigators never feel lost with the aid of global positioning system (GPS) devices. These products rely on 24 satellites that circle the Earth twice a day in very precise orbits and transmit data back to Earth. The GPS products then use between 3 to 12 of these satellites to determine the receivers' precise geographic locations (Figure 12). Many GPS devices include color mapping capability that gives detail for any United States city. GPS modules also are available for handheld computers.

Step 1:

GPS satellites orbit Earth. Every one thousandth of a second, each satellite sends a signal that indicates its current position to the GPS receiver.

Step 2:

A GPS receiver (such as in a car, a wearable device, a smart phone, a handheld device, or a collar) determines its location on Earth by analyzing at least 3 separate satellite signals from the 24 satellites in orbit.

Figure 12 How GPS works.

Wireless Technology and Education

Wireless networking is becoming commonplace in institutions of higher education. According to a recent Campus Computing Survey of the Campus Computing Project, most of the institutions that were surveyed reported the use of WLANs, and wireless networks now reach half (51.2 percent) of college classrooms. "Wireless is a great thing," says Kenneth C. Green, founding director of The Campus Computing Project. "It fosters access, mobility, and collaborative work among students and faculty."

For example, the University of Central Florida (UCF) has made wireless networking available over its entire campus—in classroom buildings, the library, administrative offices, the student union, residence halls, and even outdoor learning locations where students gather (Figure 13). In addition, students who visit the UCF library can use their wireless-enabled notebook computers or they can check out wireless notebook computers for use in the library.

Today, schools and institutions of higher learning use wireless networks to access the same applications used on wired networks: e-mail, Web access, and instant messaging. The main advantage that wireless brings is flexibility, which allows users to access e-mail and the Web at anytime and from any location. Wireless networks also offer other unique benefits, such as the ability to easily set up temporary locations, network buildings that would be difficult or impossible to

UCF photos.

Figure 13 The campus of the University of Central Florida and all new classroom buildings are designed to take advantage of the benefits of wireless networking, allowing students access to information, their classes, and each other from any campus location.

wire, or provide connections to every student in a classroom, auditorium, or outdoor setting. Some schools and school districts are also finding that setting up a wireless network is cheaper than hardwiring buildings. In some cases, a wireless cart or lab is wheeled from classroom to classroom for internet access as needed. Cost and convenience are driving more school to choose wireless network access rather than to hardwire particular buildings or an entire campus.

K-12 Schools

Every day, schools all over the world are discovering new benefits and advantages of using wireless networks and wireless technologies. The following are just a few of the emerging wireless technologies that are beginning to transform our K-12 schools.

WIRELESS CLASSROOMS Teachers can now use interactive wireless computers to determine how well students comprehend class material. They can ask students to respond to a multiple-choice or true-false question using a wireless keypad resembling a remote control (Figure 14). Within seconds, a receiver captures students' responses, and a computer tabulates

the results and tracks their scores and progress daily. Students react exceedingly well to this type of interactivity in the assessment process. Another interactive device is the CPS Chalkboard that gives teachers the ability to turn the computer into a presentation system and the ability to interact with the computer and teach from anywhere in the classroom.

WIRELESS PROJECTS Programs, such as the LEGO MINDSTORMS Education NXT, enable students to discover physics, science, technology, engineering, and math in a fun, engaging, and hands-on way (Figure 15). The project combines sensor capabilities, interactive motors, programming software, and wireless Bluetooth technology. Students design, build, and program fully functional robots. The students become young scientists as they carry out simple investigations, calculate and measure, and then record and present their results. Students use techniques that are used in the real world of science, engineering, and design. Finally, students are able to command the robot's functions through wireless technology. Projects that involve wireless functionality are another way that wireless is impacting education.

Figure 14 Every student is involved in the learning process when using Classroom Performance System response pads and **Exam**View ® educational products by eInstruction ® Corporation.

Figure 15 Hundreds of wireless tools for education are being developed for teachers to use with today's students. Shown is MINDSTORMS from LEGO.

WIRELESS GAMES Wireless technology is expanding the types of games available and the ability to incorporate more than one learner at a time. For example, the Wii from Nintendo uses wireless technology that allows users to be physically active while using the game. As a result of these advances, wireless games are another wireless trend impacting education.

WIRELESS SCHOOL BUSES Today, school districts are installing wireless Internet access in their school busses. The long dull ride on a school bus is being transformed into a mobile classroom and providing opportunities for learning. One idea from a professor at Vanderbilt University is to have students download lessons and work on the assignments while riding on the bus. These emerging trends are especially beneficial for students that live in isolated areas or congested cities, whose bus ride many last an hour or more. In addition, some school districts are adding GPS capability to their school buses, which allows districts to better manage drivers, routes, and cost (Figure 16). In addition, districts can monitor in real time exactly where all of their school busses are, which ones are running late due to weather or traffic, provide peace of mind to parents, and more. The majority of school buses could be GPS equipped and provide Internet access for students in just a few years.

This trend may also extend past the school buses, by extending the wireless revolution to all kinds of commuters and providing Internet access on public buses and trains. Even automobiles have the capability to be connected to a wireless network. Companies that provide wireless computer systems are marketing their products to parents and teachers as a back-seat learning tool. Soon students will be able to use the car ride as a time for learning.

Wireless Connectivity — Any Place, Any Time, and Any Path

As technology advances and as the Internet becomes more integrated into the personal lives of students, this new "wireless generation" wants always-on access. Students need to access instruction in meaningful learning environments, and they need this access from any place, any time, and any path — in the classroom, on the school bus, in the library, in the car, or at home with parents.

Figure 16 Internet access and GPS tracking are emerging trends for school buses. Shown is a company that specializes in providing GPS equipment and access to districts for their school buses

Wireless Summary

Your pockets, purses, book bags, and backpacks may be overflowing with small electronic devices, but the wireless revolution is making headway to combine some of these products and simplify your life. Wireless networks are growing throughout the world, driven by convenience, cost, and access and are changing forever the ways people communicate and learn and how they work at home, school, or the office. At one time, computing abilities were limited by the length of wires; now communications and computing have no physical limitations. Wireless communication has removed the wires and opened the doors to anyplace, anytime communications and connectivity — creating a world without boundaries and a world without wires.

Communications, Networks, the Internet, and the World Wide Web

Objectives

After completing this chapter, you will be able to do the following:
[ISTE NETS-T Standards I A-B, II B-E, III A-D, IV B, V A-D, VI A-E]

- Define communications

- Identify the basic components of a communications system

- Describe how and why network computers are used in schools and school districts

- Explain how the Internet works

- Describe the World Wide Web portion of the Internet

- Explain how Web documents are linked to one another

- Explain the use of Web browser software

- Explain how to use a Web search tool to find information

- Identify several types of multimedia products available on the Web

- Explain how Internet services such as e-mail, newsgroups, chat rooms, and instant messaging work

- Describe the educational implications of the Internet and the World Wide Web

- Describe different ways to connect to the Internet and the World Wide Web

Communications and networks are the fastest growing areas of computer technology and digital media. Adding tremendously to this growth is the popularity of the Internet and the World Wide Web (also called the Web), which is a service of the Internet that supports graphics and multimedia. Together, the Internet and the World Wide Web represent one of today's most exciting uses of networks. Already, these networks have changed the way people gather information, conduct research, shop, take classes, and collaborate on projects dramatically.

Businesses encourage you to browse their Web-based catalogs, send them e-mail for customer service requests, and buy their products online. The government publishes thousands of informational Web pages to provide individuals with materials such as legislative updates, tax forms, and e-mail addresses for members of Congress. Colleges have virtual tours of their campuses on the Web, accept applications online, and offer thousands of classes on the Internet.

Web Info

For more information on how the Web is expanding student learning, visit the Teachers Discovering Computers Web site (*scsite.com/tdc5*), click Chapter 2, click Web Info, and then click Expanding Student Learning.

Today, communications media and networks are breaking down the walls of a classroom, allowing students to view the world beyond where they live and learn. The Internet continues to expand student learning beyond the covers of a textbook to include interactive, up-to-date, Web-based content. Never before has any technology opened so many opportunities for learning.

The future will bring even more exciting applications of these technologies. Federal and state governments, private businesses, and organizations are investing billions of dollars in Internet-related hardware and software for K-12 schools. As a result of this substantial investment, most public schools are equipping their classrooms with multimedia computers and providing teachers and students with access to the Internet. This chapter discusses communications, networks, the Internet, and the World Wide Web; explains how they work; and reviews how students, teachers, and administrators can use these technologies to communicate, obtain almost unlimited educational information, and enhance student learning.

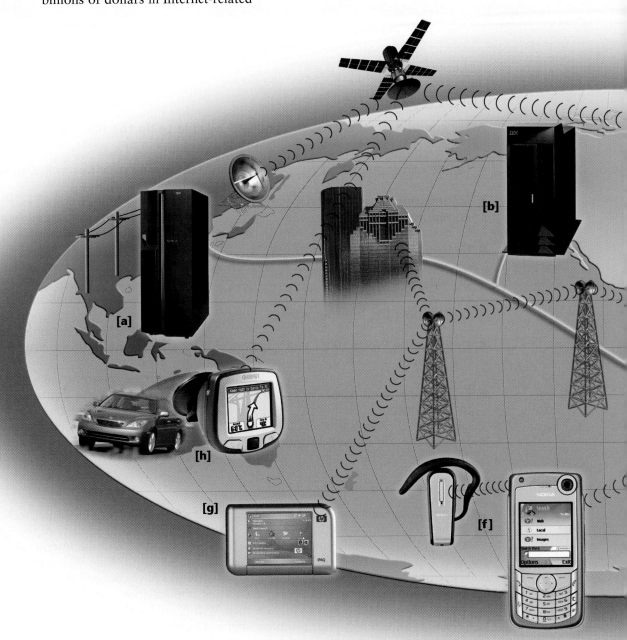

What Is Communications?

Communications, sometimes called **telecommunications**, describes a process in which two or more computers or devices transfer data, instructions, and information. The ability to communicate information instantly and accurately has changed the way people conduct business and interact with each other, and the way students learn. Electronic mail (e-mail), voice mail, facsimile (fax), telecommuting, online services, videoconferencing, the Internet, and the World Wide Web are examples of applications that rely on communications technology.

Communications Networks

Computers were stand-alone devices when first introduced. As computers became more widely used, companies designed hardware and software so computers could communicate with one another. Originally, developers created communication capabilities only for large computers. Today, even the smallest computers and handheld devices can communicate with each other. Figure 2-1 shows a sample communications system, which can contain all types of devices.

Integration Strategies

To explore ideas on integrating 21st century communications tools in your curriculum, visit the Teachers Discovering Computers Web site (*scsite.com/tdc5*), click Chapter 2, and then click Digital Media Corner.

[c]

[d]

[e]

Figure 2-1 An example of a communications system. Some devices that serve as sending devices and receiving devices are [a] mainframe computers, [b] servers, [c] desktop computers, [d] notebook computers, [e] Tablet PCs, [f] smart phones, [g] Internet-enabled PDAs, and [h] GPS receivers. The communications channel consists of telephone and power lines, cable television and other underground lines, microwave stations, and satellites.

Web Info

For more information on communications networks, visit the Teachers Discovering Computers Web site (*scsite.com/tdc5*), click Chapter 2, click Web Info, and then click Communications Networks.

A communications **network** is a collection of computers and other equipment organized to share data, information, hardware, and software. A basic communications system consists of the following equipment:

- Two computers, one to send and one to receive data

- Communications devices that send and receive data

- A communications channel over which data is sent

This basic model also includes **communications software**, which are programs that manage the transmission of data between computers.

A **communications channel** is the path that data follows as the data is transmitted from the sending equipment to the receiving equipment in a communications system.

Communications channels are made up of **transmission media**, which are the physical materials or other means used to establish a communications channel. The most widely used transmission medium is twisted-pair cable. **Twisted-pair cable** consists of pairs of plastic-coated copper wires twisted together (Figure 2-2). Standard telephone lines in your home also use twisted-pair cables. Other examples of transmission media include coaxial cable, fiber-optic cable, microwave transmission, communications satellites, and wireless transmissions.

Digital signals are individual electrical pulses that a computer uses to represent data. Telephone equipment originally was designed to carry only voice transmission, which comprises a continuous electrical wave called an **analog signal**. For telephone lines to carry data, a communications device called a **modem** converts digital signals into analog signals.

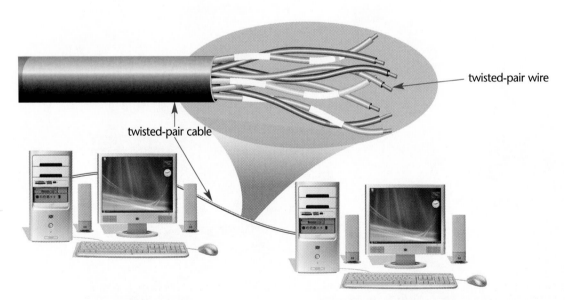

twisted-pair wire

twisted-pair cable

Figure 2-2 Twisted-pair cables often are used to connect personal computers to one another or a personal computer to a regular telephone line. They are inexpensive and easily installed.

The word modem comes from a combination of the words modulate, to change a digital signal into sound or analog signal, and demodulate, to convert an analog signal into a digital signal (Figure 2-3a). Computers at both the sending and receiving ends of this communications channel must have a modem for data transmission to occur. At the sending computer, a modem converts digital signals from the computer to analog signals for transmission over regular telephone lines. At the receiving computer, a modem converts analog signals back to digital signals.

A number of different kinds of modems are in use today. Most computers purchased for home use include internal modems that can transmit data at rates up to approximately 56,000 bits per second (56K modem). An **internal modem** is built on a circuit board that is installed inside a computer and attaches to a telephone socket using a standard telephone cord. Today, many home and small business users are using cable modems and DSL modems, also called digital modems, which provide significantly higher data access rates than 56K (Figure 2-3b). Cable modems provide

[a] digital to analog to digital communications channel

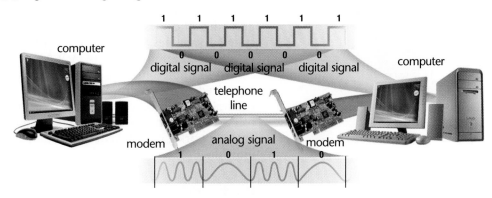

[b] all digital communications channel

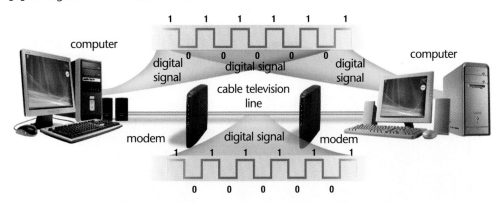

Figure 2-3 A modem connects a communications channel, such as a telephone line or a cable television line, to a sending or receiving device such as a computer. Depending on the type of communications channel, a modem may need to convert digital signals to analog signals (and vice versa) before transferring data, instructions, and information to or from a sending or receiving device.

broadband access over a cable television (CATV) network and DSL modems provide broadband access over telephone lines. These newer types of modems are discussed later in this chapter. Networked computers contain a network interface card (Figure 2-4). **Network interface cards (NICs)** connect computers directly to a school or business network without using a modem. Networks are classified as either local area networks or wide area networks.

Figure 2-4 Network cards are available for both desktop and notebook computers.

LOCAL AREA NETWORKS

A **local area network (LAN)** is a communications network that covers a limited geographical area, such as a school, office, building, or group of buildings. A LAN consists of a number of computers connected to a central computer, or server. A **server** manages the resources on a network and provides a centralized storage area for software programs and data. A **wireless LAN (WLAN)** is a LAN that uses no wires. Instead of wires, a WLAN uses wireless media, such as radio waves.

WIDE AREA NETWORKS

A **wide area network (WAN)** covers a large geographical region (such as a city or school district) and uses regular telephone lines, digital cables, microwaves, wireless systems, satellites, or other combinations of communications channels. A WAN can consist of numerous local area networks organized into one larger network. For example, a large school district may establish a WAN that consists of dozens of local area networks, each LAN representing an individual school.

HOME NETWORKS

If you have multiple computers in your home or home office, you can connect all of them together with a **home network** (Figure 2-5). Some advantages to having a home network

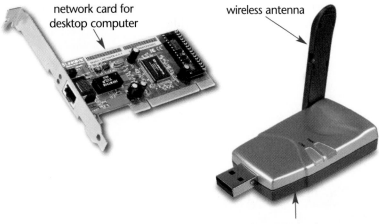

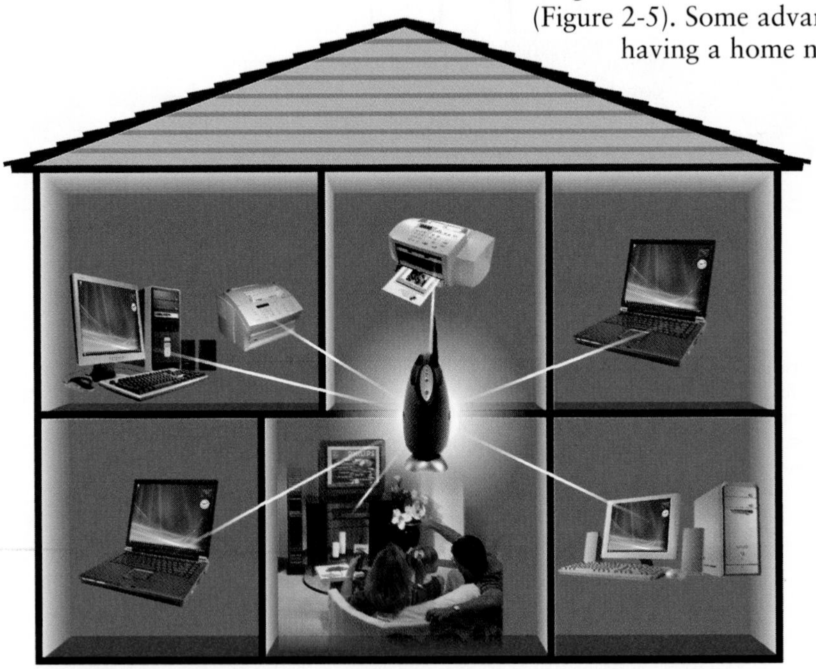

network card for desktop computer

wireless antenna

USB network adapter

Figure 2-5 An example of a home network.

include the following: all computers in the house can be connected to the Internet at the same time, each computer can access files and programs on the other computers, and all computers can share the same peripherals, such as a scanner, printer, or DVD drive.

Home networks can be either wired or wireless. To network computers and devices that span multiple rooms or floors in a home, it may be more convenient to use a wireless network. Local cable and other Internet service providers will help you set up a wireless home network for free or for a minimal installation charge. Monthly fees usually include the rental fee for a wireless modem. You can learn more about wireless networks in the special feature, A World Without Wires, that follows Chapter 1.

Networking the Classroom, School, and District

Due to extensive federal, state, and local funding, virtually all schools and school districts in the United States have networked their computers. Schools have

installed networks for three reasons: (1) to share hardware and software resources, (2) to enable communications among schools and other organizations, and (3) to connect students and teachers to the Internet.

A school network server connects all of the computers located within a school. A server manages the resources on a network and provides a centralized storage area for software programs and data. Typically, any teachers and students who use the network can access software and data on the server, although school or network administrators can limit access to specific records and software applications.

As an example of how a school district might network its computers, consider the Washington County Public School District, which consists of one high school (Ridgedale High School), two middle schools (Dresden and Fall Hills Middle Schools), and three elementary schools (Acorn, Johnson, and Martin Luther King Elementary Schools).

Martin Luther King Elementary School is a small school with 14 classrooms. Each classroom has three Macintosh computers and a printer connected to the school's local area network (Figure 2-6). Also

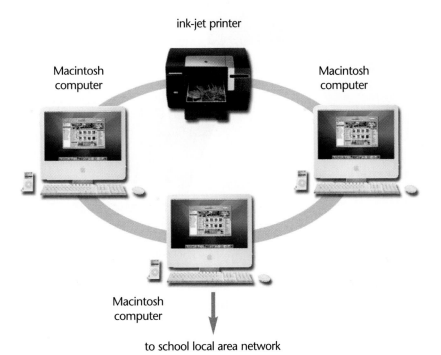

ink-jet printer

Macintosh computer

Macintosh computer

Macintosh computer

to school local area network

Figure 2-6 In each classroom, three Macintosh computers and a printer are connected to the school's local area network.

connected to Martin Luther King Elementary's local area network is a computer lab that contains 24 networked Macintosh computers and 4 additional computers that are used by school administrators and staff. In total, Martin Luther King Elementary's local area network consists of Macintosh computers and numerous printers all connected to a central server (Figure 2-7).

The local area network at Martin Luther King Elementary and the district's five other school LANs are connected to a large-capacity server and its associated equipment located at the Washington County Public School District's Central Office, which includes PCs. Together, these networks form a wide area network that contains more than 600 networked Macintosh computers and PCs (Figure 2-8).

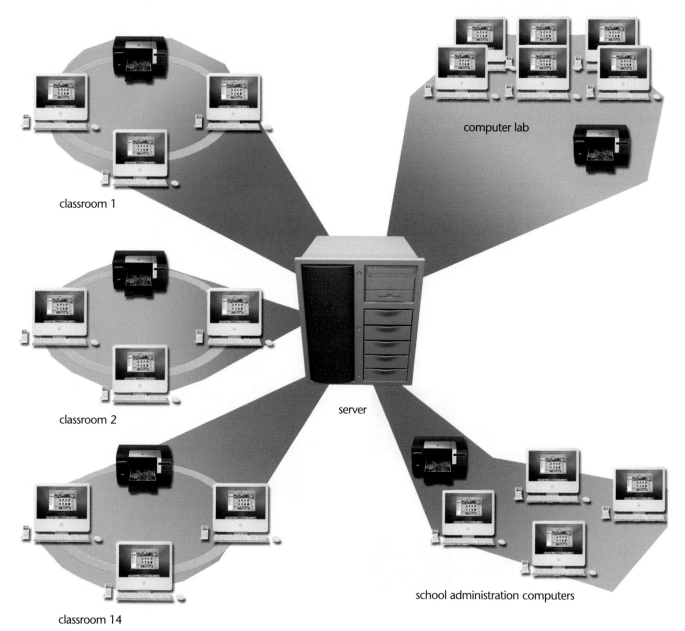

Figure 2-7 The school's local area network consists of computers in 14 classrooms, in the computer lab, and four school administration computers.

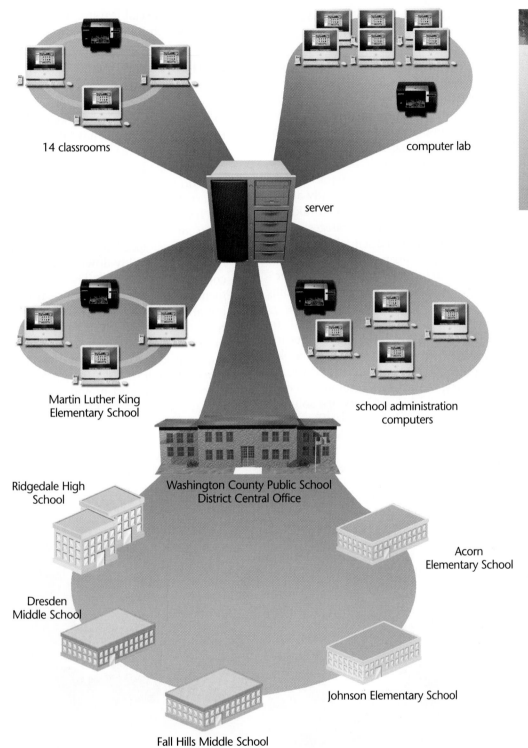

Integration Strategies

For information on how to deal with censoring in today's rapidly growing school networks, visit the Teachers Discovering Computers Web site (*scsite.com/tdc5*), click Chapter 2, and then click Education Issues.

14 classrooms

computer lab

server

Martin Luther King Elementary School

school administration computers

Ridgedale High School

Washington County Public School District Central Office

Acorn Elementary School

Dresden Middle School

Johnson Elementary School

Fall Hills Middle School

Figure 2-8 The school district's wide area network consists of the local area networks of six member schools all connected to a server located at the district's central office.

WIRELESS SCHOOLS AND CLASSROOMS

Not long ago, teachers used traditional telephones that were connected to a telephone company by cables to communicate with friends, family, and fellow teachers. Today, wireless technology allows you to keep in touch with friends and family from anywhere in the world, using a variety of devices: a smart pager, a smart phone, a handheld computer, or a notebook computer with high-speed Internet access.

Teachers and students already are part of the wireless revolution that is taking place in education. Many colleges, universities, and K-12 schools have installed wireless networks and are utilizing wireless notebook computers and other wireless devices. Many experts, including Steve Jobs, CEO of Apple Computers, believe that the future of educational computing, in both K-12 and higher education, is wireless networks, wireless notebook computers, and other wireless devices.

Today, most major computer manufacturers provide wireless network solutions and devices for K-12 schools (Figure 2-9). Devices include wireless keyboards, wireless notebook computers, wireless mobile labs, and many other devices. The use of wireless networks and devices in K-12 schools and classrooms is discussed in future chapters and in the special feature, A World Without Wires, which follows Chapter 1.

HIGH-SPEED OR BROADBAND ACCESS

Over the past 5 to 10 years, school districts have concentrated on installing local and wide area networks so that their teachers and students have Internet access in their classrooms or at the point of instruction. Many school networks, however, do not provide their classroom computers with continuous high-speed access to the Internet; access speeds vary greatly. Students and teachers must be provided continuous high-speed access to allow them to find and quickly download complex, content-rich resources. The federal government recognizes this and is spearheading initiatives to provide broadband access to K-12 schools. Networks and media that use **broadband** technologies transmit signals at much faster speeds than traditional network configurations. A recent federal report to the president and Congress stated that the promise of widely available, high-quality, Web-based education is made possible by technological and communications trends that could lead to important digital media–based educational applications over the next few years.

Figure 2-9 An example of a mobile wireless lab. Instead of taking your students to a school's computer lab, the lab is brought to your students.

The Benefits of Computer Networks in Education

One benefit of networking is that administrators, teachers, and students can share computer hardware, software, and data resources available throughout the school district. For example, administrators can maintain all student records and information securely at one central location. Teachers and administrative staff who have a need for access to student records can access various student information databases from just about any networked computer at any location.

By far, the most important benefit of networking school computers is that administrators, teachers, and students can access the unlimited educational resources available on the Internet and communicate with other educators and students all over the world instantly (Figure 2-10). In brief, networking provides schools with limitless possibilities for teaching and learning. Without question, the introduction of networks and the Internet into today's schools has had and continues to have a dramatic impact on the current generation of teachers and students.

Figure 2-10 The Internet is useful as a tool to hold students' attention and even amaze them.

What Is the Internet?

You have learned that a network, such as the one installed at Martin Luther King Elementary School, is a collection of computers and devices connected via communications devices and media. Recall also that the world's largest network is the **Internet**, which is a worldwide collection of networks that link together millions of businesses, governments, educational institutions, and individuals using modems, telephone lines, and other communications devices and media (Figure 2-11). Each of these networks provides resources and data that add to the abundance of goods, services, and information accessible via the Internet.

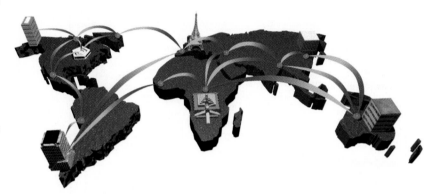

Figure 2-11 The world's largest network is the Internet, which is a worldwide collection of networks that link together millions of businesses, governments, educational institutions, and individuals.

Networks that constitute the Internet, also called the **Net**, consist of federal, regional, local, and international networks. Public or private organizations own individual networks that constitute the Internet; no single organization owns or controls the Internet. Each organization on the Internet is responsible only for maintaining its own network.

Today, more than one billion users around the world connect to the Internet for a variety of reasons. Figure 2-12 on the next page illustrates sites on the Internet that represent some of the following uses:

- Access a wealth of information, news, research, and educational material.

- Conduct business or complete banking and investing transactions.

- Access sources of entertainment and leisure, such as online games, magazines, and vacation-planning guides.

- Shop for goods and services.

- Explore virtual worlds.

Web Info

For tips and ideas on using the Internet with digital kids, visit the Teachers Discovering Computers Web site (*scsite.com/tdc5*), click Chapter 2, click Web Info, and then click Internet.

■ Meet and converse with people around the world through discussion groups, instant messaging, blogs, wikis, or chat rooms.

■ Access other computers and exchange or share files.

■ Send messages to or receive messages from other connected users.

■ Download and listen to music or download and watch movies.

■ Take a course or access educational materials.

To allow you to perform these and other activities, the Internet provides a variety of services, such as the World Wide Web, e-mail, File Transfer

[a] Web

[b] (e-mail)

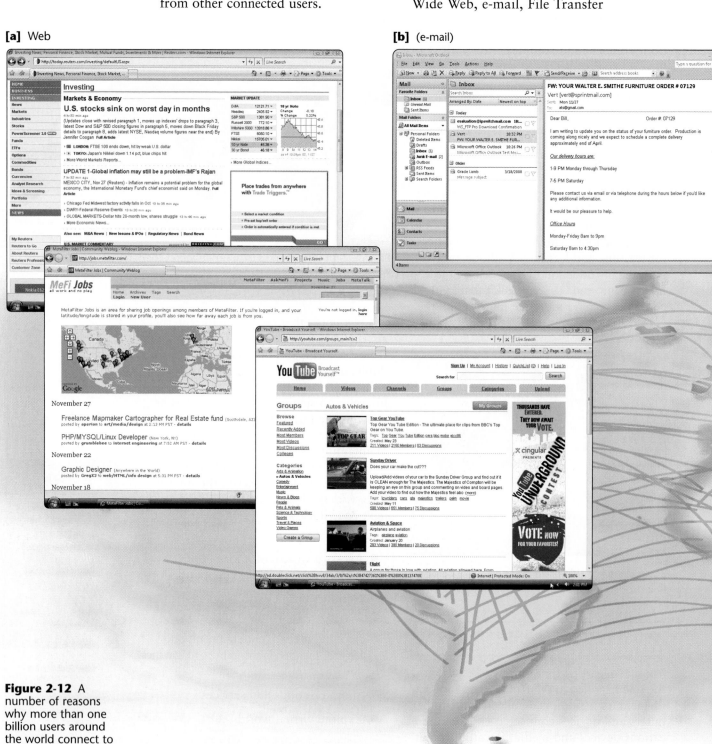

Figure 2-12 A number of reasons why more than one billion users around the world connect to the Internet.

Protocol (FTP), newsgroups, mailing lists, instant messaging, chat rooms, and Internet telephony. These services, along with a discussion of the history of the Internet and how the Internet works, are explained in the following sections.

History of the Internet

Although the history of the Internet is relatively short, its growth has been explosive. The Internet has it roots in a networking project of the U.S. Department of Defense's **Advanced Research Projects Agency** (**ARPA**). ARPA's goal was to build

[c] (FTP – File Transfer Protocol)

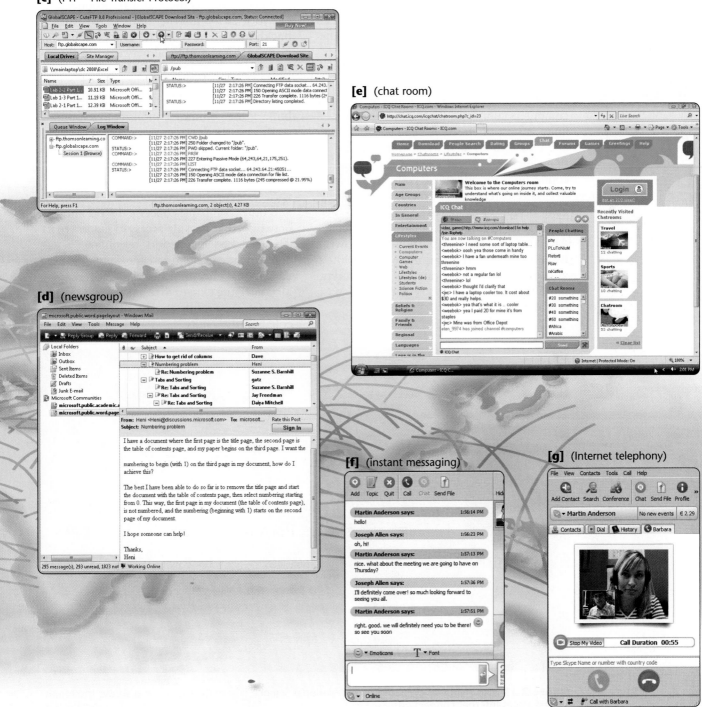

[d] (newsgroup)

[e] (chat room)

[f] (instant messaging)

[g] (Internet telephony)

Web Info

For the history of the Internet, visit the Teachers Discovering Computers Web site (*scsite.com/tdc5*), click Chapter 2, click Web Info, and then click History.

a network that (1) would allow scientists at different locations to share information and collaborate on military and scientific projects and (2) could function even if part of the network was disabled or destroyed by a disaster, such as a nuclear war. That network, called **ARPANET,** became functional in September 1969, effectively linking together scientific and academic researchers in the United States.

The original ARPANET was a wide area network consisting of four main computers, located at the University of California at Los Angeles, the Stanford Research Institute, the University of California at Santa Barbara, and the University of Utah. Each of these four computers served as the network's host. A **host** is the main computer in a network of computers connected by communications links. A host often stores and transfers data and messages on high-speed communications lines and provides network connections for additional computers.

As researchers and others realized the great benefit of using ARPANET's electronic mail to share information and notes, ARPANET underwent phenomenal growth. By 1984, ARPANET had more than 1000 individual computers linked as hosts (today, more than 350 million host computers exist on the Internet).

To take further advantage of the high-speed communications offered by ARPANET, organizations decided to connect entire networks to ARPANET. In 1986, for example, the **National Science Foundation (NSF)** connected its huge network of five supercomputer centers, called **NSFnet,** to ARPANET. This configuration of complex networks and hosts became known as the Internet (Figure 2-13).

Because of its advanced technology, NSFnet served as the major backbone network of the Internet until 1995. A **backbone** is a high-speed network that connects regional and local networks to the Internet. Other computers then connect to these regional and local networks to access the Internet. A backbone thus handles the bulk of the communications activity, or **traffic,** on the Internet.

In 1995, NSFnet terminated its backbone network on the Internet to return to its purpose as a research network. Today, a variety of corporations, commercial firms, and other companies operate the backbone networks that provide access to the Internet. These backbone networks, telephone companies, cable and satellite companies, educational institutions, and the government all contribute extensive resources to the Internet. As a result, the Internet is a truly collaborative entity.

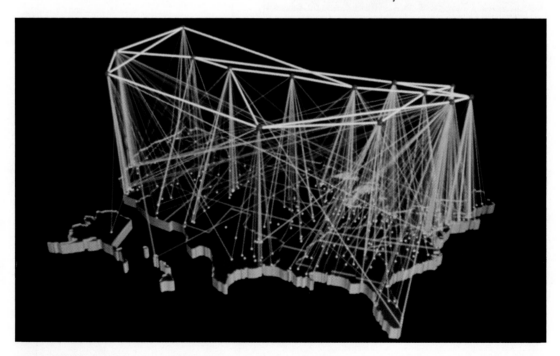

Figure 2-13 This map was prepared by the National Science Foundation (NSF) and shows the major United States Internet connections.

Over the years, the total number of computers connected to the original network increased steadily and within the last few years, explosively. Today, experts estimate that hundreds of millions of computers distribute information over the Internet, including those at virtually all K-12 schools.

A new Internet, called **Internet2 (I2)**, is an extremely high-speed network that develops and tests advanced Internet technologies for research, teaching, and learning. Members of Internet2 include more than 200 U.S. universities in cooperation with 70 leading corporations, 45 government agencies, laboratories and other institutions of higher learning, as well as over 50 international partner organizations.

How the Internet Works

Computers and other digital devices connected to the Internet work together to transfer data around the world. When a computer sends data over the Internet, the computer's software divides the data into small pieces, called **packets**. The data in a packet might be part of an e-mail message, a file, a document, a graphic, or a request for a file. Each packet contains the data, as well as the recipient (destination), origin (sender), and sequence information needed to reassemble the data at the destination. Packets travel along the fastest path available to the recipient's computer via hardware devices called **routers** (Figure 2-14).

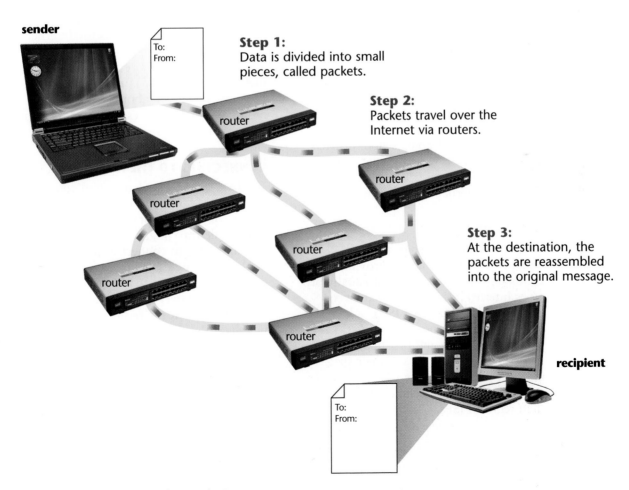

sender

Step 1:
Data is divided into small pieces, called packets.

Step 2:
Packets travel over the Internet via routers.

Step 3:
At the destination, the packets are reassembled into the original message.

recipient

Figure 2-14 How data travels over the Internet.

If the most direct path to the destination is overloaded or not operating, routers send the packets along alternate paths. Although each packet may arrive out of sequence, the destination computer uses the sequence information contained in each packet to reassemble the original message, file, document, or request. **Packet switching** is the technique of breaking a message into individual packets, sending the packets along the best route available, and reassembling the data.

For a technique such as packet switching to work, all of the devices on the network must follow certain standards or protocols. A **communications protocol** specifies the rules that define how devices connect to each other and transmit data over a network. The protocol used to define packet switching on the Internet is **Transmission Control Protocol/Internet Protocol (TCP/IP)**.

Data sent over the Internet travels over networks and communications lines owned and operated by many companies. You can connect to these networks in one of several ways. Some users connect to the Internet through an Internet service provider (ISP) or an online service provider (OSP), often using a modem to establish a connection. Organizations such as schools and businesses provide Internet access for students and employees by connecting their own network to an ISP. Some school districts and states also provide Internet services for teachers and administrators so they can access the Internet from their homes.

ACCESS PROVIDERS

An **Internet service provider (ISP)** is a regional or national access provider. A **regional ISP** is a business that usually provides Internet access to a specific geographic area. A **national ISP** is a business that provides Internet access in cities and towns nationwide and broadband access in many locations. Because of their size, national ISPs offer more services and generally have a larger technical support staff than regional ISPs.

Like an ISP, an **online service provider (OSP)** also provides access to the Internet, but such online services have members-only features that offer special content and a variety of services. Typical content and services include news, weather, educational information, financial information, hardware and software guides, games, entertainment, news, and travel information. For this reason, the fees for using an online service usually are slightly higher than fees for an ISP. Popular OSPs are America Online (AOL) and Microsoft Network (MSN).

A **wireless Internet service provider (WISP)** is a company that provides wireless Internet access to computers with wireless modems or access devices or to Internet-enabled mobile computers or devices. Internet-enabled mobile devices include PDAs, smart phones, and smart watches. An antenna on the computer or device typically sends signals through the airwaves to communicate with a wireless ISP. Some examples of wireless ISPs include AT&T Wireless, Cingular Wireless, T-Mobile, and Verizon Wireless.

Users and schools access the Internet through regional or national ISPs, OSPs, and WISPs using a variety of connection methods (Figure 2-15). Individual user accounts vary from about $7 to $25 per month for dial-up access to $20 to $55 per month for higher-speed access.

CONNECTING TO THE INTERNET

Teachers and students often connect to the Internet through their school network. When connecting from home or from the road while traveling, some individuals use dial-up access to connect to the Internet. With **dial-up access**, you use your computer and a modem to dial into an ISP or online service over regular telephone lines. The computer at the receiving end, whether at an ISP or online service, also uses a modem. Dial-up access has traditionally been an easy way for mobile and home users to connect to the Internet to check e-mail, read the news, and access other information. Because dial-up access

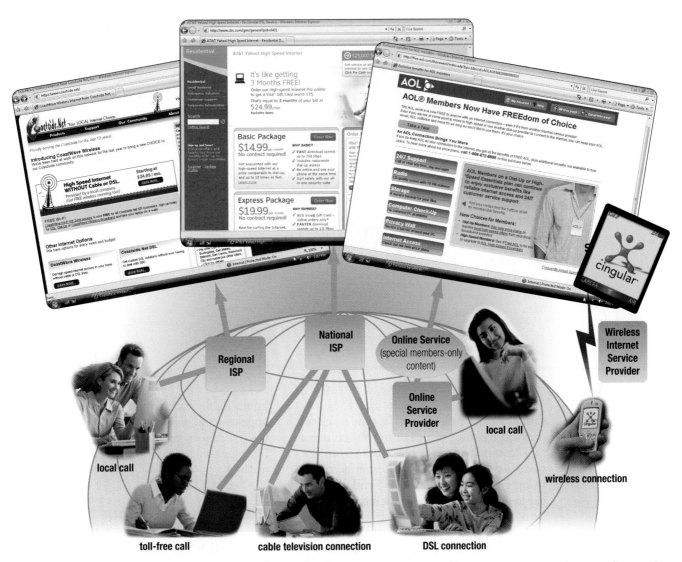

Figure 2-15 Common ways to access the Internet are through a regional or national Internet service provider, an online service provider, or a wireless Internet service provider.

uses standard telephone lines, the speed of the connection is limited.

Because dial-up access is slow-speed technology, many home and business users either already have or are opting for higher-speed broadband Internet connections through DSL, cable television networks, satellite, and power lines.

With more than 100 million homes wired for cable television, it is not surprising that more and more users are getting Internet access from their cable company. Road Runner is a popular high-speed CATV

online service provided by AOL Time Warner. CATV uses a high-speed **cable modem** that sends and receives data over the cable television network.

As shown in Figure 2-16 on the next page, CATV service enters your home through a single line and then is split between your television and your cable modem, which, in turn, is connected to your computer. Access speeds using CATV can be significantly faster than access speeds using dial-up, in many cases 20 to 50 times faster.

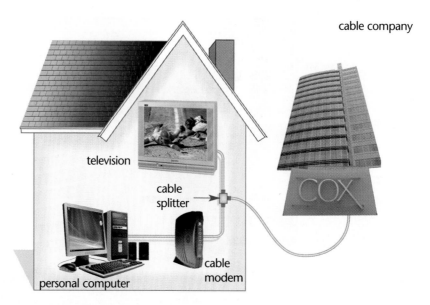
cable company

television

cable splitter

cable modem

personal computer

Figure 2-16 A typical cable modem installation.

Another high-speed alternative is a **digital subscriber line (DSL)** that transmits data on existing standard telephone lines. DSL can provide Internet access from 25 to 150 times faster than Internet access using a dial-up connection. Similar to a cable or DSL modem, a **satellite modem** provides high-speed Internet connections. It communicates with a satellite via a satellite dish. Installation and monthly access fees for DSL, CATV, and satellite services vary.

All three — cable, DSL, and satellite modems — use broadband technologies. In addition to access speed, another advantage of using CATV, DSL, and satellite services is that they are dedicated or always-on connections to the Internet, unlike a dial-up connection, which must be reestablished each time it is used.

Finally, a new and emerging way to connect to the Internet is based on **power line communications (PLC)** technology that allows broadband Internet connectivity from any home, school, or office using an electrical outlet.

Many hotels and airports provide dial-up or broadband Internet connections for a usage or per-day fee; others provide these services for free. In many public locations, people connect wirelessly to the Internet through a **public Internet access point**. Public Internet access points are appearing in airports, hotels, shopping malls, schools, and coffee shops providing Internet access either for a usage fee or for free.

THE INTERNET BACKBONE

The inner structure of the Internet works much like a transportation system. Just as highways connect major cities and carry the bulk of the automotive traffic across the country, the main communications lines that have the heaviest amount of traffic (data packets) on the Internet are collectively referred to as the **Internet backbone**. In the United States, the communications lines that make up the Internet backbone intersect at several different points. National ISPs use dedicated lines to connect directly to the Internet. Smaller, regional ISPs lease lines from local telephone companies to connect to national networks. These smaller, slower-speed networks extend from the backbone into regions and local communities like roads and streets extend to major interstates. Figure 2-17 illustrates how all of the components of the Internet work together to transfer data over the Internet to and from your computer using a cable modem connection.

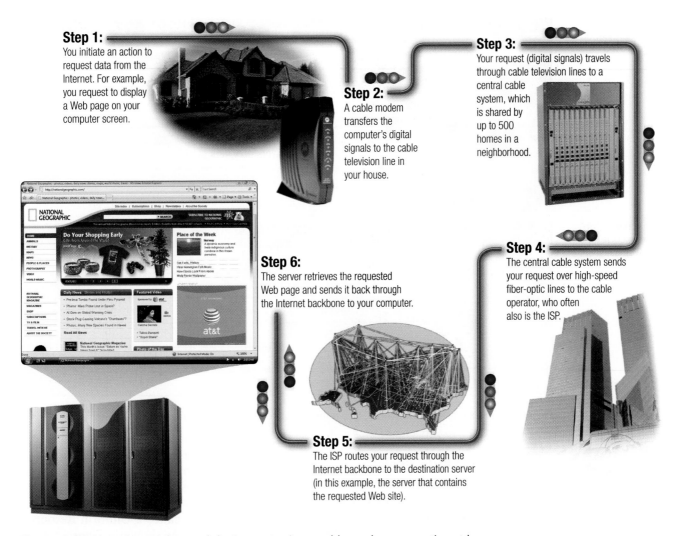

Step 1:
You initiate an action to request data from the Internet. For example, you request to display a Web page on your computer screen.

Step 2:
A cable modem transfers the computer's digital signals to the cable television line in your house.

Step 3:
Your request (digital signals) travels through cable television lines to a central cable system, which is shared by up to 500 homes in a neighborhood.

Step 4:
The central cable system sends your request over high-speed fiber-optic lines to the cable operator, who often also is the ISP.

Step 5:
The ISP routes your request through the Internet backbone to the destination server (in this example, the server that contains the requested Web site).

Step 6:
The server retrieves the requested Web page and sends it back through the Internet backbone to your computer.

Figure 2-17 How data might travel the Internet using a cable modem connection at home.

INTERNET ADDRESSES

The Internet relies on an addressing system much like that of the postal system to send data to a computer at a specific destination. Each computer's location on the Internet has a specific numeric address consisting of four groups of numbers. Because these all-numeric computer addresses are difficult to remember and use, the Internet supports the use of text-based names that represent the numeric address. The text version of a computer address is called a **domain name**. Figure 2-18 shows both the numeric address and the domain name of the Shelly Cashman Series Web site. The components of a domain name are separated by periods, each of which is referred to as a dot.

For domestic Web sites, the rightmost portion of the domain name contains a domain type abbreviation that identifies the type of organization that maintains the Web site. The rightmost portion of a university Web site, for example, is .edu, which denotes it as a site operated by an educational institution. The domain names for some K-12 school sites include the abbreviation, .k12, followed by the abbreviation for the school's state. For international Web sites, the domain name also includes a country code, such as .us for the United States and .uk for the United Kingdom. Figure 2-19 on the next page lists common domain type abbreviations, as well as lists several country code abbreviations.

Figure 2-18 The numeric address and domain name for the Shelly Cashman Series® Instructional Web site.

numeric address

198.80.146.30

domain name

www.scsite.com

[a] This table lists domain abbreviations commonly used today.

Domain Abbreviation	Type of Organization
com	Commercial organizations, businesses, and companies
edu	Educational institutions
gov	Government institutions
mil	Military organizations
net	Network providers
org	Nonprofit organizations
k12	K-12 schools

[b] A partial listing of country code abbreviations.

Abbreviation	Country	Abbreviation	Country
au	Australia	jp	Japan
ax	Antarctica	nl	Netherlands
ca	Canada	se	Sweden
de	Germany	th	Thailand
dk	Denmark	uk	United Kingdom
fr	France	us	United States

Figure 2-19 Examples of domain abbreviations and country code abbreviations.

Web Info

For an overview of the World Wide Web, visit the Teachers Discovering Computers Web site (*scsite.com/tdc5*), click Chapter 2, click Web Info, and then click WWW.

FAQ

How do I change my Web browser's home page?

To change the home page in Microsoft Internet Explorer, click Tools, click Internet Options, click the General tab, type or paste the URL for the desired Web page, and then click the OK button.

The World Wide Web

Although many people use the terms World Wide Web and Internet interchangeably, the World Wide Web is just one of the many services available on the Internet. The Internet has been in existence since the late 1960s, but the World Wide Web came into existence in the early 1990s. Since then, however, it has grown phenomenally to become the most widely used service on the Internet.

The **World Wide Web,** or simply **Web,** consists of a worldwide collection of electronic documents that have built-in hyperlinks to other related documents. These **hyperlinks,** also called **links,** allow users to navigate quickly from one Web page to another, regardless of whether the Web pages are located on the same computer or on different computers in different countries. A **Web page** is an electronic document viewed on the Web. A Web page can contain text, graphics, sound, and video, as well as hyperlinks to other Web pages. A **Web site** is a collection of related Web pages. Most Web sites have a starting point, called a **home page,** which is similar to a book cover or table of contents for the site and provides information about the site's purpose and content.

Each Web page on a Web site has a unique address, called a **Uniform Resource Locator (URL).** As shown in Figure 2-20, a URL consists of a protocol, domain name, and sometimes the path to a specific Web page. Most Web page URLs begin with **http://,** which stands for **Hypertext Transfer Protocol,** the communications protocol used to transfer pages on the Web. You access and view Web pages using a software program called a Web browser, or browser.

Some Web pages are static (fixed); others are dynamic (changing). All visitors to a **static Web page** see the same content. In contrast, visitors to a **dynamic Web page** can customize some or all of the viewed content, such as stock quotes, weather for a region, or ticket availability for flights, which means visitors see content unique to their settings. Some industry experts use the terms **Web 2.0** and **participatory Web** to refer to Web sites that allow users to modify Web site content, provide a means for users to share personal information, and have application software built into the site for visitors to use.

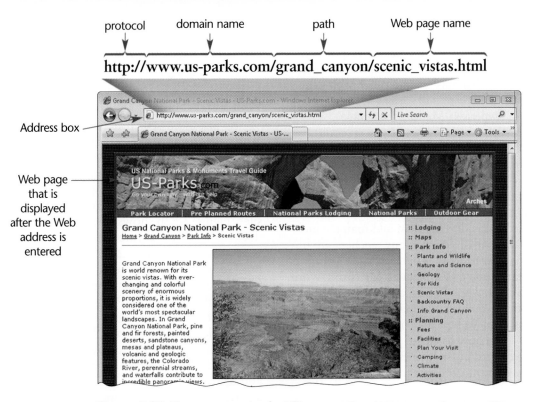

protocol   domain name   path   Web page name

http://www.us-parks.com/grand_canyon/scenic_vistas.html

Address box

Web page that is displayed after the Web address is entered

Figure 2-20 The components of a URL.

FAQ

How does a person or company obtain a domain name?

You register for a domain name from a registrar, which is an organization that maintains a master list of names for a particular top-level domain, .com, for example. Some registrars also offer Web site hosting.

The Web pages that constitute a Web site are stored on a server, called a Web server. A **Web server** is a computer that delivers (serves) requested Web pages. For example, when you enter the URL *scsite.com/tdc5* in your browser, your browser sends a request to the server whose domain name is *scsite.com*. The server then fetches the page named tdc5 and sends it to your browser. Web servers can store multiple Web sites. For example, many ISPs grant their subscribers storage space on a Web server for their personal, school, or company Web site.

HOW A WEB PAGE WORKS

A Web page (Figure 2-21) is a hypertext or hypermedia document residing on an Internet computer. A Web page can contain text, graphics, video, and sound. A **hypertext** document contains text hyperlinks to other documents. A **hypermedia** document contains text, graphics, video, or sound hyperlinks that connect to other documents.

Three types of hyperlinks exist. **Target hyperlinks** link to another location in the same document. **Relative hyperlinks** link to another document on the same Internet computer. **Absolute hyperlinks** link to another document on a different Internet computer that could be across the country or across the world.

Hypertext and hypermedia allow students to learn in a nonlinear way. Reading a book from cover to cover is a linear way of learning. Branching off and investigating related topics as you encounter them is a nonlinear way of learning, also known as **discovery learning**. As students' interest inspires them to learn more, the Web allows them to continue to explore for additional sources of information on any given topic. **Web surfing** is displaying pages from one Web site after another and is like using a remote control to jump from one TV channel to another.

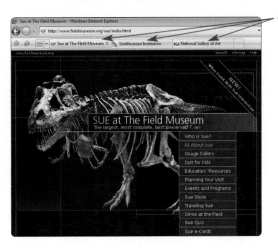

tabbed browsing

Figure 2-21 Internet Explorer, like most new versions of browsers, allows tabbed browsing.

A **Webmaster** is the person responsible for developing Web pages and maintaining a Web site. Webmasters and other Web page developers create and format Web pages using **Hypertext Markup Language (HTML),** which is a set of special codes, called **tags,** that define the placement and format of text, graphics, video, and sound on a Web page. Because HTML can be difficult to learn and use, many other user-friendly tools exist for **Web publishing,** which is the development and maintenance of Web pages. Today, many teachers are utilizing user-friendly programs, such as Dreamweaver, WebBlender, Microsoft Word, Publisher, AppleWorks, and many other programs to publish and maintain their own classroom Web pages (Figure 2-22a). You will learn how to create your own Web page using Word in Chapter 3. You also will learn how to create and integrate Web-based

curriculum pages into your lesson plans in Chapters 6 and 7.

WEB BROWSER SOFTWARE

As just discussed, you access and view Web pages using a software program called a Web browser. A **Web browser, or browser,** is a program that interprets HTML and displays Web pages and enables you to link to other Web pages and Web sites. Figure 2-22b shows the HTML source document, used to create the teacher's Web page shown in Figure 2-22a. Your Web browser translates the source document, which includes HTML tags, into a functional and beautiful Web page with many interactive features.

Besides HTML, current Web development tools utilize newer languages like eXtensible Markup Language (XML) and eXtensible HTML (XHTML). **XML** is a format increasing in popularity that allows Web page authors to create customized tags known as schema. The tags are stored in libraries and can be used in Cascading Style Sheets. A **Cascading Style Sheet (CSS)** is a simple mechanism for adding style (e.g. fonts, colors, spacing) to Web documents and defines style and formatting properties which are applied to HTML and/or XML-based Web pages. **XHTML** is flexible and also enables Web pages to be displayed on PDAs and smart phones.

Figure 2-22 The HTML code (Figure 2-22b) for the top portion of the Web page (Figure 2-22a). Web browser software interprets the HTML tags and displays the text, graphics, and hyperlinks.

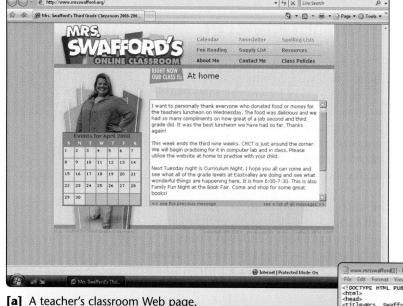

[a] A teacher's classroom Web page.

[b] HTML source document.

The first Web browsers used only text commands and displayed only text-based documents. In 1993, Marc Andreessen, a student at the University of Illinois, created a graphical Web browser called Mosaic. **Mosaic** displayed documents that included graphics and used a graphical interface. The graphical interface made it easier and more enjoyable to view Web documents and contributed to the rapid growth of the Web. Andreessen later developed the Netscape Navigator Web browser.

Before you can use a Web browser to view pages on the World Wide Web, your computer or handheld device has to connect to the Internet through an ISP or online service. When the browser program opens, it retrieves and displays a home page. As discussed earlier, a home page often is used to describe the first page at a Web site. The same term, home page, describes the Web page designated as the page to display each time you start your browser. Most browsers utilize their own Web page as the default home page, but you may change your browser's home page at any time. Many teachers, for example, set their school's home page as their browser's home page so it is the first page they see when they start their browser.

After the browser retrieves a Web page using the page's URL, it can take anywhere from a few seconds to several minutes to display the page on your computer screen. The speed at which a Web page displays depends on the speed of the Internet connection and your computer and the amount of graphics on the Web page. Many current Web browsers support **tabbed browsing**, where the top of the browser displays a tab (similar to a file folder tab) for each Web page you open (refer back to Figure 2-21). Click a tab to move from one open Web page to another.

Browsers display hyperlinks to other documents either as underlined text of a different color or as a graphical image (Figure 2-23). When you position the mouse pointer over a hyperlink, the mouse pointer changes to a small hand with a pointing finger. Some browsers also display the URL of the hyperlinked document at the bottom of the screen. You can display the document by clicking the hyperlink with a pointing device or by typing the URL in the location or Address text box of the Web browser. To remind you that you have seen a document, some browsers change the color of a text hyperlink after you click it.

Two ways to keep track of Web pages you have viewed are a history list and a favorites or bookmark list. A **history list** records the pages viewed during the time you are online, also known as a session. If you think you might want to return to a page in a future session, you can save its location as a favorite or bookmark. A **favorite** or **bookmark** consists of the title and URL of a page. Favorite lists, also called **bookmarks**, are stored on your computer, and may be used in future Web sessions. Favorites, bookmarks, and history lists allow you to display a Web page quickly by clicking the name in the list.

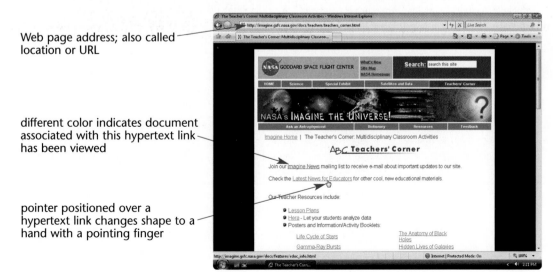

Web page address; also called location or URL

different color indicates document associated with this hypertext link has been viewed

pointer positioned over a hypertext link changes shape to a hand with a pointing finger

Figure 2-23 An example of a Web page.

WEB SITE CATEGORIES

Figure 2-24 summarizes twelve categories of Web sites. Many Web sites fall into more than one of these categories. Today's digital generation is actively involved and interacting with many newer features of the World Wide Web on a daily basis, including podcasting using both audio and video, social networks, wikis, Role-Playing Games (RPG), Massively Multiplayer Online Role-Playing Games (MMORGs), facebooks, and blogs to name just a few. Understanding the impact of these Web-based technologies on today's

digital generation is critically important to your success as a classroom teacher.

You will learn more about these Web-based features that are so important to today's digital generation in the Special Feature that follows Chapter 3, *Creating Web pages, Blogs, Wikis, and More*. In addition, you will increase your understanding of these new technologies, their impact and influence on your students, and how to integrate these technologies in the Special Feature that follows Chapter 7, *Integrating Web pages, Blogs, Wikis, and More*.

Category	Web Site Description
Portal	A **portal** is a Web site that offers a variety of Internet services from a single, convenient location. Most portals offer free services including search engine and/or subject directory, news, sports and weather, and many other services. Many portals have **online communities**, which are Web sites that join specific groups of people with similar interests or relationships.
News	A news Web site contains newsworthy material including stories and articles relating to current events, life, money, sports, and the weather.
Informational	An informational Web site contains factual information. Many United States government agencies have informational Web sites providing information such as census data, tax codes, and the congressional budget.
Business	A business Web site contains content that promotes or sells products or services and most businesses have a business/marketing Web site. Many of these companies also allow you to purchase their products or services online.
Education	An educational Web site offers exciting and challenging avenues for formal and informal teaching and learning. Many of the Web sites included as links at this textbook's companion Web site are educational Web sites.
Entertainment	An entertainment Web site offers an interactive and engaging environment. Popular entertainment Web sites offer music, videos, sports, games, ongoing Web episodes, sweepstakes, chats, and more. Sophisticated entertainment Web sites often partner with other technologies. For example, you can cast your vote about a topic on a television show.
Advocacy	An advocacy Web site contains content that describes a cause, opinion, or idea. These Web sites usually present views of a particular group or association.
Blog	A **blog**, short for **Weblog**, is an informal Web site consisting of time-stamped articles, or posts, in a diary or journal format, usually listed in reverse chronological order. A blog that contains video clips is called a **video blog**, or **vlog**.
Wiki	A **wiki** is a collaborative Web site that allows users to create, add to, modify, or delete the Web site content via their Web browser. Most wikis are open to modification by the general public.
Online Social Network	An **online social network**, also called a social networking Web site, is a Web site that encourages members in its online community to share their interests, ideas, stories, photos, music, and videos with other registered users. Most include chat rooms, newsgroups, and other communications services. Popular social networking Web sites include Facebook, Friendster, MySpace, and Google's YouTube.
Content Aggregator	A content aggregator is a business that gathers and organizes Web content and then distributes, or feeds, the content to subscribers for free or a fee. Examples of distributed content include news, music, video, and pictures.
Personal	A private individual or a family not usually associated with any organization that maintains a personal Web site or just a single Web page.

Figure 2-24 Web site categories.

SEARCHING FOR INFORMATION ON THE WEB

Searching for information on the Web can be challenging due to the sheer volume of content on the Web. In addition, no central menu or catalog of Web site content and addresses exists. Many Web sites, however, do provide search tools and maintain organized directories of Web sites to help you locate specific information. **Search tools** enable users to locate information found at Web sites all over the world. Two basic types of search tools exist: search engines (Figure 2-25) and subject directories.

A **search engine** is a specific type of search tool that finds Web sites, Web pages, and Internet files that match one or more keywords you enter. Some search engines look for simple word matches and others allow for more specific searches on a series of words or an entire phrase. Search engines do not actually search the entire Internet (such a search would take an extremely long time). Instead, they search an index or database of Internet sites and documents. Search tool companies continuously update their databases. Because of the explosive growth of the Internet and because search engines scan different parts of the Internet and in different ways, performing the same search using different search engines often yields different results.

Many search engines also provide subject directories. A **subject directory** is a type of search tool that allows users to navigate to areas of interest without having to enter keywords. Surfing subject directories is a simple matter of selecting topics and following the links for that topic. Subject directories are usually organized in categories such as education, sports, entertainment, or business. The special feature, Guide to World Wide Web Sites, Searching Techniques, and Search Tools, at the end of this chapter includes extensive information on using search tools. Also included is information on and links to a number of popular educational search tools.

MULTIMEDIA ON THE WEB

Most Web pages include more than just formatted text and hyperlinks. In fact, some of the more exciting Web developments involve **multimedia**, which is the combination of graphics, animation, audio, video, and virtual reality (VR). A Web page that incorporates color, sound, motion, and pictures with text has much more appeal than one with text on a plain background. Combining text, audio, video, animation, and sound brings a Web page to life, increases the types of information available on the Web, expands the Web's potential uses, and makes the Internet a more entertaining place to explore. Although multimedia Web pages often require more time to open because they contain large files such as video or audio clips, the pages usually are worth the wait.

Most browsers have the capability to display multimedia elements on a Web page. Sometimes, however, your browser needs an additional program called a plug-in. A **plug-in** is a program that extends the capability of the browser.

You can download or copy plug-ins free from many Web sites (Figure 2-26 on the next page). In fact, Web pages that use multimedia elements often include links to Web sites containing the required plug-in. Most browsers include commonly used plug-ins, but users often have to update their browsers as new plug-ins become available. Some plug-ins run on mobile devices as well as computers. Others have special versions for mobile devices.

The following sections discuss Web developments in the multimedia areas of graphics, animation, audio, video, and virtual reality.

Web Info

For links to many popular education-related search engines, visit the Teachers Discovering Computers Web site (*scsite.com/tdc5*), click Chapter 2, click Web Info, and then click Search Tools.

Web Info

For more information on plug-ins, visit the Teachers Discovering Computers Web site (*scsite.com/tdc5*), click Chapter 2, click Web Info, and then click Plug-ins.

Figure 2-25 Google is a popular search engine.

Plug-In Application	Description	Web Address
Acrobat Reader	View, navigate, and print Portable Document Format (PDF) files — electronic documents that retain their formatting when printed	adobe.com
Flash Player	View dazzling graphics and animation, hear outstanding sound and music, display Web pages across an entire screen	macromedia.com
QuickTime	View animation, music, audio, video, and VR panoramas and objects directly in a Web page	apple.com
RealOne Player	Listen to live and on-demand near-CD-quality audio and newscast-quality video; stream audio and video content for faster viewing; play MP3 files; create music CDs	real.com
Shockwave Player	Experience dynamic interactive multimedia, 3-D graphics, and streaming audio	macromedia.com
Windows Media Player	Listen to live and on-demand audio; play or edit WMA and MP3 files; burn CDs; watch DVD movies	microsoft.com

Figure 2-26 Plug-ins can extend the multimedia capability of Web browsers. Users usually can download them free from the developers' Web sites.

GRAPHICS A **graphic**, or **graphical image**, is a digital representation of non-text information such as a drawing, chart, or photograph. Graphics were the first medium used to enhance the text-based Internet. The introduction of graphical Web browsers allowed Web page developers to incorporate illustrations, logos, and other images into Web pages. Today, many Web pages use colorful graphical designs and images to convey messages (Figure 2-27).

Figure 2-27 The use of colorful graphic designs and images enchances the visual appeal of the Web page and helps to convey the messages.

Two common file formats for graphical images found on the Web are JPEG (pronounced JAY-peg) and GIF (pronounced jiff or giff). Figure 2-28 lists these and other file formats used on the Internet.

Acronym/ File Extension	Name
BMP/.bmp	Bit map
GIF/.gif	Graphics Interchange Format
JPEG/.jpg	Joint Photographic Experts Group
PCX/.pcx	PC Paintbrush
PNG/.png	Portable Network Graphics
TIFF/.tif	Tagged Image File Format

Figure 2-28 Graphics formats used on the Web.

The Web contains thousands of image files on countless subjects that you can download at no cost and use for noncommercial purposes. Because some graphical files can be time-consuming to download, some Web sites use thumbnails on their pages. A **thumbnail** is a small version of a larger graphical image that usually you can click to display the full-sized image (Figure 2-29).

ANIMATION Animation is the appearance of motion created by displaying a series of still images in rapid sequence. Animated graphics make Web pages visually more interesting and draw attention to important information or links. For example, text that is animated to scroll across the screen, called a **marquee** (pronounced mar-KEE), can serve as a ticker to display stock updates, news, school sports scores and events, or weather.

One popular type of animation, called an **animated GIF**, is a group of several images combined into a single GIF file. An abundance of education-related animations are available on the Web, many that you can download or copy at no cost.

Web Info

To explore a site that provides free animated GIF files, visit the Teachers Discovering Computers Web site (*scsite.com/tdc5*), click Chapter 2, click Web Info, and then click Animated GIF.

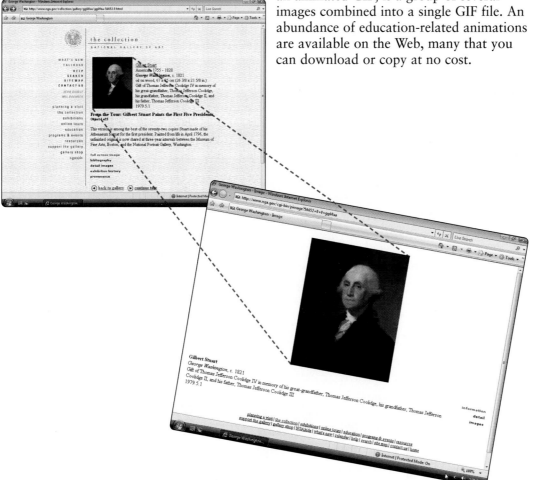

Figure 2-29 After the visitor clicks the thumbnail of the George Washington painting in the top screen, a full-sized image of the painting appears in a separate window.

Integration Strategies

To learn more about animation and how to integrate Google's Digital Earth, visit the Teachers Discovering Computers Web site (*scsite.com/tdc5*), click Chapter 2, and then click Teaching Today.

AUDIO On the Web, you can listen to prerecorded audio clips and live audio. **Audio** is music, speech, or any other sound. Simple Web audio applications consist of individual sound files that are available for downloading to a computer. After being downloaded, you can play or listen to the contents of these files. Audio files exist in a variety of formats, including MP3, WAV, WMA (Windows Media Audio), RealAudio, and QuickTime. Audio files are compressed to reduce their file sizes. For example, the MP3 format reduces an audio file to about one-tenth of its original size, while preserving the original quality of the sound.

Controversy concerning copyright infringement has surfaced due to the ease with which music can be transferred across the Internet. Users can download copyrighted music legally only if the copyright holder of the music has granted permission for users to download and play it. Many music publishers allow users to purchase and download an entire CD of music tracks to their hard disk.

Most current operating systems contain a program, called a **player**, that can play audio files on your computer. Windows Media Player, RealPlayer, and iTunes are popular players. If your player will not play a particular audio format, you can download the necessary player free from the Web.

More advanced Web audio applications use streaming audio. **Streaming** is the process of transferring data in a continuous and even flow. Streaming is important because most users do not have fast enough Internet connections to download large audio files quickly. **Streaming audio** enables you to listen to the sound file as it downloads to your computer. Many radio and television stations use streaming audio to broadcast music, interviews, talk shows, sporting events, music videos, news, live concerts, and other segments.

Podcasting is another popular method of distributing audio. A **podcast** is recorded audio, usually an MP3 file, stored on a Web site that can be downloaded to a computer or a portable media player such as an iPod. Examples of podcasts include music, radio shows, news stories, classroom lectures, political messages, and television commentaries (Figure 2-30). Users subscribe to a feed and receive new audio files automatically by using **Really Simple Syndication (RSS)**, which is a protocol that allows users to automatically receive the feeds. In education, podcasting can be very useful for teachers who want to automatically send class content, announcements, and so on to their students. A growing number of digital students who own iPods or other similar devices are using these digital communication tools on a daily basis.

Figure 2-30 Apple provides extensive podcast related resources for educators, including podcast tools, tutorials, and even free server space.

VIDEO Video consists of full-motion images that are played back at various speeds. Many Web sites include real-time video to enhance your understanding of information or for entertainment (Figure 2-31).

You can use the Web to watch live and/or prerecorded coverage of your favorite television programs or enjoy a live performance of your favorite vocalist. You can upload, share, or view video clips at a video sharing Web site such as YouTube. Educators, politicians, and businesses are using video blogs blogs to engage students, voters, and consumers.

Like audio, Web video applications consist of individual video files, such as movies or television clips, that a user must download completely before viewing. Because video segments usually are large and take a long time to download, they often are short.

Streaming video allows you to view longer or live video images as the video file downloads to your computer. Windows Media Player, RealPlayer, and Apple QuickTime can play downloaded or streaming video files.

Streaming video is creating new possibilities for teaching and learning and is having a profound impact on today's digital generation. As the speed of the Internet increases dramatically over the next few years, students from even the most remote schools will have access to thousands of full-motion videos from all over the world and covering an almost endless multitude of topics.

VIRTUAL REALITY Virtual reality (VR) is the simulation of a real or imagined environment that appears as a three-dimensional (3-D) space. On the Web, VR involves the display of 3-D images that you can explore and manipulate interactively. Using special VR software, a Web developer can create an entire 3-D site that contains infinite space and depth called a **VR world**. A VR world, for example, might show a room with furniture. You can walk through such a VR room by moving your pointing device forward, backward, or to the side. To view a VR world, you may need to update your Web browser by downloading a VR plug-in program.

Games are a popular use of virtual reality by K-12 digital students, but VR has many practical applications as well. Companies can use VR to showcase products or create advertisements. Architects create VR models of buildings and rooms to show their clients how a construction project will look before construction begins. Virtual reality also opens up a world of learning opportunities. Science educators, for example, can create VR models of molecules, organisms, and other

Figure 2-31 The Web contains thousands of videos that you can use with your digital students.

structures for students to examine (Figure 2-32). Students also can take virtual tours of historic sites located all over the world. Several schools even use VR to allow parents to take a virtual tour of the school from their home.

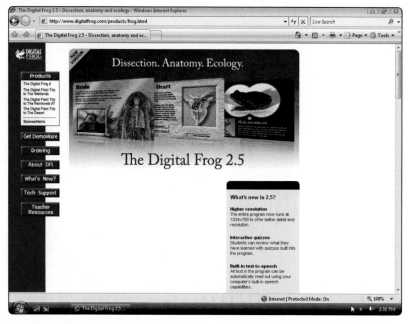

Figure 2-32 This instructional software uses VR so students can conduct virtual dissections.

Other Internet Services

Although the World Wide Web is the most talked about service on the Internet, many other Internet services are available. These services include e-mail, FTP, newsgroups, message boards, mailing lists, instant messaging, chat rooms, and Internet telephony. Each of these services is discussed in the following sections.

E-MAIL

E-mail (**electronic mail**) is the transmission of messages and files via a computer network. E-mail was one of the original features of the Internet, enabling scientists and researchers working on government-sponsored projects to communicate with their colleagues at other locations. Today, e-mail enables administrators, teachers, and students to communicate with millions of Internet users all over the world. E-mail has become a primary communications method for both personal and business use.

Using an **e-mail program,** you can create, send, receive, forward, store, print, and delete messages. E-mail messages can be simple text or can include attachments such as word processing documents, graphics, audio or video clips, and even family pictures (Figure 2-33).

When you receive an e-mail message, your ISP's software stores the message in your personal **mailbox** on its mail server. A **mail server** is a server that contains users' mailboxes and associated e-mail messages. Most ISPs and online services provide an Internet e-mail program and a mailbox on a mail server as a standard part of their Internet access services. You also can use free e-mail services such as Hotmail or Yahoo! Mail.

An **e-mail address** is a combination of a username and a domain name that identifies the user so he can both send and receive messages (Figure 2-34). Your **username** is a unique combination of characters that identifies you, and it must differ from other usernames located on the same mail server. Your username sometimes is limited to eight characters and often is a combination of your first and last names, such as the initial of your first name plus your last name. You may choose a nickname or any combination of characters for your username, but unusual combinations might be harder to remember.

Although no complete listing of Internet e-mail addresses exists, several Internet sites list addresses collected from public sources. These sites also allow you to list your e-mail address voluntarily so others may find it. The site might prompt you for other information, such as the high school or college from which you graduated, so others can determine if you are the person they want to reach.

Integration Strategies

To learn more about using and integrating e-mail with your students, visit the Teachers Discovering Computers Web site (*scsite.com/tdc5*), click Chapter 2, and then click Teaching Today.

Figure 2-33
E-mail message
with attached
JPEG picture file.

Send
button

icon for JPEG file
attached to message

Attach
button

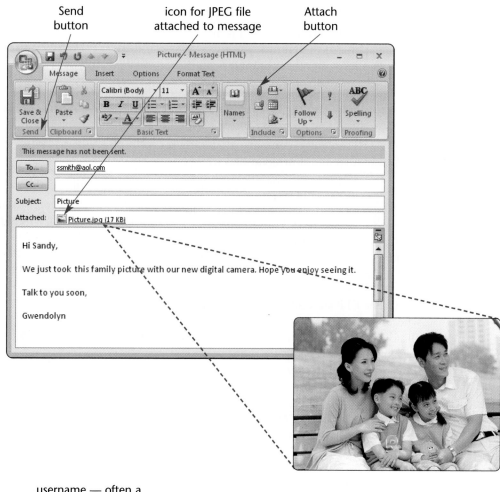

username — often a
combination of a person's
first initial and last name

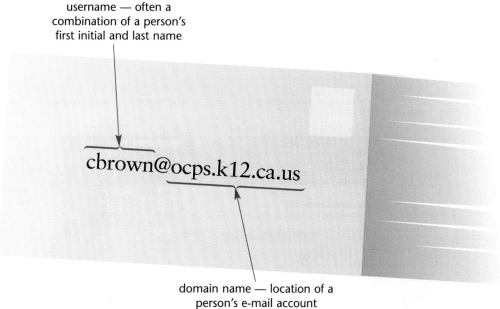

cbrown@ocps.k12.ca.us

domain name — location of a
person's e-mail account

Figure 2-34 An example of an Internet e-mail address. Sometimes, the underscore character or a period separates sections of the user's name; for example, cindy_brown@ocps.k12.ca.us.

FILE TRANSFER PROTOCOL (FTP)

File Transfer Protocol (FTP) is an Internet standard that allows you to exchange files with other computers on the Internet. For example, if you click a link on a Web page in your browser window that begins to download a file to your hard disk, you probably are using FTP (Figure 2-35).

An **FTP server** is a computer that allows users to upload and download files using FTP. An FTP server contains one or more FTP sites. An **FTP site** is a collection of files, including text, graphics, audio, video, and program files. Some FTP sites limit file transfers to individuals who have authorized accounts (usernames and passwords) on the FTP server. Many corporations, for example, maintain FTP sites for their employees.

Other FTP sites allow **anonymous FTP**, whereby anyone can transfer some, if not all, available files. Many educational sites, for example, have FTP sites that use anonymous FTP to allow educators to download lesson plans and other files. Many program files located on anonymous FTP sites are freeware or shareware programs. Many FTP sites allow users to download educational and other application software for a free 30-day evaluation period. This allows teachers, administrators, and other users to evaluate software for content and appropriateness before purchasing.

To view or use an FTP file, first you must **download**, or copy, it to your computer.

In most cases, you click the filename to begin the download procedure. Large files on FTP sites often are compressed to reduce storage space and download transfer time. Before you use a compressed file, you must expand it with a decompression program, such as WinZip or Stuffit. Such programs usually are available at the FTP site or are packaged with the file you download.

In some cases, you may want to **upload**, or copy, a file to an FTP site. To upload files from your computer to an FTP site, you use an FTP program. Many ISPs include an FTP program when you subscribe to their service. Several FTP programs also are available on the Web. In addition, many operating systems such as Windows Vista have built-in FTP capabilities.

NEWSGROUPS AND MESSAGE BOARDS

A **newsgroup** is an online area in which users conduct written discussions about a particular subject. To participate in a discussion, a user sends a message to the newsgroup and other users in the newsgroup read and reply to the message. The entire collection of Internet newsgroups is called **Usenet**, which contains thousands of newsgroups on a multitude of topics. Some major topic areas include education, news, recreation, business, and computers.

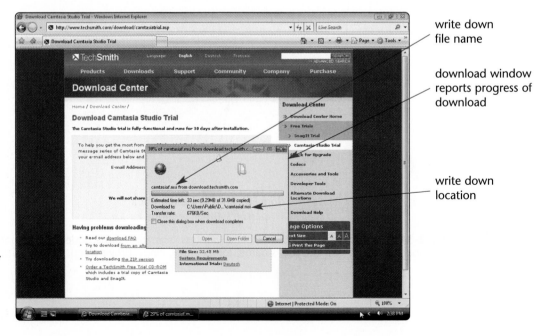

write down file name

download window reports progress of download

write down location

Figure 2-35
To ensure you can find the file when the download is complete, you should write down the file's name and the location to where the file is being saved.

A **news server** is a computer that stores and distributes newsgroup messages. Most universities, corporations, ISPs, online services, and other large organizations have a news server. Some newsgroups require you to enter your username and password to participate in the discussion. These types of newsgroups are used when the messages on the newsgroup are to be viewed only by authorized members, such as students taking a college course.

To participate in a newsgroup, you must use a program called a **newsreader**, which is included with most browsers. The newsreader enables you to access a newsgroup to read a previously entered message, called an **article**, and add an article of your own, called **posting**. A newsreader also keeps track of which articles you have and have not read.

Newsgroup members often post articles as a reply to another article — either to answer a question or to comment on material in the original article. These replies often cause the author of the original article, or others, to post additional articles related to the original article. The original article and all subsequent related replies are called a **thread** or **threaded discussion**. A thread can be short-lived or continue for some time, depending on the nature of the topic and the interest of the participants.

Using the newsreader, you can search for newsgroups discussing a particular subject, such as a type of musical instrument, brand of sports equipment, or educational topic. If you like the discussion in a particular newsgroup, you can **subscribe** to it, which means your newsreader saves the location so you can access it easily in the future.

A popular Web-based type of discussion group that does not require a newsreader is a message board. **Message boards** also are called discussion boards and typically are easier to use than newsgroups. Many Web sites provide message boards for their users (Figure 2-36).

MAILING LISTS

A **mailing list** is a group of e-mail names and addresses given a single name. When a user sends a message to a mailing list, every person on the list receives a copy of the message in her mailbox. To add your e-mail name and address to a mailing list, you subscribe to it; to remove your name, you **unsubscribe** from the mailing list. **LISTSERV** is a popular software program used to manage many educational mailing lists.

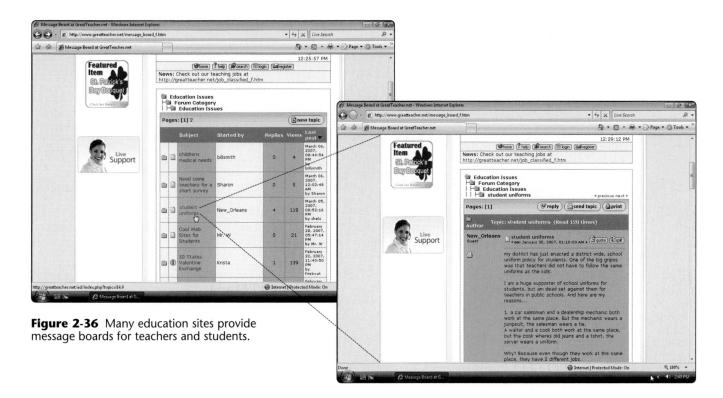

Figure 2-36 Many education sites provide message boards for teachers and students.

The basic difference between a newsgroup and a mailing list is that users on the mailing list discuss topics using e-mail, whereas newsgroup members use a newsreader for discussions. Thousands of mailing lists exist on a variety of topics in areas of entertainment, business, computers, society, culture, health, recreation, and education. To locate a mailing list dealing with a particular topic, you can use your Web browser to search for mailing lists or LISTSERV.

INSTANT MESSAGING

Instant messaging (IM) is a real-time Internet communications service (Figure 2-37) that notifies you when one or more people are online and then allows you to exchange messages or files, or join a private chat room (discussed next) with them. Many IM services can alert you to information, such as calendar appointments, stock quotes, weather, or sport scores. Some IM services support voice and video conversations.

People use IM on all types of computers, including handheld computers and Web-enabled devices. Although popular with all age groups, instant messaging services, such as AOL Instant Messenger, have become a staple of teenage life for tens of millions of

middle and high school students from around the world.

While not an Internet service, **text messaging**, known formally as **Short Message Service (SMS)** is a service that permits the sending and receiving of short messages and that is available on most digital mobile phones and other mobile devices. Text messaging is similar to instant messaging, except text messaging is most often associated with cell phones whereas instant messages are usually sent and received using personal computers. The number of text messages sent worldwide has exploded the past few years; experts estimate that the total number of text messages sent daily exceeds the population of the planet, over 7 billion messages daily. Instant messaging and text messaging are the basic forms of communications for the digital generation and between your students and their friends.

CHAT ROOMS

A **chat** is a real-time typed conversation that takes place on a computer. **Real time** means that something occurs immediately. With chat, when you enter a line of text on your computer screen, your words

Integration Strategies

For more information on instant messaging and its use in education, visit the Teachers Discovering Computers Web site (*scsite.com/tdc5*), click Chapter 2, and then click Digital Media Corner.

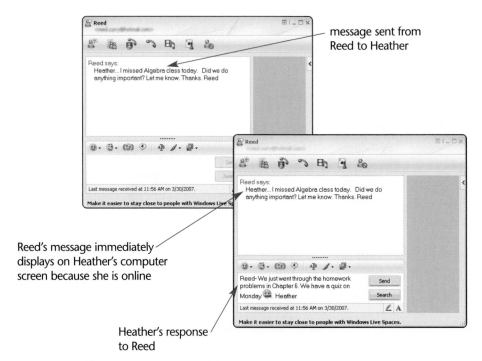

message sent from Reed to Heather

Reed's message immediately displays on Heather's computer screen because she is online

Heather's response to Reed

Figure 2-37 Instant messaging is a very popular means of communication used by today's digital students.

immediately display on one or more participant's screens. To conduct a chat, you and the people with whom you are conversing must be online at the same time.

A **chat room** refers to the communications medium, or channel, that permits users to chat with each other. Anyone on the channel can participate in the conversation, which usually deals with a specific topic.

To start a chat session, you must connect to a chat server through a **chat client**, which is a program on your computer. Today's browsers usually include a chat client. If yours does not, you can download a chat client from the Web. Some chat clients are text-based only, whereas others support graphical and text-based chats. Some chat rooms support voice or video chats that allow users to hear and see each other.

After you install a chat client, you then can create or join a conversation on a chat server. The channel name should indicate the topic of discussion. The person who creates a channel acts as the channel operator and has responsibility for monitoring the conversation and disconnecting anyone who becomes disruptive. Users can share operator status or transfer operator status to someone else.

Numerous controlled and monitored chat rooms are available for K-12 students and teachers. Several Web sites also exist for the purpose of conducting chats. Some chat sites even allow participants to assume the role or appearance of a character.

INTERNET TELEPHONY

Internet telephony, also called **Voice over** IP (Internet Protocol), enables users to speak to other users over the Internet using their desktop computer, mobile computer, or mobile device. That is, Internet telephony uses the Internet (instead of traditional telephone networks) to connect a calling party to one or more local or long-distance parties.

As you speak into a microphone or telephone connected to your computer, the Internet telephone software and the computer's sound card or the telephone adapter convert your spoken words (analog signals) to digital signals and then transmit the digitized audio over the Internet to the people you are calling. Software and equipment at the receiving end reverse the process so the receiving parties can hear what you said. Figure 2-38 illustrates a user's equipment configuration for Internet telephony.

Web Info

For more information on Internet telephony, visit the Teachers Discovering Computers Web site (*scsite.com/tdc5*), click Chapter 2, click Web Info, and then click Internet Telephony.

cable/DSL modem

Internet

telephone adapter

personal computer

telephone

Figure 2-38 Equipment configuration for a user making a call via Internet telephony.

Netiquette

Netiquette, which is short for **Internet etiquette**, is the code of acceptable behaviors users should follow while on the Internet — that is, the conduct expected of individuals while online. Netiquette includes rules for all aspects of the Internet, including the Web, e-mail, FTP, newsgroups and message boards, chat rooms, and instant messaging. Figure 2-39 outlines the rules of netiquette.

Internet Security

Any time a school district or business connects its private network to a public network such as the Internet, it must consider security concerns such as unauthorized access to confidential information. To prevent unauthorized access, schools and businesses implement one or more layers of security. A **firewall** is a general term that refers to both hardware and software used to restrict access to data on a network. Firewalls deny network access to unauthorized personnel. For example, firewalls restrict students from access to inappropriate materials or sensitive information such as student grades and attendance records.

Even with netiquette guidelines, the Internet still opens up the possibility for inappropriate behaviors and content. For example, amidst the wealth of information and services on the Internet, some content may be inappropriate for certain people. Some Web sites, newsgroups, and chat rooms, for instance, contain content or discussions that are unsuitable for children. Schools need to ensure that students do not gain access to inappropriate or objectionable materials.

To assist schools and parents with these types of issues, many browsers include software that can screen out unacceptable content. You also can purchase stand-alone Internet **filtering software**, which allows parents, teachers, and others to block access to certain materials on the Internet.

Schools help protect students from the negative aspects of the Internet by using filtering software, firewalls, and teacher observation. Most schools also use an **Acceptable**

Netiquette

Golden Rule: *Treat others as you would like them to treat you.*

1. In e-mail, newsgroups, and chat rooms:
   - Keep messages brief using proper grammar and spelling.
   - Be careful when using sarcasm and humor, as it might be misinterpreted.
   - Be polite. Avoid offensive language.
   - Avoid sending or posting **flames**, which are abusive or insulting messages. Do not participate in **flame wars**, which are exchanges of flames.
   - Avoid sending spam, which is the Internet's version of junk mail. **Spam** is an unsolicited e-mail message or newsgroup posting sent to many recipients or newsgroups at once.
   - Do not use all capital letters, which is the equivalent of SHOUTING!
   - Use **emoticons** to express emotion. Popular emoticons include

:)	Smile	:\	Undecided
:(	Frown	:o	Surprised
:|	Indifference		

   - Use abbreviations and acronyms for phrases such as

BTW	by the way
FYI	for your information
FWIW	for what it's worth
IMHO	in my humble opinion
TTFN	ta ta for now
TYVM	thank you very much

   - Clearly identify a **spoiler**, which is a message that reveals a solution to a game or ending to a movie or program.

2. Read the **FAQ** (frequently asked questions) document, if one exists. Many newsgroups and Web pages have a FAQ.

3. Use your username for your personal use only.

4. Do not assume material is accurate or up to date. Be forgiving of others' mistakes.

5. Never read someone's private e-mail.

Figure 2-39 The rules of netiquette.

Use Policy (AUP), which is an outline of user standards that reminds teachers, students, and parents that they are guests on the Internet and that they need to use it appropriately. Most schools require students, teachers, and parents to sign AUPs. Chapter 8 discusses these and other security issues in greater detail.

The Impact of the Internet and the World Wide Web on Education

More than 500 years ago, Johannes Gutenberg developed a printing press that made the written word accessible to the public and revolutionized the way people shared information. The World Wide Web is the Gutenberg printing press of modern times — opening doors to new learning resources and opportunities and allowing the sharing of information and knowledge such as never before. Just a few years ago, most students were unable to visit the Grand Canyon, the White House, the Smithsonian Institution, the National Art Gallery, or the Louvre Museum. Today, students around the world can visit these historic places and thousands of others on the Web, exploring these locales on interactive and sometimes even virtual tours.

Not only does the Internet provide access to extensive text and multimedia resources, it also allows teachers and students to communicate with other teachers and students all over the world. For example, **ePALS** Classroom Exchange is a project designed to enable digital students to develop an understanding of different cultures through student exchanges using many of the Internet-based tools discussed in this chapter (Figure 2-40). The mission of ePALS is to have students creatively write in primary and secondary languages, as well as do research and gather information about other cultures and individuals. Project ePALS is adaptable for any grade level in any country.

As the Internet expanded and evolved from a text-based communications system into the powerful multimedia communications system of today, educators quickly recognized the tremendous potential of the Internet — and especially the Web — to revolutionize the classroom. By providing a variety of learning tools, the Internet and the Web are transforming the way teachers instruct and the way students learn basic skills and core subjects. These changes have brought the Web to the forefront of instructional strategies in education in a very short period.

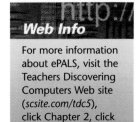

Web Info

For more information about ePALS, visit the Teachers Discovering Computers Web site (*scsite.com/tdc5*), click Chapter 2, click Web Info, and then click ePALS.

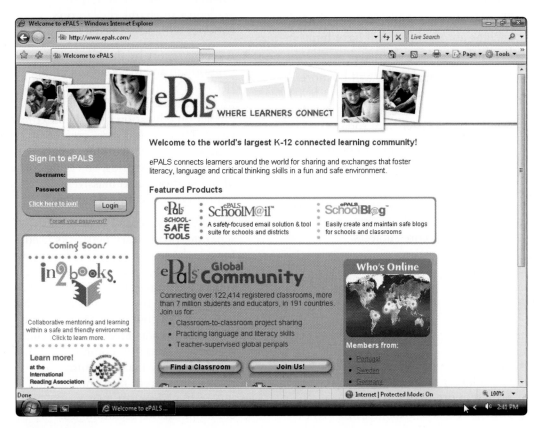

Figure 2-40 An online project, ePALS, allows millions of students from all over the world to communicate with each other.

Throughout this textbook, hundreds of links and dozens of exercises will help you understand the incredible possibilities the Web offers for K-12 education in general and your classroom in particular.

Integration Strategies

For more information on Your Web, Your Way and Web 2.0, visit the Teachers Discovering Computers Web site (*scsite.com/tdc5*), click Chapter 2, and then click Digital Media Corner.

FAQ

What is Wi-Fi?

Wi-Fi is wireless fidelity and outlines standards for wireless technology. To learn more about Wi-Fi and the wireless revolution, review the special feature, A World Without Wires, which follows Chapter 1.

The Future of the Internet and the World Wide Web

What is the future of the Internet and the World Wide Web? Without question, the Web will continue to evolve as the primary communications channel for people around the world. As the Web grows in size and operates at higher speeds, it will continue to have a major influence on restructuring K-12 education. Other predictions regarding the future of the Internet and the World Wide Web and its impact on education include the following:

- By 2009, more than one billion wireless communication devices will be in use worldwide, and most of these products will have the ability to access the Web wirelessly.

- Devices that use embedded computers, such as automobiles, will have built-in Internet access capabilities.

- Web search capabilities will be more intelligent and focused. Within a few years, the Web will operate at speeds 10,000 times faster than today.

- Businesses will continue to be the driving force behind the Web's expansion.

- The Web will become an integral part of education, revolutionizing the way students learn core subjects.

- The way we interact will change based on a new Web technology called **telepresence systems**, which bring people together to interact and collaborate whether they are physically across the street or across the globe.

- The Internet of the future will be much larger, helping Web surfers browse more than 250 million anticipated Web sites.

- Use and creation of Web-based video by today's digital generation will continue to grow explosively during the next few years.

- Researchers predict image searches will be common on the Internet in less than 15 years and will include a voice interface, a thesaurus, and customized results. For example, facial recognition technology could identify pictures based on facial features, such as blue eyes or dimples. Once an individual is identified, the search engine then could search for other pictures of that person stored on a computer or on the Internet.

- Tens of millions of kids from developing countries will join the digital generation in the next 2–3 years due to the nonprofit One Laptop Per Child organization; started by Massachusetts Institute of Technology's (MIT) Media Lab. This initiative is providing millions of $150 laptops to underprivileged students from countries around the world. These laptops connect to the Internet, have audio and video capabilities, and are waterproof. Students can charge the laptop's batteries with a foot pedal.

- A recent report by the New Media Consortium and the nonprofit group EDUCAUSE identified six technologies they predict will have a significant impact on education over the next few years. These include user-created content, social networking, smart phones, virtual worlds, emerging forms of publications, and massively multiplayer educational gaming.

- Finally, many experts believe that separate, proprietary networks used for telephone, television, and radio will merge with the Internet. Eventually, a single, integrated network will exist, made up of many different media that will carry all communications traffic. This is known as **media convergence**, which is a theory in communications in which every mass medium eventually merges into one medium due to the advent of new communications technologies.

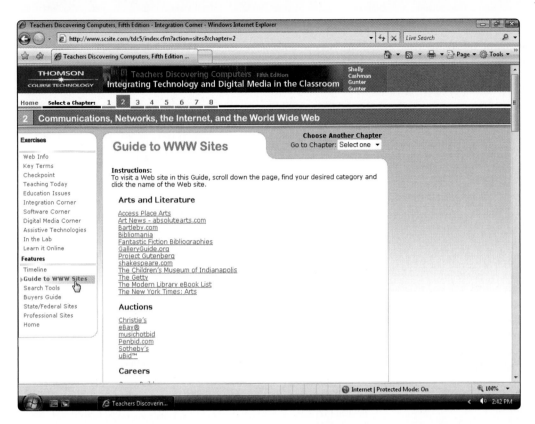

Figure 2-41 Guide to WWW Sites special feature displayed at this textbook's Web site.

Guide to World Wide Web Sites, Search Techniques, and Search Tools for Education

At the end of this chapter is a special feature that contains links to and information about more than 200 popular up-to-date Web sites. This special feature also introduces you to using search tools and contains links and information on popular education-specific search tools.

The best way to learn how to use the Internet and the World Wide Web is to log on and explore. Choose a subject and use a search tool to see what is on the World Wide Web. To display this interactive special feature, use your browser to go to *scsite.com/tdc5* to open the textbook's Web site, click Chapter 2, and then click Guide to WWW Sites on the left sidebar (Figure 2-41). Click the links to access the various Web sites. To link to the education search Web sites discussed in the special feature, click Search Tools on the left sidebar of the textbook Web site.

Summary of Communications, Networks, the Internet, and the World Wide Web

Communications will continue to impact how you work, learn, teach, access information, and use computers. Because of communications technology, individuals, schools, and organizations no longer are limited to local data resources; they can obtain information instantly from anywhere in the world. Communications networks are just one way that school districts will use communications technology to meet current instructional and management challenges. In just a few years, the Internet and World Wide Web may redefine education, just as it has transformed modern businesses and today's society. As educators all over the world integrate the Internet and the World Wide Web into their classroom curriculum, their efforts are creating an educational revolution in today's schools — one that is having a significant positive impact on the quality of graduating students.

Integration Strategies

To learn more about teaching your students how to effectively use search engines, visit the Teachers Discovering Computers Web site (*scsite.com/tdc5*), click Chapter 2, and then click Teaching Today or Digital Media Corner.

Key Terms

INSTRUCTIONS: Use the Key Terms list to help focus your study of the terms used in this chapter. To further enhance your understanding of the Key Terms in this chapter, visit scsite.com/tdc5, click Chapter 2 at the top of the Web page and then click Key Terms on the left sidebar. Read the definition for each term and then access current and additional information about the term from the Web.

Exercises

Web Info
Key Terms
Checkpoint
Teaching Today
Education Issues
Integration Corner
Software Corner
Digital Media Corner
Assistive Technologies Corner
In the Lab
Learn It Online

Features

Timeline
Guide to WWW Sites
Search Tools
Buyer's Guide
State/Federal Sites
Professional Sites

absolute hyperlink [79]
Acceptable Use Policy (AUP) [94]
Advanced Research Projects Agency (ARPA) [71]
analog signal [62]
animated GIF [85]
animation [85]
anonymous FTP [90]
ARPANET [72]
article [91]
audio [86]

backbone [72]
bandwidth [68]
blog [82]
bookmark [81]
broadband [68]
browser [80]

Cascading Style Sheets [80]
cable modem [75]
chat [92]
chat client [93]
chat room [93]
communications [61]
communications channel [62]
communications protocol [74]
communications software [62]

dial-up access [74]
digital signal [62]
digital subscriber line (DSL) [76]
discovery learning [79]
domain name [77]
download [90]
dynamic Web page [78]

e-mail address [88]
e-mail program [88]
electronic mail (e-mail) [88]
emoticon [94]
ePALS [95]

facebook [97]
FAQ [94]
favorite [81]
File Transfer Protocol (FTP) [90]
filtering software [94]
firewall [94]
flame [94]
flame war [94]
FTP server [90]
FTP site [90]

graphic [84]
graphical image [84]

history list [81]
home network [64]
home page [78]
host [72]
http:// [78]
hyperlink [78]
hypermedia [79]

hypertext [79]
Hypertext Markup Language (HTML) [80]
Hypertext Transfer Protocol [78]

instant messaging (IM) [92]
internal modem [63]
Internet [69]
Internet2 (I2) [73]
Internet backbone [76]
Internet etiquette [94]
Internet service provider (ISP) [74]
Internet telephony [93]

link [78]
LISTSERV [91]
local area network (LAN) [64]

mail server [88]
mailbox [88]
mailing list [91]
marquee [85]
media convergence [96]
message board [91]
modem [62]
Mosaic [81]
multimedia [83]

national ISP [74]
National Science Foundation (NSF) [72]
Net [67]
netiquette [94]
network [62]
network interface card (NIC) [64]
news server [91]
newsgroup [90]
newsreader [91]
NSFnet [72]

online community [82]
online service provider (OSP) [74]
online social network [82]

packet [73]
packet switching [74]
participatory Web [78]
player [86]
plug-in [83]
podcast [86]
portal [82]
posting [91]
power line communications (PLC) [76]
public Internet access point [76]

real time [92]
Really Simple Syndication (RSS) [86]
regional ISP [74]
relative hyperlink [79]
routers [73]

satellite modem [76]
search engine [83]
search tool [83]

server [64]
Short Message Service (SMS) [92]
spam [94]
spoiler [94]
static Web page [78]
streaming [86]
streaming audio [86]
streaming video [87]
subject directory [83]
subscribe [91]

tabbed browsing [81]
tags [80]
target hyperlink [79]
telecommunications [61]
telepresence systems [96]
text messaging [92]
thread [91]
threaded discussion [91]
thumbnail [85]
traffic [72]
Transmission Control Protocol/ Internet Protocol (TCP/IP) [74]
transmission media [62]
twisted-pair cable [62]

Uniform Resource Locator (URL) [78]
unsubscribe [91]
upload [90]
Usenet [90]
username [88]

video [87]
video blog [82]
virtual reality (VR) [87]
vlog [82]
Voice over IP (VoIP) [93]
VR world [87]

Web [78]
Web 2.0 [78]
Web browser [80]
Web page [78]
Web publishing [80]
Web server [79]
Web site [78]
Web surfing [79]
Weblog [82]
Webmaster [80]
wide area network (WAN) [64]
Wi-Fi [96]
wiki [82]
wireless LAN (WLAN) [64]
wireless Internet service provider (WISP) [74]
World Wide Web [78]

XML [80]
XHTML [80]

Checkpoint

INSTRUCTIONS: Use the Checkpoint excercises to check your knowledge level of the chapter. To complete the Checkpoint exercises interactively, visit scsite.com/tdc5, click Chapter 2 at the top of the Web page, and then click Checkpoint on the left sidebar.

1. Label the Figure

Instructions: Identify the components of a communications system.

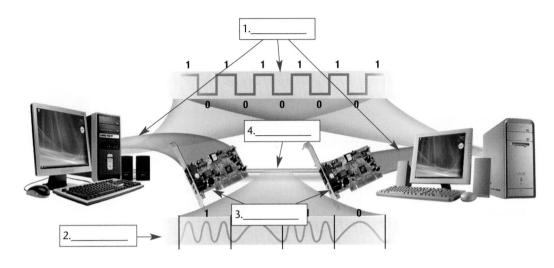

2. Matching

Instructions: Match each term from the column on the left with the best description from the column on the right.

____ 1. e-mail

____ 2. Webmaster

____ 3. network

____ 4. filtering software

____ 5. search tool

a. an individual responsible for developing Web pages and maintaining a Web site

b. a collection of computers and other equipment organized to share data, hardware, and software

c. the transmission of messages and files via a computer network

d. enables users to locate information found at Web sites all over the world

e. allows parents, teachers, and others to block access to certain materials on the Internet

3. Short Answer

Instructions: Write a brief answer to each of the following questions.

1. How are local area networks (LANs) different from wide area networks (WANs)?

2. What is a Web page? What purpose do hyperlinks have on a Web page? What is Hypertext Markup Language (HTML)?

3. Explain the process of streaming over the Web. How are streaming audio and streaming video similar? For what purposes is streaming used?

4. What is a firewall? What is filtering software? What is an Acceptable Use Policy (AUP)? Why is the use of firewalls, filtering software, and AUPs so important for K-12 networks?

5. What is a search tool? Name the two basic types of search tools and describe how each of these works. Which would you use to search for links in the category, Education?

Teaching Today

INSTRUCTIONS: Teaching Today provides teachers with integration strategies and ideas for teaching and, more importantly, reaching today's digital generation. Each numbered segment contains one or more links that reinforce the information presented in the segment. To display this page from the Web, visit scsite.com/tdc5, click Chapter 2 at the top of the Web page, and then click Teaching Today on the left sidebar.

1. Digital Earth

Today's digital students need digital tools that can offer them unique and interactive learning experiences through which they can explore and discover the world using virtual environments. Google Earth is an online, virtual globe, 3D program that allows students to develop critical thinking skills on how everyday decisions affect our environment as they travel and explore the globe, communicate with other students and teachers through Google Community. There are different levels through which you and your students can get involved in the virtual community, explore the different regions of the world, architecture, terrain, climates, and much more.

2. Search Engines

You have started using the computer lab to work on classroom projects with your digital students, which is a great opportunity for all students to get hands-on experiences with different technologies. Scanners, videos, CDs, DVDs, and many other technologies are available from which to choose. Students also can access the Internet. Managing your students in the lab while they explore these different technologies is a challenge. You decide to design a project so your students will work in groups to research a famous person in history. Before students begin their research your might reflect on the following questions: Do students need guidance on how to use a search engine to perform a proper search? Do they need help to avoid getting lost using the various technologies? Do they understand that asking the correct question or questions an important part of the solution for finding the correct answer? What about searching reference materials? Are students using primary and secondary resources? How can I design research projects that go beyond the standard writing of a paper to engage your digital students in using many different types of technologies in a collaborative way?

3. Electronic Mail

Electronic mail (e-mail) has become a preferred means of communications for many businesses, schools, and individuals. Whether using an internal network or the Internet for e-mail, you should be aware of netiquette guidelines to help ensure that recipients understand the intent behind your e-mail messages. Some users, for example, add emoticons to an e-mail message to communicate intended emotions (by adding a smiley face to a funny comment, for instance). How is using e-mail different from writing a letter? What are the similarities, if any? How might you use e-mail in your classroom with your digital students? What benefits might your students experience from using e-mail?

4. Rules and Regulations

The Internet and the Web contain thousands of wonderful sites for educators and students of all ages. Unfortunately, the Web has sites that are inappropriate for children, and some that collect information that invade the privacy of adults and children. The Federal Trade Commission's Children's Online Privacy Protection Act (COPPA) was passed by Congress in October 1998 to protect children from those who would steal personal information. COPPA also provides information on how to locate sites that have been reviewed by experts and rated as safe for children. All teachers, students, and parents should become knowledgeable about the rules and regulations that exist to protect their identity. How can you ensure student privacy on the Internet? As a teacher, what can you do to teach your students about Internet safety, information privacy, and more?

Education Issues

INSTRUCTIONS: Education Issues provides several scenarios that allow you to explore controversial and current issues in education. Each numbered segment contains one or more links that reinforce the information presented in the segment. To display this page from the Web, visit scsite.com/tdc5, click Chapter 2 at the top of the Web page, and then click Education Issues on the left sidebar.

1. Digital Equity

More people are connected to the Internet than ever before, but a large population of users is still not connected or only have dial up access. Students do not always have access to technology, the Internet, and the World Wide Web and this creates a division between the technology haves and have-nots, known as the digital divide. Digital equity is the goal of ensuring that everyone in our society has equal access to technology tools, computers and the Internet. You design a project that requires your students to work in groups and conduct research on a specific content area. Knowing that only a portion of your students have computers at home or have dial-up access, how can you design meaningful homework assignments that take into account students who do not have access to computers or high-speed Internet at home?

2. Banning Cell Phones in School

Most people would never consider cutting in line at the cafeteria or stealing somebody else's personal parking space in the parking lot. This courtesy seems to elude many people when it comes to cellular phone etiquette. People take calls during class, meetings, doctor appointments, or other inappropriate times. Psychologists have found that it may not be the cell phone users' speech volume that annoys us, but rather that the person is having a seemingly one-way conversation with no one, which is a much more difficult background noise for the brain to filter out. Recently, cell phones have taken on a new personality in schools — some students have been using phones to plan disturbances, fights, and gatherings — students call or text message each other and a situation quickly escalates from involving two students to involving twenty or more students. Many schools have told students they must leave their cell phones in their lockers and only use them during breaks; other schools have completely banned cell phones usage on school campus. Should cell phone use in schools be banned or limited in their use? Why or why not? Should simple rules of etiquette for cell phone use be more publicized or enforced? Why or why not? If so, by whom?

3. Virtual High Schools

Today, many high schools, especially small rural high schools, have difficulty offering classes such as AP biology, Latin, AP calculus, and other similar classes due to budget constraints, classroom overcrowding, lack of qualified teachers, and other important issues. Currently, many school districts and states are addressing these problems by offering a variety of online classes. Most educators agree that the Internet has great potential for education and that online classes need to be part of the K-12 learning environment. Some districts have opened 100 percent online or virtual high schools, which has generated a heated debate among educators about the effectiveness and  even appropriateness of such schools. Do you think 100 percent online high schools are an effective solution? Why or why not? Substantiate your answer.

4. Net Censoring

Each day, schools, organizations, and individuals across the country continue in an ongoing debate about Internet censorship. A number of organizations, including the American Library Association (ALA), oppose the use of Internet filtering software programs. Many schools are blocking their students from viewing popular Web sites like Wikopedia, YouTube, and even the Weather Channel. Some people feel that schools are censoring valuable information and that students would be better off with unlimited access, coupled with strict teacher observation and guidelines. Others, however, are very concerned about the use of the Internet in schools and do not want children using the Internet — even if filtering programs and Acceptable Use Policies (AUPs) are in place. Do you think schools should limit or ban Internet usage? How could you use the Internet effectively in your classroom without offending or angering parents?

Integration Corner

INSTRUCTIONS: Integration Corner provides extensive ideas and resources for integrating technology into your classroom-specific curriculum. To display this page from the Web and its links to approximately 100 educational Web sites, visit scsite.com/tdc5, click Chapter 2 at the top of the Web page, and then click Integration Corner on the left sidebar.

Integration Corner is designed for teachers and other educators who are looking for innovative ways to integrate technology into their content-specific curriculum. Integration Corner not only provides great Web sites with current information, but it also shows what other educators are doing in the field of educational technology. These Corners are designed for all educators regardless of their area of interest. Be sure to review information and sites outside of your teaching area because many great integration ideas in one area can be modified easily for use in other curricular areas.

Teachers and administrators will find other colleagues in their areas with whom to connect and share the successes and hurdles of integrating technology in a classroom or an entire school system. Consider this your one stop for integration ideas and resources. Links to educational Web sites are organized in the following 12 Corners, and different Web resources are available for each chapter. Figure 2-42 shows examples of the Web resources provided in the Chapter 2 Elementary Corner.

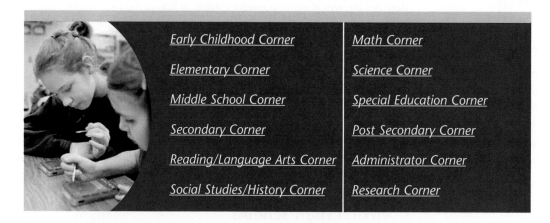

Early Childhood Corner   *Math Corner*

Elementary Corner   *Science Corner*

Middle School Corner   *Special Education Corner*

Secondary Corner   *Post Secondary Corner*

Reading/Language Arts Corner   *Administrator Corner*

Social Studies/History Corner   *Research Corner*

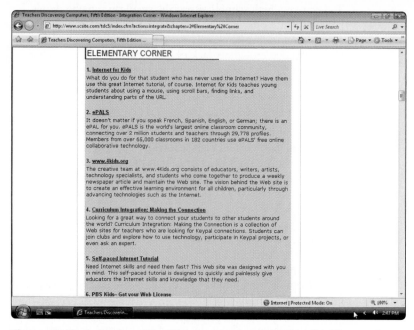

Figure 2-42 Examples of the Web resources provided in the Chapter 2 Elementary Corner.

Software Corner

INSTRUCTIONS: Software Corner provides information on popular software programs. Each numbered segment discusses specific software programs and contains a link to additional information about these programs. To display this page from the Web, visit scsite.com/tdc5, click Chapter 2 at the top of the Web page, and then click Software Corner on the left sidebar.

1. WebWhacker

If you have concerns about students accessing inappropriate Web sites while surfing the Internet, take a look at the software program, WebWhacker, which allows educators to *whack* Web sites and save them to a hard drive or a USB flash drive. With WebWhacker, you simply determine how many levels of the Web site you need for your students to access and then save the necessary Web pages. Students will not even realize they are not on the Internet right away because the program saves the Web sites exactly as they look, complete with links, buttons, animations, and all other features intact and working. WebWhacker is a super way for you to download information, while keeping your students on task and protecting them from unsuitable Web information.

2. Bailey's Book House

Bailey's Book House, produced by EDMARK, provides seven activities for prekindergarten to second grade students to learn letters and their sounds, words, common adjectives, rhyming, story-telling, and more. Students can enjoy rhymes and give them zany endings just for fun. This software also allows students to create their own storybooks and greeting cards. Bailey's Book House is an excellent tool for teaching important beginning skills to preschoolers.

3. InspireData

As a teacher, you are always looking for ways to improve data literacy by helping your students to make connections between data and real world applications. Through the use of data visualizations, students develop a more meaningful understanding of content knowledge, develop critical thinking skills, strengthen the inquiry process, and learn to analyze data. InspireData applies the proven strategies of visual learning to data literacy, inspiring students to discover significance of data as they collect and explore data in an active inquiry process. One InspireData feature is a Time Series animation, which represents data as it changes over time. This feature assists students in understanding trends and making future predictions.

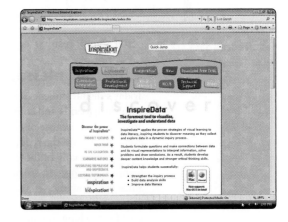

4. Encarta Reference Library

Finding information for students to complete research papers and multimedia projects is made easy with the help of reference software; and it is easy to use. Simply type keywords and search. The Encarta Reference Library combines nine great resources that include Encarta Encyclopedia Deluxe, Encarta Interactive World Atlas, Learning Tools, and more. It also includes an almanac, a dictionary, and an authoritative resource on many topics that enhance reports and multimedia presentations in classrooms of all ages.

5. Virtual Dissecting Software

High school students and teachers will enjoy using the different virtual dissection software packages being offered as an alternative to former dissection techniques that is not only fun but also clean — no disgusting smell of formaldehyde! Several companies offer teachers and students a complete virtual dissection lab on CD or DVD, which allows dissections including a frog, squid earthworm, rat, pig, crayfish, perch, and more. You can also see demos and practice your dissections on the Web with online versions.

Digital Media Corner

INSTRUCTIONS: Today's K-12 digital students need their learning to be meaningful and relevant to their lives. Digital Media Corner provides videos, ideas, and examples of how you can use digital media to enhance your teaching and your students' learning. To access the videos and links to additional information, visit scsite.com/tdc5, click Chapter 2 at the top of the Web page, and then click Digital Media on the left sidebar.

1. Your Web, Your Way

Web 2.0 is creating a new set of tools to empower educators, consumers, and businesses. Software producers have long used version numbers to designate upgrades to their products. Using the term "Web 2.0" implies a series of enhancements and the term Web 2.0 derives its meaning from improvements to the basic infrastructure of the programs and servers supporting access to Web content. For all of us using the Web, the result of these enhancements is increased functionality of Web-based applications for uses in databases and general computing capabilities needed to make the Web work faster and more efficiently. The exciting news not only for education in particular but also for society as a whole is that these improvements have permitted new technologies for everyday users to create their own products, like classroom Weblogs, media sharing programs, social network Web sites, multiplayer online games, information catalogs, personal radio stations, and bookmark sharing programs.

2. Searching the Web

As you know, getting your students to understand information literacy and efficiently searching the Web can be a daunting task. One of the many benefits of using emerging Web services is the ability for new and advanced search capabilities. So you can go above and beyond basics with greatly improved searches, Google has added customization capabilities to its search engine so your students and you can get better search results.

3. Instant Messaging from Anywhere

Today's digital students use instant messaging (IM) as an essential tool to stay in touch with their friends and communicate with parents and teachers. People all over the world are using IM because of its quick and synchronous way to communicate with other people. Now, you can even take IM on the road, without the wires. Do you ever wonder what it really means to IM? This article will answer many of those questions. As a teacher, you need to know about the newest technology developments. Click here to see how IM works. Students can spend hours talking to their friends over the Internet. Since we know they enjoy chatting over IM, why not use IM as a classroom reading and writing activity. At this Web site, you will find some great ideas on how to turn instant messaging into an instructional tool for teaching in your classroom.

4. Flash

Most people know about Flash as a plug-in that allows users to view digital media enhancements on the Web. Flash is also a popular software application. It is a dynamic digital media-creation program that can be used to create interactive animations, Web sites, presentations, games, Flash movies, and much more. There are great examples of Web sites using Flash designed for today's digital students that include extensive lessons and other resources for teaching and learning subjects like mathematics, science, and more. The Center for Technology Teacher Education (CTTE) offers a rich catalog of instructional aides that utilize Flash as a part of its programs.

5. TWICE: Two Way Interactive Connections in Education

As you learned in Chapter 1, the majority of U.S. public schools have implemented United Streaming's digital video library capabilities, but some schools are at the forefront of utilizing the speedy Internet for interactive education. TWICE, which stands for Two Way Interactive Connections in Education, promotes collaborative connections both nationally and regionally. For example, students sheltered from snowy weather in Detroit can visit NASA for a launch in tropical Cape Canaveral, Florida. While on their virtual field trip, students have the full attention of a NASA employee who receives and answers their questions in real time!

Assistive Technologies Corner

INSTRUCTIONS: Assistive Technologies Corner provides information on current hardware, software, and peripherals that will assist you in delivering instruction to students with physical, cognitive, or sensory challenges. To access extensive additional information, visit scsite.com/tdc5, click Chapter 2 at the top of the Web page, and then click Assistive Technologies on the left sidebar.

1. How Does a Person Who is Deaf or Hard of Hearing Use the Telephone?

A student who is mildly hard of hearing may choose to use an amplified telephone, one that makes telephone communication louder and more understandable. Persons who are deaf or more severely hard of hearing have used teletypwriter (TTY) or Telecommunication Devices for the Deaf (TDD) for many years. A TTY has a keyboard, a text display, and a coupler. A regular phone connection is established between two users and both users must have a TTY. The phone handset is placed into the coupler fitted for both parts of the handset. One user begins typing. The words appear on the text display for both users and the conversation proceeds. At one time, these were large bulky machines; however, today's TTYs are portable and can connect to cell phones.

Another and newer tool allows high-quality video relay such as that provided by Sorenson Video Relay Service (VRS). The VRS uses a sign language interpreter to translate voice and sign communication. A user connects with the video relay service. The interpreter places the call, and all communication goes through the interpreter. One user with a video display and camera signs to the interpreter, who translates simultaneously to the voice telephone user. When the voice user speaks, the interpreter signs, and the message is viewed on the signer's video display. Wireless communication devices with QWERTY keyboards and the associated services have brought communication freedom to the deaf and hard of hearing. The wireless services of blackberry.com, for example, provide solutions, including instant messaging and wireless e-mail.

2. How Can a Blind or Visually Impaired Person Access the Graphical Web?

The graphical nature of today's Web provides the biggest obstacle to students with a visual disability. We can make accommodations through assistive technology. Visual impairments vary in severity and in type. A slight impairment may be accommodated by activating the built-in accessibility features of the browser. For most browsers, you can increase the size of the text that is viewed on the screen.

Blind users, however, require special software installed on their computers such as a screen reader that renders text to voice. Two popular screen readers are Freedom Scientific's JAWS and GW Micro's Window Eyes. Screen reader programs read all text that appears on the computer screen. Screen reader programs provide equal access for students. Because a blind user does not use a mouse, the screen reader requires keyboard skills. These programs are somewhat expensive. Somewhat less expensive is IBM's Homepage Reader, which is a talking browser. A blind user opens the browser and the Homepage Reader software reads the contents of the Web page aloud. A different voice indicates a link, and the user selects the link using the keyboard.

3. What About Web Page Accessibility?

A screen reader, a talking browser, or any assistive device can work well only with Web pages that are accessible, that is, they met the criteria for standards that allow smooth integration of technologies. However, many Web sites are not fully accessible because the code used to create them does not follow accessibility guidelines, or they use technologies that are simply not accessible. To determine if a Web page is accessible for the student, a teacher may visit WebXACT, which is a free site that allows users to test Web sites to verify that they are accessible.

Follow the instructions at the top of this page to display additional information and this chapter's links on assistive technologies.

In the Lab

INSTRUCTIONS: In the Lab provides word processing exercises that are divided into two areas, productivity and integration. To access the links to tutorials, productivity ideas, integration examples and ideas, and more, visit scsite.com/tdc5, click Chapter 2 at the top of the Web page, and then click In the Lab on the left sidebar.

PRODUCTIVITY IN THE CLASSROOM

Introduction: All students and teachers need to know how to write a professional cover letter as well as how to develop a résumé. Many of the popular word processing applications provide wizards and templates that take users through the steps of creating these special documents. Learning how to use these wizards and templates will save you time and provide useful guidance.

1. Using a Letter Wizard to Create a Cover Letter

Problem: As a recent graduate from a Master's program in Educational Technology, you are seeking a position as a technology coordinator at a local middle school. Open your word processing software and create a cover letter as described in the following set of steps. Use the letter shown in Figure 2-43 as an example. (*Hint:* if you do not have the suggested font, use any appropriate font.)

Instructions: Perform the following tasks.

1. Create a cover letter using a Letter Wizard. If possible, use a similar letterhead style as shown in Figure 2-43. Insert your own name and address when requested by the wizard.
2. Modify the cover letter so the font is 12-point Times or Times New Roman. Use today's date in the date line. Modify the inside address and message by personalizing the information to your specific situation.
3. Create a numbered list highlighting at least two of your qualifications.
4. Check the cover letter for spelling and grammar errors.
5. Save the cover letter on a USB flash drive. Use an appropriate filename.
6. Print the cover letter.
7. Follow your instructor's directions for handing in the assignment.

2. Using a Résumé Wizard to Create a Résumé

Problem: You have prepared the cover letter in Figure 2-43 and now you are ready to create a résumé similar to the one shown in Figure 2-44 to send to the director of technology. You want your information to be clearly presented and to highlight your qualifications. Use a Résumé Wizard or template. (*Hint:* if you do not have the suggested font, use any appropriate font.)

Instructions: Perform the following tasks.

1. Use a Résumé Wizard to create a résumé. Use your name and address information.
2. Personalize the résumé using your specific information.
3. Check the résumé for spelling and grammar errors.
4. Save the résumé on a USB flash drive using an appropriate filename.
5. Print a copy of the résumé.
6. Follow your instructor's directions for handing in the assignment.

Exercises

Web Info
Key Terms
Checkpoint
Teaching Today
Education Issues
Integration Corner
Software Corner
Digital Media Corner
Assistive Technologies Corner
In the Lab
Learn It Online

Features

Timeline
Guide to WWW Sites
Search Tools
Buyer's Guide
State/Federal Sites
Professional Sites

JON MARC BOWERS

692 East First Street
Chapel Hill, NC 27516
(919) 555-4332

August 5, 2009

Ms. Roz Seguero
Director of Technology
Chapel Hill City School District
1452 Fort King Street
Chapel Hill, NC 27514

Dear Ms. Seguero,

I would like to be considered for the position of Technology Coordinator at Blue Ridge Middle School. I believe my training and experiences will greatly assist the staff and students to effectively use and integrate technology.

I have been an educator for the past seven years and I have organized and led numerous staff development workshops on a variety of software applications. I also have extensively integrated technology throughout my classroom curriculum.

I would like to mention my most important qualifications:

1. Nationally Board Certified Educator 2009
2. Recently completed a Master's degree in Educational Technology
3. MCAS Certified in Microsoft Word, Excel, and PowerPoint

I look forward to meeting with you to discuss this position further. Please contact me at (919) 555-4432 or e-mail me at jmbowers@spms.k12.nc.us.

Sincerely,

Jon Marc Bowers

Figure 2-43

In the Lab

Exercises

Web Info
Key Terms
Checkpoint
Teaching Today
Education Issues
Integration Corner
Software Corner
Digital Media Corner
Assistive Technologies Corner
In the Lab
Learn It Online

Features

Timeline
Guide to WWW Sites
Search Tools
Buyer's Guide
State/Federal Sites
Professional Sites

Jon Marc Bowers
692 East First Street
Chapel Hill, NC 27516
(919) 555-4332
jmbowers@spms.k12.nc.us

OBJECTIVE: To obtain a position as Technology Coordinator to assist administrators and teachers in learning how to effectively integrate technology throughout their classroom curriculum to positively impact student achievement.

QUALIFICATIONS

During my tenure at Orange Grove Middle School, I organized and led numerous technology staff development workshops on a variety of software applications including Microsoft Word, PowerPoint, Excel, Access, Inspiration, Photoshop, and Dreamweaver. I also created and maintained the school Web site and assisted other teachers in creating, posting, and maintaining their classroom Web pages. I also assisted teachers with basic troubleshooting on both hardware and software. As a part of my graduate program of study, I completed a 40 hour internship with the district technology coordinator and assisted with installing a new computer lab at a local elementary school.

EDUCATION

2006-2008 Master of Arts, Educational Technology, University of Central Florida, Orlando, FL
1998-2002 Bachelor of Arts, Middle Grades Education, University of North Carolina at Chapel Hill, Chapel Hill, NC

EMPLOYMENT

2006-Present
Math Teacher, Blue Ridge Middle School
Responsible for teaching all aspects of the 7th grade math curriculum for gifted students and regular education students. Develop and teach pre-algebra curriculum in a combination 7th/8th grade class.

2002-2006 Math Teacher, Orange Grove Middle School
Responsible for teaching all aspects of the 7th grade math curriculum including pre-algebra and regular curriculum courses. Team leader for 7th grade Math department. Organized meetings, reviewed curriculum and served on textbook adoption committee. Technology committee member for 3 years and also was teacher representative on School Advisory Counsel. Organized and sponsored Math Wizards after-school program that provided student tutoring, homework help, and mentoring.

AWARDS and PROFESSIONAL ACTIVITIES

2009 - 2000 Member of the National Council of Teachers of Mathematics
2009 - National Board Certification
2008 - Teacher of the Year Orange Grove Middle School
2003 - Rookie Teacher of the Year

Figure 2-44

INTEGRATION IN THE CLASSROOM

1. As a follow-up activity to career day at your school, you have your students locate job advertisements online. The students select a job they would be interested in and then use a wizard or template to write a cover letter. Use the cover letter shown in Figure 2-43 on the previous page as an example of the type of information the students should include in the first two paragraphs. The students also should include a numbered list highlighting two of their accomplishments or qualifications and then a closing paragraph with contact information. Create a cover letter to use as an example for your students. Include today's date, your name, and address.

2. Using the job they selected from the Internet, the students will create a résumé to go along with their cover letter. Create a résumé to use as an example for your students. Modify the résumé you created. Change the information in the résumé to match the cover letter in Integration in the Classroom number 1 above.

3. Your students have just finished reading a book of their choice and they are ready to begin working on their book reports. To make it more interesting, you want the students to select a character from their book, choose a job for the character, and write a cover letter and résumé based on the character's life. Choose one of your favorite characters from a book and create a sample cover letter and résumé for your students. Use today's date and your name and address as the potential employer.

Learn It Online

INSTRUCTIONS: Use the Learn It Online exercises to reinforce your understanding of the chapter concepts and increase your computer, information, and integration literacy. To access step by step online tutorials, videos, practice tests, learning games, and more, visit scsite.com/tdc5, click Chapter 2 at the top of the Web page, and then click Learn It Online on the left sidebar.

1. At the Movies

Click the At the Movies link to review a video about creating your own blog.

2. At the Movies

Click the At the Movies link to review a video about using File Transfer Protocol (FTP) software.

3. Expanding Your Understanding

When you buy a new computer, the computer manufacture often sets the default home page so the company's Web page displays every time you open your browser. Click the Expanding Your Understanding link to learn how to change your Web browser's home page to display your school districts home page, your Web site, or any other site.

4. Using Favorites

Click the Using Favorites link and complete the exercise that appears on the screen. Print just the first page of this Web site. On the back of the printout, write a brief summary explaining how to organize your favorites or bookmarks. If required, submit your results to your instructor.

5. Search Engine Tutorial

Click the Search Engine Tutorial link and complete the exercise that appears on the screen. Print just the first page of this Web site. On the back of the printout, write a brief summary of three new things that you learned about Web searching. If required, submit your results to your instructor.

6. Practice Test

Click the Practice Test link. Answer each question. When completed, enter your name and click the Grade Test button to submit the quiz for grading. Make a note of any missed questions. If required, submit your score to your instructor.

7. Who Wants to Be a Computer Genius?

Click the Computer Genius link to find out if you are a computer genius. Directions about how to play the game will be displayed. When you are ready to play, click the Play button. If required, submit your score to your instructor.

8. Wheel of Terms

Click the Wheel of Terms link to reinforce important terms you learned in this chapter by playing the Shelly Cashman Series version of this popular game. Directions about how to play the game will be displayed. When you are ready to play, click the Play button. If required, submit your score to your instructor.

9. Crossword Puzzle Challenge

Click the Crossword Puzzle link. Complete the puzzle to reinforce skills you learned in this chapter. Directions about how to play the game will be displayed. When you are ready to play, click the Play button. If required, submit the completed puzzle to your instructor.

Special Feature: Guide to World Wide Web Sites, Search Techniques, and Search Tools for Education

As you learned in Chapter 2, the World Wide Web is an exciting and highly dynamic medium that has revolutionized the way people access information. The riches of the World Wide Web are yours and your students if you can locate and utilize them effectively. You can display information on virtually any topic you can imagine, if you know the URL. Finding the information you and your students want can be a massive chore if you and your students do not know the URL or how to use Web search tools.

To help you locate information and useful Web sites, this special feature provides three resources:

1. **Guide to World Wide Web Sites:** This section provides specific information about a variety of Web pages organized in 15 different areas of interest. These are designed to provide you with an overview of what is

available on the Web. Web exercises are included at the end of each category to reinforce the material and help you and your students discover Web sites that may add a treasure trove of authentic and discovery learning. As you explore these sites, constantly ask yourself how you can integrate these sites and the information they provide into your curriculum in order to better prepare your digital students for lifelong learning and employment in the 21st century.

2. **Search Techniques:** This section provides an introduction to searching techniques, including how to use both subject directories and search engines to find educationally appropriate Web sites. Included is a list of portals with their search capabilities.

3. **Search Tools for Education:** This section provides an extensive list of popular education search tools with a brief description of each.

Fun and Entertainment

Consumers place great significance on buying entertainment products for fun and recreation. Nearly 10 percent of the United States's economy is spent on attending concerts and buying DVDs, CDs, reading materials, sporting goods, and toys.

Many Web sites supplement our cravings for fun and entertainment. For example, you can see and hear the musicians inducted into the Rock and Roll Hall of Fame and Museum (Figure 1). If you need an update on your favorite reality-based television program or a preview of an upcoming movie, E! Online and Entertainment Tonight provide the latest features on television and movie stars. The Internet Movie Database contains credits and reviews of more than 849,000 titles.

Watch the surfers riding the waves in Washington and romp with pandas at the San Diego Zoo. Web cams, which are video cameras that display their output on Web pages, take armchair travelers across the world for views of natural attractions, historical monuments, colleges, and cities. Many Web sites featuring Web cams are listed in the table in Figure 2.

Figure 1 Visitors exploring the Rock and Roll Hall of Fame and Museum Web site will find history, programs, exhibitions, and information about the inductees.

Web Cams	Web Address
AfriCam Virtual Game Reserve	africam.com
CamVista.com	camvista.com
Discovery Kids — Live Cams	kids.discovery.com/cams/cams.html
EarthCam — Webcam Network	earthcam.com
Iowa State Insect Zoo Live Camera	zoocam.ent.iastate.edu
NOAA ESRL Global Monitoring — Division South Pole Live Camera	www.cmdl.noaa.gov/obop/spo/livecamera.html
Panda Cam San Diego Zoo	sandiegozoo.org/zoo/ex_panda_station.html
Westport, Washington Surfcam	westportlodging.com/westport_web_cams.html
Wild Birds Unlimited Bird FeederCam	wbu.com/feedercam_home.htm
WorldLIVE	worldlive.cz/en/webcams

Entertainment	Web Address
AMG All Music Guide	allmusic.com
E! Online	eonline.com
Entertainment Weekly's EW.com	ew.com/ew
The Internet Movie Database (IMDb)	imdb.com
MSN Entertainment	entertainment.msn.com
Old Time Radio (OTR) — Radio Days: A Soundbite History	otr.com
Rock and Roll Hall of Fame and Museum	rockhall.com
World Radio Network (WRN)	wrn.org
Yahoo! Entertainment	et.tv.yahoo.com

For an updated list and links, click Guide to WWW sites in the Features section at scsite.com/tdc5.

Figure 2 When you visit Web sites offering fun and entertainment resources, you can be both amused and informed.

Fun and Entertainment Web Exercises

1. Visit the WorldLIVE site listed in Figure 2. View two of the Web cams closest to your hometown and describe the scenes. Then, visit the Discovery Kids — Live Cams Web site and view one of the animal cams in the Live Cams. What do you observe? Visit another Web site listed in Figure 2 and describe the view. What are the benefits of having Web cams at these locations throughout the world?

2. What are your favorite movies? Use The Internet Movie Database Web site listed in Figure 2 to search for information about two of these films and write a brief description of the biographies of the major stars and director for each movie. Then, visit one of the entertainment Web sites and describe three of the featured stories.

Travel

When you are ready to arrange your next travel adventure or just want to explore destination possibilities, the Internet provides ample resources to set your plans in motion.

To discover exactly where your destination is on this planet, cartography Web sites, including MapQuest and Maps.com, allow you to pinpoint your destination. View your exact destination using satellite imagery with Google Maps (Figure 3) and Windows Live Local.

Some good starting places are general travel Web sites such as Expedia Travel, Cheap Tickets, and Travelocity, which is owned by the electronic booking service travel agents use. These all-encompassing Web sites, including those in Figure 4, have tools to help you find the lowest prices and details on flights, car rentals, cruises, and hotels.

Figure 3 Google Maps provides location information and satellite imagery for many regions on this planet.

General Travel	Web Address
Cheap Tickets	cheaptickets.com
Expedia Travel	expedia.com
Orbitz	orbitz.com
PlanetRider Travel Directory	planetrider.com
Travelocity	travelocity.com
Cartography	**Web Address**
Google Maps	maps.google.com
MapQuest	mapquest.com
Maps.com	maps.com
Windows Live Local	local.live.com
Travel and City Guides	**Web Address**
Frommers	frommers.com
Greatest Cities	greatestcities.com
U.S.-Parks US National Parks Adventure Travel Guide	us-parks.com
VirtualTourist.com	virtualtourist.com
For an updated list and links, click Guide to WWW sites in the Features section at scsite.com/tdc5.	

Figure 4 These travel resources Web sites offer travel information to exciting destinations throughout the world.

Travel Web Exercises

1. Visit one of the cartography Web sites listed in Figure 4 and obtain the directions from your school to one of these historical destinations: the White House in Washington, D.C.; the Grand Canyon near Flagstaff, Arizona; or the Mount Rushmore National Monument in Keystone, South Dakota. Compute how many miles it is to your destination as well as the estimated drive time. Generate a list of 20 questions to ask resident experts.

2. Visit one of the travel and city guide Web sites listed in Figure 4 and choose a destination for a getaway this coming weekend. Write a one-page paper giving details about this location, such as its history, expected weather, population, local universities, parks, and tours. Explain why you chose this destination, how you plan on getting there and back, as well as an expected total cost. Provide a list of URLs used to complete this exercise.

Finance

You can manage your money with advice from financial Web sites that offer online banking, tax help, personal finance, and small business and commercial services.

If you do not have a personal banker or a financial planner, consider a Web adviser to guide your investment decisions. The Yahoo! Finance Web site (Figure 5) provides financial news and investment information.

If you are ready to ride the ups and downs of the NASDAQ and the Dow, an abundance of Web sites listed in Figure 6, including Reuters and Morningstar.com, can help you pick companies that fit your interests and financial portfolio.

Claiming to be the fastest, easiest tax publication on the planet, the Internal Revenue Service Web site contains procedures for filing tax appeals and contains IRS forms, publications, and legal regulations.

Figure 5 Yahoo! Finance Web site contains charting features that graphically depict information related to financing and investing.

Advice and Education	Web Address
Bankrate.com	bankrate.com
LendingTree	lendingtree.com
Loan.com	loan.com
The Motley Fool	fool.com
MSN Money	moneycentral.msn.com
Wells Fargo	wellsfargo.com
Yahoo! Finance	finance.yahoo.com
Stock Market	**Web Address**
AIG VALIC	valic.com
E*TRADE Financial	us.etrade.com
Financial Engines	financialengines.com
Merrill Lynch Direct	mldirect.ml.com
Morningstar.com	morningstar.com
Reuters	investor.reuters.com
Vanguard	vanguard.com
Taxes	**Web Address**
H&R Block	hrblock.com
Internal Revenue Service	irs.gov
Jackson Hewitt	jacksonhewitt.com
Liberty Tax Service	libertytax.com

For an updated list and links, click Guide to WWW sites in the Features section at scsite.com/tdc5.

Figure 6 Financial resources Web sites offer general information, stock market analyses, and tax advice, as well as guidance and money-saving tips.

Finance Web Exercises

1. Visit three advice and education Web sites listed in Figure 6 and read their top business world reports. Write a paragraph about each, summarizing these stories. Which stocks or mutual funds do these Web sites predict as being sound investments today? What are the current market indexes for the DJIA (Dow Jones Industrial Average), S&P 500, and NASDAQ, and how do these figures compare with the previous day's numbers?

2. Visit two of the stock market Web sites listed in Figure 6 and search for information about Microsoft, Adobe Systems, and one other software vendor. Write a paragraph about each of these stocks describing the revenues, net incomes, total assets for the previous year, current stock price per share, highest and lowest prices of each stock during the past year, and other relevant investment information.

Online Social Networks and Media Sharing

Do you ever wonder what your friends are doing? What about your friends' friends? Over the past several years, the popularity of online social networks has increased dramatically. Online social networks such as MySpace and AIM Pages allow you to create a personalized profile that others are able to view online. These profiles may include information about you such as your hometown, your age, your hobbies, and pictures. You also may create links to your friends' pages, post messages for individual friends, or bulletins for all of your friends to see. Online social networks are great places not only to keep in touch with your friends, but also to reconnect with old friends and meet new friends!

If you would like to post pictures and videos and do not require the full functionality of an online social network, you might consider a media sharing Web site, which is a type of online social network. Media sharing Web sites such as YouTube and Phanfare (Figure 7) allow you to post media, including photos and videos, for others to view, print, and/or download. Media sharing Web sites, like those listed in Figure 8, which may be free or charge a fee, provide a quick, efficient way to share photos of your last vacation or videos of your brother's high school graduation.

Figure 7 The Phanfare Web site allows subscribers to share their photos and videos with others.

Online Social Networks	Web Address
AIM Pages Social Network	*aimpages.com*
Facebook	*facebook.com*
Friendster	*friendster.com*
MySpace — a place for friends	*myspace.com*
Media Sharing	**Web Address**
flickr	*flickr.com*
iFeeder Media Sharing Portal	*ifeeder.com*
Phanfare	*phanfare.com*
Picasa Web Albums	*picasa.com*
Shutterfly * Shutterfly Studio	*shutterfly.com*
Twango	*twango.com*
Yahoo! Video	*video.yahoo.com*
YouTube	*youtube.com*

For an updated list and links, click Guide to WWW sites in the Features section at scsite.com/tdc5.

Figure 8 Online social networks and media sharing Web sites are popular ways to share.

Online Social Networks and Media Sharing Web Exercises

1. Visit two online social networks listed in Figure 8. Create a profile on each site. If you find a Web site that charges a fee to sign up, choose another Web site. How easy is the sign-up process? Does either Web site ask for any personal information you are uncomfortable sharing? If so, what information? Once you sign up, search for the profiles of some friends on each sites. Browse each site and make a list of its features. In your opinion, which site is better? Explain why.

2. Media sharing Web sites make it extremely easy to share photos and videos with friends, family, and colleagues. Before choosing an online media sharing Web site to use, you should do some research. Visit two media sharing Web sites in Figure 8. Is there a fee to post media to these Web sites? If so, how much? How do you post media to these Web sites? Summarize your review of these Web sites in a few paragraphs.

Blogs

Internet users are feeling the need to publish their views, and they are finding Weblogs, or blogs for short, the ideal vehicle. The blogosphere began as an easy way for individuals to express their opinions on the Web. Today, this communication vehicle has become a powerful tool for individuals, groups, and corporations, who are using blogs to promote their ideas and advertise their products. It is not necessary to have a background in Web design to be able to post to a blog.

Bloggers generally update their Web sites frequently to reflect their views. Their posts range from a paragraph to an entire essay and often contain links to other Web sites. The more popular blogs discuss politics, lifestyles, and technology.

Individuals easily may set up a blog free or for a fee, using Web sites such as Blogger, Cooeey (Figure 9), and TypePad. In addition, online social networks may have a built-in blogging feature. Be cautious of the information you post on your blog, especially if it is accessible to everyone online.

Corporate blogs, such as The GM FastLane Blog, discuss all aspects of the company's products, whereas all-encompassing blogs, such as the Metafilter Community Weblog and others in Figure 10, are designed to keep general readers entertained and informed.

Blogs are affecting the manner in which people communicate, and some experts predict they will one day become our primary method of sharing information.

Figure 9 The Cooeey Web site allows members to share their insights by posting to their personal blogs.

BLOG	Web Address
A List Apart	alistapart.com
Blog Top Sites — Internet Blogs	blogtopsites.com/internet
Blog.com	blog.com
Blogger	blogger.com
Bloglines	bloglines.com
Blogstream	blogstream.com
Boing Boing: A Directory of Wonderful Things	boingboing.net
Cooeey	www.cooeey.com
Davenetics * Politics + Media + Musings	davenetics.com
Geek News Central	geeknewscentral.com
GM FastLane Blog	fastlane.gmblogs.com
kottke.org: home of fine hypertext products	kottke.org
MetaFilter Community Weblog	metafilter.com
Scripting News	scripting.com
TypePad	typepad.com
For an updated list and links, click Guide to WWW sites in the Features section at scsite.com/tdc5.	

Figure 10 These blogs offer information about technology, news, politics, and entertainment.

Blogs Web Exercises

1. Visit three of the blog Web sites listed in Figure 10. Make a table listing the blog name, its purpose, the author, its audience, and advertisers, if any, who sponsor the blog. Then, write a paragraph that describes the information you found on each of these blogs.

2. Many Internet users read the technology blogs to keep abreast of the latest developments. Visit the Geek News Central and Scripting News blogs listed in Figure 10 and write a paragraph describing the top story in each blog. Read the posted comments, if any. Then, write another paragraph describing two other stories found on these blogs that cover material you have discussed in this course. Write a third paragraph discussing which one is more interesting to you. Would you add reading blogs to your list of Internet activities? Why or why not?

Government

When it is time to buy stamps to mail your correspondence, you no longer need to wait in long lines at your local post office. The U.S. Postal Service has authorized several corporations to sell stamps online.

You can recognize U.S. Government Web sites on the Internet by their .gov top-level domain abbreviation. For example, The Library of Congress Web site is loc.gov. The Time Service Department Web site will provide you with the correct time. If you are looking for a federal document, FedWorld (Figure 11) lists thousands of documents distributed by the government on its Web site. For access to the names of your congressional representatives, visit the extensive Hieros Gamos Web site. Government and military Web sites offer a wide range of information, and some of the more popular sites are listed in Figure 12.

Figure 11 The FedWorld Web site contains a wealth of information disseminated by the federal government.

Postage	Web Address
Endicia	*endicia.com*
Pitney Bowes	*pb.com*
Stamps.com	*stamps.com*

Government	Web Address
FedWorld	*www.fedworld.gov*
Hieros Gamos — Worldwide Legal Directories	*hg.org*
The Library of Congress	*loc.gov*
National Agricultural Library	*nal.usda.gov*
The National Archives	*archives.gov*
THOMAS Legislative Information	*thomas.loc.gov*
Time Service Department	*tycho.usno.navy.mil*
U.S. Department of Education	*ed.gov*
United States Department of the Treasury	*treas.gov*
U.S. Government Printing Office	*www.access.gpo.gov*
United States National Library of Medicine	*www.nlm.nih.gov*
United States Patent and Trademark Office	*www.uspto.gov*
USAJOBS	*usajobs.opm.gov*
The White House	*whitehouse.gov*

For an updated list and links, click Guide to WWW sites in the Features section at scsite.com/tdc5.

Figure 12 These Web sites offer information about buying U.S.-approved postage online and researching federal agencies.

Government Web Exercises

1. View the three postage Web sites listed in Figure 12. Compare and contrast the available services at each one. Consider postage cost, necessary equipment, shipping services, security techniques, and tracking capability. Explain why you would or would not like to use this service.

2. Visit the Hieros Gamos Web site listed in Figure 12. What are the names, addresses, and telephone numbers of your two state senators and your local congressional representative? On what committees do they serve? Who is the chief justice of the Supreme Court, and what has been this justice's opinion on two recently decided cases? Who are the members of the president's cabinet? Then, visit two other Web sites listed in Figure 12. Write a paragraph about each Web site describing its content and features.

Shopping and Auctions

From groceries to clothing to computers, you can buy just about everything you need with just a few clicks of your mouse. Electronic retailers (e-tailers) are cashing in on cybershoppers' purchases. Books, computer software and hardware, and music are the hottest commodities.

The two categories of Internet shopping Web sites are those with physical counterparts, such as Wal-Mart and Best Buy, and those with only a Web presence, such as Amazon.com and Buy.com (Figure 13). Popular Web shopping sites are listed in Figure 14.

Another method of shopping for the items you need, and maybe some you really do not need, is to visit auction Web sites, including those listed in Figure 14. Categories include antiques and collectibles, automotive, computers, electronics, music, sports, sports cards and memorabilia, and toys. Online auction Web sites can offer unusual items, including *Star Wars* props and memorabilia and a round of golf with Tiger Woods. eBay is one of thousands of Internet auction Web sites and is the world's largest personal online trading community.

Figure 13 Buy.com is a popular electronic retailer that sells a variety of products.

Auctions	Web Address
craigslist	*craigslist.org*
eBay®	*ebay.com*
Sotheby's	*sothebys.com*
uBid.com	*ubid.com*
Yahoo! Auctions	*auctions.yahoo.com*
Books and Music	**Web Address**
Amazon.com	*amazon.com*
Barnes & Noble.com	*bn.com*
BookFinder.com	*bookfinder.com*
Computers and Electronics	**Web Address**
BestBuy	*bestbuy.com*
Buy.com	*buy.com*
Crutchfield	*crutchfield.com*
Miscellaneous	**Web Address**
drugstore.com	*drugstore.com*
Froogle	*froogle.com*
Sharper Image	*sharperimage.com*
Walmart.com	*walmart.com*

For an updated list and links, click Guide to WWW sites in the Features section at scsite.com/tdc5.

Figure 14 Making online purchases can help ease the burden of driving to and fighting the crowds in local malls.

Shopping and Auctions Web Exercises

1. Visit two of the computers and electronics and two of the miscellaneous Web sites listed in Figure 14. Write a paragraph describing the features these Web sites offer compared with the same offerings from stores. In another paragraph, describe any disadvantages of shopping at these Web sites instead of actually visiting a store. Then, describe their policies for returning unwanted merchandise and for handling complaints.

2. Using one of the auction Web sites listed in Figure 14, search for two objects pertaining to your hobbies. For example, if you are a sports fan, you can search for a complete set of Upper Deck cards. If you are a car buff, search for your dream car. Describe these two items. How many people have bid on these items? Who are the sellers? What are the opening and current bids?

Weather, Sports, and News

Rain or sun? Hot or cold? Weather is the leading online news item, with at least 10,000 Web sites devoted to this field. Millions of people view the WX.com Web site (Figure 15) each month.

Baseball may be the national pastime, but sports aficionados yearn for everything from auto racing to cricket. The Internet has more than one million pages of multimedia sports news, entertainment, and merchandise.

The Internet has emerged as a major source for news, with one-third of Americans going online at least once a week and 15 percent going online daily for reports of major news events. Many of these viewers are using Really Simple Syndication (RSS) technology to be notified when new stories about their favorite topics are available on the Internet. Popular weather, sports, and news Web sites are listed in Figure 16.

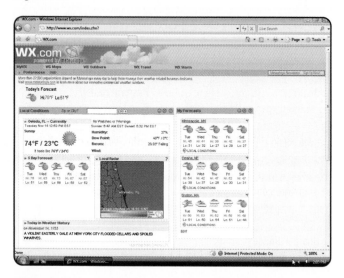

Figure 15 Local, national, and international weather conditions and details about breaking weather stories are available on WX.com.

Weather	Web Address
Infoplease Weather	infoplease.com/weather.html
Intellicast.com	intellicast.com
National Weather Service	www.crh.noaa.gov
STORMFAX	stormfax.com
The Weather Channel	weather.com
WX.com	wx.com
Sports	**Web Address**
CBS SportsLine.com	cbs.sportsline.com
ESPN.com	espn.com
NCAAsports.com	ncaasports.com
OFFICIAL WEBSITE OF THE OLYMPIC MOVEMENT	olympic.org
SIRC — A World of Sport Information	sirc.ca
Sporting News Radio	radio.sportingnews.com
News	**Web Address**
Google News	news.google.com
MSNBC	msnbc.com
New York Post Online Edition	nypost.com
onlinenewspapers.com	onlinenewspapers.com
Privacy.org	privacy.org
SiliconValley.com	siliconvalley.com
Starting Page	startingpage.com/html/news.html
USATODAY.com	usatoday.com
washingtonpost.com	washingtonpost.com

For an updated list and links, click Guide to WWW sites in the Features section at scsite.com/tdc5.

Figure 16 Keep informed about the latest weather, sports, and news events with these Web sites.

Weather, Sports, and News Exercises

1. Visit two of the sports Web sites in Figure 16 and write a paragraph describing the content these Web sites provide concerning your favorite sport. Visit news.google.com and then search for stories about this sports team or athlete. Then, create a customized news page with stories about your sports interests. Include RSS feeds to get regularly updated summaries on this subject.

2. Visit the onlinenewspapers.com and Starting Page Web sites listed in Figure 16 and select two newspapers from each site. Write a paragraph describing the top national news story featured on each of these four Web pages. Then, write a paragraph describing the top international news story at each Web site. In the third paragraph, discuss which Web site is the most interesting in terms of story selection, photographs, and Web page design.

Learning

While you may believe your education ends when you finally graduate from college, learning is a lifelong process. For example, enhancing your culinary skills can be a rewarding endeavor. No matter if you are a gourmet chef or a weekend cook, you will be cooking in style with the help of online resources, including those listed in Figure 17.

Cooking	Web Address
Betty Crocker	bettycrocker.com
recipecenter.com	www.recipecenter.com
Internet	**Web Address**
Learn the Net	learnthenet.com
Search Engine Watch	searchenginewatch.com
Wiredguide	wiredguide.com
Technology and Science	**Web Address**
CBT Nuggets	cbtnuggets.com
HowStuffWorks	howstuffworks.com
ScienceMaster	sciencemaster.com
General Learning	**Web Address**
Bartleby.com: Great Books Online	bartleby.com
Blue Web'n	www.kn.pacbell.com/ wired/bluewebn
MSN Encarta	encarta.msn.com

For an updated list and links, click Guide to WWW sites in the Features section at scsite.com/tdc5.

Figure 17 Resources, such as these, help you find answers to your questions.

If you would rather sit in front of the computer than stand in front of the stove, you can increase your technological knowledge by visiting several Web sites with tutorials on building your own Web sites, the latest news about the Internet, and resources for visually impaired users.

Have you ever wondered how to make a key lime pie? How about learning how to cook some easy, low-calorie dishes? Are you seeking advice from expert chefs? The recipecenter.com Web site (Figure 18) is filled with information related to recipes.

Figure 18 The RecipeCenter.com Web site provides access to over 100,000 recipes, as well as software to help manage your recipes.

Learning Web Exercises

1. Visit one of the cooking Web sites listed in Figure 17 and find two recipes or cooking tips that you can use when preparing your next meal. Write a paragraph about each one, summarizing your discoveries. What are the advantages and disadvantages of accessing these Web sites on the new Web appliances that might someday be in your kitchen?

2. Using one of the technology and science Web sites and one of the other Web sites listed in Figure 17, search for information about communications and networks. Write a paragraph about your findings. Then, review the material in the general learning Web sites listed in Figure 17, and write a paragraph describing the content on each Web site that is pertinent to your major.

Science

For some people, space exploration is a hobby. Building and launching model rockets allow these scientists to participate in exploring the great frontier of space. For others, space exploration is their life. Numerous Web sites, including those in Figure 19, provide in-depth information about the universe.

Periodicals	Web Address
Archaeology Magazine	archaeology.org
Astronomy.com	astronomy.com
NewScientist.com	newscientist.com
OceanLink	oceanlink.island.net
Science / AAAS	sciencemag.org
Scientific American.com	sciam.com
Resources	**Web Address**
Department of Education & Training, Victoria, Australia	www.education.vic.gov.au
National Science Foundation (NSF)	nsf.gov
Science.gov: FirstGov for Science	science.gov
Science Community	**Web Address**
American Scientist, The Magazine of Sigma Xi, The Scientific Research Society	amsci.org
Federation of American Scientists	fas.org
Librarians' Internet Index	lii.org
NASA	www.nasa.gov
Sigma Xi, The Scientific Research Society	sigmaxi.org

For an updated list and links, click Guide to WWW sites in the Features section at scsite.com/tdc5.

Figure 19 Resources available on the Internet offer a wide range of subjects for enthusiasts who want to delve into familiar and unknown territories in the world of science.

NASA's Astronaut Flight Lounge Web site contains information about rockets, the space shuttle, the International Space Station, space transportation, and communications. Other science resources explore space-related questions about astronomy, physics, the earth sciences, microgravity, and robotics.

Rockets and space are not the only areas to explore in the world of science. Where can you find the latest pictures taken with the Hubble Space Telescope? Do you know which cities experienced an earthquake today? Have you ever wondered what a 3-D model of the amino acid glutamine looks like? You can find the answers to these questions and many others through the Science.gov Web site (*science.gov*) shown in Figure 20.

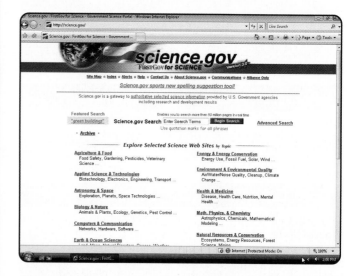

Figure 20 The Science.gov Web site provides easy access to the information in various federal science databases.

Science Web Exercises

1. Visit the NASA Web site listed in Figure 19. View the links about spacecraft, the universe, or tracking satellites and spacecraft, and then write a summary of your findings. Think of ways to tie this into an astronomy unit in which your students plan a space journey to their favorite planet or lunar body and write about what they expect to find when they land.

2. Visit the Librarians' Internet Index listed in Figure 19. Click the Technology link and then click the Inventions & Inventors topic. View the Web site for the Greatest Engineering Achievements of the Twentieth Century. Pick two achievements, read the history of each, and write a paragraph summarizing each of these accomplishments. Then, view two of the science Web sites listed in Figure 19 and write a paragraph about each of these Web sites describing the information each contains.

Environment

From the rain forests of Africa to the marine life in the Pacific Ocean, the fragile ecosystem is under extreme stress. Many environmental groups have developed Web sites, including those listed in Figure 21, in attempts to educate worldwide populations and to increase resource conservation. The

GreenNet Web site (Figure 22) contains information for people who would like to help safeguard the environment.

On an international scale, the Environmental Sites on the Internet Web page developed by the Royal Institute of Technology in Stockholm, Sweden, has been rated as one of the better ecological Web sites. Its comprehensive listing of environmental concerns range from aquatic ecology to wetlands.

The U.S. federal government has a number of Web sites devoted to specific environmental concerns. For example, the U.S. Environmental Protection Agency (EPA) provides pollution data, including ozone levels and air pollutants, for specific areas. Its AirData Web site displays air pollution emissions and monitoring data from the entire United States and is the world's most extensive collection of air pollution data.

NAME	Web Address
Central African Regional Program for the Environment (CARPE)	carpe.umd.edu
Earthjustice	earthjustice.org
EarthTrends: The Environmental Information Portal	earthtrends.wri.org
Environmental Defense	edf.org
Environmental Sites on the Internet	www.ima.kth.se/im/ envsite/envsite.htm
EPA AirData — Access to Air Pollution Data	epa.gov/air/data
Global Change and Environmental Education Resources	gcrio.org/educ.html
GreenNet	gn.apc.org
New American Dream	newdream.org
University of Wisconsin — Milwaukee Environmental Health and Safety Resources	www.uwm.edu/Dept/ EHSRM/EHSLINKS
USGS Acid rain data and reports	bqs.usgs.gov/acidrain
World-Wide Web Virtual Library: Botany / Plant Biology	ou.edu/cas/botany-micro/ www-vl/
For an updated list and links, click Guide to WWW sites in the Features section at scsite.com/tdc5.	

Figure 21 Environment Web sites provide vast resources for ecological data and action groups.

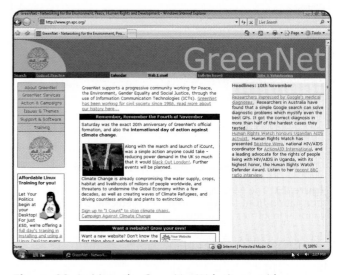

Figure 22 A visit to the GreenNet Web site provides information about people who work to support the environment.

Environment Web Exercises

1. Using the link listed in Figure 21, visit the New American Dream Web site and write a paragraph stating how many trees are leveled each year to provide paper for bulk mailings, how many garbage trucks are needed to haul the bulk mail waste, and other statistics. Read the letters that you can use to eliminate your name from bulk mail lists. To whom would you mail these letters? How long does it take to stop these unsolicited letters?

2. Visit the EPA AirData Web site. Read two reports about two different topics, such as acid rain and air quality, and summarize their findings. Include information about who sponsored the research, who conducted the studies, when the data was collected, and the impact of this pollution on the atmosphere, water, forests, and human health. Whom would you contact for further information regarding the data and studies?

Health

More than 70 million consumers use the Internet yearly to search for health information, so using the Web to store personal medical data is a natural extension of the Internet's capabilities. Internet health services and portals are available online to store your personal health history, including prescriptions, lab test results, doctor visits, allergies, and immunizations. Web sites such as MedlinePlus (Figure 23) provide free health information to consumers.

In minutes, you can register with a health Web site by choosing a user name and password. Then, you create a record to enter your medical history. You also can store data for your emergency contacts, primary care physicians, specialists, blood type, cholesterol levels, blood pressure, and insurance plan. No matter where you are in the world, you and medical personnel can obtain records via the Internet or fax machine. Some popular online health database management systems are shown in Figure 24.

Figure 23 The MedLine Plus Web site provides health information from the U.S. Library of Medicine and the National Institutes of Health.

Medical History	Web Address
PersonalMD	personalmd.com
Practice Solutions	practicesolutions.ca
Records for Living, Inc — PersonalHealth and Living Management	recordsforliving.com
WebMD	webmd.com
General Health	**Web Address**
Centers for Disease Control and Prevention	www.cdc.gov
familydoctor.org	familydoctor.org
healthfinder	healthfinder.gov
HealthWeb	healthweb.org
Medical Library Association Consumer and Patient Health Information Section (CAPHIS)	caphis.mlanet.org/consumer
MedlinePlus	medlineplus.gov
PEC: Health and Nutrition Web Sites	pecentral.org/websites/ healthsites.html
www.health.gov	health.gov

For an updated list and links, click Guide to WWW sites in the Features section at scsite.com/tdc5.

Figure 24 These health Web sites allow you to organize your medical information and store it in an online database and also obtain information about a variety of medical conditions and treatments.

Health Web Exercises

1. Access one of the health Web sites listed in Figure 24. Register yourself or a family member, and then enter the full health history. Create an emergency medical card if the Web site provides the card option. Submit this record and emergency card to your instructor. If you feel uncomfortable disclosing medical information for yourself or a family member, you may enter fictitious information.

2. Visit three of the health Web sites listed in Figure 24. Describe the features of each. Which of the three is the most user-friendly? Why? Describe the privacy policies of these three Web sites. Submit your analysis of these Web sites to your instructor.

Research and Resources

A recent Web Usability survey conducted by the Nielsen Norman Group found that 88 percent of people log onto a computer and then use a search engine as their first action. Search engines require users to type words and phrases that characterize the information being sought. Yahoo! (Figure 25), Google, and AltaVista are some of the more popular search engines. The key to effective searching on the Web is composing search queries that narrow the search results and place the most relevant Web sites at the top of the results list.

Keep up with the latest developments by viewing online dictionaries and encyclopedias that add to their collections of computer and product terms on a regular basis. Shopping for a new computer can be a daunting experience, but many online guides can help you select the components that best fit your needs and budget. If you are not confident in your ability to solve a problem alone, turn to online technical support. Web sites often provide streaming how-to video lessons, tutorials, and real-time chats with experienced technicians. Hardware and software reviews, price comparisons, shareware, technical questions and answers, and breaking technology news are found on comprehensive portals. Figure 26 lists popular research and resources Web sites.

Figure 25 The Yahoo! News search results for the phrase, computer, lists more than 26,000 stories.

Research	Web Address
A9.com	a9.com
AlltheWeb	alltheweb.com
Ask.com	ask.com
Citizendium	citizendium.org
Google	google.com
HotBot	hotbot.com
Overture	overture.com
Windows Live	live.com
Yahoo!	yahoo.com
Resources	**Web Address**
CNET.com	cnet.com
eHow	ehow.com
PC911	pcnineoneone.com
TechBargains	techbargains.com
Webopedia	webopedia.com
ZDNet	zdnet.com

For an updated list and links, click Guide to WWW sites in the Features section at scsite.com/tdc5.

Figure 26 Web users can find information by using research and resources Web sites.

Research and Resource Web Exercises

1. Use two of the search engines listed in the Research category in Figure 26 to find three Web sites that review the latest digital cameras. Make a table listing the search engines, Web site names, and the cameras' model numbers, suggested retail price, megapixels, memory, and features. Summarize which you would buy and why.

2. Visit the TechBargains Web site to choose the components you would buy if you were building a customized desktop computer. Create a table, listing the computer manufacturer, processor model name or number and manufacturer, clock speed, RAM, cache, number of expansion slots, and number of bays. Does this Web site provide enough information? Do you need to visit another Web site and create another table with comparative information before making any decisions? Summarize your findings in a brief paper.

Careers

While your education gives you valuable training to prepare you for a career, it rarely teaches you how to begin that career. You can broaden your horizons by searching the Internet for career information and job openings.

First, examine some of the job search Web sites. These resources list thousands of openings in hundreds of fields, companies, and locations. For example, the U.S. Department of Labor Web site, shown in Figure 27, allows you to find information for different types of jobs. In addition, state Departments of Education Web sites provide extensive information for future teachers.

When a company or school contacts you for an interview, learn as much about it as possible before the interview. Many of the Web sites listed in Figure 28 include detailed company profiles and links to their corporate Web sites.

Job Search	Web Address
BestJobsUSA.com	bestjobsusa.com
CareerBuilder	careerbuilder.com
CareerNet	careernet.com
CAREERXCHANGE	careerexchange.com
College Grad Job Hunter	collegegrad.com
EmploymentGuide.com	employmentguide.com
Job.com	job.com
JobBank USA	jobbankusa.com
JobWeb.com	www.jobweb.com
Monster	monster.com
Spherion	spherion.com
USAJOBS	usajobs.opm.gov
VolunteerMatch	volunteermatch.org
Yahoo! HotJobs	hotjobs.yahoo.com
Company/Industry Information	**Web Address**
Career ResourceCenter.com	resourcecenter.com
Forbes.com	forbes.com/careers
FORTUNE	fortune.com
Hoover's	hoovers.com
Occupational Outlook Handbook	stats.bls.gov/oco

For an updated list and links, click Guide to WWW sites in the Features section at scsite.com/tdc5.

Figure 27 The Occupational Outlook Handbook provides career information to those searching for jobs.

Figure 28 Career Web sites provide a variety of job openings and information about major companies worldwide.

Careers Web Exercises

1. Click the State/Federal Sites in the Features section at *scsite.com/tdc5* and then access your state's Department of Education. Review job opportunities in your state's school districts.

2. Explain to your students that it is a good idea to acquire information before graduation about the industry in which they would like to work. Are they interested in the automotive manufacturing industry, the restaurant service industry, or the financial industry? Students should use two of the company/industry information Web sites listed in Figure 28 to research a particular career related to their interests. Have students write a paragraph naming the Web sites and the specific information they found, such as the nature of the work, recommended training and qualifications, employment outlook, and earnings.

Arts and Literature

Brush up your knowledge of Shakespeare, grab a canvas, or put on your dancing shoes. Visual arts and literature Web sites, including those in Figure 29, are about to sweep you off your cyberfeet.

Arts	Web Address
accessplace arts	accessplace.com/arts.htm
Art News — absolutearts.com	absolutearts.com
The Children's Museum of Indianapolis	childrensmuseum.org
GalleryGuide.com	galleryguide.com
The Getty	getty.edu
Louvre Museum	louvre.fr
Montreal Museum of Fine Arts	mmfa.qc.ca
The New York Times: Arts	nytimes.com/pages/arts/index.html
Virtual Library museums pages (VLmp)	vlmp.museophile.com
Literature	**Web Address**
Bartleby.com	bartleby.com
Bibliomania	bibliomania.com
Fantastic Fiction	fantasticfiction.co.uk
Literary History	literaryhistory.com
The Modern Library eBook List	randomhouse.com/modernlibrary/ebookslist.html
Project Gutenberg	gutenberg.org
William Shakespeare at eNotes	shakespeare.com
For an updated list and links, click Guide to WWW sites in the Features section at scsite.com/tdc5.	

Figure 29 Discover culture throughout the world by visiting these arts and literature Web sites.

The full text of hundreds of books is available online from the Bibliomania and Project Gutenberg Web sites. Shakespeare.com provides in-depth reviews and news of the world's most famous playwright and his works. The Bartleby.com Web site features biographies, definitions, quotations, dictionaries, and indexes.

When you are ready to absorb more culture, you can turn to various art Web sites. Many museums have images of their collections online. Among them are the Getty Museum in Los Angeles (Figure 30), the Montreal Museum of Fine Arts, and the Louvre Museum in Paris.

The accessplace arts and The New York Times Web sites focus on the arts and humanities and provide fascinating glimpses into the worlds of dance, music, performance, cinema, and other topics pertaining to creative expression.

Figure 30 Permanent and temporary exhibitions, educational activities, and a bookstore are featured on the Getty Museum Web site.

Arts and Literature Web Exercises

1. Visit The Modern Library eBook List Web site listed in Figure 29 and view one book in the 20th Century Novels, 19th Century Novels, British Literature, and History sections. Create a table with columns for the book name, author, cost, online store, local store, and description. Then, read the excerpt from each of the four books and write a paragraph describing which of these four books is the most interesting to you. What are the advantages and disadvantages of reading classic literature electronically?

2. Using the arts Web sites listed in Figure 29, search for three temporary exhibitions in galleries throughout the world. Describe the venues, the artists, and the works. What permanent collections are found in these museums? Visit the museums' gift stores. View and describe three items for sale.

Successful Searching

Successful searching of the Web involves two key steps:

1. Briefly describe the information you are seeking. Start by identifying the main idea or concept in your topic and determine any synonyms, alternate spellings, or variant word forms for the concept.

2. Use the brief description with a search tool to display links to pages containing the desired information.

The two most common search tools are subject directories and search engines. You use a **subject directory** by clicking through its collection of categories and subcategories until you reach the information you want. You use a **search engine** to search based on a keyword. The following sections describe how to use a subject directory and a search engine.

Some Web sites offer the functionality of both a subject directory and a search engine. Yahoo! and Google, for example, are widely used search engines that also provide a subject directory.

Using a Subject Directory

A subject directory provides categorized lists of links. These categorized lists are arranged by subject and then displayed in a series of menus. Using this type of search tool, you can locate a particular topic by starting from the top and clicking links through the different levels, going from the general to the specific. Each time you click a category link, the search tool displays a page of subcategory links from which you again choose. You continue in this fashion until the search tool displays a list of Web pages on the desired topic. Browsing a subject directory requires that you make assumptions about the topic's hierarchical placement within the categorized list.

For the following example, assume you have been assigned the task of conducting research on the Web to find out if there are any Web sites that will allow you and your students to ask questions about reading or math issues. The assignment requires that you include at least one Web page citation. This example uses the Yahoo! (yahoo.com) search directory to locate information on reading for your assignment.

1. Start your browser and then enter the URL `www.free.ed.gov` in the Address text box. When the Federal Resources for Educational Excellence (FREE) home page is displayed, point to the Language Arts link, as shown in Figure 1.

Language Arts link

Figure 1 Federal Resources for Educational Excellence home page.

2. Click Language Arts. When the Language Arts page is displayed, point to the Reading link, as shown in Figure 2. Each time you click a category link, you move closer to the topic.

Reading link

Figure 2 Language Arts categories.

3. Click Reading. When the Reading page is displayed, point to SEE ALL, as shown in Figure 3.

SEE ALL link

Figure 3 Reading categories.

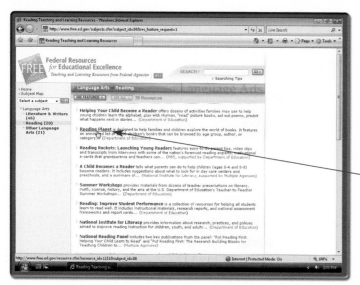

Figure 4 List of reading sites.

4. Click SEE ALL and then point to Reading Planet. Notice that there are numerous other links to resources on reading.

Reading Planet link

Figure 5 The Reading Planet Web page.

5. Click Reading Planet, read the brief description of the Reading Planet Web site, and then click GO TO THIS WEBSITE. When the page appears as shown in Figure 5, explore the site to see if this type of Web site can help you with your assignment.

With just a few clicks, the Federal Resources for Educational Excellence search directory displays information on a number of reading Web sites. The major problem with a subject directory is deciding which categories to choose as you work through the menus of links presented.

Next, you will use Google as a search engine to locate information for another research assignment.

Using a Search Engine

Search engines require that you enter search text or keywords (single word, words, or phrase) that define what you are looking for, rather than clicking through menus of links. Search engines often respond with results that include thousands of links to Web pages, many of which have little or no bearing on the information you are seeking. You can eliminate the superfluous pages by carefully choosing a keyword (or words) that limits the search. Assume you have been assigned the task of finding Web sites that will allow you and your students to ask questions about math issues. The following example uses the Google search engine to search using the phrase "ask math questions."

1. Start your browser and then enter the URL www.google.com in the Address text box. When the Google home page is displayed, type ask math questions in the Search text box and then point to the Google Search button, as shown in Figure 6.

To use Google as a subject directory, click the more link on the Google home page (see Figure 6).

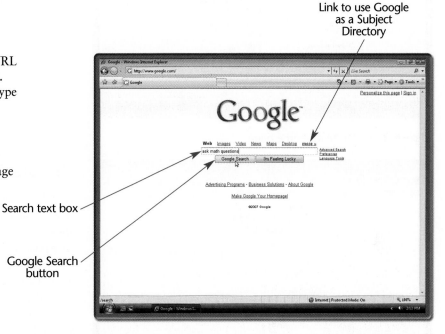

Link to use Google as a Subject Directory

Search text box

Google Search button

Figure 6 Google home page.

2. Click the Google Search button. When the results of the search are displayed, scroll through the links and read the descriptions. Point to The Math Forum - Ask Dr. Math link, as shown in Figure 7. The results in Figure 7 include more than 4.5 million links to Web pages concerning mathematics.

Most search engines sequence the results based on how close the keywords are to one another in the Web page titles and their descriptions. Thus, the first few links probably contain more relevant information.

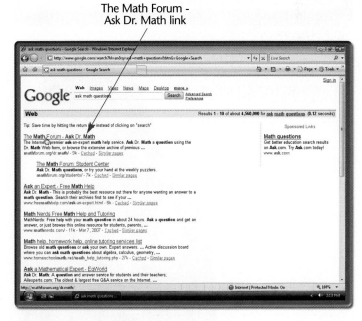

The Math Forum - Ask Dr. Math link

Figure 7 Google search results.

Figure 8 Ask Dr. Math home page.

3. Click the Math Forum – Ask Dr. Math link to display the Ask Dr. Math home page (Figure 8). With just one click, the Google search provided links to an amazing number of math Web site resources. The major problem with using a search engine is knowing which key words to enter to obtain the best search results.

Figure 9 Google Scholar Web page.

Google Scholar

Google provides Google Scholar, a new search engine (www.scholar.google.com) (Figure 9). This search engine allows users to search for scholarly literature, including peer-reviewed papers, thesis, books, preprints, abstracts, and technical reports from broad areas of research. You use Google Scholar to find articles from a wide variety of academic publishers, professional societies, preprint repositories and universities, as well as scholarly articles available across the Web.

Limiting the Search

If you enter a phrase with spaces between the keywords, most search engines return links to pages that include all of the words. Figure 10 lists some common operators, commands, and special characters you can use to refine your search.

Operator	Keyword Examples	Description
AND (+)	art AND music smoking health hazards fish +pollutants +runoff	Requires both words to be in the page. No operator between words or the plus sign (+) are shortcuts for the Boolean operator AND.
OR	mental illness OR insane canine OR dog OR puppy flight attendant OR stewardess OR steward	Requires only one of the words to be in the page.
AND NOT (–)	auto AND NOT SUV AND NOT convertible computers – programming shakespeare – hamlet – (romeo+juliet)	Excludes pages with the word following AND NOT. The minus sign (–) is a shortcut for the Boolean operator AND NOT.
( )	physics AND (relativity OR einstein)	Parentheses group portions of Boolean operators together.
" "	"harry potter" "19th century literature"	Requires the exact phrase within quotation marks to be in the page.
*	writ* clou*	The asterisk (*) at the end of words substitutes for any combination of characters.

Figure 10 Search engine keyword operators.

Guidelines to Successful Searching

You can improve your Web searches by following these guidelines.

1. Use nouns as keywords, and put the most important terms first.
2. Use the asterisk (*) to find variations of words. For example: retriev* returns retrieves, retrieval, retriever, and any other variation.
3. Type keywords in lowercase to find both lowercase and uppercase variations.
4. Use quotation marks to create phrases so the search engine finds the exact sequence of words.
5. Use a hyphen alternative. For example, use email OR e-mail.
6. Limit the search by language.
7. Use uppercase characters for Boolean operators in your search statements to differentiate between the words and operators.
8. Read a search engine's help section before you use it.
9. The Internet contains many search engines. If your search is unsuccessful with one search engine, try another.

Popular Search Sites

Most search sites include both a search engine and subject directory. Figure 11 contains a list of popular search sites and their URLs where you can access search engines and subject directories to search the Web.

Search Tool	Web Address	Subject Directory	Search Engine
A9.com	a9.com		X
AlltheWeb	alltheweb.com		X
AltaVista	altavista.com		X
AOL Search	search.aol.com	X	X
Ask.com	ask.com		X
Dogpile	dogpile.com		X
Excite	excite.com	X	X
Gigablast	gigablast.com	X	X
Google	google.com	X	X
Live Search	live.com		X
LookSmart	looksmart.com	X	X
Lycos	lycos.com		X
MSN	msn.com	X	X
Netscape Search	search.netscape.com		X
Open Directory Project	dmoz.org	X	X
Overture	overture.com		X
WebCrawler	webcrawler.com		X
Yahoo!	yahoo.com	X	X

Figure 11 Widely used search sites.

A number of outstanding search tools are tailored for use by K-12 educators. Figure 12 contains a list of the more popular education search tools. Many of these search tools contain both search engines and subject directories. In addition, a number of these search tools are reviewed by experienced educators to ensure the content and links are appropriate for K-12 students. To gain access to the Search Tools for Education, visit *scsite.com/tdc5*, click any chapter at the top of the Web page, and then click Search Tools on the left sidebar.

Ask for Kids
www.askforkids.com

Ask for Kids (formerly known as Ask Jeeves for Kids) is a fast, easy, and kid-friendly way for kids to search online. Designed to be a fun destination site focused on learning and edutainment, Ask for Kids uses natural-language technology that allows kids to ask questions and perform Web searches, such as "When did Hawaii become a state?" in the same way they would ask a parent, friend, or teacher.

Awesome Library
awesomelibrary.org

Awesome Library organizes 33,000 carefully reviewed links that are useful for teachers, students (kids or teens), parents, librarians, or college students. This Web site also allows users to browse in 9 different languages.

Ben's Guide to U.S. Government for Kids
bensguide.gpo.gov

This government-sponsored site provides learning tools for K-12 students, parents, and teachers. It includes resources on how the United States government works and other related topics.

Blue Web'N
www.kn.pacbell.com/wired/bluewebn

Blue Web'N is a searchable database containing thousands of outstanding Internet learning Web sites categorized by subject, grade level, and format. It also includes lessons, activities, projects, resources, references, tools, and more.

Busy Teachers' WebSite K-12
www.ceismc.gatech.edu/busyt

This Web site is designed to offer teachers direct source materials, lesson plans, and classroom activities. Teachers learning how to use the Internet will have an enjoyable and rewarding experience navigating through this Web site.

Education Search Engines
www.searchengineguide.com/pages/Education/

This site provides an alphabetical listing of dozens of education search engines, portals, and directories.

Education World
www.education-world.com

Visit this complete, online resource guide where educators can access a search engine that identifies educational Web sites. You also will be able to connect to lesson plans, research materials, daily features and columns, monthly site reviews, employment listings, and articles written by education experts.

Figure 12

EduHound
www.eduhound.com

EduHound is a highly specialized educational directory with built-in resource links for educators, students, and parents. This wonderful Web site seeks to harness the vast informational resources on the World Wide Web, while enabling educators to use the Internet as a classroom tool.

emTech
www.emtech.net

This Web site contains more than 15,000 resources organized by topics for teachers, students, parents, and other education professionals.

Federal Resources for Educational Excellence (FREE)
www.free.ed.gov

FREE makes it easier to find teaching and learning resources from the federal government and contains more than 1,500 federally supported teaching and learning resources from dozens of federal agencies. New sites are added regularly.

FirstGov for Kids
kids.gov

This is the U.S. government interagency kids' portal and provides links to federal kids' Web sites along with some of the best kids' sites from other organizations, all grouped by subject. This is an outstanding site for kids to search for government resources.

Google for Educators
www.google.com/educators

Google for Educators is a great source for teaching resources, everything from blogging and collaborative writing to geographical search tools and 3D modeling software.

Great Web Sites for Kids
www.ala.org/alsc/children_links.html

Looking for something fun and educational on the World Wide Web? You are likely to find it on this list of kids' Web sites compiled by the American Library Association.

Kathy Schrock's Guide for Educators
school.discovery.com/schrockguide

Kathy Schrock's Guide for Educators is a categorized list of Web sites that are useful for enhancing curriculum and professional growth. It is updated often to include the best Web sites for teaching and learning.

KidsClick!
sunsite.berkeley.edu/KidsClick!

This Web site for kids is compiled by librarians and contains a database of more than 5,000 sites organized into more than 600 subjects.

Kid's Search Tools
www.rcls.org/ksearch.htm

This site allows kids to search using a variety of kid-safe search engines from a single page.

Figure 12 *(continued)*

Learning Page
learningpage.com

This site contains a large collection of instructional materials that you can download and print, including lesson plans, books, worksheets, and many other materials.

Pedagonet
www.pedagonet.com

This Web site is a learning material and resource center where teachers can peruse a searchable database for sites related to their area plus teachers can submit requests to the site to publish needed resources.

Sites for Teachers
www.sitesforteachers.com

Sites for Teachers includes links to Web sites that contain teacher resources and educational materials. Web sites are ranked according to popularity.

STEM-NET Theme Pages for Elementary Students and Teachers
www.stemnet.nf.ca/CITE/themes.html

This Web site contains a general listing of theme-related links on a broad range of educational topics, such as the solar system, bats, sea life, weather, inventions, and much, much more.

The Educator's Reference Desk
www.eduref.org

The Educator's Reference Desk presents many useful resources, such as 2,000+ lesson plans, 3,000+ links to online education information, and 200+ question archive responses.

The Gateway to Educational Materials (GEM)
www.thegateway.org

The Gateway to Educational Materials is a consortium effort to provide educators with quick-and-easy access to thousands of educational resources, such as lesson plans and curriculum units found on various federal, state, university, nonprofit, and commercial Web sites.

Yahooligans!
kids.yahoo.com/

Yahooligans is a browsable, searchable directory of Web sites for kids and teens. Each Web site has been carefully checked by experienced educators to ensure that the content and links are age-appropriate.

Figure 12 *(continued)*

Application Software Productivity Tools for Educators

Objectives

After completing this chapter, you will be able to do the following:

[ISTE NETS-T Standards I A-B, II A-E, III A-D, IV A-D, V B-D, VI B-E]

- Explain the role of an operating system and list the main operating systems used on today's computers

- Define and describe a user interface and a graphical user interface

- Identify the important features of widely used software applications

- Describe the advantages of software suites

- Explain how to create documents

- Discuss why the use of video authoring and editing software is important for K-12 schools

- List and describe learning aids and support tools that help you use and learn software applications

- Explain how to work with different versions of software applications

An essential aspect of building computer literacy is learning about software, which is the series of instructions that tell computer hardware how to perform tasks. Having a solid understanding of software — especially application software — will help you comprehend how administrators, teachers, students, and other individuals use personal computers in today's society. It also will help you use your computer and other technologies to be more productive, organized, and well informed.

Application software such as word processing, spreadsheets, and e-mail programs can help you perform tasks such as creating documents, doing research, and managing projects. Before discussing various software applications used by teachers and students, however, this chapter provides a basic overview of the operating system and the user interface used on both Macintosh computers and PCs. The user interface controls how you work with any software, including application software.

Understanding application software can help advance your personal and professional goals by helping you manage student records, teach students with different academic needs, and work more productively. This chapter introduces you to the learning aids and tools available to help you and your students learn to use software applications. You can refer back to this chapter as you learn more about how computers are used today and how they can help you in your teaching career.

The Operating System

As with most computer users, you are probably somewhat familiar with application software. To use any application software, however, your computer must be running another type of software — an operating system.

THE ROLE OF THE OPERATING SYSTEM

Software can be categorized into two types: system software and application software. **System software** consists of programs that control the operations of the computer and its devices. System software serves as the interface between you (the user), your application software, and your computer's hardware (Figure 3-1). One type of system software, the **operating system**, contains instructions that coordinate all of the activities of the hardware devices in a computer.

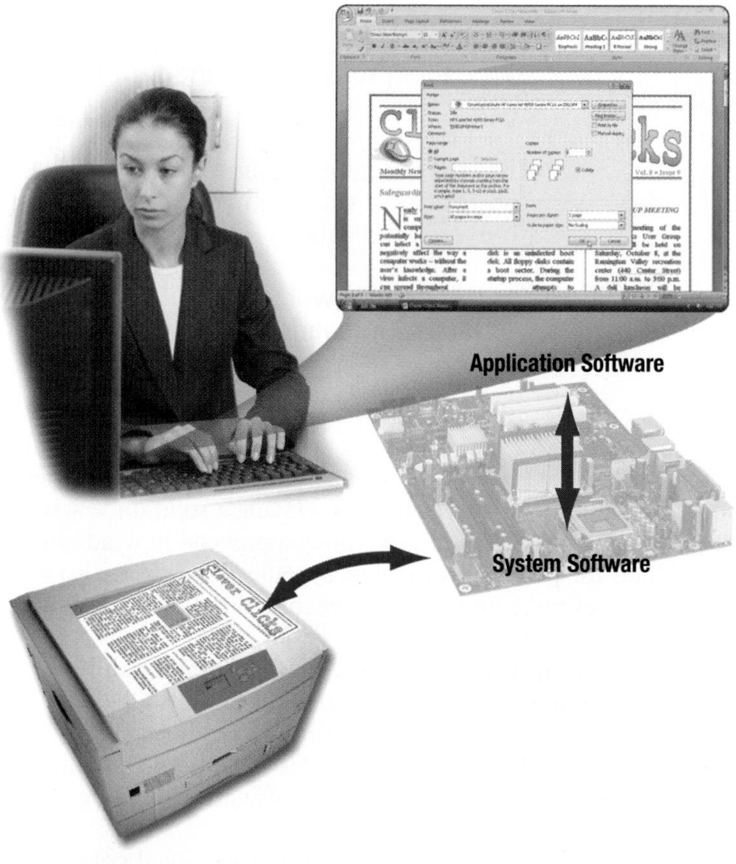

Application Software

System Software

Figure 3-1 System software is the interface between the user, the application software, and the computer's hardware. In this example, a user instructs the word processing software to print a document, the word processing software sends the print instructions to the system software, and the system software sends the print instructions to the printer.

The operating system also contains instructions that allow you to run application software.

Before either a Macintosh computer or a PC can run any application software, the operating system must be loaded from the hard disk into the computer's memory. Each time you start your computer, the operating system is loaded, or copied, into memory from the computer's hard disk. After the operating system is loaded, it tells the computer how to perform functions, such as processing program instructions or transferring data between input and output devices and memory. The operating system, which remains in memory while the computer is running, allows you to communicate with the computer and other software, such as word processors, grade books, and other application programs. The operating system continues to run until the computer is turned off.

USING DIFFERENT OPERATING SYSTEMS

Each new release of an operating system contains new features that make computers more powerful and easy to use. In addition, the newest operating systems provide enhanced integration with the World Wide Web and increase the multimedia capabilities of computers. Due to budget constraints and other factors, however, schools and home users do not always upgrade their computers every time a new version of an operating system is released. As a result, a number of different versions of operating systems currently are running on school and home computers.

MICROSOFT WINDOWS Microsoft Windows, which often is referred to simply as Windows with a capital W, is the most used operating system in the world. A brief summary of the versions of Microsoft Windows that are in use today follows.

WINDOWS XP Windows XP, released in late 2001 and upgraded in 2004, is a fast, reliable Windows operating system, providing quicker startup, better performance, increased security, and a simpler visual look than previous Windows versions. Windows XP is available in four main editions: Home Edition, Professional (Figure 3-2a), Media Center Edition, and Tablet PC Edition.

WINDOWS VISTA Windows Vista, the successor to Windows XP and released in 2007, is Microsoft's fastest, most reliable, and most efficient operating system to date, offering quicker application start up, built-in diagnostics, automatic recovery, improved security, and enhanced searching and organizing capabilities (Figure 3-2b). Windows Vista is available in five main editions: Windows Vista Home Basic, Windows Vista Home Premium, Windows Vista Ultimate, Windows Vista Business, and Windows Vista Enterprise.

- **Windows Vista Home Basic** is designed for basic home use. It includes the Windows Vista Basic interface and allows users to do each of the following easily: search for files; protect their computer from unauthorized intruders and unwanted programs; and set parental controls to monitor the use of games, the Internet, instant messaging, and other communications programs.

- **Windows Vista Home Premium** includes all the capabilities of Windows Vista Home Basic and also offers the Windows Aero interface. It also provides tools to create DVDs and edit movies, record and watch television shows, connect to a game console, securely connect to Wi-Fi networks, work with a Tablet PC, and quickly view messages on a powered-off, specially equipped notebook computer.

- **Windows Vista Ultimate** includes all features of Windows Vista Home Premium and provides additional features designed to make mobile users' computers more secure and easier to network.

MACINTOSH OPERATING SYSTEM OR MAC OS Most users of Macintosh computers use one of two versions of Mac OS.

- Mac OS, version 9.1 — Older Apple and Macintosh school computers use **Mac OS, version 9.1**.

- Mac OS X — The **Mac OS X** version of the Macintosh operating system, released in 2001, upgraded in 2004 and again in 2007, is a significant upgrade to the Macintosh operating system in both appearance and use. Included with the latest version, called Leopard (see Figure 3-5 on page 146) are new and enhanced features like Time Machine, Mail 3, iChat, Spaces, Dashboard, and Spotlight to name just a few.

OTHER OPERATING SYSTEMS Two other common operating systems are UNIX and Linux.

- UNIX — **UNIX** is a multitasking operating system developed for mainframe computers in the early 1970s by scientists at Bell Laboratories, a subsidiary of AT&T. Today, versions of UNIX are available for computers of all sizes.

- Linux — **Linux** is a popular, multitasking UNIX-based operating system that is one of the faster growing operating systems in use today. Unlike Windows and Mac OS, both of which are proprietary systems, Linux is **open source**

[a]

[b]

Figure 3-2 Figure 3-2a shows Windows XP and Figure 3-2b shows Windows Vista Ultimate.

software, which means its code is available free to the public.

THE ROLE OF THE USER INTERFACE

All software, including the operating system, is designed to communicate with the user in a certain way, through a user interface. A **user interface** controls how you enter data or instructions (input) and how information is presented on the screen (output).

One of the more common user interfaces is a graphical user interface. A **graphical user interface**, or **GUI** (pronounced gooey), combines text, graphics, and other visual cues to make software easier to use. In 1984, Apple introduced a new operating system based on a graphical user interface. Recognizing the value of this easy-to-use interface, many software companies followed suit by developing software that incorporates a graphical user interface.

Application Software

Recall that **application software** consists of programs designed to perform specific tasks for users. Application software, also called **application programs**, can be used for the following purposes:

- As a productivity/business tool
- Assisting with graphics and multimedia projects
- Supporting school and professional activities

- Helping with home and personal activities
- Facilitating communications

The table in Figure 3-3 categorizes popular types of application software by their general use. These five categories are not all-inclusive nor are they mutually exclusive; for example, e-mail can support productivity, a software suite can include Web page authoring tools, and tax preparation software can be used by a business. In the course of a day, week, or month, you are likely to find yourself using software from many of these categories, whether you are at school, home, or work. Even though you may not use all of the applications, you should at least be familiar with their capabilities.

Communications applications, such as e-mail, Web browsers, and others, were discussed in Chapter 2. This chapter gives a general overview of each of the other four categories and provides specific examples of applications in each category that are used on both PCs and Macintosh computers.

A wide variety of application software, such as word processing, is available as packaged software that can be purchased from software vendors in retail stores or on the Web. A particular software product, such as Microsoft Word, often is called a **software package**. Many application software packages also are available as shareware, freeware, and public-domain software; these packages, however, usually have fewer capabilities than retail software packages.

FAQ

Can I simply turn the computer off when I am finished?

No! You must use the operating system's shut-down procedure so various processes are closed in sequence and items in memory are released properly.

Figure 3-3 The five major categories of popular application software. You likely will use software from more than one of these categories.

Categories of Application Software

Productivity Business	Graphic Design/ Multimedia	School	Home/Personal	Communications
• Word Processing	• Desktop Publishing	• School/Student Management	• Personal Finance	• E-Mail
• Spreadsheet	• Paint/Image Editing	• Grade Book	• Tax Preparation	• Web Browser
• Presentation Graphics	• Multimedia Authoring	• Education/Reference	• Legal	• Chat Rooms
• Database	• Web Page Authoring	• Special Needs	• Entertainment	• Newsgroups
• Personal Information Management		• Note Taking		• Instant Messaging
• Software Suite				• Blogs
				• Wikis

STARTING A SOFTWARE APPLICATION

To use application software, you must instruct the operating system to start the program. Figure 3-4 illustrates how to start and then interact with the Paint program on a PC using Microsoft Windows Vista.

Both Mac OS and Microsoft Windows use the concept of a desktop to make the computer easier to use. The **desktop** is an on-screen work area that uses common graphical elements such as icons, buttons, windows, menus, and dialog boxes to make it easy and intuitive for users to interact with the computer.

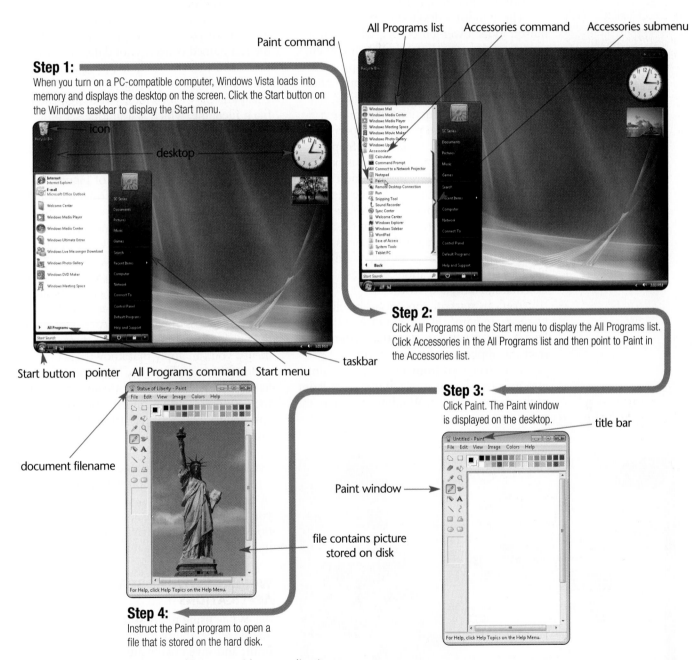

Step 1:
When you turn on a PC-compatible computer, Windows Vista loads into memory and displays the desktop on the screen. Click the Start button on the Windows taskbar to display the Start menu.

Step 2:
Click All Programs on the Start menu to display the All Programs list. Click Accessories in the All Programs list and then point to Paint in the Accessories list.

Step 3:
Click Paint. The Paint window is displayed on the desktop.

Step 4:
Instruct the Paint program to open a file that is stored on the hard disk.

Figure 3-4 How to start and interact with an application.

Integration Strategies

To learn more about how to integrate content-specific software applications, such as Kidspiration, Tessellation, and Thinkology, visit the Teachers Discovering Computers Web site (*scsite.com/tdc5*), click Chapter 3, and then click Software Corner.

An **icon** is a small image that represents a program, an instruction, or some other object. A **button** is a graphical element (usually a rectangular or circular shape) that when selected, causes a specific action to take place. To select a button, typically you click it using a pointing device, such as a mouse. You also can select a button using the keyboard. Icons, text, or a combination of both are used to identify buttons.

The Windows desktop contains a Start button in its lower-left corner, which can be used to start an application. When you click the Start button, the Start menu opens on the desktop. A **menu** is a list of commands from which you can make a selection. **Commands** are instructions that cause a computer program to perform a specific action. For example, as shown in Steps 1 and 2 of Figure 3-4 on the previous page, when you click the Start button and click the All Programs command on the Start menu, the All Programs list is displayed. Clicking the Accessories folder in the All Programs list displays the Accessories list. As shown in the Accessories list, Windows includes several applications, such as Calculator, Paint, and WordPad.

You can start an application by clicking its program name on a menu or in a list. Doing so instructs the operating system to start the application by transferring the program's instructions from a storage medium into memory. For example, if you click Paint in the Accessories list, Windows transfers the program instructions from the computer's hard disk into memory.

Once started, an application is displayed in a window on the desktop. A **window** is a rectangular area of the screen that is used to display a program, data, and/or information (see Step 3 of Figure 3-4 on the previous page). The top of a window has a **title bar**, which is a horizontal space that contains the window's name.

Any document on which you are working or you have saved exists as a file. A **file** is a named collection of data, such as a document that you create, a program, or a set of data used by a program. To distinguish among various files, you assign each file a **filename**, which is a unique set of letters, numbers, and other characters that identifies the file. The title bar of the document window usually displays a document's filename, as shown in Step 4 of Figure 3-4 on the previous page. Also shown in Step 4 of Figure 3-4 is the contents of the file Statue of Liberty displayed in the Paint window. The Statue of Liberty file contains an image photographed with a digital camera.

One of the major advantages of a graphical user interface is that elements such as icons, buttons, and menus, usually are common across applications. After you learn the purpose and functionality of these elements, you can apply that knowledge to several software applications. Many of the features just described also are applicable to the desktop of the Macintosh operating system (Figure 3-5), which is arranged somewhat differently than the desktop of a PC.

The features of a graphical user interface make it easier for users to communicate with a personal computer. You will see examples of these features and how they are used as you learn about various software applications used by schools, businesses, and individuals.

WORKING WITH SOFTWARE APPLICATIONS

While using many software applications, you have the ability to create, edit, format, print, and save documents. A **document** is a piece of work created with an application and saved on a storage medium with a unique filename. Many users think of documents as files created using word processing software. To a computer, however, a

Figure 3-5 The Mac OS X desktop contains features similar to a PC desktop, however, the arrangement of the features is different.

document is nothing more than a collection of characters, so a spreadsheet or graphic is as much a document as a letter or report. During the process of developing a document, you likely will switch back and forth among the following activities.

Creating involves developing the document by entering text or numbers, designing graphics, and performing other tasks using an input device, such as a keyboard or mouse. If you design a map using the graphics tools in Paint, for example, you are creating a document.

Editing is the process of making changes to the document's existing content. Common editing tasks include inserting, deleting, cutting, copying, and pasting items in a document. For example, using Paint, you can **insert**, or add, text to the map, such as the names of key landmarks. When you **delete**, you remove text or objects. To **cut** involves removing a portion of the document and electronically storing it in a temporary storage location called the **Clipboard**. When you **copy**, a portion of the document is duplicated and stored on the Clipboard. To place whatever is stored on the Clipboard into the document, you **paste** it into the document.

Formatting involves changing the appearance of a document. Formatting is important because the overall look of a document can significantly affect its ability to communicate effectively. For example, you might want to increase the size of the text to improve readability.

One often-used formatting task involves formatting text by changing the font, font size, or font style of text. A **font** is a name assigned to a specific design of characters. Arial and Times New Roman are examples of fonts. The **font size** specifies the size of the characters in a particular font. Font size is gauged by a mea-surement system called **points**. A single point is about 1/72 of an inch in height. The text you are reading in this book is 10.5 point. Thus, each character is about 10/72 of an inch in height. A **font style** is used to add emphasis to a font. Examples of font styles are **bold**, *italic*, and underline. Examples of these and additional formatting features are shown in Figure 3-6.

While you are creating, editing, and formatting a document, it is held temporarily in memory. As you work, you normally save your document for future use. **Saving** is the process of copying a document from memory to a storage medium, such as a

Figure 3-6
Examples of formatting features available with many productivity programs.

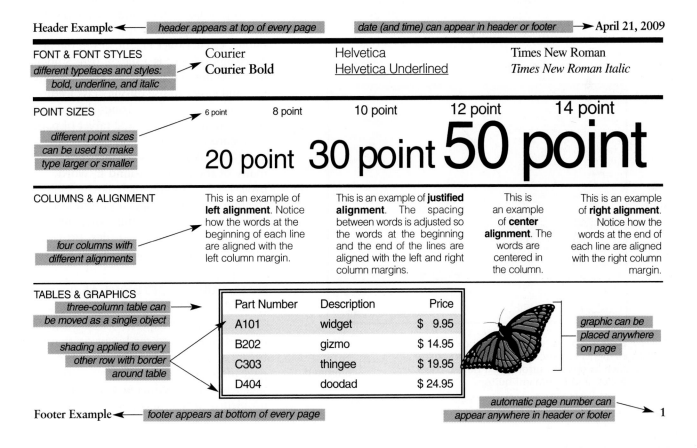

Header Example ← header appears at top of every page   date (and time) can appear in header or footer → April 21, 2009

| FONT & FONT STYLES | Courier | Helvetica | Times New Roman |
| different typefaces and styles: bold, underline, and italic | **Courier Bold** | Helvetica Underlined | *Times New Roman Italic* |

POINT SIZES
different point sizes can be used to make type larger or smaller

6 point   8 point   10 point   12 point   14 point

20 point 30 point 50 point

| COLUMNS & ALIGNMENT | This is an example of **left alignment**. Notice how the words at the beginning of each line are aligned with the left column margin. | This is an example of **justified alignment**. The spacing between words is adjusted so the words at the beginning and the end of the lines are aligned with the left and right column margins. | This is an example of **center alignment**. The words are centered in the column. | This is an example of **right alignment**. Notice how the words at the end of each line are aligned with the right column margin. |

four columns with different alignments

TABLES & GRAPHICS
three-column table can be moved as a single object
shading applied to every other row with border around table

Part Number	Description	Price
A101	widget	$ 9.95
B202	gizmo	$ 14.95
C303	thingee	$ 19.95
D404	doodad	$ 24.95

graphic can be placed anywhere on page

USB thumb drive or hard disk. You should save the document frequently while working with it so your work will not be lost if the power fails or the computer crashes. Many applications also have an optional **AutoSave** feature that automatically saves open documents at specified time periods. You should save your work frequently, however, and not rely on the AutoSave feature.

After you have created a document, you can print it many times, with each copy looking just like the first. **Printing** is the process of sending a file to a printer to generate output on a medium, such as paper. You also can send the document to others electronically, if your computer is connected to a network.

In some cases, when you instruct a program to perform an activity such as printing, a dialog box opens. A **dialog box** is a special window displayed by a program to provide information, present available options, or request a response using command buttons, option buttons, text boxes, and check boxes (Figure 3-7). A Print dialog box, for example, gives you many printing options, such as printing multiple copies or using different printers.

FAQ

Will a document print as it looks on the screen?

Usually, yes, because most current application software is WYSIWYG (what you see is what you get). The application software embeds invisible codes around the text and graphics, which instruct the printer how to present the information.

VOICE RECOGNITION

Many software applications support voice recognition. **Voice recognition**, also called **speech recognition**, is the computer's capability of distinguishing spoken words. You speak into the computer's microphone and watch your words display on your screen as you talk. You also can edit and format a document by speaking or spelling instructions.

NOTE TAKING SOFTWARE

Note taking software is application software that enables users to enter typed text, handwritten comments, graphs, drawings, or sketches anywhere on a page and then save the page as part of an electronic notebook. The software can convert handwritten comments to typed text or store the notes in a handwritten form. Users also can include audio recordings as part of their notes.

After notes are captured (entered and saved), users can organize them, reuse them, and share them easily. The software allows the users to search through saved notes for specific text. Users can search through an entire notebook. Users can flag important notes with color, highlight, and shapes. On a desktop or notebook computer, users enter notes primarily via the keyboard or microphone. On a Tablet PC, however, the primary input device is a digital pen. Students may find note taking software more convenient and easier to use during class lectures, in libraries, and in other settings that previously required a pencil and tablet of paper for recording thoughts and discussions.

Note taking software incorporates many of the features found in word processing software, such as checking spelling, changing fonts and font sizes, adding colors, recognizing voice input, inserting audio and video files, providing research capabilities, and so much more.

NOTE TAKING SOFTWARE AS A DIGITAL TOOL FOR DIGITAL KIDS

Did you ever experience the frustration of not being able to read your written notes before a test? Have you searched through page after page of your written notes for the answer to specific questions? These problems, so typical of the experiences of

Figure 3-7 This Print dialog box shows elements common to many dialog boxes, such as option buttons, text boxes, check boxes, and command buttons.

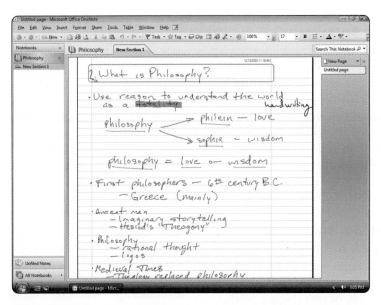

Figure 3-8 With note taking software, digital students and other mobile users can handwrite notes, draw sketches, type text, send handwritten e-mails, and more.

Integration Strategies

To learn more about how to use and integrate Microsoft's note taking software, OneNote, visit the Teachers Discovering Computers Web site (*scsite.com/tdc5*), click Chapter 3, and then click Digital Media Corner.

digital immigrant teachers may be a thing of the past for today's digital kids. In fact, note taking software for this digital generation may be a perfect solution both inside and outside the classroom. By using note taking software (Figure 3-8), students can have digital documents that are legible, searchable, and editable; however, most students are still taking notes the traditional way, with paper and pencil. Although more and more K-12 students are bringing their laptops to class and typing their notes, many of these students cannot type as fast as they can write. With the power of note taking software, students can increase their

comprehension and capture more of the content.

Many experts are predicting that as Tablet PCs and other mobile note taking devices become mainstream, printed school and college textbooks will become obsolete. Instead, digital students will interact with digital versions of their textbooks (Figure 3-9). Currently, several publishers are perfecting various ways of providing their content via the Web, Tablet PC, and traditional printed versions of their textbooks to determine which one is successful with students.

Figure 3-9 Education will reap many benefits as Tablet PCs and the multitude of software products being developed for them become mainstream.

Web Info

For more information about Microsoft Works, visit the Teachers Discovering Computers Web site, (scsite.com/tdc5), click Chapter 3, click Web Info, and then click Microsoft Works.

Productivity Software

Productivity software is designed to make people more effective and efficient while performing daily activities. Productivity software includes applications such as word processing, spreadsheet, database, presentation graphics, personal information management, and software suites. The features and functions of each of these applications are discussed in the following sections.

WORD PROCESSING SOFTWARE

One of the more widely used application software is **word processing software**, which is used to create, edit, and format documents that consist primarily of text (Figure 3-10). Millions of people use word processing software every day to create documents such as letters, memos, reports, fax cover sheets, mailing labels, and newsletters. The more popular word processing programs used in schools today are Microsoft Word, WordPerfect, and the word processing applications included with AppleWorks and Microsoft Works. By acquiring solid word processing skills, teachers can increase their productivity significantly by using word processing software to create written documents, such as lesson plans, handouts, parent communications, and student tests.

In addition to supporting basic text, word processing software has many formatting features to make documents look professional and visually appealing. When developing a newsletter, for example, you can change the font and font size of headlines and headings, change the color of characters, or organize text into newspaper-style columns. Any colors used for characters or other formatting will print

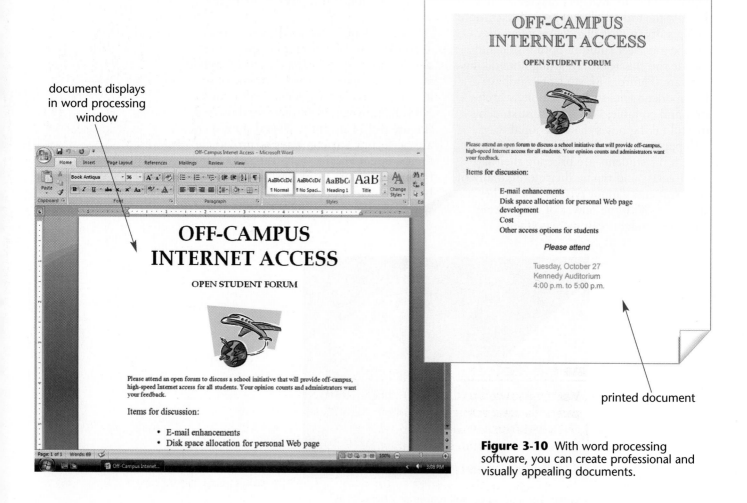

document displays in word processing window

printed document

Figure 3-10 With word processing software, you can create professional and visually appealing documents.

as black or gray unless you have a color printer.

Most word processing software also can incorporate many types of graphics. For example, you can enhance a document by adding a **border**, which is a decorative line or pattern along one or more edges of a page or graphic. One type of graphic commonly included with word processing software is **clip art**, which is a collection of drawings, diagrams, and photographs that can be inserted in other documents. **Clip art collections**, which can contain several hundred to several thousand images, usually are grouped by type, such as buildings, people, or nature (Figure 3-11). If you want to use clip art not included in your word processing software package, you can create clip art and other graphics using Paint or other applications and **import** (bring into) the clip art into a word processing document. Paint and image editing software are discussed later in this chapter. After you insert, or import, a clip art image or other graphic into a document, you can move, resize, rotate, crop, and adjust its color.

All word processing software provides basic capabilities to help you create, edit, and format documents. For example, you can define the size of the paper on which to print, as well as the **margins** — that is, the portion of the page outside the main body of text, on the top, bottom, left, and right sides of the paper. The word processing software automatically readjusts any text so it fits within the new definitions.

If you type text that extends beyond the page margin or window boundary, the word processor uses **wordwrap** to automatically position text at the beginning of the next line. Wordwrap allows you to type words in a paragraph continually without pressing the Enter key at the end of each line.

In some instances, for example if you create a multipage document, you can view only a portion of a document on the screen at a time. As you type more lines of text than can be displayed on the screen, the top portion of the document moves upward, or scrolls, off the screen. **Scrolling** is the process of moving different portions of the document into view on the screen.

A major advantage of using word processing software is that you can change easily what you have written. You can insert, delete, or rearrange words, sentences, or entire sections. You can use the **find** or **search** feature to locate all occurrences of a particular character, word, or phrase. This feature can be used in combination with the **replace** feature to substitute existing characters or words with new ones. Current word processing software packages even have a feature that automatically corrects errors and makes word substitutions as you type text.

To review the spelling of individual words, sections of a document, or the entire document, you can use a **spelling checker**, also called a **spell checker**.

Web Info

For samples of clip art available on the Internet, visit the Teachers Discovering Computers Web site, (*scsite.com/tdc5*), click Chapter 3, click Web Info, and then click Clip Art.

Web Info

For details about spelling bees, visit the Teachers Discovering Computers Web site, (*scsite.com/tdc5*), click Chapter 3, click Web Info, and then click Spelling.

Lion 1
Iris
Puppy
Puffin
Conch 1
Trout
Mammoth

Figure 3-11 Clip art consists of previously created illustrations that can be added to documents. Clip art collections include graphic images that are grouped by type. These clip art examples are from an animals and nature collection.

Spelling checker compares the words in the document with an electronic dictionary that is part of the word processing software (Figure 3-12). You can customize the electronic dictionary by adding words, such as names of companies, schools, streets, and cities, and personal names, so the software can spell check those words as well. Many word processing software packages allow you to check the spelling of a whole document at one time or check the spelling of single words as you type.

Figure 3-12 Spell checkers are included with most word processors. Shown is the spell checker included with AppleWorks.

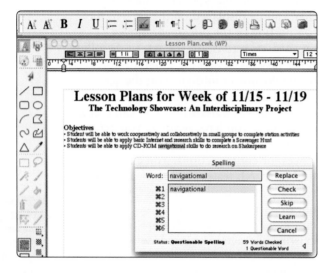

You also can insert headers and footers into a word processing document. A **header** is text you want at the top of each page; a **footer** is text you want at the bottom of each page. Page numbers, as well as company and school names, report titles, or dates are examples of items frequently included in headers and footers.

Many word processing programs make it quick and easy for teachers and students to create personalized documents using templates and special programs called wizards. A **template** is a document that contains the formatting necessary for a specific document type. A **wizard**, or **assistant**, is an automated tool that helps you complete a task by asking you questions and then automatically performing actions based on your answers. Many software applications include wizards. Word processing software, for example, uses wizards and templates to help you create blogs, memorandums, meeting agendas, letters, and other professional looking documents (Figure 3-13).

In addition to these basic features, most current word processing packages provide many other features, some of which are listed in the table in Figure 3-14 on the next page.

[a] AppleWorks

[b] Microsoft Word

Figure 3-13 A wizard, called an assistant in AppleWorks, allows teachers and students to create personalized flyers, newsletters, certificates, and more quickly. Figure 3-13a shows some of the assistants available in AppleWorks, and Figure 3-13b shows some of the templates available in Microsoft Word.

Some Word Processing Features

AutoCorrect	As you type words, the AutoCorrect feature corrects common spelling errors. AutoCorrect also corrects capitalization mistakes.
AutoFormat	As you type, the AutoFormat feature automatically applies formatting to the text. For example, it automatically numbers a list or converts a Web address to a hyperlink.
Collaboration	Collaboration includes discussions and online meetings. Discussions allow multiple users to enter comments in a document and read and reply to each other's comments. Through an online meeting, users share documents with others in real time and view changes as they are being made.
Columns	Most word processing software can arrange text in two or more columns to look like a newspaper or magazine. The text from the bottom of one column automatically flows to the top of the next column.
Grammar Checker	The grammar checker proofreads documents for grammar, writing style, sentence structure errors, and reading statistics.
Ink Input	Ink input supports input from a digital pen. Word processing software that supports ink input incorporates a user's handwritten text and drawings in a word processing document. Ink input is popular on Tablet PCs.
Macros	A *macro* is a sequence of keystrokes and instructions that a user records and saves. When you want to execute the same series of instructions, execute the macro instead.
Mail Merge	Mail merge creates form letters, mailing labels, and envelopes.
Reading Layout	For those users who prefer reading on the screen, reading layout increases the readability and legibility of an on-screen document by hiding unnecessary toolbars, increasing the size of displayed characters, and providing navigation tools.
Research	Some word processing software allows you to search through various forms of online and Internet reference information — based on selected text in a document. Research services available include a thesaurus, English and bilingual dictionaries, encyclopedias, and Web sites that provide information such as stock quotes, news articles, and company profiles.
Smart Tags	*Smart Tags* automatically appear on the screen when you perform a certain action. For example, typing an address causes a Smart Tag to appear. Clicking this Smart Tag provides options to display a map of the address or driving directions to or from the address.
Tables	Tables organize information into rows and columns. In addition to evenly spaced rows and columns, some word processing programs allow you to draw tables of any size or shape.
Templates	A *template* is a document that contains the formatting necessary for a specific document type. Templates usually exist for memos, fax cover sheets, and letters. In addition to templates provided with the software, users have access to many online templates through the software manufacturer's Web site.
Thesaurus	With a thesaurus, a user looks up a synonym (word with the same meaning) for a word in a document.
Tracking Changes	If multiple users work with a document, the word processing software highlights or color-codes changes made by various users.
Voice Recognition	With some word processing programs, users can speak into the computer's microphone and watch the spoken words appear on the screen as they speak. With these programs, users edit and format the document by speaking or spelling an instruction.
Web Page Development	Most word processing software allows users to create, edit, format, and convert documents to be displayed on the World Wide Web.

Figure 3-14 Some of the features included with word processing software.

SPREADSHEET SOFTWARE

Another widely used software application is **spreadsheet software,** which allows you to organize numeric data in rows and columns. These rows and columns collectively are called a **spreadsheet,** or **worksheet.** Manual spreadsheets created using pencil and paper have long been used to organize numeric data. The data in an electronic spreadsheet is organized in the same manner as it is in a manual spreadsheet (Figure 3-15 on the next page).

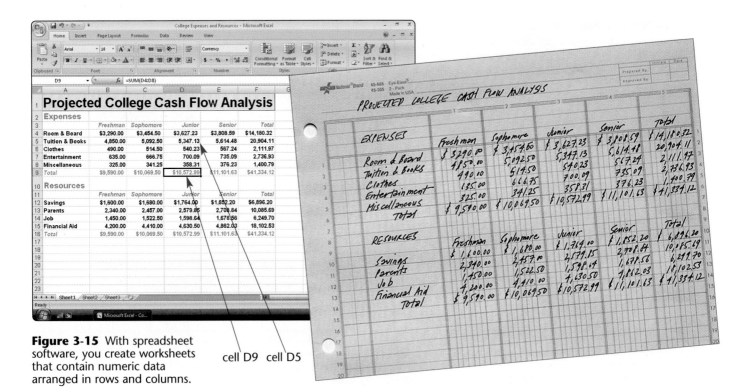

Figure 3-15 With spreadsheet software, you create worksheets that contain numeric data arranged in rows and columns.

cell D9   cell D5

Individuals who frequently work with numbers, such as financial statements and payroll, use spreadsheets. Many teachers interact with spreadsheet programs on a daily basis. Every time teachers enter students' grade or attendance information into a computer, they are entering information into a special spreadsheet program, called an electronic grade book. K-12 grade book programs are discussed later in this chapter.

As with word processing software, most spreadsheet software has basic features to help you create, edit, and format electronic spreadsheets. These features, which are included in several popular spreadsheet packages, are described below. Spreadsheet software included in Microsoft Works and AppleWorks, as well as Microsoft Excel that is packaged with Microsoft Office, are the programs typically used in schools.

Spreadsheet files normally have thousands of columns and rows. Each column is identified by a letter, and each row is identified by a number. The column letters begin with A and row numbers begin with 1. Only a small fraction of these columns and rows are displayed on the screen at one time. You can scroll to view different parts of a worksheet on your screen.

The intersection of a column and row is called a **cell**. Cells are identified by the column and row in which they are located. For example, the intersection of column D and row 5 is referred to as cell D5. In Figure 3-15, cell D5 contains the number 5,347.13, which represents Junior year Tuition & Books expenses.

Cells may contain three types of data: labels (text), values (numbers), and formulas. The text, or **label**, entered in a cell is used to identify the data and help organize the spreadsheet. Using descriptive labels, such as Room & Board, Tuition & Books, and Clothes, helps make a spreadsheet more meaningful.

Many of the spreadsheet cells shown in Figure 3-15 contain a number, or a **value**. Other cells, however, contain formulas that are used to generate values. A **formula** performs calculations on the numeric data in the spreadsheet and displays the resulting value in the cell containing the formula. In Figure 3-15, for example, cell D9 contains the formula to calculate the projected total expenses for the student's junior year.

A **function** is a predefined formula that performs common calculations, such as adding the values in a group of cells. For example, instead of using the formula =D4+D5+D6+D7+D8 to calculate the projected total expenses for the student's sophomore year, you should use the function =sum(D4:D8), which adds, or sums, the contents of cells D4, D5, D6, D7, and D8.

Another standard feature of spreadsheet software is the capability of turning numeric data into a **chart** that graphically illustrates the relationship of the numeric data. Visual representation of data in charts often makes it easier to analyze and interpret information. Most charts are variations of three basic chart types — line charts, column charts, and pie charts, as shown in Figure 3-16. It is important to pick the chart type that provides the best visualization for your data. To improve their appearance, most charts can be displayed or printed in a three-dimensional format.

As with word processing software, you can create professional looking spreadsheets quickly using wizards. Using the wizards in most popular spreadsheet packages is easy and allows you to create grade books, classroom and school schedules, charts, and more. Spreadsheet software also incorporates many of the features of word processing software, such as a spelling checker, font formatting, and the capability of converting an existing spreadsheet document into the standard document format for the World Wide Web. Because individual rows, columns, cells, or any combination of cells can be formatted, school districts and businesses often use spreadsheet programs to create their standardized forms.

DATABASE SOFTWARE

A **database** is a collection of data organized in a manner that allows access, retrieval, and use of that data. In a manual system, schools record information on paper and store it in a filing cabinet (Figure 3-17). In a computerized database, such as the one shown in Figure 3-20 on page 151, data is stored in an electronic format on a storage medium. **Database software** allows you to create a computerized database; add, change, and delete data; sort and retrieve data from the database; and create forms and reports using the data in the database.

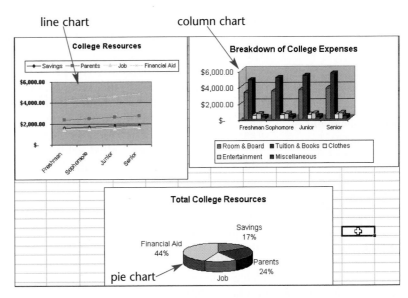

Figure 3-16 Three basic types of charts provided with spreadsheet software are line charts, column charts, and pie charts. The line chart, column chart, and pie chart shown were created from the data in the worksheet in Figure 3-15.

Database software is used extensively by businesses and other organizations to organize data and information about customers, employees, equipment, product inventory, sales information, and more. Schools use databases to organize data and information about students, staff members, school policies, equipment inventories, book inventories, purchases, and more. Database programs typically used in schools include Microsoft Access,

Figure 3-17 A database is similar to a manual system in which related data items are stored in files.

Web Info

For an example of how athletes use databases for training purposes, visit the Teachers Discovering Computers Web site, (*scsite.com/tdc5*), click Chapter 3, click Web Info, and then click Athlete.

FileMaker Pro, and the database software included in Microsoft Works and AppleWorks.

When you use a database, you need to be familiar with the terms file, record, and field. Just as in a manual system, a **database file** is a collection of related data that is organized in records. Each **record** contains a collection of related facts called fields. A **field** is the smallest unit of information you can access in a database. For example, a student database file might consist of records containing names, address information, and parental or guardian information. All of the data that relates to one student is considered a record. Each fact in a record, such as the street address or telephone number, is called a field.

Figures 3-18 through 3-20 present the development of a database containing basic information about students enrolled in Ms. Eileen Tanner's second grade class at Martin Luther King Elementary School. This simple database contains the following information about each student: first name, last name, guardian's address, name, and telephone number.

Before you begin creating a database, make a list of the data items you want to organize (Figure 3-18). Each set of related information will become a record. Each item will become a field in the database. A field entry screen from Microsoft Works is shown in Figure 3-19. To identify the different fields, assign each field a unique name that is short, yet descriptive. For example, the field name for a student's last name could be Last Name, the field name for a student's first name could be First Name, and so on. Database programs differ slightly in how they require the user to enter or define fields.

After the database structure is created by defining the fields, data for individual database records can be entered. After data for all records is entered, the database can be used to produce information. Figure 3-20 shows the database after the information about the students has been entered.

As with word processing and spreadsheet software, database software includes wizards that allow teachers and students to create databases for use as address books, directories of parents and students, equipment and book inventories, and so on.

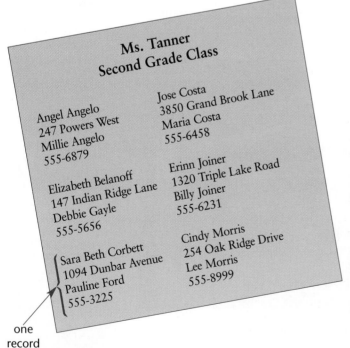

one record

Figure 3-18 This figure shows a partial list of the student information Ms. Tanner will be entering in her student database.

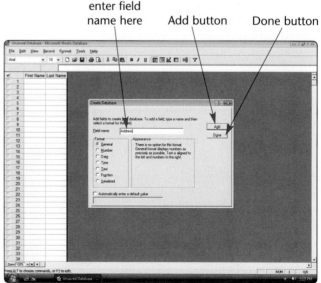

enter field name here   Add button   Done button

Figure 3-19 To create database fields in Microsoft Works, you simply type in each field name and then click the Add button. After entering all the fields you need and clicking the Done button in the Create Database dialog box, you are ready to enter the data in the new database.

fields

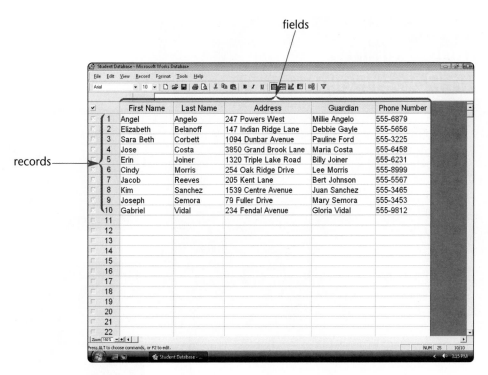

records

Figure 3-20 After data has been entered into a database, the records can be arranged in any order specified by users. In this example, the records have been organized alphabetically based on students' last names.

PRESENTATION GRAPHICS SOFTWARE

Using **presentation graphics software**, you can create documents called **presentations**, which you then use to communicate ideas, messages, and other information to a group, such as a class or auditorium of people. The presentations can be viewed as **slides** that are displayed on a large monitor or projected onto a screen. Slides also can be made into traditional overhead transparencies or printed and given to students as a handout (Figure 3-21 on the next page).

Presentation programs typically used in schools are the presentation software included with AppleWorks, Keynote, and Microsoft PowerPoint packaged with Microsoft Office.

Presentation graphics software typically provides an array of predefined presentation formats that define complementary colors for backgrounds, text, and other special effects. Presentation graphics software also provides a variety of layouts for each individual slide so

you can create a title slide, a two-column slide, a slide with clip art, and others. Any text, charts, and graphics used in a slide can be enhanced with 3-D and other effects such as shading, shadows, and textures.

With presentation graphics software, you can incorporate objects from the clip art/image gallery into your slides to create multimedia presentations. A **clip art/image gallery** includes clip art images, pictures, videos, and audio files. A clip art/image gallery can be stored on a hard disk, a CD, or a DVD; you can also access clip art/image galleries on the Web. As with clip art collections, a clip art/image gallery typically is organized by categories, such as academic, business, entertainment, and transportation. For example, the transportation category may contain a clip art image of a bicycle, a photograph of a locomotive, a video of an airplane in flight, and an audio of a Model T car horn.

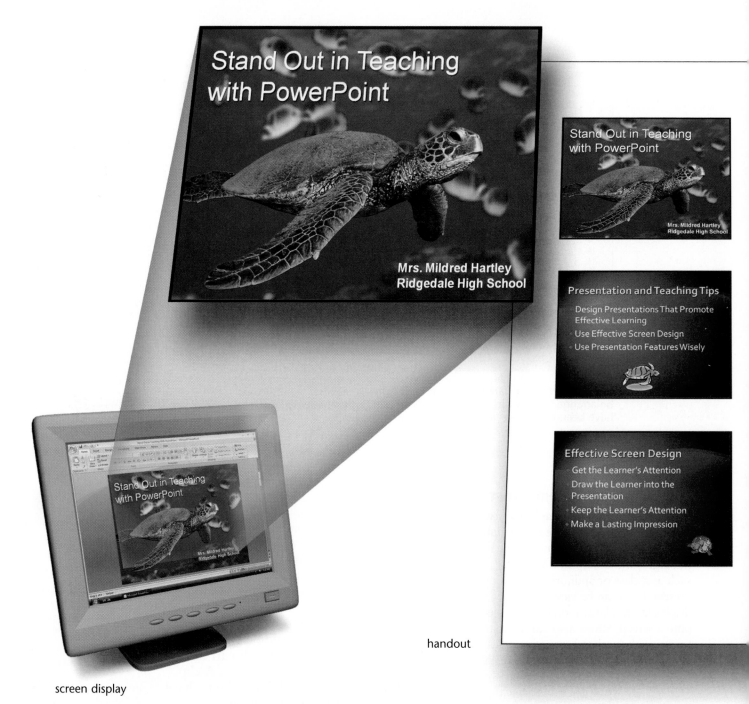

screen display

handout

Figure 3-21 Teachers and students use presentation graphics software to create electronic slides. The slides can be displayed on a computer, projected on a screen, printed and handed out, or made into transparencies.

When building a presentation, you can set the slide timing so the presentation automatically displays the next slide after a predetermined delay. You also can apply special effects to the transition between each slide. For example, one slide might slowly dissolve as the next slide comes into view.

To help organize the presentation, you can view small versions of all the slides in a slide sorter. A **slide sorter** presents a screen view similar to how 35mm slides look on a photographer's light table. The

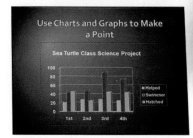

transparency

Web Info

For tips on using graphics effectively in a presentation, visit the Teachers Discovering Computers Web site, (*scsite.com/tdc5*), click Chapter 3, click Web Info, and then click Presentation.

slide sorter allows you to arrange the slides in any order or display them one at a time by clicking the mouse or pressing a key on the keyboard (Figure 3-22 on the next page).

Presentation graphics software also incorporates some of the features provided in word processing software, such as spell checking, formatting, and converting an existing slide show into a format that can be viewed on the World Wide Web.

Presentation graphics programs are important software programs for K-12 schools. Teachers can create and integrate electronic presentations into any classroom curriculum as an exciting alternative to the

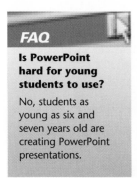

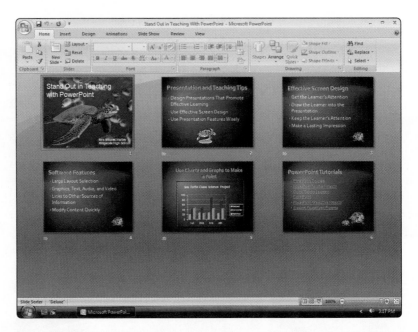

Figure 3-22 This slide sorter screen shows a small version of each slide. Using a pointing device or the keyboard, users can rearrange the order of the slides.

traditional lecture-only teaching style (Figure 3-23). Students take great pride in creating their own presentations using presentation graphics software. Later chapters provide real-life examples of how teachers integrate presentation graphics software into their instruction and curriculum. A unique feature of presentation graphics software is that it allows you to create a presentation that presents information in a nonlinear format. When using overhead transparencies, teachers traditionally show one transparency after another in a predetermined order — that is, linear teaching and learning.

With presentation graphics software programs, teachers and students can create presentations easily with links to a variety of information sources. Teachers and students, for example, can create presentations

Figure 3-23 Electronic slide presentations are an exciting alternative to the traditional lecture-only teaching style.

with links to other slides, other presentations, other files and software programs, animations, videos, audio files, and even sites on the World Wide Web (Figure 3-24) if the presentation computer is connected to the Internet. Using these links, teachers and students can branch off in a nonlinear fashion at any point in a presentation, to display or access additional information.

The ability to modify presentation content according to student interest makes presentation graphics software a powerful teaching and learning tool. The In the Lab end-of-chapter section in Chapter 5 discusses using and integrating Microsoft PowerPoint in more depth.

PERSONAL INFORMATION MANAGERS

A **personal information manager (PIM)** is a software application installed on PDAs that includes an appointment calendar, address book, notepad, and other features to help you organize personal information such as appointments, task lists, and more. A PIM allows you to take information that you tracked previously in a weekly or daily calendar, and organize and store it on your

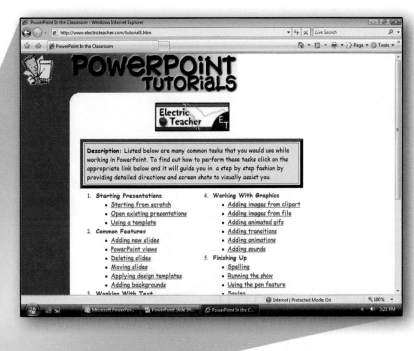

hyperlinks
to the Web

Figure 3-24 By clicking a hyperlink in a PowerPoint presentation, teachers and students can access another slide, slide presentation, sound files, videos, or a Web site if connected to the Internet.

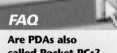

FAQ

Are PDAs also called Pocket PCs?

Only some of them. A **Pocket PC** is a type of PDA that uses the Pocket PC operating system software developed by Microsoft; only a PDA that uses the Pocket PC software is called a Pocket PC.

computer. PIMs can manage many different types of information, such as telephone messages, project notes, reminders, task and address lists, and important dates and appointments (Figure 3-25).

An **appointment calendar** allows you to schedule activities for a particular day and time. With an **address book**, you can enter and maintain names, addresses, and telephone numbers of coworkers, family members, and friends. Instead of writing notes on a piece of paper, you can use a **notepad**

to record ideas, reminders, and other important information.

Most PDAs contain many other features and built-in software programs in addition to those shown in Figure 3-25, including e-mail, Web browsing, instant messaging, and more. One of these features allows users to **synchronize**, or transfer, information and programs from the PDA to a personal computer and vice versa. Some PDAs transfer information wirelessly and others connect to the computer with a

Address Book/Contacts

Contacts	◀ 10:02 ok
Name:	Kathie Flood
Job title:	Senior Editor
Department:	Technical Books
Company:	Lucerne Publishing
Work tel:	(617) 555-8646
Work fax:	(617) 555-8680
Work addr:	
E-mail:	kathie@lucernepublish...
Mobile tel:	

Details | Notes

To-Do List

To Do	▼ All
☑ 1	Send out email re: job titles.	3/18
☐ 1	Send flowers to Cath for Anniversary	3/24
☑ 2	Build web page re: new handheld products.	3/18
☐ 3	Drop off suit to dry cleaners.	3/19
☐ 3	Pick up milk and cereal at store.	—
☐ 4	Mow yard.	3/24

(New) (Details...) (Show...)

Memos/Notepad

Notes   ◀ 11:51 ok

write notes in your own handwriting

That automatically convert to text

New Edit Tools

Datebook/Calendar

Calendar   ◀ 2:48 ✕

July 2004

S M T W T F S

Calculator

8000

% 7 8 9 +/-
MC 4 5 6 ÷
MR 1 2 3 −
M+ 0 . = +
CE
C

Figure 3-25 Most PDAs come equipped with an address book, notepad, calendar, calculator, and to-do list.

Figure 3-26 Most PDAs allow the user to synchronize, or transfer, information and programs from a personal computer to the PDA and vice versa.

Web Info

For updated links to these and other PDA software sites, visit the Teachers Discovering Computers Web site, (*scsite.com/tdc5*), click Chapter 3, click Web Info, and then click PDA Software.

cable (Figure 3-26). Many PDAs allow you to transfer information to another PDA by a process called beaming. **Beaming** is a method of transferring data through an infrared port. As with personal computers, PDAs require an operating system. Common PDA operating systems include Palm OS, PocketPC, and Linux.

PDA SOFTWARE

In addition to PIMs or installed software, a large selection of software is available for PDAs for a variety of uses, including personal productivity, business, communications, medical, scientific, travel, global positioning, entertainment, games, multimedia, and education. You can download PDA applications from the Web (Figure 3-27) or purchase them at computer and electronic stores.

Downloading and installing programs is an easy process. First, you download the software program to your personal computer, and then you install the software on your PDA using your PDA's synchronization software. A significant number of PDA software programs are available as shareware, freeware, or trial editions and can be found at a number of Web sites (Figure 3-28).

Students and teachers can benefit from PDA software designed for educational uses. Figure 3-29 on the next page describes a few of the hundreds of PDA software programs that are designed for teachers and students both in K-12 schools and institutions of higher education.

Figure 3-27 PalmGear.com is a reseller of PDA software programs.

Figure 3-28 Download.com is a popular Web site for downloading shareware and freeware programs, including popular programs for PDAs.

Education Software for PDAs

Application	Description	Examples	Web Links
Teacher Management Tools	Tools that manage grading, attendance, rosters, curriculum standards, planning, assessment, reporting, contact information, and more.	• eStandards (Media-X) • Tracker and Seeker • Handango Teacher Suite	www.media-x.com/products/estandards/index.php www.schoolid.com/ www.handango.com/
Reference Materials and Other Teaching Applications	Different types of sources for information containing useful facts or information.	• Merriam-Webster® Dictionary • Formulas for Palm OS®	www.m-w.com www.standalone.com/palmos/formulas/
ERIC Reference List on PDAs	A bibliography presenting information on the educational uses of PDAs with Web links.	• Educational Resources Information Center (ERIC) search for CRIB on PDAs	www.eric.ed.gov/
Curriculum-Specific Applications	Applications designed to support specific curriculum needs and standards.	• ImagiMath • ImagiProbe • Quizzler • Mental Math • Scholastic Wireless • Palm	www.pasco.com/palm/ www.pasco.com/palm/ www.quizzlerpro.com/ www.aaamath.com/men.html teacher.scholastic.com/wireless/ www.palm.com/us/education

Figure 3-29 Shown are just a few of the hundreds of ideas and software programs that can be used to benefit both students and teachers.

SOFTWARE SUITES

A **software suite** is a collection of individual application software packages sold as a single package. The most popular software suite used in businesses, universities, and K-12 schools is Microsoft Office available both for PC and Macintosh computers (Figure 3-30). Microsoft Office 2007, the latest version of Office is available in a number of versions including Ultimate, Professional, Small Business, Standard, and a less expensive version for Home and Student.

For many school, home, and personal users, the capabilities of a less expensive software suite more than meet their needs. Popular inexpensive software suites include **Microsoft Works** for PCs and **iWork**, formerly **AppleWorks**, for Macintosh computers (Figure 3-31).

When you install the suite, you install the entire collection of applications at once,

Figure 3-30 Microsoft Office is available in versions for both PC and Macintosh computers.

Figure 3-31 Two popular inexpensive software suites. Microsoft Works often is found on PCs and contains word processing, spreadsheet, database, and communications software. Apple's iWork, formerly AppleWorks, is used on Macintosh computers and contains word processing, spreadsheet, database, paint, and presentation software.

rather than installing each application individually. At a minimum, suites typically include word processing, spreadsheet, database, and presentation graphics. Each application in a software suite is designed specifically to work as part of a larger set of applications and to share common features.

Software suites offer two major advantages: lower cost and ease of use. Typically, buying a collection of software packages in a suite costs significantly less than purchasing the application packages separately. Software suites provide ease of use because the applications within a suite normally use a similar interface and have some common features. Thus, after you learn how to use one application in the suite, you are familiar with the other applications in the suite. For example, after you learn how to print using the suite's word processing program, you can apply the same skill to the spreadsheet, database, and presentation graphics programs in the suite.

Graphics and Multimedia Software

In addition to productivity software, many individuals also work with software designed specifically for their fields of work. For example, engineers, architects, desktop publishers, and graphic artists often use powerful software that allows them to work with graphics and multimedia. Types of graphics and multimedia software include desktop publishing software, paint/image editing software, multimedia authoring tools, Web page authoring software, and many others. The features and functions of some of these applications are discussed in the following sections.

DESKTOP PUBLISHING SOFTWARE

Desktop publishing (DTP) software allows you to design, produce, and deliver sophisticated documents that contain text, graphics, and brilliant colors. Although many word processing packages have some of the capabilities of DTP software, professional designers and graphic artists use

DTP software because it is designed specifically to support **page layout**, which is the process of arranging text and graphics in a document. DTP software is ideal for the production of high-quality color documents, such as newsletters, marketing literature, catalogs, and annual reports. In the past, documents of this type were created by slower, more expensive traditional publishing methods, such as typesetting. Today's DTP software also allows you to convert a color document into a format for use on the World Wide Web.

Many home, school, and small business users use a much simpler, easy-to-understand DTP software designed for individual desktop publishing projects. Using this DTP software, you can create newsletters and brochures, postcards and greeting cards, letterhead and business cards, banners, calendars, logos, and other such documents (Figure 3-32). Personal DTP software guides you through the development of these documents by asking a series of questions, offering numerous predefined layouts, and providing standard text you can add to documents. As you enter text, the personal DTP software checks your spelling. You can print your finished publications on a color printer or place them on the Web.

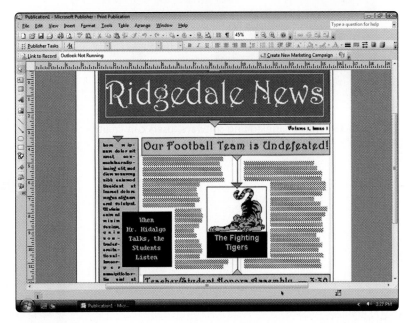

Figure 3-32 Teachers and students use desktop publishing software, such as Microsoft Publisher, to create flyers, certificates, newsletters, and other types of documents.

Integration Strategies

To learn more about how to use Adobe Photoshop Elements with your students, visit the Teachers Discovering Computers Web site (*scsite.com/tdc5*), click Chapter 3, and then click Software Corner.

PAINT/IMAGE EDITING SOFTWARE

Graphic artists, multimedia professionals, desktop publishers, and many others use paint software and image editing software to create and modify graphics (Figure 3-33), such as those used in DTP documents and Web pages. **Paint software** allows you to draw pictures, shapes, and other graphics using various tools on the screen, such as a pen, brush, eye dropper, and paint bucket. **Image editing software** provides the capabilities of paint software as well as the capability of modifying existing graphics. For example, you can retouch photographs, adjust or enhance image colors, and add special effects such as shadows and glows.

Many home, school, and small business users opt for personal paint/image editing software. Personal paint/image editing software provides a much easier-to-use interface and usually has simplified capabilities, with functions tailored to the needs of the home and small business user. Personal paint image editing software includes various simplified tools that allow you to draw pictures, shapes, and other graphics. Professional paint image editing software provides more sophisticated tools for drawing and modifying pictures, shapes, and other images.

One popular type of image editing software, called **photo editing software**, allows you to edit digital photographs by removing red-eye, adding special effects, or creating electronic photo albums. When the photograph is complete, you can print it on labels, calendars, business cards, and banners; or place it on a Web page. Popular photo editing programs used by educators include Photo Story and iPhoto.

CLIP ART/IMAGE GALLERY

Although many applications include clip art, you may find that you want a wider selection of graphics. One way to obtain them is to purchase a clip art/image gallery, which is a collection of clip art and photographs. In addition to clip art, many clip art/image galleries provide fonts, animations, sounds, videos, and audio files (Figure 3-34). You can use the images, fonts, and other items from the clip art/image gallery in all types of documents, such as letters, flyers, and class projects.

Figure 3-33 With image editing software, users can create and modify a variety of graphic images.

Figure 3-34 Clip art/image galleries provide thousands of clip art images and photographs for use in documents such as letters, newsletters, greeting cards, class projects, and presentations.

MULTIMEDIA AUTHORING SOFTWARE

Multimedia authoring software is used to create electronic presentations, simulations, and software demonstrations that can include text, graphics, video, audio, animation, and screen captures. While many multimedia authoring software programs are available, two popular programs used by educators are Camtasia Studio and Adobe Captivate. These easy to use multimedia authoring programs help educators create video presentations. Educators can use these programs even if they do not have programming knowledge or multimedia skills.

Camtasia Studio is a great solution for recording, editing, and sharing high-quality videos on the Web, CDs, DVDs, and portable media players, including Apple's iPod and Microsoft's Zune. **Adobe Captivate** allows users to create engaging and interactive Flash videos. You will learn more about Camtasia Studio in the special feature that follows this chapter, *Creating Web Pages, Blogs, Wikis, and More*.

VIDEO AND AUDIO EDITING SOFTWARE

Video consists of full-motion images played back at various speeds. With video editing software, you can modify a segment of a video, called a clip (Figure 3-35). For example, you can add and remove clips, or add special effects like sounds, banners, credits, and more. Video editing programs normally allow you to either edit or add audio components. Current PC and Macintosh computers include extensive audio and video editing capabilities; you and your students can even make your own videos. Popular programs used by educators include iMovie, Movie Maker, and Final Cut.

Integration Strategies

To learn more about using and integrating various multimedia authoring software programs, visit the Teachers Discovering Computers Web site (*scsite.com/tdc5*), click Chapter 3, and then click Digital Media Corner.

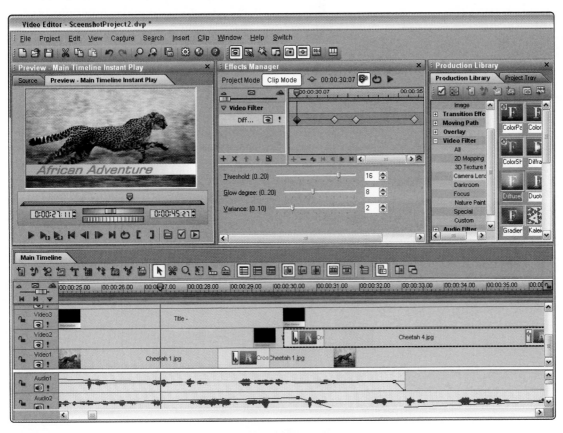

Figure 3-35 Users can use video editing software to modify video images.

WEB PAGE AUTHORING SOFTWARE

Web page authoring software is designed specifically to help you create Web pages, in addition to organizing, managing, and maintaining Web sites. As noted in previous sections, many application software packages include Web page authoring features that you can use to create Web pages and Web sites or that you can use to save a document as a Web page. For example, Figure 3-36 shows you how to convert a word processing document automatically into the standard document format for the World Wide Web by saving it as a Web page. After being saved, the document can

be published to the Web and viewed in any Web browser. Word processing programs, for example, contain enough features to satisfy the formatting and layout needs of teachers and students for building curriculum pages and other Web documents, as shown in Figure 3-37. A **curriculum page** is a teacher-created document containing hyperlinks to teacher-selected Web sites that assist in teaching content-specific curriculum objectives. Students can access teacher-created curriculum pages from home, school, the public library, or anyplace they are connected to the Internet. The ability to access these resources from such a wide variety of places provides students with just-in-time support.

Web page authoring software features allow you to create sophisticated multimedia Web pages that include graphics, video, audio, animation, and other special effects. Most word processors can be used to create Web pages. Other popular programs used by teachers and students to develop Web pages include **Microsoft Publisher**, **WebBlender**, and **Adobe Dreamweaver**. Many of these companies provide resources, tutorials, and more for teachers and students (Figure 3-38).

The special feature following this chapter provides you with access to step-by-step instructions for creating a teacher's Web page using Microsoft Word.

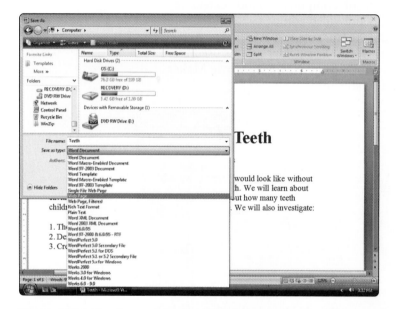

Figure 3-36 The figure shows you how to convert a word processing document automatically into the standard document format for the World Wide Web by saving it as a Web page. After being saved, the document can be published to the Web and viewed in any Web browser.

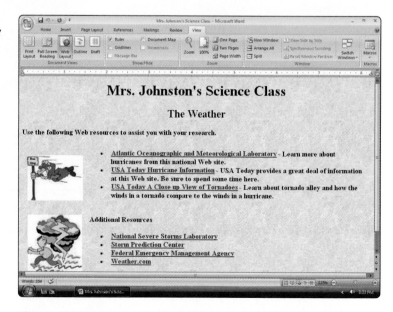

Figure 3-37 An example of a teacher-created curriculum page.

Figure 3-38 Most popular Web page authoring programs provide resources, tutorials, and more for teachers and students. In addition, many companies like Macromedia provide curriculum and integration ideas for teachers.

Software for School Use

Many school districts have undergone a period of transition in how they maintain student records and other pertinent information. An important factor driving this transition is the installation of networks.

Having networks in schools allows schools to manage and maintain information about students and teachers in a centralized way. At the lower technological end, some schools still maintain all student records manually or in software programs on individual computers. Teachers and other school personnel then periodically input student records manually into student management software that stores grades and attendance records. At the higher technological end, some schools maintain district-wide student management programs.

Software for schools and professional use includes school management software, student management software, grade book software, educational and reference software, and software for students with special needs. Each of these types of software are discussed in more detail in the sections that follow.

SCHOOL AND STUDENT MANAGEMENT SOFTWARE

Schools that have networked at least one computer in each classroom usually install school and student management software. When standardized throughout the school district, these programs can improve a school's ability to manage and analyze daily operations, budgets, and student information dramatically.

School management software is a centralized program that allows district and school personnel to manage the school district operations, such as budgeting, inventory, technology, and expenses. Most school management software packages allow a school district to keep a database of all district assets, salaries and benefits, and food services inventory; manage other school and department budgets; and track transportation vehicle maintenance and use. Some school management software also includes databases for attendance and other student information and has other functions similar to student management software. **Student management software** is a centralized program that allows administrators, teachers, and other staff to manage and track information about students, which includes attendance and academic records.

Recall from Chapter 2, Washington County Public Schools has networked all of its classroom computers (Figure 3-39). Teachers throughout the district enter attendance information into the district's student management software program shortly after classes begin. Within a few minutes, district and school administrators know exactly how many students are present. Teachers also enter student grades into the same grade book and attendance

program installed on all district computers. Record keeping at Washington County Schools thus is fully automated.

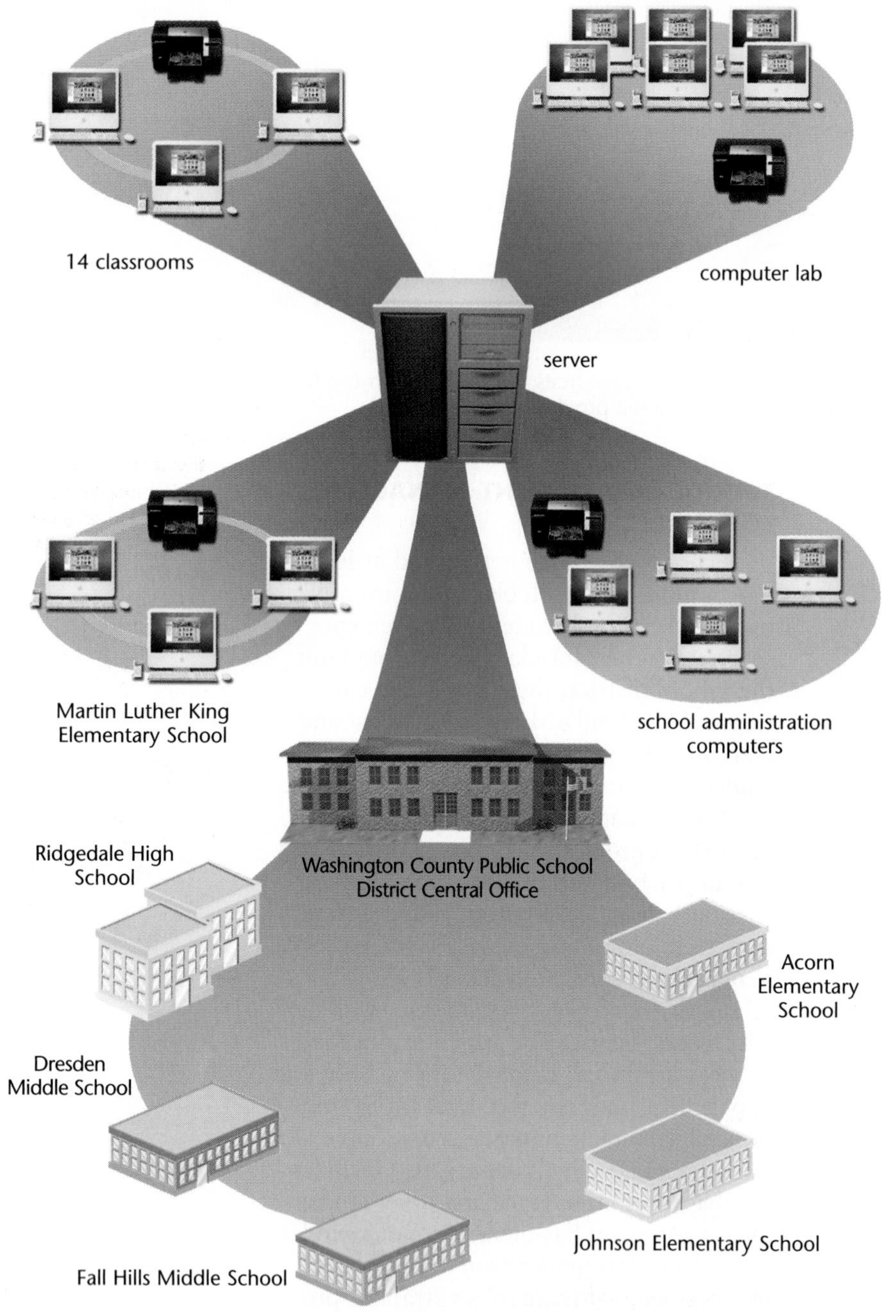

GRADE BOOK SOFTWARE

Grade book software allows teachers to track and organize student tests, homework, lab work, and other scores. Most grade book software allows you to track thousands of students and hundreds of assignments within the same grade book and sort students by name, student number, or current average. Most programs allow teachers to weight various scores automatically, apply grading curves, adjust letter grade cutoffs, or use a customized grading scale, such as Fair, Good, Excellent, and so on. Grades can be displayed and entered as points, percentages, letter grades, or in a customized grading scale.

Grade book software also integrates with other software packages. Schools that use network-based or online testing programs, for example, can import student scores directly into the grade book. Teachers also can import and export grades and rosters to a word processing, spreadsheet, or database program.

At some schools, teachers enter attendance and student grades into the same grade book program, which is installed on all district computers. Not all schools have one, district-wide grade book program for teachers to use, however; so many teachers choose their own grade book program. Numerous outstanding grade book and attendance programs are available for teachers. Some of these are shareware programs; others have trial versions that you can download from the Web for evaluation purposes. Popular grade book programs include Engrade, MicroGrade, GradeQuick, WebGrader, Easy Grade Pro, and Gradebook Plus. You also can create a basic grade book using the wizards and templates in Microsoft Excel, AppleWorks, and other programs (Figure 3-40).

14 classrooms

computer lab

server

Martin Luther King Elementary School

school administration computers

Ridgedale High School

Washington County Public School District Central Office

Acorn Elementary School

Dresden Middle School

Fall Hills Middle School

Johnson Elementary School

Figure 3-39 Washington County Public Schools uses its wide area network that connects all district classrooms to track student attendance records, grades, and more.

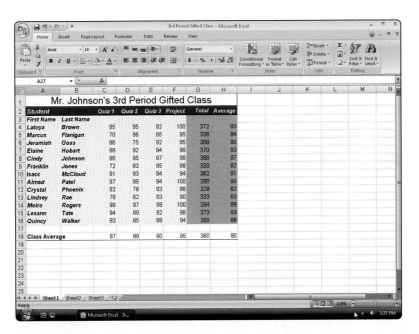

Figure 3-40 An example of a grade book that teachers can create using Microsoft Excel.

EDUCATIONAL AND REFERENCE SOFTWARE

Educational software supports learning objectives and goals. Educational software exists for just about any subject, from learning a foreign language to learning how to cook. Preschool to high school learners can use educational software to assist them with subjects such as reading and math or to prepare them for class or college entrance exams.

Educational software is covered in greater depth in later chapters. You also can find information about Web links to dozens of popular educational software programs in Software Corner and Digital Media Corner at the end of each chapter.

Reference software (Figure 3-41) provides valuable and thorough

Figure 3-41 Reference software provides valuable and thorough information for all types of users. For example, Grolier Online includes articles, lesson plans, pictures, and videos on thousands of topics.

information for everyone in an educational setting and in the family. Popular reference software includes encyclopedias, dictionaries, health/medical guides, and travel directories. Chapter 5 covers many types of educational and reference software applications and discusses their features in detail.

SPECIAL NEEDS SOFTWARE

Special needs software is designed specifically for students with physical impairments or learning disabilities to assist them in completing school assignments and everyday tasks (Figure 3-42). Special needs software includes such programs as **speech synthesis software**, text enlargement programs, talking calculators, and more.

Today, teachers have many software options available to use as tools to enhance teaching and learning of students with special needs. Many software applications discussed in this chapter and educational multimedia applications discussed in Chapter 5 also can be used to assist students with special needs. When students use these software programs in combination with assistive devices, such as touch screens and adaptive keyboards, their ability to succeed increases. These and other special input and output devices designed for use by students with special needs are discussed in Chapter 4. Examples of how teachers can integrate special needs software into their curriculum are covered in Chapters 5–7.

Web Info

For more information about a popular and free text-to-speech software program, visit the Teachers Discovering Computers Web site, (*scsite.com/tdc5*), click Chapter 3, click Web Info, and then click ReadPlease.

Recall that the textbook Web site includes an end-of-chapter section called Integration Corner. Included with Integration Corner for each chapter is Special Education Corner, where you will find dozens of links to special needs software programs and information on how other teachers are integrating technology to help special needs students. Finally, the Assistive Technologies Corner at the end of this chapter and on the Web provides extensive information and links to special needs software programs.

Software for Home and Personal Use

Many software applications are designed specifically for home or personal use. Personal software includes personal finance software, tax preparation software, legal software, entertainment software, and more. Most of the products in this category are relatively inexpensive, often priced at less than $50. The features and functions of some of these applications are discussed in the following sections.

PERSONAL FINANCE SOFTWARE

Personal finance software is a simplified accounting program that helps you pay bills, balance your checkbook, track your personal income and expenses, such as credit card bills; track investments; evaluate financial plans; and maintain a home inventory (Figure 3-43). Popular personal finance software includes Quicken and Microsoft Money.

Using personal finance software can help you determine where, and for what purpose, you are spending money so you can manage your finances. Reports can summarize transactions by category (such as dining), by payee (such as the electric company), or by billing period (such as the last two months). Bill-paying features include the ability to print checks on your printer or have an outside service print your checks.

Personal finance software packages usually offer a variety of online services, which require access to the Web. For example, you can track your investments

Figure 3-42 Using assistive technology software, teachers help students with disabilities learn subject-related content.

Figure 3-43 Many home users work with personal finance software to assist them with tracking personal expenses, paying bills, maintaining a home inventory, and more.

online, compare insurance rates from leading insurance companies, and even do your banking online. **Online banking** offers access to account balances, provides bill payment services, and allows you to download transactions and statements from the Web directly to your computer. In addition, with online banking, you can transfer money electronically from your checking to savings or vice versa. To obtain current credit card statements, bank statements, and account balances, you download transaction information from your bank using the Web.

Financial planning features include analyzing home and personal loans, preparing income taxes, and managing retirement savings. Other features in many personal finance packages include budgeting and tax-related transactions.

TAX PREPARATION SOFTWARE

Tax preparation software guides individuals, families, or small businesses through the process of filing federal taxes (Figure 3-44). Popular tax preparation software includes TurboTax and TaxCut. These software packages offer money-saving tax tips, designed to lower your tax bill. After you answer a series of questions and complete basic forms, the tax preparation software creates and analyzes your tax

forms to search for potential errors and missed deduction opportunities. After the forms are complete, you can print any necessary paperwork. Most tax preparation software packages even allow you to file your tax forms electronically.

Figure 3-44 Tax preparation software can assist you in preparing your federal and state tax returns efficiently and accurately. You even can file your return electronically using the Internet.

Web Info

For more information on legal software, visit the Teachers Discovering Computers Web site (*scsite.com/tdc5*), click Chapter 3, click Web Info, and then click Legal Software.

LEGAL SOFTWARE

Legal software assists in the preparation of legal documents and provides legal advice to individuals, families, and small businesses (Figure 3-45). Legal software provides standard contracts and documents associated with buying, selling, and renting property; estate planning; and preparing a will. By answering a series of questions or completing a form, the legal software tailors the legal document to your needs.

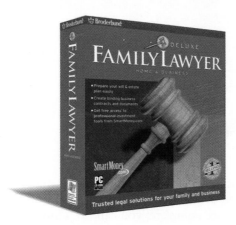

Figure 3-45 Legal software provides legal advice to individuals, families, and small businesses and assists in the preparation of legal documents.

After the legal document is created, you can file the paperwork with the appropriate agency, court, or office; or you can take the document to your attorney for her review and signature.

ENTERTAINMENT SOFTWARE

Entertainment software includes interactive games, videos, and other programs designed to support a hobby or just provide amusement and enjoyment. For example, you can use entertainment software to play games, make a family tree, compose music, or simulate flying an aircraft.

Learning Aids and Support Tools

Learning how to use an application software package effectively involves time and practice. To aid you in that learning process, your school may offer professional development classes or in-service workshops. In addition to these learning opportunities, many software applications and Web sites provide Help, tutorials, and FAQs. Thousands of books also are available to help you learn specific software packages. Many tutorials are packaged with software or are available free on the Web.

USING HELP

Help is the electronic equivalent of a user manual; it usually is integrated into an application software package (Figure 3-46). Help provides assistance that can increase your productivity and reduce your frustrations by minimizing the time you spend learning how to use an application software package.

In most programs, a function key or a button on the screen starts the Help feature. When using a program, you can use the Help feature to ask a question or access the Help topics in subject or alphabetical order. In most cases, Help has replaced the user manual altogether, which means software developers no longer include user manuals with the software.

Most Help also links to Web sites that offer **Web-based Help**, which provides updates and more comprehensive resources

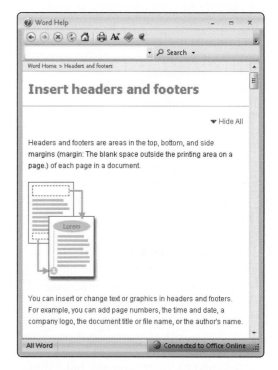

Figure 3-46 Help provides assistance from within your application, or by connecting to the Internet and accessing Web-based help if the computer is connected to the Internet.

to respond to both technical and non-technical issues about software. You can often search Help Web sites for answers to your questions, which you can enter in complete sentences or simply using keywords. Some Help Web sites contain chat rooms, in which a user can talk directly with a technical support person or join a conversation with other users who may be able to answer questions or solve problems.

OTHER LEARNING RESOURCES

If printed documentation is included with a software package, often it is organized as reference material rather than structured for learning. This makes it helpful after you know how to use a package, but difficult to use when you are first learning. For this reason, many **trade books** are available to help you learn to use the features of software application packages. These books are available where software is sold, in regular bookstores (Figure 3-47), or online. Web pages that contain an **FAQ (frequently asked questions)** section about application software abound on the Internet and help you find answers to common questions.

Tutorials are step-by-step instructions using real examples that show you how to

Figure 3-47 Many bookstores sell trade books to help you learn to use the features of personal computer application packages.

use an application. Some tutorials are printed manuals; others are software-based or Internet-based, thus allowing you to use your computer to learn about an application software package.

Many colleges and K-12 school districts provide training on many of the applications discussed in this chapter. If you want more direction than is provided in Help, trade books, FAQs, and tutorials, contact your college or school district for a list of workshops and continuing education courses that they offer.

In addition to those discussed here, many other software programs are available for use in schools, homes, and businesses. In the following chapters, you will learn more about other types of educational software, including how-to guides, computer-assisted instructional software, educational games, tutorials, educational simulations, multimedia authoring software, as well as multimedia applications.

Software Versions and Upgrades

Software programs, including operating systems, usually are designated by a **version** number. A new version of a software product designed to replace an older version of the same product is called an **upgrade**. As software manufacturers develop a newer version of a software package, the newer version usually is assigned higher numbers.

Most manufacturers designate major software releases by increasing the version number by a whole number, for example, version 4.0 to 5.0. To designate minor software improvements, manufacturers usually change the version number by less than a whole number change, such as version 4.0 to 4.2.

Sometimes manufacturers switch their naming convention. For example, Microsoft Office XP was replaced with Office 2003 which in turn was replaced with Office 2007. Similar versions of software can have different designations when used on Macintosh computers and PCs. Microsoft Office 2004 for Macintosh computers, for example, is basically the same as Microsoft Office 2003 for Windows.

If not prompted automatically by your operating system or software program, you should check periodically for critical updates to your operating system and other software programs. Most critical updates and minor software upgrades are usually free of charge.

USING DIFFERENT SOFTWARE VERSIONS

Because of the cost of software, most schools do not upgrade their software each time a manufacturer releases a new version. When schools purchase new computers, however, the latest versions of operating systems and application software often are preinstalled on the computers.

Teachers and students should know which versions of software applications are installed on their school, classroom, and home computers. Many software programs include an About or Information command on the Help menu to indicate the software version. Often, teachers and students have different versions of the same software on their home and classroom computers; a teacher might have PowerPoint 2003 on a two-year old classroom computer and PowerPoint 2007 on a new home computer.

When working with different versions of the same software, two general rules can help make your work easier. First, an older version of a software package may not open a file created in a newer version of the software. Second, newer versions usually open files created in older versions.

To help alleviate this problem, most software programs allow you to save a document in a format compatible with earlier versions of the same software or in a different file format that can be read by another software program.

MICROSOFT OFFICE 2007 Microsoft Office 2007 introduced new file formats called **Microsoft Office Open XML**. These formats are based on XML. The new file formats are applied to Word 2007, Excel 2007, and PowerPoint 2007. Figure 3-48 summaries some of the benefits of the Office Open XML Formats. File extension names also are different in Office 2007. For example, earlier versions of Word saved files with a .doc extension; the default extension for most Word 2007 files is .docx, where the "x" designates an XML file.

Benefit	Description
Compact Files	Files are automatically compressed and can be up to 75 percent smaller in some cases. The Office Open XML Formats uses zip compression technology to store documents, offering potential cost savings as it reduces the disk space required to store files and decreases the bandwidth needed to send files via e-mail, over networks, and across the Internet. When you open a file, it is automatically unzipped. When you save a file, it is automatically zipped again.
Improved Damaged File Recovery	Files are structured in a modular fashion that keeps different data components in the file separate from each other. This allows files to be opened even if a component within the file (for example, a chart or table) is damaged or corrupted.
Better Privacy and More Control Over Personal Information	Documents can be shared confidentially, because personally identifiable information and business-sensitive information, such as author names, comments, tracked changes, and file paths can be easily identified and removed using the Document Inspector feature.

Figure 3-48 Some of the many benefits of Microsoft Office 2007 Open XML Formats.

Figure 3-49 summaries the common file extension differences between Office 2007 and earlier versions of Office.

Program	Office 2007 Files	Office 97-2003 Files
Word	.docx	.doc
Excel	.xlsx	.xls
PowerPoint	.pptx	.ppt

Figure 3-49 This figure shows the basic file extensions for Word, Excel, and PowerPoint 2007 compared to earlier versions of these programs.

Because of the new XML formats, earlier versions of Office will not automatically open Word, PowerPoint, and Excel files created in 2007 XML format. There are two options to solve this compatibility issue.

- You can save your Office 2007 file in the format that was used by earlier versions of Office. Figure 3-50 shows how to save a Word 2007 file in the earlier Word 97-2003 document or .doc format.

Figure 3-50 Using Microsoft Word 2007, you can save a Microsoft Word 2007 file in the format that was used by earlier versions of Word.

- You can open and edit a file created using Office 2007 in an earlier version of Word, Excel, or PowerPoint by downloading the necessary file converters. On the computer with an earlier version of

Office, go to the Microsoft download center and download the Microsoft Office Compatibility Pack for 2007 Office Word, Excel and PowerPoint File Formats. Important Note: For the converters to work, your version of Microsoft Office must already be updated with the latest service pack. You can check to see if your version of Office is current at the Microsoft download center and if not, you can download the latest service pack.

Web Info

To update earlier versions of Microsoft Office with the 2007 Compatibility Pack, visit the Teachers Discovering Computers Web site (*scsite.com/tdc5*), click Chapter 3, click Web Info, and then click Compatibility Pack.

Chapter 3 Special Feature

At the end of this chapter is a special feature that provides you with access to links that provide instructions on how to create your own teacher's Web page. You also will learn how to create blogs, wikis, and other digital tools that you can use with your digital students. The special feature that follows Chapter 7 provides you with additional skills, as you learn how to integrate Web pages, blogs, wikis, and more.

Summary of Application Software Productivity Tools for Educators

In this chapter, you learned about user interfaces and several software applications used in schools, businesses, and homes. You also read about some of the learning aids and support tools that are available for application software. Understanding these software applications increases your computer literacy and helps you to understand how personal computers can help in your career as a teacher, in your classroom instruction, and at home. The next chapter introduces you to computer hardware; future chapters provide information on additional software applications used by educators and show you how to integrate various software applications into your classroom curriculum.

Key Terms

Exercises

Web Info
Key Terms
Checkpoint
Teaching Today
Education Issues
Integration Corner
Software Corner
Digital Media Corner
Assistive Technologies Corner
In the Lab
Learn It Online

Features

Timeline
Guide to WWW Sites
Search Tools
Buyer's Guide
State/Federal Sites
Professional Sites

address book [156]
Adobe Captivate [161]
Adobe Dreamweaver [162]
AppleWorks [158]
application program [138]
application software [138]
appointment calendar [156]
assistant [146]
AutoSave [142]

beaming [157]
border [145]
button [140]

Camtasia Studio [161]
cell [148]
chart [149]
clip art [145]
clip art collection [145]
clip art/image gallery [151]
Clipboard [141]
command [140]
copy [141]
creating [141]
curriculum page [162]
cut [141]

database [149]
database file [150]
database software [149]
delete [141]
desktop [139]
desktop publishing (DTP) software [159]
dialog box [142]
document [140]

editing [141]
educational software [165]
entertainment software [168]

FAQ (frequently asked questions) [169]
field [150]
file [140]
filename [140]
find [145]
font [141]
font size [141]
font style [141]
footer [156]

formatting [141]
formula [148]
function [148]

grade book software [164]
graphical user interface (GUI) [138]

header [146]
Help [168]

icon [140]
image editing software [160]
import [145]
insert [141]

label [148]
legal software [168]
Linux [137]

MAC OS, version 9.1 [137]
MAC OS X [137]
margin [145]
menu [140]
Microsoft Office Open XML Formats [170]
Microsoft Publisher [162]
Microsoft Windows [136]
Microsoft Works [158]
multimedia authoring software [161]

note taking software [142]
notepad [156]

online banking [167]
open source software [131]
operating system [136]

page layout [159]
paint software [160]
paste [141]
personal finance software [166]
personal information manager (PIM) [155]
photo editing software [160]
Pocket PC [156]
point [141]
presentation [151]
presentation graphics software [151]
printing [142]
productivity software [154]

record [150]
reference software [164]
replace [145]
saving [143]
school management software [169]
scrolling [145]
search [145]
slide sorter [152]
slide [151]
software package [138]
software suite [158]
special needs software [166]
speech recognition [142]
speech synthesis software [166]
spell checker [145]
spelling checker [145]
spreadsheet [147]
spreadsheet software [147]
student management software [163]
synchronize [156]
system software [136]

tax preparation software [167]
template [146]
title bar [140]
trade book [169]
tutorial [169]

UNIX [137]
upgrade [169]
user interface [138]

value [148]
version [169]
video [161]
voice recognition [142]

Web-based Help [168]
Web page authoring software [162]
WebBlender [162]
window [140]
Windows Vista [137]
Windows Vista Home Basic [137]
Windows Vista Home Premium [137]
Windows Vista Ultimate [137]
wizard [144]
word processing software [150]
wordwrap [145]
worksheet [147]

Checkpoint

INSTRUCTIONS: Use the Checkpoint exercises to check your knowledge level of the chapter. To complete the Checkpoint exercises interactively, visit scsite.com/tdc5, click Chapter 3 at the top of the Web page, and then click Checkpoint on the left sidebar.

1. Label the Figure

Instructions: Identify each component of the Print dialog box.

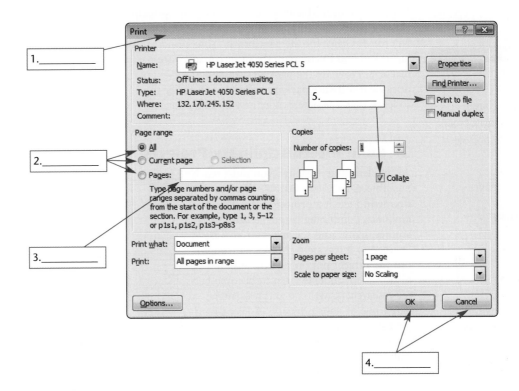

2. Matching

Instructions: Match each term from the column on the left with the best description from the column on the right.

_____ 1. Clipboard

_____ 2. database

_____ 3. record

_____ 4. commands

_____ 5. cell

a. collection of related fields

b. instructions that cause software to perform specific actions

c. temporary storage location

d. where a column and row meet

e. collection of data organized in a manner that allows access, retrieval, and use of that data

3. Short Answer

Instructions: Write a brief answer to each of the following questions.

1. What is a graphical user interface? Describe some common features of both the Windows and Macintosh graphical user interface.

2. Name and describe four different types of productivity software used by K-12 teachers. Which productivity software program do you use the most? Why?

3. What are the advantages of software suites? Describe three popular software suites used in K-12 schools.

4. What is a database? How are databases used in K-12 schools?

5. What are the advantages of using presentation graphics software programs? What are the disadvantages? How are teachers and students using presentation graphics programs?

Teaching Today

INSTRUCTIONS: Teaching Today provides teachers with integration strategies and ideas for teaching, and more importantly, reaching today's digital generation. Each numbered segment contains one or more links that reinforce the information presented in the segment. To display this page from the Web, visit scsite.com/tdc5, click Chapter 3 at the top of the Web page, and then click Teaching Today on the left sidebar.

1. Software Suites

Your school uses Macintosh computers. Your principal is considering purchasing AppleWorks for all classroom and lab computers. You have never used AppleWorks; however, you are familiar with Microsoft Office for the Macintosh. Your principal also is interested in open source software. He has asked you to compare the different software packages and make a presentation to the school's teachers. How are the packages the same? How are the packages different? What type of support does each software package offer? Is one easier to use than the other? Why or why not? Is one easier to learn than the other? Why or why not?

2. Build Interdisciplinary Projects

As an elementary teacher, you must teach all subjects to your students. You have decided to teach a project that is interdisciplinary, combining language arts, social studies, math, and science. You also have decided to integrate technology throughout the project not only to do research but also to help students learn to become better researchers, writers, and presenters. The topic of your project is Ancient Egypt. You start by using the Media Center to gather books, CDs, DVDs, reference materials, Web sites, and more. Develop a project focused on Ancient Egypt that uses the Internet, reference software, word processing software, your curriculum-specific software, and presentation graphics software. 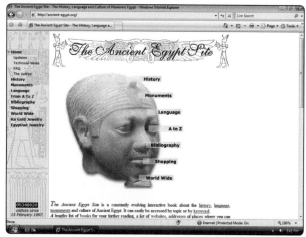 Where could you locate sample lesson plans to help you get started? Explain your plan to integrate these software applications into an interdisciplinary project that includes two or more curriculum areas.

3. Lesson Plans

Using the Internet in the classroom has numerous benefits for teachers, who can use it to find current information, online resources for lesson plans and Web-based projects, and interactive content that engages all types of learners. What are some other benefits of using the Internet in the classroom? Are there disadvantages or problems you might encounter in using Internet resources? How might you avoid or solve these problems?

4. Software Vendors

Most state Departments of Education negotiate one-year or multiyear contracts with various vendors for educational software products. This enables schools to acquire software products at substantial discounts. Contact a school in your district or access your state's Department of Education Web site and find out about a few of the software products available through the state purchasing program. Compare these prices with purchasing the same software either online or at a local computer store. What kind of discounts are the schools receiving? How many titles are available through the state catalog? What procedures does a teacher have to go through to purchase software not in the catalog?

Education Issues

INSTRUCTIONS: Education Issues provides several scenarios that allow you to explore controversial and current issues in education. Each numbered segment contains one or more links that reinforce the information presented in the segment. To display this page from the Web, visit scsite.com/tdc5, click Chapter 3 at the top of the Web page, and then click Education Issues on the left sidebar.

1. Wikis and Education

Some wikis are tightly controlled with a limited number of contributors and expert editors, these usually focus on narrowly-defined, specialized topics. Large online wikis, such as Wikipedia, often involve thousands of editors, many of whom remain anonymous. Recently, an entry on Wikipedia was maliciously altered to suggest that a prominent journalist was involved in the assassination of John F. Kennedy. As the number of Wikis has grown and the source of the content is often unknown, some educators and librarians have shunned wikis as valid sources of research. Many wikis provide information stating they have adequate controls to correct false or misleading content. Citizendium, is a wiki project started by a founder of Wikipedia that aims to improve the credibility of wikis by requiring contributors to use their real names; although anyone still can change content. Should you allow your students to use wikis as valid sources for academic research? Why or why not? Would you allow your students to submit a paper to you that cites a wiki as a source? Why or why not? What policies could wikis enforce that could garner more confidence from the public?

2. Reading Problems

You teach middle school, and this year you have the most challenging group of students you have ever had. Many of your students seem completely uninterested in learning or even in coming to school for that matter. As a result, you have continuous discipline problems and spend a lot of time sending students to the principal's office. After a few days, you become convinced that a deeper problem must exist, so you do a little research and find out that many of the students are below the 30th percentile in reading. You wonder how these students got this far without knowing how to read. Traditional reading programs obviously have not worked for these students. Using the Internet and other sources, do research to find out whether reading software programs and educational technology might be able to help them. Continue your

research to investigate alternative techniques using technology that might motivate these students and help them to learn to read. Where could you locate software and innovative teaching strategies that could help you help these students learn to read?

3. Database Software and Critical Thinking

Increasingly sophisticated software applications have impacted not only business, entertainment, and recreation, but education as well. Database software can give students the opportunity to record, track, and analyze data on virtually any subject matter. Learning about database software also provides students with knowledge of an important software program that is used extensively in business and on the Web. Does learning and using database software help students develop higher-order thinking and problem-solving skills? What other advantages does using database software offer? What are some disadvantages to using database software in the classroom? How might another application described in this chapter be used to teach higher-order thinking skills or problem solving?

4. Computer Use in the Classroom

With the explosion of educational software, multimedia, digital media, and the Internet, educators still are learning the best use for computers in the classroom. Drill and practice? Problem solving? Games? A growing number of educators feel that students should be taught the software applications they will have to know to succeed in the workplace. From the applications presented in this chapter, make a list of five applications you think every student should learn, from more important to less important. Explain your ranking. At what level do you think each application should be taught? Why?

Integration Corner

INSTRUCTIONS: Integration Corner provides extensive ideas and resources for integrating technology into your classroom-specific curriculum. To display this page from the Web and its links to approximately 100 educational Web sites, visit scsite.com/tdc5, click Chapter 3 at the top of the Web page, and then click Integration Corner on the left sidebar.

Exercises

Web Info
Key Terms
Checkpoint
Teaching Today
Education Issues
Integration Corner
Software Corner
Digital Media Corner
Assistive Technologies Corner
In the Lab
Learn It Online

Features

Timeline
Guide to WWW Sites
Search Tools
Buyer's Guide
State/Federal Sites
Professional Sites

Integration Corner is designed for teachers and other educators who are looking for innovative ways to integrate technology into their content-specific curriculum. Integration Corner not only provides great Web sites with current information but also shows what other educators are doing in the field of educational technology. Integration Corner is designed for all educators regardless of their interests. Expand your resources by reviewing information and Web sites outside of your teaching area because many great integration ideas in one area can be modified easily for use in other curricular areas.

Teachers and administrators will find other colleagues in their areas with whom to connect and share the successes and hurdles of integrating technology in a classroom or an entire school system. Consider Integration Corner your one stop for integration ideas and resources. Links to educational Web sites are organized in the following 12 Corners, and different Web resources are available for each chapter. Figure 3-51 shows examples of the Web resources provided in the Chapter 3 Middle School Corner.

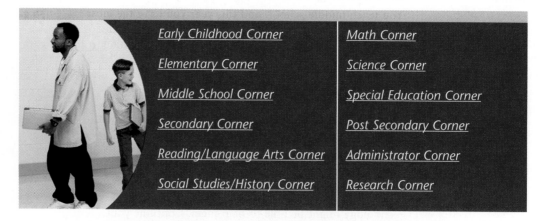

Early Childhood Corner   *Math Corner*

Elementary Corner   *Science Corner*

Middle School Corner   *Special Education Corner*

Secondary Corner   *Post Secondary Corner*

Reading/Language Arts Corner   *Administrator Corner*

Social Studies/History Corner   *Research Corner*

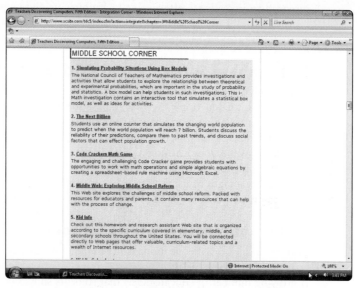

Figure 3-51 Examples of the Web resources provided in the Chapter 3 Middle School Corner.

Software Corner

INSTRUCTIONS: Software Corner provides information on popular software programs. Each numbered segment discusses specific software programs and contains a link to additional information about these programs. To display this page from the Web, visit scsite.com/tdc5, click Chapter 3 at the top of the Web page, and then click Software Corner on the left sidebar.

1. PrimeTime Math

Teachers of exceptional students will find the PrimeTime Math series excellent support software for the math curriculum. PrimeTime Math engages students by providing stories about real-world professionals using math in real-life situations, that include titles like Adrift!, Cliffbound!, Fire!, Lost!, Emergency!, and Stakeout! This software meets the National Council of Teachers of Mathematics (NCTM) standards by building mathematical understanding through use of stories about crimes, medical emergencies, fires, and wilderness search and rescues, while at the same time assisting students in realizing the importance of math in the world in which they live.

2. Adobe Photoshop Elements

Adobe Photoshop Elements allows you and your students to edit pictures from resources, such as those downloaded from digital cameras and the Internet. You can use these edited pictures to create multimedia digital projects, unique reports, personalized calendars, student bulletin boards for classroom instruction, post to blogs, and much more. Using Adobe Photoshop Elements helps your classroom photos have a professionally finished look without a lot of hassle and the price is perfect for education!

3. Thinkology

Developing students' critical thinking skills and creating learning opportunities that engage higher-order thinking skills always have been a struggle for teachers. Thinkology by Heartsoft helps K-3 students master essential critical thinking skills while having fun! Students are guided through a critical-thinking-skills journey with a cast of clever animated characters. Students learn to reason through concepts and are asked questions such as, does this make sense?

4. Kidspiration

Ever had trouble getting young learners to organize their thoughts and develop their great ideas into understandable concepts? Kidspiration is an excellent visual learning tool for teaching K-5 students to organize and express those great ideas through visual learning! Created for inexperienced readers and writers, Kidspiration helps students increase their confidence as they learn to understand concepts, organize information, write stories, and convey and share their thoughts. Brainstorming, visual mapping, thought webs, and other visual tools are used to enhance students' comprehension of concepts and information.

5. Tessellation Exploration

Do you want to make teaching tessellations to your middle and high school students fun and easy? One piece of software that makes the concept of tessellations easier to teach and allows students to practice is Tessellation Exploration by Tom Snyder Productions. The software includes an extensive tutorial on the concept of tessellations. Teachers can use the software as a tool to present the concept of tessellations. Next, students use Tessellation Exploration to construct their own tessellations, by selecting a base shape and moves, such as slides, flips, and turns; students watch their tessellation form before their eyes. Students can create slide shows with the tessellations or print them out.

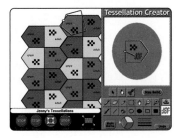

Digital Media Corner

INSTRUCTIONS: Today's K-12 digital students need their learning to be meaningful and relevant to their lives. Digital Media Corner provides videos, ideas, and examples of how you can use digital media to enhance your teaching and your students' learning. To access the videos and links to additional information, visit scsite.com/tdc5, click Chapter 3 at the top of the Web page, and then click Digital Media on the left sidebar.

1. Microsoft Movie Maker

Movie Maker is a free Windows-based video editing software program that provides tools you and your students can use to create, edit, and publish movies. You can edit and produce a movie from video clips, pictures, and audio files by dragging and dropping various digital media components into timelines and then adding special effects, transitions, and voice-overs. Movie Maker is a great product for creating digital storytelling projects with your students. A Movie Maker finished movie can be published in a variety of way, including to the Web, on a CD or DVD, or downloaded to a camera for playback on a TV.

2. Microsoft Photo Story

Photo Story, also a free download for Windows, brings your digital photos to life. You can add stunning special effects, soundtracks, and your own voice narrations and much more to your photos and your digital storytelling projects. You can add dramatic eye-catching special effects to your photo stories and then personalize them with titles and captions. Files can be made small so you can attach and send your stories in an e-mail, publish them on the Web, burn them on a CD so you can watch them on any computer or Windows-based portable device. You can add enhanced photos you create in Photo Story with your own special effects and narratives to your Movie Maker videos — the two products work great together and the best part is both are free.

3. Microsoft Producer

Microsoft Producer is an add-on for Microsoft Office PowerPoint 2003 and 2007 that can help you easily capture, synchronize, and publish audio, video, slides, and images as digital media rich interactive PowerPoint presentations. Producer has content authoring features for your presentations that you and your students can easily learn to use.

4. Adobe Software

A popular digital media production software application package is Adobe Creative Suite. The Adobe Creative Suite includes the widely used image editing program PhotoShop, the illustration creator Illustrator, the page publisher InDesign, Adobe Acrobat, and a number of other applications. Adobe's popularity is due in part to its high performance on both Windows and Macintosh platforms as well as its industry standard Portable Document Format or .pdf file format.

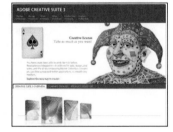

5. OneNote

Microsoft's OneNote is an easy-to-use note taking and information management program that is a natural fit for today's digital generation. You and your students can use OneNote to capture your handwritten thoughts and ideas in electronic notebooks. OneNote allows you to organize, search, and share your notes. You can share your notes, even with people who do not have OneNote. You can e-mail notes pages or publish entire notebooks to a Web site. Using a Tablet PC and OneNote, you can convert your handwritten notes to Word files. OneNote comes with a variety of templates to help you customize your pages and sections. You can choose from decorative backgrounds, watermarks, and more that you can easily customize.

Assistive Technologies Corner

INSTRUCTIONS: Assistive Technologies Corner provides information on current hardware, software, and peripherals that will assist you in delivering instruction to students with physical, cognitive, or sensory challenges. To access extensive additional information, visit scsite.com/tdc5, click Chapter 3 at the top of the Web page, and then click Assistive Technologies on the left sidebar.

1. Should Special Needs Software Be Available for All Teachers?

Yes! The educator's primary concern is to fit the software to the learner, and not the other way around. You can choose the appropriate assistive technology software when you consider the particular disability of the learner, the learner's strengths, and the learner's academic needs. A challenged student may need assistance with reading, or with communication, or with organizing and processing new information.

In the Chapter 1 Assistive Technologies Corner, you learned that operating systems have built-in accessibility features. Some of these features may be further enhanced with system software that affects the behavior of the computer across all other programs. You may choose to add new voices to the speech software built into the operating system of the computer or to add new large mouse pointers, for example, which will display whether your students are using Microsoft Word or Internet Explorer. To change the size of the mouse pointer in Windows, click the Start button on the Windows taskbar and then click Control Panel. When the Control Panel window opens, double-click the Mouse icon or link. When the Mouse Properties dialog box opens, click the Pointer tab. Numerous mouse pointer options are available by clicking the Scheme list arrow.

2. What is Speech Synthesis Software?

Many application tools are available to increase student productivity. Speech synthesis software allows students with speech and vocal muscle disorders to participate in classroom discussions. Students assign shortcut keys to reproduce specific, frequently used phrases. Then, they use the shortcut keys to type in a response quickly; the word processing software reads the response in a computerized voice. Students with visual impairments may use software with text enlargement features. Other helpful software applications include an on-screen talking calculator that features big, colorful number buttons and high-quality speech synthesis.

3. What is Speech-to-Text Software?

Speech-to-text software is used by many nondisabled users to control computers and produce documents. In the classroom, this type of software assists learners with disabilities to produce a printed document. ScanSoft is speech-to-text dictation software for both Windows (Dragon Naturally Speaking) and Macintosh (IBM Via Voice) environments. As the student speaks, the software types. These software packages "learn" to respond to the voice of the user. iCommunicator puts the speech-to-text program in an enhanced environment that also provides sign language. Although not a substitute for a sign language interpreter, this software provides an alternative for students with unique communication challenges.

4. What is Text-to-Speech Software?

Software programs that read text aloud are called text-to-speech software. Kurzweil 3000 is a robust system available for struggling learners. With the Kurzweil system, any text from books or documents can be scanned and read aloud to the student. In addition to this enhanced text-to-speech feature, the Kurzweil system allows students to complete tests and worksheets. A built-in word processor displays the test, and the student types in responses. In addition, many freeware and shareware text-to-speech programs are available on the Internet.

Follow the instructions at the top of this page to display additional information and this chapter's links on assistive technologies.

In the Lab

INSTRUCTIONS: In the Lab provides spreadsheet exercises that are divided into two areas, productivity and integration. To access the links to tutorials, productivity ideas, integration examples and ideas, and more, visit scsite.com/tdc5, click Chapter 3 at the top of the Web page, and then click In the Lab on the left sidebar.

PRODUCTIVITY IN THE CLASSROOM

Introduction: Spreadsheets have many uses for both students and teachers in the classroom. Spreadsheets are a great teacher productivity tool. Grade books, lesson plans, rubrics, classroom inventory, textbook inventory, and many other time-saving documents can be created in a spreadsheet. Students can creatively display data using a spreadsheet's charting feature, in addition to sorting and manipulating data, thereby using higher-order thinking skills.

Many of the productivity software suites have spreadsheet programs. Excel is a part of the Microsoft Office suite. Microsoft Works and AppleWorks also have a spreadsheet program. Lotus 1-2-3 and Quattro Pro also are popular spreadsheet programs.

Spreadsheets are not just for math class. It is possible to integrate spreadsheets effectively into many different curriculum areas in ways that excite students and empower their learning.

1. Building a Grade Book Spreadsheet

Problem: Keeping a grade book by hand can be a tedious task. To save time, you have created your grade book in a spreadsheet program so you can calculate percentages and grades quickly, as shown in Figure 3-52. Open your spreadsheet software and create the grade book as described in the following steps. Use the grade book shown in Figure 3-52 as an example. (*Hint:* Use the program's Help feature to better understand the steps. If you do not have the suggested font, use any appropriate font.)

Instructions: Perform the following tasks.

1. Use the names and numbers displayed in Figure 3-52 to create a spreadsheet, then complete the remaining steps to format the spreadsheet.
2. Calculate the total and average for each student and for the entire class.
3. Personalize the spreadsheet title by inserting your name and curriculum area. Format the spreadsheet title in 16-point, Arial Black font and centered over columns A through H.
4. Apply a table style to cells A2:H16. The numbers appear in the Number format with 0 decimal places.
5. Bold the Class Average label in cell A18, and then verify that the column headings in row 2 are bold. Calculate the individual student total and averages, as well as the class averages and class total as indicated in Figure 3-52. Add a solid black border to the bottom of cells A18:H18.

	A	B	C	D	E	F	G	H
1	Mr. Radcliff's 4th Period Language Arts Class							
2	Student		Book Report	Vocab Quiz	Poem	Essay	Total	Average
3	First Name	Last Name						
4	Jenny	Carlson	98	100	100	97	395	99
5	Leah	Chambers	80	70	85	90	325	81
6	Brittany	Cook	70	80	75	75	300	75
7	Oliver	Flint	78	80	90	95	343	86
8	Maria	Gomez	94	80	85	92	351	88
9	Ema	Granger	100	90	95	100	385	96
10	Chelsea	Jackson	85	100	75	90	350	88
11	Cho	Ling	92	90	85	95	362	91
12	Devon	McBride	75	90	85	90	340	85
13	Justin	Pillman	95	100	92	95	382	96
14	Carlos	Ramirez	93	90	95	95	373	93
15	Harry	Rollins	96	90	95	100	381	95
16	Juan	Sanchez	88	80	90	85	343	86
17								
18	Class Average		88	88	88	92	356	89

Figure 3-52

In the Lab

6. Create a custom header to show your name in the left-aligned, course number or title center-aligned, and the current date right-aligned.
7. Save the spreadsheet to the location of your choice using an appropriate filename.
8. Print the spreadsheet.
9. Follow directions from your instructor for turning in the assignment.

2. Building a Student Council Fund-Raiser Spreadsheet

Problem: You are the teacher sponsor of the student council at your high school. To raise money, student council members sell various items throughout the day and at special school functions. You want to see which items are the most profitable for the group and what time of day is the most successful, so you keep track of sales for four weeks. Using a spreadsheet program, prepare the spreadsheet and chart shown in Figures 3-53 and 3-54. (*Hint:* Use Help to better understand the steps. If you do not have the suggested font or color, use any appropriate font or color.)

Instructions: Perform the following tasks.

1. Create the spreadsheet shown in Figure 3-53 using the numbers as displayed.
2. Calculate the total sales for each period, each item, and for the four weeks.
3. Personalize the spreadsheet title by inserting the name of your school. Add a gray, solid pattern to the foreground of cells A1:E1. Format the title in row 1 as 16-point, Arial, bold, purple font and centered over columns A through E.
4. Format the subtitle, Student Council Fund-Raisers (Feb 1 – Feb 28), as 12-point, Arial, bold, black font and centered over columns A through E. Add a border around cells A2:E2.
5. Apply a table style to the remaining portion of the spreadsheet. Display the numbers using the Currency format with two decimal places.
6. Create a custom header to show your name left-aligned, course number or title center-aligned, and the current date right-aligned.
7. Print the spreadsheet.
8. Create the 3-D Column chart from the spreadsheet data, as shown in Figure 3-54. Add the title, Student Council Fund-Raisers, to the chart.

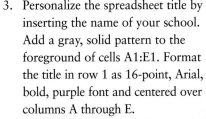

	A	B	C	D	E
1		**Ridgedale High School**			
2		**Student Council Fund-Raisers (Feb 1 - Feb 28)**			
3	*Item*	*Before School*	*Lunch*	*After School*	*Total*
4	Lollipops	$100.00	$25.00	$175.00	$300.00
5	Flowers	$175.00	$250.00	$75.00	$500.00
6	Pizza	$0.00	$0.00	$450.00	$450.00
7	Pencils	$300.00	$100.00	$50.00	$450.00
8	**Total**	$575.00	$375.00	$750.00	$1,700.00

Figure 3-53

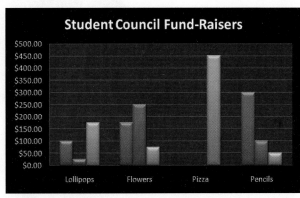

Figure 3-54

In the Lab

9. Create a custom header to show your name left-aligned, course number or title center-aligned, and the current date right-aligned. Print the 3-D Bar chart.

10. Save the spreadsheet and chart to the location of your choice using an appropriate filename.

11. Follow directions from your instructor for turning in the assignment.

INTEGRATION IN THE CLASSROOM

1. You are working on the concept of categorizing with your third-grade students. To meet state technology standards for students and to assist them with understanding this concept, you introduce spreadsheets and charts. Together with the class, you create a spreadsheet to show your students' favorite colors. You then create a 3-D Column chart to show their favorite colors graphically. Create a sample spreadsheet and 3-D Column chart to demonstrate the project for the students. Before submitting this assignment, include a custom header to show your name left-aligned, course number or title center-aligned, and the current date right-aligned.

2. As a part of your Health Education class, you decide to have your students keep track of the total fat grams they consume daily during breakfast, lunch, dinner, and snacks for one week. You encourage students to examine the labels on products and nutrition tables for all foods consumed, including fast food. The students will create a spreadsheet including totals for each day of the week and each meal of the week to determine which days and meals are the healthiest. The students will also include a bar graph to illustrate their data. Create a sample spreadsheet and Bar chart to demonstrate the project for the students. Before submitting this assignment, include a custom header to show your name left-aligned, course number or title center-aligned, and the current date right-aligned.

3. Now that the students are aware of their total fat grams consumed, you want them to explore exercise options and burning calories. Students will select three types of aerobic exercise that they will participate in for 30 minutes, three times a week. They will need to determine how many calories each type of exercise will burn. (*Hint:* Have the students search the World Wide Web.) The students will prepare a spreadsheet to record the total minutes spent exercising weekly and chart the number of calories each type of exercise burned over a one-week period. Create a sample spreadsheet and Pie chart to demonstrate the project for the students. Include a custom header to show your name left-aligned, course number or title center-aligned, and the current date right-aligned.

Learn It Online

INSTRUCTIONS: Use the Learn It Online exercises to reinforce your understanding of the chapter concepts and increase your computer, information, and integration literacy. To access dozens of interactive student labs, practice tests, learning games, and more, visit scsite.com/tdc5, click Chapter 3 at the top of the Web page, and then click Learn It Online on the left sidebar.

Exercises

Web Info
Key Terms
Checkpoint
Teaching Today
Education Issues
Integration Corner
Software Corner
Digital Media Corner
Assistive Technologies Corner
In the Lab
Learn It Online

Features

Timeline
Guide to WWW Sites
Search Tools
Buyer's Guide
State/Federal Sites
Professional Sites

1. At the Movies

Click the At the Movies - Wiki link to review a video about creating your own Wiki.

2. At the Movies

Click the At the Movies – Camtasia link to review a video about creating your own videos using Camtasia.

3. Expanding Your Understanding

Click the Expand Your Understanding link to expand your understanding of Microsoft products and their use in K-12 classrooms. Microsoft seeks to help teachers and students use its products by maintaining an extensive array of user-friendly resources. Research this Web site and write a report summarizing your findings. If required, submit your report to your instructor.

4. Installing and Removing Software Programs

Click the Installing and Removing Software Programs link to learn how to install new software programs and how to uninstall previously installed software programs. Print just the first page of this Web page. On the back of the printout, write a brief summary explaining how to uninstall a program. If required, submit your results to your instructor.

5. Practice Test

Click the Practice Test link. Answer each question. When completed, enter your name and click the Grade Test button to submit the quiz for grading. Make a note of any missed questions. If required, submit your score to your instructor.

6. Who Wants to Be a Computer Genius?

Click the Computer Genius link to find out if you are a computer genius. Directions about how to play the game will be displayed. When you are ready to play, click the Play button. If required, submit your score to your instructor.

7. Wheel of Terms

Click the Wheel of Terms link to reinforce important terms you learned in this chapter by playing the Shelly Cashman Series version of this popular game. Directions about how to play the game will be displayed. When you are ready to play, click the Play button. If required, submit your score to your instructor.

8. Crossword Puzzle Challenge

Click the Crossword Puzzle link. Complete the puzzle to reinforce skills you learned in this chapter. Directions about how to play the game will be displayed. When you are ready to play, click the Play button. If required, submit the completed puzzle to your instructor.

Special Feature: Creating Web Pages, Blogs, Wikis, and More

As you have learned so far, today's digital generation is profoundly different than the generations that preceded it. Students today crave all things digital and their world often revolves around the Web and all the wonderful digital tools and devices that they have at their fingertips.

To teach, and more importantly, to reach today's digital generation, you need to be able to integrate these new digital tools into your classroom curriculum. In this special feature, you learn about Web pages, blogs, wikis, and podcasts, as well as how to create these digital tools. In addition, you learn how to add video and audio to your creations. Finally, you will learn about multimedia authoring programs, such as Camtasia Studio—one user-friendly program that you and your students can use to develop student-centered video creations.

So let's get started!

Creating a Teacher's Web Page

As you learned in Chapter 2, **Web publishing** is the development and maintenance of Web pages. Today, teachers and students do not have to learn programming skills to create Web pages and Web sites. Instead, user-friendly Web development programs allow teachers, students, and other users to create their own Web pages using basic word processing skills. Popular Web development tools and editors used by educators include Adobe GoLive, Adobe Dreamweaver, Microsoft Publisher, WebBlender, Apple's iWeb (Figure 1), and Microsoft Word to name just a few.

Creating well designed Web pages takes a little practice, but once you get the hang of it, it is a lot of fun. The first step is to decide what you want to publish on your Web page. If you've been teaching for any length of time, you have already collected a great deal of material. Maybe you want to publish stories your students have written, share student projects, promote the activities of an after-school club, communicate with parents, or create an electronic magazine or e-book for your grade level. Whatever you want to put on your Web page, the activities in this special feature will show you the basics of how to do it. Before you begin, review Figure 2, which provides tips for organizing your Web pages.

As you have learned, Microsoft Word is a full-featured word processing program that allows teachers and students to create and revise professional looking documents, such as letters, announcements, memos, newsletters, flyers, brochures, reports, and much more. What you may not know is that Word also provides many tools that you and your students can use to create Web pages quickly and easily.

Web Info

For more information about Apple's iWeb, visit the Teachers Discovering Computers Web site (*scsite.com/tdc5*), click Chapter 3, click Web Info, and then click iWeb.

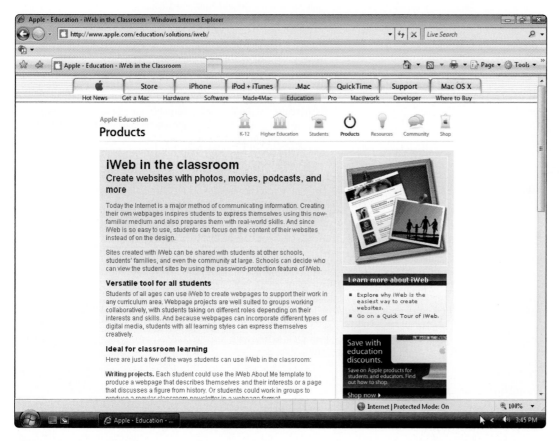

Figure 1 Apple's iWeb is one of many Web development tools that teachers and students can use to create Web pages.

Tip	Details
Web pages should be easy to read.	Make sure font types and colors are easy to read. Choose your background color and designs so they work well with fonts you use and so they make the text easy to read. Avoid flashy effects since these can distract the visitor from the purpose of your Web page.
Web pages should be easy to navigate.	Navigation is very important! If your hyperlinks are not clear to your visitors, they get lost. Always be sure visitors can easily return to your Home page. Graphic images, such as buttons or tabs, should be clearly labeled and easy to read. Navigation bars should appear in the same place on each home page for ease of use. Do not underline text for emphasis because underlined text usually denotes a link.
Web pages should be well-organized.	Organization is the key to good content delivery! A well-organized Web page leads to a well-organized Web site, and that is important. Limit graphics and links per page, use only what is essential, and do not have too much white space. Messy Web pages will take away from your content instead of adding to it. Avoid lengthy, run-on content that requires visitors to scroll. If a long article is part of the Web page, provide a list of topic links at the start of the article so visitors can quickly jump to a topic of interest. Also, once a visitor starts reading an article, provide links throughout the article that allow visitors to get back to the list of topic links at the beginning of the article.
Layout and design should be consistent on all Web pages in a Web site.	Consistency and unity will make your Web pages look more professional. All graphic images and elements, typefaces, headings, theme elements, navigation elements, and so on should remain consistent from Web page to Web page.
Web sites should be easy to locate.	Web sites are located by search engines using key words. Usually, the developer of the Web site determines the key words associated with the Web site — the words the search engine uses to find your site — be sure to associate key words visitors might use to find your Web site. Also, make your contact information easy to find on the Home page.
Web pages graphics should be small files.	Make sure graphics are small in file size. The larger a graphic file size, the longer it takes for the image to appear in your Web site. Readers get frustrated waiting for the graphics to load, and they may not stick around long enough to see your graphics load.
Web pages should be interactive.	Good interactivity engages the user and makes your Web site memorable. Try to find ways to make the Web site engaging. Be sure to update the content often.
Web pages should be quick to download.	Studies have shown that most visitors lose interest in a Web site if it does not load quickly. If you must include a file you know will take a long time to load, provide a warning at the top of the Web page so visitors know why the page is taking so long to load. Also consider providing a way for visitors to by-pass the download.

Figure 2 Some tips for creating Web pages.

As part of this special feature, you can create a basic teacher's Web page using Microsoft Word called Mr. Handley's Home Page (Figure 3.) Mr. Handley is a history teacher at Ridgedale High School.

In this project, you learn how to download graphics from the World Wide Web, open a new Word Web page, select a background image, create a title, insert and format text and headings, insert horizontal lines and graphics, create a linked list of favorite places, create an e-mail link, save the Web page, and view Mr. Handley's Home Page in your browser.

Complete step-by-step instructions for completing this project are at the textbook Web site. To download the instructions and create Mr. Handley's Home page using Microsoft Word, visit the Teachers Discovering Computers Web site (*scsite.com/tdc5*), click Chapter 3, and then click Chapter 3 Special Feature.

Creating Blogs

This section is about blogging and how to create classroom blogs for you and your students. Using a Web-based blogging program, like Blogger or EduBlog, you can create a blog in minutes!

What Is a Blog?

Recall from Chapter 2 that a **blog**, short for **Weblog**, is an informal Web site consisting of time-stamped articles, or posts, in a diary or journal format, usually listed in reverse chronological order. Recall also that a blog that contains video clips is called a **video blog**, or **vlog**. Blogs can subject specific, open to the public or private, and entertaining or educational.

Because a blog entry is like a traditional journal or diary entry, it typically includes a date, ideas on a topic of interest, and a signature. Students can use blogs to practice writing

FAQ

What is the difference between a Web site and a blog?

A blog is a Web site. Most companies view their Web sites as digital brochures. Blogs, in contrast, are dialogues between readers as each and every page or article on a blog invites and can display feedback from readers.

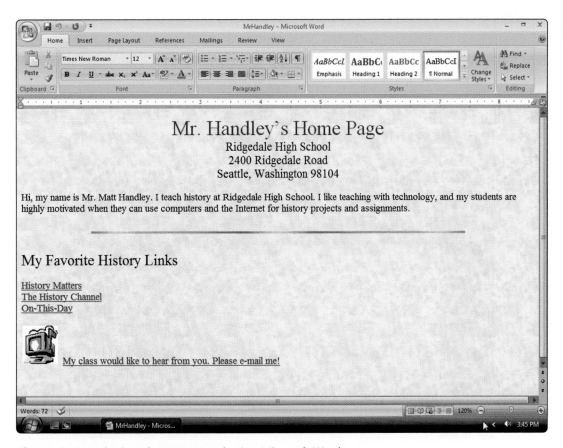

Figure 3 A teacher's Web page created using Microsoft Word.

and communication skills (Figure 4a). Teachers can use them to post daily or weekly assignments, generate thoughts, stimulate classroom discussion, connect with parents, and much more (Figure 4b).

There are many sites that you can use to create blogs similar to the ones shown in

Figure 4. Best of all, blogs are easy to create and maintain! To watch a video with step-by-step instructions for creating a classroom blog using a popular blog tool, visit the Teachers Discovering Computers Web site (*scsite.com/tdc5*), click Chapter 3, and then click Chapter 3 Special Feature.

[a]

[b]

Figure 4 Figure 4a shows a teacher-directed student blog and Figure 4b shows a teacher's blog.

In addition, you can easily post blogs and create your own classroom blog using Microsoft Word 2007.

Blogging and Word 2007

When you click the Office button and then click New in Word 2007, a New Document dialog box is displayed (Figure 5). Notice that Word defaults to two options that you can create, a Blank document or a New blog post. To open a New blog post document, double-click the New blog post icon. Word 2007 opens a new blog post document window and displays the Register a Blog Account dialog box (see Figure 6 on the next page). You then register or select your blog, create your blog post in Word, and then click the Publish button to automatically post your blog. Do not forget to fix your spelling errors before posting your blog.

Using Word 2007 to post a blog post is a simple process and your blog post can contain links, graphics, photos, and much more. In addition to posting blogs, you also can create a new blog site, such as a classroom blog site, using Word 2007. You create your classroom blog site using the Register a Blog Account dialog box (see Figure 6). You can use the free hosting service provided by Microsoft or you can select a different blog hosting site from a list (see Figure 7 on the next page).

To watch a video with step-by-step instructions for posting a blog or creating your classroom blog using Microsoft Word 2007, visit the Teachers Discovering Computers Web site (*scsite.com/tdc5*), click Chapter 3, and then click Chapter 3 Special Feature.

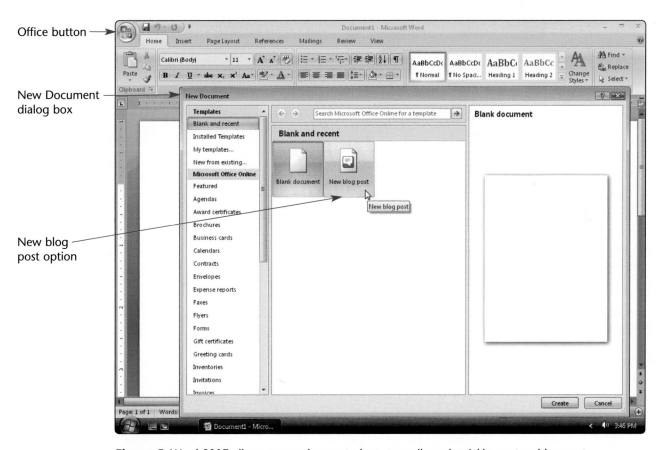

Figure 5 Word 2007 allows you and your students to easily and quickly create a blog post.

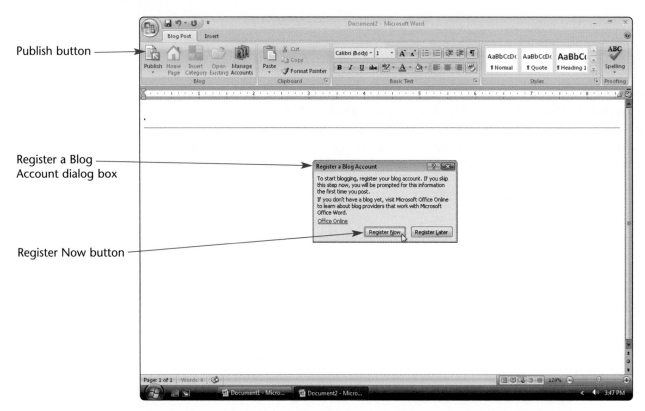

Publish button

Register a Blog
Account dialog box

Register Now button

Figure 6 Word creates a new Blog Post document and displays a dialog box that lets you register the blog to an account of your choice so you can start blogging.

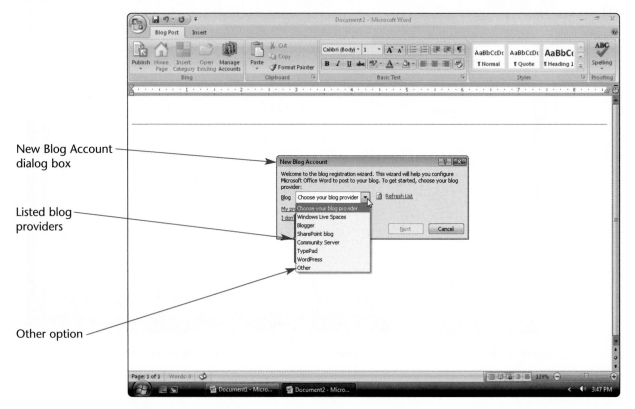

New Blog Account
dialog box

Listed blog
providers

Other option

Figure 7 The New Blog Account dialog box provides links to popular blog hosting sites, where you can register your blog. Use the Other option to register with a blog provider that is not listed.

Benefits of Using Blogs in Education

There are many benefits to using classroom blogs with your students. In short, blogs can bring today's students into the world of writing and many other curriculum areas. Below are just some of the many benefits of classroom blogging. Using blogs, your students can:

- keep a diary on their reading, projects, or classroom discussions

- embed links in their blogs as they research subjects and then report on their findings

- keep track of project-related tasks that need to be completed

- write up their findings on scientific experiments daily

- copy and paste ideas or quotes from other sources, making sure to quote or link to their source, and then personally reflect on the topic

- create cross-classroom prompts, thus being part of a network of readers and writers

- create classroom storyboards with ongoing storytelling

- log chronological events for social studies and research projects

- learn math and mentor other students having difficulties with math concepts and assignments

- ask others, such as friends, family members, librarians, and even local business professionals, to edit their blogs, or provide feedback

Learning More about Blogging

Blogging is exciting. You can use blogging to engage your digital students in powerful learning activities using the Web-based tools, such as Blogger, that they relate to. Figure 8 lists additional resources that you can use to review examples of blogs, to learn more about blogging, and to help you in your blogging adventure.

Blogging Do's

Blogging, like many other technologies you use and integrate into the curriculum, has some risks. Although you cannot review all blog entries before they are published, you can take steps to lessen the risks of inappropriate entries.

- Do know your school and district Acceptable Use Policies (AUP) and convey them to your students.

- Do get parental permission before allowing students to blog if blogging is not part of your school's Acceptable Use Policy (AUP).

- Do avoid blogging sites that require students to include their full names or e-mail addresses.

- Do avoid sites that request personal information from students.

- Do review what is permissible and appropriate with your students.

- Do remind students of the importance of netiquette and being respectful.

Web Info

For more information about the benefits of using classroom blogs, visit the Teachers Discovering Computers Web site (*scsite.com/tdc5*), click Chapter 3, click Web Info, and then click Benefits of Blogging.

BLOG	URL
EduBlog.com	*www.edublog.com/*
TypePad	*www.typepad.com/*
Blog.com	*blog.com*
Blogger	*blogger.com*
Academic Blogs	*www.blogtopsites.com/academics/*
Blogstream	*blogstream.com*
Google Blog Search	*blogsearch.google.com/*
Weblogg-ed	*www.weblogg-ed.com/*
Infinite Thinking	*www.infinitethinking.org/*
Windows Live Spaces	*spaces.live.com/*
WorldPress	*www.worldpress.org/blogs.htm*

To see an updated list with links to these and other blog sites, visit the Teachers Discovering Computers Web site (scsite.com/tdc5), click Chapter 3, and then click Chapter 3 Special Feature.

Figure 8 Popular blog sites.

- Do have rules of appropriate behavior and consequences of misbehavior.

- Do provide examples of model blogs for students to review.

- Do remind your students that blogging is a privilege and appropriate behavior will ensure continued use.

Finally, do find out if your school district allow teachers to create classroom blogs that reside on the school or district server, which, in turn can be evaluated in a safe environment using peer evaluation.

Creating a Wiki

In this section, you learn about wikis, how to create a wiki, and how to use wikis with your students.

What Is a Wiki?

Recall from Chapter 2 that a **wiki** is a collaborative Web site that allows users to create, add to, modify, or delete the Web site content via their Web browser. Most wikis are open to modification by anyone, and wikis are especially suited for collaborative

writing. Wikis also allow for linking among any number of pages. This ease of interaction and operation makes a wiki a great tool for group authoring—a powerful tool for use in teaching students team work, writing skills, and so much more.

The term wiki also can refer to the collaborative software itself, called a **wiki engine**, which facilitates the operation of wiki sites. A popular online wiki is Wikipedia (Figure 9). A **single page** in a wiki is referred to as a wiki page, while the entire body of pages, which are usually highly interconnected via hyperlinks, is the wiki. A wiki is actually a very simple, easy-to-use, user-maintained database for creating, browsing, and searching for information. The bottom line about wikis is that anyone can edit anything at anytime and add to the content of a wiki.

Create Your Own Wiki

Creating your own wiki is as easy as 1-2-3! Wikis are fun, engaging, and powerful teaching and learning tools! There are numerous Web sites that will walk you through creating a wiki and will even host your wiki for free. In fact, numerous wiki sites are dedicated to helping

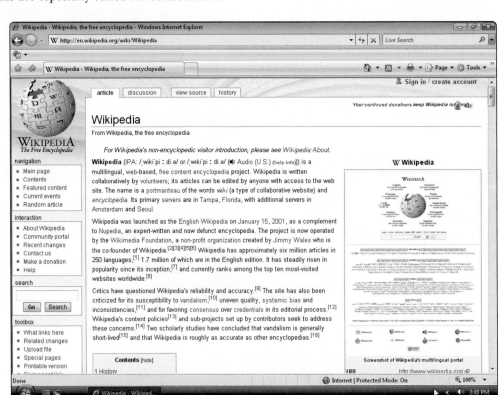

Figure 9 Wikipedia is a free encyclopedia used daily by millions of people.

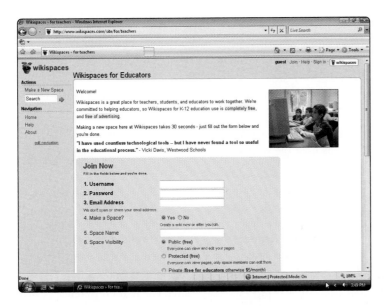

Figure 10 Wikispaces is a popular site for creating classroom wikis.

teachers and students create their own wikis (Figure 10 above). To watch a video with step-by-step instructions for creating your own wiki, visit the Teachers Discovering Computers Web site (*scsite.com/tdc5*), click Chapter 3, and then click Chapter 3 Special Feature. Figure 11 lists popular wiki creation sites and sample classroom wikis.

Wiki Tools	URL
Wikispaces	*www.wikispaces.com*
PBwiki	*pbwiki.com/edu.html*
MediaWiki	*www.mediawiki.org/wiki/MediaWiki*
Seed Wiki	*www.seedwiki.com*
Wiki Search Engine	*www.qwika.com*
Scribe Post Hall of Fame	*thescribepost.pbwiki.com*
Sample Education Wikis	**URL**
Neighborhood School Wiki	*theneighborhoodschool.org/wiki*
High School Online Collaborative Writing	*schools.wikia.com/wiki/Main_Page*
8th Grade Social Studies Wiki	*http://gps8socialstudies.pbwiki.com/*
Bud the Teacher Wiki	*www.budtheteacher.com/wiki/index.php?title=Main_Page*
Penn State Epoche Wiki	*epochewiki.pbwiki.com*

To see an updated list with links to these and other wiki sites, visit the Teachers Discovering Computers Web site (scsite.com/tdc5), click Chapter 3, and then click Chapter 3 Special Feature.

Figure 11 Popular wiki tools and sample education wikis.

Wiki Uses

The following are just a few of the many ways that wikis can be used in education:

■ to help create an easy, simple student-centered Web site

■ to facilitate group authoring and collaboration

■ as a repository for content, which can be viewed at any time from any place with an Internet connection by any student in your class

■ to provide storage for data collection, which can be accessed as needed

■ to display student projects

■ to provide a vehicle for sharing reviews

■ to share presentations, which students can view again for clarification or for the first time if they missed the class when a presentation was made

Wiki Strategies

The following provide a few strategies that you and your students can implement when using wikis.

Web Info

For more information about Citizendium, visit the Teachers Discovering Computers Web site (*scsite.com/tdc5*), click Chapter 3, click Web Info, and then click Citizendium.

To Promote Reading Skills

- Have students check the wiki history! They can tell how active a particular wiki is by clicking the recent or history links. Remind students, however, that more activity does not equate to better quality.

- Have students read reviews of the wiki to get a sense of who has used the wiki and their reactions to it.

- Encourage students to read a wiki and think critically about what they just read. Have students decide if what they read is fact or opinion, and how they might determine which it is if they don't know for sure.

- Invite students to research facts they read in a wiki. Remind students that just because something is on the Internet does not mean it is correct. Tell students they must verify what they read, especially when they read it in wikis.

To Promote Writing Skills

- Tell students that if they know something that is not included, they could add it!

- Tell students if they see something wrong, they should consider fixing it!

- Remind students to provide sources for facts they add to a wiki and always to use proper spelling and grammar.

Wiki Challenges for Educators

Because of how open most wikis are, some educators find them unsuitable for education. Critics agree that a wiki's strength, the fact that anyone can post or edit a listing, is also its greatest weakness. Wikipedia material can be written or edited by just about anyone, regardless of his or her level of subject matter expertise. In most cases, Wikipedia authors do not have to submit any identifying information. This lack of accountability has led the creators of Wikipedia to create Citizendium (Figure 12).

Citizendium has the same functionality of Wikipedia. Authors are still able to edit, delete, or modify content that has been placed on the site. The main difference between Citizendium and Wikipedia is that Citizendium requires authors to register their names and affiliation before editing any information. Citizendium also has subject matter experts from academia and private industry, who are content editors. By including an authoritative presence, a direct increase to the credibility of the information cited in wikis is projected.

One final note when using and creating wikis is to evaluate wiki hosting sites carefully before making a decision. Some free wiki hosting sites require banner ads to be placed on your wiki, which, in most cases, are not appropriate for wikis you create for use with your students.

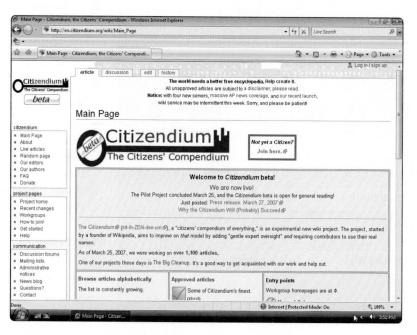

Figure 12 A wiki site started by the creators of Wikipedia.

Creating a Podcast

The term podcast is derived from Apple's portable music player, the iPod (Figure 13). Podcasts are a popular way people share information on the Web verbally. A **podcast** is recorded audio stored in a file on a Web site. The host or author of a podcast is often called a **podcaster**. A video podcast, or **vodcast**, is a podcast that contains video and usually audio. A podcast can be downloaded to a computer or a portable media player, such as a Zune or an iPod. Basically a podcast is an Internet-based radio show and, like the term radio, the term podcasting can refer either to the content and the method of syndication or to how it is downloaded.

A podcast is distinguished from other digital media formats by its ability to be downloaded automatically, using software capable of reading feed formats, such as RSS or Atom, and programs called feed readers or aggregators. Users subscribe to a feed by supplying a link to the feed. The reader program can then check the user's subscribed feeds to see if any of those feeds have new content since the last time it checked, and if so, retrieve that content and present it to the user.

At a convenient time and location, the user listens to the downloaded podcast or watches the downloaded vodcast. Examples of podcasts include music, radio shows, news stories, classroom lectures, political messages, and television commentaries. Some Web sites, such as podcast.net, specialize in podcast distribution. Others, such as National Public Radio (Figure 14), have incorporated a podcast component in their existing Web site.

Figure 13 Apple's iPod is used by millions of digital students to listen to music and podcasts.

Figure 14 National Public Radio is just one of thousands of Web sites that provide podcasts and vodcasts for their users on a variety of topics.

Web Info

For more information on how to create a podcast for an Apple iPod, visit the Teachers Discovering Computers Web site (*scsite.com/tdc5*), click Chapter 3, click Web Info, and then click Creating Podcasts.

Implications for Education

Podcasting is a technology that is quickly becoming popular in education and already is popular with your digital students. Podcasts enable students and teachers to share all kinds of information with anyone at anytime. In education, podcasts typically are produced (1) by students for use by other students or their friends; (2) by teachers for use by their students; and (3) by universities, corporations, education consortiums, and the government to provide resources and professional development for teachers and students (Figure 15).

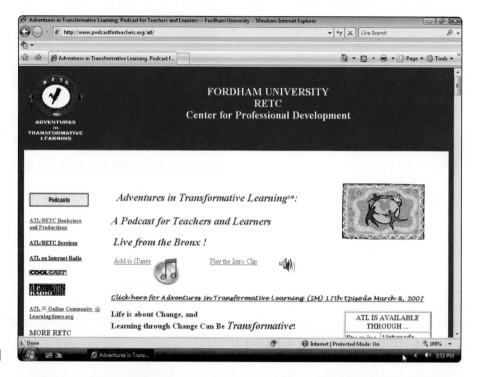

[a]

[b]

Figure 15 Figure 15a shows links to education podcasts developed, produced, and hosted by Fordham University's Regional Educational Technology Center. Figure 15b shows links to education podcasts in iTunes.

Podcast Sites	URL
Directory of Podcast Sites	www.podcast.net/
Education Podcast Network	www.epnweb.org/
Popular Podcast Communities	www.voxmedia.org/wiki/Podcast_Directories
Higher Education Podcast Repository	ed-cast.org/
Education and Professional Podcast Directory	www.learnoutloud.com/Podcast-Directory/Education-and-Professional
Yahoo Education Podcasting	groups.yahoo.com/group/Podcasting-Education/
Apple Podcasting	www.apple.com/education/products/ipod/podcasting.html
Fordham University	www.podcastforteachers.org/atl/
UCF Digital Media Podcast	sulley.dm.ucf.edu/~podcast/

To see an updated list with links to these and other podcast sites, visit the Teachers Discovering Computers Web site (scsite.com/tdc5), click Chapter 3, and then click Chapter 3 Special Feature.

Figure 16 Popular podcast sites.

You can create podcasts of a lesson or a block of instruction and, if a student is absent, he or she can download the podcast of the recorded lesson. Teachers or administrators can create podcasts to communicate curriculum, assignments, sample tests, and other information to parents. Using podcasts, teachers and students can create book talks, vocabulary or foreign language lessons, international pen pal letters (podcast pals!), music performances, interviews, student presentations, debates, and so many other things — the uses are limitless.

To watch a video with step-by-step instructions for creating a classroom podcast, visit the Teachers Discovering Computers Web site (*scsite.com/tdc5*), click Chapter 3, and then click Chapter 3 Special Feature. To help you learn more about podcasts, refer to Figure 16 above, which lists a number of popular podcast sites and education information podcast sites.

Multimedia Authoring Software

In the previous sections, you learned about creating Web pages, blogs, wikis, and podcasting. In this section, you learn about an exciting and easy to use multimedia authoring software program.

As you have already learned, **multimedia authoring software** is used to create electronic presentations, simulations, and software demonstrations that can include text, graphics, video, audio, animation, and screen captures. Some of these software programs, sometimes called video editing programs, are free and others must be purchased. Many of these software programs are covered in other parts of this textbook, especially in the Digital Media and Software Corners that follow each chapter. In this section, you learn about one of these programs that is already being used extensively in higher education and is becoming more and more popular in K-12 education, Camtasia Studio.

A number of software programs help teachers and students easily create video screencasts and then add enhancements like Webcam videos and music tracks. A **screencast** is a digital recording of a computer's screen output, often containing audio. Just as a screenshot is a picture of a computer screen, a screencast is a movie of what a user sees on the monitor. For example, you can use a program like Camtasia Studio to record anything you do on your computer, including mouse movements, which allows you to show students how to use Inspiration, demonstrate how to do Web searching, and more. The following are just some of the ways you and your students can

Web Info

For information and links for over 20 multimedia authoring software programs, visit the Teachers Discovering Computers Web site, (*scsite.com/tdc5*), click Chapter 3, click Web Info, and then click Multimedia Authoring Software.

use screencasts as digital representations of traditional printed materials:

- create digital student-centered and student-created tutorials

- teach lessons using PowerPoint presentations with voice-over and digital enhancements so the presentation becomes a video presentation

- develop short how-to-do videos and video-based, narrated demonstration

- create digital storytelling projects

- provide digital reviews of software, rubrics, classroom rules, school policies, and so on

- present an explanation of detailed content-specific materials that students can watch over and over again from any place using a variety of media devices

- create animated whiteboard-type presentations

Camtasia Studio

Camtasia Studio (Figure 17) is a powerful, yet easy to use solution for you and your students to record, edit, and share high-quality instructional videos, student created video-based projects, and

more on the Web, CDs, DVDs, and portable media players, including iPods. Camtasia includes many powerful features, including the following:

- Use the Record the Screen feature in Camtasia to record your screencast and include audio (music and/or narration) if desired. You even can record yourself along with the screen video using an inexpensive Webcam and display yourself as a picture in a picture.

- Use the Record PowerPoint feature to create a narrated presentation literally with two clicks of your mouse. To stop the recording, you press the Esc key on your keyboard, save the file as you would any file, edit the video if necessary, and then produce the video as learning supplements for your students.

- Use Camtasia to create a podcast or vodcast. For example, you can create an audio podcast using your computer's microphone or an inexpensive USB microphone. You can edit your podcast if necessary, and then produce and upload your podcast. You can even upload your podcast using Camtasia's hosting service, Screencast.com.

Figure 17 Camtasia Studio allows teachers and students to easily create all types of screencasts and videos.

Camtasia Studio makes it easy to produce and distribute your videos in a number of different formats (see Figure 18). Your students can view your videos and their videos truly anytime and anyplace, using the following ways:

- on any computer using the storage medium on which the video is stored, such as the hard drive, a USB flash drive, a CD, or a DVD

- streaming from the Web; even users that have dial up access can view your videos if you save them as Flash (.swf) files, which are significantly smaller than other video formats

- on any TV using a DVD player, a portable media player such as an iPod connected to the TV, or wirelessly from your PC, Macintosh computer, or portable media player using Apple TV or similar device connected to a TV

- on portable video media players, such as a video iPod or Zune, which allows students to watch your videos on the bus, during lunch, after school, or for that matter from just about any location and at anytime they choose

To watch a video with step-by-step instructions for creating and distributing a Camtasia video, visit the Teachers Discovering Computers Web site (*scsite.com/tdc5*), click Chapter 3, and then click Chapter 3 Special Feature. Camtasia Studio is one example (there are many others) of new or recently updated software programs that allow you to easily and quickly create and distribute true digital instructional solutions to meet the needs of today's digital generation.

Web Info

For more information on Camtasia, including how to download a 30 day free trial, visit the Teachers Discovering Computers Web site (*scsite.com/tdc5*), click Chapter 3, click Web Info, and then click Camtasia Studio.

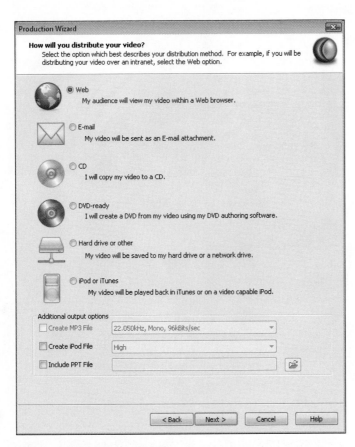

Figure 18 Using the Camtasia Production Wizard, you can produce and distribute your videos in a number of different formats.

Summary and Implications for Education

Today's digital generation crave all things digital, not traditional instructional materials printed on paper. Recent Web developments that allow students to view videos from any place and any time and easy-to-use programs like Camtasia have the potential to impact education in many positive ways; most importantly, these newer technologies allow teachers to teach today's digital students more effectively. These tools and developments can help you not just teach, but reach today's students in ways only dreamed of just a few years ago.

In this special feature, you not only learned about, but also how to create, Web pages, blogs, wikis, podcasts, and other digital media tools that you can use with your students. You will learn more about these tools and how to integrate them into your curriculum in the special feature that follows chapter 7, *Integrating Web Sites, Blogs, Wikis, and More.*

Hardware
for Educators

4

Objectives

After completing this chapter, you will be able to do the following:
[ISTE NETS-T Standards I A-B]

- Describe the system unit

- Define the term bit and describe how a series of bits are used to represent data

- Identify the major components of the system unit and explain their functions

- Explain how the CPU uses the four steps of a machine cycle to process data

- Describe the four types of input as well as various input devices and pointing devices

- List the characteristics of a keyboard and identify various types of keyboards

- Differentiate among the four types of output

- Identify the different types of output devices

- Explain differences among various types of printers

- Differentiate between storage and memory

- Identify types of storage media and devices

- Differentiate between CDs and DVDs

During your teaching career or personal endeavors, you most likely will decide to purchase a new computer or upgrade an existing one. To be effective in this decision-making process and to be an informed teacher, you should possess a general knowledge of major computer components and how various computer components interact. In addition, the International Society for Technology in Education (ISTE) has developed a series of K-12 National Technology Standards (NETS) and skills that K-12 students need to learn throughout their education. One of these technology standards recommends that graduating K-12 students demonstrate a sound understanding of technology concepts, systems, and operations. To help you better understand these concepts, so that you in turn can help your students understand them, this chapter presents a brief look at some of the hardware components used for input, processing, output, and storage. Because Macintosh computers and PCs use similar, and in many cases identical, hardware components, the majority of information presented in this chapter applies to both computer platforms. In instances in which Macintosh computers and PCs use slightly different hardware, these differences are explained.

Web Info

For more information about the National Educational Technology Standards for Students (NETS-S), visit the Teachers Discovering Computers Web site (*scsite.com/tdc5*), click Chapter 4, click Web Info, and then click NETS-S.

The System Unit

The **system unit** is a boxlike case that houses the electronic components a computer uses to process data. All types and sizes of computers have a system unit. (Figure 4-1). The system unit is made of metal or plastic and protects the electronic components from damage. On a personal computer, these components and most storage devices reside inside the system unit; other devices, such as a keyboard and monitor, usually are located outside the system unit. Notebook computers, PDAs, and other mobile devices contain almost all of their components in the system unit, including the keyboard and monitor or display.

The following explanation of how data is represented in a computer will help you understand how the components housed in the system unit process data.

Data Representation

To understand fully how the various components of the system unit work together to process data, you need a basic understanding of how data is represented in a computer. Human speech is **analog**, meaning that it uses continuous signals to represent data and information. Most computers, by contrast, are **digital**, meaning that they understand only two discrete states: on and off. Computers are electronic devices powered by electricity, which has only two states: on or off. These two states

Figure 4-1 All types and sizes of computers have a system unit.

are represented by electronic circuits using two digits; 0 is used to represent the electronic state of off (absence of an electric charge) and 1 is used to represent the electronic state of on (presence of an electric charge) (Figure 4-2).

BINARY DIGIT (BIT)	ELECTRONIC CHARGE	ELECTRONIC STATE
0		OFF
1		ON

Figure 4-2 A computer circuit represents the binary digits 0 or 1 electronically by the absence or presence of an electronic charge.

When people count, they use the digits 0 through 9, which are digits in the decimal system. Because a computer understands only two states, it uses a number system that has just two unique digits, 0 and 1. This numbering system is referred to as the **binary** system. Using just these two numbers, a computer can represent data electronically by turning circuits off or on.

Each off or on digital value is called a **bit** (short for **bi**nary dig**it**), and represents the smallest unit of data the computer can handle. By itself, a bit is not very informative. When eight bits are grouped together as a unit, they are called a **byte**. A byte is informative because it provides enough different combinations of 0s and 1s to represent 256 individual characters, including numbers, uppercase and lowercase letters of the alphabet, and punctuation marks (Figure 4-3).

The combinations of 0s and 1s used to represent characters are defined by patterns called a coding scheme. The most widely used coding scheme to represent data on many personal computers is the **American Standard Code for Information Interchange,** called **ASCII** (pronounced ASK-ee). Coding schemes, such as ASCII, make it possible for humans to interact with digital computers that recognize only bits. When you press a key on a keyboard, the keyboard converts that action into a scan code, which in turn is converted into a binary form the computer understands. That is, every character is converted to its corresponding byte. The computer then processes that data in terms of bytes, which actually is a series of off/on electrical states. When processing is finished, the computer converts the bytes back into numbers, letters of the alphabet, or special characters to be displayed on a screen or printed (Figure 4-4 on the next page). All of these conversions take place so quickly that you do not even realize they are occurring.

Web Info

For more information about the American Standard Code for Information Interchange, visit the Teachers Discovering Computers Web site (*scsite.com/tdc5*), click Chapter 4, click Web Info, and then click ASCII.

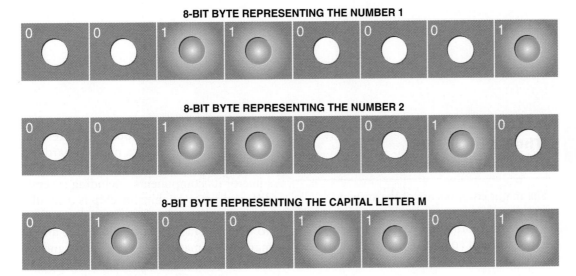

8-BIT BYTE REPRESENTING THE NUMBER 1

8-BIT BYTE REPRESENTING THE NUMBER 2

8-BIT BYTE REPRESENTING THE CAPITAL LETTER M

Figure 4-3 Eight bits grouped together as a unit are called a byte. A byte is used to represent a single character to the computer.

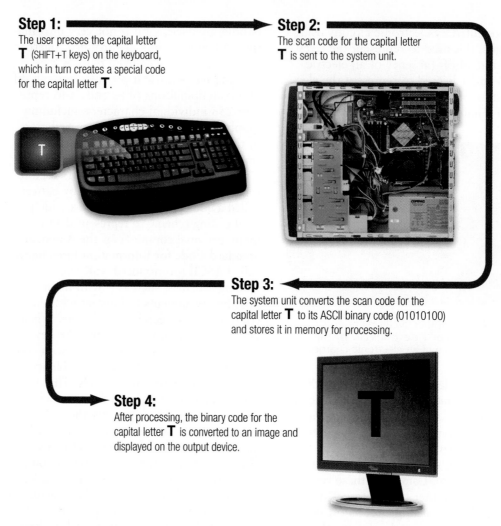

Step 1:
The user presses the capital letter
T (SHIFT+T keys) on the keyboard,
which in turn creates a special code
for the capital letter **T**.

Step 2:
The scan code for the capital letter
T is sent to the system unit.

Step 3:
The system unit converts the scan code for the
capital letter **T** to its ASCII binary code (01010100)
and stores it in memory for processing.

Step 4:
After processing, the binary code for the
capital letter **T** is converted to an image and
displayed on the output device.

Figure 4-4 Converting a letter to ASCII binary code form and back.

Web Info

For a more detailed
description of
motherboards, visit the
Teachers Discovering
Computers Web site
(*scsite.com/tdc5*), click
Chapter 4, click Web
Info, and then click
Motherboard.

The Components of the System Unit

The major components of the system
unit discussed in the following sections
include the motherboard, CPU, memory,
and ports and connectors.

THE MOTHERBOARD
Many of the electronic components
in the system unit reside on a circuit
board called the **motherboard**. Figure 4-5
shows a photograph of a motherboard
used in a personal computer and identifies
some of its components, including several
different types of chips. A **chip** is a small
piece of semiconducting material usually
no bigger than one-half-inch square and is
made up of many layers of circuits and
microscopic components that carry electronic signals. The motherboard in the system unit contains many different types of
chips. Of these, one of the most important
is the central processing unit (CPU).

adapter cards

processor

memory module (RAM chips)

expansion slots for adapter cards

memory slots

motherboard

Figure 4-5 The motherboard in a personal computer contains many chips and other electronic components.

THE CPU

The **central processing unit (CPU)** interprets and carries out the basic instructions that operate a computer. The CPU, also called the **processor** or **microprocessor**, manages most of a computer's operations. Most of the devices that connect to a computer communicate with the CPU to carry out tasks (Figure 4-6).

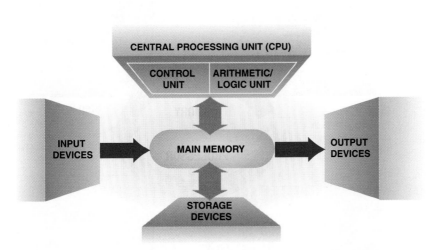

CENTRAL PROCESSING UNIT (CPU)

CONTROL UNIT | ARITHMETIC/ LOGIC UNIT

INPUT DEVICES

MAIN MEMORY

OUTPUT DEVICES

STORAGE DEVICES

Figure 4-6 Most of the devices connected to a computer communicate with the CPU to carry out a task. The arrows in this figure represent the flow of data, instructions, and information.

FAQ

What is the difference between a chip and an integrated circuit?

A computer chip is a small piece of material, usually silicon, on which integrated circuits are etched. An integrated circuit contains many microscopic pathways that carry electrical current, as well as millions of electronic components.

In a personal computer, a single chip known as the processor contains the CPU (Figure 4-7). Several processor chip manufacturers now offer dual-core and multi-core processors. A **dual-core processor** is a single chip that contains two separate processors. Similarly, a **multi-core processor** is a single chip with two or more separate processors.

Xeon

Celeron D

Core 2 Duo

Athlon 64 FX

Core 2 Extreme

Figure 4-7 Most high-performance PCs use Core 2 Duo processors. Basic PCs have a Celeron processor. Macintosh computers use the Dual 2 Core or the G5 processor.

A processor contains a number of components, including a control unit, an arithmetic/logic unit, and a system clock. The following sections describe how these components work together to perform processing operations.

THE CONTROL UNIT The **control unit**, one component of the CPU, directs and coordinates most of the operations in the computer. The control unit has a role much like a traffic cop. The control unit interprets each instruction issued by a program and then initiates the appropriate action to carry out the instruction. For every instruction, the control unit operates by repeating a set of four basic operations: (1) fetching an instruction, (2) decoding the instruction, (3) executing the instruction, and, if necessary, (4) storing the result.

Fetching is the process of obtaining a program instruction or data item from memory. **Decoding** is the process of translating the instruction into commands the computer understands. **Executing** is the process of carrying out the commands. **Storing** is the process of writing the result to memory. Together, these four instructions comprise the **machine cycle** or instruction cycle (Figure 4-8).

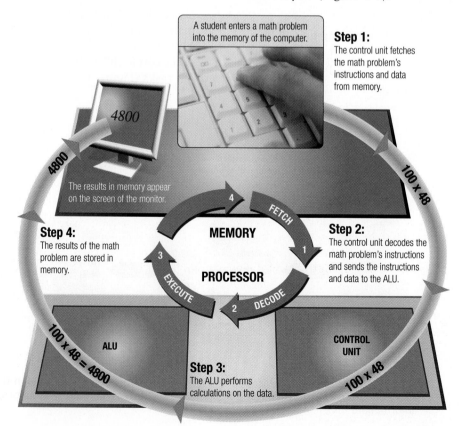

A student enters a math problem into the memory of the computer.

Step 1:
The control unit fetches the math problem's instructions and data from memory.

The results in memory appear on the screen of the monitor.

Step 4:
The results of the math problem are stored in memory.

MEMORY

PROCESSOR

FETCH

DECODE

EXECUTE

Step 2:
The control unit decodes the math problem's instructions and sends the instructions and data to the ALU.

ALU

100 X 48 = 4800

CONTROL UNIT

100 X 48

Step 3:
The ALU performs calculations on the data.

Figure 4-8 This figure shows the steps involved in a machine cycle for a student wanting to solve a math problem on a computer. After the result is in memory, it can be displayed on a monitor, printed, or stored on a storage medium.

THE SYSTEM CLOCK   The control unit relies on a small chip called the **system clock** to synchronize, or control the timing of, all computer operations. Just as your heart beats at a regular rate to keep your body functioning, the system clock generates regular electronic pulses, or ticks, that set the operating pace of components in the system unit. Think of the components of the CPU as members of a marching band that take their steps to the beat of the system clock drummer.

Clock speed is the speed at which a processor executes instructions and is measured in gigahertz (GHz). Giga is a prefix that stands for one billion, and a hertz is one cycle per second. Thus, one **gigahertz** equates to one billion ticks of the system clock in one second. A computer that operates at 4 GHz has 4 billion clock cycles, or ticks, in one second. The faster the clock speed, the more instructions the CPU can execute per second.

THE ARITHMETIC/LOGIC UNIT   The **arithmetic/logic unit (ALU)**, another component of the CPU, performs the execution part of the machine cycle. Specifically, the ALU performs arithmetic, comparison, and logical operations.

Arithmetic operations include addition, subtraction, multiplication, and division. **Comparison operations** involve comparing one data item with another to determine if the first item is greater than, equal to, or less than the other. Depending on the result of the comparison, different actions may occur. For example, to determine a student's letter grade, the student's numeric grade is compared with a set of numbers corresponding to various letter grades (for example, a numeric grade equal to or greater than 90 equates to a letter grade of A). If the student's numeric grade is equal to or greater than 90, then a letter grade of A is given; if the numeric grade is less than 90, a letter grade of A is not given and more

comparisons are performed until a letter grade can be assigned. **Logical operations** work with conditions and logical operators such as AND, OR, and NOT. For example, if you wanted to search a job database for part-time work in the admissions office, you would search for any jobs classified as part-time AND listed under admissions.

MEMORY

While performing a processing operation, a processor needs a place to store data and instructions temporarily. A computer uses **memory** to store data and information. The memory chips on the circuit boards in the system unit perform this and other functions.

Memory stores three basic items: (1) the operating system and other system software that control the computer equipment; (2) the application software designed to carry out a specific task, such as word processing; and (3) the data being processed by the application software. When a computer transfers program instructions and data from a storage medium into memory, the computer stores them as bytes. The computer stores each byte in a precise location in memory, called an address. An **address** is simply a unique number identifying the location of the byte in memory. The illustration in Figure 4-9 shows how seats in a stadium are similar to addresses in memory: (1) a seat holds one person at a time and an address in memory

Figure 4-9 This figure shows how seats in a stadium are similar to addresses in memory: (1) a seat holds one person at a time and an address in memory holds a single byte, (2) both a seat and an address can be empty, and (3) a seat has a unique identifying number and so does an address.

	Term	Abbreviation	Approximate Memory Size	Exact Memory Amount	Approximate Pages of Text
	Kilobyte	KB or K	1 thousand bytes	1024 bytes	1/2
	Megabyte	MB	1 million bytes	1,048,576 bytes	500
	Gigabyte	GB	1 billion bytes	1,073,741,824 bytes	500,000
	Terabyte	TB	1 trillion bytes	1,099,511,627,776 bytes	500,000,0001

Figure 4-10 This table outlines terms used to define storage size.

holds a single byte, (2) both a seat and an address can be empty, and (3) a seat has a unique identifying number and so does an address. To access data or instructions in memory, the computer references the addresses that contain bytes of data.

Recall that a computer stores a character as a series of 0s and 1s, called a byte. A byte is the basic storage unit in memory. Because a byte is such a small amount of storage, several terms have evolved to define storage size for memory and storage devices (Figure 4-10 above). A **kilobyte** of memory, abbreviated **KB** or **K**, is equal to 1024 bytes, but is usually rounded to 1000 bytes. A **megabyte**, abbreviated **MB**, is equal to approximately 1 million bytes. A **gigabyte**, abbreviated **GB**, is equal to approximately 1 billion bytes. A **terabyte** (**TB**) is equal to approximately 1 trillion bytes.

The system unit contains two types of memory: volatile and nonvolatile. The contents of **volatile memory** are lost (erased) when the computer's power is turned off. The contents of **nonvolatile memory**, on the other hand, are not lost when a computer is turned off or power to the computer is interrupted. RAM (random access memory) is an example of volatile memory. ROM (read-only memory) and flash memory are examples of nonvolatile memory. The following sections discuss each of these types of memory.

RANDOM ACCESS MEMORY (RAM) Some memory chips in the system unit are called **random access memory** (**RAM**). When the computer is powered on, certain operating system files, such as the files that determine how your desktop is displayed, are loaded from a storage device, such as a hard disk, into RAM. As long as the power remains on, these files remain in RAM. Because RAM is volatile, the programs and data

stored in RAM are erased when the power to the computer is turned off. Any files or data created by a user that will be needed for future use must be copied from RAM to a storage device, such as a hard disk, before the power to the computer is turned off.

The most common form of RAM used in personal computers is **synchronous dynamic RAM**, or **SDRAM**. Today, most RAM is installed by using a **dual inline memory module (DIMM)**. A DIMM is a small circuit board that contains multiple RAM chips (Figure 4-11). Common DIMM sizes can hold 256 and 512 megabytes or 1 to 2 gigabytes of memory. DIMM chips are installed in special sockets on the motherboard and can be removed and replaced easily with higher-capacity RAM chips or with additional RAM chips. The amount of memory a computer can handle depends on the motherboard.

dual inline memory module

memory chip

Figure 4-11 This photo shows a dual inline memory module (DIMM).

Integration Strategies

To learn more about how to teach your students about how RAM and other computer components work, visit the Teachers Discovering Computers Web site (scsite.com/tdc5), click Chapter 4, and then click Learn It Online.

The amount of RAM a computer requires often depends on the types of applications to be used on the computer. Remember that a computer can manipulate only data that is in memory. RAM is similar to the workspace you have on the top of your desk. Just as a desktop needs a certain amount of space to hold papers, pens, and your computer, a computer needs a certain amount of memory to store programs and files.

The more RAM a computer has, the more programs and files it can work on at once. Having sufficient RAM (1 GB or higher) is important for memory-intensive tasks, such as manipulating graphics; downloading music, videos, and movies; and creating and editing sound, digital images, and video.

A software package usually indicates the minimum amount of RAM and other system requirements. For an application to perform optimally, you usually need more than the minimum specifications on the software package.

READ-ONLY MEMORY (ROM) Read-only memory (ROM) chips store information or instructions that do not change. Manufacturers permanently record instructions and data on ROM chips. Unlike RAM, ROM memory is nonvolatile because it retains its contents even when the power is turned off. In addition to personal computers, manufacturers install ROM chips in automobiles, home appliances, toys, educational games, and thousands of other items used by people everyday.

FLASH MEMORY Flash memory is a type of nonvolatile memory that can be erased electronically and rewritten on. Most computers use flash memory to hold startup instructions because it allows the computer to update its contents easily. For example, when the computer changes from standard time to daylight saving time, the contents of a flash memory chip (and the real-time clock chip) change to reflect the new time. Flash memory chips are also used to store data and programs on many mobile computers and devices, such as PDAs, smart phones, printers, digital cameras, digital voice recorders, and pagers. When you enter names and addresses in a PDA or smart phone, a flash memory chip stores the data. Some portable media players store music on flash memory chips (Figure 4-12); others store music on tiny hard disks or flash memory cards.

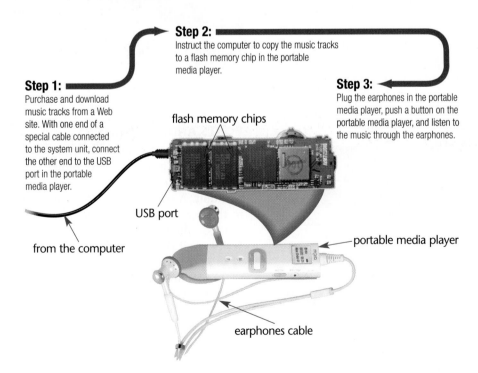

Step 1:
Purchase and download music tracks from a Web site. With one end of a special cable connected to the system unit, connect the other end to the USB port in the portable media player.

Step 2:
Instruct the computer to copy the music tracks to a flash memory chip in the portable media player.

Step 3:
Plug the earphones in the portable media player, push a button on the portable media player, and listen to the music through the earphones.

flash memory chips

USB port

from the computer

portable media player

earphones cable

Figure 4-12 How a portable media player might store music in flash memory.

EXPANSION SLOTS AND EXPANSION CARDS

An **expansion slot** is a socket on the motherboard that can hold an adapter card. An **adapter card**, sometimes called an **expansion card**, is a circuit board that enhances functions of a system component and/or provides connections to peripherals. A **peripheral** is a device that connects to the system unit and is controlled by the processor in the computer. Most of today's computers support **Plug and Play**, which means the computer can configure devices automatically as they are installed.

REMOVABLE MEMORY DEVICES

Four widely used types of removable flash memory devices include flash memory cards, USB flash drives, PC Cards, and ExpressCard modules. You can change a removable flash memory device without having to open the system unit or restart the computer. This feature, called **hot plugging**, allows you to insert and remove the removable flash memory while the computer is running.

A **flash memory card** is a removable flash memory device that you insert and remove from a slot in a computer or mobile device. Many consumer devices, such as PDAs and digital cameras use these memory cards. Some printers and computers have built-in slots that read flash memory cards. Flash memory cards are available in a variety of shapes and sizes (Figure 4-13). Storage capacities of flash memory cards range from 32 MB to 8 GB.

Integration Strategies

To learn more about how to integrate flash drives and similar devices, visit the Teachers Discovering Computers Web site (*scsite.com/tdc5*), click Chapter 4, and then click Teaching Today.

A **USB flash drive** is a flash memory storage device that plugs in to a USB port on a computer or portable device. USB flash drives are available in a variety of shapes and sizes with storage capacities ranging from 32 MB to 64 GB. USB flash drives up to 2 GB in storage (Figure 4-13) are available at stores for less than $30.

A **PC Card** is a thin, credit card-sized removable flash memory device that is used primarily to enable notebook computers to access the Internet wirelessly. An **ExpressCard module**, which can be used as a removable flash memory device, adds memory, communications, multimedia, and security capabilities to computers. Many computers have a **PC Card slot** or an **ExpressCard slot**, which is a special type of expansion slot that holds a PC Card or an ExpressCard module, respectively (Figure 4-14).

ExpressCard module

Figure 4-14 An ExpressCard module slides in an ExpressCard slot on a computer.

PORTS AND CONNECTORS

Cables are often used to attach external devices, such as a keyboard, monitor, printer, mouse, and microphone, to the system unit. A **port** is the point of attachment to the system unit. Most computers contain ports on the back as well as the front of the system unit (Figure 4-15).

Ports use different types of **connectors** that come in various sizes and shapes and that are usually male or female. Male connectors have one or more exposed pins, like the end of an electrical cord you plug into the wall. Female connectors have matching receptacles to accept the pins, like an electrical wall outlet.

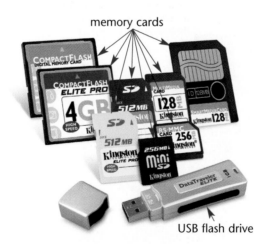

memory cards

USB flash drive

Figure 4-13 Removable flash memory devices are inserted in a slot in a computer or mobile device; a USB flash drive plugs into a USB port.

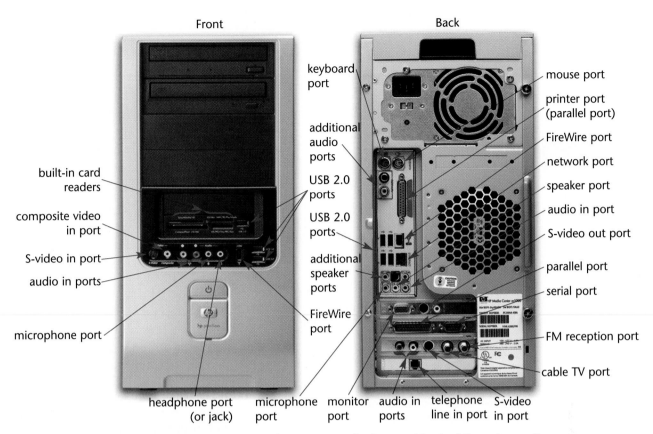

Front   Back

keyboard port
additional audio ports
USB 2.0 ports
USB 2.0 ports
additional speaker ports
FireWire port

mouse port
printer port (parallel port)
FireWire port
network port
speaker port
audio in port
S-video out port
parallel port
serial port
FM reception port
cable TV port

built-in card readers
composite video in port
S-video in port
audio in ports
microphone port

headphone port (or jack)   microphone port   monitor port   audio in ports   telephone line in port   S-video in port

Figure 4-15 Most computers have ports on the front and back of the system unit. Shown are the ports available on a PC. Macintosh computers have similar ports.

Two newer ports are USB and FireWire ports. The **Universal Serial Bus (USB) port** can connect up to 127 different peripheral devices with a single connector type. Newer personal computers typically contain six to eight USB ports either on the front or back of the system unit. The latest version, called the **USB 2.0 port,** is more advanced and faster, with speeds 40 times faster than the original USB port. The USB 2.0 port is used for devices that transfer a large amount of data, such as portable media players, DVD drives, and removable hard disks.

Similar to a USB port, a **FireWire port** can connect devices that require faster data transmission speeds, such as digital video cameras, digital VCRs, color printers, and DVD drives to a single connector type. The FireWire port is found on newer PCs and Macintosh computers. Figure 4-16 shows how FireWire and USB ports are replacing other traditional ports.

Bluetooth technology uses radio waves to transmit data between two devices. Many computers, peripheral devices, PDAs, smart phones, cars, and other consumer

TRADITIONAL PORTS

SCSI   Parallel   Audio   Serial   Keyboard   Mouse

FireWire   USB 2.0   USB 2.0

NEW PORTS

Figure 4-16 FireWire and USB ports are replacing traditional ports.

electronics are Bluetooth-enabled, which means they contain a small chip that allows them to communicate with other Bluetooth-enabled computers and devices.

Web Info

To search for a solution to a specific hardware problem for a PC, visit the Teachers Discovering Computers Web site (*scsite.com/tdc5*), click Chapter 4, click Web Info, and then click Search.

What Is Input?

Input is what you enter into the memory of a computer. As soon as input is in memory, the CPU can access it and process the input into output. Input can be categorized into four types: data, programs, commands, and user responses (Figure 4-17).

- **Data** is a collection of unprocessed items. A computer manipulates and processes data into information that is useful, such as words, numbers, pictures, sounds, and so on. Although a single item of data should be called a datum, the term data commonly is used and accepted as both the singular and plural form of the word.

Figure 4-17
Input can be categorized as data, programs, commands, and user responses.

- **A program** is a series of instructions that tells a computer how to perform

the tasks necessary to process data into information. Programs are kept on storage media such as a hard disk, CD, or DVD. Programs respond to commands issued by users.

- **A command** is an instruction given to a computer program. Commands can be issued by typing keywords or pressing special keys on the keyboard. A **keyword** is a special word, phrase, or code that a program understands as an instruction. Many programs also allow you to issue commands by selecting graphical objects. Today, most programs have a graphical user interface that uses icons, buttons, and other graphical objects to issue commands.

- Sometimes a program asks a question, such as "Do you want to save the changes you made?" that requires a **user response**. Based on your response, the program performs specific actions. For example, if you answer Yes to this question, the program saves your file to a storage medium.

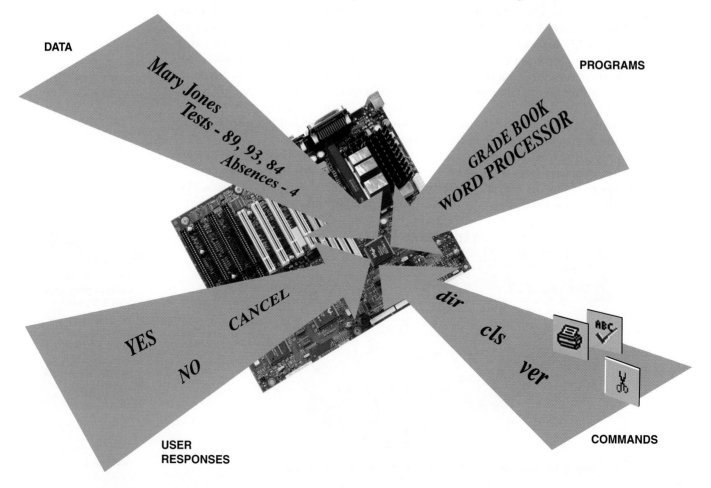

DATA

PROGRAMS

Mary Jones
Tests - 89, 93, 84
Absences - 4

GRADE BOOK
WORD PROCESSOR

YES
CANCEL
NO

dir
cls
ver

USER
RESPONSES

COMMANDS

What Are Input Devices?

An **input device** is any hardware component that allows you to enter data, programs, commands, and user responses into a computer. Input devices include keyboards, pointing devices, scanners and reading devices, digital cameras, audio and video input devices, and input devices for students with special needs. Many of these input devices are discussed in the following pages.

THE KEYBOARD

One of the primary input devices used with a computer is the keyboard. A **keyboard** is an input device that contains keys users press to enter data and instructions into a computer. Most keyboards are similar to the ones shown in Figure 4-18. You enter data, commands, and other input into a computer by pressing keys on the keyboard.

Personal computer keyboards usually contain from 101 to 105 keys; keyboards for smaller computers, such as notebook computers, contain fewer keys. A keyboard includes keys that allow you to type letters, numbers, spaces, punctuation marks, and other symbols such as the dollar sign ($) and the asterisk (*). A keyboard also contains special keys that allow you to enter data and instructions into the computer.

All computer keyboards have a typing area that includes the letters of the alphabet,

Web Info

To learn more about keyboards, visit the Teachers Discovering Computers Web site (*scsite.com/tdc5*), click Chapter 4, click Web Info, and then click Keyboard.

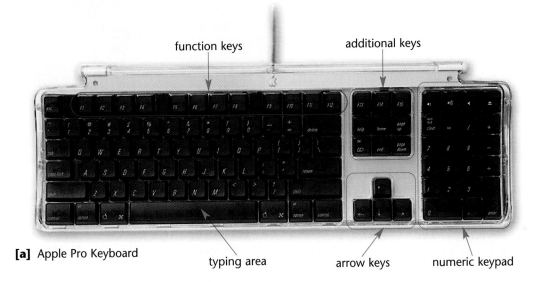

function keys additional keys

typing area arrow keys numeric keypad

[a] Apple Pro Keyboard

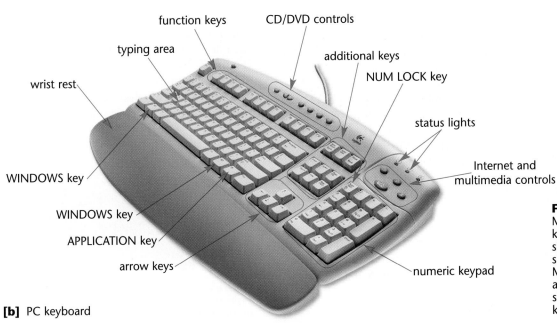

function keys CD/DVD controls

typing area additional keys

wrist rest NUM LOCK key

status lights

WINDOWS key Internet and multimedia controls

WINDOWS key

APPLICATION key

arrow keys numeric keypad

[b] PC keyboard

Figure 4-18
Macintosh and PC keyboards are similar. Figure 4-18a shows a typical Macintosh keyboard and Figure 4-18b shows a typical PC keyboard.

numbers, punctuation marks, and other basic keys. Because of the layout of its typing area, a standard computer keyboard sometimes is called a QWERTY keyboard, pronounced KWER-tee. This keyboard layout is named after the first six letters on the top-left alphabetic line of the keyboard.

Many desktop computer keyboards also have a numeric keypad located on the right side of the keyboard. A **numeric keypad** is a calculator-style arrangement of keys representing numbers, a decimal point, and some basic mathematical operators. The numeric keypad is designed to make it easier to enter numbers.

Keyboards also contain arrow keys that can be used to position the insertion point on the screen. The **insertion point**, or cursor, is a symbol that indicates where the next character you type will appear on the screen. Depending on the program, the symbol may be a vertical bar, a rectangle, or an underline. These arrow keys allow you to move the insertion point right, left, up, or down. Most keyboards also contain keys such as HOME, END, PAGE UP, and PAGE DOWN that you can press to move the insertion point to the beginning or end of a line, page, or document.

Most keyboards also include toggle keys, which can be switched between two different states. The NUM LOCK key, for example, is a toggle key found on computer keyboards. When you press it once, it locks the numeric keypad so you can use it to type numbers. When you press the NUM LOCK key again, the numeric keypad is unlocked so the same keys serve as arrow keys that move the insertion point. The caps lock key is another example of a toggle key and is used on both PCs and Macintosh computers. Many keyboards have status lights in the upper-right corner that light up to indicate that a toggle key is activated.

Newer keyboards include specialized buttons that allow you to access and use your CD/DVD drive, adjust speaker volume, open your e-mail program, start your Web browser, and more. Most keyboards attach to a serial port on the system unit via a cable. On notebook computers and handheld computers, the keyboard often is built onto the top of the system unit (Figure 4-19).

Figure 4-19 On notebook computers and mobile devices, the keyboard often is built onto the top of the system unit. Some keyboards can be detached or even virtual.

A popular keyboard used in K-12 classrooms is a **wireless keyboard**, also called a **cordless keyboard**. A wireless keyboard is a battery-operated device that transmits data using wireless technology, such as radio waves or infrared light waves (Figure 4-20). Wireless keyboards are available for use on both Macintosh computers and PCs. Some wireless keyboards come packaged with a wireless pointing device.

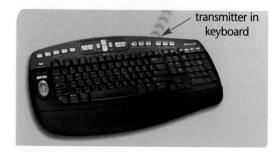

transmitter in keyboard

Figure 4-20 Wireless keyboards can be passed easily from student to student while they work on group projects.

POINTING DEVICES

A **pointing device** is an input device that allows you to control a pointer on the screen. In a graphical user interface, a pointer, or mouse pointer, is a small symbol on the monitor's screen. A pointer often takes the shape of a block arrow (↳), an I-beam (I), or a pointing hand (👆). Using a pointing device, you can position the pointer to move or select items on the screen. For example, you can use a pointing device to move the insertion point; select text, graphics, and other objects; and click buttons, icons, links, and menu commands. Common pointing devices include the mouse, touchpad and pointing stick, trackball, joystick, wheel, and touch screen.

MOUSE A mouse is the most widely used pointing device because it takes full advantage of a graphical user interface. Designed to fit comfortably under the palm of your hand, a **mouse** is an input device used to control the movement of the pointer on the screen and to make selections from the screen. The top of the mouse usually has one or two buttons; some have a small wheel. The mouse used with PCs usually is a two-button mouse (Figure 4-21); a one-button mouse is used with Macintosh computers (Figure 4-22). The first type of mouse, and the one often still used in schools, is a mechanical mouse. The bottom of a mechanical mouse is flat and contains a multidirectional mechanism, usually a small ball, which senses movement of the mouse.

The mouse often rests on a **mouse pad**, which usually is a rectangular rubber or foam pad that provides better traction for the mouse than the top of a desk. The mouse pad also protects the ball mechanism from a build up of dust and dirt, which could cause it to malfunction.

An optical mouse or a wireless mouse (also called a cordless mouse) can be used with most new computers. An **optical mouse** has no moving mechanical parts; instead, it emits and senses light to detect the mouse's movement. A **wireless mouse** or **cordless mouse** is a battery-powered device that transmits data using wireless technology, such as radio waves or infrared light waves. Many wireless keyboards come packaged with a separate wireless mouse.

As you move the mouse across a flat surface or a mouse pad, the pointer on the screen also moves. For example, when you move the mouse to the left, the pointer moves left on the screen. When you move the mouse to the right, the pointer moves right on the screen, and so on.

By using the mouse to move the pointer on the screen and then pressing, or **clicking**, the buttons on the mouse, you can perform actions such as pressing toolbar buttons, making menu selections, editing a document, and moving, or **dragging**, data from one location in a document to another. To press and release a mouse button twice without moving the mouse is called **double-clicking**. Double-clicking can be used to perform actions such as starting

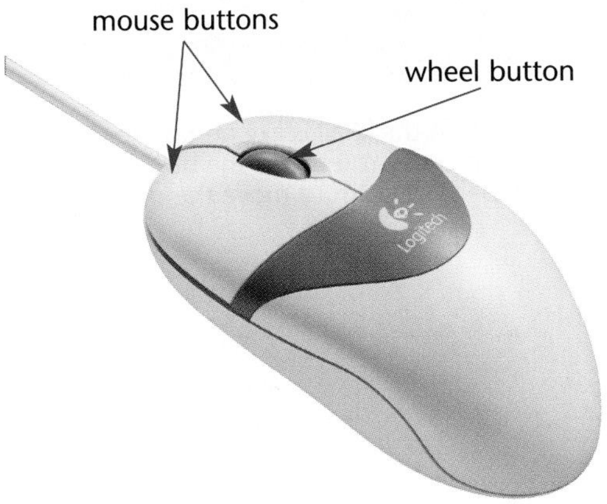

FAQ

What can I do to reduce chances of experiencing repetitive strain injuries?

Do not rest your wrist on the edge of a desk; use a wrist rest. Keep your forearm at wrist level so your wrist does not bend. Do hand exercises every fifteen minutes. Keep your shoulders, arms, hands, and wrists relaxed while you work. Keep your feet flat on the floor, with one foot slightly in front of the other.

FAQ

How do I use a wheel on a mouse?

Roll it forward or backward to scroll up or down. Tilt it to the right or left to scroll horizontally. Hold down the CTRL key while rolling the wheel to make the text on the screen bigger or smaller. These scrolling and zooming functions work with most software, including Web browsers.

mouse buttons

wheel button

Figure 4-21 A typical two button optical mouse with a wheel.

Figure 4-22 A Macintosh mouse usually has only one button.

a program or opening a document. The function of the buttons on a two-button mouse can be changed to accommodate right- and left-handed individuals.

TOUCHPAD AND POINTING STICK

A **touchpad** is a small, flat, rectangular pointing device that is sensitive to pressure and motion. Most touchpads have one or more buttons near the pad that work like mouse buttons. Touchpads often are found on notebook computers (Figure 4-23). To avoid using both a keyboard and a mouse with desktop computers, some schools purchase special keyboards that include a touchpad.

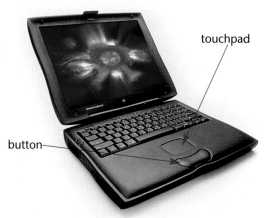

Figure 4-23 Many notebook computers have a touchpad that can be used to control the movement of the pointer.

touchpad

button

A **pointing stick** is a pressure-sensitive pointing device shaped like a pencil eraser that is positioned between keys on the keyboard (Figure 4-24). Some notebook computers contain both touchpads and pointing sticks.

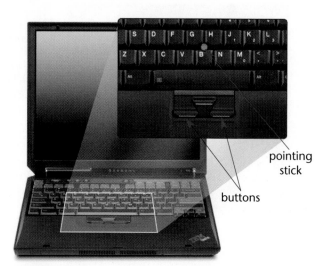

pointing stick

buttons

Figure 4-24 Some notebook computers use a pointing stick to control the movement of the pointer.

TRACKBALL

Some users opt for pointing devices other than a mouse, such as a trackball. Whereas a mouse has a ball mechanism on the bottom, a **trackball** is a stationary pointing device with a ball mechanism on its top (Figure 4-25).

The ball mechanism in a larger trackball is about the size of a Ping-Pong ball; notebook computers have small trackballs about the size of a marble. To move the pointer using a trackball, you rotate the ball mechanism with your thumb, fingers, or palm of your hand. Around the ball mechanism, a trackball usually has one or more buttons that work just like mouse buttons.

A trackball requires frequent cleaning because it picks up oils from fingers and dust from the environment. If you have limited desk space or use a notebook computer, however, a trackball is a good alternative to a mouse because you do not have to move the entire device.

Figure 4-25 A trackball is like an upside-down mechanical mouse. You rotate the ball with your thumb, fingers, or palm to move the pointer.

JOYSTICK AND WHEEL Users running game software, such as driving or flight simulation software, may prefer to use a joystick or wheel as their pointing device. A **joystick** is a vertical lever mounted on a base (Figure 4-26). You move the lever in different directions to control the actions of a vehicle or a player. The lever usually includes buttons, called triggers, that you can press to activate certain events. Some joysticks also have additional buttons that you can set to perform other actions.

A **wheel** is a steering-wheel type input device. You turn the wheel to simulate driving a car or other vehicle. Most wheels also include foot pedals for acceleration and breaking action. A joystick and wheel typically attach via a cable to the game port on a sound card or game card, or to a USB port.

Figure 4-26 Joysticks and wheels are used with game software to control the actions of a player or a vehicle.

TOUCH SCREEN A monitor that has a touch-sensitive panel on the screen is called a **touch screen**, which is a touch-sensitive display device. You interact with the computer by touching areas of the screen with your finger (Figure 4-27). In this case, the screen is the input device. To enter data, instructions, and information, you touch words, pictures, numbers, or locations identified on the screen. A touch screen often is used as the input device for a **kiosk**, which is a freestanding computer that provides information to the user. Visitors at museums, for example, can use a kiosk to access and print maps, facts on tours and exhibits, and other information.

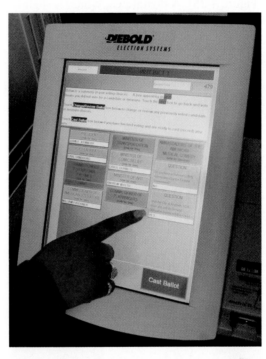

Figure 4-27 A voter uses a kiosk touch screen to cast ballots in an election.

OPTICAL SCANNERS

An optical scanner, usually called a **scanner**, is an input device that captures an entire page of text or images, such as photographs or artwork electronically. A scanner converts the text or image on the original document into digital data that can be stored on a storage medium and processed by the computer. The digitized data can be printed, displayed separately, or merged into another document for editing. Handheld devices that scan only a portion of a page at a time also are available.

Web Info

To learn more about optical scanners, visit the Teachers Discovering Computers Web site (*scsite.com/tdc5*), click Chapter 4, click Web Info, and then click Scanner.

Integration Strategies

To learn more about Tablet PCs and how they are being integrated with K-12 students, visit the Teachers Discovering Computers Web site (*scsite.com/tdc5*), click Chapter 4, and then click Teaching Today.

PEN INPUT

Mobile users often enter data and instructions with a pen-type device. With pen input, users write, draw, and tap on a flat surface to enter input. The surface may be a monitor, a screen, or a special type of paper. Two devices used for pen input are the stylus and digital pen. A **stylus** is a small metal or plastic device that looks like a tiny ink pen but uses pressure instead of ink (Figure 4-28). A **digital pen**, which is slightly larger than a stylus, is available in two forms: some are pressure-sensitive, whereas others have a built-in digital camera.

Figure 4-28 PDAs and smart phones use a stylus.

Some mobile computers and nearly all mobile devices have touch screens. Instead of using a finger to enter data and instructions, most of these devices include a pressure-sensitive digital pen or stylus. You write, draw, or make selections on the screen by touching the screen with the pen or stylus. For example, Tablet PCs use a pressure-sensitive digital pen (Figure 4-29) and PDAs use a stylus. Computers and mobile devices often use handwriting recognition software that transmits the handwritten letters and symbols into characters that the computer or device can process.

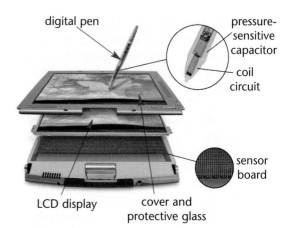

Figure 4-29 Tablet PCs use a pressure-sensitive digital pen.

Digital pens that have built-in digital cameras work differently from pressure-sensitive digital pens. These pens look like ballpoint pens. In addition to a tiny digital camera, these pens contain a processor, memory, and an ink cartridge. As you write or draw on special digital paper with the pen, it captures every handwritten mark by taking more than 100 pictures per second and then stores the images in the pen's memory. You transfer the images from the pen to a computer (Figure 4-30) or mobile device, such as a smart phone. Some pens have a cradle for transferring images, whereas others communicate wirelessly using Bluetooth.

Figure 4-30 Some digital pens have a built-in digital camera that stores your handwritten marks and allows you to transfer your handwriting to a computer.

DIGITAL CAMERAS

A **digital camera** allows you to take pictures and store the photographed images digitally instead of on traditional film (Figure 4-31). After you have taken a picture or series of pictures, you download, or transfer a copy of, the pictures to your computer. As soon as the pictures are stored on your computer, they can be edited with photo editing software, printed, posted on a Web site, and more.

AUDIO AND VIDEO INPUT

Although characters (text and numbers) still are the primary forms of input into a computer, individuals are increasingly using other types of input, such as images, audio, and video. In the previous sections, you learned about a variety of ways to input image data. The next sections discuss methods used to input audio and video data into a computer. Audio and video data often are stored on a computer's hard disk.

Audio input is the process of entering any sound into the computer, such as speech, music, and sound effects. Most personal computers sold today are equipped with a sound card necessary to record high quality sound. Recorded sound is input via a device, such as a microphone or a CD/DVD player. The most popular way to input recorded sounds today is to download audio files from the Web.

With a microphone plugged into the microphone port on the sound card, you can record sounds using the computer. After you save the sound as a file, you can play it, add it to a document, or edit it using audio editing software.

Another use for a microphone is speech recognition. **Speech recognition**, also called **voice recognition**, is the capability of a computer to distinguish spoken words. Speech recognition programs do not understand speech; but they can be trained to recognize certain words. The vocabulary of speech recognition programs can range from two words (such as Yes and No) to more than two million words. Experts agree that voice recognition eventually will be added to all software programs.

Video input is the process of capturing or downloading full-motion images and storing them on a computer's storage medium, such as a hard disk or DVD. To capture video, you plug a digital video

Figure 4-31 A digital camera is used to take pictures so images can be stored on a computer.

camera, Webcam, or similar device directly into a USB or FireWire port. To download music videos, TV shows, and movies directly from the Web, you use your Web browser. There are a variety of Web sites, for example iTunes, that provide access to videos, usually for a fee. After the video is saved, you can play or edit it using video editing software.

Recent advances in audio and video technologies are allowing users to easily create and edit audio files and video. The creation, use, and integration of audio and video in K-12 education are helping teachers address the needs of today's digital generation. Creating and editing audio and video on both Macintosh computers and PCs is covered in greater detail in the special features that follow Chapters 3, 5, and 7, as well as the Digital Media and Software Corners at the end of each chapter.

PDAs, SMART PHONES, AND MEDIA PLAYERS INPUT

Increasingly more people, including many teachers and students, are using a variety of mobile devices, such as PDAs, smart phones, and media players. A large variety of input alternatives are available for these devices and computers. Figure 4-32 on the next page provides examples of devices that can be used to input data into a PDA.

Voice is the traditional method of input for smart phones. Today, however, text messaging, instant messaging, and picture messaging have become popular methods of entering data and instructions into a smart phone.

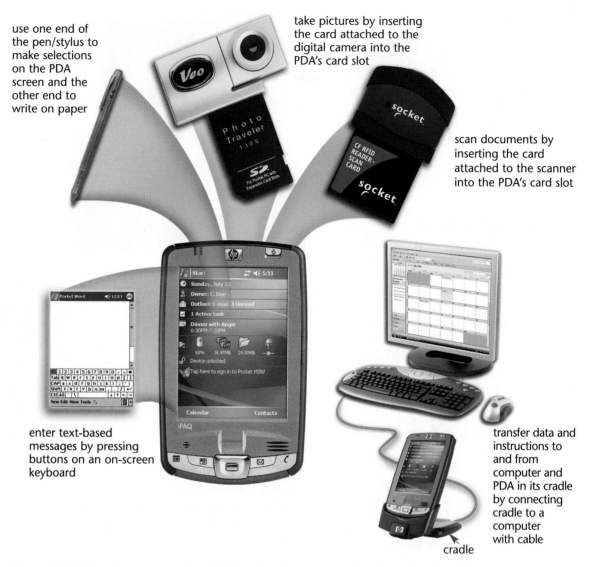

use one end of the pen/stylus to make selections on the PDA screen and the other end to write on paper

take pictures by inserting the card attached to the digital camera into the PDA's card slot

scan documents by inserting the card attached to the scanner into the PDA's card slot

enter text-based messages by pressing buttons on an on-screen keyboard

transfer data and instructions to and from computer and PDA in its cradle by connecting cradle to a computer with cable

cradle

Figure 4-32 Users have many options for inputting data into a PDA.

The **touch-sensitive pad** on a portable media player is an input device that enables users to scroll through and play music, view pictures, watch videos or movies, adjust volume, and customize settings. Touch-sensitive pads typically contain buttons and/or wheels that are operated with a thumb or finger. For example, users rotate a **Click Wheel** to browse through song, picture, or movie lists, and they press the buttons on the Click Wheel to perform actions, such as play media, pause media, or display a menu (Figure 4-33).

Additional input devices used in businesses, homes, and schools are described in Chapters 5 through 7, in Digital Imaging and Video Technology (the special feature that follows Chapter 5), and A World Without Wires (the special feature

that follows Chapter 1). Input devices for students with special needs are covered in this chapter's Assistive Technologies Corner.

Figure 4-33 You use your thumb to rotate or press buttons on a Click Wheel.

What Is Output?

Output is data that has been processed into a useful form called information. That is, a computer processes input into output. Computers generate several types of output, depending on the hardware and software being used and the requirements of the user. Four common types of output are text, graphics, audio, and video (Figure 4-34).

- **Text** consists of characters that are used to create words, sentences, and paragraphs. A character is a letter, number, punctuation mark, or any other symbol that requires one byte of computer storage space.

- **Graphics** are digital representations of nontext information, such as images, drawings, charts, pictures, and photographs. Displaying a series of still graphics creates an animation, a graphic that has the illusion of motion.

- Many of today's software programs support graphics; others are designed specifically to create and edit graphics. Graphics programs, called image editors, allow you to alter graphics by including enhancements, such as blended colors, animation, and other special effects.

- **Audio** is any music, speech, or other sound that is stored and produced by the computer. Recall that sound waves, such as the human voice or music, are analog. To store such sounds, a computer converts them from a continuous analog signal into a digital format.

- **Video** consists of photographic images that are played back at speeds that provide the appearance of full motion in real time. Software and Web sites often include videos to enhance understanding. Vodcasts and video blogs, for example, add a video component to the traditional podcast and blog.

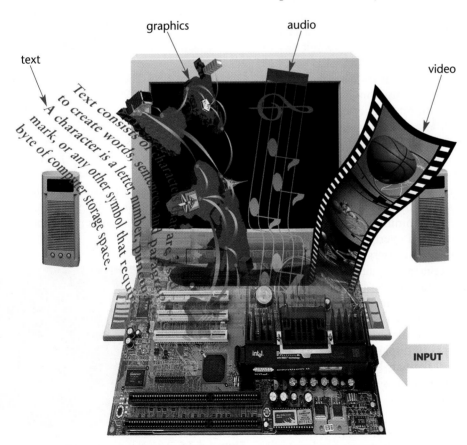

Figure 4-34 Four common types of output are text, graphics, audio, and video.

What Are Output Devices?

An **output device** is any computer component capable of conveying information to a user. Commonly used output devices include display devices, printers, data projectors, facsimile machines, multifunction devices, speakers, headphones, and earphones. Each of these output devices is discussed in the following pages.

DISPLAY DEVICES

A **display device** is an output device that displays text, graphics, and video information. A **monitor** is a display device that is packaged as a separate peripheral. Information shown on a display device often is called **soft copy** because the information exists electronically and is displayed for a temporary period.

Monitors for personal computers are available in a variety of sizes, with the more common sizes being 15, 17, 19, and 21 inches. The size of a monitor is measured diagonally, from corner to corner. The monitor size and the viewable size do not always match. For example, a monitor listed as a 17-inch monitor may have a viewable size of only 15.7 inches. Determining what size monitor to use depends on what the monitor will be used for. A larger monitor allows you to view more information at once, but it is usually more expensive. If you work on the Web or use multiple applications at one time, however, you may want to invest in at least a 19-inch monitor.

Most monitors have a tilt-and-swivel base that allows users to adjust the angle of the screen to minimize neck strain and reduce glare from overhead lighting. Monitor controls permit users to adjust the brightness, contrast, positioning, height, and width of images. Some have integrated speakers. Most mobile computers and devices integrate the display and other components into the same physical case.

Two types of display devices are CRT monitors and flat-panel displays. The following sections discuss each of these display devices.

CRT MONITORS

Like an older television set, the core of some monitors is a large glass tube called a **cathode ray tube (CRT)** (Figure 4-35). The screen, which is the front of the tube, is coated with tiny dots of phosphor material that glow when electrically charged. The CRT moves an electron beam back and forth across the back of the screen, causing the dots to glow, which produces an image on the screen. CRT monitors are still found in many homes and schools, although most new computers now come with flat panel displays.

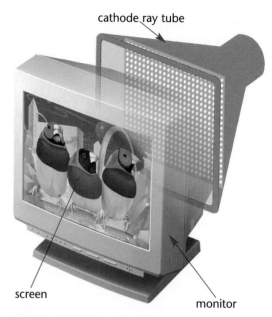

Figure 4-35 The core of most older PC monitors is a cathode ray tube.

Each dot, called a **pixel** (short for picture element), is a single point in an electronic image (Figure 4-36). Monitors consist of hundreds, thousands, or millions of pixels arranged in rows and columns that can be used to create pictures. The pixels are so close together that they appear connected.

Figure 4-36 A pixel is a single dot of color, or point, in an electronic image.

FLAT-PANEL DISPLAYS   A flat-panel display is a lightweight display device with a shallow depth and flat screen that typically uses LCD (liquid crystal display) or gas plasma technology. Types of flat-panel displays include LCD monitors, LCD screens, and plasma monitors.

LCD MONITORS AND SCREENS   An LCD **monitor**, also called a **flat panel monitor**, is a desktop monitor that uses a liquid crystal display to produce images (Figure 4-37). These monitors produce sharp, flicker-free images and do not take up much desk space.

Figure 4-38 Many portable devices, such as Tablet PCs. ultra personal computers, portable media players. smart phones, and PDAs, have built-in LCD screens.

Figure 4-37 An LCD monitor is thin and lightweight.

Mobile computers, such as notebook computers and Tablet PCs, and mobile devices, such as ultra personal computers, portable media players, smart phones, and PDAs, often have built-in LCD screens (Figure 4-38). Notebook computer screens are available in a variety of sizes, with the more common being 14, 15, and 17, and 20 inches. Tablet PC screens range from 8 inches to 14 inches. Typical screen sizes of ultra personal computers are 5 inches to 7 inches. Portable media players usually have screen sizes from 1.5 inches to 3 inches. PDA screens average 3.5 inches. On smart phones, screen sizes range from 2.5 to 3.5 inches.

LCD monitors use a technology called **liquid crystal display (LCD)**, which uses a liquid compound to present information on a display device. The quality of an LCD monitor or LCD screen depends primarily on its resolution, response time, brightness, dot pitch, and contrast ratio.

PLASMA MONITORS   Some businesses, universities, and schools use plasma monitors, which often measure more than 60 inches wide (Figure 4-39). A **plasma monitor** is a display device that uses gas plasma technology, which sandwiches a layer of gas between two glass plates. When voltage is applied, the gas releases ultraviolet (UV) light. This UV light causes the pixels on the screen to glow and form an image. Plasma monitors offer larger screen sizes and richer colors than LCD monitors but are more expensive. Like LCD monitors, plasma monitors can hang directly on a wall.

Figure 4-39 Large plasma monitors can measure more than 60 inches wide.

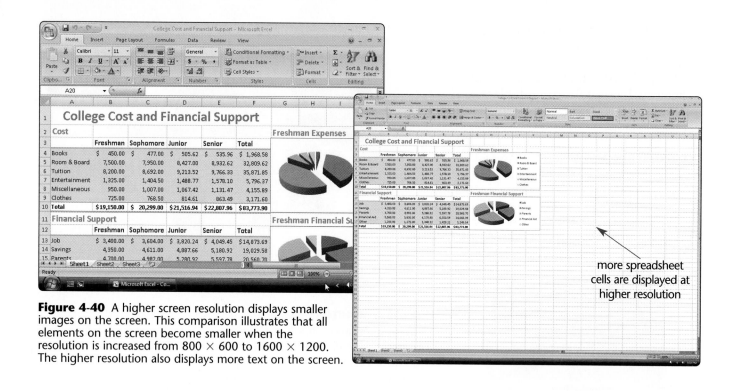

more spreadsheet cells are displayed at higher resolution

Figure 4-40 A higher screen resolution displays smaller images on the screen. This comparison illustrates that all elements on the screen become smaller when the resolution is increased from 800 × 600 to 1600 × 1200. The higher resolution also displays more text on the screen.

RESOLUTION Resolution is the number of horizontal and vertical pixels in a display device. For example, a monitor that has a 1600 × 1200 resolution displays up to 1600 pixels per horizontal row and 1200 pixels per vertical column, for a total of 1,920,000 pixels to create a screen image. A higher resolution uses a greater number of pixels and thus provides a smoother, sharper, and clearer image. As you increase the resolution, however, some items on the screen appear smaller (Figure 4-40 above). With LCD monitors and screens, resolution generally is proportional to the size of the device. For example, a 17-inch LCD monitor typically has a resolution of 1280 × 1024, while a 20-inch LCD monitor has a resolution of 1600 × 1200.

TELEVISIONS The output device for game consoles, such as Microsoft's Xbox 360, Nintendo's Wii, and Sony's PlayStation 3, often is a television. Users plug one end of a cable in the game console and the other end in the video port on the television. Although some game consoles include a small LCD screen (usually 5 inches or smaller), home users often prefer the larger television displays for game playing, watching movies, and browsing the Internet on a television, which can be achieved by connecting the television to a game console.

PRINTERS

A **printer** is an output device that produces text and graphical information on a physical medium, such as paper or transparency film. Printed information is called **hard copy** because it is a more permanent form of output than that presented on a monitor. Users can print a hard copy of a file in either portrait or landscape orientation. A page with **portrait orientation** is taller than it is wide, with information printed across the shorter width of the paper. A page with **landscape orientation** is wider than it is tall, with information printed across the widest part of the paper.

Because printing requirements vary greatly among users, manufacturers offer printers with varying speeds, capabilities, and printing methods. Until a few years ago, printing a document required connecting a computer to a printer with a cable via a USB or parallel port on the computer. Although many users today continue to print using this method, a variety of printing options are available, as shown in Figure 4-41.

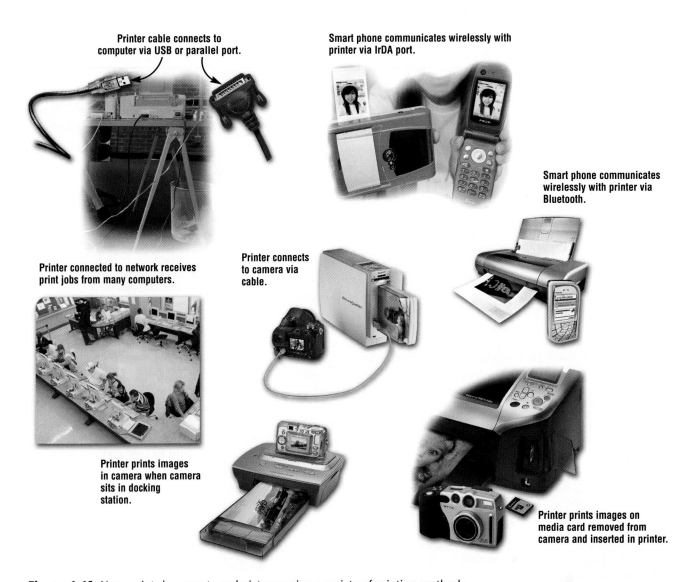

Printer cable connects to computer via USB or parallel port.

Smart phone communicates wirelessly with printer via IrDA port.

Smart phone communicates wirelessly with printer via Bluetooth.

Printer connected to network receives print jobs from many computers.

Printer connects to camera via cable.

Printer prints images in camera when camera sits in docking station.

Printer prints images on media card removed from camera and inserted in printer.

Figure 4-41 Users print documents and pictures using a variety of printing methods.

NONIMPACT PRINTERS A nonimpact **printer** forms marks on a piece of paper without actually striking the paper. Two common types of nonimpact printers are ink-jet and laser printers.

Because of their reasonable cost and print quality, ink-jet printers often are used in homes and schools. An **ink-jet printer** is a type of nonimpact printer that forms marks by spraying tiny drops of liquid ink onto a piece of paper. Ink-jet printers can produce high-quality text and graphics in both black-and-white and color on a variety of media such as paper, envelopes, labels, or transparencies. Ink-jet printers use small ink cartridges that are replaced easily or may be refilled using inexpensive ink-jet refill kits. In addition, many ink-jet printers include software to help you create items such as announcements, banners, cards, and so on.

A **photo printer** is a color printer that produces photo lab quality pictures (Figure 4-42). Many photo printers use ink-jet technology and can print photos in various sizes.

Figure 4-42 Ink-jet photo printers are a popular type of color printer used at home.

A **laser printer** is a high-speed, high-quality nonimpact printer. Operating in a manner similar to a copy machine, a laser printer uses powdered ink, called toner, which is packaged in a cartridge. When electrically charged, the toner sticks to a special drum inside the printer and then is transferred to the paper through a combination of pressure and heat (Figure 4-43). When the toner runs out, you simply replace the cartridge.

Laser printers, in a manner similar to ink-jet printers, usually use individual sheets of letter and legal-size paper stored in a removable tray that slides into the printer case. Most printers also have a manual feed slot where you can insert individual sheets, transparencies, and envelopes.

Although laser printers cost more than ink-jet printers, laser printers print very high-quality black-and-white text and graphics quickly. Although color laser printers are available, they are expensive and rarely found in K-12 schools.

Other nonimpact printers include thermal printers, portable printers, label and postage printers, plotters, and large-format printers.

DATA PROJECTORS

A **data projector** projects the image that displays on a computer screen onto a large screen, so that an audience, such as a classroom or school assembly, can see the image clearly (Figure 4-44). Data projectors range

Figure 4-43 A laser printer operates similarly to a copy machine. Electrically charged toner sticks to a special drum inside the printer and then is transferred to the paper through a combination of pressure and heat.

in size from large devices attached to a ceiling or wall in an auditorium to smaller, portable devices. Two types of smaller lower-cost units are LCD projectors and DLP (digital light processing) projectors. An LCD projector, which also uses liquid crystal display technology, attaches directly to a computer and uses its own light source to display the information shown on the computer screen. A digital light processing (DLP) projector uses tiny mirrors to reflect light, producing crisp, bright, colorful images that remain in focus and can be seen clearly even in a well-lit room.

Web Info

For more information about data projectors and how they are used in K-12 classrooms, visit the Teachers Discovering Computers Web site (*scsite.com/tdc5*), click Chapter 4, click Web Info, and then click Data Projectors.

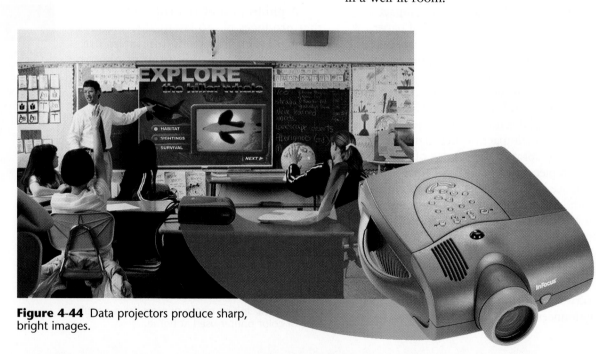

Figure 4-44 Data projectors produce sharp, bright images.

FACSIMILE (FAX) MACHINE

A **facsimile (fax) machine** is a device that transmits and receives documents over telephone lines. The documents (called faxes) can contain text, graphics, or photos, or can be handwritten. A fax machine scans the original document, converts the image into digitized data, and transmits the digitized image (Figure 4-45). A fax machine at the receiving end reads the incoming data, converts the digitized data into an image, and prints or stores a copy of the original image.

Figure 4-45 A stand-alone fax machine.

The fax machine just described is a stand-alone fax machine. You also can add fax capability to your computer via a fax modem. A fax modem is a communications device that allows you to send and receive electronic documents as faxes. A fax modem transmits electronic documents, such as a word processing letter or digital photo. A fax modem is like a regular modem except that it transmits documents to a fax machine or to another fax modem. When you receive a fax on your computer, you can view the document on the screen or print it using special fax software.

MULTIFUNCTION DEVICES

A **multifunction device (MFD)** is a single piece of equipment that provides the functionality of a printer, fax machine, copier, and scanner (Figure 4-46). The features of multifunction devices vary widely. For example, some use color ink-jet printer technology, while others use a black-and-white laser printer. Small businesses, home offices, and school administrative offices use multifunction devices because they take up less space and cost less than a separate printer, scanner, copy machine, and fax machine. Quality multifunction devices are available for less than $150.

Figure 4-46 This multifunction device is an all-in-one device that includes a color printer, scanner, fax, and copy machine.

SPEAKERS, HEADPHONES, AND EARPHONES

Electronically produced voice output is growing in popularity. **Voice output** occurs when you hear a person's voice or when the computer talks to you through the speakers on the computer. In some programs, the computer can speak the contents of a document through voice output. On the Web, you can listen to (or download and then listen to) interviews, talk shows, sporting events, news, recorded music, and live concerts from many radio and television stations. Some Web sites dedicate themselves to providing voice output, where you can

Web Info

For more information about multifunction devices, visit the Teachers Discovering Computers Web site (*scsite.com/tdc5*), click Chapter 4, click Web Info, and then click Multifunction Devices.

hear songs, quotes, historical lectures, speeches, and books (Figure 4-47). In order to take advantage of voice output, users need an audio output device connected to their computers.

Figure 4-47 Through this Web site, users can purchase and then download a book in digital audio format to a storage medium. Once downloaded, users then listen to the book's contents via their computer's speakers or a portable media player, such as an iPod, via earphones.

An **audio output device** is a component of a computer that produces music, speech, or other sounds, such as beeps. Three commonly used audio output devices are speakers, headphones, and earphones.

Most personal computers have a small internal speaker that usually emits only low-quality sound. For this reason, many personal computers are sold with stereo speakers. **Speakers** can be separate devices placed on either side of the monitor or they can be built in to the monitor or the system unit. Stereo speakers are connected to ports on the sound card. Most speakers have tone and volume controls. Some users add surround sound speakers to their computers to generate a higher-quality sound for playing games, interacting with multimedia presentations, listening to music CDs, and viewing DVDs.

When using speakers, anyone within listening distance can hear the output. Speakers are not always practical in classrooms and computer labs. Often, teachers and students use headphones or earphones that can be plugged into a port on the sound card, in a speaker, or on the front of the system unit.

By using headphones or earphones, students can concentrate better on the sound from their computers and they will not be disturbed by sounds on nearby computers or disturb other students. The difference is that **headphones** cover or are placed outside of the ear (Figure 4-48), whereas **earphones**, or **earbuds** (shown in Figure 4-33) rest inside the ear canal.

Figure 4-48 Headphones or earphones are used to help students focus on sounds coming from their computers and to prevent them from being disturbed by sounds coming from nearby computers.

What Is Storage?

Storage refers to the media on which data, instructions, and information are kept, as well as the devices that record and retrieve these items. To understand storage, you should understand the difference between how a computer uses memory and how it uses storage. As discussed earlier in this chapter, RAM temporarily stores data and programs that are being processed. RAM is volatile because data and programs stored in memory are lost when the power is turned off or a power failure occurs.

Storage stores data, instructions, and information when they are not being processed. Think of storage as a filing cabinet used to hold file folders, and memory as the top of your desk (Figure 4-49). When you need to work with a file, you remove it from the filing cabinet (storage) and place it on your desk (memory). When you are finished with the file, you return it to the filing cabinet (storage). Storage is nonvolatile, which means that data, instructions, and information in storage are retained even when power is removed from the computer.

Figure 4-49 Think of storage as a filing cabinet used to hold file folders and memory as the top of your desk. When you need to work with a file, you remove it from the filing cabinet (storage) and place it on your desk (memory). When you are finished with the file, you return it to the filing cabinet (storage).

Storage Media and Devices

A **storage medium** (media is the plural), also called **secondary storage**, is the physical material on which data, instructions, and information are kept. One commonly used storage medium is a **disk**, which is a round, flat piece of plastic or metal on which items such as data, instructions, and information can be encoded. A **storage device** is the mechanism used to record and retrieve these items to and from a storage medium. Examples of storage media are hard disks, floppy disks, CDs and DVDs, PC Cards and ExpressCard modules, flash memory cards, USB flash drives, and smart cards.

Storage devices can function as sources of input and output. For example, each time the CPU transfers data, instructions, and information from a storage medium into memory — a process called reading — the storage device functions as an input

source. When the CPU transfers these items from memory to a storage medium — a process called writing — the storage device functions as an output source.

The size, or capacity, of a storage device is measured by the amount of bytes (characters) it can hold. Storage capacity usually is measured in megabytes or gigabytes. Some devices can hold thousands of bytes, whereas others can store trillions of bytes. For example, a reasonably priced USB flash drive can store up to 512 MB of data (approximately 512 million bytes) and a typical hard disk has 250 GB (approximately 250 billion bytes) of storage capacity.

Storage requirements among users vary greatly. A teacher, for example, might have a list of names, test scores, and average grades for 30 students that requires several hundred bytes of storage. Users of larger computers, such as banks or libraries, might need to store trillions of bytes worth of historical or catalog records. To meet the needs of a wide range of users, numerous types of storage media and storage devices exist, many of which are discussed in the following sections.

MAGNETIC DISKS

A **magnetic disk** uses magnetic patterns to store data, instructions, and information on the disk's surface. Depending on how the magnetic particles are aligned, they represent either a 0 bit or a 1 bit. Recall that a bit (binary digit) is the smallest unit of data a computer can process. Most magnetic disks are read/write storage media; that is, you can access (read) data from and place (write) data on a magnetic disk any number of times.

Before data can be read from or written to a magnetic disk, the disk must be formatted. **Formatting** is the process of preparing a disk for reading and writing by organizing the disk into storage locations called tracks and sectors (Figure 4-50). A **track** is a narrow storage ring around the disk — similar to the annual rings on a tree. A **sector** is a pie shaped section of the disk, which breaks the tracks into small arcs.

Three types of magnetic disks are 3.5-inch disks, Zip disks, and hard disks. From the early 1980s through the first few years of the 21st century, the most common form of inexpensive portable magnetic

Integration Strategies

To learn more about storing digital data so you can help your students understand how to transfer current knowledge to learning of new technologies, visit the Teachers Discovering Computers Web site (*scsite.com/tdc5*), click Chapter 4, and then click Education Issues.

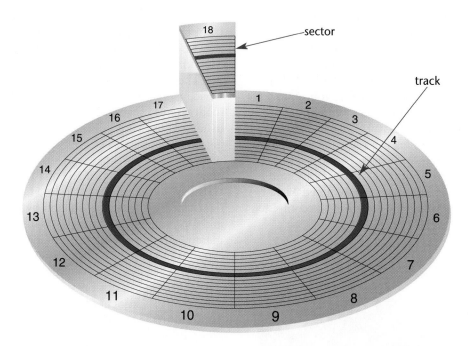

Figure 4-50 A track is a narrow recording band that forms a full circle on the surface of a disk. The disk's storage locations then are divided into pie-shaped sections, which break the tracks into small arcs called sectors.

disks for home and school were floppy disks (first 5.25-inch and then 3.5-inch) and the more expensive and greater capacity Zip disks. While these magnetic disks are still used by some users and in some schools, USB flash drives have quickly replaced them as the preferred portable storage medium.

glass, or ceramic and is coated with a material that allows data to be magnetically recorded on its surface. Although removable hard disks do exist, the hard disks in most personal computers are housed permanently inside the system unit and are enclosed in an airtight, sealed case to protect the platters from contamination (Figure 4-51).

HARD DISKS

When personal computers were introduced, software programs and their related files required small amounts of storage and files fit easily on floppy disks. As software became more complex and included graphical user interfaces and multimedia, file sizes and storage requirements increased. Today, hard disks, which provide for larger storage capacities, are the primary media for storing software programs and files. Current personal computer hard disks can store from 80 GB to 750 GB or more of data, instructions, and information.

A **hard disk** usually consists of several inflexible, circular disks, called platters, on which items, such as data, instructions, and information, are stored electronically. A **platter** in a hard disk is made of aluminum,

hard drive installed in system unit

Figure 4-51 The hard disk in a personal computer normally is housed permanently inside the system unit.

Step 2:
A small motor spins the platters while the computer is running.

Step 3:
When software requests a disk access, the read/write heads determine the current or new location of the data.

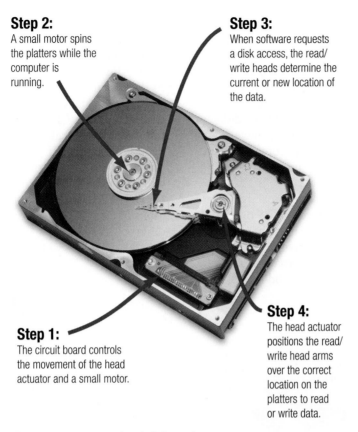

Step 1:
The circuit board controls the movement of the head actuator and a small motor.

Step 4:
The head actuator positions the read/write head arms over the correct location on the platters to read or write data.

Figure 4-52 How a hard disk works.

Recall that a hard disk is a magnetic disk that stores data, instructions, and information using magnetic patterns. Hard disks also are read/write storage media; that is, you can both read from and write to a hard disk any number of times. Figure 4-52 above shows how a hard disk works. Before you can write data, instructions, or information to a hard disk, the hard disk must be formatted. Usually, hard disk manufacturers format hard disks before they are installed in computers. Typically, a hard disk is designated drive C on PCs and as the HD Disk on Macintosh computers.

For many years, PC computers came standard with two floppy disk drives, one for 5.25-inch disks that was designated drive A and one for 3.5-inch disks that was designated drive B. Computer hard drives were normally designated as drive C. Floppy disk drives are no longer installed

on PCs and computer manufactures have retained the designation of drive C for the hard drive so as to not confuse users — drives A and B are no longer used.

MINIATURE HARD DISKS Many mobile devices and consumer electronics include miniature hard disks, which provide users with greater storage capacities than flash memory. These tiny hard disks are found in devices, such as media players, digital cameras, smart phones, and PDAs. Miniature hard disks have storage capacities that range from 4 GB to 160 GB or more (Figure 4-53).

Figure 4-53 Miniature hard disks are used in a variety of electronic devices.

PORTABLE HARD DISKS Two types of portable hard disks are external hard disks and removable hard disks (Figure 4-54). An **external hard disk** is a separate hard disk that connects to a USB or FireWire port by a cable. External hard disks can store 750 GB or higher. **Removable external hard disks** use cartridges that you insert and remove from an external hard disk drive. Some external hard drives insert into a special bay in the system unit.

Sale prices for medium-capacity portable hard drives have dropped to $75 or less. Many teachers and other users have purchased a portable hard drive to supplement their home and school internal hard drives and to back up their home and school files.

removable hard disk

external hard disk

Figure 4-54 Examples of large-capacity portable hard disks.

OPTICAL DISCS

An **optical disc** is a type of storage medium that consists of a flat, round, portable disc made of metal, plastic, and lacquer that is written and read by a laser. Optical discs used in personal computers are 4.75 inches in diameter. Smaller computers and devices, however, use mini discs that have a diameter of 3 inches or less.

CDs AND DVDs

CDs and DVDs are a type of optical storage media that consists of a flat, round, portable, plastic disc with a protective metal coating. The term *disk* is used for magnetic media and *disc* is used for optical media.

CDs and DVDs primarily store music, movies, digital photographs, and software programs. Just about every personal computer today includes some type of CD

Web Info

For more information about DVDs, visit the Teachers Discovering Computers Web site (*scsite.com/tdc5*), click Chapter 4, click Web Info, and then click DVD.

or DVD drive (Figure 4-55). Some CD and DVD drives are read only, meaning you cannot write (save) to the media. Others are read/write, which allows users to save to the disc just as they save to a hard disk.

On personal computers, the drive designation of a CD or DVD drive usually follows alphabetically after that of the hard disk. For example, if your hard disk is drive C, then the CD or DVD drive usually will be drive D. When you place a CD or DVD in a Macintosh computer, an icon that looks like a CD appears on the computer desktop.

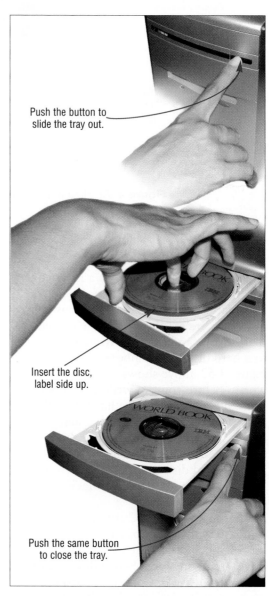

Push the button to slide the tray out.

Insert the disc, label side up.

Push the same button to close the tray.

Figure 4-55 To use CD and DVD drives, you push a button to open a tray, which causes the tray to slide out, insert the disc with the label side up, and then push the same button to close the tray.

CHARACTERISTICS OF CDs AND DVDs

CDs and DVDs are optical media that store data, information, music, and video in microscopic pits on the bottom portion of the disc. A high-powered laser light creates the pits. A lower-powered laser light reads items from the disc by reflecting light through the bottom of the disc, which usually is either gold or silver in color. The reflected light is converted into a series of bits the computer can process. Most manufacturers place a silk-screened label on the top of the disc.

CARE OF OPTICAL DISCS   Manufacturers guarantee that a properly cared for CD or DVD will last five years, but could last up to 100 years. Figure 4-56 outlines some guidelines for the proper care of CDs and DVDs. Never bend a disc. Exposing discs to extreme temperatures or humidity could cause them to warp. Stacking discs, touching the underside of discs, or exposing them to any type of contaminant may scratch the discs. If a disc becomes warped or if its

surface is scratched, data on the disc may be unreadable. Always place a CD or DVD in a protective case, such as a jewel box or disc storage case, when you are finished using it.

CDs and DVDs are available in a variety of formats. The following sections discuss many of these formats.

TYPES OF OPTICAL DISCS

Many different formats of optical discs exist today. Two general categories are CDs and DVDs, with DVDs having a much greater storage capacity than CDs. Specific formats include CD-ROM, CD-R, CD-RW, DVD-ROM, DVD-R, DVD+R, DVD-RW, DVD+RW, DVD+RAM, BD-RE, and HD DVD-RW. Figure 4-57 on the next page identifies each of these optical disc formats and specifies whether a user can read from the disc, write to the disc, and/or erase the disc. The following sections describe characteristics unique to each of these disc formats.

Do not expose the disc to excessive heat or sunlight.

Do not eat, smoke, or drink near a disc.

Do not stack discs.

Do not touch the underside of the disc.

Do store the disc in a jewel box or other protective covering when not in use.

Do hold a disc by its edges.

Figure 4-56 Some guidelines for the proper care of CDs and DVDs.

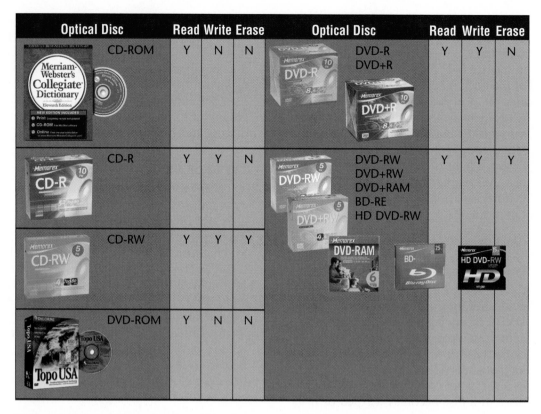

Optical Disc	Read	Write	Erase	Optical Disc	Read	Write	Erase
CD-ROM	Y	N	N	DVD-R DVD+R	Y	Y	N
CD-R	Y	Y	N	DVD-RW DVD+RW DVD+RAM BD-RE HD DVD-RW	Y	Y	Y
CD-RW	Y	Y	Y				
DVD-ROM	Y	N	N				

Figure 4-57 Manufacturers sell CD-ROM and DVD-ROM media prerecorded (written) with audio, video, and software. Users cannot change the contents of these discs. Users, however, can purchase the other formats of CDs and DVDs as blank media and record (write) their own data, videos, and information to these discs.

CD-ROM Compact disc read-only memory (CD-ROM; pronounced SEE-DEE-rom) is a type of optical disc that uses the same laser technology that audio CDs use for recording music. Unlike an audio CD, a CD-ROM can contain text, graphics, animation, and video, as well as sound. The contents of standard CD-ROMs are written, or **recorded**, by the manufacturer and only can be read and used; that is, they cannot be erased or modified — hence, the name read-only.

Because audio CDs and CD-ROMs use the same laser technology, you can use your CD drive to listen to an audio CD while working on your computer.

A CD-ROM can hold from 650 MB to 1 GB of data, instructions, and information. Because CD-ROMs have such high storage capacities, they are used to store and distribute today's complex software, such as children's, education, game, and reference programs (Figure 4-58). Most of today's software programs are sold on CD, DVD, or are downloaded from the Web. Some programs even require that the disc be in the drive each time you use the program.

Figure 4-58 Encyclopedias, games, simulations, and many other programs are distributed on CD-ROM.

PICTURE CDs   A Kodak **Picture CD** is a type of compact disc that stores digital versions of a single roll of film using a .jpg file format. Many film developers offer Picture CD service when consumers drop off film to be developed. In addition to printed photographs and negatives, you also receive a Picture CD containing your pictures. The additional cost for a Picture CD varies, but often is only $3 per roll of film.

Most optical drives can read a Picture CD. Using photo editing software and the photographs on the Picture CD, you can remove red eye, crop the photographs, enhance colors, and edit just about any aspect of the photograph. In addition, you can print photos from a Picture CD on glossy paper with an ink-jet printer. Many stores have kiosks at which you can print pictures from a Picture CD (Figure 4-59).

CD-R AND CD-RW   Many computers today include either a CD-R or a CD-RW drive as standard equipment. Unlike standard CD-ROM drives, these new drives allow you to record your own data onto a CD-R or CD-RW disc.

A **compact disc-recordable (CD-R)** is a compact disc onto which you can record your own information, such as text, graphic, and audio. With a CD-R, you can write on part of the disc at one time and another part at a later time. You can write on each part only one time, and you cannot erase the disc's content. To write on a CD-R disc, you must have CD-R software and a CD-R drive.

A **compact disc-rewritable (CD-RW)** is an erasable disc you can write on multiple times. With CD-RW, the disc acts like a 3.5-inch or hard disk. You can easily write and rewrite data multiple times. To write on a CD-RW disc, you must have CD-RW software and a CD-RW drive.

A popular use of CD-RW and CD-R discs is to create audio CDs. The steps in Figure 4-60 on the next page illustrate techniques for copying the song(s) from an existing CD or downloading the song(s) from the Web, in most cases for a fee.

Step 1:
Drop off the film to be developed. Mark the Picture CD box on the film-processing envelope.

Step 2:
When you pick up prints and negatives, a Picture CD containing digital images of each photograph is included.

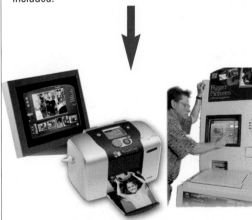

Step 3:
At home, view images on your monitor and print images from the Picture CD on your ink-jet or photo printer. At a store, print images from the Picture CD at a kiosk.

Figure 4-59 How a Picture CD works.

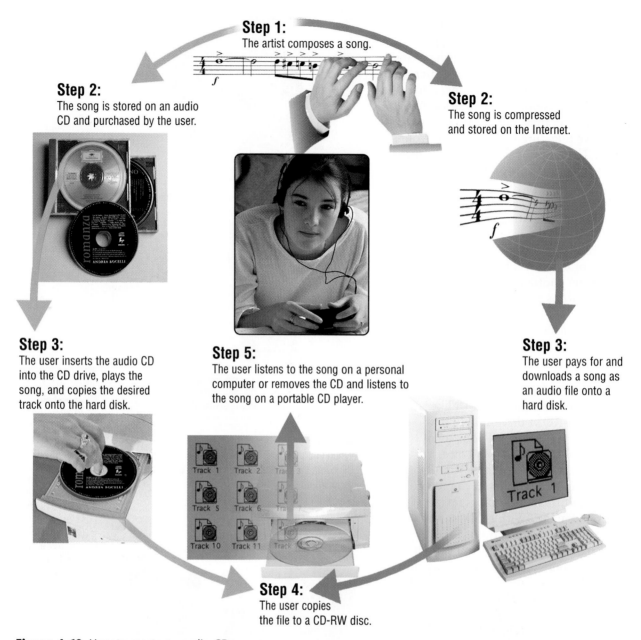

Step 1:
The artist composes a song.

Step 2:
The song is stored on an audio CD and purchased by the user.

Step 2:
The song is compressed and stored on the Internet.

Step 3:
The user inserts the audio CD into the CD drive, plays the song, and copies the desired track onto the hard disk.

Step 5:
The user listens to the song on a personal computer or removes the CD and listens to the song on a portable CD player.

Step 3:
The user pays for and downloads a song as an audio file onto a hard disk.

Track 1   Track 2   Track 3
Track 5   Track 6   Track
Track 10 Track 11 Track

Track 1

Step 4:
The user copies the file to a CD-RW disc.

Figure 4-60 How to create an audio CD.

DVD, BD, AND HD DVD Although CDs have large storage capacities, even these are not large enough for many of today's complex programs. To meet the tremendous storage requirements of today's software, the digital video disc read-only memory (DVD-ROM) format was developed.

A **digital video disc read-only memory** (**DVD-ROM**) is a high-capacity optical disc capable of storing from 4.7 GB to 17 GB (Figure 4-61). Not only is the storage capacity greater than a CD, but the quality of a DVD far surpasses that of a CD. To read a DVD-ROM, you must have a **DVD drive**. Many computers now are sold with DVD drives that will

read both CDs and DVDs, including audio CDs.

DVDs are available in a variety of formats, including one which stores motion pictures. Many computers that contain a DVD drive allow you to connect your computer directly to your television. Users also can purchase recordable (DVD-R) and rewritable (DVD+RW) versions of DVDs, which are similar to CD-R and CD-RW in the way they operate.

Many new computers come with a standard combination DVD-ROM/CD-RW drive or optional DVD-R/CD-RW. The DVD-R/CD-RW drive is called a SuperDrive on newer Macintosh computers.

DVD drive

DVD

Figure 4-61 A DVD-ROM is a high-capacity compact disc capable of storing 4.7 GB to 17 GB.

Two newer, more expensive competing DVD formats are Blu-ray (BD) and HD DVD, both of which are higher capacity and better quality than standard DVDs. A **Blu-ray Disc** has storage capacities of 100 GB, with expectations of exceeding 200 GB in the future. Blu-ray drives and players are backward compatible with DVD and CD formats. Some game consoles include a Blu-ray drive. The **HD DVD disc**, which stands for high-density DVD, has storage capacities up to 60 GB with future projections of 90 GB capacities. HD DVD drives and players are backward compatible with DVD formats. Some game consoles work with an HD DVD drive.

A mini-DVD that has grown in popularity is the UMD, which works specifically with the PlayStation Portable handheld game console. The UMD (Universal Media Disc), which has a diameter of about 2.4 inches, can store up to 1.8 GB of games, movies, or music.

Chapter 5 and the Digital Imaging and Video Technology special feature that follows Chapter 5 discuss in detail the processes of using CD-R, CD-RW, and DVD+RW technology at home and in education to create and edit CDs and DVDs.

MINIATURE MOBILE STORAGE MEDIA

Miniature mobile storage media allow mobile users to transport digital images, music, or documents to and from computers and other devices easily (Figure 4-62).

miniature mobile storage media

Figure 4-62 Many types of computers and devices use miniature mobile storage media.

Many computers, Tablet PCs, PDAs, smart phones, digital cameras, and media players have built-in slots or ports to read from and write to miniature mobile storage media. For computers or devices without built-in slots, users insert the media in separate peripherals, such as a card reader/writer which typically plugs into a USB port.

PDAs, digital cameras, media players, smart phones, and many other devices use miniature mobile storage media. The following sections briefly discuss the widely used miniature storage media: flash memory cards, USB flash drives, and smart cards.

FLASH MEMORY CARDS   A **flash memory card** is a type of solid-state media, which means it consists entirely of electronic components and contains no moving parts.

Common types of flash memory cards include CompactFlash (CF), Secure Digital (SD), xD Picture Card, and Memory Stick.

The table in Figure 4-63 compares storage capacities and uses of these media. Depending on the device, manufacturers claim miniature mobile storage media can last from 10 to 100 years. Flash memory cards are quite expensive compared to other storage media.

To view, edit, or print images and information stored on miniature mobile storage media, you transfer the contents to your desktop computer or other device. Some printers have slots to read flash memory cards. If your computer or printer does not have a built-in slot, you can purchase a **card reader/writer**, which is a device that reads and writes data, instructions, and information stored on flash memory cards. Card reader/writers usually connect to a USB port or FireWire port on the system unit. The type of card you have determines the type of card reader/writer you need.

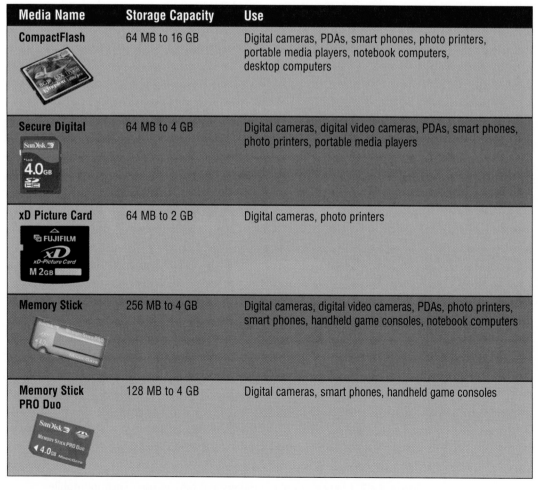

Media Name	Storage Capacity	Use
CompactFlash	64 MB to 16 GB	Digital cameras, PDAs, smart phones, photo printers, portable media players, notebook computers, desktop computers
Secure Digital	64 MB to 4 GB	Digital cameras, digital video cameras, PDAs, smart phones, photo printers, portable media players
xD Picture Card	64 MB to 2 GB	Digital cameras, photo printers
Memory Stick	256 MB to 4 GB	Digital cameras, digital video cameras, PDAs, photo printers, smart phones, handheld game consoles, notebook computers
Memory Stick PRO Duo	128 MB to 4 GB	Digital cameras, smart phones, handheld game consoles

Figure 4-63   A variety of flash memory cards.

USB FLASH DRIVES   A USB flash drive, sometimes called a pen drive or thumb drive, is a flash memory storage device that plugs into a USB port on a computer or mobile device. USB flash drives are convenient to use because they are small and lightweight enough to be transported on a keychain or in your pocket (Figure 4-64). With a USB flash drive, you and your students easily can transfer documents, pictures, music, and videos from one computer to another. Current USB flash drives have storage capacities ranging from 128 MB to 64 GB. USB flash drives have become the primary portable storage device, making the floppy disk nearly obsolete, because USB flash drives have much greater storage capacities, are much more convenient to carry, and are the preferred portable storage device for students and other computer users.

Figure 4-64 USB flash drives are popular with teachers and students and are small enough to be carried on a keychain.

SMART CARDS   A smart card, which is similar in size to a credit card or ATM card, stores data on a thin microprocessor embedded in the card. Smart cards contain a processor and have input, process, output, and storage capabilities. When you insert the smart card in a specialized card reader, the information on the smart card is read and, if necessary, updated.

Use of smart cards include storing medical records, vaccination data, and other healthcare and identification information; tracking information such as customer purchases or employee attendance, storing a prepaid amount of money, such as for student purchases on campus; and authenticating users, such as for Internet purchases. In addition, smart cards can double as an ID card.

Buyer's Guide

At the end of this chapter is a special feature that introduces you to purchasing, installing, maintaining, and troubleshooting a desktop or notebook computer.

A World Without Wires

A revolution in wireless technology and wireless devices is rapidly changing the way people work, play, and learn. To learn more about this wireless revolution and its potential impact on society and education, review the special feature A World Without Wires that follows Chapter 1.

Summary of Hardware for Educators

In this chapter, you learned about the various hardware components used in schools, businesses, and homes. First, you learned about some of the major components of the system unit. Next, you learned how to identify several types of input devices and how they operate. Third, you reviewed various output devices and learned how to identify and use them. Finally, you learned about storage devices.

After reading this chapter, you should have a good understanding of the information processing cycle and how various hardware devices are used in education. Now that you have a good working knowledge of computer hardware, you can use your newly gained knowledge to help your students understand technology concepts, systems, and operations. Because technology changes so quickly, you also need to stress to your students the importance of being able to transfer current knowledge when learning new technologies, which is one of the core national technology standards for students.

Key Terms

INSTRUCTIONS: Use the Key Terms to help focus your study of the terms used in this chapter. To further enhance your understanding of the Key Terms in this chapter, visit scsite.com/tdc5, click Chapter 4 at the top of the Web page, and then click Key Terms on the left sidebar. Read the definition for each term, and then access current and additional information about the term from the Web.

adapter card [210]
address [207]
American Standard Code for Information Interchange (ASCII) [203]
analog [202]
arithmetic/logic unit (ALU) [207]
arithmetic operations [207]
audio [221]
audio input [219]
audio output device [228]

binary [203]
bit [203]
Blu-ray Disc BD [237]
byte [211]

card reader/writer [238]
cathode ray tube (CRT) [222]
central processing unit (CPU) [205]
chip [204]
Click Wheel [220]
clicking [215]
clock speed [207]
command [212]
compact disc read-only memory (CD-ROM) [234]
compact disc-recordable (CD-R) [235]
compact disc-rewritable (CD-RW) [235]
comparison operations [207]
connector [210]
control unit [206]
cordless keyboard [214]
cordless mouse [215]

data [212]
data projector [226]
decoding [206]
digital [202]
digital camera [219]
digital pen [218]
digital video disc read-only memory (DVD-ROM) [236]
disk [229]
display device [222]
double-clicking [215]
dragging [215]
dual inline memory module (DIMM) [208]
dual-core processor [206]
DVD drive [236]

earbuds [228]
earphones [228]
executing [206]
expansion card [210]
expansion slot [210]
ExpressCard module [210]

ExpressCard slot [210]
external hard disk [232]

facsimile (fax) machine [227]
fetching [206]
FireWire port [211]
flash memory [209]
flash memory card [210]
flat panel monitor [223]
flat-panel display [223]
formatting [229]

gigabyte (GB) [208]
gigahertz (GHz) [207]
graphics [221]

hard copy [224]
hard disk [230]
headphones [228]
HD DVD-ROM disc [237]
hot plugging [210]

ink-jet printer [225]
input [212]
input device [213]
insertion point [214]

joystick [217]

keyboard [213]
keyword [212]
kilobyte (K or KB) [208]
kiosk [217]

landscape orientation [224]
laser printer [226]
LCD monitor [223]
liquid crystal display (LCD) [223]
logical operations [207]

machine cycle [206]
magnetic disk [229]
megabyte (MB) [208]
memory [207]
microprocessor [205]
monitor [222]
motherboard [204]
mouse [215]
mouse pad [215]
multi-core processor [206]
multifunction device (MFD) [227]

nonimpact printer [225]
nonvolatile memory [208]
numeric keypad [214]

optical disc [232]
optical mouse [215]
output [221]
output device [222]

PC Card [210]
PC Card slot [210]
peripheral [210]

photo printer [225]
Picture CD [235]
pixel [222]
plasma monitor [223]
platter [230]
Plug and Play [210]
pointing device [215]
pointing stick [214]
port [210]
portrait orientation [224]
printer [224]
processor [205]
program [212]

random access memory (RAM) [208]
read-only memory (ROM) [209]
recorded [234]
refresh rate [232]
removable external hard disk [232]
resolution [224]

scanner [217]
secondary storage [229]
sector [229]
smart card [239]
soft copy [222]
speakers [228]
speech recognition [219]
storage [229]
storage device [229]
storage medium [229]
storing [206]
stylus [218]
synchronous dynamic RAM (SDRAM) [208]
system clock [207]
system unit [202]

terabyte (TB) [208]
text [221]
touch screen [217]
touch-sensitive pad [220]
touchpad [214]
track [229]
trackball [214]

Universal Serial Bus (USB) port [211]
USB 2.0 port [211]
USB flash drive [239]
user response [212]

video [221]
video input [219]
voice output [227]
voice recognition [219]
volatile memory [208]

wheel [217]
wireless keyboard [214]
wireless mouse [215]

Checkpoint

INSTRUCTIONS: Use the Checkpoint exercises to check your knowledge level of the chapter. To complete the Checkpoint exercises interactively, visit scsite.com/tdc5, click Chapter 4 at the top of the Web page, and then click Checkpoint on the left sidebar.

1. Label the Figure

Instructions: Identify these areas or keys on a typical desktop computer keyboard.

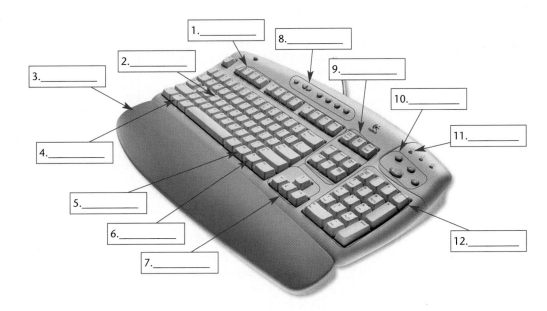

2. Matching

Instructions: Match each term from the column on the left with the best description from the column on the right.

____ 1. byte

____ 2. scanner

____ 3. output

____ 4. smart card

____ 5. chip

a. small piece of semiconducting material usually no bigger than one-half-inch square

b. eight bits grouped together as a unit

c. data that has been processed into a useful form, called information

d. an input device that can capture an entire page of text electronically

e. stores data on a thin embedded processor

3. Short Answer

Instructions: Write a brief answer to each of the following questions.

1. What are the components of the system unit? What is the purpose of the central processing unit and system clock?
2. How are RAM and ROM similar? How are they different? What terminology is used to describe the storage capacity of RAM chips?
3. Which type of printer is used commonly in schools? What are some differences between ink-jet and laser printers?
4. What are two types of digital pens? What kind of digital pen does a Tablet PC use? What kind of digital pen does a PDA use?
5. What is an optical disc? What are the two general categories of optical discs? Which optical disc has the largest storage capacity?

Teaching Today

INSTRUCTIONS: Teaching Today provides teachers with integration strategies and ideas for teaching and, more importantly, reaching today's digital generation. Each numbered segment contains one or more links that reinforce the information presented in the segment. To display this page from the Web, visit scsite.com/tdc5, click Chapter 4 at the top of the Web page, and then click Teaching Today on the left sidebar.

1. Graphing Calculators

Teachers are always looking for new technology tools to integrate in their classrooms. Math teachers have known for years that graphing calculators are excellent tools for teaching math. Students can use them not only to solve math problems, but also to see the solutions more graphically. Providing graphing calculators also can help students solve problems relating to other areas, such as geometry, algebra, and art. Use the Internet to research other ways to integrate graphing calculators into non-math teaching areas. Write a list of ideas that you discover in your research.

2. Portable Storage Media

Because of the need to move files from location to location, various portable storage media are used by students in K-12 schools and in universities. One advantage to using these devices is that you and your students can take all of your files with you. This means students can be working on projects in groups in the media center, in your class, and at home and keep all their files on one device. These devices' biggest advantage, small size, may also be their biggest disadvantage — they can be easily lost. What can you do help your students keep from losing their portable storage devices? Besides USB flash drives, are there other portable storage devices that you and your students might use in your classroom? Can you think of ways to use portable storage devices in your classroom? What are the advantages of using them?

3. Tablet PCs

Tablet PCs have been integrated into K-20 classrooms all over the country in almost every subject area. Tablet PCs come with Windows Tablet PC Edition, which includes all of the Windows features and the following additional features, to name just a few: (1) Use a digital pen on the write-on screen to issue instructions. (2) Save documents in handwritten form or convert them to text. (3) Add handwritten notes to documents and digital textbooks. (4) Enter text and instructions by speaking into the Tablet PC.

The potential benefits of using Tablet PCs, including note taking and speech recognition capabilities, to improve teaching and learning in all areas of education are enormous. Do you see a use for this digital tool in your classroom? Explain. How can you use this creative interactive computer with your students and what types of learners would benefit the most from this digital tool? What lessons could you create using the Tablet PC?

4. Ink-Jet Printers

Last year, you received a color ink-jet printer — a Hewlett-Packard DeskJet — for your classroom. Until recently, the printer worked flawlessly. Lately, however, when you print a document, the ink is smearing and the print quality is poor. No one at your school can provide technical assistance or support. Where else might you find technical support? Which type of support would you prefer? Visit Hewlett-Packard's Web site and use its Web-based technical support to determine how to fix the printer problem described previously. How does Web-based support differ from face-to-face support or support via telephone? What are some advantages and disadvantages of Web-based support?

Education Issues

INSTRUCTIONS: Education Issues provides several scenarios that allow you to explore controversial and current issues in education. Each numbered segment contains one or more links that reinforce the information presented in the segment. To display this page from the Web, visit scsite.com/tdc5, click Chapter 4 at the top of the Web page, and then click Education Issues on the left sidebar.

1. Reading Comprehension

Over the last five years, reading scores have continued to drop in one of your local school districts. Knowing that reading is one of the more crucial life skills that all students must have to be successful, the district competed for and received a $1.3 million grant to help students become better readers. The grant focuses on integrating handheld devices, such as PDAs, in the classroom as a way to fuel students' enthusiasm for reading, which could improve reading literacy throughout the district. What do you think? Can PDAs be used to help teach students to be better readers? Should there be a mix? Are lesson plans available that support using PDAs? Defend your opinion.

2. Digital Age Learners

Research suggests that what many of us refer to as Attention Deficit Disorder (ADD) is really nothing more than a skill developed by some children that have been raised in the digital age. As a result, these research findings are revealing that the learning environment these students are placed in does not match their cognitive or digital learning style, which then affects motivation and achievement. Have some of these students rewired their brains to multitask? Can they can read e-mails, send instant messages and text messages over handheld devices, speak to one another in short sentences, and continue to watch movies and participate in multiple conversations, all while finishing their homework? When we try to place these students in the traditional learning environment, are we working against their cognitive or digital learning style? What are your thoughts about this theory for this new generation of digital kids? Do you see the differences in their learning? What suggestions do you have for reaching them? Give some suggestions and defend your answer.

3. Computers for All Students

Around the world, governments have begun to supply school children with notebook computers. The United Nations endorses a plan known as One Laptop per Child to supply $150 notebook computers to developing countries — some of which already pledged to purchase millions of the devices for their school children. The device, which recharges with a hand crank, includes Wi-Fi networking and a simple, intuitive user interface. Supporters of these plans maintain that computer literacy and electronic communication are vital skills in today's world. Those who oppose this plan claim that technology detracts from traditional educational subjects. Should schools supply computers to all students? Why or why not? Should the One Laptop per Child program be limited to only those children in developing countries? Why or why not?

4. Digital Data Lasts Forever

Up to 75% of today's data never existed on paper. Historical data from thousands of years ago still exists because it was written down. Although written documents can be read hundreds of years after they were created, rapid changes in computer technology can make digital records inaccessible. Loss of access to data that is stored on aging media threatens the integrity of data retrieval. A major state university recently admitted that almost 3000 student and school files could not be accessed due to lost or outdated software. Is the potential unavailability of digital data a problem? What can be done to keep today's digital information available for future generations?

Integration Corner

INSTRUCTIONS: Integration Corner provides extensive ideas and resources for integrating technology into your classroom-specific curriculum. To display this page from the Web and its links to approximately 100 educational Web sites, visit scsite.com/tdc5, click Chapter 4 at the top of the Web page, and then click Integration Corner on the left sidebar.

Integration Corner is designed for teachers and other educators who are looking for innovative ways to integrate technology into their content-specific curriculum. Integration Corner not only provides great Web sites with current information but also shows what other educators are doing in the field of educational technology. Integration Corner is designed for all educators regardless of their interests. Expand your resources by reviewing information and Web sites outside of your teaching area because many great integration ideas in one area can be modified easily for use in other curricular areas.

Teachers and administrators will find other colleagues in their areas with whom to connect and share the successes and hurdles of integrating technology in a classroom or an entire school system. Consider Integration Corner your one stop for integration ideas and resources. Links to educational Web sites are organized in the following 12 Corners, and different Web resources are available for each chapter. Figure 4-65 shows examples of the Web resources provided in the Chapter 4 Secondary Corner.

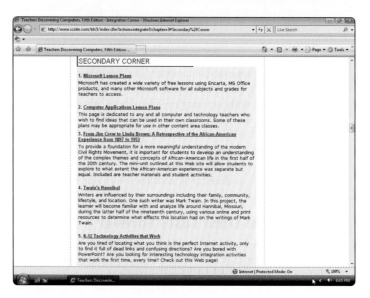

Figure 4-65 Examples of the Web resources provided in the Chapter 4 Secondary Corner.

Software Corner

INSTRUCTIONS: Software Corner provides information on popular software programs. Each numbered segment discusses specific software programs and contains a link to additional information about these programs. To display this page from the Web, visit scsite.com/tdc5, click Chapter 4 at the top of the Web page, and then click Software Corner on the left sidebar.

1. The Graph Club

The Graph Club, by Tom Snyder Productions, is an easy-to-use graphing tool every elementary classroom should have! You can create activities in which your students conduct research and graph their findings. The Graph Club allows students to construct and interpret pie, line, picture, and bar graphs. Students learn to use graphs to analyze data and solve problems, as well as write about graphs they create. Graphs can be printed by the page or even made in poster size for classroom use. The Graph Club is an innovative way to help your students understand and interpret graphs and is an excellent resource for standardized test preparation.

2. The Oregon Trail

Award-winning Oregon Trail® expands your curriculum to cover history, geography, and social studies by letting your students walk in the footsteps of courageous pioneers through compelling 3-D simulation adventures. With Oregon Trail, your students use logical reasoning and critical thinking to develop real-life decision making as they select their wagon party, supplies, read maps, plan their route, and guide their team through the wilderness. Students develop solutions to help their teams of friends and family survive the dangers of the long journey with a different scenario every time that can include attacks from wild animals, sickness, raging rivers, starvation, and more. Your students get the opportunity to not only read about a story, but also be part of the story by travelling across the Oregon Trail — with the triumphs, trials, and tribulations of a cast of characters that seems to come alive.

3. Make-A-Story

Your students can learn to interact and write stories about Timmy & His Friends with Make-A-Story. Students choose different characters, settings, and actions, and then they can hear the stories read aloud in English or a foreign language. Students can work through 18 exciting activities to gain an appreciation of different cultures while comparing those cultures through number and word activities, stories, songs, games, and crafts. This is excellent software for developing cross-curricular activities for language arts, math, social studies, and creativity.

4. Grolier Multimedia Encyclopedia

Teachers and students need to work successfully on research reports and multimedia projects. Grolier Multimedia Encyclopedia can assist your students in creating awesome multimedia presentations with thousands of links, images, full audio features, videos, animations, dynamic maps, and panoramas of amazing sites. Research reports will be a snap for students with more than 100,000 articles and the Millennium feature, which chronicles important world events for the last 1,000 years as well as Internet links. Grolier Multimedia Encyclopedia is an excellent resource for any classroom.

5. Geometer's Sketchpad

With Geometer's Sketchpad, by Key Curriculum Press, your students can explore and analyze geometric figures and concepts they are learning in the classroom. While preserving the geometric relationships of the shapes, students can manipulate the geometric figures created in Geometer's Sketchpad. Use Geometer's Sketchpad for presentations or allow your students to work alone or in groups. This software is extremely versatile and can be used from grades 5 through college. The software comes with an instructional video and documentation. The documentation includes tutorials and sample classroom activities. Extensive Internet resources also are available.

Digital Media Corner

INSTRUCTIONS: Today's K-12 digital students need their learning to be meaningful and relevant to their lives. Digital Media Corner provides videos, ideas, and examples of how you can use digital media to enhance your teaching and your students' learning. To access the videos and links to additional information, visit scsite.com/tdc5, click Chapter 4 at the top of the Web page, and then click Digital Media on the left sidebar.

1. Buying the Right Digital Camera

If you are buying your first digital camera to get started in the world of digital photography or to replace your old camera, a single digital camera that is perfect for every user simply does not exist. When making the decision about which model of digital camera to purchase, you must consider how and where you will use the camera, what results you would like, and what you can afford. What options are important to consider? To learn more about buying the right digital camera and how they work you should always do your research and learn what is best for you or your classroom needs.

2. USB 2.0 or Firewire?

You want to use an external hard drive to store data, but you are not sure which connection type to pick, USB 2.0 or Firewire. That choice needs to be made based on what you are planning to store on your drive. For convenience and compatibility between multiple computers, a USB 2.0 external hard drive is probably the better choice, especially if you are only using it to back up Word documents, PowerPoint Presentation, Web pages, grade books, etc. However, if you are planning activities requiring sustained throughput (how fast data can be transferred), such as rendering a video or music, a FireWire portable hard drive provides the best performance. Firewire portable hard drives are usually more expensive and often have to be ordered as they are not always stocked by your local computer or outlet store.

3. Maintaining Your CDs

Just because your favorite CD has a few annoying skips is not enough of a reason to discard it. A few options are available to help you continue to use those scratched CDs. How do you remove minor scratches from CDs? When a CD skips it may not always be the fault of the CD itself. In fact, it may not have a scratch on it at all. Sometimes just playing the CD in an alternate player will remedy the situation. Another way to get rid of annoying skips is to make a copy of the CD. A series of instructions and an FAQ on the Ins and Outs of making CD copies can be found on the Computer Support Website.

4. Reaching All Students

Look around your classroom, school, or mall, and you will see that most of today's digital kids have cell phones. Newer cell phones have photo, music, and video taking capabilities that could serve as a good digital technology alternative in the classroom by providing access to all students. This form of digital technology is a super way for all students to be able use their own cell phones to take photos for their digital media presentation. Third-party software vendors like Apple and others provide a means to transfer the photos from the camera to the Web. These services also allow classroom teachers and students a location to store photo albums online for a small fee.

Assistive Technologies Corner

INSTRUCTIONS: Assistive Technologies Corner provides information on current hardware, software, and peripherals that will assist you in delivering instruction to students with physical, cognitive, or sensory challenges. To access extensive additional information, visit scsite.com/tdc5, click Chapter 4 at the top of the Web page, and then click Assistive Technologies on the left sidebar.

1. Why Have Specialized Hardware in the Classroom?

The growing presence of computers in everyone's lives has generated an awareness of the need to address computing requirements for those with physical limitations. Today, the Americans with Disabilities Act (ADA) requires that all schools ensure that students with all types of special needs are not excluded from participation in, or denied access to, educational programs or activities. In addition to speech recognition, which is ideal for students who are visually impaired or who have physical or cognitive limitations, other input devices are available.

2. Are There Alternatives to Keyboards?

Students with limited hand mobility who want to use a keyboard have several options. One option is to use a keyguard. A keyguard, when placed over the keyboard, prevents the student from inadvertently pressing keys and provides a guide so the student strikes only one key at a time. Another option is a screen-displayed keyboard, in which a graphic of a standard keyboard is displayed on the student's screen. Students then use a pointing device to press the keys on the screen-displayed keyboard.

Another type of input device is a touch window, or a touch screen. This is a device that attaches to the front of a monitor that allows students to select items by touching instead of using a keyboard. Yet another alternative input device is the Intellikeys keyboard. This powerful tool has a flexible design permitting teachers to customize the keyboard with special overlays or templates that fit over the keyboard. Using Intellikeys, students with mobility issues or with cognitive disabilities can participate independently in classroom learning activities.

3. What Other Input Devices Can Benefit Students with Special Needs?

A variety of input devices are available for students with motor disabilities. Joysticks and small trackballs that can be controlled with a thumb or one finger can be attached to a table, mounted to a wheelchair, or held in a student's hand. Students with limited hand mobility can use a head-mounted pointer to control the pointer or insertion point. A switch is used much as a mouse button is used. Switches are made in a vast array of colors, shapes, and sizes. They can be operated by a tap, a kick, a swipe, or a puff, and they integrate well with other devices such as Intellikeys.

Many of these input devices now are connected to computers by USB. The computer recognizes them instantly, which means setup time is minimal. Learning how to integrate software programs and hardware devices into your curriculum that allow students with special needs to use computers as tools for learning is covered in Chapters 6 and 7.

Follow the instructions at the top of this page to display additional information and this chapter's links on assistive technologies.

In the Lab

INSTRUCTIONS: In the Lab provides database exercises that are divided into two areas, productivity and integration. To access the links to tutorials, productivity ideas, integration examples and ideas, and more, visit scsite.com/tdc5, click Chapter 4 at the top of the Web page, and then click In the Lab on the left sidebar.

PRODUCTIVITY IN THE CLASSROOM

Introduction: Database software allows you to create, store, sort, and retrieve data. Databases enable computer users to manipulate large amounts of data to produce different results. A classic example of a database is your local telephone directory.

Many database programs have wizards that walk you through creating a database, often called a database table. When you first create a database, it may look very similar to a spreadsheet in layout and design. This often is referred to as Datasheet view or List view. In this view, you can see a number of the records in the database at one time. The rows in the database are called records. Records can contain information about a person, product, or event. The columns in the database are called fields. Fields contain a specific piece of information within a record. Most database applications have a Design view, also called Form view, where information is added one record at a time and only one record is displayed at a time. Be sure to use the Help feature of your database software, such as Microsoft Access, FileMaker Pro, Microsoft Works, and AppleWorks, to learn more about the different views and features.

1. Creating and Formatting a Student Information Database

Problem: At the beginning of every school year, students are asked to fill out information cards. To save time and to begin teaching the students about databases, create a database that contains the fields shown in Figure 4-66. Then have the students enter their information into the database, keeping it updated throughout the year. This allows you always to have the most current information available.

Open your database software and create the Student Information Database. Use the field names shown in Figure 4-66. (*Hint*: Use Help to better understand the steps.)

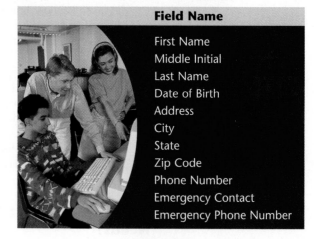

Field Name

First Name
Middle Initial
Last Name
Date of Birth
Address
City
State
Zip Code
Phone Number
Emergency Contact
Emergency Phone Number

Figure 4-66

Instructions: Perform the following tasks.

1. Create the database using the field names listed in Figure 4-66.
2. Determine the proper field widths and types so the information displays properly.
3. Enter student information to create 10 records. Enter your name for the first record.
4. Save the database to the location of your choice using an appropriate filename.
5. Print the database as a table or list.
6. Create a cover sheet using word processing software that includes your name, the current date, and the course title.
7. Follow the directions from your instructor for handing in this assignment.

In the Lab

2. Creating and Formatting a Hardware Inventory Database

Problem: At the end of every school year, you must turn in your classroom technology inventory. Creating the inventory by hand is time-consuming and tedious. Entering the information into a database allows you to update the information quickly and generate the necessary reports. Create a database that contains information regarding the technology in your classroom. The contents of the database are shown in Figure 4-67. (*Hint*: Use Help to understand the steps better.)

Manufacturer	Hardware	Serial Number	Year	Used By
Compaq	17" Monitor	023BA64WF389	2006	Students
Compaq	System Unit	CM29M-KY9KJ-TPBXJ-GRCCC-WVQRD	2007	Students
Compaq	17" Monitor	036ZV21LP912	2007	Students
Compaq	System Unit	CM21X-NY6NJ-PTAYK-BNUIU-MCWRD	2007	Students
Sony	19" Flat Screen Monitor	977AX56VR311	2008	Students
Dell	System Unit	00JKXW-KR2RR-JJ8870	2006	Students
Dell	Notebook Computer	6D3CJC58380WB	2008	Teacher
Compaq	Presario Notebook Computer	6D3CJC58380WB	2007	Students
Apple	iBook	CJ54404K39X	2008	Students
Apple	iMac	XA6352RG7Y7	2005	Students
Hewlett-Packard	Printer	SBG94AGWQK	2005	Teacher
Compaq	Printer	1M05DG2VXBP	2007	Students
Apple	Printer	CC552AAQ69O	2008	Students
Visioneer	Scanner	052C00900D1	2007	Students
Kodak	Digital Camera	144527D3	2008	Students

Figure 4-67

Instructions: Perform the following tasks.

1. Create the database using the five fields in Figure 4-67. Format the fields so the information is displayed properly.
2. Enter the data for the first 15 records from Figure 4-67 into the database.
3. Personalize the database by adding three additional records — the manufacturer, type of hardware, serial number (create a number if necessary), year purchased, and who uses the hardware item.
4. Save the database to the location of your choice using an appropriate filename.
5. Print the database as a table or list.
6. Create a cover sheet using word processing software that includes your name, the current date, and the course title.
7. Follow the directions from your instructor for handing in this assignment.

In the Lab

INTEGRATION IN THE CLASSROOM

1. Your science class is studying the <u>solar system</u>. The class is divided into groups and each group will gather the facts about their assigned planet. You have the students create a class database with the following fields: planet name, distance from the sun, number of moons, average temperature in Fahrenheit, length of year, size, atmosphere, and gravity at the surface. The students enter their findings and then compare and contrast the planets based on the different characteristics. Create a sample database selecting one planet and enter the appropriate information to demonstrate the project for the students. Include a header with your name and a footer with the current date.

2. Your third grade class is taking a field trip to the zoo. You want the students to have the opportunity to learn about animals in a creative way. Students will gather information about their <u>animals</u> from books, the Internet, and multimedia CD-ROMs. With the help of a parent volunteer, the students will enter their information into a simple database. You have selected the following fields for the database: animal name, country of origin, habitat, food, weight/size, and number of babies. Create a sample database selecting at least two zoo animals and enter the appropriate information to demonstrate the project for the students. Include a header with your name and a footer with the current date.

3. In math class, you have students work in groups to invest $5000 in a six-month certificate of deposit (CD). Students will use the Internet to gather information from local <u>banks and credit unions</u> and make a list of the current interest rates, minimum investment amounts, and total amounts earned in six months. The students then will create a database showing the name of the financial institution, its address and telephone number, the interest rate, the total value of the CD in six months, and the amount of interest earned. Create a sample database to demonstrate the project for the students. Include a header with your name and a footer with the current date.

Learn It Online

INSTRUCTIONS: Use the Learn It Online exercises to reinforce your understanding of the chapter concepts and increase your computer, information, and integration literacy. To access step-by-step online tutorials, videos, practice tests, learning games, and more, visit scsite.com/tdc5, click Chapter 4 at the top of the Web page, and then click Learn It Online on the left sidebar.

1. At the Movies

Have you ever wondered how a computer works? Click the At the Movies - Computer Tour link to view a video about how RAM, optical drives, video cards, and other computer components work.

2. At the Movies

Click the At the Movies - Camcorder link to review a video about how a video camcorder works.

3. Purchasing and Installing Memory in a Computer

One of the less expensive and more effective ways to speed up a computer, that is make it capable of processing more programs at the same time and enable it to more effectively handle graphics, gaming, and other high-level programs, is to increase its amount of memory. Click the Purchasing and Installing Memory link to learn how to purchase and install new memory in your computer. Print just the first page of this Web page. On the back of the printout, write a brief summary explaining how to purchase and install memory in a computer. If required, submit your results to your instructor.

4. Expanding Your Understanding

Every computer today contains a sound card and associated hardware and software that allow you to play and record sound. Click the Expanding Your Understanding link to learn how to adjust the sound on your computer.

5. Practice Test

Click the Practice Test link. Answer each question. When completed, enter your name and click the Grade Test button to submit the quiz for grading. Make a note of any missed questions. If required, submit your score to your instructor.

6. Who Wants to Be a Computer Genius?

Click the Computer Genius link to find out if you are a computer genius. Directions about how to play the game will be displayed. When you are ready to play, click the Play button. If required, submit your score to your instructor.

7. Wheel of Terms

Click the Wheel of Terms link to reinforce important terms you learned in this chapter by playing the Shelly Cashman Series version of this popular game. Directions about how to play the game will be displayed. When you are ready to play, click the Play button. If required, submit your score to your instructor.

8. Crossword Puzzle Challenge

Click the Crossword Puzzle link. Complete the puzzle to reinforce skills you learned in this chapter. Directions about how to play the game will be displayed. When you are ready to play, click the Play button. If required, submit the completed puzzle to your instructor.

Special Feature: Buyer's Guide

How to Purchase a Personal Computer

At some point, perhaps while you are taking this course, you may decide to buy a personal computer. The decision is an important one and will require an investment of both time and money. Like many buyers, you may have little computer experience and so you may find yourself unsure of how to proceed. You can get started by talking to your friends, coworkers, and instructors about their computers. What type of computers did they buy? Why? For what purposes do they use their computers? You also should answer the following questions to help narrow your choices to a specific computer type.

Do You Want a Desktop Computer or Mobile Computer?

A desktop computer (Figure 1a) is designed as a stationary device that sits on or below a desk or table in a location such as a home, office, or dormitory room. A desktop computer must be plugged into an electrical outlet to operate. A mobile computer, such as a notebook computer or Tablet PC (Figure 1b), is smaller than a desktop computer, more portable, and has a battery that allows you to operate it for a period without being connected to an electrical outlet.

Desktop computers are a good option if you work mostly in one place and have plenty of space in your work area. Desktop computers generally give you a better dollar value in terms of performance than notebook computers.

Increasingly, more schools are buying mobile computers to take advantage of their portability for students and teachers. The past disadvantages of mobile computers, such as lower processor speeds, poor-quality monitors, weight, short battery life, and significantly higher prices, have all but disappeared. Today, hard drive speed, capacity, processor speed, and graphics capability in notebook computers are equal to, if not better than, desktop computers; however, notebooks computers generally do still cost more than desktop computers similar in performance.

If you are thinking of using a mobile computer to take notes in class or in business meetings, then consider a Tablet PC with handwriting and drawing capabilities. Typically, note-taking involves writing text notes and drawing charts, schematics, and other illustrations. By allowing you to write and draw directly on the screen with a digital pen, a Tablet PC eliminates the distracting sound of the notebook keyboard tapping and allows you to capture drawings. Some notebook computers can convert to Tablet PCs.

Mobile computers used to have several drawbacks, including the lack of high-end capabilities. Today's high-end notebook computers include most of the capabilities of a good desktop computer. Manufacturers have made great strides in improving durability and battery life. Most notebook computers are 1.5 to 2 inches thick and weigh less than 10 pounds, making them very portable and easy to carry.

[a] desktop computer

[b] mobile computer (notebook or tablet PC)

Figure 1

Why do You Need a Computer?

Having a general idea of why you need a computer, that is, how do you intend to use it, will help you decide on the type of computer to buy. At this point in your research, it is not necessary to know the exact application titles or version numbers you might want to use. Knowing that you plan to use the computer primarily to create word processing, spreadsheet, database, and presentation documents, however, will point you in the direction of a desktop or notebook computer. If you want the portability of a smart phone or PDA but you need more computing power, then a Tablet PC may be the best alternative. You also must consider that some application programs run only on a Mac, while others run only on a PC with the Windows operating system. Still other software may run only on a PC running the UNIX or Linux operating system.

Should the Computer be Compatible with the Computers at School or Work?

If you plan to bring work home, telecommute, or take distance education courses, then you should purchase a computer that is compatible with those at school or work.

Compatibility is primarily a software issue. If your computer runs the same operating system version, such as Microsoft Windows Vista, and the same application software, such as Microsoft Office, then your computer will be able to read documents created at school or work and vice versa. Incompatible hardware can become an issue if you plan to connect directly to a school or an office network using cable or wireless technology. You usually can obtain the minimum system requirements from the Information Technology department at your school or workplace.

After evaluating the answers to these three questions, you should have a general idea of how you plan to use your computer and the type of computer you want to buy. Once you have decided on the type of computer you want, you can follow the guidelines presented in this Buyer's Guide to help you purchase a specific computer, along with software, peripherals, and other accessories.

This Buyer's Guide concentrates on recommendations for purchasing a desktop computer, notebook computer, Tablet PC, and a personal mobile device. Many of the desktop computer guidelines presented also apply to the purchase of a notebook computer and a Tablet PC. Later in this Buyer's Guide, sections on purchasing a notebook computer or Tablet PC address additional considerations specific to those computer types.

How to Purchase a Desktop Computer

Once you have decided that a desktop computer is most suited to your computing needs, the next step is to determine specific software, hardware, peripheral devices, and services to purchase, as well as where to buy the computer. The guidelines that follow provide information to help you make your preliminary decisions.

Determine the Specific Software You Want to Use on Your Computer.

Before deciding to purchase software, be sure it contains the features necessary for the tasks you want to perform. Rely on the computer users in whom you have confidence to help you decide on the software to use. The minimum requirements of the software you select may determine the operating system (Microsoft Windows Vista, Linux, UNIX, Mac OS X) you need. If you have decided to use a particular operating system that does not support software you want to use, you may be able to purchase similar software from other manufacturers.

Many Web sites and trade magazines, such as those listed in Figure 2, provide reviews of software products. These Web sites frequently have articles that rate computers and software on cost, performance, and support.

Type of Computer	Web Site	Web Address
PC	CNET Shopper	shopper.cnet.com
	PC World Magazine	pcworld.com
	BYTE Magazine	byte.com
	PC Magazine	pcmag.com
	Yahoo! Computer	computers.yahoo.com
	MSN Shopping	shopping.msn.com
	Dave's Guide to Buying a Home Computer	css.msu.edu/PC-Guide
Mac	Macworld Magazine	macworld.com
	Apple	apple.com
	Switch to Mac Campaign	apple.com/switch

*For an updated list and links, click Buyer's Guide in the Features section at the Teachers Discovering Computers Web site (*scsite.com/tdc5*).*

Figure 2 Resources for hardware and software reviews.

Your hardware requirements depend on the minimum requirements of the software you will run on your computer. Some software requires more memory and disk space than others, as well as additional input, output, and storage devices. For example, suppose you want to run software that can copy the content of one CD or DVD directly to another CD or DVD, without first copying the data to your hard disk. To support that, you should consider a desktop computer or a high-end notebook computer, because the computer will need two CD or DVD drives: one that reads from a CD or DVD, and one that reads from and writes on a CD or DVD. If you plan to run software that allows your computer to work as an entertainment system, then you will need a CD or DVD drive, quality speakers, and an upgraded sound card.

Know the System Requirements of the Operating System.

After deciding the software you want to run on your new computer, you need to determine the operating system you want to use. If, however, you purchase a new computer, chances are it will have the latest version of your preferred operating system (Windows Vista, Linux, UNIX, or Mac OS X). Figure 3 lists the minimum computer requirements of Windows Vista versions.

Look for Bundled Software.

When you purchase a computer, it may come bundled with software. Some sellers even let you choose which software you want. Remember, however, that bundled software has value only if you would have purchased the software even if it had not come with the computer. At the very least, you probably will want word processing software and a browser to access the Internet. If you need additional applications,

Windows Vista Versions	Minimum Computer Requirements
Windows Vista Home Basic	• 800 MHz processor • 512 MB of RAM • DirectX 9 capable graphics processor
Windows Vista Home Premium **Windows Vista Ultimate** **Windows Vista Business** **Windows Vista Enterprise**	• 1 GHz processor • 1 GB of RAM • DirectX 9 capable graphics processor with WDDM driver and 128 MB of graphics memory • 40 GB of hard disk capacity (15 GB free space) • DVD-ROM drive • Audio output capability • Internet access capability

Figure 3 Hardware requirements for Windows Vista.

such as spreadsheet, database, or presentation graphics, consider purchasing Microsoft Works, Microsoft Office, OpenOffice.org, or Sun StarOffice, which include several programs at a reduced price.

Avoid Buying the Least Powerful Computer Available.

Once you know the application software you want to use, you then can consider the following important criteria about the computer's components: (1) processor speed, (2) size and types of memory (RAM) and storage, (3) types of input/output devices, (4) types of ports and adapter cards, and (5) types of communications devices. You also need to consider if the computer is upgradeable and to what extent you are able to upgrade. For example, all manufacturers limit the amount of memory you can add. The information in Figure 4 (on the next page) can help you determine what system components are best for you.

Computer technology changes rapidly, meaning a computer that seems powerful enough today may not serve your computing needs in a few years. In fact, studies show that many users regret not buying a more powerful computer. To avoid this, plan to buy a computer that will last you for two to three years. You can help delay obsolescence by purchasing the fastest processor, the most memory, and the largest hard disk you can afford. If you must buy a less powerful computer, be sure you can upgrade it with additional memory, components, and peripheral devices as your computer requirements grow.

Consider Upgrades to the Mouse, Keyboard, Monitor, Printer, Microphone, and Speakers.

You use these peripheral devices to interact with your computer, so you should make sure they are up to your standards. Review the peripheral devices listed in Figure 4 and then visit both local computer dealers and large

retail stores to test the computers on display. Ask the salesperson what input and output devices would be best for you and whether you should upgrade beyond what comes standard. Consider purchasing a wireless keyboard and wireless mouse to eliminate bothersome wires on your desktop. A few extra dollars spent on these components when you initially purchase a computer can extend its usefulness by years.

Determine Whether You Want to Use Telephone Lines or Broadband (Cable or DSL) to Access the Internet.

If your computer has a modem, then you can access the Internet using a standard telephone line. Ordinarily, you call a local or toll-free 800 number to connect to an ISP. Using a dial-up Internet connection is relatively inexpensive but slow.

DSL and cable connections provide much faster Internet connections, which are ideal if you want faster file download speeds for software, digital photos, and music. As you would expect, they also are more expensive. DSL, which is available through local telephone companies or ISPs/OSPs, also may require that you subscribe to an ISP. Cable is available through your local cable television provider and some online service providers (OSPs). If you get cable, then you probably would not use a separate Internet service provider or online service provider.

If You are Using a Dial-Up Connection to Connect to the Internet, then Select an ISP or OSP.

You can access the Internet via telephone lines in one of two ways: an ISP or an OSP. Both provide Internet access for a monthly fee that ranges from $6 to $25. Local ISPs offer Internet access to users in a limited geographic region, through local telephone numbers. National ISPs provide access for users nationwide (including mobile users) through local and toll-free telephone numbers and cable.

CD/DVD Drives: Most computers come with a CD-RW drive. A CD-RW drive allows you to create your own custom data CDs for data backup or data transfer purposes. It also allows you to store and share video files, digital photos, and other large files with other people who have access to a CD-ROM drive. An even better alternative is to upgrade to a DVD/RW combination drive. It allows you to read DVDs and CDs and to write data on (burn) a DVD or CD. A DVD has a capacity of at least 4.7 GB versus the 650 MB capacity of a CD. An HD DVD has a minimum capacity of 45 GB.

Card Reader/Writer: A card reader/writer is useful for transferring data directly to and from a removable flash memory card, such as the ones used in your camera or audio player. Make sure the card reader/writer can read from and write on the flash memory cards that you use.

Digital Camera: Consider an inexpensive point-and-shoot digital camera. They are small enough to carry around, usually operate automatically in terms of lighting and focus, and contain storage cards for storing photographs. A 5-megapixel camera with a 512 MB storage card is fine for creating images for use on the Web or to send via e-mail.

Digital Video Capture Device: A digital video capture device allows you to connect your computer to a camcorder or VCR and record, edit, manage, and then write video back on a VCR tape, a CD, or a DVD. To create quality video (true 30 frames per second, full-sized TV), the digital video capture device should have a USB 2.0 or FireWire port. You also will need sufficient storage: an hour of data on a VCR tape takes up about 5 GB of disk storage.

External Hard Disk: An external hard disk can serve many purposes: it can serve as extra storage for your computer, provide a way to store and transport large files or large quantities of files, and provide security by allowing you to keep all of your data on the external disk without leaving any data on the computer. External hard disks can be purchased with the same amount of capacity as any internal disk. If you are going to use it as a backup to your internal hard disk, you should purchase an external hard drive with at least as much capacity as your internal hard disk.

Hard Disk: It is recommended that you buy a computer with 60 to 80 GB if your primary interests are browsing the Web and using e-mail and Office suite-type applications; 80 to 100 GB if you also want to edit digital photographs; 100 to 200 GB if you plan to edit digital video or manipulate large audio files even occasionally; and 200 to 500 GB if you will edit digital video, movies, or photography often; store audio files and music; or consider yourself to be a power user. It also is recommended that you use Serial ATA (SATA) as opposed to Parallel ATA (PATA). SATA has many advantages over PATA, including support for Plug and Play devices.

Joystick/Wheel: If you use your computer to play games, then you will want to purchase a joystick or a wheel. These devices, especially the more expensive ones, provide for realistic game play with force feedback, programmable buttons, and specialized levers and wheels.

Keyboard: The keyboard is one of the more important devices used to communicate with the computer. For this reason, make sure the keyboard you purchase has 101 to 105 keys, is comfortable and easy to use, and has a USB connection. A wireless keyboard should be considered, especially if you have a small desk area.

Microphone: If you plan to record audio or use speech recognition to enter text and commands, then purchase a close-talk headset with gain adjustment support.

Modem: Most computers come with a modem so that you can use your telephone line to access the Internet. Some modems also have fax capabilities. Your modem should be rated at 56 Kbps.

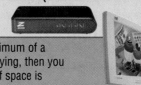

Monitor: The monitor is where you will view documents, read e-mail messages, and view pictures. A minimum of a 17" screen is recommended, but if you are planning to use your computer for graphic design or game playing, then you may want to purchase a 19" or 21" monitor. The LCD flat panel monitor should be considered, especially if space is an issue.

Figure 4 Hardware guidelines.

Ports: Depending on how you are using your computer, you may need anywhere from 4 to 10 USB 2.0 ports. USB 2.0 ports have become the connection of choice in the computer industry. They offer an easy way to connect peripheral devices such as printers, digital cameras, portable media players, etc. Many computers intended for home or professional audio/video use have built-in FireWire ports. Most personal computers come with a minimum of six USB 2.0 ports and two FireWire ports.

Port Hub Expander: If you plan to connect several peripheral devices to your computer at the same time, then you need to be concerned with the number of ports available on your computer. If your computer does not have enough ports, then you should purchase a port hub expander. A port hub expander plugs into a single FireWire port or USB port and gives several additional ports.

Printer: Your two basic printer choices are ink-jet and laser. Color ink-jet printers cost on average between $50 and $300. Laser printers cost from $200 to $2,000. In general, the cheaper the printer, the lower the resolution and speed, and the more often you are required to change the ink cartridge or toner. Laser printers print faster and with a higher quality than an ink-jet, and their toner on average costs less. If you want color, then go with a high-end ink-jet printer to ensure quality of print. Duty cycle (the number of pages you expect to print each month) also should be a determining factor. If your duty cycle is on the low end — hundreds of pages per month — then stay with a high-end ink-jet printer, rather than purchasing a laser printer. If you plan to print photographs taken with a digital camera, then you should purchase a photo printer. A photo printer is a dye-sublimation printer or an ink-jet printer with higher resolution and features that allow you to print quality photographs.

Processor: For a PC, an Intel Core 2 Duo processor at 2.66 GHz is more than enough processor power for home and small office/home office users. Game, large business, and power users should upgrade to faster processors.

RAM: RAM plays a vital role in the speed of your computer. Make sure the computer you purchase has at least 512 MB of RAM. If you have extra money to invest in your computer, then consider increasing the RAM to 1 GB or more. The extra money for RAM will be well spent.

Scanner: The most popular scanner purchased with a computer today is the flatbed scanner. When evaluating a flatbed scanner, check the color depth and resolution. Do not buy anything less than a color depth of 48 bits and a resolution of 1200 × 2400 dpi. The higher the color depth, the more accurate the color. A higher resolution picks up the more subtle gradations of color.

Sound Card: Many computers come with a standard sound card that supports Dolby 5.1 surround and is capable of recording and playing digital audio. Make sure it is suitable in the event you decide to use your computer as an entertainment or gaming system.

Speakers: Once you have a good sound card, quality speakers and a separate subwoofer that amplifies the bass frequencies of the speakers can turn your computer into a premium stereo system.

PC Video Camera: A PC video camera is a small camera used to capture and display live video (in some cases with sound), primarily on a Web page. You also can capture, edit, and share video and still photos. The camera sits on your monitor or desk. Recommended minimum specifications include 640 × 480 resolution, a video with a rate of 30 frames per second, and a USB 2.0 or FireWire port.

USB Flash Drive: If you work on different computers and need access to the same data and information, then this portable miniature mobile storage device is ideal. USB flash drive capacity varies from 16 MB to 4 GB.

Video Card: Most standard video cards satisfy the monitor display needs of application home and small office users. If you are a game user or a graphic designer, you will want to upgrade to a higher quality video card. The higher refresh rates will further enhance the display of games, graphics, and movies.

Wireless LAN Access Point: A wireless LAN access point allows you to network several computers, so they can share files and access the Internet through a single cable modem or DSL connection. Each device that you connect requires a wireless card. A wireless LAN access point can offer a range of operations up to several hundred feet, so be sure the device has a high-powered antenna.

Figure 4 Hardware Guidelines. *(continued)*

Because of their size, national ISPs generally offer more services and have a larger technical support staff than local ISPs. OSPs furnish Internet access as well as members-only features for users nation-wide. Figure 5 lists several national ISPs and OSPs. Before you choose an ISP or OSP, compare such features as the number of access hours, monthly fees, available services (e-mail, Web page hosting, chat), and reliability.

Use a Worksheet to Compare Computers, Services, and Other Considerations.

You can use a separate sheet of paper to take notes on each vendor's computer and then summarize the information on a worksheet. Most companies advertise a price for a base computer that includes components housed in the system unit (processor, RAM, sound card, video card), disk drives (hard disk, CD-ROM, CD-RW, DVD-ROM, and DVD ± RW), a keyboard, mouse, monitor, printer, speakers, and modem. Be aware, however, that some adver-tisements list prices for computers with only some of these components. Monitors and printers, for example, often are not included in a base computer's price. Depending on how you plan to use the computer, you may want to invest in additional or more powerful com-ponents. When you are comparing the prices of computers, make sure you are comparing identical or similar configurations.

Company	Service	Web Address
America Online	OSP	aol.com
AT&T Worldnet	ISP	www.att.net
Comcast	OSP	comcast.net
CompuServe	OSP	compuserve.com
EarthLink	ISP	earthlink.net
Juno	OSP	juno.com
NetZero	OSP	netzero.com
MSN	OSP	msn.com
Prodigy	ISP/OSP	myhome.prodigy.net

For an updated list and links, click Buyer's Guide in the Features section at the Teachers Discovering Computers Web site (scsite.com/tdc5).

Figure 5 National ISPs and OSPs.

If You are Buying a New Computer, You Have Several Purchasing Options: Buying From Your School Bookstore, a Local Computer Dealer, a Local Large Retail Store, or Ordering by Mail via Telephone or the Web.

Each purchasing option has certain advantages. Many college bookstores, for example, sign exclu-sive pricing agreements with computer manufac-turers and, thus, can offer student discounts and technical support. Local dealers and local large retail stores also can provide hands-on support. Some mail-order companies that sell computers by telephone or online via the Web (Figure 6) have started to provide next-business-day, on-site services.

Figure 6 Mail-order companies, such as Dell, sell computers online.

A credit card usually is required to buy from a mail-order company. Figure 7 lists some of the more popular mail-order companies and their Web site addresses.

If You Have a Computer and are Upgrading to a New One, then Consider Selling or Trading in the Old One.

If you are purchasing a replacement computer, your older computer still may have value. If you cannot sell your old computer through the classified ads, via a Web site, or to a friend, then ask if the computer dealer will buy your old computer. An increasing number of companies are taking trade-ins, but do not expect too much money for your old computer. Other companies offer free disposal of your old PC.

If You are Buying a Used Computer, Stay with Name Brands such as DELL, Gateway, Hewlett-Packard, and Apple.

Although brand-name equipment can cost more, most brand-name computers have longer, more comprehensive warranties, are better supported, and have more authorized centers for repair services. As with new computers, you can purchase a used computer from local computer dealers, local large retail stores, or mail order via the telephone or the Web. Figure 8 lists several major used computer brokers and their Web site addresses. Classified ads and used computer sellers offer additional outlets for purchasing used computers.

Be Aware of Hidden Costs.

Before purchasing, be sure to consider any additional costs associated with buying a computer, such as a USB flash drive, additional telephone line, a cable or DSL modem, an uninterruptible power supply (UPS), computer furniture, paper, and computer training classes you may want to take. Depending on where you buy your computer, the seller may be willing to include some or all of these in the computer purchase price.

Consider More than Just Price.

The lowest-cost computer may not be the best long-term buy. Consider such intangibles as the vendor's time in business, the vendor's regard for quality, and the vendor's reputation for support. If

Type of Computer	Company	Web Address
PC	CNET Shopper	shopper.cnet.com
	Hewlett-Packard	hp.com
	CompUSA	compusa.com
	TigerDirect	tigerdirect.com
	Dell	dell.com
	Gateway	gateway.com
Mac	Apple Computer	store.apple.com
	ClubMac	macconnection.com
	PC & MacExchange	macx.com

For an updated list and links, click Buyer's Guide in the Features section at the Teachers Discovering Computers Web site (scsite.com/tdc5).

Figure 7 Computer mail-order companies.

Company	Web Address
Amazon.com	amazon.com
TECHAGAIN	techagain.com
American Computer Express	americancomputerex.com
U.S. Computer Exchange	usce.org
eBay	ebay.com

For an updated list and links, click Buyer's Guide in the Features section at the Teachers Discovering Computers Web site (scsite.com/tdc5).

Figure 8 Used computer mail-order companies.

you need to upgrade your computer often, you may want to consider a leasing arrangement, in which you pay monthly lease fees, but can upgrade or add to your computer as your equipment needs change. No matter what type of buyer you are, insist on a 30-day, no-questions-asked return policy on your computer.

Avoid Restocking Fees.

Some companies charge a restocking fee of 10 to 20 percent as part of their money-back return policy. In some cases, no restocking fee for hardware is applied, but it is applied for software. Ask about the existence and terms of any restocking policies before you buy.

Use a Credit Card to Purchase Your New Computer.

Many credit cards offer purchase protection and extended warranty benefits that cover you in case of loss of or damage to purchased goods. Paying by credit card also gives you time to install and use the computer before you have to pay for it. Finally, if you are dissatisfied with the computer and are unable to reach an agreement with the seller, paying by credit card gives you certain rights regarding withholding payment until the dispute is resolved. Check your credit card terms for specific details.

Consider Purchasing an Extended Warranty or Service Plan.

If you use your computer for business or require fast resolution to major computer problems, consider purchasing an extended warranty or a service plan through a local dealer or third-party company. Most extended warranties cover the repair and replacement of computer components beyond the standard warranty. Most service plans ensure that your technical support calls receive priority response from technicians. You also can purchase an on-site service plan that states that a technician will come to your home, work, or school within 24 hours. If your computer includes a warranty and service agreement for a year or less, think about extending the service for two or three years when you buy the computer.

How to Purchase a Notebook Computer

If you need computing capability when you travel or to use in lectures or meetings, you may find a notebook computer to be an appropriate choice. The guidelines mentioned in the previous section also apply to the purchase of a notebook computer. The following are additional considerations unique to notebook computers.

Purchase a Notebook Computer with a Sufficiently Large Active-Matrix Screen.

Active-matrix screens display high-quality color that is viewable from all angles. Less expensive, passive-matrix screens sometimes are difficult to see in low-light conditions and cannot be viewed from an angle. Notebook computers typically come with a 12.1-inch, 13.3-inch, 14.1-inch, 15.4-inch, or 17-inch display. For most users, a 14.1-inch display is satisfactory. If you intend to use your notebook computer as a desktop computer replacement, however, you may opt for a 15.7-inch or 17-inch display. Dell offers a notebook computer with a 20.1-inch display that looks like a briefcase when closed. Notebook computers with these larger displays weigh seven to ten pounds, however, so if you travel a lot and portability is essential, you might want a lighter computer with a smaller display. The lightest notebook computers, which weigh less than 3 pounds, are equipped with a 12.1-inch display. Regardless of size, the resolution of the display should be at least 1024×768 pixels. To compare the monitor size on various notebook computers, visit the company Web sites in Figure 9.

Type of Notebook	Company	Web Address
PC	Acer	global.acer.com
	Dell	dell.com
	Fujitsu	fujitsu.com
	Gateway	gateway.com
	Hewlett-Packard	hp.com
	Lenovo	lenovo.com/us/en/
	NEC	nec.com
	Sony	sony.com
	Toshiba	toshiba.com
Mac	Apple	apple.com

For an updated list and links, click Buyer's Guide in the Features section at the Teachers Discovering Computers Web site (scsite.com/tdc5).

Figure 9 Companies that sell notebook computers.

Experiment with Different Keyboards and Pointing Devices.

Notebook computer keyboards are far less standardized than those for desktop computers. Some notebook computers, for example, have wide wrist rests, while others have none, and keyboard layouts on notebook computers often vary. Notebook computers also use a range of pointing devices, including pointing sticks, touchpads, and trackballs. Before you purchase a notebook computer, try various types of keyboard and pointing devices to determine which is easiest for you to use. Regardless of the pointing device you select, you also may want to purchase a regular mouse to use when you are working at a desk or other large surface.

Make Sure the Notebook Computer You Purchase has a CD and/or DVD Drive.

Most notebook computers come with a CD and/or a DVD drive. Although DVD drives are slightly more expensive, they allow you to play CDs and DVD movies using your notebook computer and a headset.

If Necessary, Upgrade the Processor, Memory, and Disk Storage at the Time of Purchase.

As with a desktop computer, upgrading your notebook computer's memory and disk storage usually is less expensive at the time of initial purchase. Some disk storage is custom designed for notebook computers, meaning an upgrade might not be available in the future. If you are purchasing a lightweight notebook computer, then it should include at least an AMD or Intel Core Duo processor, 512 MB to 1 GB RAM, and 80 GB of storage.

The Availability of the Built-In Ports and a Port Extender on a Notebook Computer is Important.

A notebook computer does not have a lot of room to add adapter cards. If you know the purpose for which you plan to use your notebook computer, then you can determine the ports you will need. Most notebooks come with common ports, such as a mouse port,

IrDA port, serial port, parallel port, video port, FireWire port, and multiple USB ports. If you plan to connect your notebook computer to a TV, however, then you will need a PCtoTV port. If you want to connect to networks at school or in various offices via a network cable, make sure the notebook computer you purchase has a network port. If your notebook computer does not come with a network port, then you will have to purchase an external network card that slides into an expansion slot in your notebook computer. You will also need to purchase a network cable. While newer portable media players connect to a USB port, older ones require a FireWire port.

If You Plan to Use Your Notebook Computer for Note Taking at School or in Meetings, Consider a Notebook Computer that Converts to a Tablet PC.

Some computer manufacturers have developed convertible notebook computers that allow the screen to rotate 180 degrees on a central hinge and then fold down to cover the keyboard and become a Tablet PC (Figure 10). You then can use a stylus to enter text or drawings into the computer by writing on the screen.

Figure 10 This HP Compaq Tablet PC converts to a notebook computer.

Purchase a Notebook Computer with a Built-In Wireless Network Connection.

A wireless network connection (Bluetooth, Wi-Fi a/b/g, WiMAX, etc.) can be useful when you travel or as part of a home network. Increasingly more airports, hotels, and cafés have wireless networks that allow you to connect to the Internet. Many users today are setting up wireless home networks. With a wireless home network, one computer, such as a desktop computer, functions as the server and the other computer, such as a notebook computer, can access the desktop computer from any location in the house to share files and hardware, such as a printer, and browse the Web. Most home wireless networks allow connections from distances of 150 to 800 feet.

If You are Going to Use Your Notebook Computer for Long Periods Without Access to an Electrical Outlet, Purchase a Second Battery.

The trend among notebook computer users today is power and size over battery life, and notebook computer manufacturers have picked up on this. Many notebook computer users today are willing to give up longer battery life for a larger screen, faster processor, and more storage. In addition, some manufacturers typically sell the notebook with the lowest capacity battery. For this reason, you need to be careful in choosing a notebook computer if you plan to use it without access to electrical outlets for long periods, such as on an airplane flight. You also might want to purchase a second battery as a backup. If you anticipate running your notebook computer on batteries frequently, choose a computer that uses lithium-ion batteries, which last longer than nickel cadmium or nickel hydride batteries.

Purchase a Well-Padded and Well-Designed Carrying Case.

An amply padded carrying case will protect your notebook computer from the bumps it will receive while traveling. A well-designed carrying case will have room for accessories such as spare CDs and DVDs, a user manual, pens, and paperwork (Figure 11).

Figure 11 A well-designed notebook computer carrying case.

If You Travel Overseas, Obtain a Set of Electrical and Telephone Adapters.

Different countries use different outlets for electrical and telephone connections. Several manufacturers sell sets of adapters that will work in most countries.

If You Plan to Connect Your Notebook Computer to a Video Projector, Make Sure the Notebook Computer is Compatible with the Video Projector.

You should check, for example, to be sure that your notebook computer will allow you to display an image on the computer screen and projection device at the same time (Figure 12). Also, ensure that your notebook computer has the ports required to connect to the video projector. You also may consider purchasing a notebook computer with a built-in video camera for video conferencing purposes.

Figure 12 Many teachers are now using their notebook computers connected to a video projection system to give presentations, show videos, and more.

For Improved Security, Consider a Fingerprint Scanner.

More than half a million notebook computers are stolen or lost each year. If you have critical information stored on your notebook computer, then consider purchasing one with a fingerprint scanner (Figure 13) to protect the data if your computer is stolen or lost. Fingerprint security offers a level of protection that extends well beyond the standard password protection. If your notebook computer is stolen, the odds of recovering it improve dramatically with anti-theft tracking software. Manufacturers claim recovery rates of 90 percent or more for notebook computers using their product.

Figure 13 Fingerprint scanner technology offers greater security than passwords.

How to Purchase a Tablet PC

The Tablet PC combines the mobility features of a traditional notebook computer with the simplicity of pencil and paper because you can create and save Office-type documents by writing and drawing directly on the screen with a digital pen. Tablet PCs use the Windows Tablet Technology in the Windows Vista operating system. A notebook computer and a Tablet PC have many similarities (Figure 14). For this reason, if you are considering purchasing a Tablet PC,

review the guidelines for purchasing a notebook computer, as well as the guidelines that follow.

Figure 14 The lightweight Tablet PC with its handwriting capabilities is popular with students.

Make Sure the Tablet PC Fits Your Mobile Computing Needs.

The Tablet PC is not for every mobile user. If you find yourself in need of a computer in class or you are spending more time in meetings than in your office, then the Tablet PC may be the answer. Before you invest money in a Tablet PC, however, determine the programs you plan to use on it. You should not buy a Tablet PC simply because it is an interesting type of computer. For additional information on the Tablet PC, visit the Web sites listed in Figure 15. You may have to use the search capabilities on the home page of the companies listed to locate information about the Tablet PC.

Company	Web Address
Dell	dell.com
Fujitsu	fujitsu.com
Hewlett-Packard	hp.com
Microsoft	microsoft.com/windowsxp/tabletpc
Toshiba	toshiba.com
ViewSonic	viewsonic.com
For an updated list and links, click Buyer's Guide in the Features section at the Teachers Discovering Computers Web site (scsite.com/tdc5).	

Figure 15 Companies that sell Tablet PCs and their Web sites.

Decide Whether You Want a Convertible or Pure Tablet PC.

Convertible Tablet PCs have an attached keyboard and look like a notebook computer. You rotate the screen and lay it flat against the computer for note taking. The pure Tablet PCs are slim and lightweight, weighing less than four pounds. They have the capability of easily docking at a desktop to gain access to a large monitor, keyboard, and mouse. If you spend a lot of time attending lectures or meetings, then the pure Tablet PC is ideal. Acceptable specifications for a Tablet PC are shown in Figure 16.

Tablet PC Specifications	
Dimensions	12" × 9" × 1.2"
Weight	Less than 5 Pounds
Processor	Pentium M Processor at 2 GHz
RAM	1 GB
Hard Disk	60 GB
Display	12.1" TFT
Digitizer	Electromagnetic Digitizer
Battery	6-Cell High Capacity Lithium-Ion
USB	3
FireWire	1
Docking Station	Grab and Go with CD-ROM, Keyboard, and Mouse
Bluetooth Port	Yes
Wireless	802.11a/b/g Card
Network Card	10/100 Ethernet
Modem	56 Kbps
Speakers	Internal
Microphone	Internal
Operating System	Windows Vista
Application Software	Office Small Business Edition
Antivirus Software	Yes – 12 Month Subscription
Warranty	1-Year Limited Warranty Parts and Labor

Figure 16 Recommended Tablet PC specifications.

Port Availability, Battery Life, and Durability are Even More Important with a Tablet PC than They are with a Notebook Computer.

Make sure the Tablet PC you purchase has the ports required for the applications you plan to run. As with any mobile computer, battery life is important especially if you plan to use your Tablet PC for long periods without access to an electrical outlet. A Tablet PC must be durable because if you use it the way it was designed to be used, then you will be handling it much like you handle a pad of paper.

Experiment with Different Models of the Tablet PC to Find the Digital Pen that Works Best for You.

The key to making use of the Tablet PC is to be comfortable with its handwriting capabilities and on-screen keyboard. Not only is the digital pen used to write on the screen (Figure 17), you also use it to make gestures to complete tasks, in a manner similar to the way you use a mouse. Figure 18 compares the standard point-and-click of a mouse with the gestures made with a digital

Figure 17 A Tablet PC requires a digital pen to handwrite notes and draw on the screen.

Mouse	Digital Pen
Point	Point
Click	Tap
Double-click	Double-tap
Right-click	Tap and hold
Click and drag	Drag

Figure 18 Standard point-and-click of a mouse compared with the gestures made with a digital pen.

pen. Other gestures with the digital pen replicate some of the commonly used keys on a keyboard.

Check Out the Comfort Level of Handwriting in Different Positions.

You should be able to handwrite on a Tablet PC with your hand resting on the screen. You also should be able to handwrite holding the Tablet PC in one hand, as well as with it sitting in your lap.

Make sure the LCD display device has a resolution high enough to take advantage of Microsoft's ClearType technologies. Tablet PCs use a digitizer under a standard 10.4-inch motion-sensitive LCD display to make the digital ink on the screen look like real ink on paper. To ensure you get the maximum benefits from the new ClearType technology, make sure the LCD display has a resolution of 800×600 in landscape mode and a 600×800 in portrait mode.

Test the Built-In Tablet PC Microphone and Speakers.

Although most application software, including Microsoft Office, recognizes human speech, it is important that the Tablet PC's built-in microphone operates at an acceptable level. If the microphone is not to your liking, you may want to purchase a close-talk headset with your Tablet PC. Increasingly more users are sending information as audio files, rather than relying solely on text. For this reason, you also should check the speakers on the Tablet PC to make sure they meet your standards.

Consider a Tablet PC with a Built-in PC Video Camera.

A PC video camera adds streaming video and still photography capabilities to your Tablet PC, while still allowing you to take notes in lectures or meetings.

Wireless Access to the Internet and Your E-Mail is Essential with a Tablet PC.

Make sure the Tablet PC has wireless networking (Bluetooth, Wi-Fi a/b/g, WiMAX, etc.), so you can access the Internet and your e-mail anytime and anywhere. Your Tablet PC also should include standard network connections, such as dial-up and Ethernet.

Review the Docking Capabilities of the Tablet PC.

The Tablet Technology in Windows Vista operating system supports a grab-and-go form of docking (Figure 19), so you can pick up and take a docked Tablet PC with you, just as you would pick up a notepad on your way to a meeting.

Figure 19 A Tablet PC docked to create a desktop computer with the Tablet PC as the monitor.

Review Available Accessories to Purchase with Your Tablet PC.

Tablet PC accessories include docking stations, mouse units, keyboards, security cables, additional memory and storage, protective hand-grips, screen protectors, and various types of digital pens.

How to Purchase a Personal Mobile Device

Whether you choose a PDA, a smart phone, an ultra personal computer, a portable media player, a handheld navigation device, or a handheld game console depends on where, when, and how you will use the device. If you need to stay organized when you are on the go, then a PDA may be the right choice. PDAs typically are categorized by the operating system they run. If you need to stay organized and in touch when on the go, then a smart phone or ultra personal computer may be the right choice. Choose a handheld navigation device if you often need directions or information about your surroundings. If you plan to relax and play games, then a handheld game console may be right for you. Busy professionals who are on

Figure 20 PDAs provide users with a multitude of tools and vary in cost from being provided free with a new wireless contract to costing thousands of dollars.

the move often carry more than one personal mobile device.

This section lists guidelines you should consider when purchasing a PDA (Figure 20), a smart phone, an ultra personal computer, a portable media player, a handheld navigation device, or a handheld game console. You also should visit the Web sites listed in Figure 21 to gather more information about the type of personal mobile device that best suits your computing needs.

Determine the Programs You Plan to Run on Your Device.

All PDAs and most smart phones can handle basic organizer-type software such as a calendar, an address book, and a notepad. Portable media players and handheld navigation devices usually have the fewest programs available to run on them. Ultra personal computers usually have the most number of programs available because the devices can run almost any personal computer software. The availability of other software depends on the operating system you choose.

The depth and breadth of software for the Palm OS is significant, with more than 20,000 basic programs and more than 600 wireless programs. Devices that run Windows-based operating systems, such as Windows Mobile, may have fewer programs available, but the operating system and application software are similar to those with which you are familiar, such as Word and Excel. When choosing a handheld game console, consider whether your favorite games are available for the device. Consider if you want extras on the device, such as the capability of playing media files.

Consider How Much You Want to Pay.

The price of a personal mobile device can range from $100 to more than $2,000, depending on its capabilities. Some Palm OS devices are at the lower end of the cost spectrum, and ultra personal computers often are at the higher end. A PDA will be less expensive than a smart phone with a similar configuration. For the latest prices, capabilities, and accessories, visit the Web sites listed in Figure 21.

Web Site	Web Address
CNET Shopper	shopper.cnet.com
iPOD	ipod.com
Palm	palm.com
Microsoft	windowsmobile.com pocketpc.com microsoft.com/smartphone
Oqo	oqo.com
MobileTechReview	pdabuyersguide.com
Nintendo	nintendo.com/channel/ds
Research in Motion	rim.com
Garmin	garmin.com
Symbian	symbian.com
Wireless Developer Network	wirelessdevnet.com
Sharp	www.myzaurus.com

For an updated list and links, click Buyer's Guide in the Features section at the Teachers Discovering Computers Web site (scsite.com/tdc5).

Figure 21 Web sites with reviews and information about personal mobile devices.

Determine Whether You Need Wireless Access to the Internet and E-mail or Mobile Telephone Capabilities with Your Device.

Smart phones often give you access to e-mail and other data and Internet services. Some PDAs, smart phones, ultra personal computers, and handheld game consoles include wireless networking capability to allow you to connect to the Internet wirelessly. These wireless features and services allow users to access real-time information from anywhere to help make decisions while on the go. Most portable media players do not include the capability to access Internet services.

For Wireless Devices, Determine How and Where You will use The Service.

When purchasing a wireless device, you must subscribe to a wireless service. Determine if the wireless network (carrier) you choose has service in the area where you plan to use the device. Some networks have high-speed data networks only in certain areas, such as large cities or business districts. Also, a few carriers allow you to use your device in other countries.

When purchasing a smart phone, determine if you plan to use the device more as a phone, PDA, or wireless data device. Some smart phones, such as those based on the Pocket PC Phone operating system or the Palm OS, are geared more for use as a PDA. Other smart phones, such as those based on Microsoft Smartphone or Symbian operating systems, mainly are phone devices that include robust PDA functionality. Blackberry-based smart phones include robust data features that are oriented to accessing e-mail and wireless data services.

Make Sure Your Device has Enough Memory and Storage.

Memory (RAM) is not a major issue with low-end devices with monochrome displays and basic organizer functions. Memory is a major issue, however, for high-end devices that have color displays and wireless features. Without enough memory, the performance level of your device will drop dramatically. If you plan to purchase a high-end device running the Palm OS operating system, the device should have at least 32 MB of RAM. If you plan to purchase a high-end device running the Windows Mobile operating system, the PDA should have at least 64 MB of RAM. An ultra personal computer can have 1 GB of RAM or more while a handheld navigation device may have over 2 GB of flash memory.

Many personal mobile devices include a hard disk for storage. Portable media players, ultra personal computers, and some smart phones include hard disks to store media and other data. Consider how much media and other data you need to store on your device. The hard disk size may range from 4 GB to more than 80 GB.

Practice with the Touch Screen, Handwriting Recognition, and Built-in Keyboard Before Deciding on a Model.

To enter data into a PDA, smart phone, and some ultra personal computers and handheld game consoles, you use a pen-like stylus to handwrite on the screen or a keyboard. The keyboard either slides out or is mounted on the front of the device. With handwriting recognition, the device translates the handwriting into a computerized font. You also can use the stylus as a pointing device to select items on the screen and enter data by tapping on an on-screen keyboard. By practicing data entry before buying a device, you can learn if one device may be easier for you to use than another. You also can buy third-party software to improve a device's handwriting recognition.

Decide Whether You Want a Color Display.

PDAs, ultra personal computers, some handheld navigation devices, and some handheld game consoles usually come with a color display that supports as many as 65,536 colors. Smart phones also have the option for color displays. Having a color display does result in greater on-screen detail, but it also requires more memory and uses more power. Resolution also influences the quality of the display.

Compare Battery Life.

Any mobile device is good only if it has the power required to run. For example, smart phones with monochrome screens typically have a much longer battery life than Pocket PC devices with color screens. The use of wireless networking will shorten battery time considerably. To help alleviate this problem, most devices have incorporated rechargeable batteries that can be recharged by placing the device in a cradle or connecting it to a charger.

Seriously Consider the Importance of Ergonomics.

Will you put the device in your pocket, a carrying case, or wear it on your belt? How does it feel in your hand? Will you use it indoors or outdoors? Many screens are unreadable outdoors. Do you need extra ruggedness, such as would be required in construction, in a plant, or in a warehouse? A smart phone with a PDA form factor may be larger than a typical PDA. A smart phone with a phone form factor may be smaller, but have fewer capabilities.

Check Out the Accessories.

Determine which accessories you want for your personal mobile device. Accessories include carrying cases, portable mini- and full-sized keyboards, removable storage, modems, synchronization cradles and cables, car chargers, wireless communications, global positioning system modules, digital camera modules, expansion cards, dashboard mounts, replacement styli, headsets, microphones, and more.

Decide Whether You Want Additional Functionality.

In general, off-the-shelf Microsoft operating system-based devices have broader functionality than devices with other operating systems. For example, voice-recording capability, e-book players, and media players are standard on most Windows Mobile devices. If you are leaning toward a Palm OS device and want these additional functions, you may need to purchase additional software or expansion modules to add them later. Determine whether your employer permits devices with cameras on the premises, and if not, do not consider devices with cameras. Some handheld game consoles include the capability to access the Web. High-end handheld navigation devices may include destination information, such as information about restaurants and points of interest, an e-book reader, a media player, and a currency converter.

Determine Whether Synchronization of Data with other Devices or Personal Computers is Important.

Most devices include a cradle that connects to the USB or serial port on your computer so you can synchronize data on your device with your desktop or notebook computer. Increasingly more devices are Bluetooth and/or wireless networking enabled, which gives them the capability of synchronizing wirelessly. Many devices today also have an infrared port that allows you to synchronize data with any device that has a similar infrared port, including desktop and notebook computers or other personal mobile devices.

Summary of Buyer's Guide

This special feature provides a solid foundation of knowledge to help you make informed decisions when purchasing computers and other related technologies. Topics covered include comparing desktop to notebook computers and specific information on purchasing these types of computers. You also learned about personal mobile devices, including smart phones, PDA, and similar devices.

Recall from Chapter 1 that one of the National Educational Technology Standards for Students states that students should be able to demonstrate a sound understanding of technology concepts, systems and operations. The standard also states that students should be able to transfer current knowledge to learning of new technologies. Share the knowledge that you have learned in this special feature with your students so they can make informed decisions when the time comes for them to purchase a computer or other related technologies. Help students understand that the technologies covered in this special feature are constantly evolving, and that in order to make informed decisions, you and your students need to have a good understanding of these technologies.

Integrating Digital Media and Educational Software Applications

5

Objectives

After completing this chapter, you will be able to do the following:
[ISTE NETS-T Standards I A-B, II A-E, III A-D, V A-D, VI B]

- Explain the differences between digital media and multimedia

- Name and define the elements of multimedia and of digital media

- Explain different uses of digital media applications

- Discuss digital media applications on the Web

- Identify various K-12 software applications

- Specify what is meant by an interactive media

- Examine the uses of digital media authoring software programs

- Explain why digital media applications are important for education

Today, digital media and multimedia play an increasingly important role in education, business, and entertainment. Digital media is multimedia that has evolved into a discipline of its own. Digital media is the realization of the dream that computer engineers have had for years, that is, for the computer to evolve from being simply a device for computation into one that is a tool with which humans can communicate and learn. The concept of digital media is the next step in this evolution of the computer. **Interactivity**, which is one of the essential features of digital media applications, also allows for individualized instruction and exploration, both of which enrich the educational experience.

This chapter introduces you to many basic digital media and multimedia concepts, discusses educational applications of digital media, and describes various media elements of multimedia. First, you learn about the different types and uses of digital media applications. Next, the chapter provides examples of a few of the hundreds of outstanding digital media education software applications that are available for teaching and learning, many of which are inexpensive. You then learn how to create, design, and present digital media presentations. Finally, the chapter reinforces the potential of digital media software applications to change dramatically the way students learn.

What Is Digital Media?

The terms technology, multimedia, and digital media are not mutually exclusive. In fact, in common usage, these terms overlap and are often used interchangeably. A brief discussion of each term follows to put each term in its historic perspective.

Technology was the term first associated with computer use in the classroom. Computers found their way into schools to be used in specialized training programs, such as graphic arts and applied sciences, such as auto mechanics, used in vocational and production education, and used in the office for administrative tasks. Using the term technology to describe this use of computers was a logical step.

The term **multimedia** by definition means "more than one media." Multimedia incorporates a variety of elements, including text, graphics, audio, video, and animation. Originally, a multimedia presentation did not have to be digital. For example, multimedia might have incorporated a slide show for visuals, a tape recorder for audio, and an overhead projector for text. But as software and hardware became capable of and adept at handling more than one media, the term multimedia was coined to define computer software applications and presentations that utilized more than one media.

Recall from Chapter 1 that **digital media** is defined as those technologies that allow users to create new forms of interaction, expression, communication, and entertainment in a digital format. Digital media uses all the elements of multimedia but in a digital format (Figure 5-1). The term digital media has not superseded or outdated the usefulness of the terms multimedia or technology. The term digital media simply underlines the pervasiveness of the use of digital formats for multimedia elements. Many applications previously defined as multimedia have seamlessly made the transition to digital media because they encompass all the elements of

Figure 5-1 Interactive digital media allows students to explore the world's knowledge in ways unheard of just a generation ago.

multimedia and digital media. The term digital media is evolving, and as a result, many digital media applications are still referred to as multimedia applications.

Have your students watched the space shuttle blast into orbit in person, viewed the Mona Lisa in the Louvre Museum, traveled to Egypt, or visited this nation's capital and explored its history? With digital media, your students can interact with and become part of these learning adventures and much more without ever physically setting foot outside of the classroom. Never before have students been able to explore the world in so many visual and interactive ways. Digital media is changing the way people work, learn, and play. Extensive research conducted over a period of more than 20 years confirms that the effective integration of multimedia applications, and now digital media, into the classroom curriculum can revolutionize the way today's digital students learn core and other subjects.

Digital media software refers to any computer-based presentation or application software that uses multimedia elements. By definition, digital media includes interaction, so some, but not all, digital media is also considered **interactive digital media**. Interactive digital media, by definition, allows users to move through information at their own pace. Interactive digital media also describes a digital media application that accepts input from the user by means of a keyboard, voice, simple movements, or a pointing device such as a mouse, and performs an action in response. Technology has evolved, for example, in video games where the player can indicate a response by simply making a gesture through an input device attached to his hand or foot. Well-designed applications provide feedback in the form of responses as the user progresses through the application or completes certain tasks.

The digital media application shown in Figure 5-2, for example, allows students to interact with and learn about the human body. The ability of users to interact with a digital media application is perhaps the most unique and important feature of digital media — a feature that has the potential to change dramatically the way digital students learn. Interactive digital media allows students to define their own learning paths, investigate topics in depth, and get immediate feedback from their exploration activities. Digital media applications also tend to engage and challenge students, thus encouraging them to think creatively and independently.

With many digital media applications, you navigate through the content by clicking links. Recall from Chapter 2 that Web pages use links to allow users to navigate quickly from one document to another. In a digital media application, links serve a similar function, allowing users to access information quickly and navigate from one topic to another in a nonlinear fashion. For example, while reading about Marco Polo, the user might click the keyword Travels to display a menu allowing the user to view a map of Marco Polo's journeys or listen to a reading from his travel journals.

Web Info

For more information about digital media applications, visit the Teachers Discovering Computers Web site (*scsite.com/tdc5*), click Chapter 5, click Web Info, and then click Digital Media Applications.

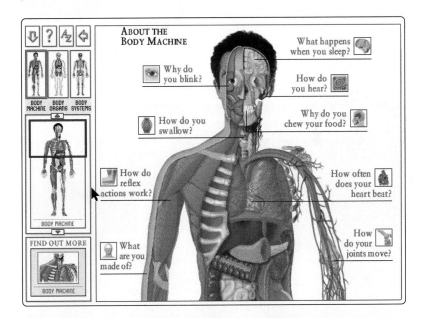

Figure 5-2 The Ultimate Human Body by Dorling Kindersley is a popular educational program that allows students to interact with and learn about the human body. Clicking the heart, for example, allows students to see and hear a video of a human heart in action.

In a digital media application, any clickable object — text, graphics, animation, and even videos — can function as a link. Figure 5-3 shows a menu of a digital media application that uses text, graphics, and animations as links to additional sources of information. Every object on the main menu is a link to discovery learning. The sections that follow provide an introduction to the different media elements contained originally in multimedia and now found in digital media applications.

barometer
image link

Integration Strategies

To learn more about integrating digital media applications, visit the Teachers Discovering Computers Web site (*scsite.com/tdc5*), click Chapter 5, and then click Digital Media Corner.

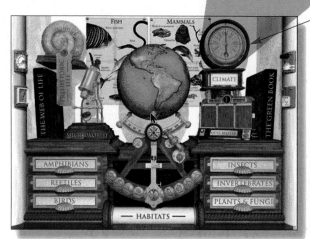

Figure 5-3 The bottom screen of the figure to the left shows a menu for one topic found in a popular nature encyclopedia. The upper-right screen shows an enlarged barometer, which opens when a user clicks the barometer and which provides additional links to other information.

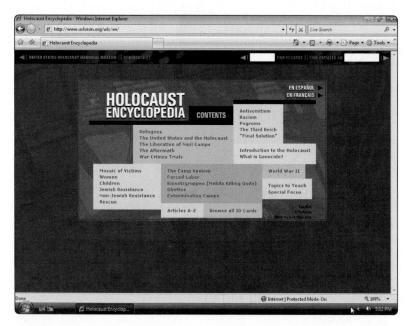

Figure 5-4 The main menu from the Holocaust Encyclopedia Web site provides text and links that allow teachers and students to access the listed topic quickly.

TEXT

Text consists of characters that are used to create words, sentences, and paragraphs and is a fundamental element used in all multimedia applications. Multimedia applications not only use ordinary text to convey basic information, they also use a variety of textual effects to emphasize and clarify information. A different font size, color, or style, for example, often is used to emphasize certain words or phrases.

Like graphics, animation, and other forms of media, text has a role in building multimedia applications. While text is easy to process visually, the use of hypertext linking has changed how we use text. Hypertext allows users to seek information that is personally meaningful.

Many multimedia and now digital media applications use text-based menus that allow you to display information on a selected topic (Figure 5-4).

GRAPHICS

Recall from Chapter 4 that a **graphic** is a digital representation of nontext information, such as a drawing, chart, or photograph. A graphic, also called a picture or image, contains no movement or animation.

In multimedia and digital media applications, graphics serve several functions. For one, graphics can illustrate certain concepts more vividly than text. A picture of Saturn, for example, clearly depicts the planet's rings in a way that text cannot. Graphics also play an important role in the learning process: many individuals — who are **visual learners** — may learn concepts faster or retain a higher percentage of material if they *see* the information presented graphically. Graphics also serve as navigational elements. Multimedia and digital media applications often use graphics as buttons that link to more information. The graphical user interfaces used on Macintosh computers, PCs, and graphical Web browsers also demonstrate the importance of graphics when using computers.

If you are creating a digital media presentation, you can obtain graphics in several ways. You can purchase a **clip art collection**, which is a set of previously created digital graphics that you can insert into a document. Many clip art collections are grouped by themes, such as Academic, Maps, and People. You also can create your own graphics using a paint or drawing program. Many presentation graphics and digital media authoring software packages, for example, include drawing tools for creating graphics, as shown in Figure 5-5. You can obtain photographs for use in digital media presentations by using a color scanner to digitize photos, taking photographs with a digital camera, or using a collection of photographs on a CD or DVD.

The lastest evolution of graphics technology is the move from two-dimensional (2D) to three-dimensional (3D) planes. Three-dimensional graphics provide the illusion of depth, creating a more realistic environment — which makes graphics more useful for simulation activities, such as flight simulators or video games.

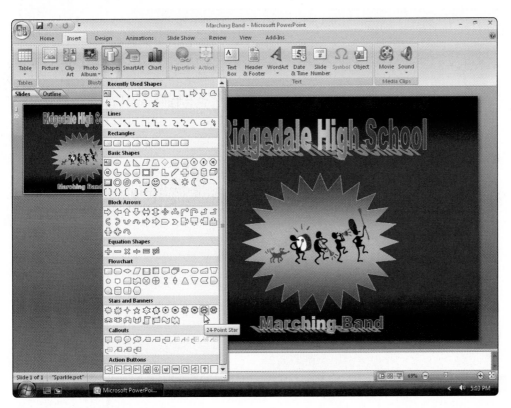

Figure 5-5 Microsoft PowerPoint provides a menu of shapes that allows you to draw a 24-point star or other shapes to include in a digital media presentation. This type of graphic image is a resizeable, movable object that can be colored in many different ways or combined with other clip art, graphics, or text.

Integration Strategies

To learn more about integrating animation, audio, and other digital media with your special needs students, visit the Teachers Discovering Computers Web site (*scsite.com/tdc5*), click Chapter 5, and then click Assistive Technologies.

ANIMATION

Displaying a series of still graphics creates an **animation**, which is a graphic that has the illusion of motion if played back at the proper framing rate. Animations range in scope from a basic graphic with a simple motion (for example, a blinking icon) to a detailed image with complex movements (such as a simulation of how an avalanche starts). As with graphics, animations can convey information more vividly than text alone. An animation showing the up-and-down movement of pistons and engine valves, as shown in Figures 5-6a through 5-6c for example, provides a better illustration of the workings of an internal combustion engine than a written explanation.

The use of animation has improved the quality of educational software dramatically and made Web sites more interesting for users. You can create your own detailed and highly dynamic animations using a graphics animation software package. In addition, you can obtain previously created animations from a CD, a DVD, or the Web.

AUDIO

Audio is any music, speech, or other sound. As with animation, audio allows digital media developers to provide information in a way that brings a concept or concepts to life. The vibration of a human heartbeat or the melodies of a symphony, for example, are concepts difficult to convey without the use of sound. Using audio in a digital media application to supplement text and graphics enhances understanding. An actor's narration added to the text of a Shakespearean play (Figure 5-7), for example, reinforces a student's grasp of the passage.

[b] piston down motion

[c] piston up motion

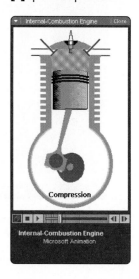

[a] snapshot

Figure 5-6 Microsoft's Encarta Encyclopedia contains numerous digital media animations, including a demonstration of how an internal combustion engine works. Figure 5-6a is a snapshot of the initial screen, Figure 5-6b shows that the piston has moved down during the intake stroke, and Figure 5-6c shows the piston moving up during the compression stroke.

Play button

Figure 5-7 Interactive encyclopedias offer students many opportunities to hear the words and passages of great historical events and literary works, such as Shakespeare's *Macbeth*. By clicking the Play button, students hear passages from *Macbeth*.

Integration Strategies

To learn more about creating and integrating video with your students, review the special feature, Digital Imaging and Video Technology, that follows this chapter.

You can obtain audio files for use in digital media applications in several different ways. One method is to capture sounds digitally using a microphone or any other audio input device that is plugged into a port on a sound card or a USB or FireWire port.

Musical Instrument Digital Interface (MIDI) is the electronic music industry's standard that defines how digital musical devices represent sounds electronically. Software programs that conform to the MIDI standard allow you to compose and edit music and other sounds. For example, you can change the speed, add notes, or rearrange the score to produce an entirely new sound. Most sound cards support the MIDI standard, so you can play and manipulate sounds on a computer that were created originally on another computer. As with graphics and animations, you also can purchase audio clips on a CD, DVD, or download them from thousands of Web sites.

VIDEO

Video consists of visual frames that are played back at speeds of 15 to 60 frames per second and provide full motion in real time. The integration of video into classroom curriculum has significantly influenced the way that students learn core subjects. Videos can reinforce lectures and readings, provide a common base of knowledge, and show things that students would not otherwise experience. For example, after reading the text of one of Martin Luther King's speeches, students can watch a video of King delivering that same speech to an enthusiastic crowd.

To use video in a digital media application, you must capture, digitize, and edit the video using special video production hardware and software. As described in Chapter 4, video often is captured digitally with a video input device such as a digital video camera.

Digital video originally required considerable amounts of storage space. With today's new video compression techniques, video can now be economically streamed, stored, and/or played on most computers. **Video compression** is accomplished in many ways. One of them is by taking advantage of the fact that only a small portion of the image changes from frame to frame. A compressed video might store all the data in the first reference frame and then, assuming that the following frames are almost identical to it, store only the data in a reference frame that specifies the changes from the first frame to the next. The compression program continues to reduce the amount of stored data in this manner.

Web Info

For an overview of digital video software, visit the Teachers Discovering Computers Web site (*scsite.com/tdc5*), click Chapter 5, click Web Info, and then click Digital Video.

Prior to viewing, the compressed video must be decompressed so that the video is restored to its original condition. The video compression software decompresses the video segment so it can be viewed. The **Motion Pictures Experts Group** (**MPEG**) has defined a set of standards for video compression and decompression called **MPEG** (pronounced em-peg). These standardized **CODEC** (**c**ompression and **dec**ompression) compression methods reduce the size of video files significantly.

Video compression and other improvements in video technology have allowed video to play a more important role in digital media applications. For example, Web sites such as Google Video and YouTube offer thousands of videos

that can be played on your computer. Technologies such as streaming video also have made video a viable part of digital media on the Web.

Digital Media Applications

A **digital media application** involves the use of digital media technology in education, business, and entertainment (Figure 5-8). Businesses use digital media, for example, in interactive advertisements and for job- and skill-training applications. Teachers use digital media applications to deliver classroom presentations that enhance student learning. Students, in turn, use digital

Figure 5-8 People use digital media applications at home, work, and school.

media applications to learn by reading, seeing, hearing, and interacting with the subject content. Digital media is used in a wide variety of computerized games and other types of entertainment, as well.

Another important application of digital media is to create **simulations**, which are computer-based models of real-life situations. Digital media simulations often replace costly and sometimes hazardous demonstrations and training in areas, such as chemistry, biology, medicine, and aviation.

The following sections provide a more detailed look at different types of well-known digital media applications, including computer-based training, electronic books and references, how-to guides, newspapers, and magazines. These sections also address the use of digital media in entertainment, virtual reality, information kiosks, and the importance of digital media on the World Wide Web. After learning about the various types of well-known digital media applications, you will learn about specific K-12 educational software applications used to improve teaching and learning by virtually all schools.

COMPUTER-BASED TRAINING (CBT)

Computer-based training (CBT) is a tool that allows individuals to learn by using and completing exercises using instructional software on computers. More recently, this type of training has been referred to as **individual-lead training (ILT)** because the training focuses more on the learner than on the instructor. Computer-based training is popular in business, industry, and education to teach new skills or enhance the existing skills of employees. Athletes, for example, use digital media computer-based training programs to practice baseball, football, soccer, tennis, and golf skills, while airlines use digital CBT simulations to train employees. School districts and universities use face-to-face and online CBT to train teachers how to teach math, reading, computer skills, and many other subjects. Interactive CBT software called **courseware** usually is available on CD, DVD, or the Web.

One important advantage of computer-based training is that it allows for flexible, on-the-spot training. Businesses and schools, for example, can set up corporate training or teacher professional development labs so employees can update their skills without leaving the workplace (Figure 5-9). Installing CBT software on an employee's computer or on the company network provides even more flexibility — allowing employees to update their job skills right at their desks, at home, or while traveling.

Computer-based training provides a unique learning experience because learners receive instant feedback — in the form of positive response for correct answers or actions, additional information on incorrect answers, and immediate scoring and results. Testing and self-diagnostic features allow instructors to verify that an individual has mastered curriculum objectives and identify students who need additional instruction or practice. Computer-based training is especially effective for teaching software skills if the CBT is integrated with the software application because it allows students to practice using the software as they learn.

Integration Strategies

To learn more about integrating digital media applications and the Web into your curriculum, visit the Teachers Discovering Computers Web site (*scsite.com/tdc5*), click Chapter 5, and then click Teaching Today.

Figure 5-9 Teachers can learn innovative uses of technology, teaching strategies, and various curriculum-related software in a school district's professional development center.

ELECTRONIC BOOKS AND REFERENCES

Imagine a library in your hands and in the hands of your students. Read your favorite *Harry Potter* or *Star Wars* novel, delete it, and download the complete works of Hemingway. The electronic book became popular several years ago making reading a digital activity for digital kids. Many analysts predict that electronic books will revolutionize the publishing industry and impact education in many positive, imaginative, and yet-to-be determined ways.

An **electronic book**, or **e-book**, is a small, book-sized computer that allows users to read, save, highlight, bookmark, and add notes to online text. To obtain the same functionality of an e-book device for your personal computer, notebook computer, Tablet PC, or PDA, you can download and install free e-book reader software programs, such as Microsoft Reader and Adobe Acrobat eBook Reader, from the Web.

iPod Books are digital books that are accessed on an iPod (Figure 5-10) using software that can be downloaded from the Apple iPod Web site. iPod Books also are available at various Web sites that provide books created by established authors as well as those created by students who author their own books and submit them for distribution.

Electronic books have many of the elements of a regular book, including pages of text and graphics. You generally turn the pages of an electronic book by clicking icons. A table of contents, glossary, and index also are available at the click of a button. To display a definition or a graphic, play a sound or video sequence, or connect to a Web site, you simply click a link (often a bold or underlined word).

E-book content is obtainable in a number of ways, from purchasing unlimited use or time-based permits, in which the e-book content disappears after the amount of time purchased has expired, to obtaining free e-book content.

Figure 5-10 In addition to songs and video, Apple's iPod can store hundreds of digital books. Students can even load their own literary creations.

For example, **Project Gutenberg** makes thousands of literary and reference books and materials available free to everyone (Figure 5-11). The e-book revolution is just beginning to impact the way people live, teach, and learn; continue to look for new ways to use and integrate e-book applications in teaching and learning.

Figure 5-11 Geoffrey Chaucer's *The Canterbury Tales* is among the thousands of public domain reference and literary works available from Project Gutenberg (*www.gutenberg.net*).

Another popular type of electronic book is an electronic reference text, such as a digital media encyclopedia on CD or DVD. An **electronic reference text**, which uses text, graphics, sound, animation, and video to explain a topic or provide additional information, is a digital version of a reference text. The multimedia encyclopedia, Microsoft Encarta, for example, includes the complete text of a multivolume encyclopedia. In addition to text-based information, Microsoft Encarta includes thousands of photos, animations, audio, and detailed illustrations. This array of digital media information is accessible via menus and links.

Electronic reference texts, such as digital media encyclopedias, also are available on the Web. Figure 5-12 lists a cross section of electronic reference texts that are available for home and school use.

Name	Publisher	URL	Description
Encarta Encyclopedia Premium	Microsoft	www.microsoft.com	Combines a number of great resources, including Encarta Encyclopedia Deluxe, Encarta Interactive World Atlas, Learning Tools, and more. Also includes translation dictionaries, homework tools, dynamic multimedia, streaming video, and updates.
Wikipedia	WikiMedia	www.wikipedia.org	The biggest multilingual free-content encyclopedia on the Internet. Over two million collaboratively written articles with thousands of images and reference links to explore.
Children's Encyclopedia	Dorling-Kindersley	www.dk.com	Delivers an interactive experience for younger students that combines fascinating and educational interactive reference materials that support learning by stimulating children's natural desire to explore.
Encyclopedia Britannica	Encyclopedia Britannica	www.britannica.com	Contains over 82,000 articles, more than 13,000 images, 1,600 clickable maps and 4,000 indexed timeline entries with Web links, videos, audio clips, and more.
American Sign Language Dictionary	Lifeprint Institute	www.lifeprint.com	Uses text, hundreds of step-by-step photos, animations, and illustrations to teach over 2,600 signs; includes curriculum workbooks, learning games, and finger spelling.

Figure 5-12 These electronic reference texts use digital media to clarify topics for students and supply additional information about thousands of subjects.

In addition to education, health and medicine are areas in which electronic references play an important role. For example, instead of using volumes of books, health professionals and students rely on electronic references for articles, photographs, illustrations, and animations that cover hundreds of health and first aid topics. Physical education, science, and medical students, for example, use the reference A.D.A.M. (Animated Dissection of Anatomy for Medicine) (Figure 5-13) to learn about the human body. A.D.A.M. includes physician-reviewed text, health visuals produced by medically trained illustrators, and multimedia interactivity which includes over 20,000 identifiable anatomical structures. Practicing physicians also use the software to communicate information to their patients.

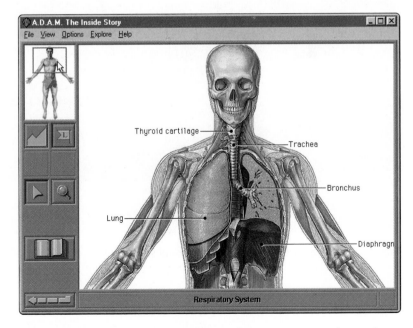

Figure 5-13 Interactive CDs or DVDs, such as A.D.A.M., can be used to study the respiratory system and other systems of the body.

Web Info

To view an online how-to guide, visit the Teachers Discovering Computers Web site (*scsite.com/tdc5*), click Chapter 5, click Web Info, and then click Guide.

HOW-TO GUIDES

Today, many interactive digital media applications are available to help individuals in their daily lives. These digital media applications fall into the broad category of how-to guides. **How-to guides** are digital media applications that include step-by-step instructions and interactive demonstrations to teach you practical new skills (Figure 5-14). Similar to computer-based training applications used by schools and businesses, how-to guides allow you to acquire new skills, become more productive, and try out your skills in a risk-free environment. The skills you learn with a how-to guide, however, usually apply to enhancing talents outside of your job.

How-to guides can help you buy a home or a car; design a garden; plan a vacation; repair your home, car, or computer; and more. Landscaping how-to guides, for example, allow you to design a landscape; place trees, shrubs, and flowers; and then add features such as pathways, fences, and retaining walls to complete the design (Figure 5-15). Many gardening how-to guides allow you to explore a database of plants with color photographs and the growth attributes of each one. Digital media how-to guides are available on CD, DVD, and the Web.

DIGITAL MEDIA NEWSPAPERS, MAGAZINES (E-ZINES), AND JOURNALS

A **digital media newspaper**, a **digital media magazine**, and a **digital media journal** are digital versions of a newspaper, magazine, or journal distributed on CD, DVD, or via the World Wide Web. An **electronic magazine**, or **e-zine**, is a digital publication available on the Web.

Digital media newspapers, magazines, and journals usually include the sections and articles found in print-based versions, such as departments, editorials, and more. Unlike printed publications, however, electronic magazines use many types of media

Name	Publisher	URL	Description
IMSI FloorPlan	Broderbund	www.broderbund.com	Customize your current floor plans or plan a new 3D Version home. Software has 2-D and 3-D editing tools.
Emily Post's Complete Guide to Weddings	M2K	www.m-2k.com	Planning the ultimate wedding, but not sure where to start? This software will help you plan and organize every detail of your wedding from guest list, to seating arrangements, to negotiating prices for photographers and musicians.
Master Landscape & Home Design	Punch! Software	www.punchsoftware.com	Design a garden or entire yard by using scanned photos of your own property; choose trees, shrubs, flowers, and vines. You also can view sample gardens, and then view the plants as they grow and change with the seasons.
MasterCook Deluxe	ValuSoft	www.mastercook.com	Prepare more than 8000 dishes based on nutritional value and ingredients on hand. Watch instructional videos and adjust the portions to the number of servings needed.
Teach Yourself PC Maintenance	Learn2.com, Inc.	www.tutorials.com	Learn computer concepts and terms and learn how to install drives and accessory hardware, such as memory, modems, maintenance tools, how to clean your keyboard, and more from interactive tutorials.

Figure 5-14 These how-to guides teach useful skills by using videos, interactive demonstrations, and animations.

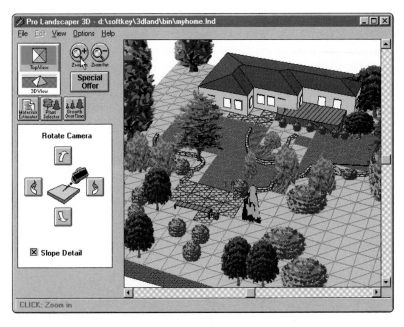

Figure 5-15 This how-to landscaping guide shows a 3-D view of a house with plants, trees, patio, and garden area.

to convey information. Audio and video clips can be included to showcase recent album releases or movies; animations can depict weather patterns or election results.

Many popular magazines and most newspapers have companion Web sites that provide digital media versions of some or all of their printed content (Figure 5-16).

Name	URL
Independent Newspapers (South Africa)	iol.co.za
Kyodo News (Tokyo)	home.kyodo.co.jp
National Geographic	nationalgeographic.com
Newsweek	newsweek.msnbc.com
The Daily Telegraph (London)	www.telegraph.co.uk
The Globe and Mail (Canada)	globeandmail.ca
The New York Times	nytimes.com
The Wall Street Journal	wsj.com
Time	time.com
USA TODAY	usatoday.com
Washington Post	washingtonpost.com

Web Info

To access an online educational magazine, visit the Teachers Discovering Computers Web site (*scsite.com/tdc5*), click Chapter 5, click Web Info, and then click Educational Magazine.

Figure 5-16 This list contains only a few of the hundreds of digital media newspapers and magazines from dozens of countries that use video and audio clips, animations, and other interactive digital media tools to bring the world to homes and classrooms.

Some digital media magazines exist only in their digital format, whereas others are simply electronic versions of existing print magazines. Up-to-the-minute news, interactive polls, and digital media elements such as audio and video clips enhance the content found in the printed magazine.

Educators also have access to hundreds of online education journals covering a variety of curriculum areas. Figure 5-17 shows a searchable Web site that provides information on and links to many education journals. Many education journals contain refereed or peer reviewed articles. **Peer review** or **refereeing** is a process of submitting an author's work or ideas to the scrutiny of others who are experts in the field. Peer reviewing is used primarily by journal editors to select and to screen manuscripts submitted for publication.

ENTERTAINMENT AND EDUTAINMENT

As described, digital media combines text, graphics, audio, video, animation, and interactivity — thus making it ideal for entertainment (Figure 5-18). Digital media **computer games**, for example, use a combination of simulation, animations, graphics, audio, and video to create a realistic and entertaining game. Often, the game simulates a real or fictitious world, in which you play the role of a character and have direct control of what happens in the game.

The music industry also sells interactive digital media applications on CDs and DVDs. Some interactive music CDs, for example, let you play musical instruments along with your favorite musician, read about the musician's life and interests, and even create your own version of popular songs. Like interactive games, these applications give you a character role and put you in control of the application. Many digital media applications are used for **edutainment**, which is an experience meant to be both educational and entertaining (Figure 5-19).

Figure 5-17 Many print-based journals and magazines have companion Web sites. This Web site provides links to and information on hundreds of education journals.

Name	Publisher	URL	Description
Backyard Baseball	Atari	http://www.atari.com/us/	Select players from 30 Major League Baseball teams or create your own team colors, ballpark, and strategy. Play online with other Windows users.
Dogz	Nintendo	www.nintendo.com	Use voice recognition to train your Dogz to sit, fetch, or roll over; create custom scenes with the Play Scene Editor.
Motocross Madness	Microsoft	www.microsoft.com	Perform stunts on your motorbike while you race up to eight opponents online via the MSN Gaming Zone.
Empire in Arms	Matrix Games	www.matrixgames.com	Play this game of grand strategy alone or with up to six other players via e-mail or on the Internet.
The Sims	Electronic Arts	www.thesims.com	Develop characters in a neighborhood, build their homes, and display your creations on the World Wide Web with these open-ended games.

Figure 5-18 Entertainment applications, rich in digital media content, provide fun for both children and adults.

Name	Publisher	URL	Description
ClueFinders	Broderbund	www.cluefinders.com	Go on amazing adventures through uncharted islands, rain forests, and other exotic locations with the ClueFinders gang. Your mission is to help the ClueFinders solve a mystery while mastering skills across the curriculum.
Harry Potter	Warner Brothers	www.harrypotter.com	Read extensive information on Harry Potter books at this official Harry Potter Web site where you can attend the Hogswarts School of Witchcraft and Wizardry, receive Quidditch training, and much more.
SimCity4	Electronic Arts	www.simcity.ea.com	Explore SimCity, one of the more widely used student edutainment games. With SimCity, you can create an entire city from the ground up.
Reader Rabbit	Broderbund	www.readerrabbit.com	Try out top-selling programs that teach young children problem solving, decision making, and logic skills. Offers help and prints reports.
The New Way Things Work	Global Software	www.learnatglobal.com	Discover how hundreds of machines work by viewing animations, illustrations, and videos.

Figure 5-19 Examples of Edutainment applications. Edutainment applications offer teachers and students both education and entertainment.

VIRTUAL REALITY

Virtual reality (VR) is the use of a computer to create an artificial environment that appears and feels like a real environment and allows you to explore space and manipulate the setting. In its simplest form, a virtual reality application displays a view that appears to be three-dimensional. The view might be of a place or an object, such as a landscape, a building, or a molecule, which users can explore. The lastest evolution in VR is **converged media**, the interaction of virtual reality with live performance. Converged media is especially useful in things like police and military training where a totally live interaction might be dangerous.

Some forms of VR software require you to wear specialized headgear, body suits, and gloves to enhance the experience of the artificial environment. The headgear displays the artificial environment in front of your eyes. The body suit and gloves sense your motion and direction, allowing you to move through and pick up and hold items displayed in the virtual environment.

Your first encounter with VR is likely to be a Web-based virtual reality game or virtual field trip. In such games, as you walk around the game's electronic landscape, the site notes your movements and changes your view of the landscape accordingly. Other VR Web sites allow you to take VR tours of a city, view hotel accommodations, tour a university, or interact with local attractions.

A popular example of virtual reality on the Web is Second Life (Figure 5-20), which is a 3-D virtual world entirely built and owned by its residents. Since opening to the public in 2003, it has grown explosively and today is inhabited by millions of students, teachers, and people from around the globe.

Figure 5-20 Second Life is a popular Web site that uses virtual reality extensively.

The United States Senate Web site provides a virtual tour of the U.S. Capitol building. Students can take a guided tour or venture out on their own to tour the Capitol (Figure 5-21).

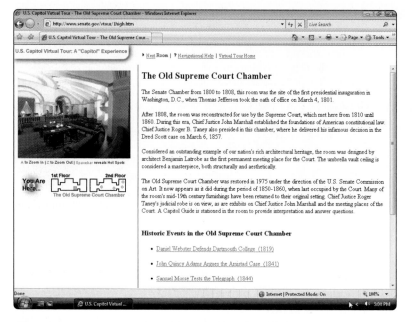

Figure 5-21 The Web allows students to take virtual tours of many historic locations all over the world.

Web Info

To take a virtual tour of a museum, visit the Teachers Discovering Computers Web site (*scsite.com/tdc5*), click Chapter 5, click Web Info, and then click Tour.

Companies use VR for more practical, commercial applications as well. Office furniture companies have created virtual showrooms in which customers wander among and inspect available products. Automobile and airplane manufacturers are using virtual prototypes to test new models and shorten product design time. Telecommunications firms and others are using computer-based VR applications for employee training. As computing power and the use of the Web increase, practical applications of VR continue to emerge for education, business, and entertainment.

INFORMATION KIOSKS

An **information kiosk** is a computerized information or reference center that allows you to select various options to browse through or find specific information. A typical information kiosk is a self-service structure equipped with computer hardware and software. Kiosks often use touch screen monitors or keyboards for input devices and have all of the data and information needed for the application stored directly on the computer.

Information kiosks provide information in public places where visitors or customers have common questions. Locations such as shopping centers, hotels, airports, colleges, and universities, for example, use kiosks to provide information on available services, product locations, maps, and other information (Figure 5-22). Museums and libraries use kiosks to allow visitors to find the location of a specific exhibit. Kiosks providing Internet access also are expected to be popular in the near future.

Figure 5-22 Airline travelers check in and print their boarding passes using a self-service kiosk.

DIGITAL MEDIA AND THE WORLD WIDE WEB

While you have explored the multitude of Web sites provided at this textbook's Web site, you might have come to the conclusion that digital media applications play an important role on the World Wide Web. In fact, much of the information on the Web today relies on digital media. Using digital media brings a Web page to life, increases the types of information available on the Web, expands the Web's potential uses, and makes the Internet a more entertaining and educational place to explore.

As described in Chapter 2, the Web uses many types of media to deliver information and enhance a user's Web experience (Figure 5-23). Graphics, animations, audio, and video reinforce text-based content and provide updated information. Many of the digital media applications described previously, including computer-based training, newspapers, e-zines, games, and virtual reality, are deliverable via the Web.

WEB-BASED TRAINING (WBT) AND DISTANCE LEARNING

Web-based training (WBT) is an approach to computer-based training that uses the technologies of the Internet and the World Wide Web. As with CBT, Web-based training typically consists of self-directed, self-paced instruction on a topic. Because it is delivered via the Web, however, WBT has the advantage of being able to offer up-to-date content on any type of computer platform. As a result, Web-based training already has replaced many traditional computer-based training applications. Over the past few years, the number of organizations using Web-based training has exploded. Today, almost every major corporation in the United States provides employees with some type of Web-based training to teach new skills or upgrade their current skills.

Web-based training also is available for individuals at home or at work. Many school districts are using the Web to deliver all types of training to their teachers. WBT offers anytime, anyplace training.

Today, anyone with access to the Web can take advantage of hundreds of digital media tutorials offered online. Such tutorials cover a range of topics, from how to change a flat tire to using (Figure 5-24) and integrating Microsoft Office in the classroom. Many of these Web sites are free; others ask you to register and pay a fee to take the complete Web-based training course.

Distance learning, also called **distance education**, **Web-based education**, and **distributed learning**, is the delivery of education from one location to another; the learning takes place at a remote location. Most colleges and universities now offer numerous distance learning courses, usually in the form of Web-based or Web-enhanced courses (Figure 5-25 on the next page).

Figure 5-23 A NASA Web server offers textual and graphical information about the AIM (Aeronomy of Ice in Mesosphere) mission.

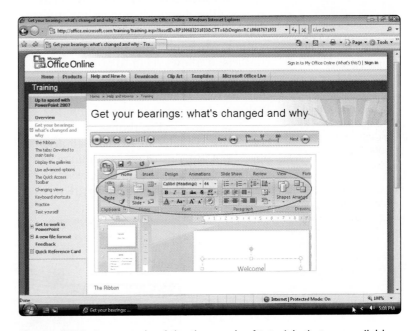

Figure 5-24 An example of the thousands of tutorials that are available on the Web.

A Web-based course, often called an **online course**, is a course that is taught mostly or completely on the Web, rather than in a traditional classroom. A **blended course** has a combination of face-to-face class meetings and online course sessions. A **Web-enhanced course** is a traditional classroom course that uses the Web to enhance the content of the course.

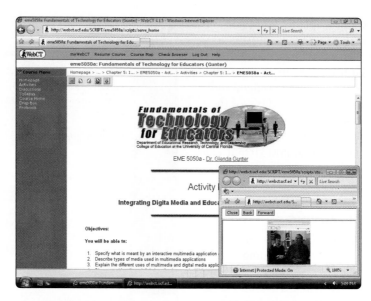

Figure 5-25 Many colleges and universities provide their online courses using Blackboard, WebCT, or eCollege learning systems, some courses incorporate instructional videos.

COLLEGES AND UNIVERSITIES Web-based courses offer many advantages for students who live far from a college or university campus, work full-time, or have scheduling conflicts; it allows them to attend class from home or other locations at any time that fits their schedule. The availability of Web-based courses has exploded in the past few years. Today, thousands of online classes are available in virtually all disciplines and millions of undergraduate and graduate students take online classes every term. Many colleges and universities now offer advanced degrees, including doctorate degrees in which all required courses are offered online. Other colleges and universities offer advanced degrees in which the majority of required courses are offered online.

In addition, a number of fully accredited universities no longer provide traditional courses; 100 percent of their courses and degrees are provided online. For example, Walden University is one of the leading fully accredited 100% online universities in the world (Figure 5-26). Walden University

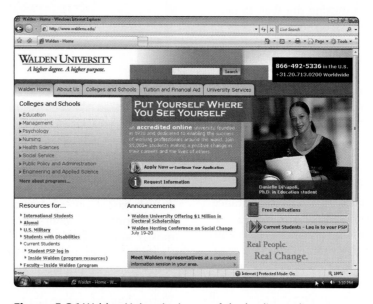

Figure 5-26 Walden University is one of the leading online universities providing graduate degrees for teachers and administrators.

provides online courses and graduate degrees in education, psychology, health and human services, management, engineering, computer science, business administration, and many other curriculum areas.

HIGH SCHOOLS   Most, if not all, states are now providing Web-based or online courses for their high school students (Figure 5-27). Web-based courses help prevent overcrowding and provide instruction for homebound students. Web-based courses also allow less-populated districts and schools in rural areas to share teachers.

By using the Web, these schools can offer specialized classes in French, Latin, calculus, and many other core and advanced subjects. By pooling resources and linking students from more than one school into a Web-based course, school districts can expand the number and type of classes they offer.

Many teachers are Web-enhancing their classes (Figure 5-28). By Web-enhancing their classes, teachers provide their students with resources to enrich their learning experience. Parents also can access the Web sites to check on homework assignments, activities, student expectations, and more.

Another benefit of using the Web in the classroom is having students interact with subject area experts. The Smithsonian Institution, for example, permits teachers and students to interact via the Web with the scientists who work for the Smithsonian. Many scientists want to increase educational opportunities for students, who someday may decide to become scientists. The special features that follow chapters 3 and 7 contains extensive information on how you can Web-enhance your classes using Web pages, blogs, wikis, podcasts, and other digital tools.

PROFESSIONAL DEVELOPMENT TRAINING
Until recently, in-service professional development training for teachers and administrators has remained basically unchanged for decades. Traditional in-service training involves teachers being trained in classrooms or labs and normally is conducted before or after school, on weekends, during in-service days, or during the summer. Schools often have to provide substitutes when teachers are required to be out of the

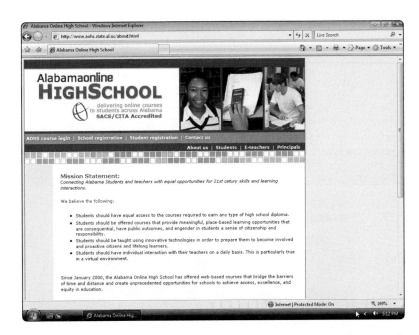

Figure 5-27 The Alabama Online High School enables principals to enroll students in online classes; for example, an individual student who needs a course that does not fit into her regular schedule or a group of students who need a course not offered in their school.

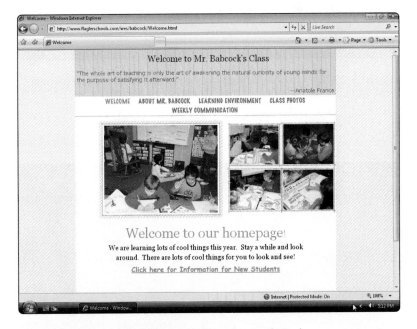

Figure 5-28 Many K-12 teachers Web-enhance their classes as a way to provide extensive resources and more for their students.

classroom to participate in extensive professional development training.

The traditional model of professional development training is undergoing a revolution — a Web-based or online revolution. Professional development training programs are being redefined in many school districts and state programs. States and school districts are adopting online training as a way to train their teachers in many areas, from technology, to English as a second language, to meeting recertification requirements, to a series of online courses leading to alternative certification. As a result of this professional development revolution, hundreds of thousands of K-12 teachers and

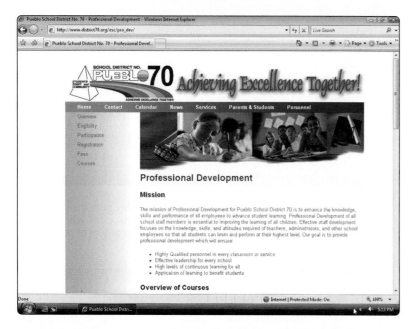

Figure 5-29 Many school districts provide extensive online professional development opportunities for their teachers and administrators.

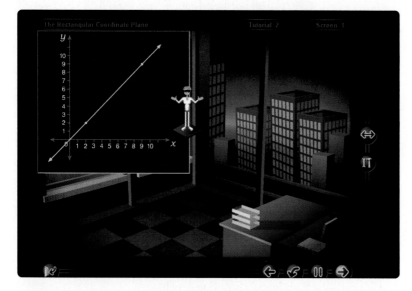

Figure 5-30 Destination Math is an example of an interactive digital media math program that provides students with nontraditional ways to master math skills correlated to state standards.

administrators now are involved in some type of online professional development training, and this is only the beginning. Currently, a great deal of in-service professional development training for teachers and administrators is being done online. A number of school districts and even some states have developed online portals for their teachers to enroll in professional development courses, access resources, and receive assistance (Figure 5-29).

Many companies now work with school districts to provide graduate courses and online professional development training for teachers and administrators. Online professional development training can be self-paced or instructor-led. Most online professional development training available for teachers is self-paced. In **self-paced training**, teachers typically sign up for a specific course or module, and after completing all the requirements, they receive credit for the training. Some self-paced training courses provide access to a Help desk or instructors who can provide assistance. In contrast, **instructor-led training** involves continuous interaction with an instructor and the courses are more structured, often including schedules and assignment due dates. Instructor-led training normally is more effective and has fewer drop-outs than self-paced training, but is considerably more expensive.

K-12 Educational Software Applications

As described in previous sections, digital media is important not only for business and entertainment, but also for education. An **educational software application** refers to computer software products used to support teaching and learning of subject-related content. Interactive digital media applications enrich the learning process by providing individualized instruction and exploration; allowing students to examine their skills in a risk-free environment; and providing instant feedback, testing, and review. Many educational software applications now are correlated to state standards (Figure 5-30).

The number and quality of educational software applications designed specifically for the K-12 learning environment have increased dramatically in the past few years. Educational software applications are available in many different designs, forms, and curriculum levels, as shown in Figure 5-31. Figure 5-31a allows teachers to pretest students' knowledge before they enter a particular level of instruction. Science Web sites, such as the biology site shown in Figure 5-31b, help students learn basic science concepts before entering the lab so they can focus on the actual hands-on experiment when in the lab.

The next sections discuss computer-assisted instruction, drill-and-practice, educational games, tutorials, educational simulations, integrated learning systems, and curriculum-specific software applications. Chapters 6 and 7 provide you with ways to integrate these types of software programs into your classroom curriculum.

COMPUTER-ASSISTED INSTRUCTION (CAI)

Computer-assisted instruction (CAI) has been used in education for more than two decades. Computer-assisted instruction is software designed to help teach facts, information, and/or skills associated with subject-related materials. At its most basic level, computer-assisted instruction is using a computer to enhance instruction. Most educators, however, do not feel that the term computer-assisted instruction accurately describes the many different computer-based educational software programs available today. With the growth of educational technology, the teaching profession has seen the emergence of other names used to refer to education software, such as computer-based instruction (CBI), computer-based learning (CBL), and computer-aided learning (CAL). For the purposes of this textbook, the term educational software applications is used as an umbrella term that emcompasses the other terms and that refers to computer software products that support teaching and learning of subject-related content (Figure 5-32).

Web Info

For links to popular education-related computer-based applications, visit the Teachers Discovering Computers Web site (*scsite.com/tdc5*), click Chapter 5, click Web Info, and then click Educational Applications.

[a] math program

[b] science Web site

Figure 5-31 Digital media applications are great tools to help teach difficult math and science concepts.

Figure 5-32 An educational multimedia application designed to teach young learners basic reading skills.

DRILL-AND-PRACTICE SOFTWARE

Drill-and-practice software is software that first supplies factual information and then through repetitive exercises allows students to continue to work on specific materials to remember or memorize the information. Another name is **skills-reinforcement software**. Drill-and-practice software is effective for learning basic skills and for remediation. **Remediation** is reviewing content many times and using alternative ways until a student grasps the concepts being taught.

One of the important features of drill-and-practice software and other educational software is that students receive instant feedback on correct and incorrect answers. Using drill-and-practice software can increase students' performance in areas that are weak. Drill-and-practice software usually has built-in features that allow the computer to move the student to the next level automatically when she masters a level. Drill-and-practice software is effective when used with students who require extra assistance in content instruction.

EDUCATIONAL GAMES

Today, the majority of educational games are available on CDs, DVDs, and on the Web. **Educational games** usually include a set of rules, and students can compete against other students or the game itself.

Games can be an effective way to teach content through repetition and practice.

Many students find educational games a fun way to learn. Various educational games create problem-solving environments forcing students to use higher-order thinking skills, for example, problem solving skills, to find solutions.

In his book *What Video Games Have to Teach Us About Learning and Literacy*, James Gee discusses how video games (especially those in which the player takes on a role of a fantasy character moving through an elaborate world) teach many things, regardless of specific content. Dr. Gee has identified up to 36 learning principles, most of them taken in a social learning context (what he refers to as "social achievement skills"), that are present in well-developed games. Video games promote and facilitate problem solving and students gladly accept the challenge, even without any lengthy introductory instruction.

Many games are provided for free to students and teachers. For example, *Ready To Learn* is an innovative learning partnership between PBS and the U.S. Department of Education. *Ready To Learn* integrates free and universally available children's educational television and online resources with community outreach to help parents and educators prepare today's digital kids for success in school. Figure 5-33 shows the PBS KIDS Web site where digital kids

Web Info

To access PBS Parents, PBS KIDS, PBS KIDS GO!, and PBS TeacherSource, visit the Teachers Discovering Computers Web site (*scsite.com/tdc5*), click Chapter 5, click Web Info, and then click Ready To Learn.

Figure 5-33 PBS KIDS is a great and safe Web resource for today's young digital kids up to 8 years old.

up to 8 years old can learn and play with all of their favorite characters through games, music, and more.

PBS also provides a Web site, PBS KIDS GO!, for digital kids ages 6–12, where they can share their opinions and stories, play games, solve puzzles, and much more (Figure 5-34). The *Ready to Learn* partnership also provides a Web site for parents (PBS Parents) and for teachers (PBS TeacherSource). To access all of these *Ready To Learn* Web sites, see the Web Info on the preceding page.

TUTORIALS

A **tutorial** is a teaching program designed to help individuals learn to use a product or concepts. Tutorials are designed to tutor, or instruct. Many software products contain built-in tutorials to teach the user how to use the software. Developers create educational tutorials that use the computer to provide an entire instructional area and are created so students can work their way through the tutorial to learn content without any help or other materials. The teaching solutions provided by tutorials range from a structured linear approach with specific content objectives to a nonlinear approach that offers alternative paths through the lesson based on students' responses, called **branching**. Branching reflects classroom learning theory by allowing students to excel at their own pace, providing feedback and remediation when needed. Figure 5-35 provides some of the features of effective educational tutorials.

EDUCATIONAL SIMULATIONS

An **educational computer simulation** or a **video game** is a computerized model of real life that represents a physical or simulated process. These programs are unique because the user can cause things to happen, change the conditions, and make decisions based on the criteria provided to simulate real-life situations. These interactive programs model some event, reality, real-life circumstances, or phenomenon. Simulations offer learners the opportunity to manipulate variables that affect the outcomes of the experience. Using simulation is not a new teaching strategy. As you learned earlier in this chapter, business and

Figure 5-34 The PBS KIDS GO! Web site provides games, digital storytelling, and much more for digital kids ages 6–12.

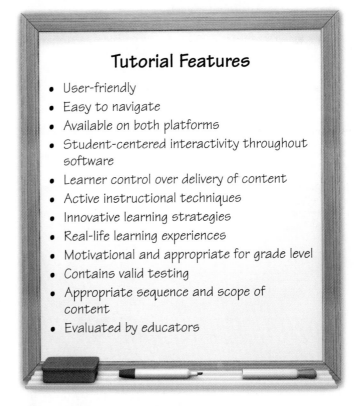

Tutorial Features

- User-friendly
- Easy to navigate
- Available on both platforms
- Student-centered interactivity throughout software
- Learner control over delivery of content
- Active instructional techniques
- Innovative learning strategies
- Real-life learning experiences
- Motivational and appropriate for grade level
- Contains valid testing
- Appropriate sequence and scope of content
- Evaluated by educators

Figure 5-35 Features of effective educational tutorials.

industry have been using simulation for many years.

Interest is growing in programs, such as SimCity, Sim Theme Park, and Sim Coaster, that let students design, interact, and provide more accurate explanations and examples of real life. **SimCity** is a very popular simulation program for education (Figure 5-36). Students design cities, communities, neighborhoods, and businesses, including infrastructure, such as telephone lines, buildings, and more. As the cities grow in size and complexity, natural disasters and other realistic problems occur continuously requiring students to use all available city resources, including financial resources, to keep the cities running.

Figure 5-36 SimCity, a popular simulation program, creates a real-life environment for development of problem-solving skills.

Figure 5-37 CompassLearning Odyssey is a popular integrated learning system.

The availability of educational computer simulations on the Web is experiencing dramatic growth. A student can learn how a building is demolished, dissect a frog, see a real human heart in action, and more.

INTEGRATED LEARNING SYSTEMS

An **integrated learning system (ILS)** is a sophisticated software program usually developed by an established educational software corporation as a complete educational software solution in one package. These software solutions provide individual student diagnostic data through pretests, instruction based on the diagnostic data, continuous monitoring of student performance with automatic adjustments in instruction when needed, a variety of formats for teaching content, and multilevels of content.

Most integrated learning systems also offer a comprehensive management solution for maintaining the software and for tracking student use and progress (Figure 5-37). Although expensive, integrated learning systems are praised as a comprehensive software solution for low-achieving schools. Integrated learning systems are appealing to school administrators, school boards, and principals because they offer a full, flexible solution in one package. Popular programs include Compass-Learning, Renaissance Learning, Pearson Digital Learning, and PLATO Learning.

A type of software application has evolved that is similar to an ILS, called an open learning system or an advanced learning system. An **open learning system** or an **advanced learning system** is an integrated learning system that includes software titles from leading publishers. What makes this type of learning system different from a traditional ILS is the number of different software titles and activities these packages include. In addition, many ILS applications prescribe the solution for the student while the new open learning systems make the teacher the key player in determining and prescribing the appropriate assessment, choosing the ideal activities, matching the software to objectives and standards, and integrating the software into their curriculum. A popular open learning system is Classworks from Curriculum Advantage.

CURRICULUM-SPECIFIC EDUCATIONAL SOFTWARE

Today, hundreds of high-quality interactive and multimedia educational programs are available for use by K-12 educators. Most of these programs are available on CD and DVD, or are installed on school networks; others are available on the Web. Many of these educational software applications are designed for curriculum-specific teaching and learning and can be organized in categories as described in the following sections. These major categories are by no means inclusive, as many software programs are available for K-12 educators that can be used in dozens of curriculum areas.

CREATIVITY   Creativity applications often have students start with a blank canvas, which allows them to use their imagination and ingenuity. Students can control the design of their projects completely, using the tools provided by the software application. Some applications provide students with ideas and premade backgrounds and images. Students typically have complete control over the design, graphics, and path they create. A number of popular software programs are available that fit in this category. Creativity software applications include Jump Start Artist (Figure 5-38), iLife, Inspiration, Kidspiration, Ultimate Writing and Creativity Center, Storybook Weaver, Cosmic Blobs, Microsoft Publisher, Paint Shop 15, Photoshop, Disney's Magic Artist Online, KidWorks, MovieWorks Deluxe, Kid Pix, and Adobe Creative Suite.

CRITICAL THINKING   Critical-thinking applications stimulate students to use critical-thinking skills (Figure 5-39). Students often are presented with a problem and a variety of ways to solve the problem. They must use critical-thinking skills to obtain the correct solution to the problem. Critical-thinking software applications include I SPY; Classroom Jeopardy; GeoSarfari Series; Building Thinking Skills; The Way Things Work; Thinkin' Things collections; Zoombinis collection; BrainCogs; SimCity; Decisions, Decisions; and Thinkology.

[a] BrainCogs

[b] The Way Things Work

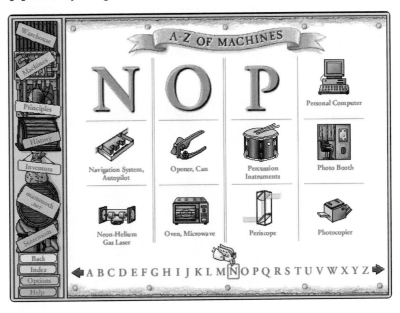

Figure 5-39
Dozens of critical-thinking applications are available for students of all ages. Figure 5-39a shows BrainCogs, which teaches higher-level thinking skills and encourages creativity. Figure 5-39b shows a popular program called The Way Things Work.

Figure 5-38 Jump Start Artist is an example of creativity software that helps young students express themselves artistically.

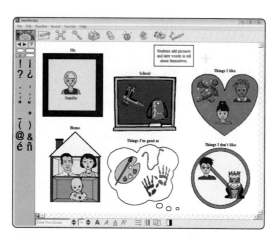

Figure 5-40 Early learning software applications are designed primarily for grades PreK-3, and provide students with a developmental head start. Displayed is a popular program called Kidspiration.

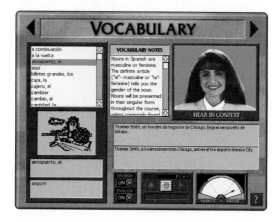

Figure 5-41 ESL and foreign language applications include software programs for Spanish, English, French, and many other languages. Shown is the popular Learn to Speak Spanish program.

Figure 5-42 Language arts software is available for all grade levels. Shown is Reader Rabbit 1, a software designed for first graders.

EARLY LEARNING Early learning **applications** are designed to provide students in grades PreK-3 with a developmental head start in reading, language arts, math, science, and other curriculum areas. Students are presented with engaging graphics, a variety of paths, and a wide variety of activities. These fun and interactive programs include Kidspiration (Figure 5-40), Millie's Math House, Living Books Library, Sammy's Science House, the JumpStart series of software titles, Reader Rabbit's Reading series, Scholastic Keys, and many more outstanding programs.

ESL/FOREIGN LANGUAGE ESL and foreign **language applications** provide K-12 students with assistance in learning English and other languages (Figure 5-41). These applications enable students to practice their skills in a nonthreatening environment. These language-specific programs include JumpStart Spanish, Heartsoft Bestsellers ESL, English for Kids, Instant Immersion series, Spanish 1a with Phonics, Rocket French, and dozens of other language programs designed for students in all grades. You also can download free translation software that lets your computer talk from the ReadPlease Web site. Other translation software allows you and your students to translate English to Spanish, French, German, and other languages.

LANGUAGE ARTS Language arts **applications**, available for all grade levels, support student learning throughout the reading and writing process (Figure 5-42). These applications try to engage students, encouraging them to learn critical skills in a fun and creative environment. Popular language arts programs include Ultimate Writing and Creativity Center, Storybook Weaver, Student Writing Center, Clicker 5, the Reader Rabbit series, Word Munchers Deluxe, Amazing Writing Machine, Reading for Meaning, Reading Blaster series, Read 180, Simon Sounds It Out, and dozens more.

MATH   Math applications help students master basic and complex mathematics and are available for all grade levels (Figure 5-43). Many applications provide students with skill practice and problem-solving activities. Math programs include the Math Advantage series, Destination Math, Mathosaurus, Geometer's Sketchpad, Math Blaster, Math Work-Shop Deluxe, MathXpert, the Mighty Math series, Math Munchers, Math Companion, Tessellation Exploration, Wild West Math, InspireData, and many more.

[a] Math Advantage - Algebra

[b] MathXpert

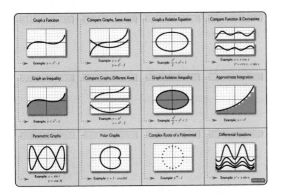

Figure 5-43 Math software engages and motivates students to learn basic and complex concepts. Figure 5-43a shows a Math Advantage Algebra 1 title, and Figure 5-43b displays MathXpert software. MathXpert is designed for high school students and covers hundreds of math concepts, including graphing.

SCIENCE   Science applications are available for all grade levels and assist students in learning a wide variety of science concepts. Multimedia science applications can assist students in mastering difficult or abstract concepts by providing visual representations.

Science applications include Thinkin' Science, Sammy's Science House, The Ultimate Human Body, I Love Science, Discovery School series, Magic School Bus series, A.D.A.M. Essentials High School Suite, BBC Science Simulations, GeoSafari (Figure 5-44), Squibs Science, Science Court, and numerous others.

Figure 5-44 Science software allows all students to explore and interact with science concepts. Shown is the GeoSafari Knowledge Pad program on marine animals.

SOCIAL STUDIES   Social studies software applications encourage higher-order thinking skills, provide reinforcement of facts, and allow students to define their own path (Figure 5-45). A few social studies programs include the Carmen Sandiego series, Oregon Trail, Amazon Trail, Time-Liner, Crosscountry USA, 3D World Atlas, Chronicle Encyclopedia of History, and the Discovery School series.

Figure 5-45 Interactive digital media software, such as the Chronicle Encyclopedia of History, allows students to understand social studies concepts.

Integration Strategies

To learn more integrating math and other software programs, visit the Teachers Discovering Computers Web site (*scsite.com/tdc5*), click Chapter 5, and then click Teaching Today or Software Corner.

Creating and Presenting Digital Media Presentations

Creating or developing **digital media presentations** involves producing various digital media elements, defining the elements' relationships to each other, and then sequencing them in an appropriate order. Many options are available for you and your students to use digital media authoring software and to present digital media presentations.

Digital media authoring software, also called multimedia authoring software, lets you create the application or presentation by controlling the placement of text and graphics and the duration of sounds, video, and animations.

Recall that a digital media presentation is interactive, meaning you can decide the amount and order of the material it contains. Digital media authoring software allows you to create interactivity by defining places in the program that respond to user input. In a digital media presentation, for example, you might include a screen where users can click buttons to play a video or skip the video and move to the next screen.

As discussed throughout this textbook, today's youth are very well connected to all that is digital. Technology is a tool they use without fear and they gravitate to it. Popular digital media authoring tools used in K-12 schools are Microsoft PowerPoint, Photo Story, and Apple iLife.

Microsoft **PowerPoint** allows teachers and students to create multimedia presentations that can incorporate text, graphics, animation, audio, video, links, and most importantly, interactivity. You can learn how to use and integrate PowerPoint in your classroom by completing the In the

Lab activities at the end of this chapter and the step-by-step project on incorporating various digital elements into a PowerPoint presentation available for download at this chapter's Digital Media Corner. In addition, review Chapter 3's Digital Media Corner for more information on Producer and Photo Story, two free add-on programs for PowerPoint that can help you and your students easily capture, synchronize, and publish audio, video, and digital images in your PowerPoint presentations.

The **iLife** integrated suite, included on all new Apple computers, is designed for the digital media revolution (Figure 5-46). Included in iLife are photo editing and manipulation, music and voice-overs, video production, DVD creation, and much more. For more information on iLife, see this chapter's Digital Media Corner.

The digital media capabilities of both PowerPoint and iLife are integrated and seamless and so easy to use that even younger students can begin producing personalized digital media projects almost immediately. The integration makes organizing projects easier because all digital elements (photos, music, and video clips, and so on) interlink. These tools help you, as the teacher, become a facilitator who guides the learning, rather than the lecturer who imparts knowledge.

Figure 5-46 Apple's iLife was created for today's digital generation.

These programs provide a wide range of opportunities for students to develop richly mediated stories, such as recording live scenes from plays as they perform; creating interactive electronic portfolios; designing and developing videos and/or slide shows of documentaries, political speeches, or historical moments; producing public service announcements that show their understanding of sensitive public policies; taking a stand by debating a topic; and/or demonstrating otherwise complex abstract concepts visually. The topics are endless, the possibilities without limits.

PRESENTING DIGITAL MEDIA

Presenting your digital media presentations, as well as having your students present their digital media projects, normally requires a projection system or electronic whiteboard so your students can see and hear the presentations and projects clearly. You also can copy students' projects to more than one computer so students can watch their presentations in small groups.

DATA PROJECTORS   Recall that a **data projector** is a device that projects the image that appears on a computer screen onto a large screen so an audience, such as students in a classroom or school assembly, can see the image clearly. Data projectors have come down in price significantly over the past couple of years and are now an affordable option for K-12 schools to use in their classrooms. Most new schools and retrofitted schools include installed digital projectors in the ceilings of their classrooms, labs, and media centers. Older schools usually have data projectors that teachers can share (Figure 5-47).

INTERACTIVE WHITEBOARDS   A teaching tool becoming increasingly popular with educators is the **interactive whiteboard**, also called an **electronic whiteboard**, which turns a computer and data projector into a powerful tool for teaching and learning. One interactive whiteboard, called a **SMART Board**, produced by Smart Technologies, is more than a presentation system (Figure 5-48). With a computer image projected onto the SMART Board, you can press on its large, touch-sensitive surface to access and control any computer application. In addition, you

can write notes, draw diagrams, and highlight information. You then can save and print your notes and hand them out to students or make them available on your school's network. Another whiteboard option is the InterWrite SchoolBoard from the GTCO CalComp. Another InterWrite option **SchoolPad** uses a Bluetooth wireless pad. SchoolPad can be used with InterWrite's interactive whiteboard or independently to create an electronic whiteboard on any wall surface. Using SchoolPad, you can control your computer from anywhere in the classroom. Other solutions include Mimio Interactive, which converts your existing whiteboard into an electronic sharing tool.

Web Info

To learn more about interactive whiteboards, visit the Teachers Discovering Computers Web site (*scsite.com/tdc5*), click Chapter 5, click Web Info, and then click Interactive Whiteboards.

Figure 5-47 Data projectors are used to project a computer's image and other digital media capabilities onto a large screen.

Figure 5-48 An electronic whiteboard is an interactive presentation system that turns a computer and data projector into a powerful tool for teaching and learning.

Why Are Digital Media and Educational Software Applications Important for Education?

Digital media applications are changing the traditional dynamics of learning in classrooms. As previously noted, interactivity is one of the major features of digital media applications. The ability of users to interact with a digital media application is perhaps the single most critical feature of digital media and has enormous potential to improve learning in K-12 schools.

As mentioned earlier, extensive research conducted over a period of more than 20 years has shown that, when properly evaluated and integrated into teaching at the point of instruction, digital media applications are highly effective teaching tools. Studies indicate that students retain approximately 20 percent of what they see; 30 percent of what they hear; and 50 percent of what they see *and* hear. When a student has a chance to hear, see, *and* interact with a learning environment, he can retain as much as 80 percent of the information. Digital media applications provide that interactive learning environment, which makes them powerful tools for teaching and learning.

One of the main reasons for teachers to utilize digital media software in the classroom is that it appeals to a variety of learning styles. Helping every student learn in her own, unique way ensures success for all students. Digital media software applications assist teachers in meeting diverse learning styles by combining interactive software integrated with teaching strategies to enhance the learning process. Furthermore, digital media software is engaging and motivational for today's digital students.

Another important reason for students' increased retention is that they become active participants in the learning process instead of passive recipients of information. Interactive digital media applications engage students by asking them to define their own paths through an application, which often leads them to explore many related topics.

Many teachers have noted that students are motivated by and enjoy the process of creating their own interactive digital media presentations using digital media authoring

software. Many students enjoy conducting research and writing when their writing projects involve the creation of digital media presentations. In addition to building skills, the completion of a digital media project is a self-esteem and confidence booster for many students.

Teachers can use digital media software both as a productivity tool and as an integration tool. You can use a multimedia software application such as PowerPoint to introduce new concepts, present lectures, as well as demonstrate effective screen design and presentation techniques. In addition, teachers can create digital media presentations to present new concepts and then provide students access to the presentations so they can easily review new information and interact directly with the software.

When teachers effectively use digital media software as a productivity tool, they are modeling for their students how to use this powerful software. This can be the first step in learning to integrate digital media software effectively into the curriculum. Teachers can have students demonstrate their learning by creating their own digital media presentations and presenting them to the class.

Using and integrating digital media can also help you manage today's digital kids in your classroom. Highly motivated students that are engaged in their learning have been directly linked to an increase in student outcomes and reduced dropout rates. Keeping students interested in learning increases student achievement. As students get older their engagement and motivation in school drops, making it even more important for us as educators to find innovative ways to keep students motivated to learn. Technology offers this opportunity, however technology can be a disruption if you do not organize, manage, and match it to your instructional objectives and strategies. The good news is technology can also assist you with classroom management if you use it correctly. Figure 5-49 covers some teaching strategies to help you manage your students in the digital classroom.

For digital media applications to reach their full potential in the classroom, teachers must evaluate digital media applications for content and appropriateness. Chapter 7

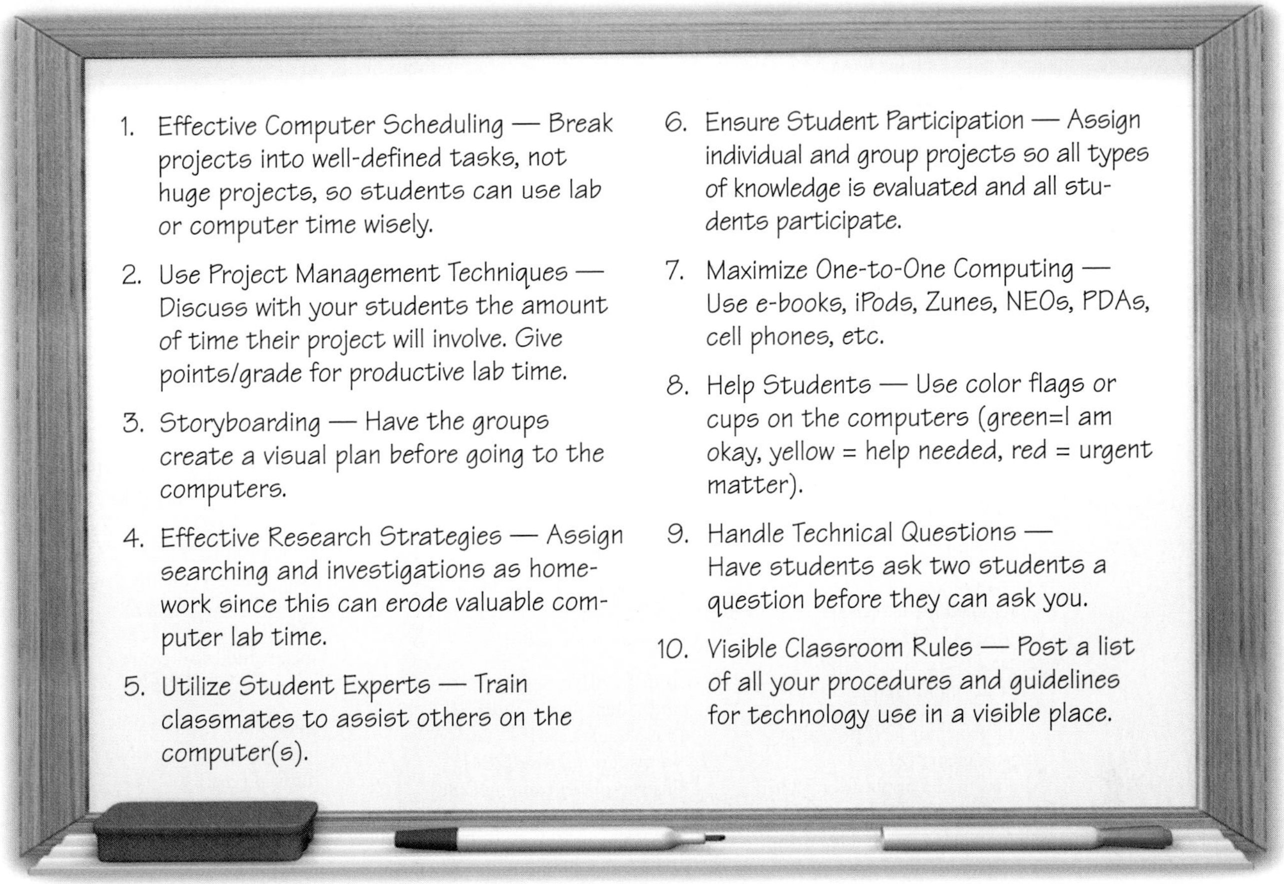

1. Effective Computer Scheduling — Break projects into well-defined tasks, not huge projects, so students can use lab or computer time wisely.

2. Use Project Management Techniques — Discuss with your students the amount of time their project will involve. Give points/grade for productive lab time.

3. Storyboarding — Have the groups create a visual plan before going to the computers.

4. Effective Research Strategies — Assign searching and investigations as homework since this can erode valuable computer lab time.

5. Utilize Student Experts — Train classmates to assist others on the computer(s).

6. Ensure Student Participation — Assign individual and group projects so all types of knowledge is evaluated and all students participate.

7. Maximize One-to-One Computing — Use e-books, iPods, Zunes, NEOs, PDAs, cell phones, etc.

8. Help Students — Use color flags or cups on the computers (green=I am okay, yellow = help needed, red = urgent matter).

9. Handle Technical Questions — Have students ask two students a question before they can ask you.

10. Visible Classroom Rules — Post a list of all your procedures and guidelines for technology use in a visible place.

Figure 5-49 Ten strategies to help you manage today's digital students in your 21st century classroom.

provides additional guidance on evaluating educational software and Web resources for the classroom.

Copyright is an important matter for you and your students to understand when using and creating digital media presentations. Copyright issues, including fair use guidelines, are covered in detail in Chapter 8. Finally, to reap the full benefits of digital media at home, you should consider investing in a high-speed DSL or cable connection to the Internet.

Digital Imaging and Video Technology

Using today's technologies, you and your digital students easily can learn how to create and edit digital graphics and video. Following this chapter is a special feature that introduces you to the world of digital imaging and video technology.

Summary of Integrating Digital Media and Educational Software Applications

This chapter examined how to use, and more importantly, how to integrate digital media and educational software applications in your classroom curriculum. First, you learned how the terms technology, multimedia, and digital media have evolved over the years. Next, you learned about the different elements used in digital media applications, the variety of digital media applications, and the growing popularity of distance learning. You then learned about educational software applications and how to create and present digital media presentations. Finally, the chapter reviewed the value of digital media in education. Effectively integrated digital media education software applications have the potential to impact education in many dramatic ways.

Key Terms

INSTRUCTIONS: Use the Key Terms to help focus your study of the terms used in this chapter. To further enhance your understanding of the Key Terms in this chapter, visit scsite.com/tdc5, click Chapter 5 at the top of the Web page, and then click Key Terms on the left sidebar. Read the definition for each term and then access current and additional information about the term from the Web.

advanced learning system [292]
animation [274]
audio [274]

blended course [285]
branching [291]

clip art collection [273]
CODEC (compression and decompression) [276]
computer-assisted instruction (CAI) [289]
computer-based training (CBT) [277]
computer game [282]
converged media [283]
courseware [277]
creativity application [293]
critical-thinking application [293]

data projector [297]
digital media [270]
digital media application [276]
digital media software [271]
digital media journal [280]
digital media magazine [280]
digital media newspaper [280]
digital media presentation [276]
digital media software [271]
distance education [285]
distance learning [285]
distributed learning [285]
drill-and-practice software [290]

early learning application [294]
e-book [278]

educational computer simulation [291]
educational game [290]
educational software application [288]
edutainment [282]
electronic book [278]
electronic magazine [280]
electronic reference text [278]
electronic whiteboard [297]
ESL and foreign language application [294]
e-zine [280]

graphic [273]

how-to guide [280]

iLife [296]
individual lead training (ILT) [277]
iPod Book [278]
information kiosk [284]
instructor-led training [288]
integrated learning system (ILS) [292]
interactive digital media [271]
interactive whiteboard [297]
interactivity [269]

language arts application [294]

math application [295]
Motion Pictures Experts Group (MPEG) [276]
multimedia [270]
Musical Instrument Digital Interface (MIDI) [275]

online course [285]
open learning system [292]

peer review [282]
PowerPoint [296]
Project Gutenberg [278]

refereeing [282]
remediation [290]

science application [295]
self-paced training [288]
SimCity [292]
simulation [277]
skills-reinforcement software [290]
SchoolPad [297]
SMART Board [297]
social studies software application [295]

technology [270]
text [272]
tutorial [292]

video [275]
video compression [275]
video games [292]
virtual reality (VR) [283]
visual learners [273]

Web-based course [285]
Web-based education [285]
Web-based training (WBT) [285]
Web-enhanced course [285]

Checkpoint

INSTRUCTIONS: Use the Checkpoint excercises to check your knowledge level of the chapter. To complete the Checkpoint exercises interactively, visit scsite.com/tdc5, click Chapter 5 at the top of the Web page, and then click Checkpoint on the left sidebar.

1. Label the Figure

Instructions: Identify each strategy tip.

1. _____
2. _____
3. _____
4. _____
5. _____
6. _____

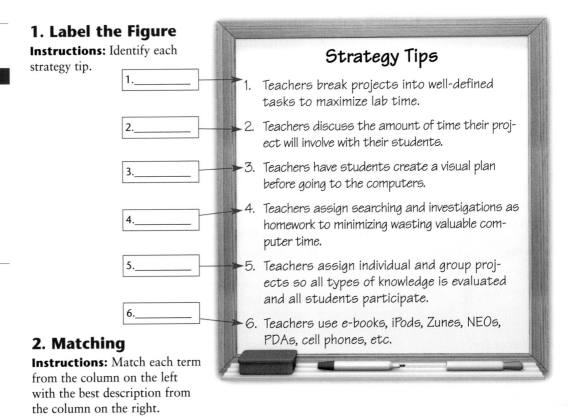

Strategy Tips

1. Teachers break projects into well-defined tasks to maximize lab time.

2. Teachers discuss the amount of time their project will involve with their students.

3. Teachers have students create a visual plan before going to the computers.

4. Teachers assign searching and investigations as homework to minimizing wasting valuable computer time.

5. Teachers assign individual and group projects so all types of knowledge is evaluated and all students participate.

6. Teachers use e-books, iPods, Zunes, NEOs, PDAs, cell phones, etc.

2. Matching

Instructions: Match each term from the column on the left with the best description from the column on the right.

____ 1. text
____ 2. graphic
____ 3. tutorial
____ 4. audio
____ 5. video

a. teaching program that helps individuals learn a product

b. photographic images played back at speeds of 15 to 60 frames per second to provide the appearance of motion in real time

c. digitized music, speech, or other sounds stored and produced by a computer

d. characters used to create words, sentences, and paragraphs; a fundamental element in multimedia

e. digital representation of nontext information, such as a drawing, chart, or photograph

3. Short Answer

Instructions: Write a brief answer to each of the following questions.

1. Briefly describe why digital media and educational software applications are important for education.
2. Name four media components of digital media software? Briefly describe each.
3. What are the differences between electronic reference books and how-to guides? Which one is used more often in education? Why?
4. What is virtual reality? How do teachers, students, and others use virtual reality? Is virtual reality available on the Web?
5. What is meant by educational software applications? Briefly describe four different categories of educational software applications.

Teaching Today

INSTRUCTIONS: Teaching Today provides teachers with integration strategies and ideas for teaching, and more importantly, reaching today's digital generation. Each numbered segment contains one or more links that reinforce the information presented in the segment. To display this page from the Web, visit scsite.com/tdc5, click Chapter 5 at the top of the Web page, and then click Teaching Today on the left sidebar.

1. Web Adventures

Many schools are using digital media applications and the Web to help students better understand the past or gain a greater appreciation of other cultures. For example, using a digital media application combined with the Web, students can immerse themselves in the content through interactive Web adventures — such as Tracking the Tiger Trade, in which they go undercover to Asia to explore the illegal trade of tiger parts; or Amazon Interactive, a project focusing on the people and geography of the Ecuadorian Amazon; or Cyberchase, an interactive and fun math adventure by PBS. Lessons using these types of digital media applications and Web adventures can be created for all grade levels. How does their use compare with traditional approaches to instruction and learning? How do you think students feel about using these types of resources? How could you best use these types of resources in your classroom? What supplemental materials would you need?

2. Multimedia Software

You think your Physical Education students would learn more and be more motivated if you integrated digital media into your curriculum. You have heard from other teachers that a wide variety of Health, Nutrition, and Physical Education software is available. Where might you locate a list of such digital media software titles that meet the standards for the district and that can assist you in teaching your students? Where might you locate such a list on the Web? Do any of the lists you find provide other teachers' reviews of the software? Do any of these resources provide information about incorporating other technologies in the curriculum? In what other ways could you use digital media to motivate your students to learn? What other actions might you take to ensure that you make an informed decision when choosing digital media software that is most effective for you and your students?

3. Virtual Field Trip

You have been teaching your students about famous eighteenth- and nineteenth-century artists. As a final activity, you want to take your students on a field trip to an art museum. The nearest museum, however, is three hours away, so the trip requires bus transportation. Due to the cost of the proposed field trip, your principal has asked you to explore other possibilities. What other options do you have? Could you take your class on a virtual field trip to an art museum? How would you and your students feel about taking that type of field trip? What are some advantages of a virtual field trip? What are some disadvantages?

4. Geography

You are teaching geography to your class. For their final project, the students are to select an area they would like to visit and then prepare a digital media presentation describing the country or region, its culture, major landmarks, and famous sites. To gather information, the students will use digital media reference books and visit geography Web sites. Using the Web for your research, list five or six reference books and Web sites that you might suggest as resources. What other digital media resources could your students use? How do digital media resources support student learning?

Education Issues

INSTRUCTIONS: Education Issues provides several scenarios that allow you to explore controversial and current issues in education. Each numbered segment contains one or more links that reinforce the information presented in the segment. To display this page from the Web, visit scsite.com/tdc5, click Chapter 5 at the top of the Web page, and then click Education Issues on the left sidebar.

1. Are We Scaring Our Kids?

We tell our kids everyone is a stranger and DO NOT talk to strangers. Turn on any news show and our children are in danger — they should never speak to strangers even when they are lost — everyone wants to harm them. Some teachers can no longer touch, hug, or comfort a child because this could be considered inappropriate behavior. Food distributors have been poisoning our children, people have been tampering with consumer items; however, many times the news stories turn out to be false or misrepresented. Are there really enemies everywhere? Have we made children suspicious of all adults? The research says these cases are rare — what do you think and how do we stop scaring our children? There are real problems but are they really on every corner, every person, in everything we eat? What do you think? Are we terrifying our children? How do you talk to your students about this?

2. Bringing the Past to the Present

A simulation on a popular digital media application lets students assume the role of a prominent Civil War general in an actual battle. Students direct and position their army. Confrontations are accompanied by video of battle reenactments. Critics argue that the use of these kinds of digital media applications lack the insight and detail of a traditional textbook. Supporters claim that, by being immersed in the battle, students gain a better understanding of the Civil War. What place do digital media applications have in learning history? Why? What are the advantages and disadvantages of digital media applications compared with traditional textbooks? In what historical studies, if any, would digital media applications be particularly appropriate? Why?

3. Information Overload

The amount of information available to people is growing every day — as scientists uncover new facts, physicians develop improved treatments, technology firms design unprecedented products, and journalists record history in the making. Technologies such as digital media CDs, DVDs, and digital media on the World Wide Web make this vast — some say overwhelming — amount of information easily available to teachers and students. As a result of this potential information overload, experts worry that students might be spending more time sifting through information than actually applying and utilizing information. What do you think? Can there ever be too much information? Why or why not? How could too much information adversely affect teachers and students? What can be done about information overload? How can teachers help students avoid this?

4. Digital Media Realism — Dealing with Tragedy

As a teacher, you are faced with helping your students deal with various types of issues. Most issues are easy to deal with and you know where to go to get advice and help. Helping students cope with tragedy, disaster, and loss is probably the most difficult. The tragic events of September 11, 2001 and April 16, 2007 at Virginia Tech University affected parents, children, friends, fellow Americans, and people around the world. Not until April 2007 had e-mail, text messaging, blogs, podcasts, cell phones, and social networks been used so extensively by people all over the world to communicate information, emotions, and sorrow resulting from a tragic event. Many agencies and Web sites exist that can provide you with information to help your students deal with this and other types of tragedies. Should you talk to your students about these issues? Where do you locate resources? How do people learn from a tragedy such as this one? Do you turn this into a teachable moment? Or do you ignore the issue? What precautions should you take to ensure that the information you provide is age appropriate?

Integration Corner

INSTRUCTIONS: Integration Corner provides extensive ideas and resources for integrating technology into your classroom-specific curriculum. To display this page from the Web and its links to approximately 100 educational Web sites, visit scsite.com/tdc5, click Chapter 5 at the top of the Web page, and then click Integration Corner on the left sidebar.

Integration Corner is designed for teachers and other educators who are looking for innovative ways to integrate technology into their content-specific curriculum. Integration Corner not only provides great Web sites with current information, but also shows what other educators are doing in the field of educational technology. These Corners are designed for all educators regardless of their area of interest. Be sure to review information and Web sites outside of your teaching area because many great integration ideas in one area can be modified easily for use in other curriculum areas.

Teachers and administrators will find other colleagues in their areas with whom to connect and share the successes and hurdles of integrating technology in a classroom or an entire school system. Consider Integration Corner your one stop for integration ideas and resources. Links to educational Web sites are organized in the following 12 Corners, and different Web resources are available for each chapter. Figure 5-50 shows examples of the Web resources provided in the Chapter 5 Special Education Corner.

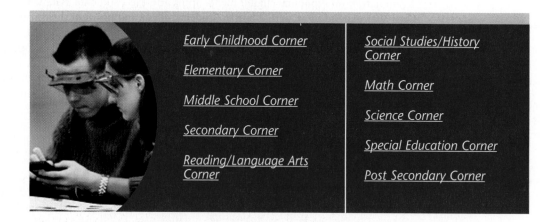

Early Childhood Corner

Elementary Corner

Middle School Corner

Secondary Corner

Reading/Language Arts Corner

Social Studies/History Corner

Math Corner

Science Corner

Special Education Corner

Post Secondary Corner

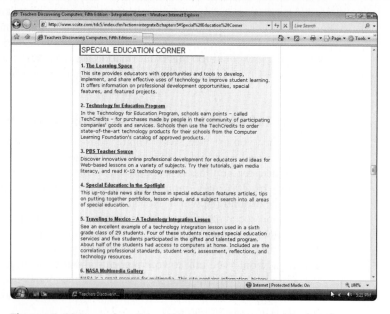

Figure 5-50 Examples of the Web resources provided in the Chapter 5 Special Education Corner.

Software Corner

INSTRUCTIONS: Software Corner provides information on popular software programs. Each numbered segment discusses specific software programs and contains a link to additional information about these programs. To display this page from the Web, visit scsite.com/tdc5, click Chapter 5 at the top of the Web page, and then click Software Corner on the left sidebar.

1. Decisions, Decisions

As a teacher, you know students always need more learning opportunities to develop critical thinking and higher-order thinking skills through decision making. Decisions, Decisions by Tom Snyder Productions creates simulations where students learn and apply the lessons of history through role-playing. Students can gather and analyze information and examine basic historical events, use illustrations from history to assess alternatives, evaluate possible outcomes, and then make decisions. The curriculum-specific areas include: ancient empires, feudalism, immigration, the Cold War, the environment, and much more.

2. ClassWorks

What if you could have 180 top software titles from leading software publishers such as Tom Snyder Productions, Knowledge Adventure, Davidson & Associates, and Scholastic Software at your fingertips with more than 10,800 activities to support your curriculum? That might be an unbelievable undertaking, but what if you also had a customized system that could set the appropriate learning paths for your students? ClassWorks Gold is an open learning system that manages your favorite software titles and integrates them into the K-8 math and language arts curriculum with a cross-curricular approach. ClassWorks is a new approach to learning that lets teachers customize the individual student's learning paths. ClassWorks has an elaborate benchmarking assessment system for reporting all student data. ClassWorks provides a great way to learn!

3. Math Blaster Series

Research confirms that the full integration of digital media math programs can improve retention of math concepts and thus math scores. Developed by educators, the Math Blaster Series from Knowledge Adventure offers interactive digital media programs for almost all age levels from pre-kindergarten to high school. Math Blaster helps students master math concepts and prepare for state and national testing. Key features include the SmartPoints reward system that motivates and helps students to achieve their personal best. Key skills covered include adding and subtracting, multiplying, understanding and using fractions, reading and understanding number patterns, reading and analyzing charts, sorting complex sets, solving problems, and enhancing logic skills.

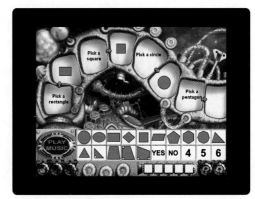

Math Blaster Ages 7-9

4. Blackboard/WebCT

Blackboard/WebCT, the world's leading provider of integrated e-learning systems for higher education, includes two of the world's top course management systems. These programs are powerful and comprehensive courseware tools used by colleges and K-12 institutions to offer online courses, professional development, and alternative types of training solutions. They automate many tasks, including scoring true/false, multiple choice, and short answer exams and tracking student progress and activity. Teachers and students can interact and collaborate online using bulletin boards and internal e-mail systems. Students can upload their own Web pages into a special area within a course. These programs provide teachers and school districts with a secure and efficient way of offering online courses to students.

Digital Media Corner

INSTRUCTIONS: Today's K-12 digital students need their learning to be meaningful and relevant to their lives. Digital Media Corner provides videos, ideas, and examples of how you can use digital media to enhance your teaching and your students' learning. To access the videos and links to additional information, visit scsite.com/tdc5, click Chapter 5 at the top of the Web page, and then click Digital Media on the left sidebar.

1. Digital Storytelling and iLife

One of the true values of digital media in education is its ability to empower teachers and students to develop stories using various forms of self expression. This is evident if you take a look at the iLife software suite that is loaded free on all Apple computers. iLife is an integration software application suite that includes support for telling stories using photographs (iPhoto), music (iTunes and Garage Band), and video (iMovie). Support for today's portable lifestyle is found on the iPod tools. Keynote, a presentation tool, can also be made to integrate with these storytelling products through its support for various forms of outputs, including QuickTime movies and Flash runtime files. What makes iLife products so powerful are their ability to integrate easily with one another and their ease of use. For example, you can start with a picture slide show set to music, then progress into full-motion video using the same content, all the while keeping true to the storyline.

2. Creating Digital Projects with PowerPoint

Microsoft PowerPoint is usually considered a linear presentation software program; however, this program has all the features a student or teacher needs to create a digital story. Students can incorporate photos, graphics, personal drawings, video, interactivity, animation, and much more to create a digital project using any content. Because PowerPoint is so easy to use, students can begin creating stories at the kindergarten level. A step-by-step project that teaches you how to incorporate various digital media elements into a PowerPoint presentation is available for download at this chapter's Digital Media Corner. In addition, a Do and Don'ts of PowerPoint presentations is provided to help you and your students create dynamic, but not overwhelming, presentations.

3. Anywhere in the World — TV on Your Computer

Slingbox is a device that enables you to view any program that plays on your TV or on a computer that has a broadband Internet connection. Produced by Sling Media, the device can redirect up to four different audio and/or video signals simultaneously from a cable box, a satellite receiver, or personal video recorder (PVR) to any computer in the world as long as it has a broadband Internet connection. This way of accessing content is known as place-shifting and is available in standard or HD formats. Software on a user's computer connects to the Slingbox and provides the user interface for viewing the video stream and changing channels. There are numerous versions of Slingbox — for PCs and Macintosh computers, and even for your cell phone.

4. Camtasia Studio

Are you looking for great ways to enhance your classes with digital media resources, tutorials, and videos where you create the content exactly like you want? Camtasia Studio is an easy to use video program that you can use to record your PowerPoint presentations, instructional videos, screencasts, and audio tracks without ever leaving your desk! Research shows that students need authentic learning through visual demonstration, which is a much more powerful form of learning than using words or text alone. You can significantly increase student learning and retention by combining visuals with auditory and textual information. With the power of interactive Camtasia Studio videos, you can deliver high-quality video content anytime and anywhere to even your most remote student. A key feature to Camtasia is the ability for recording, editing, and sharing high-quality screen video on the Web, CD, DVD, and portable media players, including iPod and Zune.

Assistive Technologies Corner

INSTRUCTIONS: Assistive Technologies Corner provides information on current hardware, software, and peripherals that will assist you in delivering instruction to students with physical, cognitive, or sensory challenges. To access extensive additional information, visit scsite.com/tdc5, click Chapter 5 at the top of the Web page, and then click Assistive Technologies on the left sidebar.

1. How Can Multimedia Software Help Students with Special Needs?

Interactive digital media software provides special learning opportunities for students with physical or learning disabilities. Because these software products engage students with various digital media, students learn using their own learning styles. Because it is interactive, they can repeat lessons independently as necessary, and review or progress at their own pace.

Some digital media software is designed specifically for students with special needs. Virtual Reality Education for Assisted Learning (VREAL) places deaf or hard-of-hearing learners in a Virtual Reality scenario to learn math, reading, language arts, and science. The characters in the VR scenarios use speech, text, and sign language to direct and instruct students to solve real-life problems. For problem readers, or students with delayed language, Clicker by Crick Software presents words in grammatical groups. Students click on a word that then moves to a position in a sentence. After clicking on several words, the student hears the new sentence read aloud.

2. What Makes Software Accessible?

Teachers purchasing or using multimedia software should look for accessibility features. At the most basic level, an accessible program gives users alternative methods of receiving information. Audible output should be provided for all visual information. Because new information often is presented in video clips, students with visual impairments will need a voice-over describing what is happening in the video. Text captioning should be provided for all audible content. Software that includes video clips, for example, should have captions on the clips, or have captions that can be turned on and off. In this way, users have access to an alternative means of understanding the narration.

Captioned media improves comprehension not only for students with hearing disabilities, but also for students with reading disabilities, as well as ESL students. Motivation, confidence, and reading comprehension improve when media captions are visible.

3. How Can I Create Accessible Media?

Classroom teachers are creating their own learning videos for and with their students. The videos easily move to PowerPoint presentations, Web pages, or other interactive digital media projects. You can make these videos accessible for all students by using features in your video editing software.

For longer clips, or extensive dialog, you may want to use a titling program. Titles are words you type that are printed on the video you are editing. Video Edit Magic, a popular Windows program, lets you type dialog from the clip directly onto your video. Apple's iMovie has a subtitle position built in to its titling feature. GeeThree's Slick Caption is an inexpensive and easy-to-use titling program available for the Macintosh platform.

You can also create captions that can be turned on and off. You will need the edited video clip, a script, and a media access program such as MAGpie, which is free from the National Center for Accessible Media. When you create media that all can use, everyone benefits!

Follow the instructions at the top of this page to display additional information and this chapter's links on assistive technologies.

In the Lab

INSTRUCTIONS: In the Lab provides Microsoft PowerPoint exercises that are divided into two areas, productivity and integration. To access the links to tutorials, productivity ideas, integration examples and ideas, and more, visit scsite.com/tdc5, click Chapter 5 at the top of the Web page, and then click In the Lab on the left sidebar.

PRODUCTIVITY IN THE CLASSROOM

Introduction: Chapter 5 introduces multimedia software applications and the positive impact they have on learning. Most schools today have a variety of multimedia applications, including Microsoft PowerPoint. Both teachers and students can use PowerPoint to create effective and interesting presentations. Students also can use PowerPoint as an authoring tool to create original stories and book reports. PowerPoint is an excellent tool for creating excitement, interest, and motivation in learning.

After working through these In the Lab activities, visit *scsite.com/tdc5/chapter5* to learn new skills or to improve your current skills by clicking the following links: Learning Microsoft PowerPoint; PowerPoint FAQ; PowerPoint Tips for Windows and Mac OS.

1. Back to School Open House

Problem: To prepare for Parent Night at your school's Open House, your principal has asked all of the teachers at your school to create a short digital media presentation outlining classroom rules, homework policies, and necessary student supplies specific to your class. You decide to create your presentation in Microsoft PowerPoint. You create the presentation shown in Figure 5-51. (*Hint:* Use Help to understand the steps better.) If you do not have a suggested template or font, use any appropriate template or font.

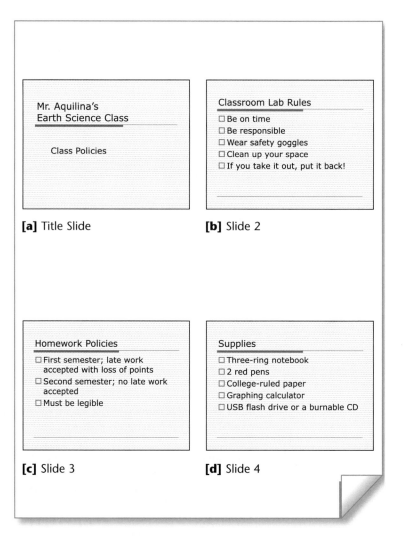

[a] Title Slide

[b] Slide 2

[c] Slide 3

[d] Slide 4

Figure 5-51

In the Lab

Instructions: Perform the following tasks.

1. Create a new presentation using an appropriate design template.
2. Create the title slide shown in Figure 5-51a using your name in place of Mr. Aquilina and the subject you teach, or intend to teach, in place of Earth Science. Increase the font size of the text, Class Policies, to 36 point.
3. Create the three bulleted list slides as shown in Figures 5-51b through 5-51d, personalizing the lists to your specific subject area or grade level.
4. Correct any spelling errors.
5. Save the presentation to a location of your choice using an appropriate filename.
6. Print the presentation.
7. Follow the directions from your instructor for handing in this assignment.

2. Adding Clip Art and Animation Effects to a Presentation

Problem: You decide to enhance your open house presentation from In the Lab 1 by adding clip art, as shown in Figure 5-52, and slide transitions. You also decide to change to a different design template. (*Hint:* Use Help to understand the steps better.) Use any appropriate clip art image.

Instructions: Use the presentation created in In the Lab 1 for this assignment. Perform the following tasks.

1. Open the presentation you created for In the Lab 1.
2. Change the design template to the Ocean design template.
3. Insert appropriate clip art on three slides.
4. Resize the clip art as necessary. Resize and relocate the text boxes as needed.
5. Apply the Dissolve slide transition effect to Slides 2, 3, and 4.
6. Save the presentation with a different file name to a location of your choice.
7. Print the presentation as a handout with four slides per page.
8. Follow directions from your instructor for handing in the assignment.

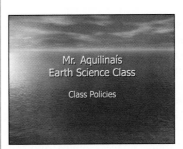

[a] Title Slide

[b] Slide 2

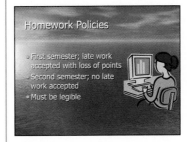

[c] Slide 3

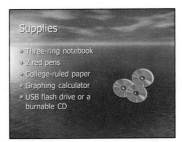

[d] Slide 4

Figure 5-52

In the Lab

3. Classroom Presentation

Problem: On the first day of school, you want to welcome your students to class and have them participate in an introduction activity. You decide to create a PowerPoint presentation to introduce yourself and provide examples of the type of information they might want to share in the activity.

Instructions: Create a PowerPoint presentation similar to the presentation illustrated in Figure 5-52 on the previous page. Use an appropriate template, attractive font style, size, and clip art images. Include the current date, your name, and e-mail address on the title slide. After you have created the presentation, save it to a location of your choice using an appropriate filename. Print the presentation and then follow your instructor's directions for handing in the assignment.

INTEGRATION IN THE CLASSROOM

1. Your fourth grade students are learning about the life cycle of a butterfly. The students will work in groups to create a research project about one species of butterfly. They will start by gathering the following information: species scientific name, common name, range, four interesting facts, stages in the life cycle, eating habits and favorite flowers or plants, one predator, and one defense against predators. Students also will locate at least two images of the butterfly. Then, they will create a digital media presentation using PowerPoint that contains a title slide and at least four additional slides. Students will use bulleted lists to present their findings. They also will include at least two images of their butterfly in their presentation, as well as other suitable clip art. Select a species of butterfly and create a sample presentation. Enter the appropriate information to demonstrate the project for the students. Include the name of the butterfly you select, your name, and the current date on your title slide.

2. Your middle school geography class is studying different countries. For a culminating project, each student selects a country and researches its economy, land formations, temperature and climate, population, and places of interest or historic significance. The students then create PowerPoint presentations to share their research with the class. The presentation should consist of a title slide and at least three other slides containing bulleted lists and images. Students need to include sound, transitions, graphic images, and Internet hypertext links in their presentations. The last slide of each presentation should list references. Prepare a PowerPoint presentation to present as an example for your students. Create a title slide and at least three additional slides with bulleted lists, graphic images, sounds, and transitions. Include your name, the current date, and the name of the country on the title slide. Include a list of references on the last slide.

3. William Shakespeare continues to influence modern theater. You want your high school drama students to understand the contributions of the past to theater and drama today. Students will be divided into four groups. Each group will research one of the following topics: the style and construction of the Globe Theater, forms of entertainment, customs of the theater, and costuming during the time of Shakespeare. Groups will create PowerPoint presentations to present their findings. The presentation should consist of a title slide, slides with bulleted lists, and images. Students also may include Internet hyperlinks. Remind students the hyperlink will only work if the computer they are using for their presentation has an active Internet connection. Prepare a presentation to present to the students as an example. Create a title slide and at least three additional slides with bulleted lists and graphic images. Include your name, the current date, and the topic on the title slide.

Learn It Online

INSTRUCTIONS: Use the Learn It Online exercises to reinforce your understanding of the chapter concepts and increase your computer, information, and integration literacy. To access dozens of interactive student labs, practice tests, learning games, and more, visit scsite.com/tdc5, click Chapter 5 at the top of the Web page, and then click Learn It Online on the left sidebar.

1. At the Movies

Click the At the Movies - iLife link to review a video about using and integrating Apple's iLife.

2. At the Movies

Click the At the Movies - PowerPoint link to review a video about creating PowerPoint 2007 presentations.

3. Bid on a Product at eBay

Online auctions have grown to be a favorite way to shop for many people. A leading online auction Web site is eBay. Have you wanted to bid on eBay but were worried that you might have difficulties? Click the eBay link to learn how to submit a bid for an item on eBay. If you submit a bid on eBay, you will see a warning message reminding you that when you bid on an item, you are entering into a contract to purchase the item if you are the successful bidder. Never make a bid unless you are prepared to make a purchase. Bidding on eBay is serious business.

4. Expanding Your Understanding

A PC video camera, sometimes called a Web cam, is a digital video camera that allows you to capture video and still images. You can use the videos in live instant messages or for live images over the Internet. You also can include the recordings of the videos on Web pages or in e-mail messages as attachments. Click the Expanding Your Understanding link to learn how to install and use a PC video camera.

5. Practice Test

Click the Practice Test link. Answer each question. When completed, enter your name and click the Grade Test button to submit the quiz for grading. Make a note of any missed questions. If required, submit your score to your instructor.

6. Who Wants to Be a Computer Genius?

Click the Computer Genius link to find out if you are a computer genius. Directions about how to play the game will be displayed. When you are ready to play, click the Play button. If required, submit your score to your instructor.

7. Wheel of Terms

Click the Wheel of Terms link to reinforce important terms you learned in this chapter by playing the Shelly Cashman Series version of this popular game. Directions about how to play the game will be displayed. When you are ready to play, click the Play button. If required, submit your score to your instructor.

8. Crossword Puzzle Challenge

Click the Crossword Puzzle link. Complete the puzzle to reinforce skills you learned in this chapter. Directions about how to play the game will be displayed. When you are ready to play, click the Play button. If required, submit the completed puzzle to your instructor.

Special Feature: Digital Imaging and Video Technology

The use of images in teaching and learning can increase student motivation, comprehension, and retention. Digital kids are visual thinkers — they see and express themselves visually. Integrating digital imaging and video technology into the curriculum has been shown to increase spatial intelligence, which is the ability to think in pictures.

Everywhere you look, people are capturing moments they want to remember. They take pictures or make movies of their vacations, birthday parties, activities, accomplishments, sporting events, weddings, and more. Because of the popularity of digital cameras and digital video cameras, increasingly more people desire to capture their memories digitally, instead of on film. With digital technology, photographers have the ability to modify and share the digital images and videos they create. When you use special hardware and/or software, you can copy, manipulate, print, and distribute digital images and videos using your personal computer and the Internet. Amateurs can achieve professional quality results by using more sophisticated hardware and software.

USB

digital camera
(input)

FireWire or USB 2.0

digital video
camera (input)

television
(output)

Figure 1 A variety of digital imaging input and output devices.

Digital photography and recordings deliver significant benefits over film-based photography and movie making. With digital cameras, no developing is needed. Instead, the images reside on storage media, such as a hard disk, DVD, or flash memory card. Unlike film, storage media can be reused, which reduces costs, saves time, and provides immediate results. Digital technology allows greater control over the creative process, both while taking pictures and video and in the editing process. You can check results immediately after capturing a picture or video to determine whether it meets your expectations. If you are dissatisfied with a picture or video, you can erase it and recapture it, again and again.

As shown in Figure 1, a digital camera functions as an input device when it transmits pictures through a cable to a personal computer via a USB port or FireWire port. Using a digital camera in this way allows you to edit the pictures, save them on storage media, and print them on a photographic-quality printer via a USB port or FireWire port.

Figure 1 also illustrates how you might use a digital video camera with a personal computer. The process typically is the same for most digital video cameras. You capture the images or video with the video camera. Next, you connect the video camera to your personal computer using a FireWire or USB 2.0 port, or you place the storage media used by the camera in the computer. The video then is copied or downloaded to the computer's hard disk. Then, you can edit the video using video editing software. If desired, you can preview the video during the editing process on a television. Finally, you save the finished result to the desired media, such as a DVD+RW or, perhaps, e-mail the edited video or post it to a media sharing Web site. As shown in the figure, a DVD player also can be used to input video.

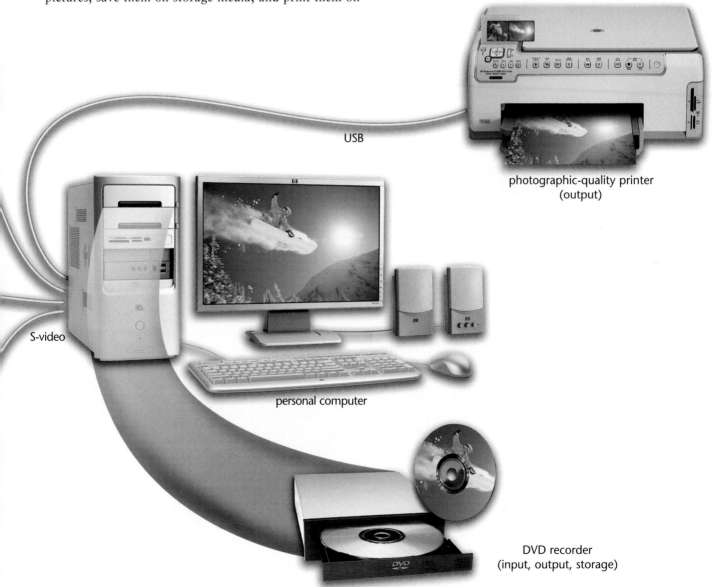

USB

photographic-quality printer
(output)

S-video

personal computer

DVD recorder
(input, output, storage)

Digital Imaging Technology

Digital imaging technology involves capturing and manipulating still photographic images in an electronic format. The following sections outline the steps involved in the process of using digital imaging technology.

Select a Digital Camera.

A digital camera is a type of camera that stores photographed images electronically instead of on traditional film. Digital cameras are divided into three categories (Figure 2) based mainly on image resolution, features, and of course, price.

[a] point-and-shoot

[b] field

[c] studio

Figure 2 The point-and-shoot digital camera (a) requires no adjustments before shooting. The field digital camera (b) offers improved quality and features that allow you to make manual adjustments before shooting and use a variety of lenses. The studio digital camera (c) offers better color and resolution and greater control over exposure and lenses.

The image resolution is measured in megapixels (million of pixels), often abbreviated as MP. The image quality increases with the number of pixels. The image resolution usually is. Features of digital cameras include red-eye reduction, zoom, autofocus, flash, self-timer, and manual mode for fine-tuning settings. Figure 3 summarizes the three categories of digital cameras.

Take Pictures.

Digital cameras provide you with several options that are set before a picture is taken. Three of the more important options are the resolution, compression, and image file format used to save the picture. While a camera may allow you to take a picture at a very high resolution, you may choose to take a picture at a lower resolution if the image does not require great detail or must be a small size, such as for use on a Web page where smaller image file sizes are beneficial.

Figure 3 Digital cameras often are categorized by image resolution, features, and price.

Type	Features	Price
Point-and-shoot cameras	Fully automatic; fits in your pocket; easy to use; ideal for average consumer usage.	Less than $300
Field cameras	Used by photojournalists; portable but flexible; provides ability to change lenses and use other attachments; great deal of control over exposure and other photo settings.	$300 to $2,000
Studio cameras	Stationary camera used for professional studio work; flexible; widest range of lenses and settings.	$1,500 and up

Compression results in smaller image file sizes. Figure 4 illustrates the image file sizes for varying resolutions and compressions under standard photographic conditions using a 6-megapixel digital camera. Figure 4 also shows the average picture size for a given resolution. The camera may take more time to save an image at lower compression, resulting in a longer delay before the camera is ready to take another picture. A higher compression, however, may result in some loss of image quality. If a camera has a 16 MB flash memory card, you can determine the number of pictures the card can hold by dividing 16 MB by the file size. Flash memory cards are available in sizes from 16 MB to 16 GB or more.

Most digital cameras also allow you to choose an image file format. Two popular file formats are TIFF and JPEG. The TIFF file format saves the image uncompressed. All of the image detail is captured and stored, but the file sizes can be large. The JPEG file format is compressed. The resolution of the image may be the same as a TIFF file, but some detail may be lost in the image.

Finally, before you take the photograph, you should choose the type of media on which to store the resulting image file. Some cameras allow for a choice of media to which you can store the image, such as a CompactFlash card or Memory Stick, while others allow for only one type of storage media. One major advantage of a digital camera is that you can erase pictures easily from its media, freeing up space for new pictures.

Transfer and Manage Image Files.

The method of transferring images from the camera to the personal computer differs greatly depending on the capabilities of both. Digital cameras use a variety of storage media (Figure 5). If your camera uses a flash memory card such as CompactFlash, Memory Stick, SmartMedia, xD Picture Card, or Secure Digital (SD), you can remove the media from the camera and place it in a slot on the personal computer or in a device, such as a card reader, connected to the personal computer.

Resolution in Pixels	COMPRESSION			Picture Size in Inches
	Low	Medium	High	
	Resulting Image File Size			
3000 × 2000	8.9 MB	3.3 MB	780 KB	16 × 20
2272 × 1704	2 MB	1.1 MB	556 KB	11 × 17
1600 × 1200	1 MB	558 KB	278 KB	8 × 10
1024 × 768	570 KB	320 KB	170 KB	4 × 6

Figure 4 Image file sizes for varying resolutions and compressions under standard photographic conditions using a 6-megapixel digital camera.

SD Card

CompactFlash Card

xD Picture Cards

Figure 5 SD Cards, CompactFlash Cards, and xD Picture Cards are popular storage devices for digital cameras.

Your camera or card reader also may connect to the personal computer using a USB, USB 2.0, or FireWire (Figure 6) port. Some personal computers include an internal card reader. When you insert the memory card or connect the camera, software on the personal computer guides you through the process of transferring the images to the hard disk. Some operating systems and software recognize a memory card or camera as though it is another hard disk on the computer. This feature allows you to navigate to the files, and then copy, delete, or rename the files while the media still is in the camera.

Figure 6 Using a USB or FireWire connection, you can add a card reader to your personal computer.

After you transfer the files to the hard disk on your personal computer, you should organize the files by sorting them or renaming them so that information, such as the subject, date, time, and purpose, is saved along with the image. Finally, before altering the images digitally or using the images for other purposes, you should back up the images to another location, such as a CD or DVD, so the original image is recoverable.

Edit Images.

Image editing software allows you to edit digital images. You should edit a copy, not the original image file, so that you always have the original file to use as a backup or for other editing projects. The following list summarizes the more common image enhancements or alterations:

- Adjust the contrast and brightness; correct lighting problems; or help give the photograph a particular feeling, such as warm or stark

- Remove red-eye

- Crop an image to remove unnecessary elements and resize it

- Rotate the image to change its orientation

- Add elements to the image, such as descriptive text, a date, a logo, or decorative items; create collages or add missing elements

- Replace individual colors with a new color

- Add special effects, such as texture, motion blurring, or reflections, to enhance the image

- Add aging to make the image appear as if it was taken a long time ago

Some popular image editing programs are Adobe Photoshop, Microsoft Digital Image Suite, and Corel Paint Shop Pro Photo. Figure 7 shows some of the effects available in Corel Paint Shop Pro X on the Artistic Effects submenu.

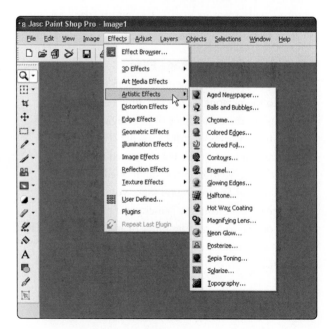

Figure 7 The capability of applying effects separates digital photography from film photography.

Print Images.

Once an image is saved, and perhaps altered digitally, it is ready to be printed. You can print images on a personal color printer or send them to a professional service that specializes in digital photo printing.

When printing the images yourself, make sure that the resolution used to create the image was high enough for the size of the print you want to create. For example, if the camera used a resolution of 640 × 480 pixels, then the ideal print size is wallet size (3 × 2 inches). If you print such an image at a size of 8 × 10 inches (instead of 3 × 2 inches), then the image will appear pixilated, or blurry. Use high-quality photo paper for the best results. A photo printer gives the best results when printing digital photography.

Many services print digital images, either over the Internet or through traditional photo developing locations and kiosks (Figure 8), such as those found in drug stores or shopping marts. Some services allow you to e-mail or upload the files to the service, specify the size, quality, and quantity of print, and then receive the finished prints via the postal service. Other services allow you to drop off flash memory cards or CD-ROMs at a photo shop and pick up the prints later, just as you do with traditional photo developing shops.

Distribute Images Electronically.

Rather than printing images, you often need to use the images electronically. Depending on the electronic use of the image, the image may require additional processing. If you use the images on a Web site or want to e-mail a photo, you probably want to send a lower-resolution image. Image editing software allows you to lower the resolution of the image, resulting in a smaller file size. Also, you should use standard file formats when distributing an electronic photo. The JPEG format is viewable using most personal computers or Web browsers. Some online services allow you to upload and share your photos free of charge and will automatically change your photos to a lower resolution and JPEG format.

You can store very high resolution photos on a DVD or a CD. DVD and CD mastering software allows you to create slide show presentations on a recordable DVD or CD that can play in many home DVD players or personal computer DVD drives. Photo sharing Web sites, such as Fotki and Flickr (Figure 9), allow you to share your photos with family and friends or with the whole world. You also can search for and view photos of others.

Finally, you should back up and store images that you distribute electronically with

Figure 8 A kiosk allows you to print digital images in high resolution on photo paper.

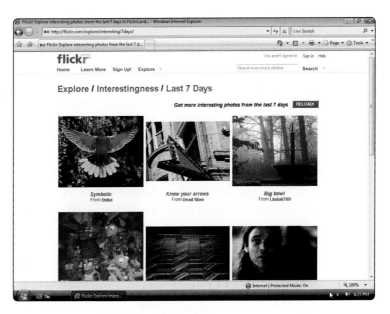

Figure 9 The Flickr photo sharing Web site allows you to share your photos, organize your photos, and search for photos.

the same care as you store your traditional film negatives. A picture paints a thousand words — using digital technology with your students gives them the opportunity to express ideas while also understanding content through their own digital eyes. Digital cameras are an easy and inexpensive way for you to begin the process of integrating digital technology in your classroom curriculum.

Digital Video Technology

Digital video technology allows you and your students to input, edit, manage, publish, and share video production projects using a personal computer. With digital video technology, you can transform home and classroom videos into Hollywood-style movies by enhancing the videos with scrolling titles and transitions, cutting out or adding scenes, and adding background music and voice-over narration. As we have discussed throughout this textbook, students learn not only technical skills, but storytelling and literacy skills by creating projects that incorporate the use of video technology. The following steps outline the process of using digital video technology.

Select a Video Camera.

Video cameras record in either analog or digital format. Analog formats include 8mm, Hi8, VHS-C, and Super VHS-C. Digital formats include Mini-DV, MICROMV, Digital8, DVD, and HDV (high-definition video format). Digital video cameras fall into three general categories: high-end consumer, consumer, and webcasting and monitoring (Figure 10). Consumer digital video cameras are by far the most popular type among consumers. Some high-end consumer models support the HDV high-definition standard; others allow you to record directly on to a DVD disc. A video recorded in high-definition can be played back on a high-definition display. Digital video cameras provide more features than analog video cameras, such as a higher level of zoom, better sound, and greater control over color and lighting.

[a] high-end consumer

[b] consumer

[c] webcasting and monitoring

Figure 10 The high-end consumer digital video camera (a) can produce professional-grade results. The consumer digital video camera (b) produces amateur-grade results. The webcasting and monitoring digital video camera (c) is appropriate for webcasting and security monitoring.

Record a Video.

Most video cameras provide you with a choice of recording programs, which sometimes are called automatic settings. Each recording program includes a different combination of camera settings, so you can adjust the exposure and other functions to match the recording environment. Usually, several different programs are available, such as point-and-shoot, point-and-shoot with manual adjustment, sports, portrait, spotlight scenes, and low light. You also have the ability to select special digital effects, such as fade, wipe, and black and white. If you are recording outside on a windy day, then you can enable the wind screen to prevent wind noise. If you are recording home videos or video meant for a Web site, then the point-and-shoot recording program is sufficient.

Transfer and Manage Videos.

After recording the video, the next step is to transfer the video to your personal computer. Most video cameras connect directly to a USB 2.0 or FireWire port on your personal computer (Figure 11). Transferring video with a digital camera is easy because the video already is in a digital format that the computer can recognize.

An analog camcorder or VCR requires additional hardware to convert the analog signals to a digital format before the video can be manipulated on a personal computer. The additional hardware includes a special video capture card using a standard RCA video cable or an S-video cable (Figure 12). S-video cables provide sharper images and greater overall quality. When you use video capture hardware with an analog video, be sure to close all open programs on your computer because capturing video requires a great deal of processing power.

When transferring video, plan to use approximately 15 to 30 gigabytes of hard disk storage space per hour of digital video. A typical video project requires about four times the amount of raw footage as the final product. Therefore, at the high end, a video that lasts an hour may require up to 120 gigabytes of storage for the raw footage, editing process, and

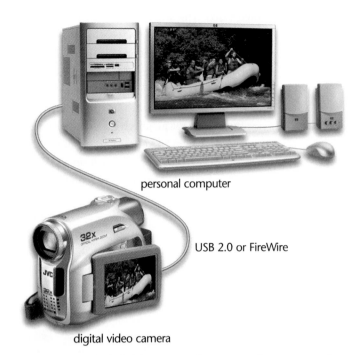

personal computer

USB 2.0 or FireWire

digital video camera

Figure 11 A digital video camera is connected to a personal computer via a FireWire or USB 2.0 port. No additional hardware is needed.

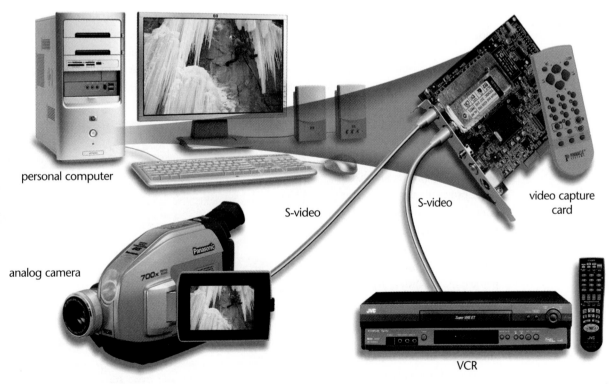

personal computer

analog camera

S-video

S-video

video capture card

VCR

Figure 12 An analog camcorder or VCR is connected to the personal computer via an S-video port on a video capture card.

final video. This storage requirement can vary depending on the software you use to copy the video from the video camera to the hard disk and the format you select to save the video. For example, Microsoft's Windows Movie Maker can save 15 hours of video in 10 gigabytes when creating video for playback on a computer, but saves only 1 hour of video in 10 gigabytes when creating video for playback on a DVD. A high-definition video file may require over 10 gigabytes per hour.

The video transfer requires application software on the personal computer (Figure 13).

Figure 13 Some video editing software allows you to transfer your video from any video source to a hard disk.

Windows Vista includes the Windows Movie Maker software that allows you to transfer the video from your video camera. Depending on the length of video and the type of connection used, the video may take a long time to download. Make certain that no other programs are running on your personal computer while transferring the video.

The frame rate of a video refers to the number of frames per second (fps) that are captured in the video. The most widely used frame rate is 30 fps. A smaller frame rate results in a smaller file size for the video, but playback of the video will not be as smooth as one recorded with a higher frame rate.

When transferring video, the software may allow you to choose a file format and a codec to store the video. A video file format holds the video information in a manner specified by a vendor, such as Apple or Microsoft. Four of the more popular file formats are listed in Figure 14.

File Format	File Extensions
Apple QuickTime	.MOV or .QT
MPEG-4 (DivX)	.DIVX
Microsoft Windows	.WMV or .ASF
Real RealMedia	.RM or .RAM

Figure 14 Popular video file formats.

File formats support codecs to encode the audio and video into the file formats. A particular file format may be able to store audio and video in a number of different codecs. A codec specifies how the audio and video is compressed and stored within the file. Figure 15 shows some options available for specifying a file format and codec in a video capture program. The dialog box in Figure 15 allows the user to determine whether the video is smoother in playback or if the video is more crisp, meaning that it includes more detail. The file format and codec you choose often is based on what you plan to do with the movie. For example, if you

Figure 15 Video editing software allows you to specify a combination of file format and codec when saving a video.

plan to upload your video to the YouTube video sharing Web site, the best choices are DivX and Xvid MPEG-4 file formats.

After transferring the video to a personal computer and before manipulating the video, you should store the video files in appropriate folders, named correctly, and backed up. Most video transfer application software helps manage these tasks.

Edit a Video.

Once the video is stored on your hard disk, the next step is to edit, or manipulate, the video. If you used a video capture card to transfer analog video to your computer, the files may require extra initial processing. When you use a video capture card, some of the video frames may be lost in the transfer process. Some video editing programs allow you to fix this problem with frame rate correction tools.

The first step in the editing process is to divide the video into smaller pieces, or scenes, that you can manipulate more easily. This process is called splitting. Most video software automatically splits the video into scenes, sometimes called clips, thus sparing you the task. After splitting, you should cut unwanted scenes or portions of scenes. This process is called pruning.

After you create the scenes you want to use in your final production, you edit each individual scene. You can crop, or change the size of, scenes. That is, you may want to cut out the top or a side of a scene that is irrelevant. You also can resize the scene. For example, you may be creating a video that will be displayed in a Web browser. Making a smaller video, such as 320 × 200 pixels

instead of 640 × 480 pixels, results in a smaller file that transmits faster over the Internet. Some video sharing Web sites recommend smaller video resolutions, such as 320 × 200 pixels.

If video has been recorded over a long period, using different cameras or under different lighting conditions, the video may need color correction. Color correction tools (Figure 16) analyze your video and match brightness, colors, and other attributes of video clips to ensure a smooth look to the video.

You can add logos, special effects, or titles to scenes. You can place a company logo or personal logo in a video to identify yourself or the company producing the video. Logos often are added on the lower-right corner of a video and remain for the duration of the video. Special effects include warping, changing from color to black and white, morphing, or zoom motion. Morphing is a special effect in which one video image is transformed into another image over the course of several frames of video, creating the illusion of metamorphosis. You usually add titles at the beginning and end of a video to give the video context. A training video may have titles throughout the video to label a particular scene, or each scene may begin with a title.

The next step in editing a video is to add audio effects, including voice-over narration and background music. Many video editing programs allow you to add additional tracks, or layers, of sound to a video in addition to the sound that was recorded on the video camera. You also can add special audio effects.

Figure 16 Color correction tools in video editing software allow a great deal of control over the mood of your video creation.

The final step in editing a video is to combine the scenes into a complete video (Figure 17). This process involves placing scenes in order and adding transition effects between scenes. Video editing software allows you to combine scenes and separate each scene with a transition. Transitions include fading, wiping, blurry, bursts, ruptures, erosions, and more.

Figure 17 In Ulead VideoStudio, scenes (shown individually in the upper-right corner), are combined into a sequence on the bottom of the screen.

Distribute the Video.

After editing the video, the final step is to distribute it or save it on an appropriate medium. You can save video in a variety of formats. Using special hardware, you can save the video on standard video tape. A digital-to-analog converter is necessary to allow your personal computer to transmit video to a VCR. A digital-to-analog converter may be an external device that connects to both the computer and input device, or it may be a video capture card inside the computer.

Video also can be stored in digital formats in any of several DVD formats, on CD, on a video sharing Web site, or on video CD (VCD). DVD or CD creation software, which often is packaged with video editing software, allows you to create, or master, DVDs and CDs. You can add interactivity to your DVDs. For example, you can allow viewers to jump to certain scenes using a menu. A video CD (VCD) is a CD format that stores video on a CD-R that can be played in many DVD players.

You also can save your video creation in electronic format for distribution over the Web or via e-mail. Popular video sharing Web sites, such as YouTube and TeacherTube, have recommendations for the best file format and codecs to use for video that you upload to them. Your video editing software must support the file format and codec you want to use. For example, Apple's iMovie software typically saves files in the QuickTime file format.

Professionals use hardware and software that allow them to create a film version of digital video that can be played in movie theaters. This technology is becoming increasingly popular. The cost of professional video editing software ranges from thousands to hundreds of thousands of dollars. Video editing software for the home user is available for a few hundred dollars or less. Some Hollywood directors believe that eventually, all movies will be recorded and edited digitally.

After creating your final video for distribution or your personal video collection, you should back up the final video file. You can save your scenes for inclusion in other video creations or create new masters using different effects, transitions, and scene order.

Summary

Using and integrating video technology in K-12 education has grown tremendously over the past few years, primarily due to decreased cost of equipment and software and the prevalence of videos on the Web. The potential of video technology to positively impact teaching and learning is limitless. Remember, digital kids crave all things digital; to engage them in your classroom, you need to use authentic activities that incorporate multiple intelligences.

Technology, Digital Media, and Curriculum Integration

6

Objectives

After completing this chapter, you will be able to do the following:
[ISTE NETS-T Standards I A-B, II A-E, III A-D, IV A-D, V A-D, VI A-E]

- Define curriculum and explain curriculum standards and learning benchmarks

- Explain technology integration, also called curriculum integration

- Describe the use of computers in computer labs versus classroom instruction

- Identify ways in which technology can positively influence learning

- Identify ways to plan for technology integration

- Explain various planning tools and instructional models

- Describe the steps of the ASSURE Model

- Identify ways to get started using technology at a new school

- Describe the use of learning centers

Throughout this textbook, you have learned about computers and other educational technologies, and you have seen the impact technology has on people's lives, schools, and classrooms. Every day, computers help many individuals accomplish job-related tasks more efficiently and effectively. For educators, computers and other technologies serve as the tools needed to implement new and evolving teaching strategies.

Chapter 1 of this textbook introduced educational technology and covered the digital generation — how they learn and what they should know. The next three chapters focused on building computer and information literacy skills. Chapter 5 introduced you to integrating digital media and education software into your curriculum. This chapter provides you with a basic understanding of how to integrate technology across the curriculum. As you learned in Chapter 1, integration literacy is the ability to use computers and other technologies combined with a variety of teaching and learning strategies to enhance students' learning. Integration literacy means that teachers can determine how to match appropriate technologies to curriculum standards, benchmarks, and outcomes. Integration literacy relies on a solid foundation of computer and information literacy, both of which are essential for helping you integrate technology into your classroom curriculum.

What Is Curriculum?

Education can be defined as all the experiences, knowledge, and skills a learner gains from both school and society. Education literature defines the term "curriculum" in many ways. Often, curriculum is defined simply as that which is taught.

For the purposes of this textbook, **curriculum** is defined as the knowledge, skills, and performance standards students are expected to acquire in particular grade levels, or through sequences or clusters based on subject matter units of instruction, such as language arts, mathematics, science, English, history, physical education, and others (Figure 6-1). Curriculum often is designed at the state or school district level by a team of curriculum specialists, instructional leaders, and other experts. For curriculum to be implemented properly, teachers must not only understand the curriculum but also be empowered to adapt the curriculum in such a way as to meet the instructional needs of their students.

Many countries have Departments of Education or educational organizations that serve as the governing association for educational regulations and reform. Agencies in the United States include the federal Department of Education (DOE), and each state has its own Department or Board of Education (Figures 6-2a and 6-2b).

The federal Department of Education is the governing body for public education in the United States. State education departments provide their school districts with policies, directives, and updates to state public education issues. In addition, state DOEs provide access to up-to-date statistics, information about standards and accountability, teacher certification, scholarships, grants and funding sources, resources, and more.

State education departments also provide their school districts with documents that describe curriculum standards and benchmarks for learning. These documents often are called **curriculum frameworks** or **curriculum guides.** Although curriculum frameworks usually include subject-specific standards, they often also include direction for specific content areas, benchmarks, activities, and forms of evaluation.

School curriculum frameworks include not only standards, but also examples that teachers can use to develop curriculum-based lesson plans. They usually are organized by subject and grade level. Curriculum frameworks can include specific curriculum standards, learning goals, and grade level expectations to assist teachers in meeting curriculum benchmarks. Many states refer to frameworks as blueprints for implementing content standards.

Integration Strategies

To access dozens of integration ideas specific to your classroom curriculum, visit the Teachers Discovering Computers Web site (*scsite.com/tdc5*), click Chapter 6, click Integration Corner, and then click your grade level corner.

Figure 6-1 Integrating technology in the classroom helps teachers achieve the learning outcomes defined by the curriculum.

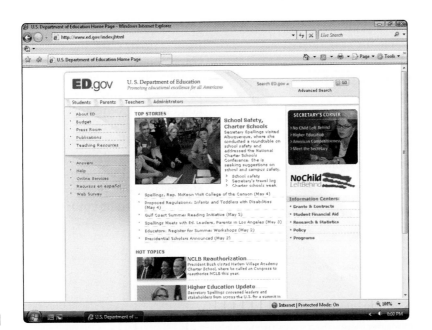

[a]

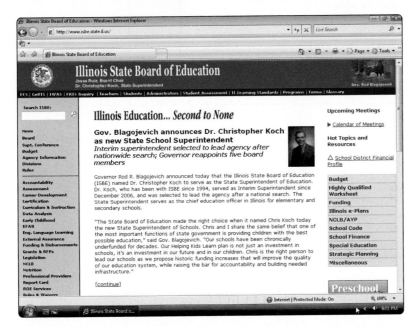

[b]

Figure 6-2 This figure shows the home page of [a] the U.S. Department of Education and [b] the Illinois State Board of Education. The U.S. government and state education agencies provide parents, educators, and students with a multitude of resources and information.

Many school districts are drafting their own interpretations of state curriculum standards to improve learning and meet the needs of students. Many districts also are creating guides to help teachers teach curriculum standards by providing examples and mastery-level checklists with curriculum standards. Teachers usually have to include these documents with their lesson plans to show how students are mastering the skills necessary to be promoted to the next level. Some states and districts are incorporating **Grade Level Expectations (GLEs)** into their curriculum. The purpose of GLEs is to show the content and skills that students are expected to master for each subject area and to assist teachers in making sure students meet the content standards for a particular subject area. Many school districts have developed **Mastery Objective Checklists**, which are skills that must be mastered by a current grade level. These skills are usually listed on a grid or table for easy reference.

CURRICULUM STANDARDS AND BENCHMARKS

A **curriculum standard**, also called a **curriculum goal**, defines what a student is expected to know at certain stages of education. Curriculum standards for K-12 education are a collection of general concepts that school districts expect students to learn as they progress through the grade levels. Curriculum standards vary from state to state and usually cover core subjects, such as language arts, mathematics, science, social studies, physical education, art, health, and foreign languages. A **benchmark**, or **learning objective**, is a specific, measurable outcome or indicator that usually is tied to a curriculum standard. Figure 6-3 lists a sample curriculum standard and appropriate, measurable benchmarks for the standards at different grade levels.

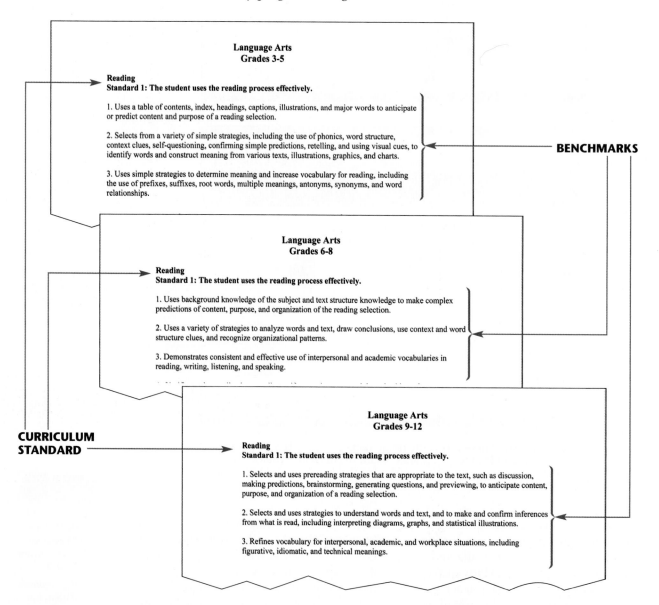

CURRICULUM STANDARD

BENCHMARKS

Language Arts Grades 3-5

Reading
Standard 1: The student uses the reading process effectively.

1. Uses a table of contents, index, headings, captions, illustrations, and major words to anticipate or predict content and purpose of a reading selection.

2. Selects from a variety of simple strategies, including the use of phonics, word structure, context clues, self-questioning, confirming simple predictions, retelling, and using visual cues, to identify words and construct meaning from various texts, illustrations, graphics, and charts.

3. Uses simple strategies to determine meaning and increase vocabulary for reading, including the use of prefixes, suffixes, root words, multiple meanings, antonyms, synonyms, and word relationships.

Language Arts Grades 6-8

Reading
Standard 1: The student uses the reading process effectively.

1. Uses background knowledge of the subject and text structure knowledge to make complex predictions of content, purpose, and organization of the reading selection.

2. Uses a variety of strategies to analyze words and text, draw conclusions, use context and word structure clues, and recognize organizational patterns.

3. Demonstrates consistent and effective use of interpersonal and academic vocabularies in reading, writing, listening, and speaking.

Language Arts Grades 9-12

Reading
Standard 1: The student uses the reading process effectively.

1. Selects and uses prereading strategies that are appropriate to the text, such as discussion, making predictions, brainstorming, generating questions, and previewing, to anticipate content, purpose, and organization of a reading selection.

2. Selects and uses strategies to understand words and text, and to make and confirm inferences from what is read, including interpreting diagrams, graphs, and statistical illustrations.

3. Refines vocabulary for interpersonal, academic, and workplace situations, including figurative, idiomatic, and technical meanings.

Figure 6-3 Each curriculum standard in the Florida Sunshine Standards has at least one measurable benchmark. The first curriculum standard for reading in language arts, for example, is the same across grades, but the benchmarks increase in difficulty from grades 3 to 12.

What Is Technology Integration?

Defining curriculum is easy when compared to defining technology integration. First, **integration** by itself is defined as bringing different parts together into a whole. Therefore, **technology integration,** also called **curriculum integration,** is the combination of all technology parts, such as hardware and software, together with each subject-related area of curriculum to enhance learning. Furthermore, technology integration is using technology to help meet the curriculum standards and learner outcomes of each lesson, unit, or activity.

Mastering the integration of technology into the curriculum is not easy. Extensive formal training and practical experiences are imperative for successful integration of technology at all levels of K-12 education. Technology cannot enhance learning unless teachers know how to use and integrate technology into curriculum-specific or discipline-specific areas.

First and foremost, teachers must remember that technology is only a tool to enhance or support instructional strategies. Educators should take steps to integrate technology throughout classroom experiences, activities, and projects, as well as find ways to use technology to teach curriculum-specific content while establishing connections between those subjects and the real world (Figure 6-4). This chapter assists you in learning the basics necessary to integrate technology into your classroom and provides the understanding needed to promote integration literacy.

A critical issue related to technology integration is that technology should not drive the curriculum. The curriculum, rather, should drive the technology; that is, teachers should use the appropriate technologies to enhance learning at the appropriate times and to teach to the standards (Figure 6-5).

In the next section, you will learn the pros and cons of using computers located in a centralized computer lab or in individual classrooms.

Figure 6-4 When a teacher integrates virtual reality technology in his classroom curriculum, students are introduced to many unique and positive learning experiences. For example, in this photo students are exploring the virtual world of 3-D modeling.

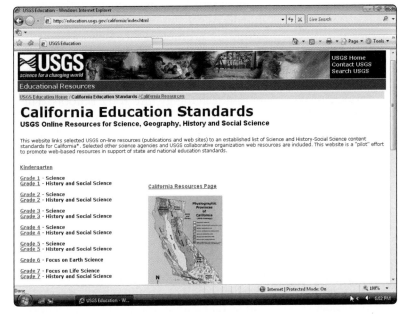

Figure 6-5 Many Web sites provide teachers with curriculum integration activities and strategies related to specific standards.

CLASSROOM INTEGRATION VERSUS COMPUTER LABS AND MEDIA CENTERS

Many educators have become advocates of integrating computers into content areas. For years, teachers and administrators have focused their efforts on getting technology or computer labs into schools. A **computer lab**, or **technology lab**, usually is a designated classroom filled with computers and technology for students to use individually or in groups (Figure 6-6). Lab computers usually are connected to the school's local area network (LAN) and provide many resources in a centralized area.

Figure 6-6 Computer labs give students access to computers and other technologies.

Teachers can schedule time in computer labs for an entire class period and use the labs for many purposes, such as whole-group instruction, small-group activities, or individual student-centered learning. In addition to computer labs, school media centers contain computers and also can be scheduled for use by classroom teachers. Computer labs are a popular approach to getting technology into K-12 schools. The primary reasons administrators usually opt for computer labs are related to cost and location. When computers are installed in the same location, they are easier to maintain and connect to a school network. Popular uses for networked school computer labs are for students to work on projects and work through tutorial software and integrated learning systems software.

Computer labs clearly provide solutions to some educational dilemmas and are an excellent addition to any school. Research shows that computers and related technologies, however, are more effective when integrated into subject content and placed in

the classroom — at the point of instruction. **Point of instruction** is having the technology in the classroom at the teachers' and students' fingertips (Figure 6-7).

Figure 6-7 This teacher knows that by using computers at the point of instruction he can enhance the students' learning experiences.

If technology is readily available, teachers and students will use the technology more. An example is an elementary teacher teaching a lesson on frogs. Students want to see and learn more about frogs, so they start asking questions. Teachers can turn to the technologies in their classrooms, such as digital media software programs or the Web, to show how a frog jumps, where frogs live, and more.

Convenience is important and so is the availability of the technology at the time of instruction. Many educators refer to this as a teachable moment. When students are interested and ready to learn more about a topic, teachers have a **teachable moment**, which is an open window of opportunity for the information to be comprehended in greater detail by students (Figure 6-8). Computers, when placed in the hands of students and teachers, provide unique, effective, and powerful opportunities for many different types of teaching and learning by engaging the students in learning experiences. Research is revealing that students retain knowledge longer when they are actively involved in using digital media

Integration Strategies

To learn more about how to integrate hardware, software, and peripherals with students who are challenged, visit the Teachers Discovering Computers Web site (*scsite.com/tdc5*), click Chapter 6, and then click Assistive Technologies Corner.

Figure 6-8 A teacher often can identify a teachable moment just by looking in the faces of excited students who are motivated to learn!

to meet learning objectives and related benchmarks.

The Classroom in Action

To illustrate the benefits of using technology at the point of instruction, this section takes you into Mr. Balado's fifth-grade classroom at Martin Luther King Elementary School. Just as Mr. Balado finished reading his class a fictional story about a mouse that barely escaped being swallowed whole by a barn owl, several students raised their hands to ask questions. "How did the barn owl see the mouse in the dark?" asked one student. Another student inquired, "Can an owl really scan the entire barn without moving off of its perch?" "What was the pellet that flew from the owl's mouth?" asked a third. Mr. Balado smiled because he expected these types of questions and knew they would open the door to a wonderful opportunity for learning. The questions clearly led to a teachable moment, which he could maximize by using his classroom technologies.

Mr. Balado's classroom contains five student computers networked to the school's local area network and the World Wide Web. In addition, Mr. Balado has an instructional computer with access to the Web that is connected to an interactive whiteboard (similar to the classroom shown in Figure 6-9). Using a projector system to display the images on an interactive whiteboard is an excellent way to allow all students to see what displays on the instructional computer's monitor, to see and hear interactive digital media applications, and to interact with the Web and educational software, while at the same time asking questions. These questions create enthusiasm and a desire for additional knowledge among the students.

Mr. Balado had planned and prepared for the integration of various technologies into his interdisciplinary lesson. First, he

FAQ

Are projection systems still too expensive for the individual classroom?

No, they have come down significantly in price and some districts are making them standard equipment in all new classroom construction and adding them to existing classrooms.

Figure 6-9 Teachers easily can connect a computer to a Smart Technologies Interactive Whiteboard to display a computer monitor's image to the entire class.

Web Info

To take a virtual tour of a museum, visit the Teachers Discovering Computers Web site (*scsite.com/tdc5*), click Chapter 6, click Web Info, and then click Virtual Tour.

had searched the Web for sites that would be appropriate for the fifth-grade curriculum and would provide detailed information and research about different owl species and their environment, their food and hunting behaviors, their anatomy, and more. Locating the Web sites in advance allowed him to identify several excellent sites and eliminated the need to waste time searching for Web sites during class instruction time. In addition, Mr. Balado evaluated all of the Web sites in advance for their content and appropriateness for his fifth-grade students. Evaluation of technology resources is an important element in technology integration and is covered in detail in Chapter 7.

While interacting with the Web sites, students asked more questions, such as the following: Where do owls fall on the food chain? What specific foods do owls eat? How do owls gather food? What happens to the food after the owls swallow it whole? Why do owls hoot? Are owls mean animals that are always on the attack? What makes owls different from other birds? This was all part of Mr. Balado's instructional plan, and his students' questions continued as Mr. Balado actively engaged them in exploration and discovery learning at selected owl Web sites (Figure 6-10). The students were genuinely excited while exploring Web sites about these birds of prey; they were discovering new concepts while Mr. Balado guided their learning.

With computers in his classroom for use at the point of instruction, Mr. Balado had his students' full attention. Together they explored interesting Web sites while traveling through interactive virtual field trips as wildlife biologists. **Virtual field trips** allow you to walk through doorways, down halls, and let you see everything in a three-dimensional world via a computer as if you were there.

Mr. Balado's students were no longer only hearing a story about a fictional owl; they were now seeing, hearing, and interacting with a variety of owl species. After they looked at many owl facts, pictures, and video clips, Mr. Balado asked his students to storyboard their narrative stories about owls, their prey, and the food chain. Later, he will take his students to a computer lab where they will use their storyboards to create narratives with text and visuals.

Integrating Technology into the Curriculum

As this example illustrates, computers and other technologies can provide unique, effective, and powerful opportunities for many different types of teaching and learning. Educators recognize that technology can serve as an extremely powerful tool that can help alleviate some of the problems of today's schools. Motivating students to learn is one area that all educators constantly are trying to achieve. Technology has the potential to increase student motivation and class attendance.

Using these technology tools with students with varying abilities has helped to address different learning styles and reach diverse learners. With the right approach, educators can integrate technologies such as computers, CDs, DVDs, digital cameras, application software, digital media applications and devices, e-books and electronic references, handheld computers, iPods, and the Web into almost any classroom situation. For technology to enhance student learning, however, it must be integrated into the curriculum.

The key to successful technology integration is identifying what you are trying to accomplish within your curriculum. First, you must consider what the standards

![Screenshot of Owls Web page in Windows Internet Explorer showing two barn owls with the title "Owls" and descriptive text about owls, followed by a list of owl species including Barn Owl, Barred Owl, Burrowing Owl, Eagle Owl, Elf Owl, Great Gray Owl, Long-eared Owl, Northern Hawk Owl, Saw-whet Owl, Snowy Owl, and Spectacled Owl.]

Figure 6-10 The Web provides vast amounts of information that allows students and teachers to discover innovative ways to enhance learning.

and related learning objectives are, and then you must identify an appropriate technology tool that will help you accomplish your instructional goals. Although this process sounds simple, complete integration of technology in all subject areas is complex and takes a great deal of planning. A later section of this chapter discusses how to plan for technology integration.

After you have determined specific standards and related learning objectives and you have identified technologies appropriate for areas of the curriculum, you then can begin to develop innovative ways to teach a diverse population of learners with different learning styles (Figure 6-11). A **learning style** refers to how individuals learn, including how they prefer to receive, process, and retain information. Learning styles vary among individuals. For example, some people learn better alone, while others learn better in groups. Many different types of learning styles exist and most individuals learn using a combination of several styles. The use of technologies, such as digital media and the Web, can help address learning styles and needs of today's digital generation.

By engaging students in different ways, technology encourages them to take a more active role in the learning process. To learn more about learning styles and

theories, read the special feature that follows this chapter: Learning Theories and Educational Research.

Changing Instructional Strategies

When students play a more active role in the learning process, the teacher's role must change. Teachers need to transition from the conventional lecture-practice-recall teaching methods — often called the sage on the stage — to a classroom in which teachers engage students in activities that allow them opportunities to construct knowledge — a new role called the guide on the side. That is, teachers should shift from being the dispenser of knowledge to being the facilitator of learning. Rather than dictating a learning process, a **facilitator of learning** motivates students to want to learn, guides the student learning process, and promotes a learning atmosphere and an appreciation for the subject.

Two main assumptions must be considered as teachers become facilitators of learning. The first is that students can create their own learning and that the teachers' role is to assist their students in this process. The second is that academic work extends beyond

Web Info

To discover more about learning styles, visit the Teachers Discovering Computers Web site (*scsite.com/tdc5*), click Chapter 6, click Web Info, and then click Learning Styles.

Figure 6-11 Technology is a tool that creates valuable learning experiences for many different types of learners.

Web Info

For more information about barriers to technology integration, visit the Teachers Discovering Computers Web site (*scsite.com/tdc5*), click Chapter 6, click Web Info, and then click Barriers.

the mere storage of information. Instead, teachers want their students to be able to assimilate information and become problem solvers.

As teachers become facilitators of learning and incorporate technology into their instructional strategies, they will progress through several developmental stages. **Wellivers Instructional Transformation Model**, for example, describes five hierarchical stages of technology integration through which all teachers must progress to integrate technology effectively (Figure 6-12).

Barriers to Technology Integration

With all change comes barriers, and technology integration is no exception.

Bill Gates stated in a speech, "In all areas of the curriculum, teachers must teach an information-based inquiry process to meet the demands of the information age. This is the challenge for the world's most important profession. Meeting this challenge will be impossible unless educators are willing to join the revolution and embrace the new technology tools available." Even after many years, these words still are true.

For more than two decades, several barriers have hindered technology integration in many schools. Such barriers include a lack of teacher training, security constraints that impede instructional strategies, lack of administration support, limited time for teacher planning, computer placement in remote locations making access difficult, budget constraints, lack of high-speed school networks, and basic resistance to change by many educators.

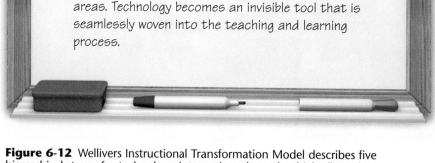

Wellivers Instructional Transformation Model

1. **Familiarization** — Teachers become aware of technology and its potential uses.

2. **Utilization** — Teachers use technology, but minor problems will cause teachers to discontinue its use.

3. **Integration** — Technology becomes essential for the educational process and teachers are constantly thinking of ways to use technology in their classrooms.

4. **Reorientation** — Teachers begin to rethink the educational goals of the classroom with the use of technology.

5. **Revolution** — The evolving classroom becomes completely integrated with technology in all subject areas. Technology becomes an invisible tool that is seamlessly woven into the teaching and learning process.

Figure 6-12 Wellivers Instructional Transformation Model describes five hierarchical stages for technology integration, through which all teachers must progress in order to integrate technology effectively.

Every educator looks at the integration of technology — and its challenges — from a different perspective. Technology coordinators view the problems of insufficient hardware, software, and training as major obstacles. Teachers consider the lack of time to develop technology-based lessons a concern. Administrators identify teachers' lack of experience using technology in instruction as yet another challenge. Teachers and administrators, however, can and are beginning to overcome these barriers with effective leadership, proper training, planning, and a commitment to enhancing teaching and learning using technology (Figure 6-13).

Technology Integration and the Learning Process

Before teachers can begin to develop integration skills, they must realize and understand how the integration of technology can enhance teaching and learning. Research shows that using technology in the classroom motivates students, encourages them to become problem solvers, and creates new avenues to demonstrate creative thinking. Teachers also have found that using computers or computer-related technologies can capture and hold students' attention. Interactive technologies, such as software applications, digital media,

With Proper Technology Training, Teachers Can Do the Following:

- Create relationships between active learning and active teaching.

- Develop an appreciation and an understanding of the potential of technology.

- Learn to be creators of digital media for self-expression.

- Develop leadership skills and become role models for successful integration.

- Understand the power of technology integration.

- Design integrated curriculum activities that develop critical thinking and problem solving skills.

- Learn the benefits of technology in the classroom.

- Develop ownership of the technology through authentic experiences.

- Learn to motivate students with digital media and other technologies.

- Achieve success by becoming informed and reflective decision makers.

- Become advocates for technology integration.

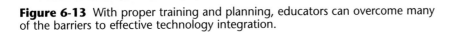

Figure 6-13 With proper training and planning, educators can overcome many of the barriers to effective technology integration.

reference guides, tutorials, animations, simulations, and the Web, are especially engaging as they allow students to determine the flow of information, review concepts, practice skills, do in-depth research, and more.

Technologies that provide interactivity, learner control, and student engagement are a natural choice for improving instruction. When used properly, technology is extremely beneficial in the learning process.

THE LEARNING PROCESS

For learning to take place, learners must be engaged in the process of education. One way to engage learners is to motivate them through authentic learning experiences. **Authentic learning** experiences are instructional activities that demonstrate real-life connections by associating the concept being taught with a real-life experience or event (Figure 6-14). For authentic learning to take place, teachers must involve students in the process of gathering, analyzing, and using information to make informed decisions that relate to real life. More than any previous generation, today's digital students look for revelancy in the content of the various subjects they are learning.

When possible, teachers should promote **active learning**, which is a type of learning that occurs when students become engaged in inquiring, investigating, reflecting, solving problems, and formulating and answering questions. Active learning also involves the process of students discussing, brainstorming, explaining, and debating issues with each other and with their teacher, both to determine solutions as well as to identify their own questions. Active learning makes learning more relevant by promoting the retention of information, motivating students to extend their learning, and giving students a sense of ownership of the information they are presenting. Active learning is especially appropriate when teaching to a wide variety of learning styles.

A lesson on the human digestive system, for example, presents concepts that are difficult for students to understand. Students have never seen the digestive system, nor can they feel or touch it. For students to understand these new concepts, they must have background information or a knowledge base on which to build. Providing a knowledge base on which students can build is called **anchored instruction**. Through anchored instruction, learning and teaching activities are designed around an anchor (or situation) that provides a scenario or problem enhanced with curriculum materials that allow exploration by the learner. Anchored

Web Info

For more information about authentic learning experiences, visit the Teachers Discovering Computers Web site (*scsite.com/tdc5*), click Chapter 6, click Web Info, and then click Authentic Learning.

Figure 6-14 Learners are motivated to learn through authentic, real-life experiences.

instruction also includes the component of **problem-based instruction**, in which students use the background (anchor) information to begin to solve and understand complex problems or concepts.

Providing students with opportunities to expand their knowledge base allows them to experience visionary exploration or discovery learning. Recall from Chapter 2 that discovery learning is a nonlinear learning process that occurs when you investigate related topics as you encounter them. Discovery learning also is an inquiry-based method of teaching and learning where students interact with their surroundings by exploring and manipulating objects, investigating and solving problems through inquiry, or performing hands-on exercises and experiments. When students discover and explore meaningful concepts on their own, they are more likely to understand and retain information. Discovery learning also helps students become better critical thinkers.

TECHNOLOGY AND THE LEARNING PROCESS

Technology can provide numerous tools to support many types of instruction and learning. To teach students about the human heart, for example, a teacher could integrate an educational software application such as Body Works or Microsoft Encarta into the lesson. **Body Works** is a digital media product for teaching related concepts about the human body. As you learned in the previous chapter, **Microsoft Encarta** is an interactive multimedia encyclopedia. These applications provide working visual models of how the various parts of the human heart interact (Figure 6-15). These applications thus allow students to see and experience clearly things they could never experience by only reading a textbook. Applications such as these also allow students to build a **cognitive scaffold**, which is a mental bridge to build an understanding of complicated concepts.

Another benefit of integrating educational applications is that they encourage students to think not only in words and pictures, but also in colors, sounds, animations, and more. When people think, their thoughts are filled with sounds, images, colors, and movements. A young child, for example, will describe a

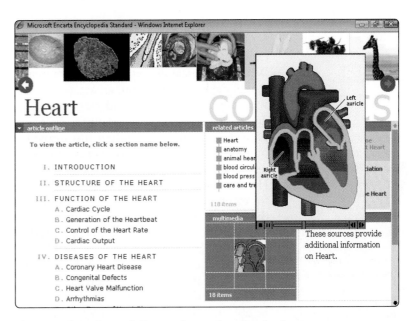

Figure 6-15 Microsoft Encarta is an educational software program that allows students to interact with a myriad of subjects. In this example, students see and hear how the human heart works.

fire engine by indicating its color and demonstrating the sounds and movements of fire engines going to a fire (Figure 6-16). Most traditional instruction, however, uses words and pictures only, often in two-color textbooks. Digital media tools allow students to have learning experiences in which concepts are brought to life with a variety of representations — videos, sounds, colors, pictures, simulations, and animations.

Figure 6-16 Everyone thinks in colors, images, sounds, and animations. A young child, for example, will describe a fire engine by imitating the sounds of a siren, indicating its color, and visualizing the sounds and movements of fire engines going to a fire.

Technology helps teachers promote active learning and create authentic learning experiences by allowing students to conduct Web-based research, explore concepts in a digital media presentation, create a slide show for a history presentation, create a database of results from a group science project, and more. Technology also provides opportunities for anchored instruction. Students can watch a Web-based video clip of a Himalayan mountain-climbing expedition, for example, and then move on to examine the history of Tibet, the Sherpa culture, the physical effects of climbing in high altitudes, or how avalanches start.

Computers, digital media, and especially the Web create numerous opportunities for discovery learning. Many students may never be able to visit an extraordinary museum, such as the Smithsonian Institution. The Web, however, can transport them to a world beyond their own, filled with infinite amounts of information — visually, audibly, and even virtually. Using discovery learning, you can break down classroom walls with technology, the Web, and most importantly — opening doors for imagination. Properly integrated technology allows students to understand concepts more clearly and learn no matter who or where they are.

The Internet and the World Wide Web have been called the **educational equalizer** — that is, they give students of all backgrounds, socioeconomic levels, learning styles, geographic locations, academic levels, and learning abilities access to the same information. Figure 6-17 illustrates how the Web brings these elements together to provide valuable learning experiences.

The Web allows students to experience educational opportunities previously not available. Students can publish their work, meet students with similar interests across the globe, and participate in shared learning experiences with classrooms worldwide. The Internet and Web also support projects in which students interact with authors, elected officials, or scientists conducting research. E-mail, blogs, wikis, podcasts, and Web-based projects are ideal for teacher-monitored school projects that involve language arts, cultural learning, history, geography, social studies, science, or communications with friends around the world (Figure 6-18).

As illustrated by these examples, computers can provide many unique, effective, and powerful opportunities for teaching and learning. Such opportunities include skill-building practice, interactive

Integration Strategies

To learn how to integrate Web pages, blogs, wikis, podcasts, and digital media screencasts, review the special feature that follows Chapter 7, *Integrating Web Pages, Blogs, Wikis, and more*

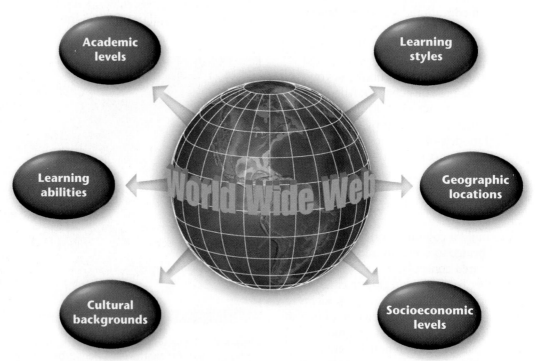

Figure 6-17 The Web, which provides access to a seemingly infinite amount of information, has the capability of addressing learner differences, and, thus, leveling the playing field for all students.

Figure 6-18 Using computers and the World Wide Web, students can join various projects to learn about other cultures and communicate with other students around the world.

learning, and linking learners to instructional technology resources. In addition, computers support communications beyond classroom walls, thus enabling schools and communities to provide an environment for cooperative learning and the development of innovative opportunities for learning.

Cooperative learning refers to a method of instruction in which students work collaboratively in groups to achieve standards and related learning objectives. Instead of working alone on activities and projects, students share ideas, learn teamwork skills, and begin to help one another to accomplish tasks or achieve objectives. **Cooperative classroom activities** are student-centered, with the teacher serving as a facilitator and the students as information seekers. **Higher-order thinking skills** are the abilities to solve problems, engage in critical thinking, and interpret and solve complex issues. Teachers need to create activities for students to promote the use of higher-order thinking skills throughout their educational experiences (Figure 6-19).

By promoting new and enhanced learning experiences, properly integrated technology offers limitless possibilities for instruction and learning. Computers, digital media, the Web, and other technologies help students to understand concepts more clearly and help

teachers develop unique activities that maximize every teachable moment. Students become knowledge seekers and active learners who acquire knowledge and find different ways to interpret what they discover. Finally, technology can help improve students' abilities as independent thinkers and encourage them to become lifelong learners.

Figure 6-19 Computers support communications beyond classroom walls, thus providing an environment that allows for cooperative learning, development of higher-order thinking skills, and solving complex problems.

Integration Strategies

To learn more about mentoring and how mentorship programs can help teachers increase their integration literacy skills, visit the Teachers Discovering Computers Web site (*scsite.com/tdc5*), click Chapter 6, and then click Teaching Today.

Strategies for Integrating Technology into Teaching

The best strategy for curriculum integration is to put the technology into the hands of trained teachers, make it easily accessible, and let them decide how best to use it at the point of instruction in their classrooms. Teachers then can use an array of teaching strategies to develop a learning environment in which students are encouraged to be independent learners and take responsibility for their own learning.

The main goal of such teaching strategies is to provide a consistent application of technology tools to support instructional curriculum areas. Also, it is important to give every student the opportunity to work with computers and related technologies. When proper strategies are used for technology integration, students enjoy learning to use technology as well as the content in the subject-related curriculum areas.

Already, many experienced educators are integrating technology into subject-specific instruction — and have seen the benefits technology integration can bring to the learning experience. One critically important element in effective technology integration is continuous planning. For technology integration to be successful, careful planning is required at all levels, which involves district-level planning, school-level planning, and classroom-level planning. Each level must plan systematically so that technology is integrated effectively and seamlessly into all facets of education.

The Role of the School District

Effective curriculum integration cannot take place if support for technology integration does not come from several sources within the school district. School district administrators must plan carefully for every aspect of curriculum integration, from purchase to installation to teacher and staff training and technical support. Almost every school district has a detailed technology plan for technology integration. A **technology plan** is an outline that specifies the school district's procedures for purchasing and maintaining equipment and software, and training teachers to use and then integrate technology

into their classroom curriculum. Because of emerging and changing technologies, many school districts update their technology plans every three to five years. Many individual school technology committees review their technology plans every couple of years to make sure they meet their district's plans.

To prepare educators to use the technology after it is implemented, administrators provide technology training with mentorship programs and follow-up staff development after training (Figure 6-20). A **mentorship program** teams new or novice teachers with experienced teachers to encourage new teachers to learn to integrate technology resources. Collaboration is promoted by sharing planning time and e-mail with other teaching professionals inside and outside the district. Experienced teachers guide new teachers by providing information and suggestions. In-house workshops are provided so teachers learn to use and integrate the available technologies in their schools and classrooms.

Figure 6-20 Mentorship programs allow teachers to learn computer and technology integration concepts from experienced teachers in a nonthreatening environment.

Today, many federal, public, and state grant funding sources are requiring that part of the funding be spent on teacher training. This funding has increased the number of teachers using and integrating technology.

In addition, numerous Web sites are dedicated to mentoring new and experienced teachers in everything from how to get started with technology to classroom management. These sites provide wonderful resources for teachers and offer an avenue for teachers to find ideas, advice, and support. Mentors can help new teachers become more effective in the classroom.

To view a school district's technology plan, visit the Teachers Discovering Computers Web site (*scsite.com/tdc5*), click Chapter 6, click Web Info, and then click Technology Plan.

Planning for Technology Integration in the Classroom

Teachers must plan carefully for the use and integration of computers and technologies in the classroom. Just as planning is essential to effective instruction, it is required for effective use and integration of technology in the classroom. One important consideration is deciding on the most appropriate technology to achieve the desired learner outcomes. Teachers must plan how they will teach the curriculum, what areas they need to cover for content, and where they can use technology to meet curriculum standards and related learning objectives.

Another important consideration in the planning stage is preparing the classroom environment (Figure 6-21). The way in which you integrate technology into the curriculum will depend largely on how much technology is in your classroom or in your school. Whether you use one computer, two computers, or thirty computers, you must plan how and when you will use those computers and how you will enable your students to use those computers. The amount of planning will vary according to the arrangement of computers in your classroom and school and the scope of your lesson. Chapter 7 discusses these and other planning issues.

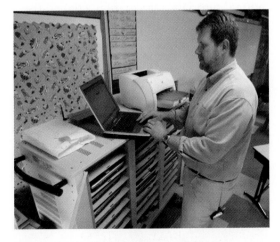

Figure 6-21 Teachers must prepare their classrooms carefully for the integration of computers and other technologies.

ONE-COMPUTER CLASSROOM

In classrooms with only one computer, teachers must plan to maximize the effectiveness of that one computer. In such classrooms, the computer most commonly is used for teacher administrative use and can be used to create letters, worksheets, puzzles, handouts, lesson plans, tests, forms, newsletters, data collection (i.e., electronic grade book, attendance, student information, mail merge), and more.

To gain full instructional benefits, you need to use your single computer in different ways. For example, you can use it for record keeping, knowledge acquisition by searching the Web, and classroom presentations. To allow students to view the presentations or demonstrations, you easily can project the monitor's content with a projector onto a projection screen, classroom wall, or interactive whiteboard, described in Chapter 5. If your school has only a few of these devices, you will have to plan ahead to schedule them for use in your classroom.

A good instructional strategy for the classroom computer is to introduce students to various types of software and create learning paths before taking the class to the computer lab. Using this instructional strategy optimizes the time students spend on computers while in the lab. Rather than spending time learning basic software skills, students can devote time to interacting with the computer to experience discovery learning.

You can turn your computer into an activity or production center and let your students use the computer as a creation tool for production and publishing when working on word processing, database, spreadsheet, graphics, and multimedia projects. You can create opportunities for group presentations created by the students to be made to the class. You can add other handheld technologies to your classroom to extend the use of your single computer.

In addition, teachers in a one-computer classroom can use the computer for the same purposes as described in the next sections on two or more computer classrooms. Many

Web Info

For additional strategies and applications for one-computer classrooms, visit the Teachers Discovering Computers Web site (*scsite.com/tdc5*), click Chapter 6, click Web Info, and then click One Computer.

Web Info

For more information about curriculum planning with technology, visit the Teachers Discovering Computers Web site (*scsite.com/tdc5*), click Chapter 6, click Web Info, and then click Curriculum Planning.

ways exist to enhance teaching and learning in the one-computer classroom. With only one computer available, however, additional planning might be required.

TWO-COMPUTER CLASSROOM

In classrooms with two computers, teachers must develop a strategy to manage their use. One computer could be used mainly for research on the Internet, presentations, Web-based projects, and e-mail. The other computer might be used as a writing center or for students to create digital media projects.

Regardless of how you use the computers, you should develop a strategy for how you will allocate computer use and how students' computer time will be managed. Questions that can assist with planning follow:

- Will both computers have the same hardware, software, and network access?

- Will one or both computers be connected to the Web?

- Will students rotate through using one or both computers on a daily basis?

- How much time will each student be allowed on each computer?

- Is it better to have the students work together on projects?

- How are you going to observe your students using the Internet?

- How will you evaluate student learning?

MORE THAN TWO COMPUTERS

Teachers who have several computers may find that arranging their classrooms in a single learning center or several learning centers, through which groups of students can rotate as they complete projects or activities, provides an environment for productive use of the computers. Other technologies also can be organized into learning centers, such as a video center in which students can use digital video cameras to record and watch themselves performing plays, creating and telling stories, or role-playing; a CD/DVD center where

students can conduct research and learn new skills by interacting with instructional CDs and DVDs; a listening or reading center; a digital media production center where students can create their own digital media projects, and much more.

Before setting up a computer center or centers, teachers should ask the planning questions previously cited, in addition to considering how many computers will be in each center and what other technologies, if any, might be included in the center. As indicated, the technologies a teacher utilizes will depend on the curriculum standards and learning objectives. Furthermore, part of preparing the classroom environment is being aware of the prerequisite skills necessary for students to be successful.

USING A COMPUTER LAB AND THE MEDIA CENTER

Because few classrooms include a computer for every student, using a computer lab allows teachers to provide learning opportunities that are not possible in a one-, two-, or even five-computer classroom. The most important advantage of using a computer lab is that all students are provided hands-on experience with the computer technology (Figure 6-22). Computer labs can be used successfully by teachers and students for one-to-one computing, tutorials, remediation, cooperative learning, computer skill instruction, digital production projects, Internet research, whole class instruction, and integrated learning systems (ILS).

Figure 6-22 By using networked computers with Internet access, students can work on different projects at the same time.

Integration Strategies

To access dozens of integration ideas that you can use with one, two, or more than two classroom computers, visit the Teachers Discovering Computers Web site (*scsite.com/tdc5*), click Chapter 6, click Integration Corner, and then click your grade level corner.

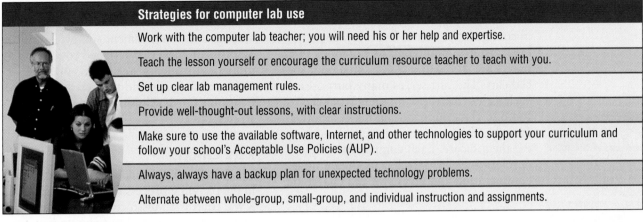

Strategies for computer lab use
Work with the computer lab teacher; you will need his or her help and expertise.
Teach the lesson yourself or encourage the curriculum resource teacher to teach with you.
Set up clear lab management rules.
Provide well-thought-out lessons, with clear instructions.
Make sure to use the available software, Internet, and other technologies to support your curriculum and follow your school's Acceptable Use Policies (AUP).
Always, always have a backup plan for unexpected technology problems.
Alternate between whole-group, small-group, and individual instruction and assignments.

Figure 6-23 Suggestions that will assist teachers in the computer lab to make the instructional lessons a successful learning experience for students.

Computer labs have an added benefit of allowing students to interact with technology and software that is student centered. Taking your class to a computer lab, however, requires careful planning and scheduling to use the allocated time efficiently and effectively. Managing instruction in a lab environment also requires that teachers carefully plan their learning strategies for this multicomputer environment.

The advantage of using a computer lab for instructional purposes is that all students have access to computers, the Internet, and software. Many times, other available technologies allow students to work on projects and develop additional technology skills, such as video production and much more. Figure 6-23 above lists some suggestions to help make your time in the computer lab a successful learning experience.

USING A WIRELESS MOBILE LAB

Today's wireless digital technology represents an evolution of products and services for businesses and education. Many innovative technologies have evolved and are being used in K-12 and higher education classrooms; these technologies provide teachers with new and exciting integration possibilities.

One use of wireless technology is a **wireless mobile lab,** also called a **computer lab on wheels** or **computers on wheels** (COW). A wireless mobile lab is a portable cart with wireless notebook computers that can be transported from one classroom to another (Figure 6-24). As you learned in previous chapters, wireless communications make technology more accessible and flexible. The wireless mobile lab uses all the advantages of wireless technology, bringing technology to digital students without having to take them to a dedicated computer or technology lab. These rolling digital learning centers can be moved almost anywhere and shared among classrooms. These mobile labs allow for expanded network capabilities and offer many instructional opportunities for teachers.

Web Info

For more information about wireless mobile labs, visit the Teachers Discovering Computers Web site (*scsite.com/tdc5*), click Chapter 6, click Web Info, and then click Wireless Labs.

Figure 6-24 A wireless mobile lab transports computers to the students instead of the students going to a computer lab.

Web Info

For another example of how to use a KWL chart, visit the Teachers Discovering Computers Web site (*scsite.com/tdc5*), click Chapter 6, click Web Info, and then click KWL Chart.

Wireless mobile labs consist of wireless notebook computers that can be purchased in configurations from just a few to as many as 36 computers. The notebook computers are stored and transported on a special cart. The cart serves many purposes, such as moving the computers from classroom to classroom, storing the computers at night, charging the computers, and keeping them secure. Each company that has developed mobile labs has its own unique configuration and ways you can charge the computers and external batteries.

Teachers and students both benefit from this access to technology. By bringing technology to the classroom at the point of instruction, wireless mobile labs effectively integrate technology into the classroom. Because of the many possibilities that wireless mobile labs can and are providing, many experts believe that wireless mobile labs eventually will replace many traditional, wired computer labs.

Planning Lessons with Technology

One of the more important parts of technology planning is developing classroom lessons and activities that utilize technology. Students begin school having varying degrees of knowledge about computers and technology. Students should, at some point, be taught basic computer concepts and operations, but they will learn many basic computer skills just from everyday use. For the digital generation, technology has always been in every aspect of their lives. Educators need to realize that by integrating digital media and related technologies, students develop their own digital literacy, while at the same time, they are given new reasons to get excited and motivated about content and learning.

When planning lessons that use technology, teachers must consider the skills and knowledge level required for students to start and complete the lesson successfully. If technology is part of the lesson, teachers need to consider student technology skills. Many different tools are available to assess students' skill levels, such as a skill assessment survey. A **skill assessment survey** is designed to identify individual students' academic and technology skill levels and then create a starting point for developing instructional strategies.

KWL CHARTS

Another simple and effective tool to help in the planning process is a KWL chart. A **KWL chart** is an instructional planning chart to assist a teacher in identifying student understanding of curriculum standards and related objectives by having students state what they already **K**now, what they **W**ant to know, and then, based on that information recording what students will **L**earn, as shown in Figure 6-25. A KWL chart is a very helpful planning tool in determining skill and knowledge levels of students before beginning almost any project. After a teacher has established the learning objectives, the KWL chart can be used as a survey tool to determine what students already know about a topic and what technology skills they will need for a project. The teacher and students then can determine what they will learn from the project and the technologies best suited to mastering the objectives.

As the project progresses, students are encouraged to list what they have learned on the KWL chart. Not only will students be learning subject-related matter, they will be learning new and different types of technology skills when using technology to accomplish tasks.

An alternative version of the KWL chart is a KWHL chart. A **KWHL chart** also is an instructional planning tool, but adds an additional component — How students will learn. This additional component creates an opportunity for students and teachers to plan for how the learning experiences will occur.

A great way to create active learning opportunities for your students is to let them create KWL and KWHL charts when you introduce a new topic or project.

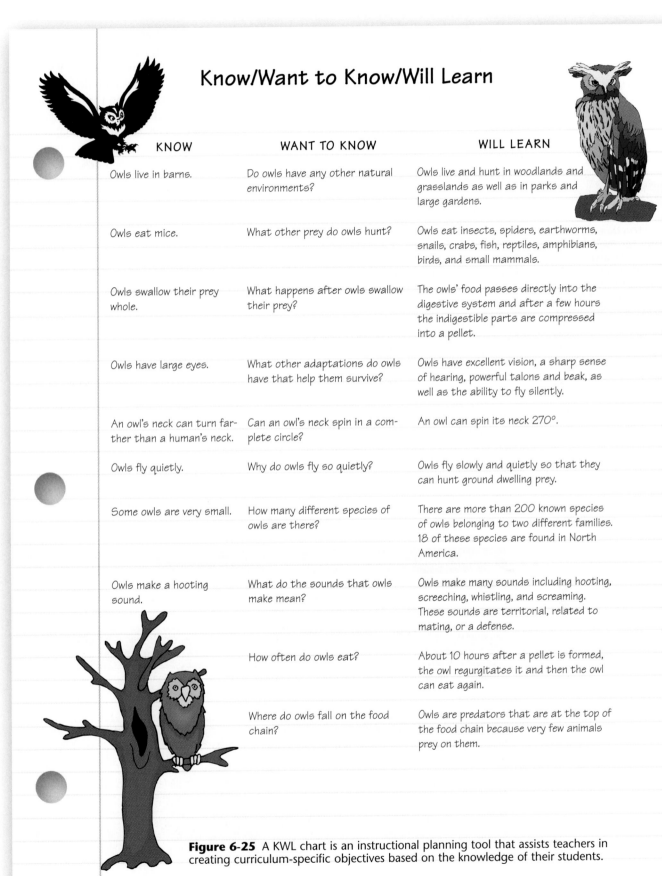

Know/Want to Know/Will Learn

KNOW	WANT TO KNOW	WILL LEARN
Owls live in barns.	Do owls have any other natural environments?	Owls live and hunt in woodlands and grasslands as well as in parks and large gardens.
Owls eat mice.	What other prey do owls hunt?	Owls eat insects, spiders, earthworms, snails, crabs, fish, reptiles, amphibians, birds, and small mammals.
Owls swallow their prey whole.	What happens after owls swallow their prey?	The owls' food passes directly into the digestive system and after a few hours the indigestible parts are compressed into a pellet.
Owls have large eyes.	What other adaptations do owls have that help them survive?	Owls have excellent vision, a sharp sense of hearing, powerful talons and beak, as well as the ability to fly silently.
An owl's neck can turn farther than a human's neck.	Can an owl's neck spin in a complete circle?	An owl can spin its neck 270°.
Owls fly quietly.	Why do owls fly so quietly?	Owls fly slowly and quietly so that they can hunt ground dwelling prey.
Some owls are very small.	How many different species of owls are there?	There are more than 200 known species of owls belonging to two different families. 18 of these species are found in North America.
Owls make a hooting sound.	What do the sounds that owls make mean?	Owls make many sounds including hooting, screeching, whistling, and screaming. These sounds are territorial, related to mating, or a defense.
	How often do owls eat?	About 10 hours after a pellet is formed, the owl regurgitates it and then the owl can eat again.
	Where do owls fall on the food chain?	Owls are predators that are at the top of the food chain because very few animals prey on them.

Figure 6-25 A KWL chart is an instructional planning tool that assists teachers in creating curriculum-specific objectives based on the knowledge of their students.

You can conduct this exercise as a large group activity in which the whole class participates, or you can break up the class in small groups and then let the groups share their results. KWL and KWHL charts can be used in all subjects from kindergarten through university-level classes.

Instructional Models

Before you start a lesson, you plan the lesson, which is a process that involves using an instructional design or model. Effective teaching with technology also involves using an instructional model. An **instructional model** is a systematic guide for planning instruction or a lesson.

When using and integrating technology, an instructional model and planning take on a more important role. Which technology you use is not the critical issue; what is important is that you integrate the technology effectively and the technology is appropriate to the learning objectives. Many instructional models are available from which you can choose. For the purpose of this textbook, the popular educational instructional model called the ASSURE Model is described.

FAQ

Are other instructional models available that can assist teachers in integrating technology into their curriculum?

Yes. Other popular instructional models include the ADDIE Model, Kemp Model, Dick & Carey Model, and Diamond Model.

THE ASSURE MODEL

The **ASSURE Model** developed in the late 1990s by Heinich, Molenda, Russell, and Smaldino is a procedural guide for planning and delivering instruction that integrates technologies and media into the teaching process (Figure 6-26). The ASSURE Model is a well-known guide for developing any instructional lessons. The following is a description of the steps of the ASSURE Model and an explanation of how to use the model in your classroom.

ANALYZE THE LEARNER Knowing your learner's skill level is important. Some students may come into your classroom with academic and technology skills that others do not possess. Teachers should plan for this situation. Know your audience and consider the diverse differences in the student population you are teaching.

STATE OBJECTIVES Student objectives are statements of the type of skills and knowledge you expect students to be able to demonstrate at the end of instruction. When you have clear student objectives, you can select your materials and determine the focus and purpose of the lesson or project more wisely. Be sure to match student objectives to curriculum standards and learning objectives.

ASSURE Model	
Analyze the Learner	• Who are the learners? • What are their skill levels? • What are their learning styles?
State Objectives	• What do you want the learners to gain knowledge of? • What are the specific learner outcomes?
Select Methods, Media, and Materials	• What methods of instruction will you use? • Which media are appropriate? • Which materials will you need?
Utilize Methods, Media, and Materials	• How will you use the methods and media? • How will you use the materials? • What is your instructional strategy?
Require Learner Participation	• What will the learners be required to do? • Will the learners engage in active or passive learning?
Evaluate and Revise	• Did the lesson meet the objectives? • How will you evaluate content and technologies used? • How will you revise and improve?

Figure 6-26 The ASSURE Model is an instructional model used by educators to develop technology-enriched lessons.

SELECT METHODS, MEDIA, AND MATERIALS

Selection of methods, media, and materials includes three steps, which are (1) decide on the method of instruction, (2) choose the media format that is appropriate for the method, and (3) select, modify, update, or design materials for the instruction. Media and materials include all items you choose to meet the curriculum standard, such as print, technology, information resources, and related components. Media can take many forms, including CD, DVD, the Internet or the Web, a video, an overhead projector, a graphing calculator, special technology devices for learning, software, digital media, or any combination of these and other items (Figure 6-27).

The first step is to decide which method best meets your needs, such as lecture, discovery, tutorials, demonstration, or creation of student projects. Next, you need to decide on the media, how you are going to use the media, and what you want the learners to do. Make sure the materials you identify are available and list what you are planning to use them for. Finally, determine if you need to modify any of the media or materials or design new media or materials.

UTILIZE METHODS, MEDIA, AND MATERIALS

Teachers should preview all media and materials they are planning to use, including videos, digital media applications, and Web sites. Although a software company may advertise that a particular software product contains the correct content for your objectives, you, as the teacher, must evaluate the content of all software. Again, refer to your learning objectives to assist you in determining this step. Next, you will need to prepare the classroom environment. Use these questions to guide you in making preparations:

- What equipment, software, or devices are required to use the media?
- Do you need to reserve extra equipment that you might not have in your classroom?
- How do you prepare your classroom to use the equipment?
- How do you prepare the students to use the media and materials?
- Do you need to schedule a computer lab or the media center?

Figure 6-27 Teachers must choose which media to use and when it is appropriate to use the technology.

Web Info

For assistance with creating lesson plans, visit the Teachers Discovering Computers Web site (*scsite.com/tdc5*), click Chapter 6, click Web Info, and then click Lesson Plans.

REQUIRE LEARNER PARTICIPATION   As previously discussed, the most effective learning situations are those that require active learning and ask learners to complete activities that build mastery toward the learning objectives. Classroom lessons should motivate students to be active learners who are involved in the process of learning, such as practicing, performing, solving, building, creating, and manipulating. As you develop these lessons, you must decide what information to include in the activities. If students are doing a research project using the Web, for example, they need guidelines of what to incorporate and how you will assess the outcome of the project. Chapter 7 discusses assessment tools in more detail.

EVALUATE AND REVISE   At the end of a project or lesson, it is important to evaluate all aspects of the lesson, instruction, or learning experience. **Evaluation** is the method of appraising or determining the significance or worth of an item, action, or outcome. This **evaluation process** includes assessing learning objectives, reviewing, critiquing the learners' work or works based on specific standards, and evaluating reviews of the media and materials used. Teachers should conduct thoughtful reflection on all aspects of the instructional process. **Reflective evaluation** is thinking back on the components of the teaching and learning process and determining the effectiveness of the learner outcomes and the use of technology during the process (Figure 6-28). Students also should be asked to reflect on their learning experiences, their perceptions on the content learned, and their evaluation of the learning process. The lesson should be revised based on the evaluations.

Critical Questions to Ask During the Evaluate and Revise Phase of the ASSURE Model

- Did students learn what you wanted them to learn?

- Can students demonstrate understanding of the content?

- Was the chosen technology effective in achieving the learning objectives?

- Were the learning objectives met using the technology?

- Should learning objectives be taught in a different format?

- Would these learning objectives be better taught without technology or with another technology?

- Can students work cooperatively with a partner on this lesson?

- Would parts of the content be better understood if students worked individually?

- What would you change?

- What would you keep the same?

- How will you revise this lesson?

Figure 6-28 Questions teachers should consider during the evaluation and revision phase.

The ASSURE Model is one popular educational model that teachers can use to plan for technology integration into instruction. Emerging technologies will expand teachers' potential to communicate effectively, to convey ideas, and to motivate, encourage, and educate students. As you revise your lesson plans, you will need to evaluate and consider using new and emerging technologies.

As you can see, planning is important on all levels — from the district, to the classroom, to individual lessons. As a new teacher, planning for technology integration will present its challenges. The next section provides information on where to go for guidance and materials to help you plan for technology integration in your classroom.

Getting Started at a New School

Suppose you are a new teacher and it is the first day of the preplanning week for teachers. You are excited to get that first glimpse of your new classroom. When you finally do, you discover you have two new networked computers and a color ink-jet printer in your classroom. Fortunately, you learned about Mac computers and PCs during your teacher education courses. Although you are comfortable using computers, you immediately wonder how to get started. Fortunately, there are many Web sites, like the one shown in Figure 6-29, that can help you as you get started finding ways to integrate these computers into your classroom curriculum. As

you start to plan for technology integration, you will need to consider many issues related to technology information and support, technology training, hardware, software, other technologies, and technology supplies.

INFORMATION ABOUT TECHNOLOGY

One of the first items to investigate is who else in the school is using technology in their classrooms. Individuals to consult are your principal, media specialist, curriculum resource teacher, technology committee members, or other teachers, especially those who teach the same grade level and subjects that you teach. These educators will know who else is integrating technology actively in their classrooms. Check to see if your school has a mentorship program.

Ascertain if your school has a technology committee and who the members are. You can get this information from your principal or assistant principal. Consult your teacher's manual for a list of various school committees and their members. A **technology committee** consists of teachers, administrators, and staff who consider, investigate, advise, and make recommendations to the principal and technology coordinator about technology-related issues. A **teacher's manual** is a booklet that contains information, rules and regulations, rights and responsibilities, and policies and procedures, including those related to all aspects of technology in the district. It should provide answers to many of your questions. Most manuals are located on the school or school district Web site.

Integration Strategies

To learn more how to get started in your new school with Limited English Proficiency students, visit the Teachers Discovering Computers Web site (scsite.com/tdc5), click Chapter 6, and then click Education Issues.

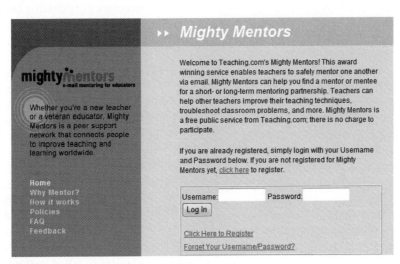

Figure 6-29 There are many Web sites dedicated to helping new teachers through online support and mentoring.

Integration Strategies

To learn more about integrating software programs like Reader Rabbit, ChemLab, Destination Math, and others, visit the Teachers Discovering Computers Web site (scsite.com/tdc5), click Chapter 6, and then click Software Corner.

Web Info

For more information about grant opportunities, visit the Teachers Discovering Computers Web site (*scsite.com/tdc5*), click Chapter 6, click Web Info, and then click Grants.

Finally, you should determine where you should go to get technology support. The principal, media specialist, school or district technology coordinator, and other teachers who use technology can offer you support or guide you to where you can find support.

TECHNOLOGY TRAINING

Take time to find out if your school offers any professional development or in-service training for using and integrating technology. Most schools and school districts offer free training for teachers. **In-service** means training teachers after they have entered the profession of teaching. Your principal, curriculum resource teacher, technology coordinator, or district instructional technology coordinators are able to provide information on in-service training opportunities. Sometimes, school secretaries also will be up to date on this information.

For information about technology workshops, talk with your principal, curriculum resource teacher, other teachers, or district technology coordinator. Let these people know you are interested in any technology or other training that becomes available. If you have students with learning disabilities in your classroom, check with the district exceptional student education program specialist about training opportunities. Many school districts post the dates and times of in-service training and workshops on the district's Web site and other Web resources.

HARDWARE

Determining how you can upgrade your classroom computers or obtain additional hardware is another item to consider. As soon as you can, join your school's technology committee. Technology committees help make the decisions on what new technologies will be purchased, where these new technologies will be placed, and how the technology plan for the school is implemented. You also may need to look into **educational grants** for additional funds. Your principal and curriculum coordinator usually receive notification of grant opportunities. Let them know you are interested in writing a grant and they will provide you with the information. If your district has a person responsible for grant writing for the district or county, he can serve as a good

source of information. In addition, you will find numerous grant opportunities on the Internet. Chapter 7 provides more information on locating and writing educational grants.

A question to consider is what type of equipment you can purchase if you receive grant funds. Before you write a grant, determine what kind of equipment you can purchase. Your principal, technology coordinator, curriculum coordinator, or members of the technology committee should be able to provide you with this information. If your school is networked, also check with the network administrator at the district level.

SOFTWARE

With hardware requirements decided, you will need to determine what kind of software is available to you and where you can find it. First, you should check your classroom computer for installed software. To learn more about the software available at your school or on the school's network, ask the school media specialist, curriculum resource teacher, technology facilitator, or district technology coordinator. If you are a special education teacher, check with your district exceptional student education coordinator, who should know what software is available for students with disabilities.

Next, determine the procedure for purchasing additional software. The school secretary or other teachers can direct you to the right person for this information. If your school is networked, it is important to check with the network coordinator before purchasing software so you can avoid buying software that already may be installed on the network or may conflict with the network. Many schools install computer-assisted instructional software programs on their network servers for use by all teachers.

Finally, you need to determine if your school district or state Department of Education has an adopted state bid list for purchasing software. Many states contract with companies to purchase specific software applications at reduced prices, and these are included on a **state bid list**. Be sure to find out if your state has a special catalog of software titles that they have adopted (Figure 6-30). Curriculum resource teachers, technology coordinators,

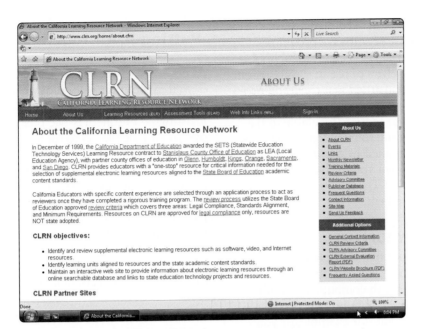

Figure 6-30 Many states provide online access to state-approved electronic learning resources.

or media specialists are good sources for this information. Your district office should maintain this information as well.

OTHER TECHNOLOGIES

Consider other technologies and where you can find them, such as a VCR, DVD player, digital camera, digital video camera, scanner, projector, or an electronic whiteboard. A school's media center can be scheduled for use by teachers and students

(Figure 6-31). Reserve early because allocation is usually based on a first-come, first-served basis. In addition, your media specialist usually handles scheduling and distribution of DVD players, VCRs, digital cameras, and other equipment. Ask about the length of time that you are allowed to keep checked-out equipment.

You also should ask where you can find a listing of educational software programs offered throughout the school or district for

Figure 6-31 A school's media center can be scheduled for teachers and students.

use in the classroom. The media specialist usually has a list of software programs available on CDs, DVDs, and the school network for teachers to use in the classroom.

A listing of instructional television programs and broadcast times, and any videos the school has or that are available to the school through interlibrary loan programs, usually is maintained by the media specialist. She can inform you of the procedures for checking out CDs, DVDs, VCR tapes, and other equipment.

TECHNOLOGY SUPPLIES

A basic, but often overlooked, question to consider is how you can obtain additional supplies for use with computers and other technologies. If the bulb in your overhead projector burns out, for example, or you need paper or ink cartridges for your printer, how do you go about replacing these supplies? Generally, the media specialist can replace burned-out bulbs and solve other supply problems with projectors. In many schools, the school secretary usually handles orders for general supplies. A good starting point is to talk to the media specialist or technology coordinator and they will direct you to the appropriate person.

Now that you have some basic knowledge of where to go for guidance and materials to help you integrate technology into your classroom, consider how one teacher is putting it all together.

Web Info

To learn how to order technology and other school supplies online, visit the Teachers Discovering Computers Web site (*scsite.com/tdc5*), click Chapter 6, click Web Info, and then click Supplies.

Putting It All Together

As described earlier in this chapter, Mr. Balado is well aware that technology can make a difference in his fifth-grade students' learning — and he has been using technology to enhance his classroom lessons. After the students completed their narratives, Mr. Balado planned a highly integrated classroom strategy for teaching the science curriculum to his fifth graders. As part of the integrated learning environment, he provided carefully planned centers, which enabled him to divide his classroom for group activities and inquiry learning through these interdisciplinary lessons.

CREATING AN INTEGRATED LEARNING ENVIRONMENT

Centers, or **learning centers,** give you the opportunity to break your classroom into many different types of learning environments without ever leaving the room. Just as an office building has different offices in which work is accomplished, learning centers allow students to rotate around the classroom to complete projects or activities (Figure 6-32). Mr. Balado had an instructional plan for how the students would work through the centers in his classroom. In Mr. Balado's Owl Exploration, students took on the role of explorer and learned what it would be like to have a career as a wildlife biologist.

Figure 6-32 Learning centers are a great way to organize a classroom to optimize learning opportunities.

Mr. Balado had five computers in his classroom for student use and 22 students. He divided the students into groups of two and three; these students would work together throughout the levels of the project. Mr. Balado then assigned each group a North American species of owl to research.

Students were excited and surprised because most did not even know that there was more than one species of owl. Their assignment was twofold. First, they were to find out as much as possible about their owl species. Second, they would use their newly acquired knowledge to help inform the public on what needs to be done to ensure the safety of North American owls and to prevent them from becoming extinct. Instead of writing a report, students would create a research-based interactive digital media project, models, and more.

Mr. Balado gave each group the same guidance and questions to think about for their project, such as the following: What does a wildlife biologist really do? Where might a wildlife biologist have to travel? What kind of education would you need to be a wildlife biologist?

Mr. Balado also instructed his students to conduct research on their species of owl, in a manner similar to the way wildlife biologists would conduct research, by answering questions such as the following: What does your owl look like? In what ecosystem would you find your owl? What does your owl eat? How large is your owl expected to grow and what is its average weight? He also asked each group to gather all the information the group wanted others in the class to understand about their particular species of owl.

Many educators teach their students to use an **essential questioning technique**, which is looking for the most important or fundamental part of a topic. In this process, students develop their own questions, find their own answers, and develop their own meaning from the information they collect. By using this essential questioning technique, students discover insight and are motivated to learn more. When students have learned how to ask the appropriate questions, they have learned how to learn. Mr. Balado knows that the ability to ask good questions leads to concrete learning opportunities; so he asked the students to formulate their own questions and find answers to them.

THE CLASSROOM CENTERS

For his lesson on North American owls, Mr. Balado set up seven learning centers in his classroom. The centers included a discovery computer center, a Web search center with a computer connected to the Internet, a modeling center, the great explorers' library center, a scanning and photo center with a computer set up for scanning pictures and other objects, a science center, and a digital media project center.

The discovery computer center included two computers and different CDs and DVDs that Mr. Balado had checked out from the media center. These cover predator and prey relationships, the food chain, and wildlife of North America. He purchased two CDs at his own expense. The Web search center has one computer that students can use to investigate various Web sites. Mr. Balado has provided links to these Web sites on his curriculum Web page. To locate these Web sites and other available media, Mr. Balado worked with the media specialist at his school. After he had collected and evaluated a list of sites for the students to conduct their research, Mr. Balado created a curriculum page so students would not be wasting time surfing the Web without supervision (Figure 6-33). Mr. Balado is quite aware of the dangers of inappropriate or inaccurate information available at some Web sites.

Web Info

For more information about creating learning centers, visit the Teachers Discovering Computers Web site (*scsite.com/tdc5*), click Chapter 6, click Web Info, and then click Learning Centers.

Figure 6-33 Teacher-created curriculum Web pages allow students to link directly to appropriate Web sites.

Web Info

For more information about the benefits of technology integration, visit the Teachers Discovering Computers Web site (*scsite.com/tdc5*), click Chapter 6, click Web Info, and then click Benefits.

The modeling center included all types of modeling tools, modeling clay, paper, rocks, and more. This center was for students to create a three-dimensional model of their owls and other objects related to the project. At the next center, the great explorers library center (Figure 6-34), Mr. Balado provided a collection of books, journals, and magazines for students to use to research owls and become great research scientists. The media specialist was instrumental in locating books and print materials through the state's interlibrary loan program, which was established by the state to assist teachers in obtaining resources from media centers throughout the state.

The scanning and photo center had a computer set up with a scanner and digital editing software that students could use to scan and manipulate pictures from books, magazines, and other sources for their projects. The science center had real owl pellets, owl pellet dissection data sheets, and bone sorting charts that Mr. Balado obtained from an Internet science company. This center also included two digital microscopes that the students could use to closely investigate their findings and take digital photographs of their discoveries. Mr. Balado set

up this center like a real science lab. He wanted to give his students authentic, hands-on experience to help them gain some understanding of what it takes to work as a scientist.

The last center was the digital media project center, which had one computer set up for students to create their digital media projects using either PowerPoint or iLife. Because the school had site licenses, PowerPoint and iLife were installed on all of the classroom computers so students could work on their projects as they progressed through the various centers. Students took the storyboard with narratives they had written about owls and combined true facts they had now learned to create their own digital video story about an owl.

Having students create the content makes the learning more memorable in two ways. First, they are learning by creating both text-based and visual content that addresses the dual coding theory as suggested by Paivio (you will learn more in the Learning Theories Special Feature at the end of this chapter). Second, because students are involved in discovery and constructivist learning, the content becomes personalized, and thus more relevant to them.

THE RESULTS OF TECHNOLOGY INTEGRATION

Students worked though the centers and created some of the most interesting and creative projects Mr. Balado had ever seen (Figure 6-35). One group had located a

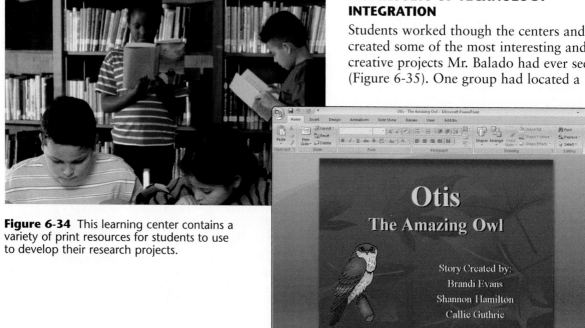

Figure 6-34 This learning center contains a variety of print resources for students to use to develop their research projects.

Figure 6-35 Students can use PowerPoint to create digital media projects.

picture of an owl soaring above its prey in a field, so for their model, they decided to create an owl flying above a field.

Most students could describe in detail all of the information they had learned about their species of owl — and, interestingly, each group had personalized its learning by giving its owl a nickname. The projects were outstanding; most of them contained many pictures and owl stories with research and details about North American owls and field wildlife biology.

Mr. Balado knew that his students were involved actively in their own learning and had interacted with numerous resources, Web sites, and software programs. By engaging in active learning at each center and using higher-order thinking skills, Mr. Balado's students, with his assistance, created their own questions, found their own answers, and created their own digital media projects. As a result of this process, Mr. Balado's students created new paths of knowledge that enhanced their learning, while achieving the unit learning objectives and benchmarks, and addressing curriculum standards.

As Mr. Balado and his students learned, technology can make a difference in the classroom if used appropriately and integrated into the curriculum. In addition, Mr. Balado noticed that his students' self-esteem, self-confidence, and writing skills improved as a result of creating their own projects (Figure 6-36). Students had prepared for the unit by reflecting on what they knew and what they wanted to know about owls (refer again to Figure 6-25 and the KWL chart). At the end of the unit, students reflected on their learning by articulating what they learned about owls.

Figure 6-36 Students feel an amazing sense of pride and ownership when they complete their own projects.

This reflection process helped Mr. Balado with his own reflective evaluation.

Learning Theories and Educational Research

At the end of this chapter is a special feature that provides information on educational learning theories and theorists. This special feature introduces you to educational terms, learning theories, educational research, and learning strategies that you should understand and apply to your own instructional strategies.

All teaching strategies have learning theories and educational research embedded within the instructional framework. Learning theories help teachers form instructional strategies and technology integration techniques by providing a basic framework for teaching and learning. Teachers learn to combine the different strategies and integration methods that are most suitable and appropriate for teaching their students.

Summary of Technology and Curriculum Integration

As you have learned in this chapter, the best strategy for technology integration is to place technology into the hands of students and trained teachers, make it easily accessible, and let them decide how best to use it in their classrooms at the point of instruction. Teachers are the content experts who should evaluate all resources used in classrooms.

This chapter first discussed curriculum and technology issues as they apply to technology integration and then provided teachers with ideas, an instructional model, and effective planning strategies. The chapter then provided an introduction to the concept of technology integration that will help you build your integration literacy skills. Finally, this chapter showed you how one teacher, Mr. Balado, fully integrated technology into an interdisciplinary project. In Chapter 7, you will build upon the skills you have learned in this chapter and increase your integration literacy skills by learning implementation strategies and integration activities that are curriculum directed.

Integration Strategies

To learn more about integrating storytelling with your students, visit the Teachers Discovering Computers Web site (*scsite.com/tdc5*), click Chapter 6, and then click Teaching Today.

Key Terms

INSTRUCTIONS: Use the Key Terms to help focus your study of the terms used in this chapter. To further enhance your understanding of the Key Terms in this chapter, visit scsite.com/tdc5, click Chapter 6 at the top of the Web page, and then click Key Terms on the left sidebar. Read the definition for each term and then access current and additional information about the term from the Web.

Exercises

Web Info
Key Terms
Checkpoint
Teaching Today
Education Issues
Integration Corner
Software Corner
Digital Media Corner
Assistive Technologies Corner
In the Lab
Learn It Online

Features

Timeline
Guide to WWW Sites
Search Tools
Buyer's Guide
State/Federal Sites
Professional Sites

active learning [334]
anchored instruction [334]
ASSURE Model [344]
authentic learning [334]

benchmark [326]
Body Works [335]

centers [350]
cognitive scaffold [335]
computer lab [328]
computer lab on wheels [341]
computers on wheels (COW) [341]
cooperative classroom activity [337]
cooperative learning [337]
curriculum [324]
curriculum framework [324]
curriculum goal [326]
curriculum guide [324]
curriculum integration [327]
curriculum standard [326]

education [324]
educational equalizer [336]
educational grant [348]
essential questioning technique [351]

evaluation [346]
evaluation process [346]

facilitator of learning [331]

Grade Level Expectations (GLEs) [325]

higher-order thinking skills [337]

in-service [348]
instructional model [344]
integration [327]

KWHL chart [342]
KWL chart [342]

learning centers [350]
learning objective [326]
learning style [331]

Mastery Objective Checklist [325]
mentorship program [338]
Microsoft Encarta [335]

point of instruction [328]
problem-based instruction [335]

reflective evaluation [346]

skill assessment survey [342]
state bid list [348]
student objective [344]

teachable moment [328]
teacher's manual [347]
technology committee [347]
technology integration [327]
technology lab [328]
technology plan [338]

virtual field trip [330]

Wellivers Instructional Transformation Model [332]
wireless mobile lab [341]

Checkpoint

INSTRUCTIONS: Use the Checkpoint excercises to check your knowledge level of the chapter. To complete the Checkpoint exercises interactively, visit scsite.com/tdc5, click Chapter 6 at the top of the Web page, and then click Checkpoint on the left sidebar.

Exercises

Web Info

Key Terms

Checkpoint

Teaching Today

Education Issues

Integration Corner

Software Corner

Digital Media Corner

Assistive Technologies Corner

In the Lab

Learn It Online

Features

Timeline

Guide to WWW Sites

Search Tools

Buyer's Guide

State/Federal Sites

Professional Sites

1. Label the Figure

Instructions: Identify the five hierarchy stages of the Wellivers Instructional Transformation Model.

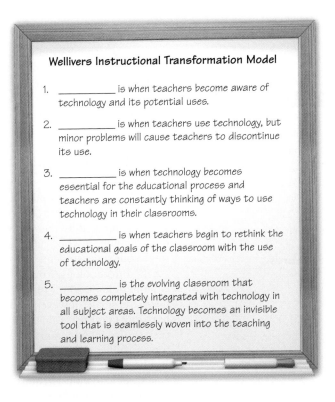

Wellivers Instructional Transformation Model

1. _____ is when teachers become aware of technology and its potential uses.

2. _____ is when teachers use technology, but minor problems will cause teachers to discontinue its use.

3. _____ is when technology becomes essential for the educational process and teachers are constantly thinking of ways to use technology in their classrooms.

4. _____ is when teachers begin to rethink the educational goals of the classroom with the use of technology.

5. _____ is the evolving classroom that becomes completely integrated with technology in all subject areas. Technology becomes an invisible tool that is seamlessly woven into the teaching and learning process.

2. Matching

Instructions: Match each term from the column on the left with the best description from the column on the right.

____ 1. ASSURE Model

____ 2. authentic learning

____ 3. curriculum standards

____ 4. mentorship program

____ 5. KWL chart

a. lessons connected to real-life events

b. instructional planning tool to assist teachers in identifying curriculum objectives

c. procedural guide for planning and delivering instruction that integrates technology

d. collection of general concepts that school districts expect their students to learn

e. when new teachers team with experienced teachers

3. Short Answer

Instructions: Write a brief answer to each of the following questions.

1. What is the difference between a curriculum standard and a benchmark? Are both curriculum standards and benchmarks measurable? Why or why not?

2. What are learning styles? How can a teacher be a facilitator of learning and at the same time address various students' learning styles?

3. Name five barriers to technology integration. In your opinion, which barrier is the most important? Why?

4. Name three people who can help teachers find information on available technologies in their schools. Describe other sources that can assist teachers in locating technology resources.

5. Name three areas teachers must address when planning for technology integration in a one-computer classroom. Can these same planning strategies also work for a two-computer classroom?

Teaching Today

INSTRUCTIONS: Teaching Today provides teachers with integration strategies and ideas for teaching and, more importantly, reaching today's digital generation. Each numbered segment contains one or more links that reinforce the information presented in the segment. To display this page from the Web, visit scsite.com/tdc5, click Chapter 6 at the top of the Web page, and then click Teaching Today on the left sidebar.

1. Lesson Plans

After using technology in your classroom, you are beginning to understand that using technology is different from integrating technology. You want to begin integrating technology into your social studies curriculum. Where do you begin? Are resources available on the Internet that can help you? Where can you locate examples of lesson plans that integrate technology but still support your curriculum? Can you modify these lessons to use in your classroom?

2. Grant Opportunities

Your school is located in a rural area, and technology funds are limited. You have used technology with students before and were encouraged by the results. You have one computer in your classroom and want to provide your students with greater access to technology. You have decided to explore possible grant opportunities. Your district is small, however, and does not have any grant programs. Very few businesses in your community offer grant opportunities. Where can you learn about other grant opportunities? Are there grants available specific to your circumstances? What are some other funding options? What other organizations in your community could you contact?

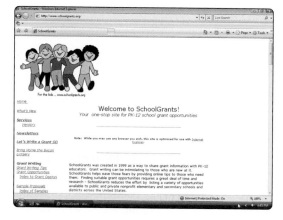

3. Mentoring

You want to integrate technology into your curriculum, but you do not know where to start. You want to provide the students with authentic learning activities and you need ideas. You consider talking to a teacher who integrates technology, but you do not know anyone. You have heard of a Web site where teachers can receive mentoring from other teachers as well as ask for advice and receive ideas. What are some advantages to finding assistance online? What are some disadvantages? Could you use this type of assistance for any subject? Why or why not? Could your students benefit from this type of interaction? Why or why not? How can you locate more resources such as this for yourself and for your students?

4. Storytelling

As a teacher, you know that by putting the technology in the hands of students you can create innovative learning experiences and increase motivation, all while teaching curriculum-specific content. You heard about an innovative project designed to get students writing stories about themselves called digital storytelling. The project is based on the principles of telling personal stories. Getting students to write is the crucial step in achieving many curriculum standards and is often one of the benchmarks associated with a standard. Getting students writing, especially about themselves, family, or community, is one way to encourage writing while strengthening writing skills. What kind of lesson plans can you develop using storytelling? What questions could you ask your students to get them thinking? What is a story circle? Could you find ways to weave a story throughout all curriculum areas? How?

Education Issues

INSTRUCTIONS: Education Issues provides several scenarios that allow you to explore controversial and current issues in education. Each numbered segment contains one or more links that reinforce the information presented in the segment. To display this page from the Web, visit scsite.com/tdc5, click Chapter 6 at the top of the Web page, and then click Education Issues on the left sidebar.

1. Bilingual Education

A recent survey of state education agencies indicates that more than five million students with Limited English Proficiency (LEP) students are enrolled in public schools and that this number is growing — dramatically, in many locations — every year. This trend poses unique challenges for educators who want to ensure that these students have the same opportunities as English-proficient students. In transitional bilingual education programs, instruction is provided for some subjects in the students' native language and part of the school day is spent on developing English skills. Bilingual education's critics argue that this approach keeps students in a cycle of native-language dependency that ultimately prevents them from making significant progress in English-language-acquisition and leads to lower test scores. These critics argue that these students must spend 100 percent of their time on task in English to master proficiency in English. What do you think? What Web site resources provide teachers with practical material for culturally diverse classrooms? What other technologies and teaching strategies can you use to enhance LEP student learning?

2. Integrated Learning System

Your school district has spent a significant amount of money on an integrated learning system that is available for all teachers throughout the district to use. This software generates tests and automatically tracks student progress. The software also includes thousands of interactive student assignments, data-driven decision-making capabilities, and the ability to create customized learning paths for your students so they can progress through the content at their own pace and path. What are some of the benefits of this type of software? What are some advantages/disadvantages? Does this type of software appeal to different learning styles? How could students with learning disabilities use this type of software?

3. Levels of Integration

It is the second month of the semester, and you are teaching seventh-grade science. The parents of one of your students contact you. They are upset because when their son was in elementary school, the majority of teachers were using technology in their classrooms. At your middle school, however, their son has not had the same opportunities. The parents are very concerned about the lack of technology. What can you do about this situation? To whom can you refer the parents? Do greater barriers to technology integration exist in middle schools than in elementary or high schools? Why or why not? How could you integrate technology into your seventh-grade science curriculum?

4. Security Versus Integration

In your school district, Internet access is available in all classrooms, the media center, and the computer lab. Most teachers at your school use the Internet for their research but due to security issues, your students are not allowed to search for information. Many Web sites, some software programs, and many basic Windows functions are blocked. Even Flash drives are blocked because of security concerns, which makes saving files and projects very difficult. Your school district offers many workshops on ways to integrate technologies, but once you get back to your school you find it difficult to implement what you have learned. How can you integrate technology when the school administration and technology coordinators will not allow you? Are there ways to use and integrate technology without using the Internet? Can you think of ways to integrate other technologies? How do you find other ways for you students to conduct research via the Web when many popular sites are blocked?

Integration Corner

INSTRUCTIONS: Integration Corner provides extensive ideas and resources for integrating technology into your classroom-specific curriculum. To display this page from the Web and its links to approximately 100 educational Web sites, visit scsite.com/tdc5, click Chapter 6 at the top of the Web page, and then click Integration Corner on the left sidebar.

Exercises

Web Info
Key Terms
Checkpoint
Teaching Today
Education Issues
Integration Corner
Software Corner
Digital Media Corner
Assistive Technologies Corner
In the Lab
Learn It Online

Features

Timeline
Guide to WWW Sites
Search Tools
Buyer's Guide
State/Federal Sites
Professional Sites

Integration Corner is designed for teachers and other educators who are looking for innovative ways to integrate technology into their content-specific curriculum. Integration Corner not only provides great Web sites with current information, but it also shows what other educators are doing in the field of educational technology. These Corners are designed for all educators regardless of their area of interest. Be sure to review information and sites outside of your teaching area because many great integration ideas in one area can be modified easily for use in other curriculum areas.

Teachers and administrators will find other colleagues in their areas with whom to connect and share the successes and hurdles of integrating technology in a classroom or an entire school system. Consider Integration Corner your one stop for integration ideas and resources. Links to educational Web sites are organized in the following 12 Corners, and different Web resources are available for each chapter. Figure 6-37 shows examples of the Web resources provided in the Chapter 6 Post Secondary Corner.

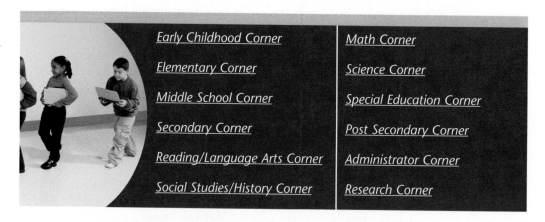

Early Childhood Corner
Elementary Corner
Middle School Corner
Secondary Corner
Reading/Language Arts Corner
Social Studies/History Corner

Math Corner
Science Corner
Special Education Corner
Post Secondary Corner
Administrator Corner
Research Corner

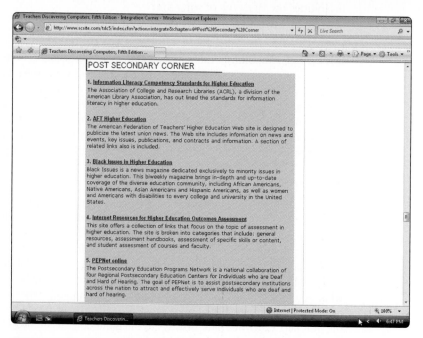

Figure 6-37 Examples of the Web resources provided in the Chapter 6 Post Secondary Corner.

Software Corner

INSTRUCTIONS: Software Corner provides information on popular software programs. Each numbered segment discusses specific software programs and contains a link to additional information about these programs. To display this page from the Web, visit scsite.com/tdc5, click Chapter 6 at the top of the Web page, and then click Software Corner on the left sidebar.

1. Destination Series

Destination Math and Reading series by Riverdeep are comprehensive software programs that provide authentic experiences when teaching mathematics and reading. Destination Math provides a curriculum that makes the connection between real world and mathematics while teaching basic skills, math reasoning, conceptual understanding, and problem solving. The Destination Reading series, for Grades 4-8, is a stimulating reading courseware that builds understanding for all learners. Destination Reading provides careful sequencing of reading and writing skill development so that each new skill builds upon prior knowledge. The Destination Series is aligned with state and national curriculum standards and is grounded in current scientific research.

2. Model ChemLab

Would you like to create experiences to let your students become scientist through challenging, authentic simulations that can be conducted in the computer lab or online? Model Science Software has several software classroom solutions that are perfect alternatives to dangerous, expensive, or environmentally hazardous labs. Model ChemLab is a unique product that integrates observations, practice, and theory with interactive simulations and a lab notebook workspace to create a working lab environment. Frequently used lab equipment and procedures are used to simulate the steps involved in performing an experiment. Students step through the actual lab procedure while interacting with equipment in a way that is similar to the real lab experience. The software has pre-designed curriculum with lab experiments and activities for general chemistry for high school and college students.

3. Reader Rabbit

Reader Rabbit's Reading Series from The Learning Company provides a playful and engaging way for elementary students to develop essential building blocks to learn to read. The program includes activities to help recognize words and phonics; learn to read, decode, and spell; and develop and enhance vocabulary skills, visual memory, and concentration. It contains four activities, each of which has four levels of difficulty. The activities in Reader Rabbit's Reading 2 for Grades 1-3 contain more than 1000 practice words and give students many opportunities to practice identifying consonant blends as well as short and long vowel sounds. A score chart tracks the number of correct responses and attempts, and displays the percentage of correct answers for each of the four levels. Included with the software is a teacher resource binder that includes a comprehensive user's guide, 17 detailed lesson plans, dozens of bonus ideas, Internet resources, a scope and sequence chart, and more.

4. Owl and Mouse Software

Help your students learn continents, countries, states, capitals, borders, physical features, historical facts, and cultural monuments with games, software (most of it free), and educational activities from Owl & Mouse Educational Software. Your students can learn geography with a free interactive map that teaches the locations of the major cultural monuments of the world. Use the world geography interactive map to teach the physical features of the world including rivers, mountains, lakes, deserts, and rainforests. Your students can learn the countries of different continents and their capitals with fun and educational map puzzle games, too.

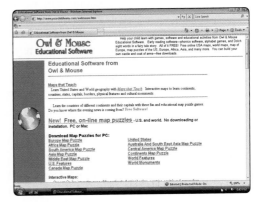

Digital Media Corner

INSTRUCTIONS: Today's K-12 digital students need their learning to be meaningful and relevant to their lives. Digital Media Corner provides videos, ideas, and examples of how you can use digital media to enhance your teaching and your students' learning. To access the videos and links to additional information, visit scsite.com/tdc5, click Chapter 6 at the top of the Web page, and then click Digital Media on the left sidebar.

1. Massive Multiplayer Online Role-Playing Game

A Massively Multiplayer Online Role-playing Game (MMORPG) is a game in which an unlimited number of players can participate. Players assume the fictional role of one of a select number of characters that interact within the fantasy setting initiated within the game. Players have limited control over the actions of their characters. MMORPGs are different from small multiplayer or single player games not only by the number of participants but also because the game's virtual world persists and evolves, even when the player is absent. The player base for MMORPGs is over 15 million, which shows their popularity worldwide. Players are not limited to children and teens. In fact, the age of players ranges from 18 to 45 years and is expanding on both ends of the scale each year.

2. Video Editing with Final Cut Studio

Are you looking for innovative ways to make professional looking videos? Well, look no further. This sensational video editing design studio produced exclusively for Apple OS X users contains six applications, which include: Final Cut Pro, Motion, Soundtrack Pro, Compressor, DVD Studio Pro, and Color a newly designed application for professional color grading. Final Cut Pro's applications encourage innovation, giving amateur and professional producers the freedom to create custom solutions and to share project data using QuickTime. Using QuickTime allows students to move media easily between computers. Projects can also be delivered via a wide range of delivery formats — including those supported by the Web, iPod, iPhone, Apple TV, and broadcast servers.

3. Web Publishing with WordPress

WordPress is a free Web publishing package. It traces its roots back to a team of programmers trying to develop a blog writing system that would be exceptionally easy for its users to manage. It shares some features that are similar to other open-source programs. Open-source software permits users to use, change, and improve the software. With WordPress, for example, users are free to extend its capabilities through ancillary programs and scripts called plug-ins. Besides its ease of use as a Web page editing system and blog writing system, WordPress capabilities are often extended through the use of plug-ins. These plug-ins allow bloggers to include pictures, video, sound, etc. in their blogs, which is more than what visitors usually expect to find in a blog. WordPress is also a content management system (one that helps developers keep track of content, images, and other media). WordPress is an outgrowth of the Web 2.0 features in which developers are looking to combine static Web pages with products that easily permit and support multiple author and end-user changes and modifications.

4. UB the Director

How do you encourage students to be interested in a book that does not relate directly to them? One technique is to use booktalking, a concept that means telling stories about the context and background in which the book is written. Digital booktalking allows students to read the content as if they were going to make a movie out of the book. Digital booktalking utilizes digital media to tell the story. Students are taught text-to-screen techniques and then learn how to pull important details from a book to create a book trailer. A book trailer is a short 2–3 minute video that encapsulates the essence of the book, main characters, metaphors, and so on. Using easy-to-use video editing software like Apple's iMovie, Microsoft's PhotoStory or Movie Maker, students can easily build their own movies. Examples of trailers can be found at Digital Booktalk. In fact, this Web site accepts student-produced work.

5. Keynote

Keynote is a digital media presentation application that comes with Apple's iWork suite. Keynote includes features such as cinema-like transitions, pre-set animated text and titling effects, photo masking, and the ability to seamlessly add video clips. Keynote is easy to use allowing today's digital students to transition to learning the essence of digital storytelling. Keynote works seamlessly with iLife applications such as iPhoto and Garageband.

Assistive Technologies Corner

INSTRUCTIONS: Assistive Technologies Corner provides information on current hardware, software, and peripherals that will assist you in delivering instruction to students with physical, cognitive, or sensory challenges. To access extensive additional information, visit scsite.com/tdc5, click Chapter 6 at the top of the Web page, and then click Assistive Technologies on the left sidebar.

1. Will Assistive Technology Help My Teaching? Yes!

Just as with students in a typical classroom, students with special needs must also attain curriculum standards. The teacher sets clear learning objectives based on the benchmarks, and plans for all students to attain those objectives, including those students with special needs. Technology helps engage all students in the learning process; however, technology can greatly enhance the learning process for students with special needs. Reminding educators that curriculum is central to instruction, the Center for Applied Special Technology (CAST) has developed the Universal Design for Learning, a theoretical curriculum design approach providing the fewest barriers to learning

In their book, *Teaching Every Student in the Digital Age: Universal Design for Learning*, Rose and Meyer remind teachers that access to information is not synonymous with access to learning, and that teachers must plan for learning, and not simply provide accessible information. Like all technology, assistive technologies need to be used at the right time and with the appropriate curriculum goals in mind to provide access to learning.

2. What Are Some Ways to Use Assistive Technology to Help Students Learn?

To better answer this question, let's read about two teachers who are using assistive technologies. Ms. Daniels at Fourth Street Elementary School has two students with dyslexia in her classroom. The class is reading *Island of the Blue Dolphins*. Ms. Daniels uses the classroom Smart Board to present an Inspiration concept map that introduces students to the story's setting and provides them with background information. She will use the same program later to illustrate plot development as the story proceeds. Her dyslexic students depend on this organization to help them comprehend the whole story.

Strengthening of reading skills for many students is challenging, but especially for those students with dyslexia. Her students with dyslexia struggle through decoding and comprehension of the text during reading class, but with the graphical map they have a framework from which to proceed. In science class, these same students often use Kurzweil 3000, their text reader, to complete assigned classroom readings. Using a text reader helps them grasp science concepts quickly, and return to the printed text as needed.

Mr. Kamla's third grade class is studying energy. One of his students, Carla, who has cerebral palsy, finds it difficult to navigate the online tutorial with captioned video clips that Mr. Kamla created for the classroom learning center. Mr. Kamla used Intellitools' Overlay Maker to create a specialized template with large navigation keys that he places over the Intellikeys keyboard. Now, Carla is able to access the same tutorial as her classmates. Because the video clips he created are captioned, they provide all students with multisensory learning opportunities.

Mr. Kamla and Ms. Daniels often collaborate on their accessibility ideas. Last year, they adapted two WebQuests for a class with several students with emotional disturbances. They located a WebQuest on the Web that would meet their curriculum goals, but realized that the special needs students would not be able to participate fully. Following Bernie Dodge's suggestions for adapting existing WebQuests, they used more prompts and more details in the directions and in the accompanying printed materials. They structured the student interaction carefully and with tasks clearly focusing on the learning objectives. Making sure the WebQuest met accessibility standards, they published the WebQuest. Planning for learning by all students is simply good practice in any classroom. Choosing the right technology tool helps instructors explore a myriad of ways to engage all learners!

Follow the instructions at the top of this page to display additional information and this chapter's links on assistive technologies.

In the Lab

INSTRUCTIONS: In the Lab provides desktop publishing exercises that are divided into two areas, productivity and integration. To access the links to tutorials, productivity ideas, integration examples and ideas, and more, visit scsite.com/tdc5, click Chapter 6 at the top of the Web page, and then click In the Lab on the left sidebar.

PRODUCTIVITY IN THE CLASSROOM

Introduction: Desktop publishing provides teachers with effective and efficient ways to communicate with students, parents, faculty, and others in a professional manner. Many word processing applications, such as Microsoft Word, AppleWorks, and Microsoft Works, provide templates enabling users to create newsletters and many other documents with ease. Many excellent desktop publishing software applications also are available. Microsoft Publisher and Adobe PageMaker are two popular programs used by educators. Exciting and innovative ways exist that allow teachers to integrate desktop publishing effectively into the curriculum. Students enjoy creating professional looking documents and finding creative ways to exhibit what they have learned.

1. Creating and Formatting a Parent Newsletter

Problem: As a kindergarten teacher, you believe it is important to send home monthly newsletters to keep parents informed of what is happening in the classroom. Open your word processing or desktop publishing software application and create a newsletter as described in the following list. Use the newsletter shown in Figure 6-38 as an example. If you are using a template, modify the newsletter design to accommodate the template. If you are using Microsoft Word, consider using tables, columns, section breaks, and text boxes to create the newsletter. (*Hint:* Use Help to understand the steps better.)

Instructions: Perform the following tasks.

1. Personalize the newsletter by inserting your name instead of Ms. Erhart's name and the grade level or subject you teach. Format the first and second heading lines in 16-point Times or Times New Roman font centered on the page.

2. Personalize the newsletter by using the current month and year. Enter the month and year (using the format Month, Year) right-aligned in 16-point Times or Times New Roman font.

3. Choose an appropriate picture, image, or clip art graphic, and then insert it on the page left-aligned.

4. Create an opening paragraph with a heading and at least three lines of text. Format the heading line in 14-point Times or Times New Roman font. Format the text in 12-point Times or Times New Roman font.

5. Create the body of the newsletter in two columns. Format section headings centered in uppercase 12-point Times or Times New Roman bold font. Format the text in 12-point Times or Times New Roman font.

6. Create a closing paragraph at the bottom of the newsletter. Format the text in 12-point Times or Times New Roman font.

7. Choose an appropriate picture, image, or clip art graphic and then insert it on the lower-right side of the newsletter.

8. Save the document to the location and with a filename of your choice. Print the document and then follow your instructor's directions for handing in the assignment.

In the Lab

Ms. Erhart's
Kindergarten Class Newsletter

February, 2009

Winter Wonders

January passed quickly for our class! February holds
many fun activities and lots of good learning. Please be
sure to join us for our Valentine's Day party and mark
February 23 on your calendar for our special Black
History event!

COME OUT AND READ

Our class is hosting a Come Out and Read
night! Students can wear pajamas and get
comfy on big pillows as they enjoy a good
book with a parent or sibling. We also will
have a special storyteller coming in to share
some exciting stories with the group. Be
sure to join us for the fun!

WHAT'S HAPPENING IN CLASS

We continue to focus on letter recognition
and letter sounds during February. We also
are studying the seasons and reading stories
about winter. These are the stories we will
use in class. Check them out from the library
to reinforce these concepts at home!

A Snowy Day, by Ezra Jack Keats
The Mitten, by Jan Brett
Little Polar Bear, by Hans de Beer
Mama, Do You Love Me?, by Barbara M.
Joosse

BLACK HISTORY MONTH

February is Black History Month, and
students will learn about the contributions of
inspirational African-Americans. To
continue our focus on reading during
February, we will be using the following
books:

The Story of Ruby Bridges, by Robert Coles
Under the Quilt of Night, by Deborah
Hopkinson
Sweet Clara and the Freedom Quilt, by
Deborah Hopkinson
*Martin's Big Words: The Life of Dr. Martin
Luther King, Jr.*, by Doreen Rappaport
Amazing Grace, by Mary Hoffman

The class will work together and create an
exciting presentation for their families on
February 23! Look for more information in
our next newsletter.

Reading is such an important skill, and together we can prepare your
children to be successful readers and lifelong learners. Please do not
hesitate to contact me if you have any questions or comments.
Remember, you are always welcome to come into our classroom and be
a part of the learning experience!

Figure 6-38

In the Lab

2. Creating and Formatting a Department Newsletter

Problem: You are a member of your high school's Foreign Language Department. Your responsibility is to communicate information to the rest of the Foreign Language Department. You decide the easiest way to share new information is by creating a newsletter. Use the newsletter shown in Figure 6-39 as an example. (*Hint:* Use Help to understand the steps better.)

Instructions: Format the first and second heading lines in 14-point Arial bold font. Insert your name in place of Mr. Schatz in 12-point Times or Times New Roman bold font. Enter the current month and year (in the format Month, Year) in 14-point Arial bold font. Create the body of the newsletter in three columns. Personalize the information in the newsletter to reflect the grade level or subject that you teach. Format the section headings in 12-point Arial bold font. Format the text in 12-point Arial font. Format the country names in 11-point Arial bold font. Enter the Web site titles in 11-point Arial font. Format the Web site addresses in 10-point Arial font. Enter the quote in 12-point Times or Times New Roman italic font. Insert appropriate pictures, images, or clip art graphics.

After you have typed and formatted the newsletter, save the newsletter to a location and with a filename of your choice. Print the newsletter and then follow your instructor's directions for handing in the assignment.

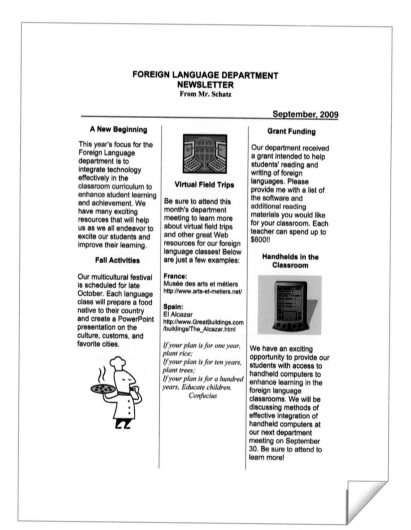

Figure 6-39

In the Lab

3. Creating and Formatting a Newsletter for a State Organization

Problem: You are the secretary for your subject area state organization. It is your responsibility to create a newsletter summarizing your state convention, providing information for the upcoming year's convention, and any other pertinent information.

Instructions: Create a newsletter similar to the newsletter illustrated in Figure 6-39. Use an appropriate layout, and then select font types and styles, font sizes, and clip art images for the newsletter. Include the current date, your name, and e-mail address. Save the newsletter to a location of your choice using an appropriate filename. Print the newsletter and then follow your instructor's directions for handing in the assignment.

INTEGRATION IN THE CLASSROOM

1. In honor of Black History Month, you have planned a cross-curricular project. You will divide students into groups and assign each group one of the following curricular areas: science, society and culture, math, art, music, or literature. Each group will choose one famous African-American to research who has made a significant contribution in the group's assigned field. Students then will create a newsletter outlining their findings. They will discuss the person's place of birth, family history, educational background, interests, and contributions to their particular field. Students will include at least one image in the newsletter. Select a famous African-American and create a sample newsletter for your students. Include your name and the current date in your sample newsletter.

2. Your high school Spanish class is studying cities in Spain. To reinforce reading and writing Spanish while learning about the country, students will create a newsletter written in Spanish. Students will work in groups and research three different cities in Spain. They will access and read online newspapers from the cities they select, gather travel and tourist information, obtain appropriate graphics that illustrate aspects of their chosen cities, and then create a newsletter in Spanish that presents the information they learned. Students will present their newsletter to the class and distribute a copy of it to each class member. Create a sample newsletter for your students. If you are not fluent in Spanish, select another foreign language. If you are not fluent in a foreign language, research three cities in Spain and create a newsletter presenting travel and tourist information written in English. Include your name, the current date, Web resources, and graphics in your sample newsletter.

3. While teaching the American Revolution, you team up with an English teacher to provide your students with a constructivist learning activity. Students will select one event that led up to the American Revolution and create a newsletter using information and images they locate from print resources and the Internet. Students will conduct their research in the history classroom and the English teacher will assist students with the layout, design, and writing techniques. Using the ideas and techniques you have learned in this In the Lab, create a sample newsletter for your students. Include your name, the current date, the course number, and course title in your newsletter.

Learn It Online

INSTRUCTIONS: Use the Learn It Online exercises to reinforce your understanding of the chapter concepts and increase your computer, information, and integration literacy. To access dozens of interactive student labs, practice tests, learning games, and more, visit scsite.com/tdc5, click Chapter 6 at the top of the Web page, and then click Learn It Online on the left sidebar.

1. At the Movies

Click the At the Movies – Publisher link to review a video about getting started with Publisher 2007.

2. At the Movies

Click the At the Movies – Windows Media Player link to review a video about getting the most from Windows Media Player in Windows Vista.

3. Maintaining Your PC's Hard Disk

You computer's hard disk is used for the majority of your storage requirements. Maintaining your hard disk can help prevent the loss of data. In addition, it is important that your hard disk operates at peak efficiency. Click the Maintaining Your PC's Hard Disk link to learn how to maintain your PC's hard drive by detecting and repairing disk errors using the Check Disk utility, removing unused files and folders using the Disk Cleanup utility, and consolidating files and folders using the Disk Defragmenter utility.

4. Expanding Your Understanding

When you print using a computer, you control printing at two different points: first, before the printing actually begins, and second, after the document has been sent to the printer. Click the Expanding Your Understanding link to learn how to set the parameters for printing.

5. Practice Test

Click the Practice Test link. Answer each question. When completed, enter your name and click the Grade Test button to submit the quiz for grading. Make a note of any missed questions. If required, submit your score to your instructor.

6. Who Wants to Be a Computer Genius?

Click the Computer Genius link to find out if you are a computer genius. Directions about how to play the game will be displayed. When you are ready to play, click the Play button. If required, submit your score to your instructor.

7. Wheel of Terms

Click the Wheel of Terms link to reinforce important terms you learned in this chapter by playing the Shelly Cashman Series version of this popular game. Directions about how to play the game will be displayed. When you are ready to play, click the Play button. If required, submit your score to your instructor.

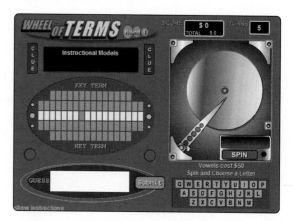

8. Crossword Puzzle Challenge

Click the Crossword Puzzle link. Complete the puzzle to reinforce skills you learned in this chapter. Directions about how to play the game will be displayed. When you are ready to play, click the Play button. If required, submit the completed puzzle to your instructor.

Special Feature: Learning Theories and Educational Research

A great deal of discussion has taken place about the definition of learning by educational theorists, researchers, and practitioners; yet, no universal definition of learning has been accepted. As a result, numerous definitions exist, and they vary greatly in describing the exact nature of learning. For this textbook, **learning** is defined as the process of gaining knowledge or skills acquired through instruction or study, or to modify behavior through exposure to a type of conditioning or form of gaining experience. A **theory** is a scientific set of principles presented to clarify or explain a phenomenon. **Learning theories** provide frameworks for interpreting the conditions and observations of teaching and learning and provide the bridge between education and research.

Educational research builds the foundation for the development of sound instructional strategies; however, it takes practice and moving the theory into practice to create the bridge that evolves into technology integration. Each new lesson you present to your students should be based on learning theory and educational research. Learning theories have been shown to enhance learning and increase motivation and student achievement. Which learning theory you use depends on what you want to teach, how you want to teach it, and who you are teaching. The latter is very important because as we have learned today's kids are totally different. The way they learn also is different.

In Chapter 1, you learned some of the characteristics of today's digital generation. In addition to describing who these kids are and how they think, their traits have implications on teaching and learning. Today's students tend to process information at what Prensky refers to as a "twitch speed." In other words, students today often fail to spend time reflecting and processing information at what Craik and Lockhart refer to as **deep processing levels**. Research has found that deep processing levels are necessary for students to make sense of information, to give meaning to the information, and to remember things for a longer period of time. Today's students' prefer graphics over text-based communications. This learning preference ties to Clark and Paivio's ideas on dual coding and how pictures interface with a person's abilities to recall information.

Today's students like to live, work, and play in digital social settings with others; this interaction is known as their **social network** (Figure 1). Even though digital students pride themselves on being individuals, they prefer instruction that involves interaction for themselves and with others. This learning preference ties directly to the work of Lev Vygotsky, Albert Bandura, and others. Recall the ARCS Motivational Model described in Chapter 1 and the ASSURE Model described early in this chapter and how both of these models are relevant to discussions about learning theories. Most models, including these, underline how important it is to know one's audience before developing class content and deciding how to mediate the instructional activities.

Figure 1 Today's digital students interact digitally in what is known as their social network, which is in total contrast to the way in which any previous generation interacted socially.

This special feature highlights some of the theories and theorists that will help you better integrate technology into your curriculum. For more information about specific learning theories and researchers, including reference materials, access the Web Info annotations located in the margins throughout this special feature. The first section discusses the behaviorism learning theory.

Behaviorism

Behaviorism is the prediction and control of human behavior in which introspection and/or independent thinking form no essential part of its methods. Behaviorism came into vogue during a period of time that coincided with the industrial revolution called **modernism** in which everything of value (including learning) was measured solely in terms of science. To a behaviorist, human learning is purely an objective and experimental branch of natural science. There is no internal cognitive processing of information.

The behaviorist recognizes no dividing line between man and animal — both learn to behave solely through a system of positive and negative rewards. For some students, this type

of conditioning works very well. Behaviorists such as Pavlov, Skinner, and Bandura have contributed a great deal to the understanding of human behavior, and an overview of their contributions are described in the following sections.

Ivan Pavlov

Ivan Pavlov (1849 – 1936) became famous for his behavioral experiments with dogs, and he won the Nobel Prize in Physiology in 1904 (Figure 2). Pavlov used conditioning to teach dogs to salivate when he rang a bell. When he provided the stimulus (food) and he achieved his desired reflex (salivation), he rang a bell. Eventually, the dogs associated the bell with food and they began to salivate when Pavlov rang the bell even if food was not present. This process was termed **classic conditioning** and refers to the natural reflex that occurs in response to a stimulus. Pavlov was a scientist, and he conducted these experiments to study digestion, but as a result, other behaviorists studied his work as an example of stimulus response. Some behaviorists felt this technique of stimulus response had human applications as well.

Web Info

For more information about Behaviorism, visit the Teachers Discovering Computers Web site (*scsite.com/tdc5*), click Chapter 6, click Web Info, and then click Behaviorism.

Web Info

For more information about Ivan Pavlov, visit the Teachers Discovering Computers Web site (*scsite.com/tdc5*), click Chapter 6, click Web Info, and then click Pavlov.

Figure 2 Ivan Pavlov's research into the physiology of digestion led him to create a science based on conditioned reflexes that won him the Nobel Prize in 1904.

B.F. Skinner

B.F. Skinner (1904 – 1990) describes another form of conditioning that is labeled as behavioral or operant conditioning (Figure 3). **Operant conditioning** describes learning that is controlled and results in shaping behavior through the reinforcement of stimulus-response patterns. Skinner conducted experiments with pigeons and rewarded them when he saw them behaving in a desired manner. When a stimulus-response pattern occurs, such as a pigeon turning (a stimulus), a reward is given (response). Eventually, Skinner was able to teach pigeons to dance using this technique. Ultimately, he taught pigeons to engage in complex tasks such as bowling in a specially constructed bowling alley.

Skinner believed that people shape their behavior based on the rewards or positive reinforcement they receive. Skinner believed human behavior, even the language development of children, is based on stimulus-response theory. He observed that when children made attempts at sounds, parents smiled and reinforced that behavior. Eventually, the child learns to say the word correctly as parents and others reinforce her efforts.

In his experiments, Skinner found that reinforcement was a powerful motivator. He conducted experiments with people as well and he even used his own infant daughter. Skinner felt that when a child produces a desirable behavior and is rewarded for it, that behavior will be repeated. In contrast, if a response is negative, the behavior will be extinguished. Many classroom management techniques are based on these principles. Figure 4 compares classic and operant conditioning.

Web Info

For more information about B.F. Skinner, visit the Teachers Discovering Computers Web site (*scsite.com/tdc5*), click Chapter 6, click Web Info, and then click Skinner.

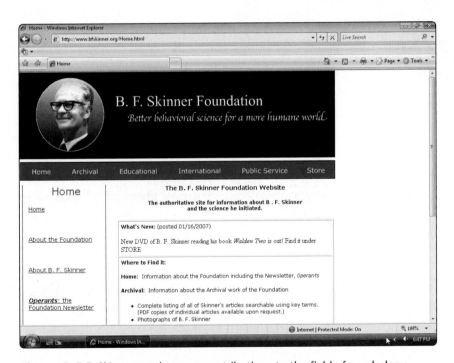

Figure 3 B.F. Skinner made many contributions to the field of psychology, including the theory of behavioral or operant conditioning.

Classic Conditioning Pavlov	Operant Conditioning Skinner
Classic conditioning introduces the stimulus and then reinforces the reflex. A neutral stimulus (the bell) becomes analogous with a reflex (salivation).	Operant conditioning begins with a stimulus (behavior) and then is reinforced with a response (reward). A bond becomes established between the operant (stimulus/behavior) and the reward.

Figure 4 Classic versus operant conditioning.

Web Info

For more information about Albert Bandura, visit the Teachers Discovering Computers Web site (*scsite.com/tdc5*), click Chapter 6, click Web info, and then click Bandura.

Many forms of computer-based instruction and educational software are based on Skinner's operant conditioning. They provide positive reinforcement when a desired behavior occurs and negative reinforcement when the student does not provide the desired behavior. For instance, when the correct answer is given, the software program provides positive verbal and visual feedback for the student's correct response. As Figure 5 shows, even young children enjoy learning and getting positive feedback.

Figure 5 Many software and hardware developers are designing products to reinforce learning for younger students.

Albert Bandura

Albert Bandura (1925 –) has studied and is famous for his ideas on **social learning**, which he renamed **Social Cognitive Theory** (Figure 6). Bandura focuses on those motivational factors and self-regulatory mechanisms that contribute to a person's behavior, rather than just environmental mechanisms, which differentiates his theories from Skinner's operant conditioning.

Bandura believes that people acquire behaviors, first, through the observation of others and then, by using those observations to imitate what they have observed. Several studies involving television commercials have supported this theory of observational modeling. **Observational modeling** is watching something and then mimicking the observed behavior. For example, when a person purchases a product advertised on TV based on claims made in the commercial (such as the idea that using a specific shampoo will increase popularity) and then uses the same mannerisms seen in the commercial (such as flipping one's hair while looking coyly over a shoulder), then that person is modeling the behavior shown in the commercial.

Social learning theory has been applied extensively in the context of behavior modification, which is widely used in training programs.

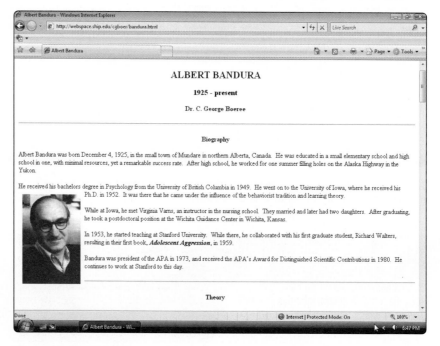

Figure 6 Albert Bandura contributed many ideas to both behaviorist and cognitive learning theories.

In later years, Bandura focused his work on the concept of self-efficacy, which ties to motivation and cognition. **Self-efficacy** is a personal observation about one's perceived ability to feel, think, and motivate oneself to learn.

As he furthered his research, Bandura began to analyze a person's personality through the interaction of three things: the environment, the behavior, and the person's psychological processes. Bandura then started to consider a person's ability to retain information through images in the mind, called **imagery**. It was at this time that he stopped being a strict behaviorist and began to join the position of the cognitivists, a new movement that was just beginning to take root. So significant were his contributions to this movement, that he often has been called the father of the cognitivist movement. In the next section, you will learn more about cognitive theory and cognitivists like Paivio, Gagne, Gardner, and Bloom.

Cognitivist

Cognitive theory is an offshoot of traditional psychological concepts of thinking, deciding, remembering, and so on. The cognitive psychologist views these activities in terms of how they underlie behavior. According to **cognitive theory**, activities like thinking and remembering seem like a behavior, thus providing an avenue to use behavior analysis to measure their effect on learning. Because cognitivist theory came about as a reaction to behaviorist thinking that was in vogue at the time, there has always been a certain amount of tension between behaviorist and cognitivist approaches to learning.

Cognitivists objected to behaviorists because they felt that behaviorists thought learning was simply a reactionary phenomenon and ignored the idea that thinking plays a role. Paivio, Gagne, Gardner, and Bloom are just a few of the cognitivists who have contributed a great deal to the understanding of cognitive theory; their contributions are discussed in the sections that follow.

Allan Paivio

Allan Paivio (1925 –) proposed that presenting information in both visual and verbal form enhances recall and recognition. He developed a considerable amount of research to support what has become referred to as the dual coding theory. **Dual coding theory** assumes that people process information in two distinctly different ways: (1) processing for images and (2) processing for language (Figure 7). This research supports the theory that today's visual learners learn in different ways depending on the medium. Dual coding theory identifies

Web Info

For more information on dual coding theory, visit the Teachers Discovering Computers Web site (*scsite.com/tdc5*), click Chapter 6, click Web Info, and then click Dual Coding Theory.

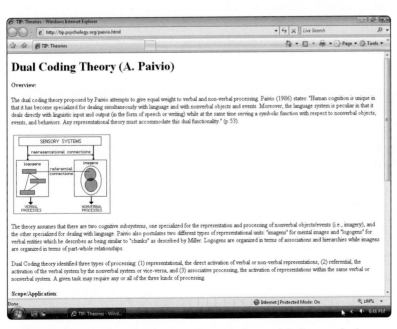

Figure 7 Allan Paivio's dual coding theory helps explain how today's digital students process information.

three subprocesses: (1) representational, in which verbal or nonverbal representations are directly influenced, (2) referential, in which the verbal system is activated by nonverbal communication forms or vice-versa, and (3) associative, in which both text-based systems and graphic representations can trigger mental associations. A given task may require any or all of the three kinds of processing and form the basis for the study of such things as learning a second language.

One of the shortcomings, according to some, is the fact that Paivio placed equal importance on verbal and nonverbal processing. Many theorists have since disputed these findings, in which they have shown that graphics tend to endure longer in one's memory but are not processed as economically. Even with its distracters, dual coding theory has long formed the basis of subsequent educational theories.

Robert Gagne

Robert Gagne (1916 – 2002), a psychologist and educator, developed his learning theories based partially on the behaviorist's and information-processing point of view. Gagne is known for his contributions in the area of cognitive learning hierarchies, which involves the development of skills based on a building-block principle. Gagne identified five major categories of learning: verbal information, intellectual skills, cognitive strategies, motor skills, and attitudes (Figure 8). He made an enormous contribution to learning theory and instructional systems design. While in the Air

Force, he began to develop some of his ideas for his comprehensive learning theory. He incorporated characteristics of both behavior modification theory and performance education.

Gagne developed three principles that he viewed as integral for successful instruction: (1) providing instruction on the set of component tasks that build toward a final task, (2) ensuring that each component task is mastered, and (3) sequencing the component tasks to ensure optimal transfer to the final task. In other words, a teacher must teach alphabet recognition so that her students can read words. After students can read words, they can read a sentence, and then two sentences, and then a paragraph, and so on. This process reflects a hierarchy of components.

Careful planning must take place so that learning is optimal and instruction can be broken down into meticulously planned lessons. Gagne believed that a variety of internal and external conditions must be present for learning to occur and he also believed that learning results in observable behavior. The internal conditions can be described as states that include attention, motivation, and recall. The external conditions are the factors surrounding a person, such as timing and place. The observable behavior is the result of the internal process of learning. Further, Gagne discussed that learners must go through a hierarchy of skills from simple to complex. Finally, he identified five areas of learning outcomes (Figure 8).

Web Info

For more information about Robert Gagne, visit the Teachers Discovering Computers Web site (*scsite.com/tdc5*), click Chapter 6, click Web Info, and then click Gagne.

Categories of Learning Outcomes	Examples of Outcomes
1. Verbal information	Learner can state what has been learned.
2. Intellectual skills: composed of concrete and defined concepts	Learner can discriminate between facts, can identify colors, and can follow directions.
3. Cognitive strategies	Learner reads books.
4. Motor skills	Learner can use a mouse or joystick.
5. Attitudes	Learner prefers reading to watching TV.

Figure 8 Gagne's five areas of learning outcomes.

Gagne sought to understand what conditions were necessary for students to learn. Instruction is an external condition for learning that leads to the internal process of learning. To maximize the potential for the internal process of learning to occur, Gagne identified **nine events of instruction** (Figure 9).

Nine Events of Instruction
1. Gain attention of the learners
2. Inform learners of the objective
3. Stimulate recall of prior learning
4. Present the stimulus or lesson
5. Provide learning guidance and instruction
6. Elicit performance
7. Provide feedback
8. Assess performance
9. Enhance retention and transfer

Figure 9 Gagne's nine events of instruction can help teachers develop technology-enriched lesson plans.

Howard Gardner

Many researchers have focused on understanding and defining intelligence. They believe that intelligence is a key to understanding how students learn. **Intelligence** is the ability to gain knowledge, apply knowledge, manipulate one's environment, and think abstractly. Howard Gardner (1943 –) developed what he called the theory of multiple intelligences (Figure 10).

Gardner, a professor at Harvard University, has conducted years of research on regular and gifted students and also studied adults with brain damage. In those who had been injured, he wanted to correlate what part of the brain had been injured and how the physical injury affected learning and other physical abilities. Through his original research, he concluded that individuals use eight different intelligences to perceive and understand the world. Gardner believes that individuals might have all of the intelligences, yet one, two, or more intelligences may be more dominant than others for each individual. Gardner's eight intelligences and suggested integration strategies are described in Figure 11 (on the next page).

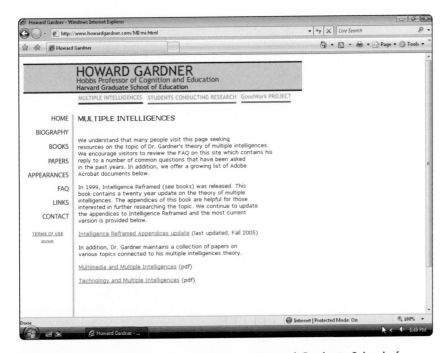

Figure 10 Howard Gardner is a professor at Harvard Graduate School of Education and is best known for his theory of multiple intelligences.

Web Info

For more information about Howard Gardner, visit the Teachers Discovering Computers Web site (*scsite.com/tdc5*), click Chapter 6, click Web Info, and then click Gardner.

Intelligence	Description	Technology Integration
Linguistic–verbal	Ease in using language; think in words; sensitivity to rhythm and order; enjoy writing, reading, telling stories, and doing crossword puzzles	Word processing programs, prompted programs, label-making programs, word game programs, and programs that require the student to read and answer questions
Logical–mathematical	Ability to engage in inductive and deductive reasoning; use numbers effectively and to categorize, infer, make generalizations, and test hypotheses	Database programs, spreadsheet programs, problem-solving software, simulations that allow students to experiment with problems and observe results, and strategy game formats
Spatial–visual	Ability to visualize objects and special dimensions, think in images and pictures, like to draw and design, and enjoy puzzles	Draw and paint programs; graphic production software; reading programs that use visual clues such as color coding, desktop publishing, multimedia, concept mapping, and atlas programs
Body–kinesthetic	Ability to move the body with skill and control, expertise in using the body to express ideas and feelings	Software requiring alternate input such as joystick, touch window, or graphics tablet; keyboarding/word processing programs; graphics programs that produce blueprints for making 3-D models; and software that includes animated graphics and/or requires physical engagement
Musical	Ability to recognize patterns and sounds; sensitivity to pitch and rhythm; the capacity to perceive, express, transform or discern musical forms; think in tones, and learn through rhythm and melody	Programs that combine stories with songs; reading programs that associate letters/sounds with music; programs that use music as a reward; programs that allow students to create their own songs, hypermedia, and multimedia
Interpersonal	Ability to understand and communicate effectively with others, understand them, and interpret their behavior	Telecommunications programs, programs that address social issues, programs that include group participation or decision making, programs that turn learning into a social activity, and games that require two or more players
Intrapersonal	An awareness of oneself, goals, and emotions; the capacity for self-knowledge of one's own feelings; and the ability to use that knowledge for personal understanding	Tutorial software, programs that are self-paced, instructional games in which the opponent is the computer, programs that encourage self-awareness or build self-improvement skills, and programs that allow students to work independently
Naturalist	An awareness of the natural world around them; can identify people, plants, and other environmental features; can develop a sense of cause and effect in relation to natural occurrences, such as weather; can formulate and test hypotheses	Problem-solving software, simulations that allow students to experiment with problems and observe results, strategy game formats, database software, concept mapping software, and weather probeware

Figure 11 Using Gardner's original eight multiple intelligences and technology integration, teachers can find ways to reach all students.

Gardner also believes that the intelligences are influenced by biological predispositions and learning opportunities in an individual's cultural context. The teacher-directed instructional method appeals strongly to the linguistic-verbal and logical-mathematical intelligences. Gardner suggests that instructional methods should include a variety of activities that support other intelligences, such as physical education, role-playing, arts, cooperative learning, reflections, and creative play.

A variety of assessment methods should be incorporated to accommodate the wide variety of student learning styles more accurately. An important observation Gardner made was identifying the need that educators take into account the differences in students' multiple intelligences and use them as a guide to personalize instruction and assessment, which results in the ability to design appropriate instructional strategies.

Benjamin Bloom

Benjamin Bloom (1913 – 1999), an educational psychologist, focused his research on students' cognitive learning domain (Figure 12). Bloom and a group of psychologists sought to classify learning behaviors to better understand how

knowledge is absorbed. Bloom classified learning into three domains: cognitive, affective, and psychomotor. Bloom defined the **cognitive domain** as a student's intellectual level, in other words, what students know and how they organize ideas and thoughts. He defined the **affective domain** as a student's emotions, interests, attitude, attention, and awareness. Finally, he categorized the **psychomotor domain**, which includes a student's motor skills and physical abilities. All of these domains can overlap in learning activities and are integrated throughout learning experiences.

Bloom wanted to develop a practical means for classifying curriculum goals and objectives. Many educators today develop their curriculum goals and objectives with these three domains in mind. Educators are responsible for planning curriculum activities that support what students already should know and what they should learn. Teachers create their instructional plans based on state standards, learning objectives, and learning theories. Teachers often arrange skills they want students to acquire using a scaffolding effect from simple to complex. Within the cognitive domain, Bloom identified six levels that can be used to acquire knowledge about a topic.

Web Info

For more information about Benjamin Bloom, visit the Teachers Discovering Computers Web site (*scsite.com/tdc5*), click Chapter 6, click Web Info, and then click Bloom.

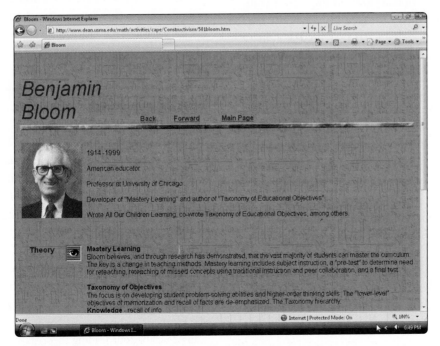

Web Info

For more information about Bloom's Taxonomy, visit the Teachers Discovering Computers Web site (*scsite.com/tdc5*), click Chapter 6, click Web Info, and then click Bloom's Taxonomy.

Figure 12 Benjamin Bloom's research focused on developing student problem-solving abilities and higher-order thinking skills. He was the creator of the concepts of Mastery Learning and Bloom's Taxonomy.

Competencies	Skills
Knowledge Learner can recall information.	Arrange, repeat, recall, define, list, match, name, order, narrate, describe
Comprehension Learner can explain and predict.	Summarize, classify, explain, discuss, give examples, identify, explain, translate
Application Learner can solve problems and use information.	Apply, demonstrate, solve, change, discover, experiment, interpret, show, present
Analysis Learner can see patterns, organize parts, and recognize hidden meanings.	Analyze, experiment, examine, compare, contrast, associate, dissect, conclude, test
Synthesis Learner can use previous ideas to create new ones, and relate ideas. from several areas	Collect, assemble, compose, develop, design, invent, create, plan, revise, role-play, theorize
Evaluation Learner can compare and discriminate between ideas, judge, and value ideas.	Compare, assess, contrast, criticize, debate, judge, value, predict, estimate, appraise

Figure 13 The six levels of Bloom's Taxonomy move from simple to complex.

Web Info

For more information about Constructivism, visit the Teachers Discovering Computers Web site (*scsite.com/tdc5*), click Chapter 6, click Web Info, and then click Constructivism.

The levels move from simple to complex and are designed to increase a student's comprehension. These levels commonly are referred to as **Bloom's Taxonomy** (Figure 13 above).

Many teachers may not realize they are creating instructional plans that only challenge students within the first two levels. For instance, if students are learning about computers and then are asked to name only the parts and describe what they do, the activity has stayed in the Knowledge and Comprehension levels. If students are asked to propose how computers have changed their lives, the assignment has moved to the Analysis level.

Bloom believed and demonstrated through his research that all children can learn. Bloom's Taxonomy has been linked to mastery learning. **Mastery learning** is defined as a model for learning in which students continue to gain information and knowledge, working through modules or teacher instruction only after they have mastered the content of the previous modules. All students can learn given the correct conditions for learning and sufficient time. The critical ingredient is changing instructional methods so students can master the content.

Constructivism

Extensive research has been conducted to assist educators in better understanding which instructional strategies will increase students' motivation to learn and determine their comprehension of a subject. Many researchers agree that traditional teacher-directed or lecture-based instruction often is limited in its effectiveness to reach today's learners. Teacher-directed instruction, however, still is used in many classrooms because of its ability to deliver information quickly; yet, students' understanding and comprehension can be low when this is the only teaching method used to address learning objectives and benchmarks.

Confucius once said, "I hear and I forget. I see and I remember. I do and I understand." Constructivists agree that students learn by doing. When students actively participate in the learning process by using critical-thinking skills to analyze a problem, they will create, or construct, their own understanding of a topic or problem. **Constructivist** theory, or **constructivism**, is based on a type of learning in which the learner forms, or constructs, much of what he or she learns or comprehends. The following sections describe four leading theorists of constructivism.

Jean Piaget

The theories of Jean Piaget (1896 – 1980) profoundly influenced the constructivist movement (Figure 14). Piaget was a psychologist who developed the cognitive learning theory after he observed children for many years. Piaget perceived that children think very differently from adults. He felt children were active learners and did not need motivation from adults to learn. Piaget believed that children were constructing new knowledge as they moved through different cognitive stages, building on what they already knew. Furthermore, children interpret this knowledge differently as they progress through different stages.

Piaget defined four cognitive stages (Figure 15). The first stage **sensorimotor** is when learning takes place primarily through the child's senses and motor actions. The second stage **preoperational** is when children begin to use symbols and images. They use language symbols and play pretend games. An object such as a cardboard box can be a container, but it also can represent a house.

Next, children move from the two egocentric stages into the third stage **concrete operational**.

Web Info

For more information about Jean Piaget, visit the Teachers Discovering Computers Web site (*scsite.com/tdc5*), click Chapter 6, click Web Info, and then click Piaget.

Figure 14 Jean Piaget was a psychologist who developed his learning theory after many years of observing children.

Cognitive Stages	Ages (Approximate)	Characteristics of Learning
Sensorimotor	Birth to 2 years	Imitation, learn through senses and motor activities, do not understand the world around them, and egocentric
Preoperational	2 to 6/7 years	Egocentric, pretend play, drawing ability, speech and communication development, concrete thinking, and intuitive reasoning
Concrete operational	6/7 to 11/12 years	Classification, logical reasoning, problem solving, and beginnings of abstract thinking
Formal operational	11/12 years through adulthood	Comparative reasoning, abstract thinking, deductive logic, and test hypotheses

Figure 15 Piaget's four cognitive stages.

In this stage, beginning about age 7, children begin to think logically. This is the stage when children are beginning to learn many facts. They also can begin to understand other points of view besides their own. Piaget called his last cognitive stage **formal operational**. During this stage, which begins at about age 12, children transition from concrete thinking to more abstract. They can formulate a hypothesis and understand cause and effect. Children or adolescents begin to formulate their own beliefs and morals.

Piaget felt that children are working cognitively toward equilibrium as they move through the four different cognitive stages. While they are learning, children create what Piaget called schema. **Schema** is their cognitive understanding or development at any given time. Piaget concluded that children assimilate new knowledge as they experience new things and learn new information, which Piaget called **assimilation**. Children fit this information or these experiences into their lives to change their knowledge base and to make sense of their environment and the world around them. Piaget called this process **accommodation**.

Through the insightful work of Piaget and others, researchers believe it is important to provide a rich learning environment for children to explore (Figure 16). Children learn by actively

investigating a topic. Piaget's theories support the use and integration of technology because of the opportunities technology supplies to reach a diverse population of learners with different learning styles. Using Web Quests, scavenger and treasure hunts, curriculum pages, and many other educational technologies, teachers can create student-centered activities that actively engage students in the learning process.

Jerome Bruner

An American psychologist and educator, Jerome Bruner (1915 –) proposed that learning is an active process in which the learner constructs new ideas or concepts based on his current or past knowledge (Figure 17). Bruner believes that constructivist learners are active learners; they are actively engaged in the learning process. Constructivism emphasizes an integrated curriculum where students learn a subject in various ways or through many different activities.

Technology offers many strategies for the constructivist learning environment. When using the constructivist approach, students may complete a variety of activities while learning about a topic. For example, if students are studying endangered species, they may research this topic by using books, videos, and other digital media in the media center, as well as informational Web

Web Info

For more information about Jerome Bruner, visit the Teachers Discovering Computers Web site (*scsite.com/tdc5*), click Chapter 6, click Web Info, and then click Bruner.

Figure 16 Student learning comes alive when teachers integrate the Internet and multimedia software into their classroom curriculum.

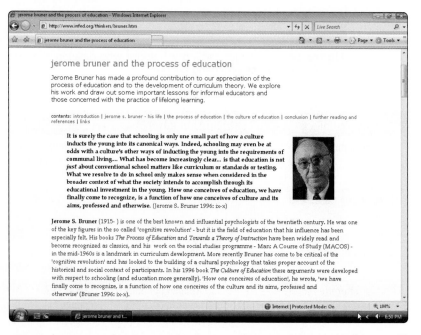

Figure 17 Jerome Bruner's constructivist theory stresses that teachers actively should engage their students in their own learning.

sites. They can then use an AlphaSmart to write up their findings in a word-processing document, study vocabulary words with electronic flash cards, create a drawing about endangered species in a paint program, create a spreadsheet to graph population changes over time, build a model with clay, and even learn songs about saving endangered animals or species.

Bruner's constructivist theory provides a framework for instruction based on the study of cognition. The theoretical concept of **cognition** suggests that an individual progresses through different intellectual stages. In constructivist theory, the learner selects and changes information to understand and make decisions, relying on higher-order thinking skills to solve a problem. An individual creates in her mind mental models that provide meaning and association to experiences that allow the individual to go beyond the given information. Bruner felt the teacher's role should be to encourage students through exploration and inquiry; in other words, learning should be discovery (Figure 18).

As far as instruction is concerned, teachers should try to encourage students to discover concepts by themselves. Teachers should engage students by providing activities that guide students and create opportunities for discussion or for using the Socratic method of learning. The **Socratic method** is when students learn how to analyze problems, to think critically about their own point of view and the opinions of others, as well as to articulate and defend their position. This method assists students in solving problems through questioning and answering techniques, which engages them in discussion. The task of the teacher is to take the materials to be learned and translate the information into a form appropriate for the learners' current level of understanding. Bruner felt that the curriculum should be organized in a spiral manner so that students continually build upon what they already have learned; this approach is called the **spiral curriculum**.

Lev Vygotsky

Lev Vygotsky (1896 – 1934), a Russian educational psychologist, also was interested in children's cognitive development (Figure 19). He developed what is known as **social cognition theory**. Although his ideas overlap in many ways with the traditional constructivists' point of view, Vygotsky believed that learning was influenced significantly by social development. He theorized that learning took place within the

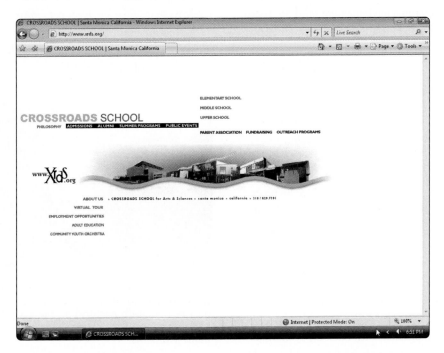

Figure 18 Many schools, such as Crossroads School for Arts & Sciences, believe students should discover their own learning paths through active learning in areas such as intuition, imagination, artistic creativity, and physical expression.

Web Info

For more information
about Lev Vygotsky,
visit the Teachers
Discovering
Computers Web site
(*scsite.com/tdc5*),
click Chapter 6, click
Web Info, and then
click Vygotsky.

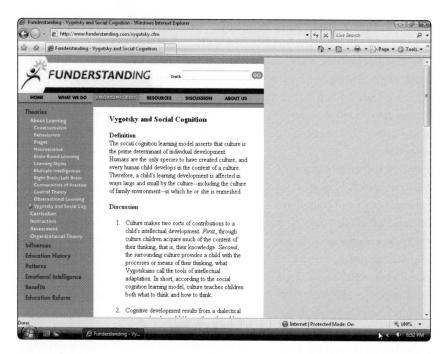

Figure 19 Lev Vygotsky was a Russian psychologist who believed that learning is influenced significantly by social development.

context of a child's social development and culture. For instance, when children vocalize, they learn that sounds have meanings and sounds become language. They learn that spoken language becomes the inner language that children use to think or develop cognitively. They also learn that gestures have meaning and are used to communicate and interact with others.

As stated earlier, Piaget believed children progressed through different stages of cognitive development and that achieving higher levels of thinking was not accomplished easily. Lev Vygotsky believed that a child's social environment could positively or negatively affect the child's cognitive development. Vygotsky proposed that children have a **zone of proximal development**, which is the difference between the problem-solving ability that a child has learned and the potential that the child can achieve from collaboration with a more advanced peer or expert, such as a teacher.

If some form of expertise challenges a child, then greater cognitive development can occur. Vygotsky theorized that if a 9-year-old child worked on a problem with an adult or another child who was advanced, the 9-year-old would be able to learn the concept or ideas that were more complex than the 9-year-old could understand on his own; this is known as **collaborative learning**. With practice, the child then would be able to apply the new cognitive skills to other situations. Vygotsky felt students should work collaboratively to share their different perspectives with each other; then they could negotiate a solution and come to a much deeper understanding of a problem or tasks (Figure 20).

Figure 20 Vygotsky believed students should work collaboratively to share their different perspectives with each other. Here, students use handheld computers to work together to solve math problems.

Furthermore, Vygotsky proposed that teachers should discover the level of each child's cognitive/social development, and build or construct their learning experiences from that point. He referred to this process as **scaffolding**. In education, a scaffold is altering of the **schemata**, which is an organized way of creating or providing a cognitive mental framework for understanding and remembering information. As teachers and other students provide information and different perspectives for each other, these sources can become a scaffold, a temporary source of knowledge. Then students assimilate this knowledge and build their own, thus removing the need for a scaffold.

Building on constructivism theory and Vygotsky's scaffolding, the Cognition and Technology Group at Vanderbilt (CTGV) developed **anchored instruction**. Anchored instruction is a model for technology-based learning and is a form of instruction where the student already has learned concepts and information, which form a basis for other information to connect to and build upon, and which is called the **anchor**. The CTGV wanted to create complex, realistic problems that students could explore and then develop potential solutions for those problems based on their exploration. When challenged with a problem, anchored instruction motivates students to build new ideas and anchor them to what they already have learned.

John Dewey

John Dewey (1859 – 1952) has influenced American education significantly (Figure 21). He was an educational psychologist, philosopher, and political activist who was an advocate for child-centered instruction. He believed that learning should engage and expand the experiences of the learners. He encouraged educators to reflect on their strategies and create activities that combine concrete and practical relevance to students' lives.

Like Vygotsky, Dewey believed that education was a social process. He viewed school as a community that represented a larger picture. In 1896, Dewey began the University Elementary School, or Laboratory School. Many educators called this school the Dewey School. The school prospered and earned national attention. Dewey felt that school should be viewed as an extension of society and students should play an active role in it, working cooperatively with each other. Dewey viewed learning as student-directed with a teacher serving as a guide for

Web Info

For more information about John Dewey, visit the Teachers Discovering Computers Web site (*scsite.com/tdc5*), click Chapter 6, click Web Info, and then click Dewey.

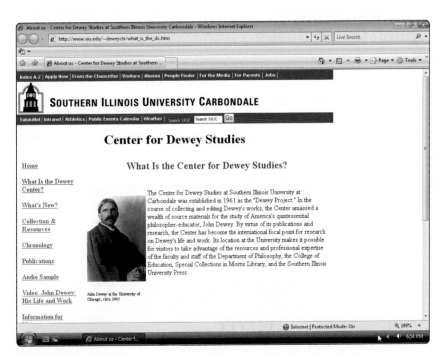

Figure 21 John Dewey, an educational psychologist and philosopher, believed that learning should engage and expand the experiences of the learners.

resources. He believed students learn by doing and should be allowed to construct, create, and actively inquire. Dewey theorized that this type of learning truly prepared students to function well in society.

Dewey was part of a movement in the early 1900s that was called **progressive education**. Progressive education focused on educating the whole child, physically, mentally, and socially, and not on just the dispensation of facts and information. John Dewey's name also has been linked to other early movements, such as **pragmatism**. Pragmatists believed that the truth of a theory could be determined only if a theory worked. In other words, theory is valuable only for its practical application.

Dewey founded several schools in addition to his Laboratory School. He advocated educational reform, pursued philosophy, and supported many political issues, such as women's suffrage. Through his observations, he proposed that education begins with experience. He has been called, by some, the Father of American Education. His influence can be seen in American classrooms today — where children explore the curriculum, conduct science experiments, use manipulatives for math, and search the Internet for information.

Web Info

For more information about game-based learning, visit the Teachers Discovering Computers Web site (*scsite.com/tdc5*), click Chapter 6, click Web Info, and then click Game-Based Learning.

Connecting with Today's Kids Through Game-Based Learning

Through the last few sections of this special feature, you have read about some, but not all, of the educational theories and theorists — helping you develop a foundation and understanding of the principles of teaching and learning. As we

have stated throughout this textbook, there is a new generation of learners — a digital generation.

Video games have been the center of considerable controversy and discussion in recent years. Many believe that the excessive use of video games has led to a general decline in the academic achievement by today's digital generation, especially those who are gamers. In some ways, they are correct. Peter Moore suggests that some digital students are prone to powering down at school to conserve energy — energy they will need for after-school gaming activities in which the players are called upon to react and interact in a highly developed and fast-paced virtual world. Why are students willing to spend hours in front of a computer screen interacting with a game that requires using search and problem-based learning techniques to wind their way through the various encounters, but these same students are not interested in using those same skills in a more traditional learning environment? Does presentation matter? Does content matter? Several studies have reported a link between supposed antisocial behaviors and violent games; however, there have not been any study results that can confirm cause and effect.

Further, stating or implying that playing games, regardless of their aggressiveness, actually promotes antisocial behaviors, has not been shown to be true. In fact, James Gee has identified 36 learning principles that can be found in all successful video games, regardless of content. The meta-learning principles are built into the makeup of video games and are supported by current research on human learning and cognition. Figure 22 lists six of these principles.

Learning Principles Found in Successful Video Games
1. How players form an identity to buy into the content
2. How players learn to connect different symbol systems (words, symbols, artifacts)
3. How players choose between various methods to solve a problem
4. How players identify, filter, and utilize different nonverbal cues
5. How players leverage their knowledge to reapply solutions learned from one situation to newly discovered ones
6. How players identify and develop a sense for story

Figure 22 This table lists just a few of the learning principles that James Gee suggests are based on human learning and cognitive science.

Games have become an important social trend. Many educators also believe that games have become an important teaching tool because they can provide a compelling context by the way they invoke interactive, engaging, and immersive activities. The fact is, however, that games have yet to effectively and continuously help classroom teachers teach subject-specific content. Yes, there have been successes in some content areas, such as science and history, but there is still room for growth in the gaming industry as it relates to education.

Simulation games have been successful in the military, business, and industry. For example, flight simulators have been very successful in increasing cost-efficient ways of teaching skills to pilots. Educators like James Gee suggest that while most games teach something, most of the positive outcomes of games used in instructional settings center on motivation, social skill-building, simulations, and changing attitudes, rather than on content-related skills. These outcomes are hard to measure and so this has caused considerable confusion among game evaluators. Evaluators often confuse the popularity of games, which is based on game-play and interactivity (which does foster positive, intrinsic, and social learning) with their educational value. Just because a game is fun to play does not mean it teaches subject-specific content or meets the curriculum standards that all students must meet each year to progress.

Several outside factors contribute to the lack of success in integrating games into the curriculum. First, many teachers feel pressure to use them despite their lack of content because their students play games so much and they receive funding to have them in their schools. Because many teachers do not play games regularly, they do not understand games and how games became so successful in the market place. Game developers also contribute to this situation because many times they are pressured to add educational content as an after-thought; and as a result, the game often does not follow good educational practices.

It is important to know what makes games successful, both commercially and as instructional aides. Certainly, one might infer that process learning or scaffolding takes place in most commercially successful games as players move from one level to another by recalling rules, game mechanics, and processes from previous levels. A few games promote these processes to the some extent to ensure they enforce higher-order learning or critical problem solving skills. Hints (or cheats, which is what they are referred to by the game industry and which is a problem term in education) are provided and can be a great form of feedback to the players/learners, but few of them are written clearly enough to ensure that they effectively resemble feedback needed in lesson situations.

So, as a teacher, how do you go about deciding whether to use a game in your classroom? How do you evaluate the game's content and play process so you can be assured that your students actually are learning what you intend them to be learning? One way is to use a rubric to evaluate the education value of a game.

Many feel educational games have the potential to revolutionize classroom instruction, so three university researchers (Gunter, Kenny, & Vick) created an evaluation rubric based upon their RETAIN (Relevance, Embedding, Transfer, Adaptation, Immersion, Naturalization) model that is shown in Figure 23. The RETAIN rubric correlates to instructional methods and learning theories that are closely aligned with generally accepted game design principles and theories, including Keller's ARCS Model and Gagne's Events of Instruction. The rubric incorporates Bloom's hierarchical structure for knowledge acquisition and Piaget's ideas on schema.

Recently, educators have been looking into games and research has been published that outlines some of the more important and credible aspects of games — those aspects that make games stand out academically. Essentially, it boils down to this: games need to be engrained and based on educational best practices or learning theories.

Web Info

To learn more about evaluating games, visit the Teachers Discovering Computers Web site (*scsite.com/tdc5*), click Chapter 6, click Web Info, and then click Evaluating Games.

	Level 0	Level 1	Level 2	Level 3
Relevance	The story/fantasy creates little stimulus for learning and is in a format that is of little interest to the players/learners nor does it utilize advanced organizers. The player/learner does not know the state of the game or the required learning content based on the choices presented.	The story/fantasy is age/content appropriate or it has a limited educational focus and little progression. The pedagogic elements are somewhat defined but occasionally players/learners are allowed by the embedded fantasy to become engaged in inappropriate content or contexts.	*In addition to overcoming limitations and/or adding to Level 1 features, the the following are also present:* Specific didactic content is targeted and learning objectives are clearly defined. Creates interest in what is to be learned and a natural stimulus and desire to learn more.	*In addition to overcoming limitations and/or adding to Level 1 & 2 features, following are also present:* Is relevant to players'/learners' lives, (real or imagined) and/or the world around them using characters and themes familiar to them. Matches the players/learners to their appropriate developmental level by providing adequate cognitive challenges.
Embedding	The "teachable" moments disrupt the player's/learner's gameplay, that is, flow of the game. Has no interactive focus/hook either on the emotional, psychological, physical, or intellectual level.	Didactic elements are both present but are not cohesively integrated — one or the other is added as an afterthought to the first. Content to be learned is exogenous to the fantasy context of the game.	*In addition to overcoming limitations and/or adding to Level 1 features, the following are also present:* Allows for extended experiences with problems and contexts specific to the curriculum. Intellectual challenges are presented to players/learners of sufficient level to keep them interested in completing the game.	*In addition to overcoming limitations and/or adding to Level 1 & 2 features, the following are also present:* Involves the players/learners both mentally and emotionally in such a way that they are conditioned to accept change and invest in the belief. Educational content is fully endogenous to the fantasy context
Transfer	Offers no anchored or scaffolded levels of challenge, no evidence of using integrated content from previous levels, or little challenges at an increasing level of difficulty. Process knowledge is not mapped to targeted academic content.	Offers levels of challenge that emphasize similar lines of thought and problem analysis to be applied to other implied contexts. Contains 3D cues and interactive animation that facilitate the transfer of knowledge during pedagogic events.	*In addition to overcoming limitations and/or adding to Level 1 features, the following are also present:* Players/learners are able to progress through the levels easily. Active problem solving is required to move to the next level. Players/learners can progress through instructional elements that are introduced in a hierarchical manner so that knowledge gained during gameplay can be transferred to other situations.	*In addition to overcoming limitations and/or adding to Level 1 & 2 features, the following are also present:* Includes authentic real life experiences that reward meaningful "post-event" knowledge acquisition. Contains "after action reviews" that offers players/learners an opportunity to teach other (computation or actual) players/learners what they have learned.

Figure 23 A comprehensive rubric you can use to evaluate the educational value of games.

(continued on next page)

	Level 0	Level 1	Level 2	Level 3
Adaptation	Fails to involve the players/learners in an interactive context. Information is not structured in a way that can be at least partially grasped by the learner. Does not sequence the material that is to be learned.	Builds upon the player's/learner's existing cognitive structures. New content is sequenced based on the principle of cognitive dissonance — as a result players'/learners' need to interpret events in order to determine what about the new content contradicts what they already know.	*In addition to overcoming limitations and/or adding to Level 1 features, the following are also present:* Instruction is designed to encourage the player's/learner's to go beyond the given information and discover new concepts for themselves. Content sequenced in such a way as to require players/learners to identify old schema and transfer it to new ways of thinking.	*In addition to overcoming imitations land/or adding to Level 1 & 2 features, the following are also present:* Makes learning an active, participatory process in which the players/learners construct new ideas based upon their prior knowledge. Presents information that focuses on external or internal characteristics that enable the learner to associate new information with previous learning.
Immersion	Provides no progressive, formative feedback during each unit of gameplay. Presents little or no opportunity for reciprocal action and active participation for players/learners.	Elements of play are not directly involved with the didactic focus, but they do not impede or compete with pedagogic elements. Presents some opportunity for reciprocal action in a defined context, that is, a context that is meaningful, repeatable, and interactive, but players/learners do not feel fully interactive in the learning.	*In addition to overcoming limitations and/or adding to Level 1 features, the following are also present:* Requires the player/learner to be involved cognitively, physically, psychologically, and emotionally in the game content. The use of mutual modeling creates a shared responsibility for learning among the participants.	*In addition to overcoming limitations and/or adding to Level 1 & 2 features, the following are also present:* Presents opportunity for reciprocal action and active participation for players/learners. Presents both the environment and the opportunity for belief creation.
Naturalization	Presents little opportunity for the mastery of facts or a particular skill. Target content/skills are rarely revisited. Little opportunity is given to build upon previous knowledge and/or skills in a logical and	Replay is encouraged to assist in retention and to remediate shortcomings. Improves the speed of cognitive response, automaticity, and/or visual processing.	*In addition to overcoming limitations and/or adding to Level 1 features, the following are also present:* Encourages the synthesis of several elements and an understanding that once one skill is learned it leads to the easier acquisition of later elements. Requires the players/learners to make judgments about ideas and materials.	*In addition to overcoming limitations and/or adding to Level 1 & 2 features, the following are also present:* Causes players/learners to be aware of the content in such a way that they become efficient users of that knowledge. Causes the player/learner to spontaneously utilize knowledge habitually and consistently.

(continued from previous page)

Figure 23 A comprehensive rubric you can use to evaluate the educational value of games.

Question	Explanation	Sample Evaluation
Is the game relevant?	In addition to presenting learning materials in a way that is relevant to your students, their needs, and their learning styles, the instructional units in the game should be relevant to one another and set in context with previously learned materials, using introductory materials that contain advanced organizers.	All games in the Carmen Sandiego series have mechanics that make them relevant to the learner. For example, the games' clues build on one another providing scaffolding content as players' progress through the games. Each level builds on previous deductions, which students use as they complete the game. A few places where relevance could be improved include the introduction to each geographic region, which is brief, and the game development, which does little to build on prior content knowledge. At the beginning of play there are no building blocks for the player to learn how to track geographic locations.
Is the content embedded into the story/fantasy?	Research has shown that the closer the learning is tied to the fantasy context the better the learning. The intent is to integrate the educational content in such a way as to make it intrinsic to the fantasy context of the game so that learning and gameplay function together seamlessly.	Each game in the Carmen Sandiego series has a compelling story line that includes geography content and vocabulary placed strategically through the story line. Throughout the game, players are attempting to track down Carmen Sandiego. Students must use the clues they gather to assess where to go next in the game. The geography content is embedded in each story in the in *Where in the World* series.
Does knowledge transfer?	The game should cause a circumstance in which the targeted knowledge is transferred to similar or new and unique situations so players/learners are able to assimilate and accommodate it. The idea of transfer is well known in educational circles as critical to higher-order learning.	Content, especially geography content students learn as they play the games, can be transferred, but the knowledge gained may not result in long term retention. Why? A player collects clues in an area, which are used for figuring out the identity of the thief being tracked and for deciding where to go next. Once those decisions are made, the player has to focus on using the next set of clues to find a new location. Students often forget the previous knowledge gained as they focus on the new content and progressing through the game.
Does the game provide for extended practice?	Extended practice creates an opportunity for what educators call automaticity or spontaneous knowledge. The game needs to be analyzed to assess whether students are able to use what they have learned habitually and whether they are able to consistently monitor their progress without thinking about it and having to devote significant mental resources to the new knowledge.	During the game, players seek out clues and new information in order to track down the thief. In *Where in the World Carmen Sandiego* clues build on an identity and solving a crime. The only way to gain more knowledge about a particular geographic area is to play the game again and see if that geographic area is part of the journey. If the thief does not go to that same geographic area, then the student will not encounter background information about that area. This will impact how much a student can learn about a particular geographic area while playing the game.

Figure 24 This figure provides an example of how to evaluate a game using components of the RETAIN rubric.

Figure 24 is an example of how to evaluate the value of games using the RETAIN rubric in Figure 23. One of the games in the Carmen Sandiego series, *Where in the World is Carmen Sandiego?*, is a game intended to teach geography. The game was originally created by Broderbund Software in the late 1980s with many updates since. The goal of the game is to track and arrest Carmen and her villains, who travel around the world. The game was not designed originally for the classroom, but when it was adopted by so many schools, the creators broadened its appeal by adding other academic content, such as math and science. The latest releases have returned to its original geographical and historical focus.

When using the questions and explanations in Figure 24 to evaluate the Carmen Sandiego series, you can see that the games do not embed content well. The series does permit considerable opportunity for players/learners to become immersed in the background and environment of each game. It also provides good levels of naturalization as well because it allows for repetitive play through its varied content and fantasy context. The second and following times one plays a game in the series, the situations in the game vary greatly, which reduces the boredom often found in games that encourage repetitive practice. Games that do not vary the content often cause the player/learner to lose interest.

There are no manuals to teach players how to play the games. They do not seem to need them or want them. The construct of the games needs to be such that the process is self-revealing. As these learning principles are implied in the construct of the games, they actually provide better opportunities to teach things to students than most of what is being used to develop lesson activities in today's classroom — classrooms being occupied by digital, game-playing students. Perhaps educators should take a look at how games are constructed and utilize many of these same principles in their own school's curriculum. The results just may be surprising for educators and education. What we are looking for are games that not only stimulate the learner but also teach content in a meaningful way — making the learning and the experience fun and successful!

Putting Theory into Practice

The next two Classroom in Action sections explore how teachers utilize learning theories in their classrooms to facilitate learning and achieve curriculum standards, while at the same time find ways to reach today's digital students. The first story, *Teaching Kids to Think – The Thinking Ladder*, shows how an elementary teacher integrates technology and Bloom's Taxonomy to help her students develop higher-order thinking skills. The second, *Digital Kids – The Sam Schugg Story*, shows how the integration of technology with learning theory can inspire today's digital generation.

The Classroom in Action
Teaching Kids to Think — The Thinking Ladder

This section explores how one teacher puts learning theories into action. Nirsa Gautier, a fourth-grade teacher, was busy working on a simple spelling rule that her class was having difficulty remembering. Suddenly, she thought of a great idea using Bloom's Taxonomy that might enhance her lesson and assist her students' learning.

Mrs. Gautier stopped her spelling lesson and drew a ladder on the whiteboard (Figure 25). She listed the six thinking levels on the ladder and then explained each level in simple terms. She told her students that for them to be successful thinkers, they needed to progress to each level. The new class goal was to get to the highest level!

Mrs. Gautier then went back to the spelling lesson. She asked her students to identify what thinking level they were operating at on the thinking ladder. Some of the students were able to tell her immediately that they were at the Knowledge level. She explained that they could

Figure 25 Mrs. Gautier's thinking ladder is based on Bloom's Taxonomy.

not move to higher levels of thinking success without mastering this basic knowledge. Now she had their attention! The class all agreed they had to remember the rule to move up the ladder.

Mrs. Gautier asked her students to work in groups collaboratively for five minutes to help each other remember the rule. She knew this was a great constructivist learning strategy. After five minutes, she randomly called on students to see if their group strategy had worked. To her amazement, every student she called on knew the rule! She congratulated the class on a job well done and then challenged them to move up to the next level of the thinking ladder.

To encourage higher-order thinking skills, Mrs. Gautier had her students develop questions based on a reading selection. The students responded in their journals and wrote three questions for the selection. Each question had to come from a different thinking level. She found that by asking students to write or construct their own thinking questions from different levels, they first must be able to think on that level. She then would have a student ask a question, another student answer the question, and a third student identify the thinking level. Mrs. Gautier found that often students created better thinking questions than she did! In addition, many of the students were thrilled to know that they were able to answer questions that required higher-order thinking skills. They liked the challenge.

After these experiences, Mrs. Gautier created a large thinking ladder using a word processing program and placed it in the center of the classroom for her students to view. She wanted to make sure that she was integrating the thinking-ladder learning strategy into every class lesson. Mrs. Gautier printed the thinking levels on cardstock, glued magnets on the back, and placed each thinking level on a rung of the ladder. This gave the students colorful visual cues as they moved along the thinking continuum to a higher thinking level. Mrs. Gautier also created a PowerPoint presentation using pictures that illustrated how the students move up the thinking ladder to thinking success (Figure 26). In the presentation, she explained in more detail each

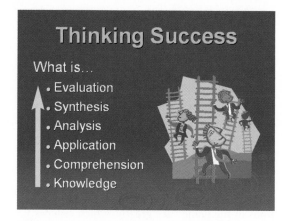

Figure 26 Mrs. Gautier uses PowerPoint to teach her students how to use higher-order thinking skills to move up the thinking ladder.

thinking level and how to apply it when the students read, solve problems, and answer questions. Mrs. Gautier had her students discuss which questions were more difficult to answer. The students began to realize that higher-order thinking involves more time and thought. Consequently, Mrs. Gautier also realized that she must give her students more time to think before answering questions. She decided to call this *think time*.

Mrs. Gautier works her thinking ladder into every subject. When the students create multimedia research projects, she makes sure to include an aspect of each thinking level in the assessment rubric used for evaluation. This guides the students to find information, analyze and evaluate what they read, and then apply it in a meaningful way. After introducing Bloom's Taxonomy into the class, Mrs. Gautier noticed a real excitement as students began to strive to move up the ladder of thinking success.

Teaching students thinking skills using Bloom's Taxonomy revolutionized the way Mrs. Gautier teaches and the way her students learn. Her students became more focused because not only were they thinking, but they were consciously developing the thinking process! They became more confident, taking more responsibility for their learning, and realizing that they must do the thinking to learn.

The Classroom in Action
Digital Kids — The Sam Schugg Story

Sam Schugg is your typical high school kid. He does not like going to high school and when he is there he does not pay attention for very long. It is almost like he is powering down in most of his classes; however, put him in front of a computer and he will pay attention for hours. He shines in his technology class in spite of the fact that he is very reserved and does not speak much. He goes to English class and cannot relate. He wants to be a game developer when he grows up and he feels that reading and writing will not be very important for him to enter that profession. He does okay in math and science but, once again, he does not see their relevance to his plans for the future. As a result, he struggles with his grades in all subjects except for his technology class. What makes matters worse is that all attempts to help remediate his weaknesses have yielded little results because previous efforts mostly centered on requiring him to read more books, to solve more word problems, and/or to conduct more experiments.

Things are about to change. His technology teacher, Bob Phelan, was just completing his studies in instructional design and felt that perhaps a new direction was needed. Banking on Sam's fondness for computers and gaming, Mr. Phelan decided to try a new way to reach Sam and many other students just like him in his technology class (Figure 27).

Figure 27 One technique to motivate today's students to read and write is for teachers to create lessons that integrate digital media.

Mr. Phelan met with Sam's English teacher, Rita Rivera, to discuss his plan. When discussing Sam's situation, Ms. Rivera said that Sam reacted like many of her students when she assigned books to be read, they always wanted to know why they had to read and not simply be allowed to watch the movie! This was frustrating to Ms. Rivera. Mr. Phelan suggested that the students produce a movie about a book. Mr. Phelan had heard of a project called Digital Booktalk. Not only would this activity utilize the students' strengths but it also could be based on many of the learning theories and ideas that Mr. Phelan wanted to put into practice. Mr. Phelan also knew that all students enjoyed stories and if he based the lessons on the premise of bringing out the concept of storytelling, this would be motivating to the students. They decided to combine their classes and teach together. Ms. Rivera could teach about storytelling and Mr. Phelan would teach them digital video editing. Mr. Phelan's students could mentor on the technical aspects of the project and learn about storytelling from the English teacher and her students.

First, they knew that most of their students were visual learners. Both teachers agreed that, even though technology would be the entry point, the activity had to result in making students better readers and writers. After the videos were created, students would write about their experiences and include related vocabulary words. The idea seemed simple — use Robert Doman's ideas about teaching to students' strengths and then remediate the weaknesses. Student learning would be reinforced because they would be working with both images and texts, which was supported by Paivio's ideas about dual coding and Craik and Lockhart's and Bloom's ideas about levels of processing.

Producing their own videos fits the constructivists' ideas about students creating their own meaning while, at the same time, students would be encouraged to retain information because they would be learning by doing and that would also ensure deeper processing of their skills. The instructional plan also follows Gagne's building-block principles.

Web Info

For more information on digital storytelling, visit the Teachers Discovering Computers Web site (scsite.com/tdc5), click Chapter 6, click Web Info, and then click Digital Storytelling.

Web Info

For more information on creating movie trailers, visit the Teachers Discovering Computers Web site (*scsite.com/tdc5*), click Chapter 6, click Web Info, and then click Digital Booktalk.

The Digital Booktalk curriculum stated that everyone in the class would read the same book. They would start with the basic premise of story, then learn text-to-screen techniques of making movies, and move into visual storytelling techniques using a camera and/or photos and a video editor. Students would discuss how to read the selected book as if they were going to make a movie out of it. The two teachers realized that making a full length movie would result in a very large project so they looked at a curriculum that has students create a video trailer about the book. **Video trailers** are short, 2–3 minute summaries of the book (similar to the movie previews shown for upcoming attractions in movie theaters). Using summarizing principles similar to what is done for book talks, the two teachers helped the students come up with their concepts. After the video trailers were produced, the teachers showed the projects, providing students the opportunity to see how others view the content of the same books. The other students would review and evaluate each other's video trailers using a rubric the two teachers designed that focused on content. When they were done, students were asked to write the essence of their video trailer in narrative style using vocabulary words that the teachers required.

When the projects were presented, Sam Schugg's project was the best in the class. The students evaluated his project with great feedback and he scored high on the rubric. He did not even complain during the writing portion of the assignment and on reflection said, "I was so surprised that I could do so well on this. I enjoyed this assignment!" The teachers could tell Sam had pride in his work.

This activity was successful because it was founded on sound instructional practices that incorporated many of the learning theories described earlier in this special feature. Students were motivated to read because they were focused on doing something with the information they obtained from the book. Now, instead of the reading being a passive activity, students are reading for a purpose and are involving themselves in the outcomes using a communication medium they are attracted to and one that is already a large part of their digital lives.

Summary of Learning Theories and Educational Research

Learning is a complex task. Understanding how students learn is an internal process that is difficult to observe. Educators can provide instruction and information, and assess how much information has been retained. Educational research and learning theories are important because they help educators to understand how students learn. From learning theories and research, teachers can improve their instruction and the way they provide information to learners, and they can improve teaching and learning environments.

Integrating technology into teaching is a very powerful way to weave these learning theories throughout the curriculum. Digital media technology appeals to a variety of learning styles and learning intelligences (Gardner). Students are more actively engaged in their learning when teachers effectively integrate technology (Bruner). Technology is effective with group projects, working in teams (Vygotsky and Dewey), and problem-solving activities requiring higher-order thinking skills that allow students to build new ideas from their current knowledge base (Bloom). Teachers even have used computer time effectively as part of a behavior management system (Pavlov and Skinner).

Learners are dynamic and no two will be the same. Theorists help teachers understand how to adapt instruction, information, and the environment for different learners. So, much is to be gained by understanding learning theories and what each theorist has contributed. Their ideas can help educators piece together the complex task of teaching all learners. Integrating learning theories and technology into classroom instructional strategies can make a difference in student motivation and also can increase student achievement in your classroom!

For information on the references used in the creation of this special feature, see Appendix A or access this special feature's Web Info segments.

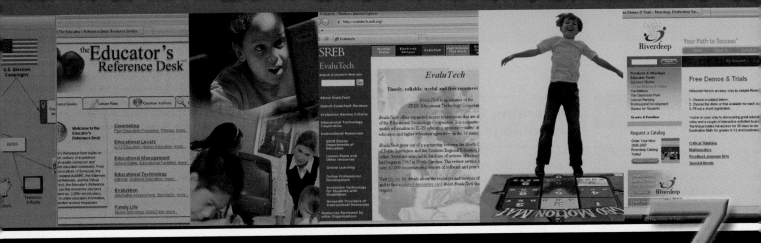

Evaluating Educational Technology and Integration Strategies

Objectives

After completing this chapter, you will be able to do the following:

[ISTE NETS-T Standards I A-B, II A-E, III A-D, IV A-C, V A-D, VI A-C]

- Identify sources of information for evaluating educational technology and digital media

- Outline the considerations and tools used to evaluate software applications

- Describe and explain the key criteria used to evaluate Web resources

- Describe the tools for evaluating the effectiveness of technology

- Compare and analyze the methods used to evaluate student projects

- Identify different technology integration strategies by classroom layout and design

- Define and describe the value of a curriculum page

- Describe ways to integrate technology into specific curriculum subject areas

- Describe authentic assessment tools for student projects

- Identify and compare possible sources of funding for classroom technology

As you learn about the various types of emerging technology and methods of integrating them into your classroom curriculum, undoubtedly, you will be called upon to evaluate the appropriateness of this technology and the effectiveness of its integration into the learning process. This chapter presents an overview of how to evaluate the many different types of technologies that are available today. It also offers specific strategies for how to integrate technology in your classroom based on the number of computers and other devices available to you and your students. Also provided are several subject-specific examples of curriculum integration activities. Finally, this chapter suggests several ways you can raise funds to pay for state-of-the-art technology in your classroom to enhance the teaching and learning experience.

Integration Strategies

To learn more about evaluating video games for use with your students, visit the Teachers Discovering Computers Web site (*scsite.com/tdc5*), click Chapter 7, and then click Education Issues.

Evaluating Educational Technology

Evaluating the appropriateness and effectiveness of educational technology is an important aspect of integrating current technologies into your classroom curriculum. To **evaluate** an item is to determine its value or judge its worth. Evaluating educational technology involves determining if the technology is appropriate and enhances the teaching and learning process. To be considered **appropriate**, educational technology must be suitable for the educational situation, must be motivational, and must promote learning at the correct levels of student ability and academic achievement. It also must address curriculum standards and related learning objectives.

Evaluating educational technology before instruction begins, during the instructional period, and after instruction has taken place is important (Figure 7-1). Before using software or sites on the World Wide Web, for example, teachers should determine if this technology meets their curriculum needs and if the product or content is developmentally and age appropriate for their classroom learning situation. Information from many sources helps teachers evaluate the appropriateness of educational technologies. Teachers should continue to evaluate the technology while it is being used and after the instruction using the technology is complete.

SOURCES OF INFORMATION

Finding the right educational technology can be difficult, especially for new users of technology because each year, developers create hundreds of new educational software packages and Web sites for K-12 classroom use (Figure 7-2). To avoid confusion in this important task, teachers might rely on a variety of resources to help them identify and evaluate the appropriateness of educational technologies. These resources include material from school districts, state Departments of Education, professional educational organizations, hardware and software catalogs, recommendations of colleagues, published evaluations, technology conferences, and Web sites.

SCHOOL DISTRICTS AND STATE DEPARTMENTS OF EDUCATION
Many school districts compile software evaluations that provide guidance on subject-specific software. In addition, many state Departments of Education provide lists of software that are recommended and evaluated by educators. Teachers can access these lists and evaluations at state-sponsored Web sites or they can request them in printed form.

To assist you in locating these sources of information from your school district and state Department of Education, contact your technology coordinator, curriculum resource specialist, media specialist, technology committee, or other teachers.

The Evaluation Cycle

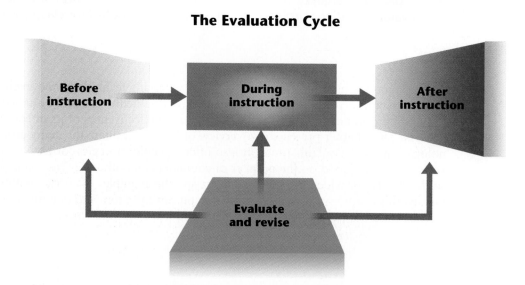

Figure 7-1 Successful technology integration requires evaluation during all phases of instruction.

Figure 7-2 Numerous high-quality educational software packages are available for classroom use.

PROFESSIONAL EDUCATIONAL ORGANIZATIONS   Many local, state, regional, national, and international educational organizations provide extensive information on how to evaluate educational resources (Figure 7-3). Many of these groups provide Web sites with information and feedback on software program levels, content, and pricing.

CATALOGS   Often, companies list hardware and software suited for educational use in their catalogs. These catalogs are a valuable resource to help identify technologies for your classroom. In addition to providing information about existing and new products, many software firms also provide information about how their products relate to curriculum and learning standards. You can order free catalogs from most companies by calling a toll-free number or completing an online form at the company's Web site. Many companies have extensive online catalogs that also provide demos of their popular software titles.

RECOMMENDATIONS OF COLLEAGUES
A good way to identify software and other technology that has potential for your classroom is to talk to other educators. Colleagues can offer advice about outstanding

products as well as about those products to avoid — advice that often is based on firsthand experience.

PUBLISHED EVALUATIONS   Departments of Education, professional organizations, and other educational groups publish evaluations of new products. Numerous software developers include evaluations completed by educators on their Web sites. Many educational publications and journals also have sections dedicated to reviews of educational technologies. In addition, many online publications, journals, and other Web sites provide educators with comprehensive evaluations and reviews of educational software and hardware.

CONFERENCES   Every year, dozens of national and state organizations host technology conferences (Figure 7-4). A **technology conference** is a meeting dedicated to providing a vast array of information and resources for educators. This gathering might be large or small and includes workshops and presentations by educators and vendors on hundreds of technology topics. In addition, software and hardware vendors usually have booths staffed by representatives to provide teachers with demonstrations and information about their products.

FAQ

How can teachers find out about technology conferences in their state or across the country?

Access T.H.E. Journal's conference calendar at: *www.theconference calendar.com* and search by month, year, state, and country.

Figure 7-3 Many local, state, regional, national, and international educational organizations maintain Web sites that provide educators with evaluations of educational technologies.

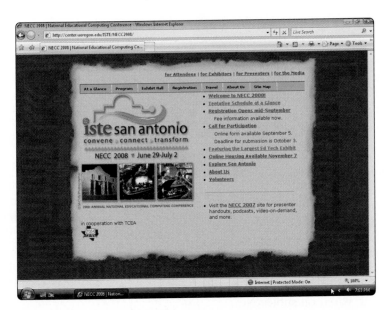

Figure 7-4 Technology conferences provide teachers with valuable resources, information, and opportunities to discuss educational technology issues with other educators and vendors.

THE WEB   By far, the Web is the most comprehensive source of tools and resources to help you evaluate educational technology. Teachers may visit thousands of Web sites dedicated to educational topics. Mailing lists, forums, newsgroups, discussion groups, listservs, wikis, blogs, and bulletin boards available on the Web also provide vast sources of information.

One of the larger well-known discussion lists is EDTECH. The **EDTECH** discussion list allows educators from many different areas — teachers, administrators, technology coordinators, media specialists, and university faculty — to exchange information,

comments, and ideas on educational issues. If you have never subscribed to a discussion list, a link on the EDTECH site provides helpful tips and guidelines (Figure 7-5).

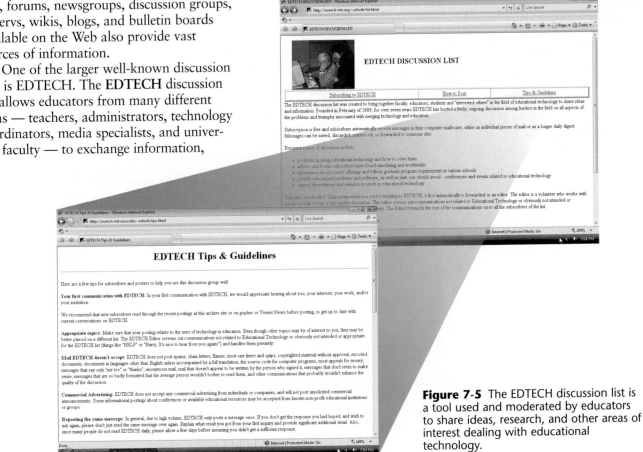

Figure 7-5 The EDTECH discussion list is a tool used and moderated by educators to share ideas, research, and other areas of interest dealing with educational technology.

Web Info

To access software reviews, visit the Teachers Discovering Computers Web site (*scsite.com/tdc5*), click Chapter 7, click Web Info, and then click Software Reviews.

Web Info

For more examples of evaluation rubrics for students, visit the Teachers Discovering Computers Web site (*scsite.com/tdc5*), click Chapter 7, click Web Info, and then click Rubrics.

EVALUATING SOFTWARE APPLICATIONS

When you identify a software package as potentially suited to your curriculum needs, you should evaluate the software for appropriateness, review the accuracy of the content, and consider its relevance to the curriculum standards and related benchmarks. A cost-effective way to evaluate software is to download a free trial copy from some of the many software companies that offer these trial versions at their Web sites (Figure 7-6). You can then use the trial version for the specified period to determine its suitability for your curriculum.

A rubric is a great tool for evaluating software. A **rubric** is a detailed scoring guide for assessment, based on subjective stated criteria.

Software evaluation rubrics help you and your students evaluate educational software. A **software evaluation rubric** is an assessment tool that provides a number of important evaluation criteria, including content, documentation and technical support, ability and academic levels, technical quality, and ease of use to help assess the quality of software or other items. A two-page Software Evaluation Rubric is shown in Figure 7-7 (on the next two pages).

Many schools develop their own software evaluation rubrics for teachers to use, while in other schools, teachers create their own software evaluation rubrics. In addition, the Web is a great resource for locating rubrics. Many different software evaluation rubrics are available on the Web for you to use or alter to fit your specific needs.

CONTENT   When evaluating educational software, content is the most important area to consider. When examining software content, you need to determine if the software is valid. **Valid** means the software has well-grounded instructional properties, meets standards, provides appropriate content, and teaches what is intended.

Most software companies and distributors provide a description of the content and learning skills addressed by their software packages; most software companies match the skills the software teaches with specific curriculum standards and related benchmarks. When evaluating the content of a software application, always relate the content to your school's and state's specific curriculum standards and related benchmarks.

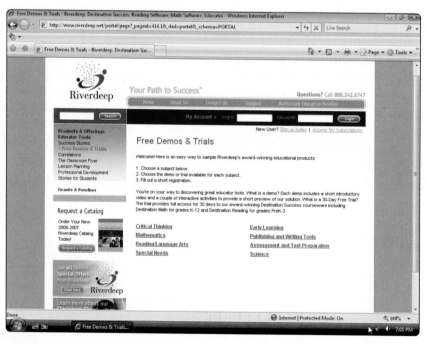

Figure 7-6 Many software companies allow you to download free evaluation copies of their software.

Rubric

Software Evaluation Rubric

Application Title:_____ Subject Area:_____

Version:_____ Producer/Publisher:_____

Date Published: _____

Curriculum Standard(s): _____

Learning Objective(s):_____

Technology Standard(s):_____

Prerequisite Skills:_____

Configuration

Hardware/System Requirements: _____

_____

Type of Drive Required: DVD _____ CD_____ Network _____

Hard Disk Space Required: _____ Memory Required:_____

Program Categories: (Check all that apply)

☐ Presentation   ☐ Drill and Practice   ☐ Educational Game

☐ Authoring   ☐ Simulation   ☐ ILS

☐ Problem Solving   ☐ Tutorial   ☐ Distance Learning

Other:_____

Skill/Ability/Grade Levels: _____

State or District Content Standard(s): _____

_____

National or State Technology Standard(s):_____

_____

Use the following system to rate the software

1 = Strongly disagree	2 = Disagree	NA = Not applicable
3 = Agree	4 = Strongly agree	

Content

1. The content is accurate and factual.	1	2	3	4	NA
2. The content is educationally appropriate.	1	2	3	4	NA
3. The content is free of errors.	1	2	3	4	NA
4. The content meets your learning goals and objectives.	1	2	3	4	NA
5. The content is age appropriate.	1	2	3	4	NA
6. The content is free of stereotypes and cultural bias.	1	2	3	4	NA
7. The content meets district and state standards.	1	2	3	4	NA

Figure 7-7 A software evaluation rubric helps teachers evaluate educational software packages.

Rubric

Software Evaluation Rubric

(1=Strongly disagree; 2=Disagree; 3=Agree; 4=Strongly agree; NA=Not applicable)

Ease of Use

1. Directions are clear.	1	2	3	4	NA
2. Students can exit the program at any time.	1	2	3	4	NA
3. Students can restart the program where they stopped.	1	2	3	4	NA
4. The software is reliable and free of disruption by system errors.	1	2	3	4	NA

Documentation and Support

1. The teacher/instructor manual is clear and thorough.	1	2	3	4	NA
2. The software has an 800/888 support number.	1	2	3	4	NA
3. Online technical support is available.	1	2	3	4	NA
4. Help and tutorials are clear and easy to use.	1	2	3	4	NA

Ability Levels

1. The user level can be set by the teacher.	1	2	3	4	NA
2. The user level automatically advances.	1	2	3	4	NA
3. The software covers a variety of ability/skill levels.	1	2	3	4	NA

Assessment

1. Software has built-in assessment and reporting tools.	1	2	3	4	NA
2. Assessment methods are appropriate and suited to learning objectives.	1	2	3	4	NA
3. Software documents and records student progress.	1	2	3	4	NA
4. Teachers easily can assess students' progress by evaluating progress reports.	1	2	3	4	NA

Technical Quality

1. Animation and graphics are used well.	1	2	3	4	NA
2. Audio (voice input/output) is used well.	1	2	3	4	NA
3. Feedback and prompts are appropriate.	1	2	3	4	NA
4. The application allows branching.	1	2	3	4	NA

Recommendation

☐ Purchase Immediately   ☐ Do Not Purchase

Comments:_____

_____

Evaluator:_____ Date:_____

Figure 7-7 (continued)

DOCUMENTATION AND TECHNICAL SUPPORT   When evaluating software, consider the technical support and documentation the software offers. **Documentation** is any printed or online information that provides assistance in installing, using, maintaining, and updating the software. You should review the documentation for readability and depth of coverage. **Technical support** is a service that hardware and software manufacturers and third-party service companies offer to customers to provide answers to questions, repairs, and other assistance. Companies usually provide technical support over the telephone or via the Web (Figure 7-8). Many firms even provide on-site support.

In addition to reviewing the available documentation and technical support, you also should determine if any other support is available, such as clear, easy-to-use aids and tutorials. Some software companies, for example, provide instructor resource guides and lesson plans to assist in integrating their software into curriculum areas.

ABILITY LEVELS AND ASSESSMENT

Educators need to evaluate whether the software can be used with more than one ability or academic level. An **ability level** refers to a student's current competency level or the skill level the student can achieve for a specific learning objective. The **academic level** is based on the grade level with increments to determine if a student is performing at the appropriate level. Several software applications, such as math and reading software, adjust the ability or grade level as students successfully move through specific skills. Numerous software applications allow you to set the academic, or ability levels at which you require students to work. Assessment is discussed starting on page 404.

TECHNICAL QUALITY AND EASE OF USE

Technical quality refers to how well the software presents itself and how well it works. Items to evaluate are the clarity of the screen design; appropriateness of feedback and student prompts; and use of graphics, animations, sound, and other media elements.

Ease of use, or user-friendliness, refers to anything that makes the software easy to use. Software should be easy for both teachers and students to use, while at

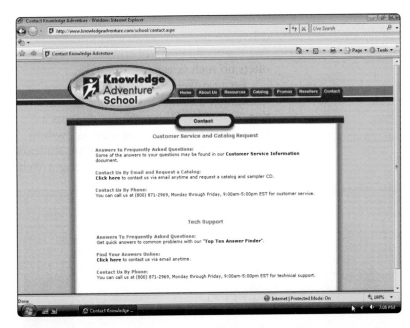

Figure 7-8 Many software manufacturers provide technical support for their products via the Web.

the same time maintaining the students' interest.

Student opinions also play an important role in successfully integrating any technology. Teachers need to be open and embrace the fact that today's digital students may be very technologically savvy. After you complete your evaluation, you might want to obtain feedback from students by allowing them to use and test the software. If students have a difficult time working through exercises, they might dislike the program and get frustrated. If students dislike the software, they will not enjoy using it even though they may learn. This dislike will limit the effectiveness of the software in classroom use. Make sure the software is easy to use and appropriate for your students' grade and ability levels.

EVALUATING WEB RESOURCES

The Web is an incredible resource for teachers. Not all of the information on the Web, however, is placed there by reliable sources. Web page authoring software has made it easy for anyone to create, or publish, a Web page or Web site that contains personal opinions, ideas, and philosophy. In contrast, before a book is published, the content is reviewed for accuracy and objectivity and the author's credentials are verified. After being published, the book's copyright

Web Info

For more details about evaluating Web sites, visit the Teachers Discovering Computers Web site (*scsite.com/tdc5*), click Chapter 7, click Web Info, and then click Web Site Evaluation.

date and table of contents allow users to determine the currency of the information and the book's depth of coverage. A Web site offers no such safeguards.

Because Web sites often contain inaccurate, incomplete, or biased information, evaluating Web resources presents a unique challenge. Teachers must know how to evaluate Web sites and teach their students how to do the same. When evaluating a Web

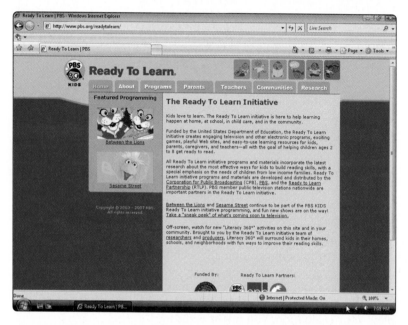

Figure 7-9 Teachers can consider this Web site authoritative because it is based on the latest research and the Web site is developed and maintained by a number of credible public and private organizations.

Figure 7-10 Information documenting the authority of a Web site often is found at the bottom of the Web site's home page.

site as an instructional source, you should consider criteria such as authority, affiliation, purpose, content, audience, and Web design.

AUTHORITY When evaluating Web sites, **authority** refers to the credibility of the person or persons who author and maintain the site. Determining authority is the first place to start in the evaluation process. If the author is not a credible source for information, the information on the site might be unreliable. A Web site on asteroids by a distinguished astronomy professor, for example, has more authority than an astronomy Web site created by an amateur stargazer. When reviewing a Web site, answer the following questions:

- Is the author clearly identified? If you cannot identify the creator of the Web page, you might want to avoid this Web site.

- Examine the credentials of the author or organization of the Web site. What evidence indicates that the author qualifies to publish on this topic? The authority of the Web page shown in Figure 7-9, for example, is based on the credibility of several organizations and corporations.

- Has the author or organization listed experience, position, education, or other credentials? If you do not see this information immediately, refer to the bottom of the home page, which often provides additional information about the author's or organization's affiliation. Can the author be contacted for clarification? Listing an e-mail address and other pertinent information is important for establishing authority.

AFFILIATION **Affiliation** refers to the professional organization, school, school district, university, company, or government office with which a particular Web site is associated (Figure 7-10). Well-known sources of information such as the U.S. government, universities, school districts, newspapers, and non-profit organizations usually have reliable facts on their Web sites. Also, it is good to examine the credentials and reputation of the organization or organizations affiliated with the Web site.

A simple way to determine a site's affiliation is to examine the URL and domain name to identify what type of organization maintains the Web page. A site with a .com domain, for example, is operated by a commercial business; a .edu domain is controlled by an educational institution (Figure 7-11).

PURPOSE AND OBJECTIVITY   Purpose is the reason the Web site was created or the intent of the Web site. As you evaluate a Web site, you must ascertain if it is being provided as a public service, if it is free from bias, and why the author or creator is providing this information.

Objectivity is the process of determining or interpreting the intent or purpose of the Web page and if it is free of bias, such as advertising. If the purpose is not clearly stated, you must attempt to determine the purpose or intent of the Web page. Is the primary intent to provide information or sell a product? Does the author want to make a political point or have fun? Determining the purpose or intent of the Web site plays a critical role in the evaluation process.

CONTENT AND LEARNING PROCESS
Content is the information a Web page provides. Web pages use a variety of media to convey facts, opinions, and news. As you evaluate the content of a Web page, consider the following questions:

- Is the content valid and appropriate? Is the content popular or academic, satiric or serious?

- Does the information on the page relate to your curriculum and instructional standards?

- What topics are covered? Is the information clearly labeled and well organized?

- For what level is the information written? How thorough is the information?

- Do the links within the site add value and assist you in meeting your instructional goals?

As you evaluate the content of a Web page, keep the learning objectives and curriculum standards of the classroom in mind. Also, take the time to check the links to ensure they work and are appropriate

Figure 7-11 The .edu domain verifies the Web site is affiliated with an educational institution, in this case, the University of Connecticut.

for your intended audience and learning process.

Learning process is when the content engages students to use higher-order thinking skills to go beyond the simple acquisition of knowledge and become active learners. This is accomplished when the content challenges students to think, compare, reflect, hypothesize, and discuss.

AUDIENCE AND CURRENCY   The audience is the individual or group intended to view and use the Web page. You should review the Web page to determine if it is suitable for an audience such as your students. Is the content appropriate for your students? Can you use this Web page in your classroom? Again, keep your learning objectives in mind as you examine the Web page. Currency is the measure of how up to date, or timely, the Web page content is and how often it is updated. A good Web page states clearly when the page was last revised or updated.

DESIGN   The design of a Web site is the way it is arranged — that is, the way it uses instructional design principles to deliver content to the user. A well-designed Web site makes it easy and enjoyable for viewers to access the site's content and information. A poorly designed site, for example, where links or elements are organized in a confusing way, can frustrate viewers because they cannot find the information they want.

An effective Web page loads in a reasonable amount of time, has a pleasing visual appearance, is easy to navigate, and has links that are well organized, clearly marked, work properly, and lead to related materials.

Both in and out of the classroom, teachers and students should evaluate Web sites critically to maximize the value of the Web. To assist in the evaluation of Web sites, teachers often find rubrics useful. A **Web evaluation rubric** is a detailed scoring guide for assessing the value and content of Web sites. As shown in the examples in Figure 7-12 and Figure 7-13,

Web evaluation rubrics typically provide a number of important evaluation criteria for specific areas such as content, learning process, and authority of the author, and then present rating levels with specific standards for each. Students and teachers benefit from using rubrics. Figure 7-12 illustrates a user-friendly, engaging Web site evaluation rubric that might be used by young students. Figure 7-13 shows a more detailed Web evaluation rubric that might be used by a teacher. No matter which method you choose, the key is to have a predetermined way of effectively evaluating Web sites.

Web Info

To learn the 10 Cs for evaluating Internet resources, visit the Teachers Discovering Computers Web site (*scsite.com/tdc5*), click Chapter 7, click Web Info, and then click 10 Cs.

Rubric

Student Web Site Evaluation Rubric

Student team members: _____

DESIGN
Can move easily from page to page
Good use of graphics (pictures and color)

CONTENT
Information is useful
Content is as good or better than that of similar sites

TECHNICAL ELEMENTS
Pages load quickly (within 15 seconds)
All links work

CREDIBILITY
Contact person is stated with his or her e-mail address
The name of the host school or organization is given
Date this site was last updated is provided

page 1 of 1

Figure 7-12 Young students enjoy rubrics that are fun and user-friendly when evaluating Web sites.

Rubric

Web Site Evaluation Rubric

Title of Web Site: _____

Curriculum Area: _____

URL: _____

Learning Objectives supported by this site: _____

_____

	Level 1	Level 2	Level 3	Level 4	Level
Authority	No author is listed and no e-mail contact is provided.	No author is listed but an e-mail contact is provided.	An author is listed with no credentials and you cannot tell if the author is the creator of the material.	An author is listed with appropriate credentials, and is the creator of the material.	
Affiliation	It is unclear what institution supports this information.	A commercial Internet provider supports the site, but it is unclear if the author has any connection with a larger institution.	The site is supported by a larger institution, but some bias is apparent in the information from the institution.	The site is supported by a reputable institution without bias in the information.	
Purpose	The purpose is unclear or cannot be determined.	The Web site has more than one purpose but meets only a few of my objectives.	The purpose is somewhat clear and meets most of my objectives.	The purpose of the Web site is clear and meets my objectives.	
Objectivity	The Web page is a virtual soapbox.	The Web site contains some bias and a great deal of advertising.	The Web site contains some advertising and minimal bias.	The Web site contains little advertising and is free of bias.	
Content	The information on the Web site does not relate to my objectives.	The information relates to my objectives, but many of the links do not work.	The information relates to my objectives, links work, but the site is not well organized.	The information relates to my objectives, the links work, and the site is well organized.	
Learning Process	The information will not challenge learners to think, reflect, discuss, compare, or classify.	The information will not challenge learners to think but does provide interesting facts for resource information.	The information at this Web site will provide some challenges for the learner to think but does not relate to my objectives.	The information challenges learners to use higher-order thinking skills, effectively engages the learner, and meets my learning objectives.	
Audience	The Web pages are not appropriate for my audience.	The Web pages are written above the level of my audience, but some of the information is useful.	The Web pages are written at an appropriate level for my audience and some of the information is useful.	The Web pages are written at an appropriate level and the information is suitable for my classroom.	
Currency	Information on the site has not been revised in the last 18 months, or no date can be located.	Information on the site has not been updated in the last year, but the information still is of good quality.	Information has been updated in the last six months and seems to reflect currency.	Information has been updated in the last three months and is accurate.	
Design	The Web site design is inappropriate for my audience.	The Web site loads slowly and the general appearance is poor.	The Web site loads well, but the site is not easy to navigate.	The Web site loads well, is easy to navigate, visually pleasing, and easy to read.	
				Total	

Figure 7-13 A rubric is helpful in evaluating the educational value of Web sites.

Integration Strategies

To learn more about integrating and evaluating technology with your special needs students, visit the Teachers Discovering Computers Web site (scsite.com/tdc5), click Chapter 7, and then click Assistive Technologies Corner.

Web Info

To explore technology assessment further, visit the Teachers Discovering Computers Web site (scsite.com/tdc5), click Chapter 7, click Web Info, and then click Assessing Technology.

Evaluating the Effectiveness of Technology Integration

Integrating technology effectively into the curriculum requires planning, time, dedication, and resources. Because it is important to determine whether integration strategies are working, teachers, schools, and school districts should take steps to evaluate the effectiveness of their technology integration.

Evaluating the effectiveness of technology can be challenging; no simple way exists to evaluate what works in all situations — all students, all technology, all schools, and all classrooms. Nor do any standard types of evaluation show the relationship between the technology and student achievement.

The first step in evaluating educational technology's impact on student achievement is to develop indicators that measure a student's performance, skills acquired, and academic and ability levels obtained. Test scores are not the only, or even the best, indicators of the successful integration of technology. The types of learning best supported by technology are those not easily measured by traditional assessments, such as standardized tests. Due to the nature of technology and the way the learning environment is changing, educators must create and use different types of evaluation tools.

ASSESSMENT TOOLS FOR EVALUATING THE EFFECTIVENESS OF TECHNOLOGY INTEGRATION

Evaluating the effectiveness of educational technology can help you assess whether the technology is appropriate for the learner, meets learning objectives, and enhances the learning process. Traditionally, teachers use many different evaluation techniques in the final stage of instruction or when assessing **student performance**. To ensure that students meet the learning objectives, teachers must use many forms of assessment to evaluate student performance. **Assessment** is any method used to understand the current knowledge a student possesses; it can range from a teacher's subjective judgment based on a single observation of a student's performance to a state-mandated standardized test.

Reliable assessments accurately estimate student performance, permits appropriate generalizations about the students' skills and abilities, and enables teachers or other decision makers to make appropriate decisions. **Traditional assessments** include testing in the form of multiple choice, fill-in-the blank, true/false, short answer, and essay questions. Traditional assessments can be used to evaluate the effectiveness of technology.

Just as technology opens many new and exciting doors for teaching and learning, technology also opens new doors for evaluating student performance. When integrating technology, some teachers and schools move toward a nontraditional approach of student assessment, known as alternative assessment.

Alternative assessment uses nontraditional methods to determine whether students have mastered the appropriate content and skill level. Authentic assessment, project-based assessment, and portfolio assessment are alternative ways to evaluate students' performances. These assessment tools can be used to determine how well and in what ways they meet curriculum standards and related benchmarks.

AUTHENTIC ASSESSMENT **Authentic assessment** can be formal or informal and aims to present students with tasks that mirror the objectives and challenges typical of their instructional activities. Students answer open-ended questions, create questions, conduct hands-on experiments, do research, write, revise and discuss papers, and create portfolios of their work over time. Authentic assessment is based on a method of learning called authentic learning. **Authentic learning** presents learning experiences that demonstrate real-life connections between students' lessons and the world in which they live.

Authentic assessment measures this learning by evaluating a student's ability to master practical benchmarks. Using authentic assessment, for example, a student may be asked to discuss historical events, generate scientific hypotheses, solve math problems, create portfolios or presentations, or converse in a foreign language.

Authentic assessment helps students not only understand concepts and subject matter, but also develop real-world skills, which they can apply outside the classroom and beyond the school environment. For example, teachers might look for evidence of good collaboration skills, the ability to solve complex problems and make thoughtful decisions, and the ability to develop and make effective presentations. Authentic assessments reflect student learning over time and provide a better view of student performance, instead of performance based on just one item or one test. A teacher then has documentation of the student's progress throughout the entire project, which provides the teacher with evidence of growth and learning.

PROJECT-BASED ASSESSMENT   **Project-based assessment** is an innovative approach to assessment that focuses on assessing student projects. It is based on a type of authentic learning called project-based learning. **Project-based learning** is a model for teaching and learning that focuses on creating learning opportunities for students by engaging them in real-world projects where they have an active role in completing meaningful tasks, constructing their own knowledge, solving problems, or creating realistic projects. Project-based learning transforms the teacher into the facilitator and the students into the doers or participants in the task at hand. When using any type of authentic learning technique, many teachers use a checklist, rating scale, or a rubric to evaluate the learning process.

PORTFOLIO ASSESSMENT   Another popular form of alternative assessment is portfolio assessment. **Portfolio assessment** evaluates student assignments or projects over a period of time. Portfolios are an effective way to match assessment with learning goals. Some educators call this **embedded assessment** because assessment tasks are part of the learning process. Through the process of creating their own assignments, students improve their abilities to assess their strengths and weaknesses and are able to apply these skills to other areas of study to become better learners. Because students work on long-term assignments, they usually have the opportunity to fix or learn from their mistakes and do a better job on future portfolio assignments.

For portfolio assessment to be successful, students must learn how to interact effectively with their teachers to ensure that they fully understand the teacher's assessment of each portfolio assignment.

When students receive guidance and support from their teachers and parents and gain an understanding of themselves as learners, they can experience amazing growth and powerful learning opportunities. The disadvantage of portfolio assessment is that creating and assessing portfolios takes longer to evaluate than a quick test and requires a great deal of work by both the student and the teacher. The results reveal, however, that portfolio assessment is well worth the investment.

In this digital age, electronic portfolios are starting to become more commonplace in K-12 and higher education. An **electronic portfolio**, or **e-folio**, is an electronically stored portfolio that contains student assignments or projects. Electronic portfolios offer a powerful way for students to create a variety of projects that contain digital media, reflective writings or narratives, drawings, audio, photos, and videos based on predetermined criteria that teachers can evaluate to assess learning.

CHECKLISTS, RATING SCALES, AND RUBRICS
A **checklist** is a predetermined list of performance criteria used in project-based and portfolio assessment. Figure 7-14 on the next page shows a Project Evaluation Checklist. After a student has met a criterion, the criterion is marked as complete. Checklists usually consist of yes and no questions used to determine if the item or items are present. Checklists allow you or your students to keep track of the items.

The benefit of a checklist for an assessment tool is that you can use this tool quickly and students understand very quickly if an item is or is not met. When creating your own checklist, you should include items that clearly show if benchmarks are being met. Another effective option is to have your students create their own checklists or add to yours.

A **rating scale** is a more complex form of a checklist that lists a numerical value, or rating, for each criterion. Assessment involves rating each student on her achievement for each criterion and specifying the total based on all criteria.

Another very popular form of alternative assessment is the rubric. As you recall, a rubric is a detailed assessment tool that makes it easy for teachers to assess the quality of an item, such as a learning project.

Integration Strategies

To learn more about alternative assessment, visit the Teachers Discovering Computers Web site (*scsite.com/tdc5*), click Chapter 7, and then click Education Issues.

Web Info

To learn more about portfolio assessment, visit the Teachers Discovering Computers Web site (*scsite.com/tdc5*), click Chapter 7, click Web Info, and then click Portfolios.

Checklist

Project Evaluation Checklist

Date: _____

Student Name(s): _____

Project Title: _____

	YES	NO
CONTENT		
The project meets all learning objectives.	☐	☐
The project is original and creative.	☐	☐
Mastery of subject is evident.	☐	☐
Use of higher-order thinking skills is evident.	☐	☐
Information is accurate and the subject matter is appropriate.	☐	☐
Information is presented in a logical sequence.	☐	☐
A variety of reliable sources are used.	☐	☐
Sources are properly cited.	☐	☐
Words are spelled correctly and sentences are grammatically correct.	☐	☐
LAYOUT		
The project is visually appealing.	☐	☐
The project is easy to navigate.	☐	☐
The text is easy to read and follow.	☐	☐
Digital media features are used effectively.	☐	☐
Color and design scheme are appropriate.	☐	☐
ORGANIZATION		
Student completed a project storyboard.	☐	☐
Planning is demonstrated.	☐	☐
Project flows smoothly.	☐	☐
Project was completed.	☐	☐

Figure 7-14 Teachers often use alternative assessment tools such as checklists (shown here) and rating scales to evaluate student performance.

Rubrics help students understand how teachers will evaluate their projects by providing a range of criteria with information about how to meet each one. Rubrics describe specific and measurable criteria for several levels of quality against which teachers can evaluate completed projects.

Rubrics can help students and teachers define the value or quality of completed assignments. Rubrics also help students critique and revise their own assignments before handing them in. For example, rubrics help students make sure they have included all required elements and have met each criteria for grading. Although a rubric is similar to a checklist and a rating scale, it describes in greater detail the criteria and components that must be achieved.

TEACHER OBSERVATION   When evaluating technology integration or curriculum integration, one of the more widely used authentic assessment techniques is teacher observation. **Teacher observation** (Figure 7-15) is the result of teachers actively observing their students during the learning process.

Teachers notice whether students are highly motivated during the learning process, that is, they observe the impact of technology used, how long the students work on a given objective, and the length of time students continue working on a task to master its content and skills. Teacher observation is a powerful assessment tool, and often it is used in combination with other assessment tools. All of these tools can be used to evaluate individual and group projects.

EVALUATING TECHNOLOGY-BASED STUDENT PROJECTS

Today, skills in technology are essential for students to learn. Technology-based student projects help facilitate integrating technology and digital media into the curriculum. In the process, students learn how to use, manage, and understand technology and how it is used to synthesize and present information on a variety of subjects. Although it might seem like a good idea, you should avoid teaching technology as a separate subject. Instead, you should integrate it into your curriculum.

Figure 7-15 This teacher knows that teacher observation is critical when integrating technology.

Some software programs, such as those provided with integrated learning systems (ILS), for example ClassWorks, automatically track student progress. Others, such as Inspiration, iMovie, and PowerPoint, do not provide assessment components. These applications, however, are ideal for students to use to create projects that are innovative and motivational. Teachers who use these software programs for technology-based student projects need to develop effective assessment tools to measure student achievement related to these tools.

Before a teacher presents a project's requirements to students, he or she should create an assessment rubric. Figure 7-16 on the next page illustrates a student project evaluation rubric that guides students on how they will be evaluated on projects. Rubrics are excellent for evaluating all types of student projects. They provide an authentic assessment of project-based learning activities. To determine the criteria to include in the rubric, ask yourself what the students should learn and how this learning will be evidenced in their projects. In the rubric, be sure to specify what students need to include in their projects and clearly inform the students how they will be evaluated.

Checklists, rating scales, and teacher observation also are valid assessment tools for technology-based student projects. Your curriculum standards and benchmarks should define and guide the selection and creation of your assessment tool.

FAQ

Is teacher observation really a powerful tool?

Yes! It is probably one of the most powerful tools that teachers use. A teacher needs to be aware of everything going on in the class room, regardless of whether it relates to technology.

Rubric

Student Project Evaluation Rubric

Team Leader:_____

Team Members: _____

Project Title:_____

	Beginning	Developing	Accomplished	Exemplary
Development Process				
Student used quality reference materials and timely Web sites in gathering information.	0 1 2	3 4 5	6 7 8	9 10
Student completed project outline/storyboard.	0 1 2	3 4 5	6 7 8	9 10
Student obtained permission to use copyrighted materials.	0 1 2	3 4 5	6 7 8	9 10
Content				
Understanding of topic is evident.	0 1 2	3 4 5	6 7 8	9 10
Information is presented in a clear manner.	0 1 2	3 4 5	6 7 8	9 10
Information is appropriate and accurate.	0 1 2	3 4 5	6 7 8	9 10
Content shows understanding of the learning objectives.	0 1 2	3 4 5	6 7 8	9 10
Student used higher-order thinking skills when analyzing and synthesizing content.	0 1 2	3 4 5	6 7 8	9 10
Important ideas related to topic are included and an understanding of important relationships is evident.	0 1 2	3 4 5	6 7 8	9 10
Includes properly cited sources.	0 1 2	3 4 5	6 7 8	9 10
Design				
The information is presented in a logical, interesting sequence.	0 1 2	3 4 5	6 7 8	9 10
Video, 3-D, and all enhancements are used appropriately.	0 1 2	3 4 5	6 7 8	9 10
Colors, images, animation, and sound enrich the content.	0 1 2	3 4 5	6 7 8	9 10
The project works and is technically sound.	0 1 2	3 4 5	6 7 8	9 10
Text is easy to read and students have followed rules of good screen design.	0 1 2	3 4 5	6 7 8	9 10
Accurate spelling and grammar are used throughout.	0 1 2	3 4 5	6 7 8	9 10
Presentation				
The student maintains eye contact with class.	0 1 2	3 4 5	6 7 8	9 10
The student speaks clearly and is easily heard.	0 1 2	3 4 5	6 7 8	9 10
The presentation is an appropriate length.	0 1 2	3 4 5	6 7 8	9 10
Technology is used well while presenting.	0 1 2	3 4 5	6 7 8	9 10

Total Possible 200   Total _____

Figure 7-16 A rubric guides students in determining how they will be evaluated on projects. This rubric, for example, is designed to evaluate students' digital media projects.

EVALUATING CONTENT   Your standards and benchmarks will help determine the content to include in student projects and how to assess this content. This should be the most important part of the project. For technology-based student projects, content may include factual information about a historical figure, key points included in a digital media math project, interactive PE presentation, biology lab data in a spreadsheet, and other pertinent information. In addition, evaluation of the content should include a review of punctuation, grammar, spelling, coverage of material, presentation of the material in a logical order, and specific information such as a title, references, and information about the author.

EVALUATING PLANNING   Effective presentations involve planning. Students also must plan a project before creating it, if it is to be effective. When assigning technology-based projects, establish how you want students to plan and what tools they will use. A software planning tool such as **Inspiration** helps students and teachers quickly develop and communicate ideas using flowcharts, concept maps, and story webs through visual learning techniques (Figure 7-17). **Visual learning techniques** are methods that present ideas and information through graphical webs. Inspiration lets you build visual diagrams to work through the process of thinking, organizing thoughts, revealing patterns, and prioritizing information.

   Flowcharts are diagrams that show the step-by-step actions that must take place by plotting a sequence of events. Flowcharts are useful in helping students outline the individual tasks that must be performed to complete an action, a story, or an experiment and the sequence in which they must be performed. A **concept map** or **story web** helps students use flowcharting to understand the attributes and relationships of the main subject and provides a visual tool for brainstorming and planning (Figure 7-18). Another useful planning tool is a **storyboard**, which is a drawing that allows students to design and lay out a project or assignment before creating it on a computer.

EVALUATING CREATIVITY When evaluating student projects, teachers should consider students' originality, imaginative and

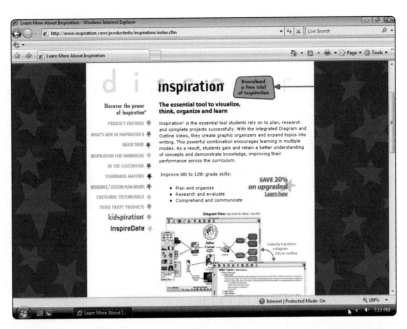

Figure 7-17 Inspiration is an excellent tool for teaching students how to organize their thoughts and ideas.

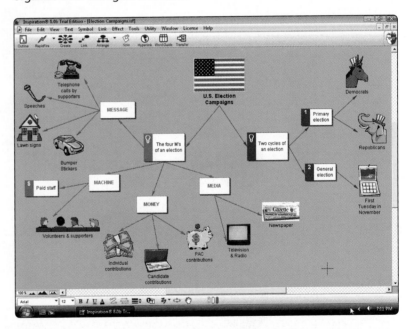

Figure 7-18 Using Inspiration software, students create a concept map to plan an undertaking such as this project on election campaigns.

innovative approach, and artistic abilities — all aspects of **creativity**. Creative student projects should be interesting and unique. Students should demonstrate an understanding of how to use the special effects offered by multimedia authoring software to enhance their projects, instead of distracting from its content. Color, clip art, and artwork should strengthen content, not distract from it.

Integration Strategies

To learn about using peer evaluation of student projects, visit the Teachers Discovering Computers Web site (*scsite.com/tdc5*), click Chapter 7, and then click Digital Media Corner.

PUTTING IT ALL TOGETHER — EVALUATING TECHNOLOGY INTEGRATION

Mrs. Vicki Osborne teaches social studies and other subjects at Fall Hills Middle School. She has one computer in her classroom and 26 students. Her middle school is on a **block schedule**, which is an alternative way of scheduling classes. This means the social studies class meets every other day for 90 minutes. Mrs. Osborne's curriculum requires that her social studies students learn about the electoral process, so she is having them research a recent presidential candidate and then prepare a digital media presentation to convey their findings to the class.

She has six goals for the lesson. The students are to do the following: (1) work cooperatively in groups with three or four students in each group; (2) use reference materials and Web resources to research their candidate; (3) identify three major campaign issues for their candidate; (4) provide personal facts about the candidate, such as education, occupation prior to politics, and military service; (5) create a group digital media presentation to present their research with either PowerPoint or iMovie; and (6) use correct grammar, spelling, and punctuation in their presentation. She uses a rubric to evaluate the students' projects.

Mrs. Osborne begins her social studies lesson by displaying her PowerPoint digital media presentation using a projector for easy viewing by all students. The first step is to brainstorm with her students about the lesson and create a concept map about the election process and the candidates (Figure 7-19).

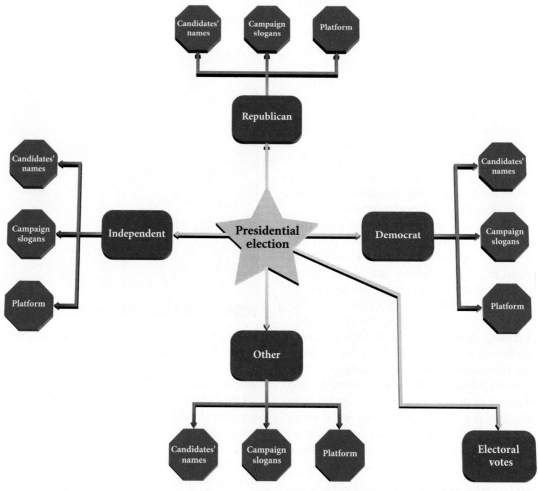

Figure 7-19 Mrs. Osborne and her students create a concept map showing their ideas on the election process and candidates.

She also hands out a copy of her evaluation rubric, discusses the rubric with her students, and answers their questions. Students then are divided into groups to complete their first task.

Students are required to create a flowchart or storyboard of their projects using concept mapping software such as Inspiration. After Mrs. Osborne approves their flowchart drawings or storyboards, the groups are ready to begin creating their projects. Before starting the projects, Mrs. Osborne borrowed an additional computer from another teacher and arranged for two groups to use computers in the media center. This allows four groups to work on computers at the same time. Groups rotate through the four computers in 40-minute blocks (Figure 7-20).

When the groups finish their projects, Mrs. Osborne has each group present their project to the class in the media center. She also invites the principal, a local politician, the media specialist, and another social studies class to view the presentations. The students are very proud of their projects and enjoy showing them to their peers, teachers, and school administrators. The school newspaper plans to highlight some

of the projects. To make this an authentic learning experience, Mrs. Osborne's students created voting boxes and arranged for the students at Fall Hills Middle School to vote in a mock election. Her students created campaign slogans and ran the campaign just like a real world political campaign.

To integrate technology successfully, teachers must continuously evaluate educational technology before instruction begins, during the instructional period, and after instruction has taken place. Technology not only changes the learning process but also changes the teaching and evaluation processes. Teachers have the responsibility to evaluate and update assignments and activities continuously — on a daily, weekly, monthly, or semester basis — depending on the project or assignment.

To make learning more effective, often only minor changes and improvements are necessary. In other instances, however, teachers need to implement major revisions to reflect content, curriculum, or technology changes. The next few sections introduce you to other integration strategies, such as using technology in various classroom configurations and developing curriculum pages.

FAQ

Are there other software programs that teachers and students can use to create concept maps or flowcharts?

Yes, concept maps, flowcharts, and diagrams can be created easily in most word processing programs, such as Microsoft Word, by using the drawing tools.

Figure 7-20 Centers allow students to work collaboratively in groups on student-centered projects.

Integration Strategies

To explore dozens of curriculum and grade specific integration strategies, visit the Teachers Discovering Computers Web site (*scsite.com/tdc5*), click Chapter 7, and then click Integration Corner.

Integration Strategies

To help meet the constant challenge of motivating students to learn, teachers must change their traditional roles and become facilitators of learning. Technology plays a key role in easing this change because it allows teachers to use technology tools to enhance the learning environment, motivate students, guide students in an active learning process, and encourage them to learn. The most effective way to integrate technology is to place the technology at the point of instruction — the classroom. Because of the ever-increasing need to motivate students to learn, teachers have a mandate to use the powerful tools of technology to enhance the learning environment.

Many different technologies, availability of computer labs, and different kinds and numbers of computers in the classroom are found in schools today (Figure 7-21). The following instructional strategies describe techniques to integrate technology into a one-computer classroom, a multicomputer classroom, and a computer lab.

ONE-COMPUTER CLASSROOM

Most classrooms are equipped with one digital media computer and are referred to as a **one-computer classroom**. Many ways exist in which to integrate educational technology with only one computer in the classroom. As you learned in Chapter 6, the most common practice is to use the computer for classroom presentations and demonstrations. By projecting the computer's image on a projection screen or classroom wall, you can use the computer to supplement and enhance your traditional lectures to accomplish whole-class instruction of learning objectives. You also can use the computer to introduce new concepts, prepare students for a lesson, describe background information for assignments, and explain evaluation criteria.

Figure 7-21 Technology can be integrated into many different classroom environments.

Another strategy permits students to work on the computer in small groups to foster collaboration and cooperative learning opportunities. Students also can use the computer to present their assignments, projects, and research activities to the entire class. In addition, you can use the computer to maintain records, create presentations and projects, do research, and communicate with other teachers (Figure 7-22).

To integrate technology in a one-computer classroom, follow these guidelines:

- Obtain Internet access. Use the Web's many educational resources, such as audio, video, and multimedia applications to enhance instruction and learning.

- Utilize educational application software. Both teachers and students can make use of the abundance of educational software available on CDs, DVDs, and school networks.

- Enhance lectures and presentations. Connect the computer to a projector, and then use the computer to enhance lectures, create and give presentations, and take students on virtual field trips.

- Use the computer as a teaching assistant. Tutor individual students by having them use drill and practice software, tutorials, simulations, and problem-solving software.

- Foster group and cooperative learning. Students can use the computer as an informational resource or a creation tool for group projects, such as digital media presentations.

- Write an ongoing story. Begin a story on the computer that serves as a creative writing center, and invite student authors to add to it daily. Before you begin, explain the rules for acceptable behavior, the types of content to be included in the story, and the types of entries that are satisfactory.

Figure 7-22 Teachers benefit from using a classroom computer to maintain grades and other important files.

- Create a class blog. Ask your students to evaluate the way we receive information today by reading and comparing two to three different Web logs about a current event. Then, have them write a response in the class blog about the Web logs they thought were most accurate and compelling.

- Start a class newsletter. Invite students to write articles and use word processing or desktop publishing software to create a class newsletter (Figure 7-23).

Figure 7-23 Students gain real-world skills by creating a class or school newsletter.

- Maintain a student database. Instead of having students fill out information forms, let them enter the information into a database on the computer. Students also can enter information on a variety of content-related subject areas, such as information on science projects, vocabulary words, historical places, and so on.

- Utilize the computer as a teacher productivity tool. The computer is an excellent medium for creating curriculum activities, lesson plans and tests, maintaining grades and attendance records, writing letters to parents, and creating achievement certificates. Purchasing gradebook or student information management software helps to streamline many daily management responsibilities.

- Use other low-cost input devices, such as AlphaSmarts and PDAs, for students to create first drafts, take notes in class, and enter data into their documents. Later, the data can be downloaded to the computer. This is a super time-saver and is ideal for student projects.

- Optimize computer lab time. Use the computer to introduce students to various types of software and thus create learning paths before taking students to the school's computer lab. This will optimize the time students spend on computers while in the computer lab.

- New emerging technologies allow you to create an exciting learning environment; for example, you can roll a complete computer lab into your classroom. If your school has a wireless mobile lab, schedule time to use the lab. This is a great way to move the technology you need into your one-computer classroom.

MULTICOMPUTER CLASSROOM

Having two or more computers in your classroom fosters additional learning opportunities that allow flexibility in computer usage and make technology integration an integral part of the

Web Info

For more information about AlphaSmarts, visit the Teachers Discovering Computer Web site (*scsite.com/tdc5*), click Chapter 7, click Web Info, and then click AlphaSmarts.

curriculum. Remember, one-computer classroom strategies also apply to a classroom with two or more computers.

One way to use two or more computers is to set up the computers as separate learning centers for student use. Teachers can divide the centers by subject area and then create activities that continuously change to match the curriculum or lessons being taught. A math center, for example, might include CDs, DVDs, and network-based tutorials to reinforce math skills. A language arts center might include word processing software for creative writing projects; iMovie, PowerPoint, and Photoshop to create digital media presentations; as well as reading and spelling software skill programs.

A social studies center might allow students to use the Web as a research tool and correspond with other classrooms via the Internet to learn more about the culture, language, history, and geography of other regions. Software programs such as Oregon Trail and MapMaker Toolkit help reinforce mapping and geography skills in relation to other curriculum areas.

Learning centers are an effective way to create a flexible learning environment with many options for students. Teachers can integrate technologies into learning centers to create specialized centers such as a video center, a listening center, and a digital production center.

To illustrate how one teacher is integrating technology into a science curriculum, consider the middle school classroom of Miss Julie Davis. At the beginning of class, she takes her students for a nature walk on school property to learn about trees, plants, changing seasons, and photosynthesis. During the nature walk, students notice a lot of trash on the school grounds. Students take their PDAs, smart phones, Neos, Pocket PCs, and Tablet PCs to enter data on a form Miss Davis created for them to fill out during their excursion. This way, the students enter their thoughts, explorations, and findings while they are in the environment, and not later, when they might have forgotten important information and findings.

She encourages her students to use digital cameras to take pictures of the trash, plants, trees, and other items of interest. In a follow-up discussion in class, the students decide the trash is a form of pollution — and they should do something to make the school cleaner. Miss Davis recognizes this as a teachable moment and asks essential questions to start the students thinking. She asks, "Can we make a difference? How can we help prevent pollution, starting at school?" The students begin brainstorming. Following the discussion, Miss Davis shows the students a short CNN video on global warming.

The next day, Miss Davis continues the learning process by dividing the students into groups to begin their research projects on waste, environmentally hazardous materials, trees, plants, and air associated with the environment. Next, the students begin working on their KWLQS charts. A **KWLQS chart** is similar to the KWL chart discussed in Chapter 6, with the additions of Q, which stands for further questioning, and S, which stands for sharing (referring to the fact that students will share their projects with their fellow students). Miss Davis and the students decide to create a survey to examine all the environmental issues at the school. From the survey results, it is clear most students are aware that the school has to dispose of trash, but most of them have never focused on the hazardous products, such as cleaners, that need to be disposed. It is also clear that none of the students had thought about the school's various types of trash, or whether the school recycles, or whether the methods used for disposing of hazardous waste could harm the environment. Miss Davis places the students in groups and assigns each group different environmental issues to research.

Miss Davis is fortunate to have four new computers in her classroom. Two of the computers are used as Web research centers, while the other two are set up as creation centers. To complete group projects, students rotate through the Web centers and use Miss Davis' curriculum pages. Miss Davis found resources on the Web (Figure 7-24) to help her create her curriculum pages. Students use the curriculum pages to locate resources from agriculture, environmental protection agencies, and other related Web sites. Then, they use the creation centers to develop presentations that suggest ways to protect the environment. The students incorporate their digital pictures into digital media projects

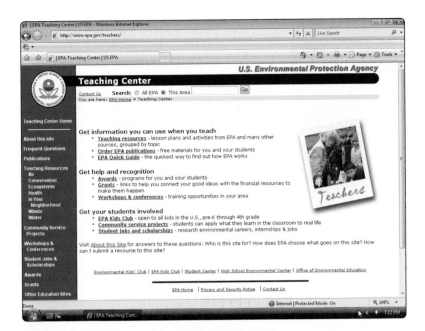

Figure 7-24 Students easily can locate information dealing with pollution, global warming, and other environmental issues on the Web.

Figure 7-25 Students can import and edit images taken with a digital camera to enhance their projects.

(Figure 7-25). While completing the projects, the students learn about citizenship and that everyone is responsible for protecting the environment.

As a result of their projects, students decide to start a schoolwide cleanup project. The class creates flyers using Microsoft Publisher and posts them throughout the school so all the students and teachers will be aware of the environment. They also

Web Info

For a tutorial on how to create Web scavenger hunts, visit the Teachers Discovering Computers Web site (*scsite.com/tdc5*), click Chapter 7, click Web Info, and then click Scavenger Hunt.

create a Web page, sharing what they have learned with the community.

As this example illustrates, using computers and other technologies in the classroom promotes active learning, involves the students, and provides a sense of ownership, or authentic learning, of the information being presented. Having two or more computers in the classroom — especially when they are used as learning centers — requires more planning and attention to detail than having just one computer. Before setting up a learning center or centers, teachers should consider how many computers will be in each center and what other technologies, if any, may be included in the center. After the centers are set up, teachers can work on managing and planning activities, scheduling rotation times through each center for the students as they complete projects and activities. Teachers can create a sign-up list or use a timing device so all students have a fair amount of time on the computers.

COMPUTER LABS

Computer labs and media centers offer teachers instructional opportunities that are not possible in a one-, two-, or even a five-computer classroom. The most important advantage of using a computer lab or a wireless mobile lab is that all students have hands-on experience using computer technology. Teachers may successfully use computer labs for drill and practice, remediation, collaborative learning, computer skill instruction (for example, word processing), Internet research, whole class instruction, and tutorials.

Students often learn technology skills or subject-specific skills in isolation from the rest of the curriculum while in school computer labs. The labs, however, can also support the technology integration that teaches curriculum standards and related benchmarks. They are not just a place to teach keyboarding, remedial math, and science drills. A lab with new computers, scanners, Web access, and other technologies makes it possible to integrate computer-related skills into subject-directed curriculum areas. Teachers, for example, can integrate specific software applications into subject-area content.

Integration Strategies

To learn more about creating and integrating curriculum pages, review In the Lab at the end of this chapter and visit the Teachers Discovering Computers Web site (*scsite.com/tdc5*), click Chapter 7, and then click In the Lab.

Teacher-created activities, such as Web scavenger hunts, also teach computer skills, while giving students direction. A **Web scavenger hunt** is an inquiry-oriented activity in which students explore the resources of the Web using discovery learning to find the answers to teacher-created questions (Figure 7-26). While searching for the answers, students use higher-order thinking skills. When teachers plan creative instructional activities in advance, the computer lab, along with other technologies and the Internet, can bring authentic excitement and enthusiasm to students who otherwise might be uninterested in their daily school work.

Curriculum Integration Activities

Many teachers already use computers and technology in their classrooms and computer labs to help meet curriculum standards. For curriculum integration to be effective, however, the curriculum should drive the technologies used in the classroom; that is, teachers should use the applicable technologies to enhance learning at the appropriate times.

As teachers use technology in the classroom, they are finding many different ways to integrate it into curriculum-specific learning objectives. Learning to integrate technology effectively, however, requires planning and practice. The more practice you have in teaching with and integrating technology, the more you will discover innovative ways to use technology to facilitate all types of instruction.

CURRICULUM PAGES

One of the main technology integration challenges that teachers face today is determining exactly how to use the Internet in their classrooms. Teachers who integrate the Internet successfully are using it in ways that engage students in problem solving, locating research information, and developing higher-order thinking skills. Supervising students and controlling Web activities with curriculum pages is crucial to the successful use of the Internet in classrooms.

Exercise

Roller Coaster Scavenger Hunt

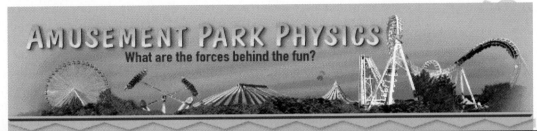

To learn more about the forces behind the fun, visit the Amusement Park Physics Web site using the following link:

www.learner.org/exhibits/parkphysics

Part A: Visit the site and read about roller coasters to answer the questions that follow.

1. Do roller coasters have engines?_____

2. What drives a roller coaster? _____

3. What is the difference between running wheels and friction wheels? _____

_____

4. How do roller coasters stop? _____

5. What is centripetal force?_____

6. What is gravitational force? _____

7. Name and explain three physics terms that relate to roller coasters. _____

Part B: Follow the online instructions to design your own roller coaster and answer the questions that follow.

8. What hill height did you choose? Why? _____

9. What hill shape did you choose? Why? _____

10. Which exit path did you choose? Why? _____

11. What did you choose for the height of your second hill? Why?_____

_____

12. What type of loop did you add? Why? _____

13. Did your roller coaster design succeed or fail? Why?_____

_____

_____

On the back of this paper, list four additional facts that you have learned.

Good Luck!

Figure 7-26 A scavenger hunt is a great way to have students explore the resources of the Web while using their higher-order thinking skills at the same time.

Recall from Chapter 3 that a **curriculum page** is a teacher-created document containing hyperlinks to teacher-selected Web sites that assist in teaching content-specific curriculum objectives. In addition, curriculum pages support learning objectives by providing students with quality Web resources, links to additional information, and opportunities to learn more. Because your curriculum page contains links that you have already researched and evaluated, students waste no time needlessly surfing instead of learning. A curriculum page can be a useful tool to ensure students spend your precious class time linking quickly to Web sites that you know will provide valuable information that is relevant to your lesson. Curriculum pages are easy to create and are a valuable teaching tool for students to use when accessing the World Wide Web.

Simple curriculum pages contain hyperlinks to teacher-selected sites. More detailed curriculum pages provide hyperlinks to Web sites and instructions for constructive and purposeful activities that students complete when they get to the selected Web sites. Using curriculum pages with these types of activities helps students find answers to teacher-created questions and helps them create and answer their own questions.

Figure 7-27 shows examples of teacher-created curriculum pages. The special feature that follows this chapter provides additional ideas on how to integrate curriculum pages, blogs, wikis, and more.

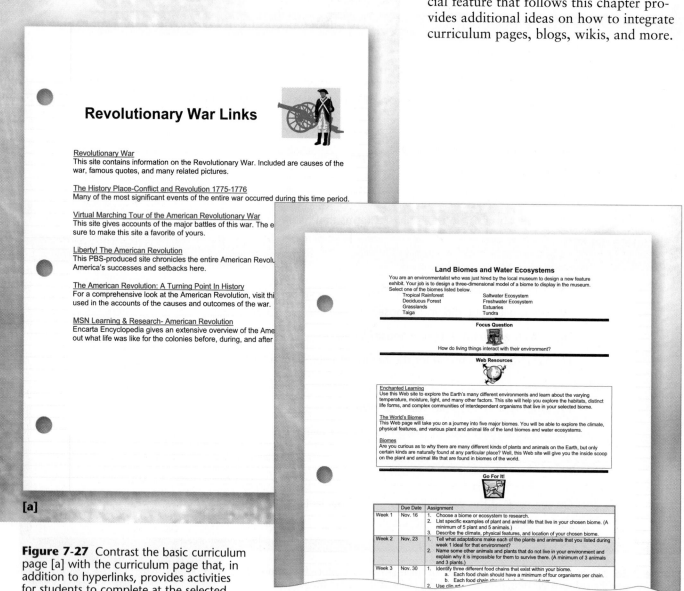

Figure 7-27 Contrast the basic curriculum page [a] with the curriculum page that, in addition to hyperlinks, provides activities for students to complete at the selected Web site [b].

CREATING LESSON PLANS

Planning is one of the most important variables for good instruction, and curriculum integration demands a great deal of planning. When first introducing technology into the classroom, many teachers try to incorporate technology into their existing lesson plans and activities. Because of the nature of the new technology tools, however, and because teaching and learning approaches must change, most teachers learn quickly this initial approach is only partially effective. To be successful in integrating technology, teachers must rethink and redesign activities and create new teaching and learning strategies as they actively integrate technology across their curriculum. In other words, new technology tools require new instructional lessons.

Teachers do not have to rely solely on their own resourcefulness to create technology-enriched lesson plans and activities. Today, teachers may receive online advice from other educators by joining educational mailing lists, forums, newsgroups, discussion groups, bulletin boards, blogs, and vlogs. Teachers also may refer to the Educator's Reference Desk, which provides thousands of resources and services to the education community (Figure 7-28).

Numerous lesson plans and activities at thousands of educational Web sites are available for teachers to use (Figure 7-29). Many such sites provide search engines to locate curriculum-specific lesson plans and activities for almost any K-12 area.

The following sections provide examples of subject-specific and interdisciplinary teacher-created curriculum integration activities. Each of these lesson plans are centered on a focus question and use a combination of learning processes and teaching strategies to assist in the delivery of the instructional process. The purpose of these curriculum integration activities is to provide a basic understanding of how to integrate technology into the classroom. You can adapt these examples to subject areas covered in your classroom or use them in other curriculum areas for thematic instruction.

Web Info

For more information about using computers as tools for learning, visit the Teachers Discovering Computers Web site (*scsite.com/tdc5*), click Chapter 7, click Web Info, and then click Learning Tools.

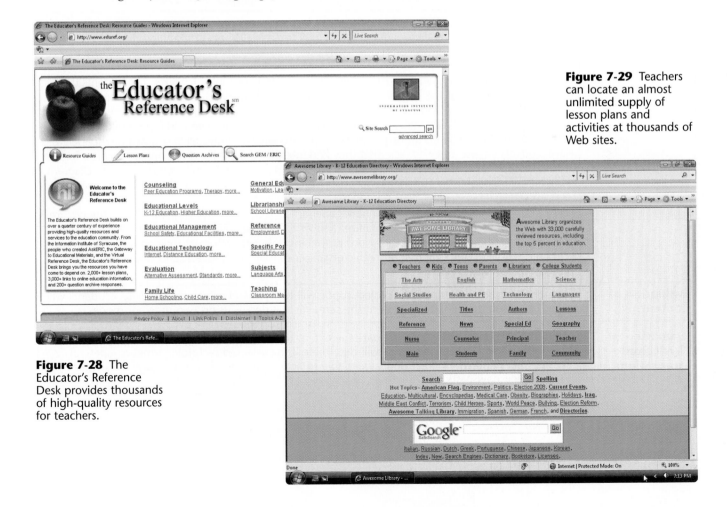

Figure 7-28 The Educator's Reference Desk provides thousands of high-quality resources for teachers.

Figure 7-29 Teachers can locate an almost unlimited supply of lesson plans and activities at thousands of Web sites.

LANGUAGE ARTS INTEGRATION Language arts curriculum usually includes instruction in reading, writing, listening, viewing, speaking, and literature. Figure 7-30 shows a curriculum integration activity, called *Extra! Extra! Know All About It*, that integrates technology into the subject areas of research and writing.

Language Arts

Curriculum Area:	Language Arts
Subject Area:	Research and Writing
Lesson Title:	Extra! Extra! Know All About It
Suggested Grade Level:	3–5, 6–8, could be adapted for any grade level
Equipment Needed:	Technology: Digital video camera, computer, microphones, TV, VCR Software: Digital video editing software Other: Teacher-created curriculum Web pages with Web resources about newscasting and news reporting; newspapers, prerecorded news stories that have been evaluated for age appropriateness, items students can use as props
Focus Question:	How can news stories help keep citizens informed?
Learning Objectives:	■ Students will find the important parts of a news story. ■ Students will analyze the news story based on point of view. ■ Students will write a news story appropriate for a newspaper article. ■ Students will use digital media to create a news story appropriate for a newscast.
Instructions:	Introduce the task by asking students, "What is the purpose of newspaper articles and television news stories?" Allow several students to respond. Then ask, "What is the main difference between a newspaper article and a television newscast?" Give each student a who, what, when, where, why, and how graphic organizer. Tell students that they are going to fill out the graphic organizer as they watch several newscasts from different anchors. Discuss their findings. Watch the newscasts again and have students determine what type of bias is presented as well as how the story would be different if it were told from a different point of view. Divide the class into groups of three or four students and give each group a newspaper. Have students choose a news article that they find interesting and fill out a graphic organizer for the article. Discuss their findings, the bias, and possible points of view. As a class, make a Venn Diagram comparing and contrasting the differences between a newspaper article and a television newscast. Give each group a photograph from a newspaper article that they have not read. Using the picture, have each group fill in the graphic organizer and write a newspaper article based on what they see. They will use Publisher or some other word processing software to format their articles. The groups will then use their photograph and graphic organizer to make a newscast. Encourage the use of props and creativity.
Evaluation of Content:	Teacher observation along with a project rubric will be used to evaluate this activity. Students will be evaluated on their ability to present the same factual details using two different modes.
Evaluation of Curriculum Integration:	Using observation, teachers will evaluate the extent to which technology assisted students to master the objectives. Teachers also will determine if the selected technology met a variety of learning styles and whether students were able to acquire the needed technology skills while creating their newscasts.

Figure 7-30 A sample lesson plan for *Extra! Extra! Know All About It*.

SOCIAL STUDIES INTEGRATION Social studies curriculum usually encompasses instruction in history, geography, civics, and economics. Figure 7-31 shows a curriculum integration activity, called *What Wonderful Webs We Weave*, that integrates technology into the subject area of ancient Egypt.

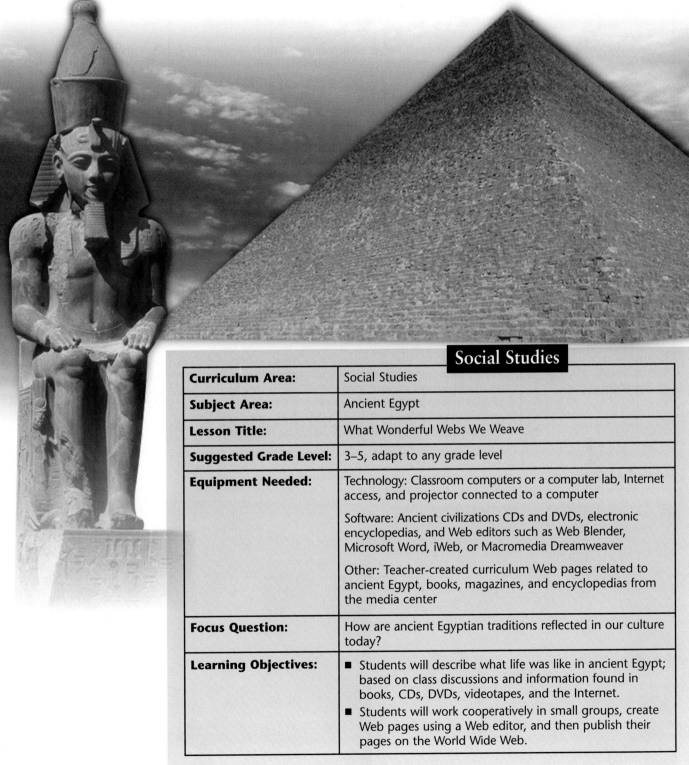

Social Studies	
Curriculum Area:	Social Studies
Subject Area:	Ancient Egypt
Lesson Title:	What Wonderful Webs We Weave
Suggested Grade Level:	3–5, adapt to any grade level
Equipment Needed:	Technology: Classroom computers or a computer lab, Internet access, and projector connected to a computer Software: Ancient civilizations CDs and DVDs, electronic encyclopedias, and Web editors such as Web Blender, Microsoft Word, iWeb, or Macromedia Dreamweaver Other: Teacher-created curriculum Web pages related to ancient Egypt, books, magazines, and encyclopedias from the media center
Focus Question:	How are ancient Egyptian traditions reflected in our culture today?
Learning Objectives:	■ Students will describe what life was like in ancient Egypt; based on class discussions and information found in books, CDs, DVDs, videotapes, and the Internet. ■ Students will work cooperatively in small groups, create Web pages using a Web editor, and then publish their pages on the World Wide Web.

Figure 7-31 A sample lesson plan for *What Wonderful Webs We Weave.*   *(continued)*

Instructions:	Introduce the activity to students by asking the focus question, then use student responses to create a KWLQS chart about ancient Egypt. As a class, decide on five or six broad topics of study relating to ancient Egypt: mummies, pyramids, Pharaohs, and so on. Connect a classroom computer to a projector and view teacher-created curriculum Web pages about ancient Egypt. Discuss what makes a Web site interesting, attractive, and relevant. Distribute an evaluation rubric for the students' Web page project. Review the rubric with students so they understand how their Web pages will be evaluated. Next, divide the class into small groups of three or four students. Have each group select one of the broad topics the class listed. Provide time for students to research their group's topic. They may use the CDs, DVDs, Web sites, books, magazines, and encyclopedias from the media center, the teacher-created curriculum Web pages, and the Internet. After students finish their research, have them complete a planning worksheet. Students plan their content, Web page layout, background, attention-getting titles, animated GIFs, pictures, and links to related Web sites. After students have created their Web pages on paper, have them use a Web editor to create their Web pages. When the Web pages are complete, they can be posted on your school's server or on a free Web server site.
Evaluation of Content:	Teacher observation along with the project rubric will be used to evaluate this activity. In addition, students' planning worksheets will be used for assessment purposes. Quality of research, the information drawn from Web sites, and the extent to which the students answered the focus question also will be assessed.
Evaluation of Curriculum Integration:	Learning to access, analyze, and apply information from different resources is a necessary skill for students and will be observed. How well students locate information, determine what information is valuable, and apply that information will be examined. Student motivation and enthusiasm when creating a Web page also will assist with evaluating the technology.

Figure 7-31 (continued)

MATHEMATICS INTEGRATION Mathematics curriculum usually includes instruction in basic number concepts, measurements, geometry, algebra, calculus, and data analysis.

Figure 7-32 shows a curriculum integration activity, called *The Business of Professional Sports*, that integrates technology into the subject areas of measurement, problem solving, and estimation.

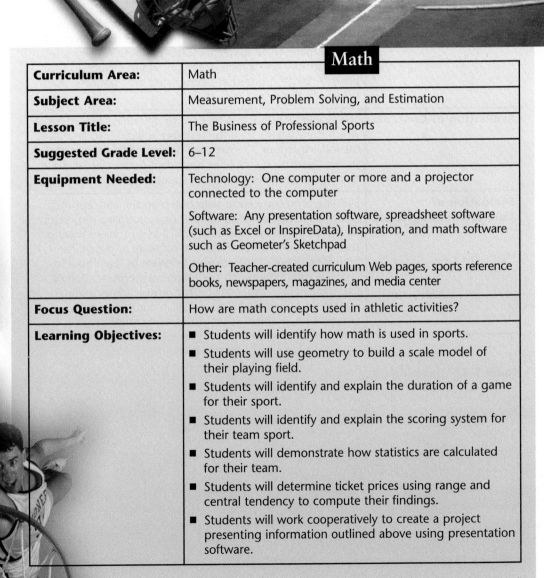

Math

Curriculum Area:	Math
Subject Area:	Measurement, Problem Solving, and Estimation
Lesson Title:	The Business of Professional Sports
Suggested Grade Level:	6–12
Equipment Needed:	Technology: One computer or more and a projector connected to the computer Software: Any presentation software, spreadsheet software (such as Excel or InspireData), Inspiration, and math software such as Geometer's Sketchpad Other: Teacher-created curriculum Web pages, sports reference books, newspapers, magazines, and media center
Focus Question:	How are math concepts used in athletic activities?
Learning Objectives:	■ Students will identify how math is used in sports. ■ Students will use geometry to build a scale model of their playing field. ■ Students will identify and explain the duration of a game for their sport. ■ Students will identify and explain the scoring system for their team sport. ■ Students will demonstrate how statistics are calculated for their team. ■ Students will determine ticket prices using range and central tendency to compute their findings. ■ Students will work cooperatively to create a project presenting information outlined above using presentation software.

Figure 7-32 A sample lesson plan for *The Business of Professional Sports*. *(continued)*

Instructions:	Have students list all the team sports they know. Create a concept map using Inspiration, projected to the class on the television monitor with Math as the center. Brainstorm with the class on how math is used in each of the sports they named, and then add these ideas to the concept map. Invite students to select their favorite team sport and then group students according to interest. Distribute an assessment rubric and discuss how it will be used to evaluate students' projects.

Students will use the rubric and follow the learning objectives to determine what elements to include in their projects. Encourage them to use the Internet for research, as well as any resources from the media center including newspapers to calculate statistics. Provide each group with a designated time to use the computer. When groups are not using the computer, they may be using other resource materials to develop their projects.

Coordinate with the media specialist students' access to other computers, or schedule time in the computer lab when the groups are working on their presentations. Have students use Geometer's Sketchpad to enter data and evaluate team statistics. Create graphs in Geometer's Sketchpad and compare. Have students create graphs using any spreadsheet software application or InspireData to include in their projects. When groups have completed their projects, share them with the class. |
| **Evaluation of Content:** | The evaluation rubric will be used to determine the extent to which the students used the learning objectives to answer the focus question. Teachers will determine the extent of student learning by the level of student motivation and a demonstrated understanding of statistics. |
| **Evaluation of Curriculum Integration:** | Evaluate problem-solving skills based on the concept map students created to visualize their brainstorming responses. Furthermore, assess technology skills and problem-solving skills acquired through the use of software applications. Evaluate the use of spreadsheet software to learn how to organize information and see graphical representation of that information. Evaluate student presentations to determine if this process reinforces skills in communication, organization, problem-solving skills, and critical-thinking skills. |

Figure 7-32 *(continued)*

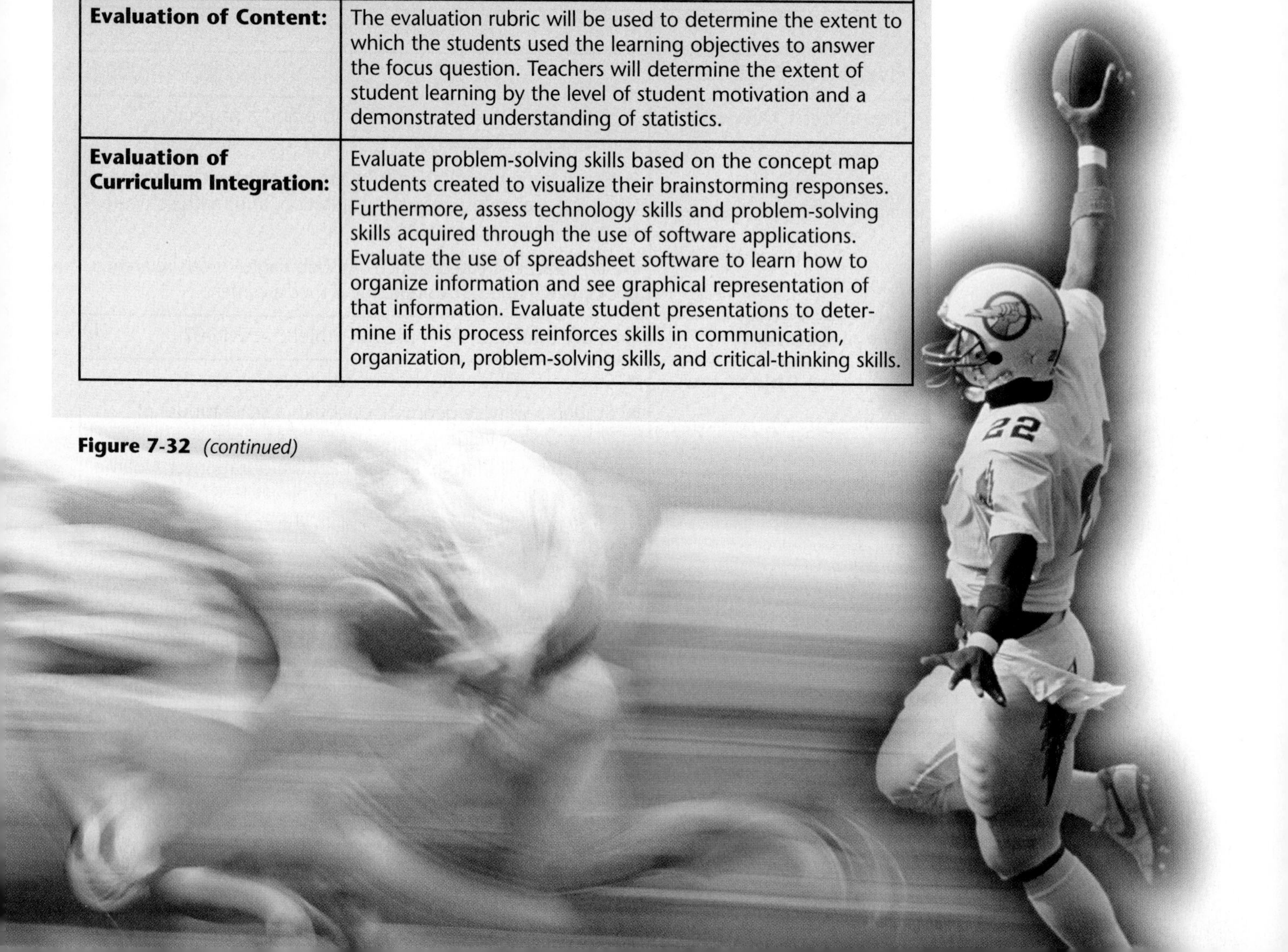

SCIENCE INTEGRATION
Science curriculum usually contains instruction in physical sciences, earth and space sciences, and life sciences. Figure 7-33 shows a curriculum integration activity, called *Let's Think as a Scientist*, that integrates technology into the subject area of life science.

Science

Curriculum Area:	Science
Subject Area:	Life Sciences
Lesson Title:	Let's Think as a Scientist
Suggested Grade Level:	K-12
Equipment Needed:	Technology: One computer and a projector/whiteboard connected to the computer Software: Thinkin' Science. This lesson can be adapted with other software-specific products. Other: Student computers if available
Focus Question:	Why is it necessary for scientists to have good observation skills?
Learning Objectives:	■ Students will practice observation and problem-solving skills. ■ Students will demonstrate understanding of content. ■ Students will interpret data. ■ Students will determine cause and effect between two events.
Instructions:	Begin this activity with a whole class discussion; use the focus question to guide the conversation. Thinkin' Science explores the earth, life, and physical sciences. Connect the computer to a projector/whiteboard. For this activity, go to Animal Tracking. Students will need to observe animals and then apply problem-solving skills. Students will explore animal behavior and then interpret data that is presented. Guide students by asking questions and drawing their attention to important events. To provide further practice of observation skills, and to increase problem-solving skills, use the activity, *What Did You See?* The students will be presented with a scene. The scene will disappear and students will have to recreate the scene. All students should tell you what needs to be placed in the scene. After you have used the software with the whole class, you can set it up in a learning center. *Note:* the software comes with a Teacher's Guide and reproducible activity sheets. You can place these in the learning center to support the students.
Evaluation of Content:	Students will be quizzed on content provided to determine if problem-solving skills and observation skills were mastered. The number of correctly answered questions from each student will determine attainment of content.
Evaluation of Curriculum Integration:	Teacher observation will be used to measure student attention and motivation. An additional evaluation will be identifying how many students utilize the software in the learning center.

Figure 7-33 A sample lesson plan for *Let's Think as a Scientist*.

PHYSICAL EDUCATION AND HEALTH INTEGRATION   Physical education and health curriculum usually includes instruction in basic health and physical education literacy. Figure 7-34 shows a curriculum integration activity, called *Eating Healthy!*, that integrates technology into the subject area of nutrition.

	Physical Education and Health
Curriculum Area:	Physical Education and Health
Subject Area:	Nutrition
Lesson Title:	Eating Healthy!
Suggested Grade Level:	3–5, could be adapted for any grade level
Equipment Needed:	Technology: Three computers, at least one with Internet access Software: PowerPoint or Keynote, database and drawing programs such as Microsoft Office, iWorks, Microsoft Works, Photoshop Elements, and Microsoft Paint Other: Teacher-created curriculum Web pages, books, nutrition brochures (from hospitals/health departments), and the Dole 5 A Day Web site (*www.dole5aday.com*)
Focus Question:	How do food choices affect your overall health?
Learning Objectives:	■ Students will use the Internet to take the Dole 5 A Day Challenge. ■ Students will create five recipes that include at least one serving of fruits/vegetables in each recipe. ■ Students will enter one of their recipes into a class cookbook database. ■ Students will work cooperatively to locate facts about their assigned fruit/vegetable using the Dole Fruit and Vegetable Encyclopedia and other resources. ■ Students will use PowerPoint or HyperStudio to create and present a multimedia project on their fruit/vegetable.
Instructions:	Individually, students will go to the Dole 5 A Day Web site to take the 5 A Day Challenge and to discover how food choices affect their health. Students will be given time to browse the Web page to learn more about why it is so important to eat at least five fruits/vegetables per day. Students will use the information from the Web site and nutrition brochures to create five recipes for their 5-day menu. Students will select their favorite recipe and add it to the class cookbook database. Students will create a creative cookbook cover using a desktop publishing or drawing program. They will print copies of the recipes to share with their families. Students will work in groups of two or three to create a digital media presentation on an assigned fruit/vegetable. Students will use books, nutrition brochures, and the Dole 5 A Day Web site to collect the information that they need to complete their projects.
Evaluation of Content:	Each student's menu item will be evaluated using a rubric (spelling and grammar included). Group projects also will be evaluated using a rubric (spelling and grammar included). Teachers will observe students as they work to determine whether students understand how food choices affect their overall health.
Evaluation of Curriculum Integration:	The effectiveness of the technology will be evaluated by testing students' content retention in a culminating quiz. Effectiveness will be apparent in student presentations. Students will gain valuable experience exploring Internet resources and learning how to use them to complete an assignment.

Figure 7-34   A sample lesson plan for *Eating Healthy!*

ARTS INTEGRATION Arts curriculum usually incorporates instruction in the visual and performing arts, including drawing, painting, dance, music, and theater. Figure 7-35 shows a curriculum integration activity, called *The Theory of Color*, that integrates technology into the subject area of color theory.

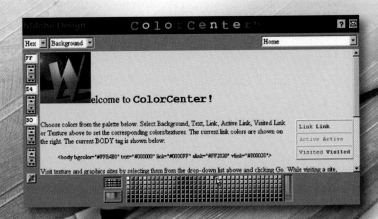

Art	
Curriculum Area:	Art (integrates Math)
Subject Area:	Color Theory — Reinforcing Basic Reading, Writing, and Math Skills
Lesson Title:	The Theory of Color
Suggested Grade Level:	3–6, easily adapted to higher levels
Equipment Needed:	Technology: Requires access to a student computer lab, requires computer connected to large monitor or TV Software: PowerPoint and any paint program
Focus Question:	How does the world around you reflect colors?
Learning Objectives:	■ Students will increase understanding of color theory. ■ Students will increase use of reading, math, and writing in the art classroom. ■ Students will demonstrate abstract conceptualization of written materials. ■ Students will demonstrate skills in computer paint accessories.

Figure 7-35 A sample lesson plan for *The Theory of Color*.   *(continued)*

Instructions:	Students are given a brief introduction explaining the goals of the lessons. They are told that an important part of the lesson is their own reading and writing skills. A simple pretest is given to allow students to demonstrate any preexisting knowledge of the content area.
	Color mixing: Using basic math skills and written directions, students prepare a series of diagrammatic color charts that teach basic color mixing and theory. The blank charts are prepared with the paint software. The color formulas will be written in a mathematical or fractional way (for example, Orange = 1/2 Yellow + 1/2 Red). Students will use eyedroppers to mix tempera paints to the proper proportion and paint samples as a permanent record in their portfolios.
	Relating reading and color theory: Based on the belief that students should be taught to visualize color as described in books or stories, students will read a series of excerpts from stories that include written descriptions of colors. Students will create color samples that show an understanding of the written excerpt and the colors described.
	Relating color to written descriptions: In contrast to the previous activity, students will be given blank lined pages for writing text. Each blank page will have a preprinted block of color. Students will be directed to create brief descriptive paragraphs that relate to each of the attached colors.
	Integrating technology: This lesson will be spread over time to allow adequate computer access time. Students will engage in a computer-oriented lesson that integrates what they have learned about colors with both reading and technology.
	Students will create a drawing with the paint program. The requirement for this piece of art will be that it clearly shows three primary colors, three secondary colors, one tint, and one shade.
Evaluation of Content:	A rubric will be used that the students easily can understand. Students will engage in critiques of each other's work. Critiques will be consolidated and students and instructors jointly will discuss the results of the exercises. The teacher also will assign individual student work. This will be based on the rubric to ensure consistency and reliability of results. Final results are compared with the pretest, where marked improvement in the students' understanding of color and color theory should be identified.
Evaluation of Curriculum Integration:	Teacher observation should be used to determine the quality of the projects. A teacher-created rubric should be used to determine the quality of the projects. Higher levels of complexity or variance in the final projects can be evaluated.

Figure 7-35 *(continued)*

COLOR MATTERS

EXCEPTIONAL EDUCATION INTEGRATION

Exceptional education curriculum, or special education curriculum, usually contains instruction in all curriculum areas with adaptations made for students with unique characteristics or special needs. These students include those who are gifted, learning disabled, physically disabled, emotionally disabled, or mentally disabled. Instruction for regular-education students and exceptional-educational students is merging as teachers find that many of the technology resources and integration activities dramatically enhance the instruction of students with special needs. Teachers easily can modify many of the integration activities illustrated in Figure 7-30 through Figure 7-35 to meet the needs of exceptional educational students. Figure 7-36 shows a curriculum integration activity, called *Rain Forests Are in Trouble,* that integrates technology into the subject area of current events and can be used for all students, including students with special needs.

Special Education

Curriculum Area:	Science, Social Studies, Math, and Language Arts for special education students
Subject Area:	Current Events
Lesson Title:	Rain Forests Are in Trouble
Suggested Grade Level:	3–5 (This lesson has been developed for grade levels 3 to 5 special education students. This lesson can be used with 3rd to 12th grade with appropriate adaptations.)
Equipment Needed:	Technology: Computer and a projector/whiteboard, Internet access and use of the Welcome to the Amazon Web site Software: Microsoft Encarta or other electronic encyclopedias, iMovie, Movie Maker, and PowerPoint. Other: Teacher-created curriculum Web pages on rain forests around the world, audio device, closed caption software, 3×5 index cards, notebooks, pencils, pens
Focus Question:	Why are rain forests worth saving?
Learning Objectives:	■ Students will collect and analyze information about the rain forests. ■ Students will describe a Web expedition to the Amazon using the Internet. ■ Students will explain current research efforts on tropical rain forests. ■ Students will demonstrate knowledge gained of tropical rain forest issues, and explore plant life cycles. ■ Students will create a digital media research report.

Figure 7-36 A sample lesson plan for *Rain Forests Are in Trouble.*   *(continued)*

Instructions:	Start the activity by asking students what they know about rain forests. Use their responses to create a KWHL chart with the students. Make sure print is large and colorful depending on needs.
	Students will work with partners and in groups of four. They will be given a list of Web sites about rain forests. They will access at least three different sites and take notes (3×5 index cards) about five different aspects of the rain forests. If an e-mail address is listed, students will write a short note asking a specific question they want to know about the rain forest.
	Students will work with their same team members and venture into the Amazon Web site. While there, they enter the options available at the Web site: Research, The Team, Map, About Netspedition, Equipment, and Venezuela. They document a brief description of each. Next, they will give a brief description about one of the butterfly surveys, indicating date, location, and what types of butterflies were caught. The team then will access the log book and choose one specific day on the calendar. They will record the date, location, the temperature, a description of one of the photographs, a description of the author's feelings, and the name of the person entering the information.
	Students continue to work in their cooperative teams taking turns at the computer, or they use other input devices such as PDAs, AlphaSmarts, and Tablet PCs. Use visual aids when needed. Each student plays the role of a scientific expert, chemist, ecologist, botanist, or taxonomist using one of four unique student reference books. Students will create a research-based video production project on the computer with drawings, maps, and so on. Consider assistive technologies for keyboard and mouse if needed.
Evaluation of Content:	The projects the students complete will indicate whether the students grasped the concepts indicated by the preceding objectives. Students will be evaluated on their ability to analyze and present factual details This project could be used as an additional or follow-up assignment.
Evaluation of Curriculum Integration:	Teacher observation will help to verify if the technology assisted in meeting various learning styles and needs of special education students. Teacher observation will determine if technology assisted in student attention and motivation. Students will be evaluated on time on task and length of time students work to master content and technology skills. An additional evaluation will be looking at each student and his individual needs throughout the lesson.

Figure 7-36 *(continued)*

INTERDISCIPLINARY INTEGRATION   An **interdisciplinary curriculum** usually includes two or more academic disciplines or curriculum areas to form a cross-discipline or subject-integrated lesson. A **cross-discipline lesson** includes a combination of curriculum-specific areas, such as math or science, that are integrated with language arts. A **subject-integrated lesson** is a lesson that integrates multiple skills, such as speaking, reading, thinking, and writing with multiple subject areas such as math, science, and language arts to create a more holistic learning experience. An interdisciplinary curriculum can combine various skills or disciplines to make a lesson more fully integrated for authentic and inquiry-based learning. Figure 7-37 shows a curriculum-integration activity, called *Natural Disasters Occur Everywhere*, that integrates technology in the subject areas of writing, research, science, social studies, health, and art. Figure 7-38 shows an activity, called *GeoMotion Learning Activity*, that integrates physical education, science, math, and geography.

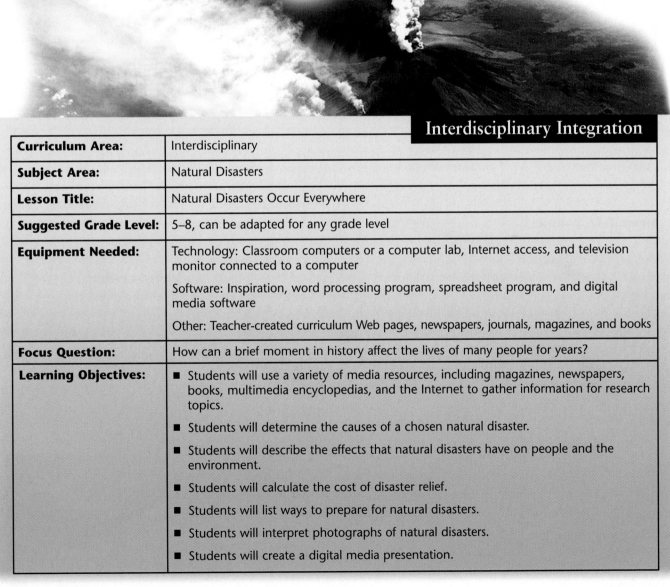

Interdisciplinary Integration

Curriculum Area:	Interdisciplinary
Subject Area:	Natural Disasters
Lesson Title:	Natural Disasters Occur Everywhere
Suggested Grade Level:	5–8, can be adapted for any grade level
Equipment Needed:	Technology: Classroom computers or a computer lab, Internet access, and television monitor connected to a computer Software: Inspiration, word processing program, spreadsheet program, and digital media software Other: Teacher-created curriculum Web pages, newspapers, journals, magazines, and books
Focus Question:	How can a brief moment in history affect the lives of many people for years?
Learning Objectives:	■ Students will use a variety of media resources, including magazines, newspapers, books, multimedia encyclopedias, and the Internet to gather information for research topics. ■ Students will determine the causes of a chosen natural disaster. ■ Students will describe the effects that natural disasters have on people and the environment. ■ Students will calculate the cost of disaster relief. ■ Students will list ways to prepare for natural disasters. ■ Students will interpret photographs of natural disasters. ■ Students will create a digital media presentation.

Figure 7-37 An interdisciplinary lesson plan for *Natural Disasters Occur Everywhere*.

(continued)

| Instructions: | Introduce the task by asking the focus question. Allow several students to respond. Introduce the term natural disaster. Create a KWL chart to determine what students know about natural disasters and what they want to learn. Divide the class into groups of three or four students and have each group go to *ndrd.gsfc.nasa.gov* to select a natural disaster that they want to research. Distribute a predetermined assessment rubric and cover the evaluation procedures for the final project.

Students will use the Internet and other resources to collect data on their chosen natural disaster. Students will use Inspiration to organize their data into a concept web; students should include information such as the type and cause of the natural disaster, where the disaster occurred, the effect on people and the environment, and the type of aid currently being sent.

Students will find and save photographs that depict the effect the natural disaster had on people and the environment.

Using the knowledge that they gained from their research, students will determine what type of aid they could put into a relief-care package for a family of four with a $100 budget. Students should also use the food pyramid as a guide to help choose healthy food items to include in their care package. Students will gather the prices of each item using newspaper ads, the Internet, and other available resources. They will use a spreadsheet program to calculate the cost of the care package with appropriate sales tax.

Using the computer lab or classroom computers, students will create a culminating multimedia presentation to present their research findings and their plans for aiding the victims. Groups will share their projects with the class. |
|---|---|
| Evaluation of Content: | Teacher observation along with the project rubric will be used to evaluate this activity. Students will be evaluated on usage of the Web and other technology tools. The quality of research and information utilized and the extent to which the focus question was answered also will be assessed. Students will also peer review projects. |
| Evaluation of Curriculum Integration: | Students' ability to access, analyze, and apply information from different resources will be observed. Students' motivation and enthusiasm when creating the digital media presentation also will assist with evaluating the technology. |

Figure 7-37 *(continued)*

Interdisciplinary Integration

Curriculum Area:	Interdisciplinary — Physical Education, Science, Math, Geography (N,S,E,W)
Subject Area:	Exercise, Heart Rate, Geometric Shapes, Math Computations, Distance in Miles, Directions
Lesson Title:	GeoMotion Learning Activity
Suggested Grade Level:	Grades 3–5, easily adaptable to 6–8
Equipment Needed:	Technology: One computer or more, projection system, Internet access, pedometers, and heart rate monitors (optional) Software: GeoFitness Children's, Hip Hop, or Motion Oke DVDs Other: GeoMats, calculator
Focus Question:	Why is your heart so important?
Learning Objectives:	■ Students will learn about the heart and be able to take and then record their resting and exercise pulse. ■ Students will perform and analyze three different physical activities, comparing heart rates and number of steps (with use of pedometer) recorded for each five minute activity. ■ Each student will have a GeoMat and follow along with the DVD, performing step patterns, directional movements, and jumping to increase their heart rate and perform meaningful movement, while reinforcing cognitive learning. ■ Students will use a calculator to convert steps to miles.
Instructions:	Students will learn about the heart and how it functions using a curriculum page created by the teacher. Students will learn to take a pulse and understand that exercise with an increase in heart rate is needed to strengthen the heart. The teacher will introduce students to the pedometer and discuss how all student steps (miles) will be logged into a Web site to show how many miles were completed by the class and the distance traveled on a map at the end of the lesson. Students will wear a pedometer to gather data for three different activities. They will record their heart rate and number of steps after each activity on a worksheet. Students will follow along and perform the activities on DVD. Each student performs each activity for five minutes with a five minute rest in-between to allow heart rate to lower to pre-exercise rate. 1. Geometric Shape Activity: Students will perform step patterns on the GeoMat named after geometric shapes and other symbols (square, rectangle, triangle, X, etc.) to music to increase their heart rate. 2. Geography / Directions Activity: Students will perform movements to the East, West, North, and South on the GeoMat to increase their heart rate. 3. Math Activity: Students will jump to the correct numbers on the GeoMat to solve addition, subtraction, multiplication, and division problems while increasing their heart rate and performing meaningful movement to learn math. At the completion of the three activities students will log all results and complete the worksheet. They will use a calculator to convert steps to miles. Next, the teacher will show students the process of logging onto a Web site to enter their miles on a map.

Figure 7-38 An interdisciplinary lesson plan for *GeoMotion Learning Activity.*   (continued)

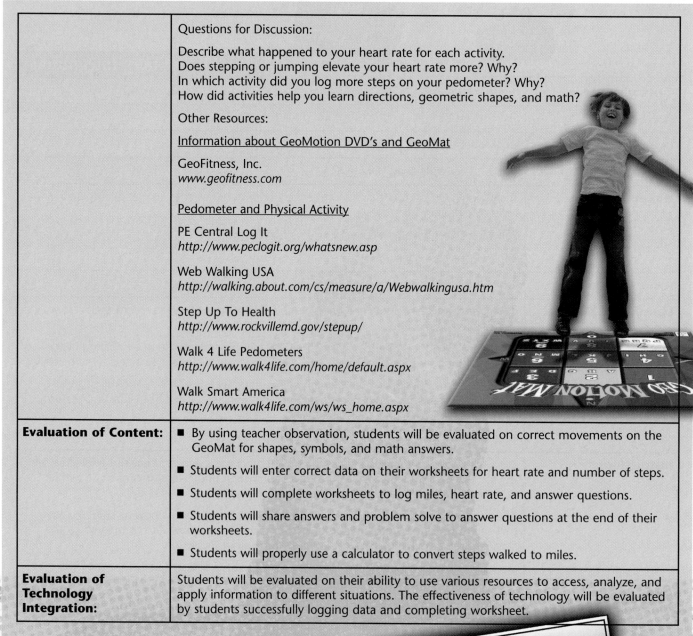

	Questions for Discussion: Describe what happened to your heart rate for each activity. Does stepping or jumping elevate your heart rate more? Why? In which activity did you log more steps on your pedometer? Why? How did activities help you learn directions, geometric shapes, and math? Other Resources: Information about GeoMotion DVD's and GeoMat GeoFitness, Inc. *www.geofitness.com* Pedometer and Physical Activity PE Central Log It *http://www.peclogit.org/whatsnew.asp* Web Walking USA *http://walking.about.com/cs/measure/a/Webwalkingusa.htm* Step Up To Health *http://www.rockvillemd.gov/stepup/* Walk 4 Life Pedometers *http://www.walk4life.com/home/default.aspx* Walk Smart America *http://www.walk4life.com/ws/ws_home.aspx*
Evaluation of Content:	▪ By using teacher observation, students will be evaluated on correct movements on the GeoMat for shapes, symbols, and math answers. ▪ Students will enter correct data on their worksheets for heart rate and number of steps. ▪ Students will complete worksheets to log miles, heart rate, and answer questions. ▪ Students will share answers and problem solve to answer questions at the end of their worksheets. ▪ Students will properly use a calculator to convert steps walked to miles.
Evaluation of Technology Integration:	Students will be evaluated on their ability to use various resources to access, analyze, and apply information to different situations. The effectiveness of technology will be evaluated by students successfully logging data and completing worksheet.

Figure 7-38 *(continued)*

Finding Funds to Support Classroom Technology Integration

One of the more difficult aspects of implementing technology in schools is finding and obtaining the funds for new technologies and the associated ongoing expenses. At present, many school districts do not have sufficient funding to incorporate technology at all levels throughout the district. For this reason, a classroom might not contain all the hardware and software to fully integrate technology and digital media into the curriculum.

Although the continued drop in computer and educational software prices lessens the problem, obtaining funding for classroom technology is still challenging. Many teachers, however, find that persistence often produces dramatic results. To increase the quantity and quality of technology in a classroom, a teacher first should ask the principal and other district administrators for additional classroom equipment and software. If you still need to obtain additional technology funding, you can turn to numerous other sources, including local school districts, public and private businesses, and government agencies.

FUND-RAISING DRIVES AND ACADEMIC CONTESTS

Class car washes, bake sales, and other activities can help raise money to purchase additional computers, hardware components, and software for classrooms. Local businesses such as banks, car dealerships, grocery stores, and department stores often respond to solicitations to improve the educational quality of the schools in their areas with donations. Corporations frequently are eager to become involved in active school technology programs — whether it is to contribute equipment, funds, or expertise. Teachers regularly write letters to local school business partners stating the school's needs to enlist their support. Even relatively small amounts of acquired funding can make a difference in the availability of technology in your classroom. Raising $100 will fund a new inkjet printer, numerous educational CDs/DVDs, or a color scanner; $1,000 will allow the purchase of a high-end multimedia computer with software or several digital cameras with software and accessories. Teachers should always get permission from the school's administration prior to raising funds. Another way to obtain hardware and software for the classroom is to enter academic contests. Teachers can locate information about hundreds of academic contests on the Web and in educational journals and magazines.

Teachers should involve the community, especially parents, in fundraising. The local school community holds its schools accountable for everything that goes on in the classroom, so enlisting the help of parents and business partners will broaden the base of support for the school's educational technology efforts. In addition, parents might have contacts or affiliations with local businesses or be able to provide further information on how to obtain funding. Another avenue for locating potential sources for technology funding is to showcase your classroom's use of technology for parents, business leaders, and school board members at your school's Parent Teacher Association (PTA), Parent Teacher Organization (PTO), or Parent Teacher Student Organization (PTSO) meetings.

Schools also should consider asking for volunteer services from the community in addition to or instead of asking for funds to pay for services. If funding for equipment maintenance is not available, for example, a local consultant might be willing to donate services. Many schools find that a combination of financial and volunteer support demonstrates the community's commitment to technology integration and strengthens the long-term community-school partnerships.

GRANTS

The majority of outside funding sources for technology fall under a general category called grants. **Grants** are funds provided by a funding source that transfers money, equipment, or services to the grantee. The **grantee** is the teacher, school, or organization to which the grant funds or equipment are transferred. Grants can be obtained from school districts, state Departments of Education, federal sources, foundations, and corporations. Grants range from a few hundred to millions of dollars. Many corporations maintain or

Web Info

For more information on how the Web is expanding student learning, visit the Teachers Discovering Computers Web site (scsite.com/tdc5), click Chapter 7, click Web Info, and then click Expanding Student Learning.

Web Info

For more information about grant opportunities for educators, visit the Teachers Discovering Computers Web site (scsite.com/tdc5), click Chapter 7, click Web Info, and then click Grants.

support foundations that provide grants, both large and small, for creative projects.

To obtain a grant, a school district, school, or teacher must submit a grant proposal in response to a request for proposal (RFP). A **request for proposal (RFP)** is a document provided by the grant source that details the information teachers and schools need to provide to write a successful grant proposal. A **grant proposal** is the document the potential grantee sends to the funding source. Grant proposals can vary from a simple one-page application to an extensive multipage document.

When writing a grant, schools can take one of several approaches. A single person might write the grant proposal; teachers might write grant proposals with other teachers, media specialists, technology coordinators, curriculum resource specialist, and school district personnel; or if the proposal is extensive, the school districts might even employ a grant-writing specialist or consultant to write the proposal to increase the availability of technology in their classrooms.

The principal, curriculum resource specialist, and technology coordinator usually receive notification of grant opportunities. In addition, teachers can locate many grant opportunities on the Web (Figure 7-39). Teachers should always receive approval from school administration before applying for any grant.

Chapter 7 Special Feature

The special feature that followed Chapter 3 provided you with information on and links to step-by-step instructions and videos for creating a teacher's Web page, blogs, wikis, podcasts, and screencasts. You learned earlier in this chapter that curriculum pages are wonderful tools for enhancing your students' learning experience. The special feature that follows this chapter builds on your knowledge and enhances your Web page development skills by providing you with step-by-step instructions for creating a teacher's Web site, including how to create a curriculum page using Microsoft Word.

You will also learn additional integration techniques and ideas for blogs, wikis, podcasts, and screencasts. As you will discover, integrating these tools can help you get your students more excited about learning, can assist you in reaching more students by addressing various learning styles, and allows you to explore ways to involve your students in their own learning.

Summary of Evaluating Educational Technology and Integration Strategies

Technology will not make a difference in the quality of students graduating from K-12 schools unless teachers learn how to integrate the use of technology into their curriculum and use it as a tool to enhance learning. This chapter first introduced the various tools and resources teachers use to evaluate the appropriateness of educational technology and the effectiveness of technology integration. Next, a number of strategies were presented for integrating technology into one-computer classrooms and other K-12 instructional settings along with subject-specific curriculum integration activities. Finally, the chapter provided information on how to obtain funding to increase the availability of technology in your classroom.

Figure 7-39 Many Web sites provide teachers and administrators with current, extensive information on grants for education.

Key Terms

INSTRUCTIONS: Use the Key Terms to help focus your study of the terms used in this chapter. To further enhance your understanding of the Key Terms in this chapter, visit scsite.com/tdc5, click Chapter 7 at the top of the Web page, and then click Key Terms on the left sidebar. Read the definition for each term and then access current and additional information about the term from the Web.

Exercises

Web Info
Key Terms
Checkpoint
Teaching Today
Education Issues
Integration Corner
Software Corner
Digital Media Corner
Assistive Technologies Corner
In the Lab
Learn It Online

Features

Timeline
Guide to WWW Sites
Search Tools
Buyer's Guide
State/Federal Sites
Professional Sites

ability level [399]
academic level [399]
affiliation [400]
alternative assessment [404]
appropriate [392]
arts curriculum [427]
assessment [404]
audience [401]
authentic assessment [404]
authentic learning [404]
authority [400]

block schedule [410]

checklist [405]
concept map [409]
content [401]
creativity [409]
cross-discipline lesson [431]
currency [401]
curriculum page [418]

design [401]
documentation [399]

e-folio [405]
ease of use [399]
EDTECH [395]
electronic portfolio [405]

embedded assessment [405]
evaluate [392]
exceptional education curriculum [429]

flowchart [409]

grant proposal [436]
grantee [435]
grants [435]

Inspiration [409]
interdisciplinary curriculum [431]

KWLQS chart [415]

language arts curriculum [420]
learning process [401]

mathematics curriculum [423]

objectivity [401]
one-computer classroom [412]

physical education and health curriculum [426]
portfolio assessment [405]
project-based assessment [405]
project-based learning [405]
purpose [401]

rating scale [405]
reliable assessment [404]
request for proposal (RFP) [436]
rubric [396]

science curriculum [425]
social studies curriculum [421]
software evaluation rubric [396]
special education curriculum [429]
storyboard [409]
story web [409]
student performance [404]
subject-integrated lesson [431]

teacher observation [407]
technical quality [399]
technical support [399]
technology conference [394]
traditional assessment [404]

valid [396]
visual learning technique [409]

Web evaluation rubric [402]
Web scavenger hunt [416]

Checkpoint

INSTRUCTIONS: Use the Checkpoint exercises to check your knowledge level of the chapter. To complete the Checkpoint exercises interactively, visit scsite.com/tdc5, click Chapter 7 at the top of the Web page, and then click Checkpoint on the left sidebar.

1. Label the Figure

Instructions: Read each description in the grid that follows. Then identify the criteria category used to evaluate Web sites that the description describes.

1. _____	2. _____	3. _____
No author is listed and no e-mail contact is provided.	It is unclear what institution supports this information.	The purpose is unclear or cannot be determined.
4. _____	5. _____	6. _____
The Web page is a virtual soapbox.	The information on the Web site does not relate to my objectives.	The information will not challenge learners to think, reflect, discuss, compare, or classify.
7. _____	8. _____	9. _____
The Web pages are not appropriate for my audience.	Information on the site has not been revised since 2005, or no date can be located.	The Web site is not appropriate for my audience.

2. Matching

Instructions: Match each term from the column on the left with the best description from the column on the right.

_____ 1. curriculum page

_____ 2. request for proposal

_____ 3. checklist

_____ 4. evaluate

_____ 5. concept map

a. to determine the value or to judge the worth

b. provides a visual tool for brainstorming and planning

c. teacher-created document that contains hyperlinks to teacher-selected Web sites

d. predetermined list of performance criteria

e. a document provided by a grant source that details the information needed to write a grant

3. Short Answer

Instructions: Write a brief answer to each of the following questions.

1. Describe four resources where teachers can find information about how to evaluate educational software. Why is it important for teachers to evaluate software before using it in the classroom?

2. Should teachers evaluate Web resources for instructional value in the same way they evaluate print resources? Why or why not?

3. Describe three techniques for evaluating student technology projects.

4. Briefly describe three uses of technology in a one-computer classroom. Why does having more than one computer in a classroom allow for more flexibility and greater integration of technology?

5. Briefly describe grant funding for K-12 schools. Why are grants so important for many K-12 schools? Describe three ways in which teachers can obtain funding for classroom technology.

Teaching Today

INSTRUCTIONS: Teaching Today provides teachers with integration strategies and ideas for teaching and, more importantly, reaching today's digital generation. Each numbered segment contains one or more links that reinforce the information presented in the segment. To display this page from the Web, visit scsite.com/tdc5, click Chapter 7 at the top of the Web page, and then click Teaching Today on the left sidebar.

1. Parent Teachers Organization

The Parent Teachers Organization (PTO) at your school has raised money to purchase software for all classes in your grade level. Your principal asks you to work with other teachers in your grade to make recommendations for software purchases to enhance the curriculum. Your principal asks you and the teachers to supply a wish list with seven to ten different titles, a detailed evaluation of each title, and pricing for each. Based on what you have learned in this chapter, what would be your next step in identifying appropriate software packages and then evaluating each? Where can you find software reviews? To what extent are these reviews helpful? What type of information can you gather about the software from these reviews? What kind of site-licensing and pricing are available for each package?

2. Integrating Blogging and Digital Teaching

So, you have heard about blogging. In fact, you may even have been doing it for personal fun, but not in your classroom. Well, why not? Your students will love it! Teachers are aware that students write better when they are engaged in authentic learning experiences — not just getting feedback from their teacher. Blogging can give your students excellent opportunities to read and write, provide effective conditions for cooperative learning, collaboration, and discussion, and be a powerful tool to enable communication skills to develop. Blogging can be highly motivating to students, especially those who otherwise might not participate in classroom discussions. Research suggests students are interested in blogging because they love to see their published works on the Web, they enjoy the rhetoric with their peers, and they are comfortable using this form of communications. What ways can you think of to integrate blogging into your curriculum? What benefits do you think this communication can provide the students?

3. More Than One Curriculum Area

You teach students with special needs in a middle school. You want to integrate software applications into your curriculum to enhance your students' learning. You are looking for software applications that can be used in more than one curriculum area. You are familiar with programs such as PowerPoint and iLife and already are using them in different curriculum areas. Describe the ways in which two other applications described in this chapter can be used in more than one curriculum area. Test drive SimCity, a popular software program. Which curriculum areas can this type of software be used in? How would you integrate this type of software into your curriculum? What curriculum standards and related benchmarks could it help teach?

4. Evaluating Student Work

As you begin to integrate technology into your curriculum, you need alternative ways to assess student performance. In this chapter, you read about the rubrics that teachers use to assess performance. Itemize the key points to remember when evaluating student work. What alternative assessment tools can you use in your classroom? When is using alternative assessment tools most appropriate? When are other types of assessment tools most appropriate?

Education Issues

INSTRUCTIONS: Education Issues provides several scenarios that allow you to explore controversial and current issues in education. Each numbered segment contains one or more links that reinforce the information presented in the segment. To display this page from the Web, visit scsite.com/tdc5, click Chapter 7 at the top of the Web page, and then click Education Issues on the left sidebar.

1. Video Games — Good or Bad?

There has been a lot of attention on whether video games are actually promoting aggressive behaviors in younger players. Studies have shown that many of today's youth spend up to 4–5 hours per day on computers. According to the Kaiser Family Foundation, 92% of American children play video games for 20 to 33 minutes per day. In his book, *What Video Games Have to Teach Us About Literacy and Learning*, James Gee is an outspoken advocate for the use of games to teach meta-learning principles. His research reveals even the so-called "shoot-em up" games can teach skills. On the other hand, there are those like Canadian psychology professor David Grossman who compares soldiers in training to children watching television. Grossman feels that both situations teach individuals to reject traditional values and create the illusion that the world is a dark and dangerous place. Grossman suggests that video games are increasingly desensitizing viewers — particularly children — to violence, and he has led a campaign in Canada to force media companies to become more accountable to this threat. Grossman is convinced that not only are media companies teaching violence but they are also teaching children to like it. What do you think? What implications might Grossman's campaign have on technology in education?

2. Evaluating Web Sites

A great deal of information exists on the Internet that is not what it appears to be. Sometimes, material seems authoritative and well written, but upon closer inspection, the material is biased, inaccurate, or out of date. Your school board feels it is a teacher's responsibility to teach students to recognize the quality and authority of information they find on the Internet. Do you agree or disagree? Why? How will you teach your students to do this? What criteria should students use when evaluating Web sites? Do students need to evaluate all Web sites? Support your answer with illustrations from existing Web sites.

3. Grants for Training

You locate a request for proposal (RFP) to fund a grant for notebook computers for all the teachers in your school. The grant will provide the notebook computers, but the school has to provide the teacher training. You want to develop the proposal with the help of the technology committee. You recognize this is a great opportunity to get technology into the hands of all teachers through the use of their own notebook computers. You think your school has an extremely good chance of being funded. The principal immediately says, "NO!" She feels the teachers should write grants only to obtain student computers. She also states that no funds are available for teacher training. Do you see a solution to this dilemma? What should you do? Where can you go to obtain more information and creative ideas for writing the grant and solving the training issues? How will you convince the principal that putting a notebook computer in each teacher's hands is an important initial step toward technology integration?

4. Alternative Assessment

Your first teaching job is at a very progressive new school that has technology in every classroom. During your college education, you learned a great deal about assessing student achievement through testing. You learned how to create appropriate traditional tests for subjects. This new school, however, has no traditional testing program. It has implemented an innovative approach to learning that uses only alternative assessment. No grades are assigned and all assessment is based on mastery learning. Do you think this is a good strategy? Support your position with reasons based on educational research. What alternative assessment tools can you use to meet the school's standards? Describe the advantages and disadvantages of this type of assessment.

Integration Corner

INSTRUCTIONS: Integration Corner provides extensive ideas and resources for integrating technology into your classroom-specific curriculum. To display this page from the Web and its links to approximately 100 educational Web sites, visit scsite.com/tdc5, click Chapter 7 at the top of the Web page, and then click Integration Corner on the left sidebar.

Integration Corner is designed for teachers and other educators who are looking for innovative ways to integrate technology into their content-specific curriculum. Integration Corner not only provides great Web sites with current information but also shows what other educators are doing in the field of educational technology. These Corners are designed for all educators regardless of their area of interest. Be sure to review information and Web sites outside of your teaching area because many great integration ideas in one area can be modified easily for use in other curriculum areas.

Teachers and administrators will find other colleagues in their areas with whom to connect and share the successes and hurdles of integrating technology in a classroom or an entire school system. Consider Integration Corner your one stop for integration ideas and resources. Links to educational Web sites are organized in the following 12 Corners, and different Web resources are available for each chapter. Figure 7-40 shows examples of the Web resources provided in the Chapter 7 Administrator Corner.

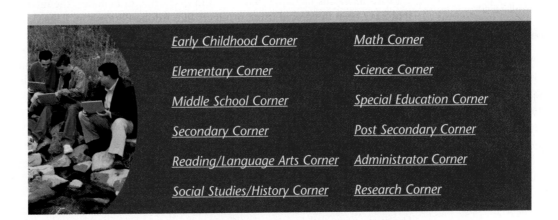

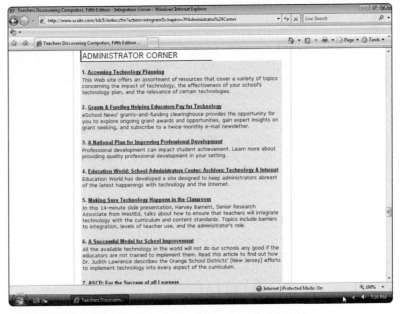

Figure 7-40 Examples of the Web resources provided in the Chapter 7 Administrator Corner.

Software Corner

INSTRUCTIONS: Software Corner provides information on popular software programs. Each numbered segment discusses specific software programs and contains a link to additional information about these programs. To display this page from the Web, visit scsite.com/tdc5, click Chapter 7 at the top of the Web page, and then click Software Corner on the left sidebar.

1. Inspiration

Inspiration is a powerful software product that allows students to think visually through webbing, concept mapping, and more. Inspiration provides students in grades 4-12 and beyond with the ability to organize and develop their thoughts before creating, reports, presentations, and video production projects. Language arts teachers will find Inspiration an awesome writing and literature tool. History and science teachers can use Inspiration to create timelines and to plan research reports and projects. Inspiration can be integrated into all areas of the curriculum and will inspire your students to new heights!

2. Adobe Acrobat

Are you looking for a way to create professional documents that can be distributed electronically via various means including the Web and that can still maintain the integrity of images and formats that have been integrated using products like Adobe Photoshop, PageMaker, or other desktop publishing software? Adobe Acrobat is the perfect solution. Whether you are a novice just beginning to design formatted documents or a skilled designer, Adobe Acrobat helps you maintain control over how, when, and by whom your documents are accessed. Create and exchange documents, collect and compare comments, and tailor the security of a file in order to distribute your documents reliably and professionally.

3. Adobe Captivate

Adobe Captivate is a software program that you can use to create online demonstrations, tutorials, scenario-based instructional videos, and software simulations. Captivate also can be used to build scenarios in which you can branch from one topic to another to create a controlled set of links and paths for users to follow. The software outputs to either Flash or PowerPoint files that can be used in podcasts. The software also lets you build interactive programs, demos, and lessons. Because it is based on several Flash technologies, the end product is a small file size that makes it very efficient to use on the Web. The ability to add hot spots within the screen allows viewers to branch to other slides and sections of the presentation, providing an interactive lesson format.

4. LeapFrog

LeapFrog products are changing the way some children learn reading, writing, and arithmetic. LeapPads, a LeapFrog product, uses books embedded with NearTouch technology, which makes any part of a page touch-interactive. By using the special pen and touching it to words on the page, the voice program reads aloud the words. Students can write, draw, and paint using story-based games, the interactive touch screen, and the pen. LeapFrog products have multiple skills levels, tailored tutorials, and an entire system with features that meet the diverse learning needs of K-4 students.

Digital Media Corner

INSTRUCTIONS: Today's K-12 digital students need their learning to be meaningful and relevant to their lives. Digital Media Corner provides videos, ideas, and examples of how you can use digital media to enhance your teaching and your students' learning. To access the videos and links to additional information, visit scsite.com/tdc5, click Chapter 7 at the top of the Web page, and then click Digital Media on the left sidebar.

1. Edutainment in Action in Education

A key component to the effectiveness of using digital media is the term *edutainment*, more specifically, using the attractive qualities and aesthetics of entertainment media for learning purposes. The essence of edutainment as well as entertainment and traditional literature is, was, and always will be identifying with the story. This book highlights how, why, and where implementing the benefits of digital storytelling can benefit your students' education and your lesson planning — everybody wins! If you need more information on edutainment, click the Edutainment in Action in Education link to learn more. After all, edutaining the youth of today about the invaluable information of the past by using the technologies of tomorrow and beyond is the future of education.

2. Game Maker

Game Maker, currently being distributed by Yo-Yo Games, is a dynamic game development program that allows non-programmers the ability to make fairly robust computer games without the need to know how to be a programmer. You or your students can create professional looking games using drag-and-drop to place user-friendly actions in your game. The game software contains backgrounds, animated graphics, music, and sound effects. There is a built-in programming language for more advanced users that provides full functionality for creating a full array of game types and 3-D graphics. The basic package is free but requires registration for access to full functionality of the programs. Game Maker comes preloaded with a collection of freeware images and sounds, making this a super media product for digital learners.

4. Digital Media in the Classroom

As you have learned throughout this textbook, digital media is everything from QuickTime movies to graphic design software applications. With so much information and technology out there, choosing the appropriate form of digital media to integrate in your curriculum can be intimidating. Evaluating digital media for appropriateness and usability is just like evaluating software, Web sites, and other technologies. The textbook presents guidelines for evaluating Web sites that include examining authority, affiliation, purpose and objectivity, content and learning process, audience and currency, and design of the digital media material encountered online, at a conference, or from peer educators. These guidelines are excellent for establishing the credibility of the digital media as well. The tools you use to conduct an evaluation of a Web site, a software application, or a digital media piece can be very similar; including the elements you evaluate!

5. Peer Evaluation of Student Projects

Many teachers believe that their main form of motivating students to participate in projects and activities is to use a project grade. An alternative assessment technique is to let student peers evaluate each other's projects. Digital media lends itself to the shared experience, in which all students can easily participate in the viewing of final projects. Teachers should develop a rubric for students to complete, including an area where peers can write constructive comments. After the students get the chance to review the peer evaluation, ask them to write a reflection about their project, discussing what they liked about it, what they might do differently, and what they learned from the peer evaluations.

Assistive Technologies Corner

INSTRUCTIONS: Assistive Technologies Corner provides information on current hardware, software, and peripherals that will assist you in delivering instruction to students with physical, cognitive, or sensory challenges. To access extensive additional information, visit scsite.com/tdc5, click Chapter 7 at the top of the Web page, and then click Assistive Technologies on the left sidebar.

1. How Can I Choose the Best Software for Students with Special Needs?

Many times, students with significant physical or mental disabilities will come to the classroom with a technology plan as part of their IEPs. When this is not the case, quality software will provide the best chance for success for a student with mild to moderate learning difficulties. To ensure a quality tool for a special needs user, the teacher might want to add some special considerations to the Software Evaluation Rubric (Figure 7-7) located in this chapter.

Technical Quality

1. Are captions available for video clips or audio files?
2. Will the software function using alternative input devices such as alternative keyboards?

Presentation of Information

1. Are directions presented using both visual and auditory means? Are directions intelligible with the sound turned off?
2. Is sufficient time given for the user to read and comprehend directions?
3. Are directions clear and are examples of user tasks provided?
4. Is text clear and easy to read? Does the user have control over text size?

Content

1. Is content presented dependent on color, or only by a single mode (auditory or visual)?
2. Does content provide logical structures for information, and is the information presented using different structures?

2. How Can I Integrate Technology in the Special Needs Curriculum?

Integration activities for students with special needs enhance learning for all students. Exciting activities for learners with special needs may include some of the following.

Using **graphic organizing** tools (Inspiration, Kidspiration), students may
- Create a flowchart or timeline to plan their learning activities
- Create a similarities/differences chart for any new concept
- Create a concept map to demonstrate understanding

Using **digital video editing software** (iMovie, MovieMaker, and others), students may
- Create video clips to illustrate and share experiences
- Title or caption the video clips

Using **digital media tools** (Keynote, PowerPoint, and so on), students may
- Author and illustrate multimedia books to retell a story
- Prepare and illustrate researched information for presentation

Using **database tools** (AppleWorks, Microsoft Office), students may
- Collect and organize information such as a Zoo Animal database
- Create database reports or tables based on information for alternative presentation of information

3. Does Technology Enhance Learning for Students with Special Learning Needs?

Technology is a tool, not a cure for learning disabilities. Used with clearly planned learning goals and appropriate instructional strategies, almost all technology tools can help level the field for students with disabilities, providing equal access to the curriculum and opportunities for success.

Follow the instructions at the top of this page to display additional information and this chapter's links on assistive technologies.

In the Lab

INSTRUCTIONS: In the Lab provides curriculum page development exercises that are divided into two areas, productivity and integration. To access the links to tutorials, productivity ideas, integration examples and ideas, and more, visit scsite.com/tdc5, click Chapter 7 at the top of the Web page, and then click In the Lab on the left sidebar.

PRODUCTIVITY IN THE CLASSROOM

Introduction: As you have learned, many kinds of curriculum pages exist. For example, a curriculum page can serve as a guide, assisting students in locating quality information on the Internet. Teachers easily can create curriculum pages using a variety of software programs and Web editors. You can use Microsoft Word to create Web pages, and Word is available on many home and school computers. Microsoft Publisher also can be used to create Web and curriculum pages. Some popular stand-alone Web editors used by educators include Adobe GoLive, WebBlender, and Macromedia Dreamweaver.

Teachers can use curriculum pages in a variety of ways. One type of curriculum page is a list of annotated links focusing on one area of the curriculum or supporting one particular project. A curriculum page also can present students with a learning task, provide guidelines for how the task will be evaluated, and provide preselected Web sites that support the task.

Utilizing curriculum pages in the classroom provides many benefits. Students develop independent thinking and working skills, as well as higher-order thinking and problem-solving skills. Furthermore, preselecting Web sites maximizes the time students spend on the Internet and helps teachers to better supervise their students. Students also can create curriculum pages to provide evidence of their learning. This can be a powerful and exciting way for students to demonstrate their newly acquired knowledge and skills.

1. Creating and Formatting a Dental Health Curriculum Page

Problem: You are beginning a unit on dental health in your first grade classroom. You want to create a curriculum page to use with and read to the class to enhance the students' learning experience. Also, by using a curriculum page, the students will be able to go back and review Web sites after the unit is finished. The curriculum page is shown in Figure 7-41 on the next page. Open Microsoft Word or any Web editing software and create the curriculum page as described in the following steps. To download the images shown in Figure 7-41, visit the Teachers Discovering Computers Web site (*scsite.com/tdc5*), click Chapter 7, and then click the link Creating a Curriculum Page using Microsoft Word or use any appropriate background and clip art image to personalize the page. (*Hint:* Use Help to understand the steps better.)

Instructions: Perform the following tasks.

1. Insert the background image.
2. Display the first heading line, Let's Learn About Teeth, in 24-point Times or Times New Roman dark blue font.
3. Display the second heading line in 18-point Times or Times New Roman dark blue, bold font. Personalize the curriculum page by inserting your name instead of Ms. Yoshimura's name.
4. Insert a table with one row and two columns. Format the table to display as shown in Figure 7-41.
5. Insert an appropriate picture, image, or clip art graphic in the left column.
6. The two paragraphs and the bulleted list in the right column display in 14-point Times New Roman dark blue, bold font.
7. The line following the table and the bulleted list display in 14-point Times New Roman dark blue, bold font.

In the Lab

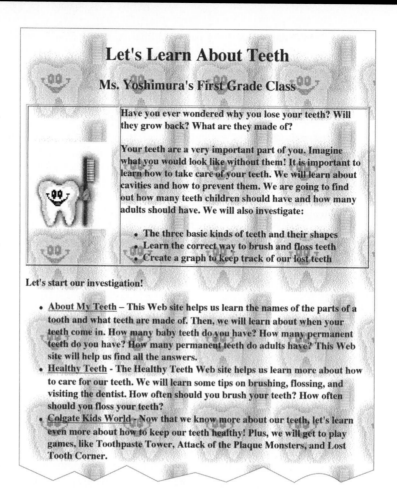

Figure 7-41

8. Link the word About My Teeth to http://www.ms-flossy.com/SmileysPlace. Link the words Healthy Teeth to http://www.healthyteeth.org. Link the words Colgate Kids World to http://www.colgate.com/app/Kids-World/US/HomePage.cvsp.

9. Save the curriculum page to the location and with a filename of your choice. Print the curriculum page and then follow your instructor's directions for handing in the assignment.

2. Creating and Formatting a Science Curriculum Page

Problem: Your eighth-grade science class has been studying the weather. As a final project, students must gather research and create a digital media presentation. You create a curriculum page to facilitate their research. The curriculum page is shown in Figure 7-42. To download the images shown in Figure 7-42, visit the Teachers Discovering Computers Web site (*scsite.com/tdc5*), click Chapter 7, and then click the link Creating a Curriculum Page using Microsoft Word or use any appropriate background and clip art image to personalize the page. (*Hint:* Use Help to understand the steps better.)

Instructions: Insert the background image. Enter the first heading line in 24-point Times or Times New Roman font. Insert your name in place of Mr. Pawliger's name. Enter the subheading The Weather in 18-point Times or Times New Roman font. Insert a table with one row and two columns and format the table as shown in Figure 7-42. Insert a graphic in the left column of the table. The text and bulleted list in the right column display in 12-point Times New Roman bold font. The line immediately below the table displays in 12-point Times New Roman bold font.

In the Lab

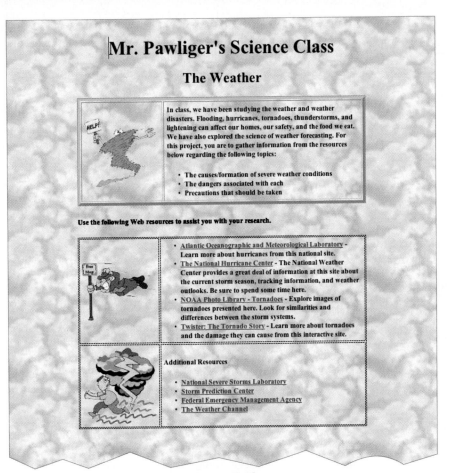

Figure 7-42

Insert a table with two rows and two columns to help organize the links. Format the table to display as shown in Figure 7-42. (*Hint:* Format the table to display without borders.) The text and bulleted lists display in 12-point Times New Roman bold font. Insert graphics and create the hypertext links using the Web site addresses (URLs) listed in the following table.

Linked Text	Web Site
Atlantic Oceanographic and Meteorological Laboratory	www.aoml.noaa.gov
National Hurricane Center	www.nhc.noaa.gov
NOAA Photo Library - Tornadoes	www.photolib.noaa.gov/nssl/tornado1.html
Twister: The Tornado Story	whyfiles.org/013tornado/index.html
National Severe Storms Laboratory	www.nssl.noaa.gov
Storm Prediction Center	www.spc.noaa.gov
Federal Emergency Management Agency	www.fema.gov
The Weather Channel	www.weather.com

In the Lab

After you have typed and formatted the curriculum page, save the curriculum page to the location and with a file name of your choice. Print the curriculum page and then follow your instructor's directions for handing in the assignment.

3. Creating and Formatting a Subject-Specific Curriculum Page

Problem: You want to create a curriculum page to support a concept you are teaching in your classroom and to provide students with preselected Internet resources.

Instructions: Create a curriculum page similar to the curriculum page illustrated in Figure 7-42 on the previous page. Use appropriate layouts, font types, font styles, font sizes, and clip art images. Include your name and the subject area you teach. After you have created the curriculum page, save the curriculum page to the location of your choice using an appropriate filename. Print the curriculum page, and then follow your instructor's directions for handing in the assignment.

INTEGRATION IN THE CLASSROOM

1. While studying the 50 states, you have your elementary students work in pairs to design and create a curriculum page about the state of their choice. They are to include their names and the name of the state at the top of the curriculum page. They also will include a graphic of either the state or the state flag, a brief paragraph about the state, and a bulleted list that includes the state capital, state bird, and state flower. The students then will include three links to Internet resources that provide additional information about their state. Create a sample curriculum page for your students using the state of your birth or the state in which you currently live. Include your name on the curriculum page.

2. To help your middle school language arts students develop reading, vocabulary, and writing skills and increase their awareness of community and global issues, you begin a unit using newspapers in your classroom. You arrange for local newspapers to be donated to your classroom so each student has a copy. You also have students explore local newspapers and news sources online. You direct students to select an article from either a local newspaper or an online news source and create a curriculum page that summarizes the news item and contains at least three links to Internet resources that support or give further information on their selected topic. Students will present their curriculum pages to the class and you will have them posted on your school's server so all students can access the information. Create a sample curriculum page for your students. Include your name and school at the top of the curriculum page. Include your e-mail address and the current date at the bottom of the curriculum page.

3. Your music class has been studying famous composers. To prepare for the end-of-unit exam, you divide the students into five groups and have each group research one composer. The groups then create a curriculum page that other students use as they study. On their curriculum pages, students are required to include a graphic image, a brief paragraph about the composer, a bulleted list of the titles of at least five famous pieces, and at least four annotated links to Web resources. The curriculum pages will be placed on the computers in the classroom, media center, and computer lab. In addition, you will post the curriculum pages on the Web to assist the students in studying at home. Select a famous composer and create a sample curriculum page for your students. Include your name on your curriculum page. Include your e-mail address and the current date at the bottom of the curriculum page.

Learn It Online

INSTRUCTIONS: Use the Learn It Online exercises to reinforce your understanding of the chapter concepts and increase your computer, information, and integration literacy. To access dozens of interactive student labs, practice tests, learning games, and more, visit scsite.com/tdc5, cick Chapter 7 at the top of the Web page, and then click Learn It Online on the left sidebar.

1. Evaluating Internet Resources

Evaluating information found on the World Wide Web is a critical skill that teachers and students must possess. Click the Evaluating Internet Resources link to complete an exercise and learn how to evaluate the quality of Internet resources.

2. Rubrics

Designing effective evaluation tools to assess student learning requires thought and preparation. One popular assessment tool is an assessment rubric. Click the Rubrics link to complete an exercise on how to create effective rubrics.

3. Expanding Your Understanding

Concept maps, flowcharts, story webs, storyboards, and other graphic organizers assist students with visualizing concepts and organizing information. Click the Expanding Your Understanding link to learn more about these concepts.

4. Practice Test

Click the Practice Test link. Answer each question. When completed, enter your name and click the Grade Test button to submit the quiz for grading. Make a note of any missed questions. If required, submit your score to your instructor.

5. Who Wants to Be a Computer Genius?

Click the Computer Genius link to find out if you are a computer genius. Directions about how to play the game will be displayed. When you are ready to play, click the Play button. If required, submit your score to your instructor.

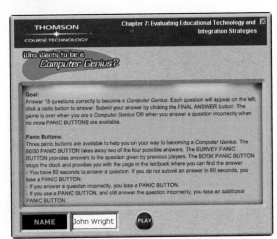

6. Wheel of Terms

Click the Wheel of Terms link to reinforce important terms you learned in this chapter by playing the Shelly Cashman Series version of this popular game. Directions about how to play the game will be displayed. When you are ready to play, click the Play button. If required, submit your score to your instructor.

7. Crossword Puzzle Challenge

Click the Crossword Puzzle link. Complete the puzzle to reinforce skills you learned in this chapter. Directions about how to play the game will be displayed. When you are ready to play, click the Play button. If required, submit the completed puzzle to your instructor.

Special Feature: Integrating Web Pages, Blogs, Wikis, and More

You have already learned what Web pages, wikis, blogs, podcasting, and screencasts are in previous chapters; you also learned how to create these tools in the special feature that follows Chapter 3. You may be wondering, "How am I going to integrate these emerging digital tools and Web-based technologies into my curriculum?"

This special feature provides you with a number of integration ideas for each of these topics. Also provided at the textbook Web site are links to additional resources, including links to teacher-created Web pages, wikis, blogs, podcasts, and video screencasts. Integrating these tools can help you transition your classroom to a more active learning environment and, therefore, create a place where students will want to be!

Shift in Learning Environments

Figure 1 shown here from Chapter 1 is important to review because the table shows the shift from traditional learning environments to new learning environments. Teachers should reflect on and strive to implement the techniques associated with the new learning environments in their classrooms. You have been learning throughout this textbook about many technologies and, more importantly, how to adapt/use technologies to accommodate these new learning environments. In other words, you have been learning about how to integrate technologies into your curriculum so it permeates all aspects of your teaching and your students' learning.

The good news is that many of the technologies we have been discussing have become mainstream in society and are just starting to have an impact in K-12 education. The even better news is that these technologies are simple to use, often free, and easy to integrate with your digital students. Perhaps the best news is that these technologies support the strategies inherent in the new learning environments, as shown in Figure 1.

From Passive Learning to Active, Exploratory, and Inquiry-Based Learning

As reported in a recent study by the NPD Group, kids are using electronic devices at earlier and earlier ages, beginning at an average age of 6.7 years compared to an average age of 8.1 years reported just two years before. As the report stated, "Kids are drawn to the latest and greatest digital devices and appear to have no fear of technology and adopt it easily and without fanfare, making these devices a part of their everyday lives."

So how, as teachers, can we change our lessons and teaching to meet the needs of today's digital students? There are many wonderful and easy-to-use technology tools that can help you both teach, and more importantly, reach today's digital kids. You have been learning different ways you can update your lessons to integrate many of these tools. Figure 2 on the next page summarizes some of these techniques.

As you begin exploring how to integrate the specific digital media tools covered in this special feature, we will focus on two overarching strategies: teacher-created content and student-assisted/created content.

Web Info

For more information on how you can adapt your teaching to the new learning environments, visit the Teachers Discovering Computers Web site (*scsite.com/tdc5*), click Chapter 7, click Web Info, and then click New Learning Environments.

Establishing New Learning Environments by Incorporating New Strategies

Traditional Learning Environments	New Learning Environments
Teacher-centered instruction	Student-centered learning
Single-sense stimulation	Multisensory stimulation
Single-path progression	Multipath progression
Single media	Multimedia
Isolated work	Collaborative work
Information delivery	Information exchange
Passive learning	Active/exploratory/inquiry-based learning
Factual, knowledge-based learning	Critical thinking and informed decision making
Reactive response	Proactive/planned action
Isolated, artificial context	Authentic, real-world context

Source: International Society for Technology in Education (ISTE)

Figure 1 This chart shows the characteristics that represent traditional approaches to learning and corresponding strategies often associated with new learning environments for your students.

Tip	Description
Plan	Plan, plan, plan. As always, planning is essential. Include a variety of digital media resources as you build your units, lessons, and activities. Remember, your students are already using these tools so let them show what they know!
Evaluate	Determine how the students will provide evidence of their learning and how you will measure the outcomes. Use rubrics to set the stage for what you expect from the lesson and guide the learning experience. Be sure to specify the types of resources, including technologies, students are expected to use for their projects.
Be flexible	Be willing to shift gears. Integrating technology always requires flexibility — both flexibility with using a variety of tools and flexibility with learning outcomes. Integrating technology can open new doors. You may be surprised at what your students learn in addition to your lesson objectives!
Involve students	Involve students in their own learning. This is incredibly motivating, engaging, and increases retention. Students need to be able to weave their learning into their own personal narratives. Allowing students to be a part of the planning process can be exciting and bring out new and creative ways of learning important concepts.
Be creative	Think outside the box and encourage your students to do the same. Start changing your own thinking from linear to non-linear. Constantly ask yourself if you are using traditional teaching techniques or techniques that are more geared toward the new learning environments as shown in Figure 1.
Be aware	Remember to be vigilant. While new technologies are fun and exciting, they also pose some risks. Be sure you are aware of these risks and proactively safeguard against them.

Figure 2 Techniques that can help you integrate various technologies.

Teacher-Created Content

The first strategy is one you are already very comfortable with — creating the instructional content yourself. Using the tools covered in this special feature enables you to create instructional content that your students can view at anytime and anyplace. In other words, you can create digital media versions of practice tests, homework assignments, project reviews, content specific lecture materials, and more. The key is that you are the one using the digital media tools to transition from traditional instructional materials, like a typical lecture, to a podcast on the topic. Creating digital media subject-specific content was not easy for most teachers to do until recently. Now you have many different tools and ways to create content in digital format. And, the best part is many of these tools are free!

You can create instructional content using Web and curriculum pages, blogs, wikis, podcasts, and video screencasts, to name just a few of the technologies that have emerged over the past few years. Most importantly is the fact that the instructional content is created by you for your students, rather than generic instructional content created by software companies. In other words, you now have the ability to tailor your educational content to meet the needs of your students in so many different ways.

Every classroom is different and in many cases, dramatically different. For example, a test or quiz review created in Camtasia by a 7th grade math teacher for her students in Miami or New York City studying estimation by using transportation costs in high population cities may not be as effective when used with 7th graders from a rural school district in the Midwest also studying estimation. The key point here is that each classroom teacher knows the needs of his or her students; now, each teacher has the resources to easily create digital media content that will work for his or her students. Using digital tools makes it easy to personalize instruction for your classroom, which makes learning more meaningful and applicable to the lives of your students.

Student-Assisted/Created Content

The second strategy for creating instructional digital media is to involve your students either partially or completely. When students are involved in the creation process, they buy into their own learning (Figure 3). You must be the guide, provide the learning objectives for the lesson, and assess the learners; but how you help your students master the content can be a plan you create with the students. Learning is a social process, and allowing students to have a voice in the process makes a tremendous difference. Research shows that when students are included in the design process, they are more engaged, involved, and take more responsibility for their learning. When students are actively engaged, they tend to retain the material longer, which improves academic achievement.

As noted above, your students may be more comfortable with the technology tools than you are. This is okay! You do not have to be the expert. Your expertise is in the planning and guidance of the learning. They can teach you the technology along the way.

Students are also incredibly creative. Allowing students to be involved in this process may give you additional ideas and methods for presenting content to future classes. Many great grant ideas are born out of student creativity and involvement. Once you tap into the creativity of your students, you will reach them and keep them connected and engaged.

You also can have your students create digital instructional content that other students can use for self study and practice. Creating instructional materials can empower as well as raise the self-esteem of your students. Involving your students in the creation of instructional material benefits everyone by giving students who create the instructional materials challenging projects on which to work and, at the same time, giving students who need a private tutor the extra help they need. In addition, it provides you the opportunity to assess how well the students developing the instructional materials really understand the learning objectives associated with the project.

Figure 3 When students are actively involved in the creation process, they buy into their own learning.

Often, students who are striving to learn or comprehend a concept get stuck. Hearing the same material presented in a digital manner by a fellow student can help them grasp the concept. And again, because the content is being presented in a manner they are more interested in and comfortable with, students respond better to it.

Let's Get Started and Have Some Fun

To summarize, all of these digital technology tools can greatly enhance your students' interest and motivation, which leads to increased academic achievement. Take time to learn how to make the tools work for you and to learn which one works best with each content area. Be sure to try something new and to involve your students in the process. You will be pleasantly surprised and pleased with the results.

Two final thoughts before we get started. First, most of the ideas covered in the following sections are adaptable for almost any grade level or subject area. Second, the concepts covered in one of the technology sections that follow are often applicable to another technology. For example, what you learn about creating screencasts using Camtasia is applicable to podcasts and blogs.

Web Info

To learn more about integrating technology, visit the Teachers Discovering Computers Web site (*scsite.com/tdc5*), click Chapter 7, click Web Info, and then click Integration Issues.

The following sections of this special feature contain integration ideas and resources for you to get a jump start on thinking about the multitude of ways to integrate Web pages, wikis, blogs, podcasts, and screencasts in your classroom curriculum and throughout your school. Figure 4 summarizes some important issues that you should consider when integrating these tools.

Integration Strategy: Creating and Integrating a Class Web Site!

Many teachers maintain class Web sites because they have found them to be valuable integration tools. Teachers use their class Web sites to post curriculum pages, assignments, information for

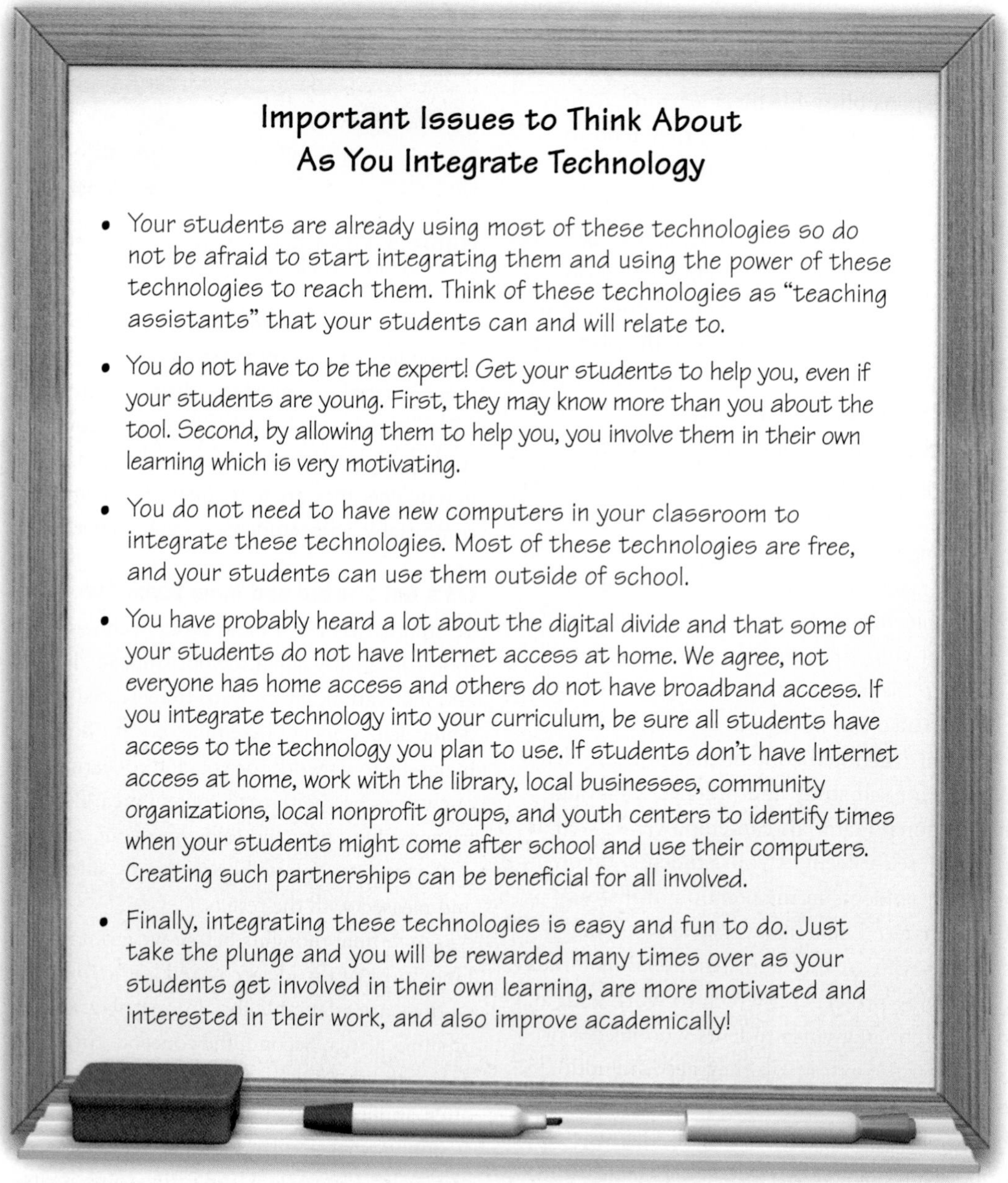

Important Issues to Think About As You Integrate Technology

- Your students are already using most of these technologies so do not be afraid to start integrating them and using the power of these technologies to reach them. Think of these technologies as "teaching assistants" that your students can and will relate to.

- You do not have to be the expert! Get your students to help you, even if your students are young. First, they may know more than you about the tool. Second, by allowing them to help you, you involve them in their own learning which is very motivating.

- You do not need to have new computers in your classroom to integrate these technologies. Most of these technologies are free, and your students can use them outside of school.

- You have probably heard a lot about the digital divide and that some of your students do not have Internet access at home. We agree, not everyone has home access and others do not have broadband access. If you integrate technology into your curriculum, be sure all students have access to the technology you plan to use. If students don't have Internet access at home, work with the library, local businesses, community organizations, local nonprofit groups, and youth centers to identify times when your students might come after school and use their computers. Creating such partnerships can be beneficial for all involved.

- Finally, integrating these technologies is easy and fun to do. Just take the plunge and you will be rewarded many times over as your students get involved in their own learning, are more motivated and interested in their work, and also improve academically!

Figure 7-4 Some important issues you should consider when first starting to integrate Web pages, blogs, wikis, and other similar technologies.

parents, and much, much more. Developing a class Web site with curriculum pages can be a very rewarding experience and one in which you can involve your students. Your class site can be tailored in a multitude of ways to meet your needs, students' needs, parents' needs, and school's needs. Figure 5 provides examples of how a class Web site can meet a variety of needs.

- Mrs. Gray's needs: Mrs. Gray can post classroom expectations (Classroom Goals/Behavior Plan link), homework assignments (Weekly Hometask link), student work (Student Essays link and Student Artwork link), and more.

- Student needs: Students can visit the class Web site for information about assignments (Weekly Hometask link) and for information they may have forgotten to bring home (Spelling Lists link), and more.

- Parent needs: Parents can visit the class Web site for information about what is happening in the classroom (Classroom Newsletter link), for information about additional help (Saxon Math Schedule link), and more.

- School needs: Mrs. Gray can provide links to important school- and district-related information (Important Current Information link), the ability to search for more school news, such as the school calendar (Search link), and more.

A class Web site benefits everyone who visits it. An important part of any class Web site is the curriculum Web page.

Curriculum Web Pages

As you have learned, a curriculum page is most effective when it is viewed in a Web browser. A curriculum page can be a stand alone Web page or it can be part of a class Web site. Curriculum pages should provide students with quality Internet resources that will enhance their learning of a particular concept. Instead of listing all information on one curriculum page, making it quite long and intimidating, many teachers elect to create separate curriculum pages and then link each one to their class home page. You link two pages together by creating a hyperlink between the two pages.

Figure 5 The possibilities are almost endless when you create your own classroom Web site.

Building Your Class Web Site

Now let's get down to the nuts and bolts of creating a curriculum page that is linked to Mr. Handley's Home Page. As you might recall, Mr. Handley's Home Page was discussed in the special feature following Chapter 3. Complete step-by-step directions for completing the home page are located at this textbook's Web site. If you have not already created the home page, you can download the instructions by visiting the Teacher's Discovering Computers Web site (*scsite.com/tdc5*), click Chapter 3, click Creating a Teacher's Web Page using Microsoft Word, and then follow the instructions to create the home page. Mr. Handley's Home Page will be used as the home page in this project.

In this project, you will use many features of Microsoft Word to create a curriculum page, called Mr. Handley's American History Class. The curriculum page provides students with assignment information and Web links for a five-day period. The curriculum page will be linked to Mr. Handley's Home Page (Figure 6).

The step-by-step instructions provide information on how to open a new Web page to create your curriculum page, select a background image, create a title, insert and format text and headings, insert a horizontal line graphic and other graphics, use tables to organize assignment information, create numerous links to teacher-selected and evaluated history Web sites, and save your curriculum page. The instructions also provide information on how to link Mr. Handley's Home Page to the curriculum page.

Complete step-by-step instructions for completing this Web site project (creating a curriculum page and linking it to a home page) are located at the textbook Web site. To download the instructions and create Mr. Handley's American History Class curriculum page, visit the Teachers Discovering Computers Web site (*scsite.com/tdc5*), click Chapter 7, and then click Creating a Curriculum Page using Microsoft Word.

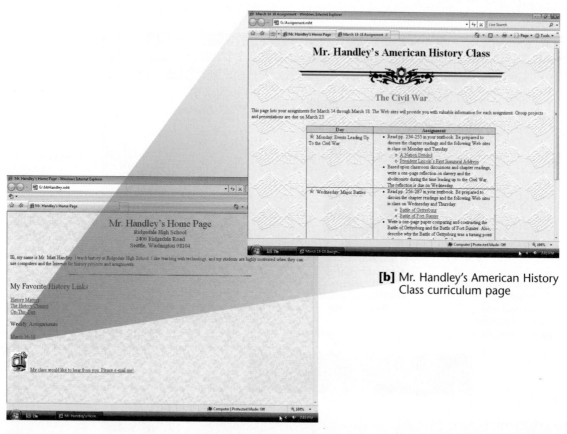

[b] Mr. Handley's American History Class curriculum page

[a] Mr. Handley's Home Page

Figure 6

A great place to get ideas for developing your own class Web page is from the class Web pages that are on the Web. Check your school district's Web site for links to other class Web pages at your school and search the Web to find class Web sites at other schools. Figure 7 lists a number of popular sites that you can use to find ideas and strategies for integrating curriculum pages.

Web Site Resources	URL
ThinkQuest	www.thinkquest.org
International Schools Cyberfair	www.globalschoolnet.org/gsh/cf/
AT&T Education	www.kn.pacbell.com/wired/wired.html
20 Sites to Help Jump Start Web Projects	www.eschoolnews.com/news/showStory.cfm?ArticleID=3647
Creating Web Pages in Class	www.k12academics.com/creating_web_pages_in_class.htm
Busy Teachers	www.ceismc.gatech.edu/busyt/tech_integ.shtml
K12 Station	www.k12station.com/k12link_library.html
KinderArt – K12	www.kinderart.com/teachers/webpage.shtml

To see an updated list with links to these and other Web site integration ideas, visit the Teachers Discovering Computers Web site (scsite.com/tdc5), click Chapter 7, and then click Chapter 7 Special Feature.

Figure 7 Sample Web sites you can explore to learn more about integrating Web and curriculum pages.

Integration Strategy: Teaching With Blogs!

As you have seen, blogging is popping up everywhere from business to medicine, for sharing important facts or just for fun. Increasingly, blogging is becoming popular in K-12 education as teachers are exploring ways to use and integrate blogs with their students. In the special feature that follows Chapter 3, you learned about creating blogs and the benefits of using blogs in education, and explored resources for creating classroom blogs. There are many ways to integrate blogs; let's explore a few ideas.

Blogging allows teachers and students to share and interact with others, and blogging allows students to enjoy seeing their work posted publically. Students today love social interactions with others. They are amazing at finding and creating social networking online. One of the ways that students interact socially is with blogs. You can integrate blogs into virtually any curriculum (Figure 8). The following sections will explore ideas, strategies, and lessons to integrate blogging.

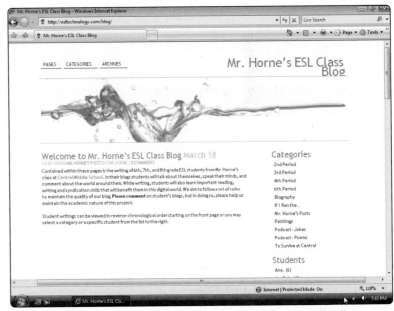

Figure 8 Blogs can be an effective integration tool in virtually all areas as shown in a middle school teacher's blog for his ESL students.

Web Info

For more information on how you can integrate blogs, visit the Teachers Discovering Computers Web site (*scsite.com/tdc5*), click Chapter 7, click Web Info, and then click Integrating Blogs.

Journaling

You can use blogs to have students create online journals. As educators, we are always looking for ways to improve students' reading and writing skills. Students are not always enthusiastic about writing assignments and often do not write unless they have an assignment that requires writing. Blogs are one way we can facilitate improving writing skills while helping students change how they feel about writing.

Students can journal on many topics. Many teachers are just beginning to realize how effective reflective journaling can be when it comes to motivating students to write. For example, after your students create individual or group projects, you can have them post their personal reflections by writing about their experiences while creating their project.

Class Blog

A class blog can be used for sharing important information, reminders, or student projects. A class blog can provide class information, assignments, and teacher-student and teacher-parent class and school information (Figure 9). Adding content to a class blog is easy—simply copy your content from any document, and then paste it into your blog.

Data Collection and Research

While working on group projects, keeping data in one location for examination by others is often difficult. One solution is to use blogs to have students report their data. Using a blog makes organization of data for teachers and students easier. Students can use blogs to organize science, math, and other data collections. Students can take photos of their data collection, such as representative samples of seashells collected at a local beach and create a table listing the types and number of shells collected. Students can use a blog to post their photos, tables, and reflective writings about their explorations and findings. For example, students and teachers can use blogs to document traditional and virtual field trips by posting field reports and other data, such as photos and drawings.

Students can use a blog to record their research, run experiments and then reflect on their findings, develop an inquiry discussion, and develop solutions. The blog becomes the students' digital record of the research process for inquiry, evaluation, observation, commentary, and review of their findings and the findings of others as well.

Student Projects

Blogs can be used with all kinds of student projects including having students create their own blog for a blog project. The project might involve students from various grade levels. For example, younger students might write a story or a poem and then older students can add the younger students' writings to the blog. Younger students brush up on their writing skills and older students learn the skills necessary to create and maintain a blog. All students who participate in the team project learn to work collaboratively.

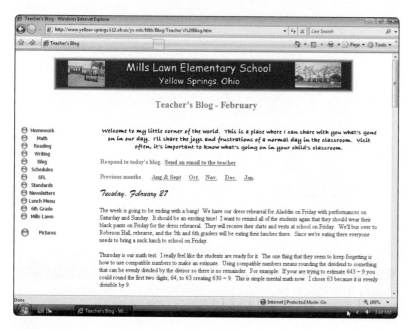

Figure 9 An elementary teacher's classroom blog.

Discussion and Collaboration Tool

Blogs are great tools for for discussions and collaborations. For example, students can review articles for discussion and create a digital discussion, similar to a book club but centered on the article selected for reading. Students can ask questions, discuss, and form opinions about various topics covered in the articles. Teachers can use the blog to set up ways for students to work alone or in groups to discuss research articles, subject-specific content, and more. A great resource is using primary sources mixed in with other classroom sources for information. The blog can extend the shared learning experience beyond the classroom environment, allowing students to work collaboratively anytime and anyplace.

Feedback and Assessment

Blogs are one way to provide feedback and assessment from peers, teachers, and others outside the classroom who should observe, comment, and mediate as needed on student work. Students can self-evaluate by reflecting on the process at the end of the assignment or project.

Presentations

Another use for blogs is to have students post presentations. For example, you can have students create a portion of a presentation, post their sections, share online, and give feedback, etc. Later they can compile the various sections into a PowerPoint presentation or another type of presentation while working collaboratively online.

Community-Based Blog

We live in a global society, and as such, students need to be aware of the world around them. Why not have your students create community-based blogs? Students need to connect beyond the walls of their classroom. You can use a blog to create ways to connect your class to their community or other communities around the world with an informational project blog. Projects have been started where students blog with seniors and community leaders. They use the blogs to communicate about issues that are important to the local government and community agencies, such things as cleaning up the community or communicating with and assisting senior citizens. Global projects, such as Save the Turtles, that your students can become involved in are readily available.

The above examples are just a few of the many ways you can integrate blogs into your curriculum. The easiest way to find ideas is to explore the ways other teachers are integrating blogs. Figure 10 lists a number of sites you can use to find additional ideas and strategies for integrating blogs. You also can use Google or another search engine to find additional examples of teachers' blogs by searching for "K-12 class blog" or "K-12 teacher blog."

Blog Resources	URL
Elementary Blog Spot	www.elementary-school.blogspot.com
Blogging? It's Elementary My Dear Watson!	www.educationworld.com/a_tech/tech/tech217.shtml
Curious Cat	engineering.curiouscatblog.net/
Blogmeister	www.classblogmeister.com
Journalism Classroom Blog	www.central.hcrhs.k12.nj.us/mcjournalism/
Anne's Write Weblog	www.itc.blogs.com/thewriteweblog/
ESOL Students Blog	esltechnology.com/blog/
Blogtopia: Blogging about Your Own Utopia	www.readwritethink.org/lessons/lesson_view.asp?id=942

To see an updated list with links to these and other blog site integration ideas, visit the Teachers Discovering Computers Web site (scsite.com/tdc5), click Chapter 7, and then click Chapter 7 Special Feature.

Figure 10 Sample Web sites you can explore to learn more about integrating blogs.

Integration Strategy: Teaching with Wikis!

Every time you look something up on the Internet most likely the first few results in your search will be from Wikipedia, one of the most popular wikis on the Web. Most of us go there to check definitions, to look for terms and information, and to find answers to questions quickly — even though we know that anyone can add, delete, and modify content in a wiki. We go there, and use the information as a springboard for additional searches. So why have wikis become so popular? Or, more importantly, why should teachers integrate wikis? As you read through the following sections, keep asking yourself these questions and determine if you can find ways to integrate wikis into your curriculum and into your student projects.

You can integrate wikis in virtually any curriculum (Figure 11). The following sections explore ideas, strategies, and lessons to integrate wikis.

Collaboration and Brainstorming

You can use wikis to build collaboration skills and to encourage brainstorming. Team work is an essential skill for your students to learn. It is a skill they will use not only now but also in their future employment in a global economy and in life. Managing your students to work together on group projects and to collaborate at the same time can be challenging. Students need to have interaction and communication between each other, and part of collaborating is learning how to negotiate decisions.

In addition to collaboration skills, students can use wikis to brainstorm. As we know, students need time to come up with creative solutions to problems and assignments. Wikis can provide an electronic working space for thought processing. A wiki can be a place where students bounce ideas off one another, helping them solidify their own thoughts in the process.

Portfolios and Authentic Assessment

A wiki is an easy way to create a Web site where students can showcase their work. Students can create electronic portfolios or e-folios to post on a wiki. Wikis create an avenue for maintaining a digital format of students' work, which can be used to track learning progress throughout the year for evaluation and assessment. In addition, students can view, assess, and collaboratively discuss each other's work and find ways to self improve.

As you learned in Chapter 7, e-folios are a great way to store students' projects and assignments. Teachers can use e-folios to assess long term achievement and follow student gains, as well as to show a variety of authentic project-based assessment techniques to students, parents, and other teachers.

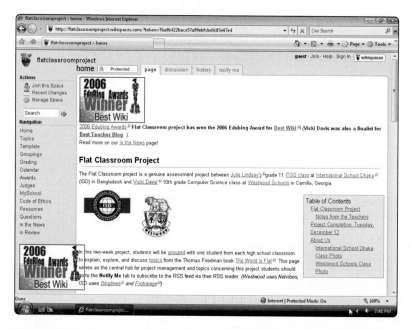

Figure 11 A great example of a teacher's Wiki, called the Flat Classroom Project, was created by a high school teacher from Georgia.

Projects

Students can post their projects to wikis. There is no subject area that wikis cannot be integrated into. A wiki can be used to record and organize data, storyboard and plan, and ultimately create projects and other classroom activities. The wiki is where students contribute ideas on the topic, build the project, and collaborate on the project (Figure 12). You become the facilitator by offering suggestions and asking probing questions to make students inquire deeper into the concepts, by keeping them on task, and by teaching them to construct their own learning through problem solving and discovery. An example is to have students create a wiki for social studies where each group analyzes the different tactics used by opposing generals during the Civil War. Another example is to create a science project where each student does research and analyzes different parts of the human body.

Literature Discussion

Use a wiki for literature discussion. For example, you can have your students read the same book and instead of writing a review or critique of the book on paper, you can have each student post his/her reflections and discussion of the book in the wiki. Students can use graphics and drawings to express the storyline, point of view, plot, and characters. In this way, the wiki becomes a round-table for peer editing and feedback, which can be used to assist students in improving their writing skills.

Journalism and Collaborative Writing

Wikis are great tools for journalism and collaborative writing. Several online newspapers started wikis to let their customers review and critique articles and current events. Why not let students do the same by starting a classroom newspaper wiki that they can use to critique newspaper stories and discuss current events? Then, let the students create their own stories with each student adding, editing, and writing parts of the story.

Published research shows that fictional books based on non-fictional events intrigue students on the topics presented in the book, which helps create opportunity to teach information

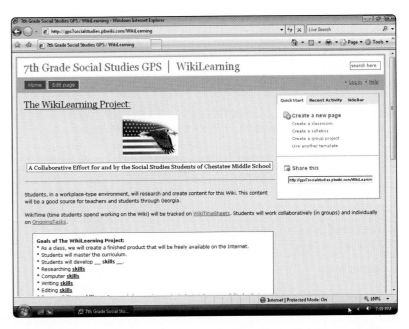

Figure 12 Student wikis are great classroom projects as shown in this social studies wiki created by 7th grade students.

about the non-fictional events and reading literacy. Students can work like an editorial board and hash out opinions, work on conflicting stories, draw conclusions about stories, decide what is important in our daily news, determine what should be introduced as a lead story, and then post all of this as a wiki.

Technology Skills

Many times we are busy focusing on the curriculum and subject-specific content, but we must not forget that students need to develop technology skills in all areas. We all know they are tech-savvy, but learning how to use the technology responsibly, as well as better ways to use the various technology tools to be productive, is important. As students work with wikis, they will hone their technology skills, for example, their search techniques and their typing skills. Integrating a wiki into your curriculum is a perfect way to incorporate technology skills into subject-specific curriculum.

The previous examples are just a few of the many ways you can integrate wikis. The easiest way to find more ideas is to explore the ways other teachers are integrating wikis. Figure 13 (on the next page) lists a number of sites that you can use to find additional ideas and strategies for integrating wikis.

Web Info

For more information on how you can integrate wikis, visit the Teachers Discovering Computers Web site (*scsite.com/tdc5*), click Chapter 7, click Web Info, and then click Integrating Wikis.

Wikis Resources	URL
Wikiteach — A Wiki Library of Lesson Plans	www.wikiteach.org
Lesson Plan 101	lessonplan101.com/index.php/Main_Page
Using Wikis Ethically Lesson	www.atozteacherstuff.com/pages/5829.shtml
The Teacher's Lounge Wiki	www.teacherslounge.editme.com
Wikis in Education	www.wikiteach.org/index.php/wikiteach/action/lessonplan/iVar/189
Wiki Lesson: A Collaboration of Sights and Sounds	www.readwritethink.org/lessons/lesson_view.asp?id=979
Sample Wikis	www.wikiplanbook.com/index.php?title=Main_Page
Flat Classroom Project	flatclassroomproject.wikispaces.com/
Wiki Comparison Site	www.wikimatrix.org/
Studying Social Studies	studyingsocietiesatjhk.pbwiki.com/

To see an updated list with links to these and other wiki site integration ideas, visit the Teachers Discovering Computers Web site (scsite.com/tdc5), click Chapter 7, and then click Chapter 7 Special Feature.

Figure 13 Sample Web sites you can explore to learn more about integrating wikis.

Integration Strategy: Teaching with Podcasts!

As you learned in the special feature that follows Chapter 3, podcasts are derived from Apple's portable music player, the iPod. Apple introduced the iPod in 2001 and to date over 100 million iPods have been sold worldwide. Many of your students probably already own an iPod or similar portable media device, which means your students do not need to have a computer at home to listen to podcasts. Instead, they can listen to podcasts or watch vodcasts anytime and anyplace using their digital media player.

While iPods are clearly the most popular portable media players, there are many other similar devices including Microsoft's Zune, which was introduced in late 2006. In addition, most smart phones available today include many of the features available on iPods and other portable media players. Plus, more and more of these devices allow users to see high quality video. In the not too distant future, most of these devices will contain video capabilities. The use and integration of these devices is exploding in education and new integrations ideas are constantly being posted on the Web (Figure 14).

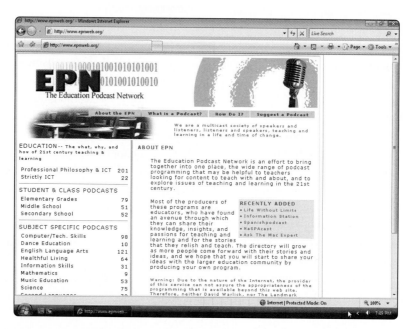

Figure 14 The Education Podcast Network is a great first place to visit to gather ideas on how to integrate podcasts.

As shown in Figure 15, portable music players, including iPods, are clearly more than just music players. In fact, they can be integrated into the curriculum in a multitude of ways, with all grade levels, and in all content areas. The following sections provide a few ideas for integrating podcasts with your students.

One-to-One Computing

Use podcasts as a way to promote one-to-one computing, which is the concept of one computer for each student. One-to-one computing is an important goal for many school districts, but is it a realistic goal for all schools due to budget and other concerns? While digital media players cannot replace computers, they can provide a means for delivering technology to more students. For example, podcasting can be an amazing audio and video tool that provides the delivery of educational content in a form that is portable and at the students' finger tips. And, since many students already have an iPod or similar type of portable media player or a cell phone that is capable of downloading and playing podcasts, this technology is readily accessible to them. Listening to content over and over can increase retention of the topic. Podcasts of classroom lectures also can help students who miss class.

Interviewing

Interviewing skills are important for students to learn, and podcasts can be used to share interviews. One technique is to either start or end projects with an interview. Students gain communication skills and techniques in learning to connect with others. For example, as part of your science curriculum when studying weather, have students interview local community leaders such as local meteorologists, and then organize the interviews together into a podcast. Another idea is to have student teams interview individuals in the community of the professions they are interested in and let each team create a group of podcasts to share their findings. They might be surprised what they learn about the community and local occupations.

Storytelling

Storytelling is the one of oldest forms of sharing, telling, and learning, and podcasts are a great way to share storytelling. Having students create and learn to tell stories not only increases motivation but also helps students retain content. One of the many things that brain research is revealing is that our brains are wired to organize, retain, and access information through storytelling. This suggests that if we teach curriculum concepts with storytelling that students will be

Web Info

To learn more about integrating podcasts with your students, visit the Teachers Discovering Computers Web site (*scsite.com/tdc5*), click Chapter 7, click Web Info, and then click Integrating Podcasts.

Figure 15 Look for resources, such as LearningInHand, to help you find ways to integrate podcasts into your curriculum.

able to retain information better, apply that information with less difficulty, and be able to transfer information to other situations.

Creating podcasts is a natural for storytelling. Here are some ways to get started with storytelling. Let students create stories by taking on a character in a story or let them create their own story. Create an on-going classroom round robin story, as each student takes a turn creating a piece of the story and adds to the story. Cut unusual photos out of the newspaper or download them from the Web and let students, who have no knowledge about the photo, tell a story about the photo. Then, share the real story about the photos. Help students turn each of these stories, no matter how they are created, into their podcast story.

Assessment

Assessment is an important concept in K-12 education, and there are a number of ways to assess students including quizzes and tests. Podcasts can be used to help your students prepare for both teachers' quizzes/tests and standardized tests. Students have always used various techniques to prepare for quizzes and tests, for example flash or flip cards. Why not introduce

digital flash card podcasts as a way for students to prepare? You also can use podcasts to create practice quizzes that students can use individually or with other students. You can even download free quiz software that you can use to create podcast quizzes (Figure 16).

Informing Parents

Use podcasts to keep parents informed. It is important to communicate classroom and school information to parents. You can use your podcast to introduce yourself at the beginning of a school year or the start of a new term, to remind parents of students' due dates for major assignments and projects, to make announcements, and to keep everyone up-to-date on the latest classroom news. Students also love to hear their own voice, and they can assist you by creating the audio and video files for the podcast. Make podcasts available on your class Web page so busy parents can download and listen to them at their convenience.

The above examples are just a few of the many ways you can integrate podcasts. Figure 17 lists a number of sites that you can use to find additional ideas and strategies for integrating podcasts.

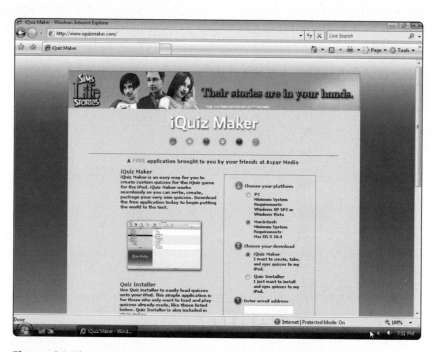

Figure 16 There are many ways to add quiz and test reviews for students to your podcasts, this site provides a free quiz development tool.

Podcasting Resources	URL
Education Podcast Network	www.epnweb.org
Exchange ideas, lesson plans, and podcasts	www.shambles.net/pages/learning/infolit/edupodcast
A Podcasting Lesson from PBS	www.pbs.org/newshour/extra/teachers/lessonplans/media/podcasting.html
Using Podcasts with ESOL Students	www.esl.about.com/od/englishlistening/a/intro_podcasts.htm
Video Podcasts – Lesson for High School Students	www.microbeworld.org/look/VideoPodcast-LessonPlans.aspx
Radio WillowWeb	www.mpsomaha.org/willow/radio
Coulee Kids	www.sdlax.net/longfellow/sc/ck/index.htm
ColeyCast	www.murrieta.k12.ca.us/tovashal/bcoley/coleycast/index.htm
Goochland County Public Schools	www.glnd.k12.va.us/podcasts/
MeFeedia K-12 Podcasts	www.mefeedia.com/tags/k12/
Podcasting with Handhelds	www.k12handhelds.com/podcasting.php
Gadsden City Schools Podcast	www1.gcs.k12.al.us/~podcast/
Podcasting ideas from Apple	www.apple.com/education/products/ipod/podcasting.html
To see an updated list with links to these and other podcast integration ideas, visit the Teachers Discovering Computers Web site (scsite.com/tdc5), click Chapter 7, and then click Chapter 7 Special Feature.	

Figure 17 Sample Web sites you can explore to learn more about integrating podcasts.

Integration Strategy — Teaching with Screencasts!

In the special feature that follows Chapter 3, you learned about using Camtasia Studio to create video screencasts. As you learned, Camtasia is an easy to use program which lets you create screencasts that can be integrated into any subject area and at any age level. Screencasts are a great way to start reaching your students through the power of digital media. Before we dive into some integration ideas, let's first discuss why screencasts may be the instructional solution you have been searching for.

Why Integrate Video Screencasts

Researchers have been reporting ways to integrate video in education for many years; however, only recently have researchers started reporting on the positive impact of integrating video screencasts with today's digital students.

We know that students learn in many different ways. You have studied and explored different theories and types of learning styles to help you better understand how students learn. Some researchers categorize students as audio, visual, and kinesthetic learners. Auditory learners prefer to learn by hearing, like a teacher's spoken words or listening to an audio book or CD. Visual learners tend to learn best when they see pictures, movies, animations, and graphics. Finally, kinesthetic learners like to do things, like projects or activities. Video screencasts created in Camtasia Studio can meet the needs of all of these types of learners. As you continue to think about integrating screencasts into your curriculum, keep these three learning styles in mind and you will discover that your screencasts and your students' screencasts can meet your students' wide range of learning styles.

Web Info

To learn more about integrating Camtasia-created screencasts, visit the Teachers Discovering Computers Web site (scsite.com/tdc5), click Chapter 7, click Web Info, and then click Integrating Camtasia.

Educators also know that, due to different learning styles, diversity, and learning abilities, some students understand a concept as soon as it is introduced by a teacher, some students need extra explanation to understand a concept, and some students need extensive review and explanation to understand the concept being presented. A major issue for educators is to find the time to meet the educational needs of all their students. By creating screencasts and making them available in multiple formats, such as Internet streaming, downloadable to portable media players, on CDs and DVDs, and other formats, students can review the concepts as many times as needed — anytime, any path, and anyplace. By viewing the screencasts that you create, your students can hear and see you and your explanations until they grasp the concept(s). In other words, teacher- and student created screencasts using Camtasia might just be the solution you have been searching for, a solution that meets the learning needs of your students and minimizes your instructional limitations due to time constraints and class size.

Camtasia has the power to transition your classroom from a place where students "may not want to be" to a classroom where students "want to be." The variety of screencasts you can create is virtually boundless and limited only by you and your student's imagination and creativity. Figure 18 lists a few of the many reasons why you should consider integrating screencasts that you and your students create.

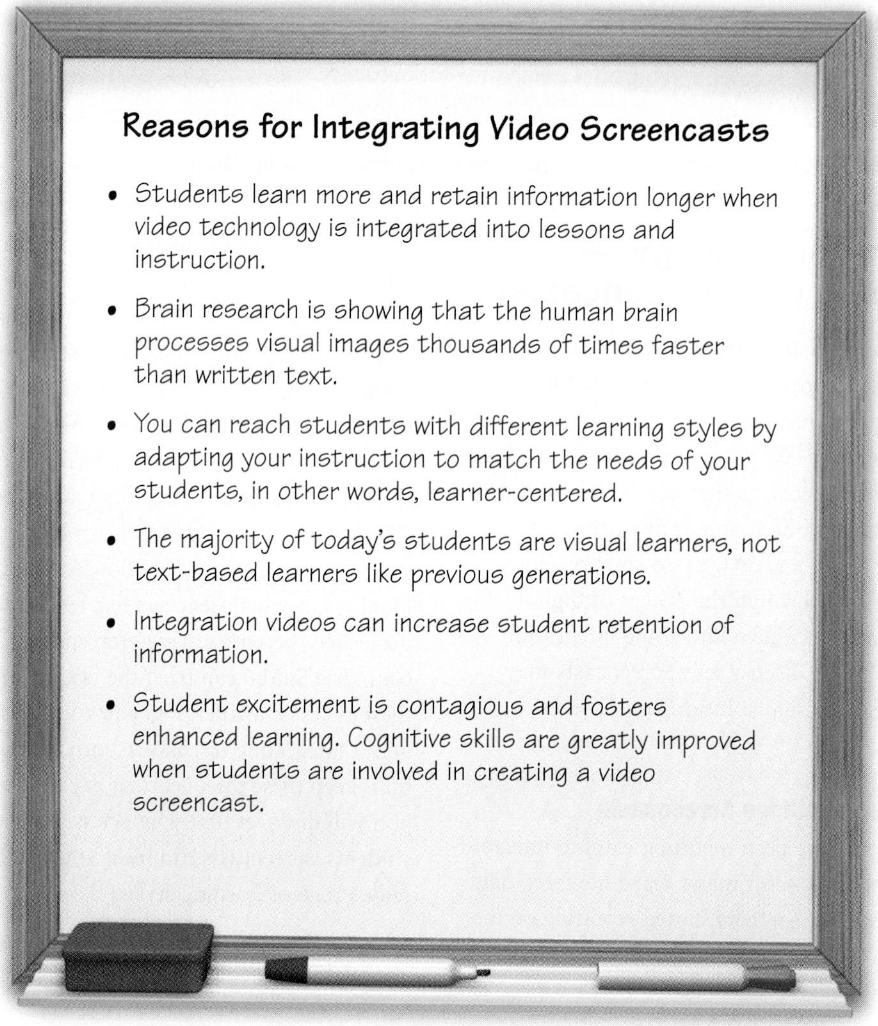

Reasons for Integrating Video Screencasts

- Students learn more and retain information longer when video technology is integrated into lessons and instruction.

- Brain research is showing that the human brain processes visual images thousands of times faster than written text.

- You can reach students with different learning styles by adapting your instruction to match the needs of your students, in other words, learner-centered.

- The majority of today's students are visual learners, not text-based learners like previous generations.

- Integration videos can increase student retention of information.

- Student excitement is contagious and fosters enhanced learning. Cognitive skills are greatly improved when students are involved in creating a video screencast.

Figure 18 Just a few of the many reasons why teachers should integrate video screencasts in their classroom curriculum.

Mathcasts and More

Mathcasts are defined by Tim Fahlberg as "screencasts for mathematics — that is, screen movies of writing with voice and/or captions that focus on mathematics." Figure 19 shows an example of a mathcast created by a teacher using Camtasia Studio. First, students see a PowerPoint slide with basic information about a math concept, in this example, positive and negative numbers. Then, as the teacher lectures, handwritten notes appear on the slide to underscore the point being made in the discussion.

Camtasia-created screencasts can be used with students from pre-K to seniors. If you are teaching history, you can use Camtasia to create screencasts focused on specific lesson topics, such as the Gettysburg Address or the signing of the Declaration of Independence, and call them historycasts; if you are teaching science, you can use Camtasia to create screencasts that present specific topic concepts, such as lab safety or cell division, and call them sciencecasts; if you are teaching vocabulary, you can use Camtasia to create screencasts that introduce new words — including how to pronounce the words, how to spell the words, how to use the word — and call them vocabularycasts; if you are reviewing grammar, you can use Camtasia to create screencasts that reinforce grammar rules and call them grammarcasts, and so on.

The use and integration of screencasts is just beginning to impact the way teachers teach and students learn. Camtasia can be used by you to create teacher-centered screencasts or by your students to create student-centered screencasts. Figure 20 lists a number of Web sites that you can use to find additional ideas and strategies for integrating screencasts.

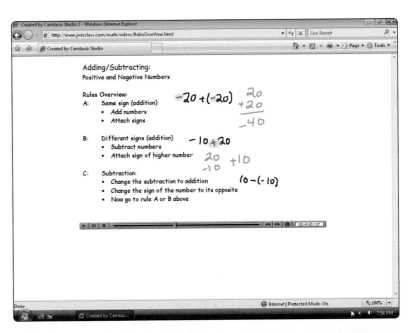

Figure 19 An example of a mathcast created by teacher and available for her students to view anytime and anyplace and as many times as needed.

Screencasts Resources	URL
Example of Camtasia in Action	www.projectstreamer.com/users/campbell79/acct_eq2/acct_eq2.html
Parent Screencast	www.dekalb.k12.ga.us/parent.portal/flash/login.html
Rockford Public Schools	techsmith.com/community/education/interview/tmcfadden.asp
Camtasia Case Studies	www.techsmith.com/community/education/k12casestudies.asp
Camtasia Can Enhance Math Centers	www.mathtv.org/currentepisode.html
Camtasia Newsletter	techsmith.com/community/subscription.asp
Best Practice — Students Win with Camtasia	techsmith.com/camtasia/interview/henriegrover.asp
Sample Camtasia — Math	www1.gcs.k12.al.us/~podcast/media/3rdgrade_math.html
What are Mathcasts	math247.jot.com/WikiHome/What%20are%20Mathcasts
To see an updated list with links to these and other screencast integration ideas, visit the Teachers Discovering Computers Web site (scsite.com/tdc5), click Chapter 7, and then click Chapter 7 Special Feature.	

Figure 20 Sample Web sites you can explore to learn more about integrating screencasts.

Summary and Implications for Education

In this special feature, we introduced integration ideas for Web pages and a number of emerging digital tools, such as blogs, wikis, podcasts, and screencasts. All of these digital tools and integration techniques allow for the student to transition from passive learning to active, exploratory, and inquiry-based learning. Integrating these tools into your curriculum can help your students become more excited about learning, assist in reaching more students by involving a variety of learning styles, and allow students to construct their own learning.

The key is to explore these tools and use the ones that work for you and for your students. You do not need to be an expert in each of the tools because you can use the expertise of your students to help you learn as they themselves learn. Many of these digital tools are already used as entertainment by your students. Why not bring these digital tools into your curriculum so you can work within the digital-rich environment these students already operate in and are already comfortable with? As we stated earlier, integrating these tools can help you transition your classroom to a more active learning environment and, therefore, create a place where students will want to be!

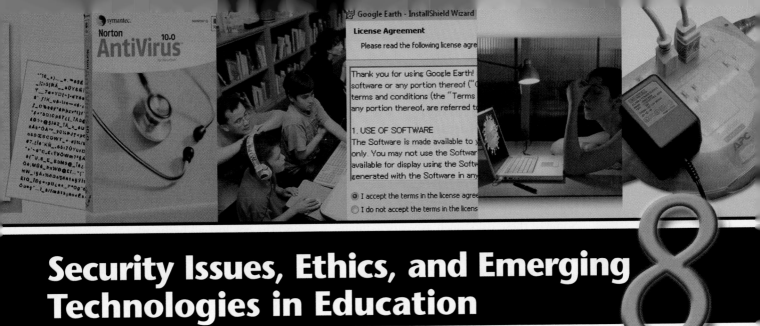

Security Issues, Ethics, and Emerging Technologies in Education

8

Objectives

After completing this chapter, you will be able to do the following:
[ISTE NETS-T Standards I A-B, II A-E, V A-D, VI A-E]

- Identify security risks that threaten home and school computers

- Describe how computer viruses and malicious software programs work and the steps you can take to prevent viruses

- Describe different ways schools safeguard computers and networks

- Explain why computer backup is important and how it is accomplished

- Define what is meant by information privacy and its impact on schools

- Identify the components of copyright that impact education

- Describe the ethical issues related to Internet usage and steps schools are taking to address them

- Identify safe and healthy uses of technology resources

- Describe the emerging technologies that will transform traditional classrooms

Every day, businesses, schools, and individuals depend on computers to perform a variety of significant tasks, such as tracking sales, recording student grades, creating reports, searching the Web, and sending e-mail. People increasingly rely on computers to create, store, and manage critical information, so it is important to ensure that computers and software are protected from loss, damage, and misuse. School districts, for example, must take precautions to guarantee that student information, such as grades, attendance rates, personal and family data, and learning problems, is protected from loss and kept confidential.

This chapter identifies some potential risks to computers and software, and describes a number of safeguards that schools, businesses, and individuals can implement to minimize these risks. The chapter also discusses information privacy, including the current laws that keep certain data confidential. The chapter then reviews concerns about the ethical use of computers and which activities are right, wrong, or even criminal. Next, the chapter covers security, privacy, and the ethical issues that relate to how teachers and students use the information they find on the Internet. Finally, the chapter concludes with a discussion about health issues and emerging technologies in education.

Web Info

For more information about computer viruses, visit the Teachers Discovering Computers Web site (*scsite.com/tdc5*), click Chapter 8, click Web Info, and then click Viruses.

Computer Security: Risks and Safeguards

Any event or action that has the potential of causing a loss of computer equipment, software, data and information, or processing capability is a **computer security risk**. Some of these risks, such as viruses, unauthorized access and use, and information theft, are a result of deliberate acts that are against the law. Any illegal act involving a computer generally is referred to as a **computer crime**. The following sections describe some of the more common computer security risks and the measures that you and your school can take to minimize or prevent their consequences.

COMPUTER VIRUSES

At 4:30 in the afternoon, Mrs. Vicki Reamy of Ridgedale High School is in her classroom making last-minute adjustments to the Excel spreadsheet she plans to use in tomorrow's third-period Business Education class. As she opens the spreadsheet file to make one last change, the top of the spreadsheet displays the message, "Something wonderful has happened, your PC is alive." Dismayed, she realizes that a computer virus has corrupted her spreadsheet and she has lost all her work.

A **virus** is a potentially damaging computer program designed to affect your computer negatively without your knowledge or permission by altering the way it works. More specifically, a virus is a segment of program code that implants itself in a computer file and spreads systematically from one file to another. Figure 8-1 answers frequently asked questions about computer viruses.

Computer viruses, however, do not generate by chance. Creators of virus programs write them for a specific purpose — usually either to spread from one file to

Figure 8-1 A virus spreads from one computer to another as illustrated in this figure.

A COMPUTER VIRUS: WHAT IT IS AND HOW IT SPREADS

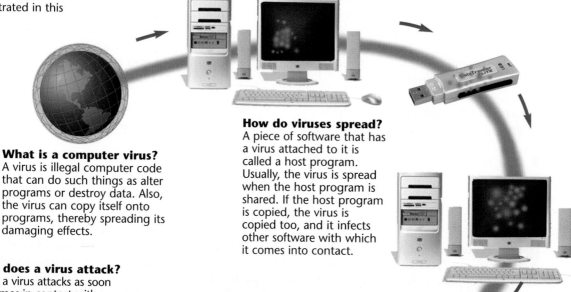

What is a computer virus?
A virus is illegal computer code that can do such things as alter programs or destroy data. Also, the virus can copy itself onto programs, thereby spreading its damaging effects.

How do viruses spread?
A piece of software that has a virus attached to it is called a host program. Usually, the virus is spread when the host program is shared. If the host program is copied, the virus is copied too, and it infects other software with which it comes into contact.

When does a virus attack?
Usually a virus attacks as soon as it comes in contact with other software or storage devices. Sometimes, a virus attacks at the time or date specified by the person who wrote the virus code. When the predetermined time or date registers on the computer's internal clock, the virus attacks. Sometimes, the virus code will display a message letting you know that the virus has done its damage.

Why are viruses not detected immediately?
People who copy and keep the host software are unaware that the virus exists because the virus is designed to hide from computer users for weeks or even months. Antivirus software can often, but not always, identify and quarantine viruses.

another, to trigger a symptom, or to cause damage. Many viruses, for example, are designed to destroy or corrupt data stored on the infected computer. The symptom or damage caused by a virus, called the **virus payload**, can be harmless or it can cause significant damage, as planned by the creator. Figure 8-2 outlines some common symptoms of virus infections.

Unfortunately, Vicki Reamy's experience is not unusual. Although viruses are a serious problem for both PC and Macintosh computer users, the majority of virus programs are intended to infect PCs. Currently, more than 180,000 known viruses or variants exist, and hundreds of new viruses or variants are identified every month. The increased use of networks and the Internet makes the spread of viruses easier than ever. Viruses commonly infect computers through e-mail attachments. Figure 8-3 on the next page shows how a virus can spread from one computer to another through an infected e-mail attachment. Before you open or execute any e-mail attachment, you should ensure that the e-mail message is from a trusted source and you should scan the attachment using antivirus software.

Although numerous variations are known, three main types of viruses exist: boot sector viruses, file viruses, and macro viruses. A **boot sector virus** replaces the boot program used to start the computer with a modified, infected version of the boot program. When the computer runs the infected boot program, it loads the virus into the computer's memory. Once a virus is in memory, it spreads to any storage media inserted into the computer. A **file virus** inserts virus code into program files; the virus then spreads to any program that accesses the infected file. A **macro virus** uses the macro language of an application, such as word processing or spreadsheet, to hide virus codes. When you open a document with an infected macro, the macro virus loads into memory. Certain actions, such as saving the document, activate the virus. Macro viruses often are part of templates, which means they will infect any document created using one of the templates.

Two common variations of computer viruses, also known as **malicious software programs**, are worms and Trojan horses. A **worm** is a program that copies itself repeatedly in a computer's memory or on a network, using up resources and possibly shutting down the computer or network. Creators of worms often play on user psychology to entice people to download and run them. As a result, a number of well-known worms have hijacked e-mail systems and sent copies of themselves around the world in a matter of hours. The notorious Melissa worm quickly spread around the world causing serious harm to millions of computers. A **Trojan horse** (named after the Greek myth) is a malicious software program that hides within or is designed to look like a legitimate program.

Some viruses are relatively harmless pranks that temporarily freeze a computer or cause it to display sounds or messages.

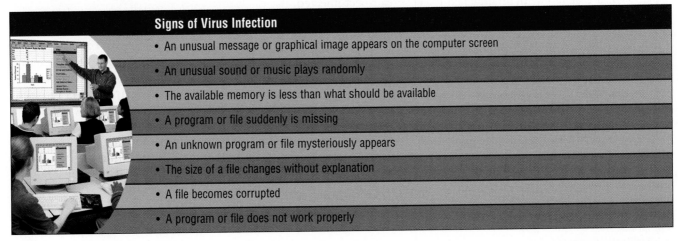

Signs of Virus Infection

- An unusual message or graphical image appears on the computer screen
- An unusual sound or music plays randomly
- The available memory is less than what should be available
- A program or file suddenly is missing
- An unknown program or file mysteriously appears
- The size of a file changes without explanation
- A file becomes corrupted
- A program or file does not work properly

Figure 8-2 Viruses attack computers in a variety of ways. Listed here are some of the more common signs of virus infections.

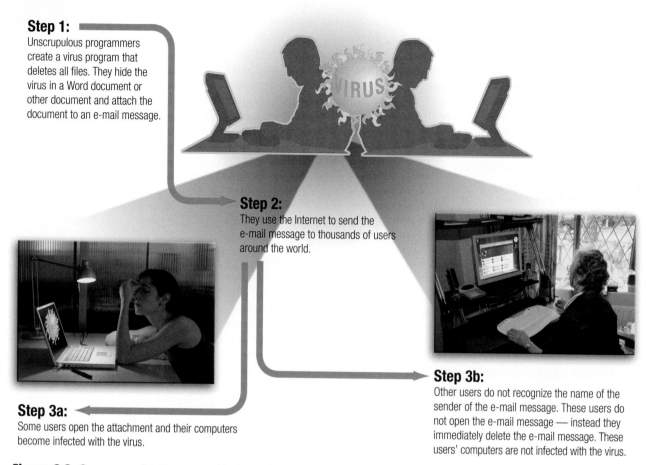

Step 1:
Unscrupulous programmers create a virus program that deletes all files. They hide the virus in a Word document or other document and attach the document to an e-mail message.

Step 2:
They use the Internet to send the e-mail message to thousands of users around the world.

Step 3a:
Some users open the attachment and their computers become infected with the virus.

Step 3b:
Other users do not recognize the name of the sender of the e-mail message. These users do not open the e-mail message — instead they immediately delete the e-mail message. These users' computers are not infected with the virus.

Figure 8-3 One way a virus can spread is through an e-mail attachment.

For example, when the Music Bug virus is triggered, the computer plays a few chords of music. Other viruses cause extensive damage to computer files and spread quickly throughout a network. For example, if a state administrator sends an e-mail message with an attached Excel spreadsheet infected with a macro virus to every school district in the state, the virus could quickly infect hundreds of computers.

Some viruses are considered logic bombs or time bombs. A **logic bomb** is a program that activates when it detects a certain condition. One disgruntled worker, for example, planted a logic bomb that began destroying files when his name was added to a list of terminated employees. A **time bomb** is a type of logic bomb that activates on a particular date. A well-known time bomb is the **Michelangelo virus**, which destroys data on your hard disk on March 6, the date of

Michelangelo's birthday. The World Wide Web is a great source for finding information about viruses and malicious software programs.

VIRUS DETECTION AND REMOVAL

Completely effective ways to keep a computer or network safe from computer viruses simply do not exist. You can, however, take precautions to protect your home and classroom computers from virus infections. Viruses normally are spread between computers by inserting an infected storage media (such as a CD or USB flash drive) in a computer or downloading an infected file from the Internet or via an e-mail attachment. Figure 8-4 lists a number of safe computing tips that can help you minimize the risk of viruses.

Safe Computing Tips

- **Purchase and install reliable antivirus software.** Most programs offer free virus definition updates. Update antivirus software virus definitions every week. The cost of antivirus software is much less than the cost of rebuilding damaged files.

- **Scan all removable media.** USB flash drives and other removable storage devices are common culprits for carrying viruses from one computer to another and spreading viruses throughout networks. If someone hands you a removable storage device that has been used in another system — scan it.

- **Scan all files downloaded from the Internet.** The number-one source for viruses is downloaded files. To be safe, download all files into a special folder on your hard drive and scan them for viruses immediately after downloading.

- **Scan all attached files before opening them.** It is possible to transfer a virus to your system by opening an attachment.

- **Turn off e-mail preview.** Although it is not likely that you will get a virus from reading your e-mail, many e-mail programs allow users to preview an e-mail message before or without opening it. Some sophisticated viruses and worms can deliver their payload when a user simply previews the message. Thus, users should turn off message preview in their e-mail programs.

- **Scan all software before using even if it is shrink-wrapped.** Viruses have been found in manufacturer-supplied software. Scan before installing software.

- **Avoid pirated, illegal copies of copyrighted software.** Not only is using them illegal, but they are a favorite source of viruses.

- **Never start your computer with removable media in the drives,** unless the media is uninfected.

- **Install a personal firewall program to help protect against unwanted incoming attacks.** As a minimum, make sure that your operating system's firewall is activated.

- **Back up your files often.** Even with the best antivirus software, realize that your computer's files can be infected. Be prepared to deal with the problem.

- **Set your antivirus program to scan automatically.** Most antivirus programs can be set up to scan the system automatically when booted and check it whenever removable media devices are accessed or files are opened.

Figure 8-4 Teachers can follow these simple steps to practice safe computing and minimize the risk of viruses.

Integration Strategies

To learn more about teaching your students safe computing, visit the Teachers Discovering Computers Web site (*scsite.com/tdc5*), click Chapter 8, and then click Teaching Today.

Integration Strategies

To learn more about teaching your students about viruses, visit the Teachers Discovering Computers Web site (*scsite.com/tdc5*), click Chapter 8, and then click Education Issues.

Web Info

For details about antivirus programs, visit the Teachers Discovering Computers Web site (*scsite.com/tdc5*), click Chapter 8, click Web Info, and then click Vaccines.

Using an antivirus program is one of the more effective ways to protect against computer viruses. An **antivirus program** is designed to detect, disinfect, and protect computers and networks from viruses. Antivirus programs, also called **vaccines**, work by looking for programs that attempt to modify the boot program, the operating system, or other programs that normally are read from but not written to (Figure 8-5).

In addition to providing protection from viruses, most antivirus programs also have utilities to remove or repair infected programs and files. If the virus has infected the boot program, however, the antivirus program may require you to restart the computer with a rescue disc. A **rescue disc** is normally a CD-ROM that contains an uninfected copy of key operating system commands and start-up information that enables the computer to restart correctly. After you have restarted the computer using a rescue disc, you can run repair and removal programs to repair damaged files and remove infected files. If the program cannot repair the damaged files, you might have to replace or restore them with uninfected backup copies of the files. Later sections in the chapter explain backup and restore procedures.

To help protect against viruses, most schools install antivirus programs on their networks and on individual computers throughout the school. Two popular antivirus programs used in schools and homes are shown in Figure 8-6.

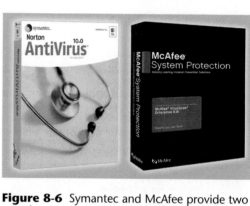

Figure 8-6 Symantec and McAfee provide two popular antivirus programs used in schools, businesses, and homes.

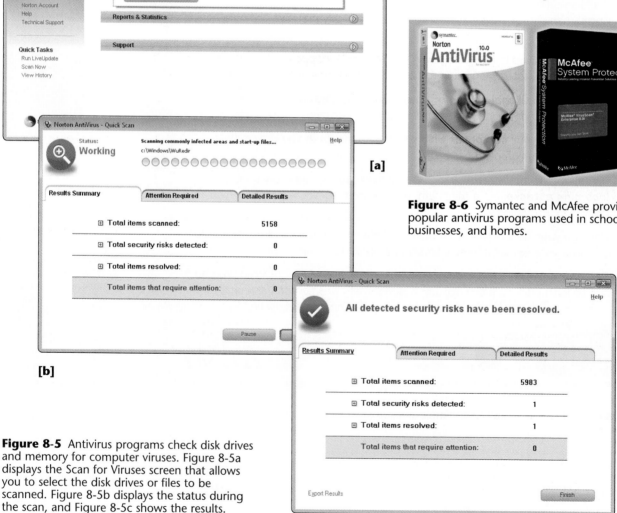

[a]

[b]

[c]

Figure 8-5 Antivirus programs check disk drives and memory for computer viruses. Figure 8-5a displays the Scan for Viruses screen that allows you to select the disk drives or files to be scanned. Figure 8-5b displays the status during the scan, and Figure 8-5c shows the results.

When you install an antivirus program, you should set up the program to monitor a computer continuously for possible viruses, including continual scans of all removable storage media and files downloaded from the Internet (Figure 8-7). You also should set the program to update virus definitions automatically every week.

False warnings about viruses often spread via e-mail and over the Internet. Known as **virus hoaxes**, these warnings describe viruses that are not actually known to exist. Given the damage viruses cause, however, you should take the time to research the validity of any virus warnings you receive, in the event the warning is real. The Symantec Security Response Hoax Web page regularly releases new virus hoax names. If you think you have received a message about a false virus, you can verify it at the Hoax Web page.

UNAUTHORIZED ACCESS AND USE

Unauthorized access is the use of a computer or network without permission. An individual who tries to access a computer or network illegally is called a **cracker** or hacker. The term, **hacker**, although originally a complimentary word for a computer enthusiast, now has a derogatory connotation because it refers to people who try to break into a computer, often intending to steal or corrupt its data. Crackers and hackers typically break into computers by connecting to the system via a modem and logging on as a user. Some intruders have no intent of causing damage to computer files; instead, they want to access data, information, or programs and use what they access for illegal purposes. Other intruders leave some evidence of their presence with a message or by deliberately altering data.

Unauthorized use is the use of a computer or data for unapproved or possibly illegal activities. Unauthorized use ranges from an employee using a company computer to send personal e-mail or to track his or her child's soccer league scores to someone gaining access to a bank system and completing an unauthorized transfer of funds.

One way to prevent unauthorized access to and use of computers is to implement **access controls**, which are security measures that define who can access a computer,

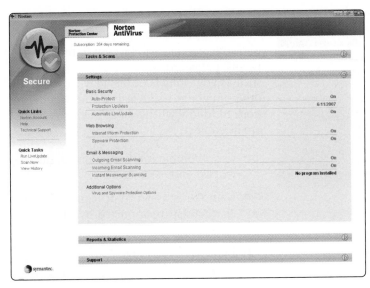

when they can access it, and what actions they can take while using the computer. To prevent unauthorized use and access to sensitive information, schools install different levels and types of access controls. Schools set up their networks so that users have access only to those programs, data, and information for which they are approved. Most schools and businesses provide authorized users with unique user identification (often called **user ID** or username) and a **password** that allows them to log on to the network to use e-mail, to transfer files, and to access other shared resources (Figure 8-8). When a user logs on to a computer or network by entering a user ID and a password, the operating system checks to see if the user ID and password match the entries stored in an authorization file. If the entries match, the computer or network grants access.

Figure 8-7 Using Norton AntiVirus Auto-Protect, users can opt for several different virus protection options.

Figure 8-8 Many schools require administrators, teachers, staff, and students to log on to the school's network with a unique user ID (or User name, as shown here) and password.

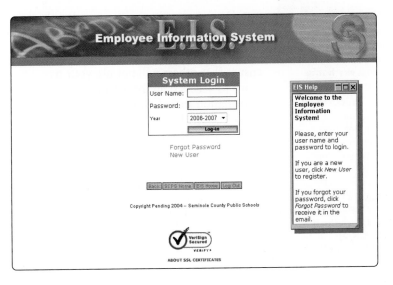

Often, you are asked to select your own password by choosing a word or series of characters that will be easy to remember. If your password is too simple or obvious, such as your initials or birthday, however, others might guess it easily. Some suggestions to follow when you create a password are listed next:

- Use a combination of letters, digits, words, initials, and dates.

- Make the password at least eight characters (if supported by the software).

- Join two words together.

- Add one or more numbers at the beginning, middle, or end of a word.

- Choose words from other languages.

- Choose family names far back in your family tree.

- Choose a password you can type without looking at the keyboard.

Generally, the more creative your password, the harder it is for someone else to figure out. Even long and creative passwords, however, do not provide complete protection against unauthorized access. Some basic precautions to take include the following:

- Do not leave written copies of your passwords near your computer.

- Use a password that is easy to remember, so that you do not have to write it down.

- Change your password frequently.

- Do not share your password with anyone, especially telemarketers.

Following these guidelines helps to ensure that others will not use your password to access data, programs, or sensitive information stored on your computer or a school network.

At many schools, each user ID and password is associated with a specific level of computer and network access. A brief description of basic access levels that schools use to prevent unauthorized access and use of sensitive information follows:

- Students usually can access only instructional materials and software.

Although many schools also provide student access to the Internet and Web — many schools install filtering software on the networks to prevent students from viewing inappropriate Web sites. Students do not have network access to grades, attendance rates, and other sensitive and personal information.

- Teachers typically have access to all the programs, data, and information to which students have access; they usually have access to selected information about their students, such as grades and attendance. Teachers normally do not have access to information about other teachers, students, or any administrative files.

- Principals and assistant principals normally have access to all information that pertains to students enrolled at their schools; they may not access information about students attending other schools in the district.

- School district administrators and superintendents usually have access to all information stored on their districts' network servers.

POSSESSED OBJECTS AND BIOMETRIC DEVICES

A **possessed object** is any item that you must carry to gain access to a computer or computer facility. Examples are badges, cards, smart cards, and keys. The card you use in an automated teller machine (ATM) is a possessed object that allows access to your bank account. Possessed objects are often used in combination with a **personal identification number** (**PIN**) that is a numeric password that provides an additional level of security.

Biometric devices authenticate a person's identity by translating a personal characteristic, such as a fingerprint, into a digital code that then is compared with a digital code stored in the computer verifying the personal characteristic. If the digital code in the computer does not match the personal characteristic code, the computer denies access to the individual.

FIREWALLS

Despite efforts to protect the data on your computer's hard disk, it still is vulnerable to attacks from hackers. A **firewall** is a security system consisting of hardware and/or software that prevents unauthorized access to data and information on a network. Schools use firewalls to deny network access to outsiders and to restrict both student and teacher access to sensitive data (Figure 8-9). Many schools route all communications through a proxy server. A **proxy server** screens all incoming and outgoing messages.

If you are using Windows Vista/XP or Mac OS X, you already have a personal firewall that protects your computer from unauthorized access by monitoring all incoming network traffic. If you use a router, you also have a hardware firewall. Hardware firewalls stop many intrusions before they break into your computer.

For enhanced firewall protection and added features, some home and business users purchase stand-alone personal firewall software. A **personal firewall** is a software program that detects and protects your personal computer and its data from unauthorized intrusions. These products constantly monitor all transmissions to and from your computer and inform you of any attempted intrusions. These easy-to-use products are definitely worth their expense, which usually is less than $40. Figure 8-10 lists popular personal firewall products.

HARDWARE THEFT AND VANDALISM

For schools, hardware theft and vandalism present a difficult security challenge. To help minimize the theft of computers and associated equipment, schools can implement a variety of security precautions. In addition to installing security systems, many schools also install additional physical security devices such as cables that lock the equipment to a desk, cabinet, or floor (Figure 8-11). Schools also normally install deadbolt locks and alarm systems to protect the equipment in their computer labs.

With the increasing use of portable equipment such as notebook computers, iPods, smart phones, PDAs, and other handheld computers, hardware theft poses a more serious risk. Increasingly, K-12 schools and

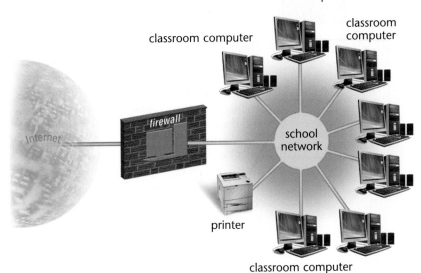

Figure 8-9 A firewall restricts unauthorized intruders from accessing data, information, and programs on networks and individual computers.

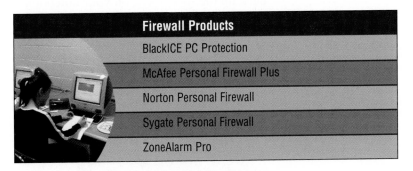

Firewall Products
BlackICE PC Protection
McAfee Personal Firewall Plus
Norton Personal Firewall
Sygate Personal Firewall
ZoneAlarm Pro

Figure 8-10 Popular personal firewall products.

Figure 8-11 Using cables to lock computers can help prevent the theft of desktop and mobile computer equipment.

colleges are providing notebook computers for teachers and loaning them to students for short periods. Some universities and colleges even require that each entering student purchase a notebook computer. Users must take special care to protect their notebook computers. The size and weight of these smaller computers make them easy to steal, and their value makes them tempting targets for thieves.

Common sense and a constant awareness of the risks are the best preventive measures against theft of notebook computers and other portable equipment. You should never, for example, leave a notebook computer unattended or out in the open in a public place, such as the cafeteria or on the seat of a car. Some schools install physical devices such as cables that temporarily lock notebook computers to a desk or table (see Figure 8-12). As a precaution in case of theft, you also should back up the files stored on your notebook computer regularly.

Figure 8-12 The size and weight of notebook computers make them easy to steal, and their value makes them tempting targets for thieves. Schools and teachers need to take special precautions to prevent the theft of their notebook computers.

Some schools purchase insurance policies to cover their notebook computers, desktop computers, and other computer equipment. In addition, schools can purchase a service that actually tracks down a stolen notebook computer. This unique system often is called by its nickname, *the Lojack of the Computer World*. As soon as a person who has stolen a notebook computer uses the computer to access the Internet, the software on the

computer sends a message regarding the location of the stolen computer to the school's system network administrator, who then notifies the police.

In addition to hardware theft, another area of concern for K-12 schools is vandalism. **Computer vandalism** takes many forms, from a student cutting a computer cable or deleting files to individuals breaking in a school and randomly smashing computers. Schools usually have written policies and procedures for handling various types of vandalism.

SOFTWARE THEFT

Like hardware theft and vandalism, software theft takes many forms — from a student physically stealing a CD to intentional piracy of software. **Software piracy** — the unauthorized and illegal duplication of copyrighted software — is by far the most common form of software theft.

When you purchase software, you actually do not *own* the software; instead, you have purchased the right to use the software, as outlined in the software license. A **software license** is an agreement that provides specific conditions for use of the software, which users must accept before using the software. Manufacturers usually print the terms of a software license on the software packaging, or in the case of software downloaded via the Web, a page at the manufacturer's site. The same agreement generally displays on a licensing acceptance screen during the software's setup program (Figure 8-13). Installation and use of the software constitutes the user's acceptance of the terms.

The most common type of license agreement included with software packages purchased by individual users is a **single-user license agreement**, or **end-user license agreement (EULA)**. An end-user license agreement typically includes numerous conditions, including the following:

- Users may install the software on only one computer. Some license agreements allow users to install the software on one desktop computer and one notebook computer.

- Users may not install the software on a network, such as a school computer lab network.

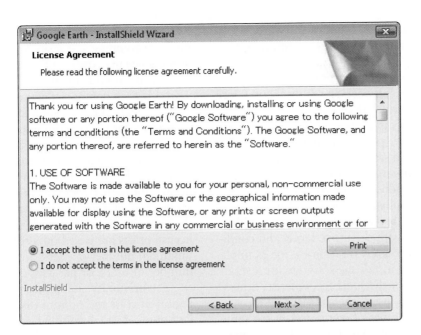

Figure 8-13 Purchasers of single-use software usually have to accept all the terms of the licensing agreement during installation of the software.

- Users may make *one* copy for backup purposes.

- Users may not give copies to friends and colleagues.

Unless otherwise specified by a software license, you do not have the right to loan, rent, or in any way distribute software you purchase. This means you cannot install the software on both your home and classroom computer or on more than one classroom or home computer. Doing so is not only a violation of copyright law, but also a federal crime.

Software piracy introduces a number of risks into the software market: it increases the chance of viruses; reduces your ability to receive technical support; and significantly drives up the price of software for all users. Experts estimate that for every authorized copy of software in use, at least one unauthorized copy is made. One recent study reported that software piracy results in worldwide losses of more than billions of dollars per year.

Software piracy continues for several reasons. Some countries do not provide legal protection for software, while other countries rarely enforce laws. In addition, many buyers believe they have the right to copy the software for which they have paid hundreds, even thousands of dollars.

Newer Microsoft Office and Windows products contain software-based product activation technology, which means you need to activate your Office and Windows products to use them. **Product activation** is an antipiracy technology designed to verify that software products have been licensed legitimately. Microsoft states that product activation is quick, simple, unobtrusive, and that it protects customer privacy.

Product activation works by verifying that a software program's product key, which you must use to install the product, has not been used on more personal computers than intended by the software's license. Software companies take illegal copying seriously and prosecute some offenders (including school districts, school administrators, and teachers) to the fullest extent of the law. Penalties include fines up to $250,000 and up to five years in jail.

Most schools have strict policies governing the installation and use of software and enforce their rules by periodically checking classroom and lab computers to ensure that all software is properly licensed. Teachers who are not completely familiar with their school's policies governing installation of software should check with the school's technology coordinator before installing any software on a classroom computer.

Web Info

For a list of freeware for the PC or Mac, visit the Teachers Discovering Computers Web site (*scsite.com/tdc5*), click Chapter 8, click Web Info, and then click PC Freeware or Mac Freeware.

Two additional types of software, shareware and freeware, also require license agreements and are protected under copyright law. As you learned in Chapter 1, **shareware** is software that is distributed free for a trial period. If you want to use a shareware program beyond the trial period, the developer (person or company) expects you to send a small fee. **Freeware**, by contrast, is software provided at no cost to a user by an individual or company. You should carefully read the license included with any shareware or freeware to familiarize yourself with the usage terms and conditions. Some shareware licenses, for example, allow you to install the software on several computers for the same fee, whereas others allow you to install the software on an unlimited number of computers in the same school for a minimal additional fee. Always scan shareware and freeware programs for viruses before installation and use.

To reduce software costs for schools and businesses with large numbers of users, software vendors often offer special discount pricing or site licensing. With discount pricing, the more copies of a program a school district purchases, the greater the discount. Purchasing a software **site license** gives the

buyer the right to install the software on multiple computers at a single site. Site licenses usually cost significantly less than purchasing an individual copy of the software for each computer; many school districts, in fact, purchase software site licenses that allow for use on computers throughout the district, thus gaining substantial savings.

Network site licenses for many software packages also are available. A **network site license** allows network users to share a single copy of the software, which resides on the network server. Network software site license prices are based on a fixed fee for an unlimited number of users, a maximum number of users, or per user.

A **community site license** gives an entire region or state the right to install an unlimited number of educational copies of a particular software program on individual computers or a network. As with other site licenses, a community site license provides substantial savings. Figure 8-14 summarizes the various types of software licenses used in education. A number of major software companies, such as Microsoft, provide site licenses for some of their software to K-12 schools at drastically reduced rates.

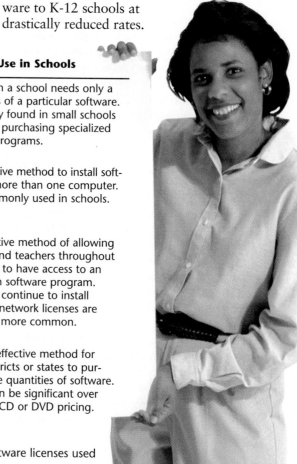

Type of License	Characteristics	Use in Schools
Single-user	Software can be installed on only one computer. Some license agreements allow users to install the software on one desktop computer and one notebook computer.	Used when a school needs only a few copies of a particular software. Commonly found in small schools and when purchasing specialized software programs.
Multiple-user	Software can be installed on a set number of computers, typically 5, 10, 50, or more. Cost varies based on number of computers.	Cost-effective method to install software on more than one computer. Most commonly used in schools.
Network License	Software is installed on the school's network. The license will specify and the software will control a specific number of simultaneous users, such as 50, 100, 250, or 500. Cost varies based on number of computers.	Cost-effective method of allowing students and teachers throughout the school to have access to an application software program. As schools continue to install networks, network licenses are becoming more common.
Community/State License	Frequently used with software distributed on CDs/DVDs. Any number of programs can be purchased for either Macintosh or PC platforms.	Very cost-effective method for school districts or states to purchase large quantities of software. Savings can be significant over individual CD or DVD pricing.

Figure 8-14 A summary of the various types of software licenses used in education.

INFORMATION THEFT

As you have learned, information is a valuable asset to an organization, such as a school district. The deliberate theft of information causes as much or more damage than the theft of hardware. Information theft typically occurs for a variety of reasons — organizations steal or buy stolen information to learn about competitors and individuals steal credit card and telephone charge card numbers to make purchases. Information theft often is linked to other types of computer crime. An individual, for example, may gain unauthorized access to a computer and then steal credit card numbers stored in a firm's accounting files.

Most organizations prevent information theft by implementing the user ID controls previously mentioned. Another way to protect sensitive data is to use encryption. **Encryption** is the process of converting readable data into unreadable characters by applying a formula that uses a code, called an **encryption key**. The person who receives the message uses the same encryption key to decrypt it (convert it back to readable data). Both the sender and receiver computers use the same encryption software. Any person illegally accessing the information sees only meaningless symbols (Figure 8-15).

School networks do contain a great deal of important and confidential information about students, teachers, and staff. Although information theft is not a major problem in schools, the potential is taken seriously. As a result, schools implement many of the security precautions described in this chapter.

SYSTEM FAILURE

Theft is not the only cause of hardware, software, data, or information loss. Any of these can occur during a **system failure**, which is a malfunction of a computer. System failures occur because of electrical power problems, hardware component failure, or software error.

One common cause of system failures in school and home computers is an abrupt variation in electrical power, which can cause data loss or damage computer components. In a school network, for example, a single power disturbance can damage multiple computers and their associated equipment. Two more common electrical power variations that cause system failures are undervoltages and overvoltages.

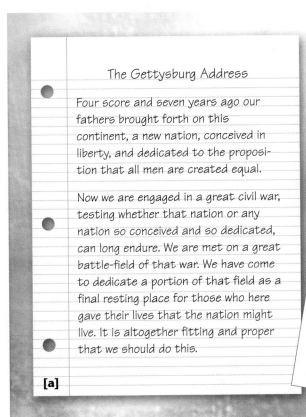

The Gettysburg Address

Four score and seven years ago our fathers brought forth on this continent, a new nation, conceived in liberty, and dedicated to the proposition that all men are created equal.

Now we are engaged in a great civil war, testing whether that nation or any nation so conceived and so dedicated, can long endure. We are met on a great battle-field of that war. We have come to dedicate a portion of that field as a final resting place for those who here gave their lives that the nation might live. It is altogether fitting and proper that we should do this.

[a]

[b]

Figure 8-15 The first two paragraphs of the Gettysburg Address in plain text [a] and after the text is encrypted [b].

An **undervoltage** occurs when the electrical power supply drops. In North America, electricity normally flows from the wall plug at approximately 120 volts. Any significant drop below 120 volts is considered an undervoltage. A **brownout** is a prolonged undervoltage; a **blackout** is a complete power failure. Undervoltages cause data loss and computer crashes but generally do not cause serious equipment damage.

An **overvoltage**, or **power surge**, occurs when the incoming electrical power increases significantly above the normal 120 volts. A momentary overvoltage, called a **spike**, occurs when the power increase lasts for less than one millisecond (one thousandth of a second). Spikes are caused by uncontrollable disturbances, such as lightning, or controllable disturbances, such as turning on a piece of equipment that uses the same electrical circuit. Overvoltages can cause immediate and permanent equipment damage.

To protect your computer equipment from overvoltages, you should use surge protectors. A **surge protector** is a device that uses special electrical components to smooth out minor voltage errors, provide a stable current flow, and keep an overvoltage from damaging computer equipment (Figure 8-16). Schools should use surge protectors for all classroom and lab computers and printers.

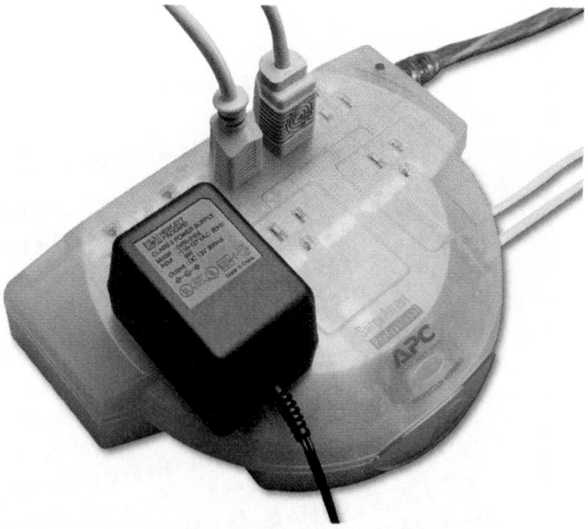

Figure 8-16 Circuits inside a surge protector safeguard equipment against overvoltages.

If your home computer connects to the Internet, you need to have surge protection not only for your computer, but also for your modem, telephone lines, DSL lines, and other Internet cables. Many surge protectors include plug-ins for telephone lines and other cables (Figure 8-17). If your surge protector does not have these plug-ins, you can purchase separate devices to protect these lines. Overall, surge protectors provide an inexpensive way to protect computers and associated equipment. Basic surge protectors cost less than $15 and surge protectors that include protection from power surges over network cables cost less than $35.

in-out network connections

Figure 8-17 Home users should purchase a surge protector that includes an in-and-out connection for telephone lines and other network cables.

Although a surge protector absorbs a small overvoltage without damage, a large overvoltage, such as that caused by a lightning strike, will cause the surge protector to fail to protect the computer components. Surge protectors also are not completely effective; large power surges can bypass the surge protector and repeated small overvoltages can weaken a surge protector permanently.

For additional electrical protection, many home and school users connect their computers and printers to an uninterruptible power supply, instead of a surge protector. An **uninterruptible power supply (UPS)** is a device that contains surge protection circuits and one or more batteries that provide power during a temporary or permanent loss of power (Figure 8-18). The amount of time a UPS allows you to continue working depends on the electrical requirements of the computer and the size of the batteries in the UPS. A less expensive UPS provides enough time for users to save their current work and properly shut down the computer after a power outage (about 10 minutes).

Figure 8-18 If power fails, an uninterruptible power supply (UPS) uses batteries to provide electricity for a limited time. A UPS also contains circuits that safeguard against overvoltages.

To ensure that their networks will continue to operate in the event of a power loss, most schools and businesses install UPSs to protect their network servers. Home users also should consider investing in a UPS, especially if they live in an area prone to power surges, power failures, and lightning strikes. For home users, the $30 to $175 investment in a UPS can prevent user frustration associated with most power-related computer problems, crashes, and loss of data. Some UPS manufacturers pay for any damage your computer sustains from power surges, including lightning strikes.

BACKING UP — THE ULTIMATE SAFEGUARD

To prevent data loss caused by a system failure or a computer virus, many schools, businesses, and home users back up their important files. A **backup** is a duplicate of a file, program, or disk that can be used if the original is lost, damaged, or destroyed. When a file is corrupted or destroyed, the backup copy is used to **restore**, or reload, the file on a computer or network file server. Schools and home users often overlook storing backup copies at another location, called an **off-site location**, as an additional precaution. This simple precaution prevents a single disaster, such as a fire, from destroying both the primary and backup copies of important files.

Most schools have a **backup procedure** that outlines a regular plan of copying and backing up important data and program files. At many schools, the backup procedures cover only essential school programs, information, and data, such as student grades, attendance, and other personal information. Schools normally do not back up the files individual teachers or students create on their classroom computers. If your school does not provide backups for the files you create in your classroom, you should make backup copies of your school files periodically and store them on a portable hard drive or CDs. Likewise, you should back up the files you create on your home computer. Whether at school or home, backing up your important files prevents loss of lesson plans, curriculum pages, handouts, tests, and more — files that represent years of work. Teachers also should teach their students how to back up their homework, projects, and other files.

Creating backup copies of your files is not a difficult procedure. The easiest way is to copy your important files from your hard disk to a CD, USB flash drive, or portable hard drive. In addition, most personal computer operating systems include an easy-to-use backup utility program (Figure 8-19). Such utilities not only allow users to back up their important files, they also compress the backed up files so they require less storage space than the original files.

Web Info

To learn more about Microsoft Backup, visit the Teachers Discovering Computers Web site (*scsite.com/tdc5*), click Chapter 8, click Web Info, and then click Backup.

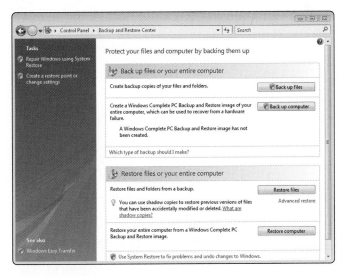

Figure 8-19 Microsoft Backup is a utility program that comes with Microsoft Windows and is an easy way to back up your important computer files.

Web Info

To explore Computer Ethics — Cyberethics, visit the Teachers Discovering Computers Web site (*scsite.com/tdc5*), click Chapter 8, click Web Info, and then click Cyberethics.

Ethics and the Information Age

As with any powerful technology, individuals can use computers for both good and bad actions. The standards that determine whether an action is good or bad are called **ethics**. **Computer ethics** are the moral guidelines that govern the use of computers, networks, and information systems (Figure 8-20). Five areas of computer ethics frequently discussed are (1) unauthorized use of computers, (2) hardware, software, and information theft, (3) information privacy, (4) copyright, and (5) the existence of objectionable materials on the Internet.

Unauthorized use of computers and hardware, copying software, and information theft were discussed earlier in this chapter. The following sections present the issues surrounding information privacy and copyright. The ethical issues related to objectionable materials on the Internet are discussed later in this chapter.

Computer Ethics for Educators

1. An educator will not use a computer to harm other people.

2. An educator will not interfere with others' computer work.

3. An educator will not look at others' computer files.

4. An educator will not use a computer to steal.

5. An educator will not use a computer to lie.

6. An educator will not copy or use software without paying for it.

7. An educator will not use others' computer resources without permission.

8. An educator will not use others' work.

9. An educator will think about the social impact of the programs he or she creates.

10. An educator always will use a computer in a way that shows respect and consideration for other people.

Modified from the *Ten Commandments for Computer Ethics* by the Computer Ethics Institute.

Figure 8-20 Computer ethics are the guidelines that govern the use of computers and information systems. This figure lists computer ethics for educators.

INFORMATION PRIVACY

Information privacy is the right of individuals and organizations to deny or restrict the collection and use of information about them. In the past, information privacy was easier to control because information was kept in separate locations, individual schools in a large school district maintained their own files, individual stores had their own credit files, government agencies had separate records, doctors had separate files, and so on.

Now it is feasible, both technically and economically, for schools, businesses, and other organizations to store large amounts of related data in a database or on one network server because of the widespread use of networks and increased storage capacity. These organizations also use computers to monitor student and employee activities. As a result, many people have concerns about how the unauthorized collection and use of data and monitoring affects their privacy. Figure 8-21 lists actions you can take to make your personal data more private.

UNAUTHORIZED COLLECTION AND USE OF INFORMATION Most individuals are surprised to learn that national marketing organizations often purchase the information individuals provide for magazine subscriptions, product warranty registration cards, contest entry forms, and other documents.

By combining this acquired data with other information obtained from public sources, such as driver's licenses and vehicle registration information, national marketing organizations create an **electronic profile** of an individual. The organizations then sell these electronic profiles to organizations that distribute information on a product, service, or cause to a specific group of individuals (for example, all sports car owners over 40 years of age living in the southeastern United States).

Direct marketing supporters say that using information in this way lowers overall selling costs, which, in turn, lowers product prices. Critics contend that the information contained in these electronic profiles reveals more about individuals than anyone has a right to know. These same individuals believe that, at a minimum, companies should inform the individuals whose personal information they intend to sell or release and give the individuals the right to deny such use.

How to Safeguard Personal Information

Fill in only required information on forms, both in print and on the Web.
Do not preprint your telephone number or Social Security number on personal checks.
Have an unlisted or unpublished telephone number.
Find out how to block your telephone number from displaying on the receiver's system if Caller ID is available in your area.
Do not write your telephone number on charge or credit receipts.
Ask merchants not to write credit card numbers, telephone numbers, Social Security numbers, and driver's license numbers on the back of your personal checks.
Purchase goods with cash instead of credit or checks.
Avoid shopping clubs and buyers' cards.
Find out why merchants want personal information before releasing the information to them.
Inform merchants that you do not want them to distribute your personal information.
Ask, in writing, to be removed from mailing lists.
Obtain your credit report once a year from each of the three major credit reporting agencies (Equifax, Experian, and TransUnion) and correct any errors.
Request a free copy of your medical records once a year from the Medical Information Bureau.
Install a cookie manager to filter cookies.
Clear your history file when you are finished browsing.
Set up a free e-mail account. Use this e-mail address for merchant forms.
Turn off File and Print Sharing on your Internet connection.
Install a personal firewall.
Sign-up for e-mail filtering through your Internet service provider or use an antispam program such as Brightmail.
Do not reply to spam for any reason. It might not be a good idea to unsubscribe to unsolicited spam; by sending back a message, you might only confirm that your e-mail account is active.
Surf the Web anonymously with programs such as Freedom Websecure or through an anonymous Web site such as Anonymizer.com.

Figure 8-21 Techniques to keep personal data private.

PHISHING Phishing is a scam in which a perpetrator sends an official-looking e-mail that attempts to obtain personal and financial information from the recipient. Some phishing e-mail messages ask the recipient to provide personal information in the reply; others direct the recipient to a phony Web site that collects the information. To help deter phishing scams and spam (discussed next), Microsoft and others are developing standards that will require e-mail messages to contain sender identification so recipients can verify the legitimacy of messages.

SPAM Spam is an unsolicited e-mail message or newsgroup posting sent to many recipients or newsgroups at once. The content of spam ranges from selling a product or service, to promoting a business opportunity, to advertising offensive materials. One study indicates the average user receives more than 1000 spam e-mail messages each year. Spam sent through an instant messaging system, instead of through e-mail, is called **spim**. Spam sent via Internet Telephony is called **split**.

You can reduce the amount of spam you receive using several techniques. Some e-mail programs have built-in settings that delete spam automatically. Other e-mail programs, such as Outlook Express, allow you to set up message rules that block all messages from a particular sender or subject. You also can sign up for e-mail filtering from your Internet service provider.

E-mail filtering is a service that blocks e-mail messages from designated sources. You can block unwanted e-mail messages by using an **antispam program** that attempts to remove spam before it reaches your inbox. The disadvantage of using e-mail filters and anti-spam programs is that sometimes they remove valid e-mail messages.

PRIVACY LAWS The concern about privacy has led to federal and state laws regarding storing and disclosing personal data and other computer-related issues (Figure 8-22). Common points in some of these laws include the following:

- A business or government agency collecting data about individuals should limit the information collected and only store what is necessary to carry out the organization's functions.

- After it has collected data about individuals, an organization must make provisions to restrict data access to only those employees who must use it to perform their job duties.

- An organization should release an individual's personal information outside the organization only after the individual has agreed to its disclosure.

- When an organization collects information about an individual, the organization must inform the individual that it is collecting data and give her the opportunity to determine the accuracy of the data.

Schools and school districts have a legal and moral responsibility to protect sensitive information, whether it is in printed form or stored electronically on school computers. Just like any other business, school districts must follow state and federal laws concerning storage and release of personal information about students, teachers, and staff personnel. For these reasons, school districts generally restrict access to sensitive information stored on their networks and in printed materials on a strict need-to-know basis.

Teachers also must follow federal and state laws concerning the storage and release of information about their students. Teachers should carefully read and make sure they understand all school district policies concerning the release of sensitive information related to their students.

EMPLOYEE AND STUDENT MONITORING

Employee monitoring uses computers to observe, record, and review an individual's use of a computer, including communications such as e-mail, keyboard activity (used to measure productivity), and Internet sites visited. A frequently discussed issue is whether an employer has the right to read an employee's e-mail messages. Actual policies vary widely, with some organizations declaring they will review e-mail messages regularly, whereas others state they consider e-mail private and will protect it just like a letter sent through the postal service.

Most schools usually have very specific rules governing the use of e-mail and school networks by teachers, administrators, staff, and students. Some schools randomly monitor e-mail messages and the Internet sites visited by teachers, administrators, staff, and students, whereas other schools do not. Some schools also randomly monitor files stored on the school network.

Teachers should become familiar with all school policies concerning e-mail and computer and Internet usage. To ensure that individuals understand these policies, most schools require that teachers, students, staff, and parents sign an Acceptable Use Policy (AUP) that provides specific guidance for using school computers, networks, and the Internet. Teachers also should ensure that students fully understand that school personnel or their future employers might monitor their use of the organization's computer resources.

COPYRIGHT LAWS

As discussed earlier in this chapter, copyright laws cover software programs to protect them from piracy. Copyright law includes many other aspects, however, that teachers need to understand. The Copyright Act of 1976 and its numerous amendments apply to all creative works. A **copyright** means the original author or creator of the work retains ownership of the work and has the exclusive right to reproduce and distribute the creative work.

Date	Law	Purpose
2003	**CAN-SPAM Act**	Gives law enforcement the right to impose penalties on people using the Internet to distribute spam.
2003	**Health Insurance Portability and Accountability Act (HIPAA)**	Describes how personal medical information can be used and disclosed. HIPAA became effective on April 14, 2003.
2002	**Dot Kids Implementation and Efficiency Act**	Establishes the Dot Kids domain that lists only Web sites that conform to policies to protect children under the age of 13. It functions similarly to the children's section of a library. Ruled unconstitutional in 2004.
2001	**Provide Appropriate Tools Required to Intercept and Obstruct Terrorism (PATRIOT) Act**	Gives law enforcement the right to monitor people's activities, including Web and e-mail habits.
2000	**Children's Internet Protection Act (CIPA)**	Protects children from obscene and pornographic materials by requiring libraries to install filtering software on their computers. Upheld by the Supreme Court in July 2003.
1998	**Children's Online Privacy Protection Act (COPPA)**	Protects personal information for children under the age of 13.
1997	**No Electronic Theft (NET) Act**	Closes a narrow loophole in the law that allowed people to give away copyrighted material (such as software) on the Internet without legal repercussions.
1996	**National Information Infrastructure Protection Act**	Penalizes theft of information across state lines, threats against networks, and computer system trespassing.
1994	**Computer Abuse Amendments Act**	Amends 1984 act to outlaw transmission of harmful computer code such as viruses.
1992	**Cable Act**	Extends privacy of Cable Communications Policy Act of 1984 to include cellular and other wireless services.
1991	**Telephone Consumer Protection Act**	Restricts activities of telemarketers.
1988	**Computer Matching and Privacy Protection Act**	Regulates the use of government data to determine the eligibility of individuals for federal benefits.
1988	**Video Privacy Protection Act**	Forbids retailers from releasing or selling video-rental records without customer consent or a court order.
1986	**Electronic Communications Privacy Act (ECPA)**	Provides the same right of privacy protection for the postal delivery service and telephone companies to the new forms of electronic communications, such as voice mail, e-mail, and cellular telephones.
1984	**Cable Communications Policy Act**	Regulates disclosure of cable television subscriber records.
1984	**Computer Fraud and Abuse Act**	Outlaws unauthorized access of federal government computers.
1978	**Right to Financial Privacy Act**	Strictly outlines procedures federal agencies must follow when looking at customer records in banks.
1974	**Privacy Act**	Forbids federal agencies from allowing information to be used for a reason other than for which it was collected.
1974	**Family Educational Rights Privacy Act**	Gives students and parents access to school records and limits disclosure of and records to unauthorized parties.
1970	**Fair Credit Reporting Act**	Prohibits credit reporting agencies from releasing credit information to unauthorized people and allows consumers to review their own credit records.

Figure 8-22 Summary of the major U.S. government laws concerning privacy.

Web Info

To learn more about fair use, visit the Teachers Discovering Computers Web site (*scsite.com/tdc5*), click Chapter 8, click Web Info, and then click Fair Use.

All educators need to understand how copyright laws impact the manner in which they and their students use information created by others. Such an understanding is important because the building blocks of education use the creative works of others: books; videos; newspapers, magazines, and other reference materials; software; and information located on the World Wide Web.

Three areas of copyright directly impact today's classrooms: (1) illegal copying or using copyrighted software programs; (2) fair use laws and their application to the use of both printed copyrighted materials and copyrighted materials accessible on the Internet; and (3) use of copyrighted materials on teacher and student Web pages. The first area (illegal copying or using licensed and copyrighted software) was covered earlier in this chapter; the following sections cover the other two areas of copyright.

FAIR USE The Copyright Act of 1976 established **fair use** and provided the guidelines that allow educators to use and copy certain copyrighted materials for nonprofit educational purposes. Figure 8-23 shows Section 107 of U.S. Copyright Law, which deals with fair use. Copyright issues are complex and sometimes the laws are vague. School districts often provide teachers with specific guidelines for using copyrighted materials in their classrooms. Schools can interpret copyright issues differently, so school policies concerning the use of copyrighted materials vary widely. Teachers need to read and understand school policies concerning copyright.

In addition to providing printed school policies on copyright issues, most schools provide teachers with information and answer questions about copyright issues. For information or answers to questions concerning software copyright issues, teachers should ask their school or district technology coordinator. For all other issues concerning copyright, fair use, and associated school district policies, teachers should speak with their media specialist. Media specialists receive training on copyright issues and deal with them on a daily basis. If in doubt, teachers should contact the creator of the work and ask for written permission to use his material.

Fair use guidelines apply to copyrighted materials on the Internet just as they apply to a copyrighted article published in a magazine. Basically, Web sites include two kinds of information: original copyrighted information and information without copyright restriction. Web pages that contain original information generally include a copyright statement on the page; the copyright statement normally contains the copyright symbol, the year, and the creator's name (Figure 8-24).

U.S. Copyright Law: Fair Use

(U.S. Code, Title 17, Chapter 1, Section 107)

§ 107. Limitations on exclusive rights: Fair use

Notwithstanding the provisions of sections 106 and 106A, the fair use of a copyrighted work, including such use by reproduction in copies or phonorecords or by any other means specified by that section, for purposes such as criticism, comment, news reporting, teaching (including multiple copies for classroom use), scholarship, or research, is not an infringement of copyright. In determining whether the use made of a work in any particular case is a fair use, the factors to be considered shall include:

(1) the purpose and character of the use, including whether such use is of a commercial nature or is for nonprofit educational purposes;

(2) the nature of the copyrighted work;

(3) the amount and substantiality of the portion used in relation to the copyrighted work as a whole; and

(4) the effect of the use upon the potential market for or value of the copyrighted work.

The fact that a work is unpublished shall not itself bar a finding of fair use if such finding is made upon consideration of all the above factors.

Figure 8-23 The Copyright Act of 1976 provides the structure for the copyright law. Section 107 of the U.S. Copyright Law defines Fair Use.

If a teacher uses copyrighted materials from the Internet, she must follow fair use guidelines, school policies, and any restrictions listed on the Web site. If the information located on the Web site does not include copyright restriction, it does not mean the creator is waiving his privileges under copyright. To be safe, you should assume everything on the Web is copyrighted. Always follow fair use guidelines and school policies when using Web materials for educational purposes. In addition, always give proper credit and use citations if appropriate.

These guidelines do not apply only to text-based materials on the Web. The Web also contains a multitude of graphics, animations, and audio and video files teachers can download and use for educational purposes or classroom presentations. When teachers download and use these materials, they must adhere to fair use guidelines, school policies, and any other restrictions noted on the Web site.

TEACHER AND STUDENT WEB PAGES

Teachers and students in school districts all over the country are creating and publishing their own Web pages (Figure 8-25). As previously discussed, **Web publishing** is the development and maintenance of Web pages. When developing these pages, teachers and students must take care to respect copyright laws and follow the guidelines outlined in the previous section.

Copyright laws do protect all original materials created by students and teachers and published on the Web. To ensure that this is clear, however, teachers and students may want to include a copyright statement at the bottom of their home page.

The use of copyrighted materials (text, graphics, animations, audio, and video) on teacher or student Web pages requires permission from the creator of the materials. Most Web pages include an e-mail link to use when asking for permission to use copyrighted materials. To use the materials on the Web, simply send a short e-mail message to the creator of the work and explain how you will use her work on your Web page. Many authors are more than willing to allow teachers to use their original text or artwork for educational purposes as long as they receive proper credit.

Figure 8-24 This educational Web page has a copyright statement. The copyright statement includes basic copyright information as well as other information.

Figure 8-25 Teachers and students in school districts all over the country are creating and publishing their own Web pages.

Many school districts have specific guidelines that teachers and students must follow when publishing Web pages on school servers. Teachers should carefully read all school rules before publishing any teacher or student Web pages. Some schools, for example, prohibit using any copyrighted materials on Web pages. In such instances, students and teachers must use only original material or material that is not copyrighted. Generally, teachers may use materials from government-sponsored Web sites, which are considered public domain (Figure 8-26). Anything considered **public domain** — including software or creative works — is free from copyright restrictions.

Most school districts purchase or have access to copyright-free CDs and DVDs or they subscribe to services that contain thousands of clip art images, photos, graphics, and audio and video clips. In addition, tens of thousands of copyright-free materials are available on the Internet for teachers and students to use on their Web pages and in class presentations and projects (Figure 8-27).

In addition to respecting copyright law, teachers also must consider other issues related to Web page publishing. Teachers, for example, must protect their students from Internet users who might want to harm them by ensuring that no personal information about students is included on the Web pages. Figure 8-28 lists some basic guidelines that teachers should consider when creating Web pages.

Finally, a broadly interpreted issue known as intellectual property rights is beginning to play an important role in public education. The major intellectual property rights issue currently being discussed is who owns online content and courses, both in higher education and K-12 education. A recent survey found that most institutions of higher education see content as the property of the instructor. More than half also believe that the instructor owns the actual course. Currently, most K-12 districts handle ownership of items such as tests, lesson plans, and other teaching materials and these districts see ownership as a non-issue. Some districts are beginning to clarify the ownership of online courses.

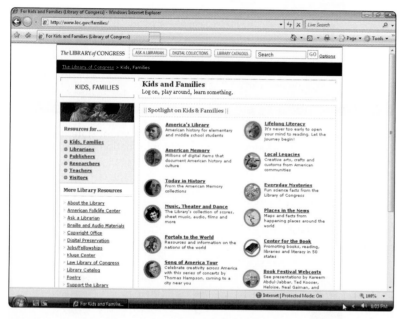

Figure 8-26 An example of a public domain government Web page. Government Web pages usually have a URL that contains or ends in .gov.

Figure 8-27 This Web page for teachers provides links to dozens of Web sites that provide free graphics, animations, and more.

Web Page Guidelines

- Always protect the identity of your students.

- Never list student last names, telephone numbers, home addresses, or e-mail addresses.

- Use only first names of students on a Web site, but never in conjunction with other identifying information, such as a photograph.

- Use caution when including digital pictures of classrooms; avoid pictures that show close-ups of students.

- Never provide links to sites that are not appropriate for K-12 students or educational settings.

- List the function of all linked Web pages. Link only to pages that inform, explain, or teach a concept or curriculum area to students. Beware of linking to Web sites that persuade students.

- Avoid providing links to sites whose primary purpose is selling noneducational products and services, unless relevant to the subject under discussion.

- Avoid linking to Web pages that are not updated on a regular basis.

- Provide links to sites that help you achieve instructional and curriculum goals.

- Avoid discussing controversial issues on your Web site or linking to Web sites that discuss controversial issues, unless these issues are part of your curriculum.

- Carefully read and follow all guidelines and policies that your school district provides.

Figure 8-28 Guidelines that teachers should consider when creating teacher and student Web pages.

Internet Ethics and Objectionable Materials

As you already have learned in this chapter, the widespread use of the Internet — especially in today's schools and classrooms — raises many issues regarding security, privacy, and ethics. Of all of these, one issue is of particular concern for teachers and parents: the availability of **objectionable material** on the Internet, including racist literature, obscene pictures and videos, gambling, and age-restricted items such as cigarettes and alcohol.

Teachers and other school personnel must be concerned with three different types of Internet materials that fall under the general term, objectionable material. The first area includes all materials that most people consider pornographic, such as obscene pictures, stories, graphics, articles, cartoons, and videos. The second area includes racist literature, controversial subjects such as gambling, and other similar materials. Teachers and parents usually easily identify Web sites that contain materials in these first two areas.

The third area includes Web sites that contain incorrect material and thus are inappropriate for K-12 students. Identifying this type of Web page is more difficult than identifying the first two. Because anyone can create and publish a Web page or Web site, some people deliberately create and publish materials on Web pages to fool unsuspecting people. Young students are extremely vulnerable to being fooled by these sites. These Web sites appear perfectly appropriate for K-12 students but contain

Web Info

For more information about Web page guidelines, visit the Teachers Discovering Computers Web site (*scsite.com/tdc5*), click Chapter 8, click Web Info, and then click Guidelines.

information that is historically and otherwise inaccurate. An elementary student might not know the difference between a site that is historically inaccurate about America's founding fathers and an educational site that is accurate.

Before the explosive growth of the Internet, it was difficult for most K-12 students to obtain and view objectionable materials, such as pornographic magazines. Today, anybody with Internet access can view a vast array of obscene and other inappropriate materials on the Web. Many people want to ban such materials from the Internet, whereas others would only restrict objectionable materials so they are not available to minors. Opponents argue that banning any material violates the constitutional right of free speech. Opponents state that instead of limiting Internet access and materials, schools should teach students right from wrong. As you integrate technologies into your classroom, you must always be vigilant. Be sure your students do not encounter objectionable material, and if they encounter objectionable material, be sure your students know what to do.

GOVERNMENT ACTIONS

Over the past two decades, many government actions have helped protect children from being exploited, including numerous Internet-related initiatives. One success story is the Children's Internet Protection Act which is covered in the next section.

CHILDREN'S INTERNET PROTECTION ACT

Congress passed the **Children's Internet Protection Act (CIPA)** in 2000 to protect children from obscene, pornographic, and other information considered harmful to minors. CIPA requires that public libraries install filtering software to block Web sites that contain obscene images or content. As you learned in Chapter 2, filtering software programs prevent browsers from displaying materials from targeted sites or sites that contain certain keywords or phrases. CIPA was challenged by opponents who argued that this law would obstruct appropriate, nonobscene material from being viewed. In July 2003, the U.S. Supreme Court upheld CIPA, arguing that it does not violate freedom of speech. As a result, all public libraries must install filters on their

computers to block access to online pornography or lose federal funding.

Many K-12 schools and parents have proactively taken steps to protect their students and children from the negative aspects of the Internet. Although only a small percentage of the information available on the Internet is unsuitable for children at home or in K-12 schools, educators agree that such materials have no place in our classrooms. Teachers and parents need to ensure that children understand that inappropriate materials exist on the Internet. Children also need to understand that some individuals might try to exploit them via e-mail messages or in chat room conversations.

A recent and emerging trend is a phenomenon called cyberbullying. **Cyberbullying** is the posting or sending of detrimental or cruel text or images using the Internet or other digital devices. Students are most often the victim of cyberbullying just as they are with traditional bullying. However, students are not the only recipients of cyberbullying; recently, teachers also have been victims of cyberbullying. Often students post cruel information about their teachers as a joke, not realizing the seriousness of their actions. All teachers need to be aware of the actions and consequences of cyberbullying and teach their students that bullying either in person or in cyberspace is wrong. Teachers also need to make sure their students understand that they can and will be held accountable for their actions, including criminal prosecution, if appropriate.

The following sections cover what we can do both as parents and educators to keep our children and students safe from the negative aspects of the Internet and digital media.

PARENTAL CONTROLS

Parents can take a number of steps to prevent children from accessing pornographic and other objectionable materials on the Internet. One option is to use the parental controls available with Windows Vista/XP and Mac operating systems. In Windows, for example, you can use parental controls to change Windows settings in order to set limits that control how your children use the computer (Figure 8-29).

Web Info

For more information on cyberbullying, visit the Teachers Discovering Computers Web site (*scsite.com/tdc5*), click Chapter 8, click Web Info, and then click Cyberbullying.

Web Info

For more information on parental controls, visit the Teachers Discovering Computers Web site (*scsite.com/tdc5*), click Chapter 8, click Web Info, and then click Parental Controls — Windows or Parental Controls — Mac OS.

Windows Settings	Additional Information
Windows Vista Web Filter	Use to set the limits for how your children use the Web. You can restrict the Web sites that children visit, check an age rating, indicate whether you want to allow file downloads, and set up which content you want the content filters to block and allow. You can also block or allow specific Web sites.
Time limits	Use to set specific time limits on your children's computer use. Time limits prevent children from logging on during specified hours, like afternoon homework time period. You can set different logon hours for every day of the week. If they are logged on when their allotted time ends, they will be automatically logged off.
Games	Use to prevent your children from playing games you do not want them to play. Allows you to control access to games, choose an age rating level (based upon the Entertainment Software Rating Board), choose the types of content you want to block, and decide whether you want to allow or block specific games.
Allow and block specific programs	Use to prevent your children from running specific programs that you do not want them to run.

Figure 8-29 Information on the various Windows settings (parental options) you can set when using Windows Vista as shown in Figure 8-30. To learn more, use Windows Help.

The first step when using Windows Vista/XP or Mac OS parental controls is to create a separate user account for each of your children and then set up the various controls, which can be different for each child and member of your household. For example, your seven year old probably should have different restrictions than your high school senior. To set up a new account for your child when using Windows, click Start, click Control Panel, and then click User Accounts. When using Mac OS, choose Apple menu, System Preferences, and then click Accounts. Figure 8-30 shows the parental control options available when using Windows Vista. Once you have set up your parental controls, you can review informative Activity Reports.

Parental controls and features available with Mac OS are similar to those for Windows users with a few additional controls including what Apple calls: (1) Securing the cookie jar or preventing your kids from many inappropriate computer issues; (2) creating a personal post office so your child can only exchange e-mail with people you know; (3) the don't talk to strangers feature that lets you decide who your children can chat with online.

Another effective approach to blocking objectionable materials is to install filtering software programs on any computer with Internet access. Many filtering software programs allow parents to filter harmful Web sites, restrict Internet access, monitor children's online activities, and prevent children from accidentally providing personal information in e-mail messages or in chat rooms (Figure 8-31).

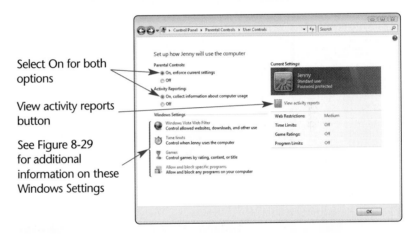

Select On for both options

View activity reports button

See Figure 8-29 for additional information on these Windows Settings

Figure 8-30 Shown are the various parental control options when using Windows Vista.

Finally, the best way for parents to protect children is to monitor their children's activities while on the Internet both by direct and indirect observations. One technique is to keep the family computer in the family room or in an area where you can observe your children while they are working on the computer.

Figure 8-31 Net Nanny is a popular Internet filtering software program that provides parents with numerous options for protecting their kids as they surf the Web.

Because it is difficult to always monitor or observe children's Internet activities directly, you can check which Internet sites children are visiting by viewing the browser's history list (Figure 8-32). This simple but effective technique is useless, however, if children are allowed to clear the history list.

Favorites Center button displays favorites, feeds, and history.   Previously accessed Web sites   History Tab   Web sites accessed Today

Figure 8-32 A browser's history list records information about all the sites visited for a predetermined period.

EDUCATIONAL CONTROLS

As you have learned, businesses and parents have several available options to control access to inappropriate Internet sites. Most school districts also control student access to objectionable materials by implementing these controls and a few additional ones. For schools, attacking this problem requires a four-pronged approach: filtering software, Acceptable Use Policies, use of curriculum pages, and teacher observation. All four prongs of the approach are discussed in the following sections.

FILTERING SOFTWARE
As previously discussed, filtering software programs prevent the browser from accepting material from targeted sites or material that contains keywords or phrases. Schools install Internet filtering software on their

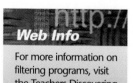
Web Info
For more information on filtering programs, visit the Teachers Discovering Computers Web site (*scsite.com/tdc5*), click Chapter 8, click Web Info, and then click Filtering Programs.

networks and then constantly update the software programs to keep them as current as possible. Although very effective, these filtering software programs do not prevent access to all objectionable and inappropriate materials. One drawback to using filtering software is that it also can block access to legitimate materials or research on controversial issues. A filtering software program is the first level of protection that many school districts use.

ACCEPTABLE USE POLICIES
Recognizing that teachers, students, administrators, and staff personnel need guidance, most schools develop specific standards for the ethical use of computers, school networks, and the Internet. These standards are called Acceptable Use Policies. As discussed in Chapter 2, an Acceptable Use Policy (AUP) is a set of rules that governs the use of school and school district computers, networks, and the Internet by teachers, administrators, staff, and students.

Acceptable Use Policies vary greatly from school district to school district. Many schools have separate AUPs for students, teachers, and staff personnel. Many school districts require both students and their parents to sign student AUPs. Some schools publish student AUPs on their Web sites, which allows new students and parents to print, review, sign, and then mail or deliver them to the school (Figure 8-33). Schools normally will not allow students or teachers to access the school's network or Internet unless a signed AUP is on file. Many AUPs contain the following guidelines:

- Notice that use of school computers, networks, and the Internet is a privilege, not a right
- Notice that students should behave as guests when on the Internet — that is, they should use good manners and be courteous
- List of rules and consequences concerning accessing objectionable Internet sites
- List of rules and consequences dealing with copyright issues
- Outline of proper use of all networks and computers

- List of rules covering online safety and release of personal information

- Notice that students who violate AUPs will face disciplinary action and possible permanent cancellation of school network and/or Internet access privileges

CURRICULUM PAGES As you learned in Chapter 7, a curriculum page is a teacher-created document or Web page that contains hyperlinks to teacher selected and evaluated Web sites. Links on a curriculum page support learning objectives by providing students with quality Web resources, links to additional information, and opportunities to learn more. Using a curriculum page offers several advantages. Students quickly link to excellent sites, instead of the various locations they might find from searching the Internet for information. Because the teacher evaluates the linked sites for content and appropriateness before posting them, a curriculum page significantly reduces the chance students will view an inappropriate site. Furthermore, by providing links for students to click, a curriculum page eliminates the need for students to type URLs. Students often make mistakes typing URLs, which, in addition to wasting time, sometimes links them to inappropriate or incorrect sites.

TEACHER OBSERVATION Teacher observation or supervision permits teachers to monitor their students actively and continuously while they are on the Internet (Figure 8-34). Teacher observation is extremely important and, in most cases, a final measure to prevent students from accessing objectionable and inappropriate materials on the Internet. For teacher observation to be effective, teachers must constantly and actively watch what their students are doing in the classroom and viewing on the Internet. Teachers should direct students that, if they access an Internet site that contains objectionable material, they should immediately click their browser's Back button to return to the previous page and if this does not work simply close the browser. Either is a quick-and-easy way to prevent objectionable material from displaying in the browser. You also might want students to notify you if such a situation arises so that you can add that site to the sites restricted by the filtering software. Some

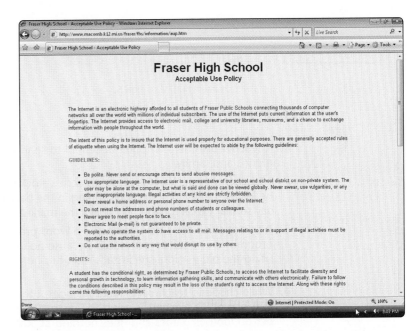

Figure 8-33 Many schools include AUPs on their Web sites so new teachers, students, and parents can print and review, sign, and then mail or deliver them to the school.

Figure 8-34 Teacher observations can prevent students from viewing objectionable or inappropriate material on the Internet.

schools have installed software programs on their lab computers, such as Apple's Remote Desktop for Macintosh computers, which enables teachers to keep an eye on all the computer screens in a classroom or lab.

As a final note, all educators should understand clearly the ethical issues covered in this chapter in order to model these concepts for their students and teach them to be ethical computer users. The questionnaire shown in Figure 8-35 on the next page will help you further understand these ethical concepts.

COMPUTER ETHICS QUESTIONNAIRE

	Ethical	Unethical	Crime
1. A teacher uses her computer at school to send e-mail to her friends and family.	☐	☐	☐
2. A teacher uses the Web at school to access stock market reports. He leaves the Web connection running in the background all day so that he can periodically check the market.	☐	☐	☐
3. A principal installs a new version of a word processing program on her office computer. Because no one will be using the old version, she installs it on her home computer so her husband and children can use it.	☐	☐	☐
4. While checking teachers' e-mail messages, the principal finds that one of his teachers is using the district's e-mail system to bet on football games and does nothing about it.	☐	☐	☐
5. A school technology facilitator has her students develop PowerPoint tutorials. When the projects are completed, she offers to sell the tutorials to another school.	☐	☐	☐
6. A principal tells a teacher to install a piece of software on numerous computers on campus. The teacher knows the software has a single-user license, but because the principal said to install it, he does.	☐	☐	☐
7. Personnel in the district's computer center occasionally monitor computer use in the schools. They monitor how often and for what length of time particular teachers are connected to the Internet, as well as what sites have been visited.	☐	☐	☐
8. The media specialist uses photo retouching software to put her school name on another school's logo.	☐	☐	☐
9. A teacher downloads a piece of shareware software. He uses it for the allotted time and when asked to pay for the software, he simply closes the window and continues to use it.	☐	☐	☐
10. An educational learning company contacts a principal requesting information about students, including names and addresses. The company offers to provide students with free learning supplements. The principal sends the company her student database.	☐	☐	☐
11. Your students are creating Web pages. They search the Internet for ideas. One of them finds a very cool home page, copies the page, changes the name, and uses it as her own.	☐	☐	☐
12. You are doing a unit on famous cartoon characters and go to the Disney Web site to get clip art for your curriculum page.	☐	☐	☐
13. Two of your students have posted cruel and malicious information about a teacher you know from another school.	☐	☐	☐

Figure 8-35 Indicate whether you think each described situation is ethical, unethical, or a crime. Discuss your answers with other teachers; use this questionnaire as a springboard for a discussion about computer ethics with your students.

Health Issues

Users are a key component in any information system. Thus, protecting teachers and students is just as important as protecting hardware, software, and data. Many health-related issues concerning computer use can be minimized by teaching students at an early age how to use computers properly so they reduce their risk of injury. The following sections discuss health risks and preventions.

COMPUTERS AND HEALTH ISSUES

The Bureau of Labor Statistics reports that work-related musculoskeletal disorders account for one-third of all job-related injuries and illnesses. A **musculoskeletal disorder** (**MSD**), also called a **repetitive strain injury** (**RSI**), is an injury or disorder of the muscles, nerves, tendons, ligaments, and joints. Computer-related RSIs include tendonitis and carpal tunnel syndrome. The largest job-related injury and illness problems in the United States today are repetitive strain injuries. For this reason, the Occupational Safety and Health Administration (OSHA) has developed industry-specific and task-specific guidelines designed to prevent workplace injuries with respect to computer usage.

Tendonitis is inflammation of a tendon due to some repeated motion or stress on the tendon. **Carpal tunnel syndrome** (**CTS**) is inflammation of the nerve that connects the forearm to the palm of the wrist. Repeated or forceful bending of the wrist can cause CTS or tendonitis of the wrist. Symptoms of tendonitis of the wrist include extreme pain that extends from the forearm to the hand, along with tingling in the fingers. Symptoms of CTS include burning pain when the nerve is compressed, along with numbness and tingling in the thumb and first two fingers.

Long-term computer use can lead to tendonitis or CTS. Factors that cause these disorders include prolonged typing and mouse usage, or continual shifting between the mouse and the keyboard.

You can take many precautions to prevent these types of injuries both for yourself and your students. Take frequent breaks during computer sessions to exercise your hands and arms (Figure 8-36). To prevent injury due to typing, place a wrist rest between the keyboard and the edge of your desk. The wrist rest reduces strain on your wrist while typing. To prevent injury while using a mouse, place the mouse at least six inches from the edge of the desk. Finally, minimize the number of times you switch between the mouse and the keyboard, and avoid using the heel of your hand as a pivot point while typing or using the mouse.

HAND EXERCISES

- Spread fingers apart for several seconds while keeping wrists straight.
- Gently push back fingers and then thumb.
- Dangle arms loosely at sides and then shake arms and hands.

Figure 8-36 To reduce the chance of developing tendonitis or carpal tunnel syndrome, take frequent breaks during computer sessions to exercise your hands and arms.

Another type of health-related condition due to computer usage is **computer vision syndrome (CVS)**. You may have CVS if you have any of these conditions: sore, tired, burning, itching, or dry eyes; blurred or double vision; distance-blurred vision after prolonged staring at a display device; headache or sore neck; difficulty shifting focus between a display device and documents; difficulty focusing on the screen image; color fringes or after-images when you look away from the display device; and increasing sensitivity to light. Although eyestrain associated with CVS is not thought to have serious or long-term consequences, it is disruptive and unpleasant. Figure 8-37 outlines some techniques you can follow to ease eyestrain.

People who spend their workday using the computer

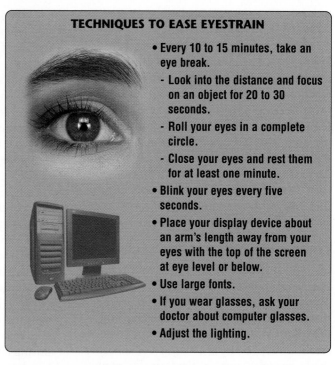

TECHNIQUES TO EASE EYESTRAIN

- Every 10 to 15 minutes, take an eye break.
  - Look into the distance and focus on an object for 20 to 30 seconds.
  - Roll your eyes in a complete circle.
  - Close your eyes and rest them for at least one minute.
- Blink your eyes every five seconds.
- Place your display device about an arm's length away from your eyes with the top of the screen at eye level or below.
- Use large fonts.
- If you wear glasses, ask your doctor about computer glasses.
- Adjust the lighting.

Figure 8-37 Following these tips can help reduce eyestrain while working on the computer.

sometimes complain of lower back pain, muscle fatigue, and emotional fatigue. Lower back pain sometimes is caused by poor posture. Always sit and have your students sit properly in the chair. Take a short break every 30 to 60 minutes — stand up, walk around, or stretch.

ERGONOMICS

Ergonomics is an applied science devoted to incorporating comfort, efficiency, and safety into the design of items in the workplace. Ergonomic studies have shown that using the correct type and configuration of chair, keyboard, display device, and work surface helps users work comfortably and efficiently, and helps protect their health (Figure 8-38).

Many display devices and keyboards have features that help address ergonomic issues. Some keyboards have built-in wrist rests and can be purchased from any computer supply store. Other keyboards are ergonomically designed specifically to prevent RSI. Display devices usually have controls that allow you to adjust the brightness, contrast, positioning, height, and width of images. Most monitors have a tilt-and-swivel base, allowing you to adjust the angle of the screen to minimize neck strain and reduce glare from overhead lighting.

viewing angle: 20° from eye to to center of screen

viewing distance: 18 to 28 inches

arms: elbows at about 90° and arms and hands approximately parallel to floor

chair: chair height should be adjustable and chair should have 4 or 5 legs for stability

keyboard: placement should be 23 to 28 inches depending on height of user

feet: flat on floor

Figure 8-38 A well-designed work area should be flexible to allow adjustments to the height and build of different individuals. Good lighting and air quality also are important considerations.

Emerging Technologies

The classrooms and schools you attended throughout your 13 years of K-12 education probably were similar to the classrooms in which your parents sat — for some of you, the schools and furniture were exactly the same. More importantly, your educational experience and the educational experiences of your parents probably were very similar, too. Unlike society, which has changed dramatically, many schools and school curricula have been slow to change during the past few decades.

Fortunately, the infusion of modern digital media computers, high-speed networks and Internet access, higher-quality educational software, and a realization by administrators that teachers must receive extensive and appropriate technology training is beginning to transform many classrooms.

Due to the infusion of informational technologies and the World Wide Web, teachers no longer are bound by the four walls of traditional classrooms and the two covers of traditional textbooks (Figure 8-39). Furthermore, technology has helped a number of schools significantly improve the quality of their graduates.

Because of the strong commitment of federal, state, and local governments, thousands of organizations dedicated to improving education, and millions of concerned parents, the infusion of technologies into schools will continue — and continue explosively. Technology has only begun to influence the way teachers instruct and students learn.

The following sections summarize seven emerging areas of educational technology that will continue to influence significantly the public education system: the digital media revolution, the World Wide Web, the next generation of software on DVDs, assistive technologies, Web- and video-enhanced digital textbooks, Web-based distance learning, and wireless technologies. Importantly, many of these emerging technologies will continue to support and reinforce state and federal curriculum and technology standards.

Figure 8-39 The Web has enormous potential to change the way teachers instruct and students learn due to the vast amount of current and education-related information available at thousands of Web sites.

DIGITAL MEDIA REVOLUTION

As you have learned throughout this textbook, today's digital kids are different and they learn differently. You have learned a lot about all that is digital media. You have read about many new and exciting software programs that thousands of students are using everyday to create digital media presentations and projects. An interactive digital media revolution is just beginning — a revolution being fueled by the needs and desires of today's digital students. This revolution will continue to profoundly impact the way teachers teach and the way today's digital students learn. To reach and motivate today's students, teachers must understand this digital media revolution and utilize current and future digital media technologies. This digital media revolution will shape a generation like never before in history, and teachers must eagerly adopt and integrate digital media technologies and create innovative teaching and learning opportunities.

Another impact of this digital media revolution is a trend to move from using traditional textbooks and curriculum to an all digital curriculum. In the fall of 2005, Vail High School in Tucson became Arizona's first all wireless, all laptop, all digital public school. Vail's digital students will not be carrying around nor using traditional textbooks, instead, its curriculum will be completely digital, including extensive use of online resources.

Integration Strategies

To learn more about the digital media revolution so you can integrate emerging tools with your students, visit the Teachers Discovering Computers Web site (*scsite.com/tdc5*), click Chapter 8, and then click Digital Media Corner.

THE WORLD WIDE WEB

The federal government is committed to ensuring that every K-12 classroom has high-speed Internet access and is investing billions of dollars to meet that goal. The following specific Internet improvements will directly influence the quality of the K-12 educational experience:

- The speed of the Internet will increase dramatically.

- The majority of PreK-12 students in most schools will be able to access thousands of full-motion videos on demand. Streaming video technology will allow teachers to bring live video footage of current and historical events into their classrooms. In addition, teachers and students will create their own high-quality videos on a multitude of topics. More students will be reviewing video productions on their iPods and other similar devices.

- Teachers and students will have instant access to tens of thousands of interactive Web-based educational software programs, including tutorials, exercises, virtual-reality tours, science experiments, games, and other subject-related activities. Many of these online educational programs will be fully interactive, thus opening up incredible opportunities for discovery learning (Figure 8-40). Because of Bluetooth and other transfer technologies, many of these programs will be accessed by students on their iPods and other similar devices.

Figure 8-40 Many educational Web sites are offering students and teachers opportunities to explore education topics interactively.

EDUCATIONAL SOFTWARE ON DVD

During the last 10 years, the influx of digital media computers with CD-ROM drives and the availability of hundreds of high-quality CD-based educational software programs impacted education significantly.

During the next five years, the availability of DVD-based education software programs will have an even greater impact on education. The large storage capacity of DVDs allows educational software developers to build programs that contain vast amounts of information, graphics, animations, video, and interactive links. These next-generation educational software programs on DVDs will include hours of high-quality full-motion video that teachers and students may access instantly.

ASSISTIVE TECHNOLOGIES

Dramatic improvements are being made in hardware, software, and Web-based tools that teachers will use to help instruct students with special needs. As you learned earlier, assistive technologies are innovative technologies that modify or adapt the classroom for special learning needs. Assistive technologies aid in teaching students who have physical, sensory, or cognitive disabilities. Emerging assistive technologies will provide teachers with innovative tools to help students with special needs overcome the disability that blocks or impedes their learning process.

Teacher education programs and K-12 schools are placing more emphasis on assistive technologies, due to the number of students with disabilities who are mainstreamed into regular classrooms. According to the Individuals with Disabilities Education Act (IDEA) Amendments of 1997, regular classroom teachers must be part of the cross-curriculum and interdisciplinary team that teaches all students. Technology is the bridge that provides new strategies for all students to learn and succeed (Figure 8-41).

Many leaders express concern that current technologies are widening the gap between the economic haves and have-nots. Federal funding, private funding, and emerging technologies will provide the funding and guidance needed to ensure that at-risk students have equal access to current and emerging technologies.

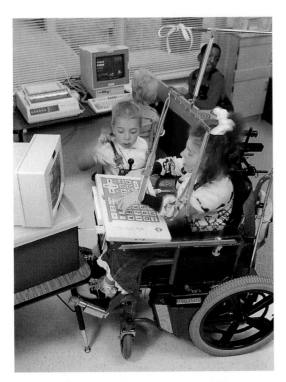

Figure 8-41 Technology can be the bridge that provides new strategies for all students to learn and succeed, including students with physical and other challenges.

FEDERAL ACCESSIBILITY INITIATIVE

In 1998, Congress amended the Rehabilitation Act to require federal agencies to make their electronic and information technology accessible to people with disabilities. Under **Section 508**, agencies must give employees with disabilities and members of the public access to technology that is comparable to the access available to others. The law applies to all federal agencies when they develop, procure, maintain, or use electronic and information technology.

Education agencies can verify easily that their Web sites and pages meet Section 508 requirements by using a software program that analyzes Web sites and pages to see if they meet the World Wide Web Consortium's (W3C) Web content Accessibilities Guidelines. For example, for a Web site to be approved, it must (partial list):

- Provide text equivalents for all nontext elements (such as images, animations, video, and audio).

- Provide summaries of graphs and charts.

- Ensure that all information displayed in color also is available without color.

WebXACT is a free software program, created by the Watchfire Corporation that allows Web authors to identify changes they need to make to their pages so users with disabilities can more easily use their Web pages. Using WebXACT is simple; Web authors enter their URL and WebXACT analyzes the Web site for compliance (Figure 8-42). Additional information is provided at this chapter's Assistive Technologies Corner.

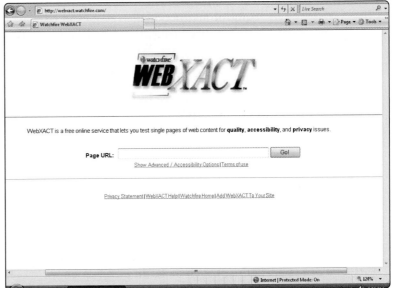

Figure 8-42 This free site allows Web authors to check their Web sites to ensure that the Web sites meet accessibility guidelines.

WEB- AND VIDEO-ENHANCED DIGITAL TEXTBOOKS

For many years, K-12 textbooks remained basically unchanged. Recently, however, this began to change as the Web became an integral part of K-12 books. Traditional textbooks will fade into history as all areas of education create increasingly interactive and extensive Web- and video-enhanced digital textbooks. Many of these books will correlate to national and state curriculum standards and benchmarks.

Imagine teaching social studies, biology, or English literature using a Web- and video-enhanced digital textbook with an extensive Web site that continuously is updated and maintained by a team of experienced educators. In addition, the digitized textbooks provide students with discovery learning avenues and information about thousands of topics from thousands of sources all over the world. Finally, a number of textbook publishers are predicting that traditional textbooks will become obsolete as more and more school districts adopt digital textbooks for their digital curriculum.

WEB-BASED DISTANCE LEARNING

Due to the increasingly diverse population of students, education is changing in an effort to meet the needs of this diverse and changing student body. These changes bring the Web to the forefront of instructional strategies in education — specifically, the use of Web-based distance learning. Web-based distance learning already has experienced phenomenal growth in institutions of higher education and K-12 schools. The more common approach for schools to take, however, is to use the Web to enhance classes and instruction.

Web-based instructional strategies offer creative solutions for homebound students, home-schooled students, at-risk students, students who are physically challenged, and teacher shortages for specialized positions. Because many small or rural schools cannot offer students courses such as Latin and French, or advanced-placement courses in math and science, states and school districts now offer students these specialized courses using the Web. Depending on the situation and school district policies, students take these Web-based courses at home, at a public library, or in a classroom — Internet access is the common agent for this remote instruction. For example, Florida Virtual School, which opened in 1997 as a two-county initiative, now provides online classes and instruction to all public, private, and home-school students in Florida and other states (Figure 8-43).

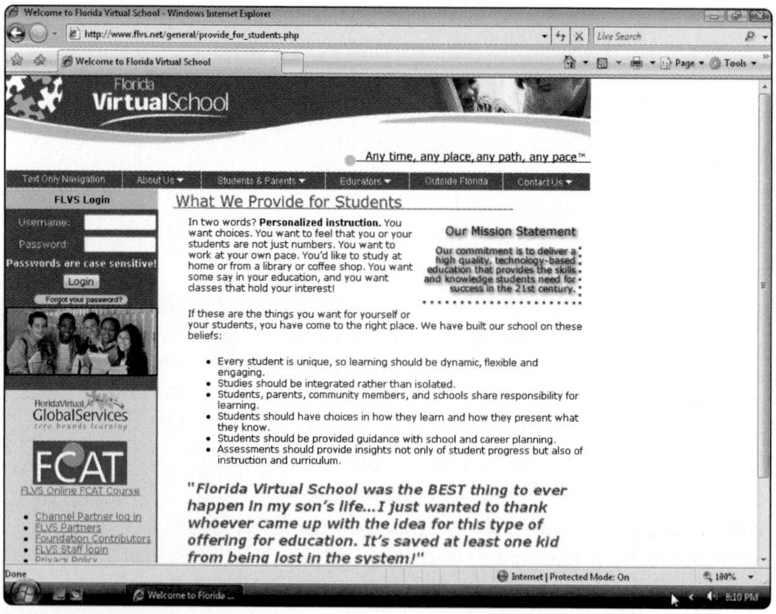

WIRELESS TECHNOLOGIES

The last decade of the twentieth century was dominated by the evolution of the World Wide Web. Although the Web will continue to evolve and mature, it is clear that the first decade of the twenty-first century is being dominated by the wireless revolution that is taking place globally. Today's wireless technology represents an evolution in products and services that quickly is transforming the way people live, work, learn, and teach. Wireless technology will continue to impact our K-12 education system dramatically in the following ways:

- Wireless communications will allow teachers and students to connect their smart phones, PDAs, notebook computers, Tablet PCs, iPods, and other wireless devices to a truly global high-speed network.

- Wireless desktop computers, Tablet PCs, mobile labs, and other devices will ensure that educational technology is used seamlessly at the point of instruction.

- Global wireless access will ensure that all children, regardless of their socioeconomic status, will have access to educational classroom materials and the world itself from their homes, their schools, and many other locations throughout their communities.

Wireless technologies already have changed the way you communicate with relatives, colleagues, and friends. Indeed, you are taking part in the wireless revolution that is sweeping the world and is just beginning to change and influence the way we teach and learn in our schools.

Web Info

To learn more about a Web-enhanced high-school class, visit the Teachers Discovering Computers Web site (*scsite.com/tdc5*), click Chapter 8, click Web Info, and then click Class.

Figure 8-43 Today, more than 40,000 high school students from all 67 Florida county school districts, charter and private schools, and other states enroll in more than 90 classes via the Florida Virtual School.

To learn more about the wireless revolution and how it will impact you, your students, and your family, review the special feature, A World Without Wires, that follows Chapter 1.

Guide to Professional, State, and Federal Educational Web Sites

The federal government, state governments and institutions, and professional educational organizations provide a multitude of resources for K-12 teachers and students. The special feature that follows this chapter provides links to and information on (1) more than 30 popular professional education organizations, all of which provide educational resources for teachers and students, (2) over 30 federal government agencies, and (3) Departments of Education for all 50 states and the District of Columbia. Updated links to the most current URLs for these resources are located at the textbook Web site.

Summary of Security Issues, Ethics, and Emerging Technologies in Education

The livelihood of businesses, schools, and individuals depends on the computers and networks in use every day. This increased reliance on computers and information sent over networks makes it essential to take steps to protect the systems and information from known risks. At the same time, employees, teachers, and students also have an obligation to use computers responsibly and not abuse the power computers provide. This responsibility presents constant challenges, which sometimes weigh the rights of the individual against increased efficiency and productivity. Schools have the added responsibility and challenge of protecting their students from unethical practices and people. Educational technologies are tools, and their effectiveness is determined by the knowledge, skill, experience, level of training, and ethics of the user. The educational technology knowledge you acquire should help you participate more effectively in

decisions on how to use computers and other educational technologies, and how to use the Internet efficiently and ethically.

Summary of Teachers Discovering Computers

To be effective in using educational technology in their classrooms, teachers must be computer literate, information literate, and most importantly, integration literate. This textbook provided you with knowledge and skills in all three areas. What you have learned is only a beginning.

Teachers must continuously update their technology and technology integration skills. Teachers have an incredible responsibility — a far greater responsibility than any previous generation of teachers. The amount of knowledge that teachers must instill in their digital students is enormous and continues to expand at a phenomenal rate. To continue to prosper in the twenty-first century, educational institutions must provide today's digital students with a solid foundation of the basic skills and other core subjects. Used as instructional and productivity tools, current and emerging technologies help teachers make a difference in the quality of their students' education. Teachers can use and integrate technology to influence future generations in immensely positive ways (Figure 8-44).

Figure 8-44 Teachers make a difference in the quality of their students' education when they integrate technology effectively.

Key Terms

Instructions: Use the Key Terms to help focus your study of the terms used in this chapter. To further enhance your understanding of the Key Terms in this chapter, visit scsite.com/tdc5, click Chapter 8 at the top of the Web page, and then click Key Terms on the left sidebar. Read the definition for each term and then access current and additional information about the term from the Web.

Exercises

Web Info
Key Terms
Checkpoint
Teaching Today
Education Issues
Integration Corner
Software Corner
Digital Media Corner
Assistive Technologies Corner
In the Lab
Learn It Online

Features

Timeline
Guide to WWW Sites
Search Tools
Buyer's Guide
State/Federal Sites
Professional Sites

access control [475]
antispam program [486]
antivirus program [474]

backup [483]
backup procedure [483]
biometric device [476]
blackout [482]
boot sector virus [471]
brownout [482]

carpal tunnel syndrome (CTS) [497]
Children's Internet Protection Act (CIPA) [492]
community site license [480]
computer crime [470]
computer ethics [484]
computer security risk [470]
computer vandalism [478]
computer vision syndrome (CVS) [498]
copyright [486]
cracker [475]
cyberbullying [492]

electronic profile [484]
e-mail filtering [486]
employee monitoring [486]
encryption [481]
encryption key [481]
end-user license agreement (EULA) [478]
ergonomics [498]
ethics [484]

fair use [488]
file virus [471]
firewall [477]
freeware [480]

hacker [475]

information privacy [484]

logic bomb [472]

macro virus [471]
malicious software programs [471]
Michelangelo virus [472]
musculoskeletal disorder (MSD) [497]

network site license [480]

objectionable material [491]
off-site location [483]
overvoltage [482]

password [475]
personal firewall [477]
personal identification number (PIN) [476]
phishing [485]
possessed object [476]
power surge [482]
product activation [479]
proxy server [477]
public domain [490]

repetitive strain injury (RSI) [497]
rescue disc [474]
restore [483]

Section 508 [501]
shareware [480]
single-user license agreement [478]
site license [480]
software license [478]
software piracy [478]
spam [485]
spike [482]
spim [485]
split [485]
surge protector [482]
system failure [481]

teacher observation [495]
tendonitis [497]
time bomb [472]
Trojan horse [471]

unauthorized access [475]
unauthorized use [475]
undervoltage [482]
uninterruptible power supply (UPS) [475]
user ID [474]

vaccine [474]
virus [470]
virus hoax [475]
virus payload [471]

Web publishing [489]
worm [471]

Checkpoint

Instructions: Use the Checkpoint exercises to check your knowledge level of the chapter. To complete the Checkpoint exercises interactively, visit scsite.com/tdc5, click Chapter 8 at the top of the Web page, and then click Checkpoint on the left sidebar.

1. Label the Figure

Instructions: Identify each type of software license.

Type of License	Characteristics	Use in Schools
1._____	Software can be installed on only one computer. Some license agreements allow users to install the software on one desktop computer and one notebook computer.	Used when a school needs only a few copies of a particular software. Commonly found in small schools and when purchasing specialized software programs.
2._____	Software can be installed on a set number of computers, typically 5, 10, 50, or more. Cost varies based on number of computers.	Cost-effective method to install software on more than one computer. Most commonly used in schools.
3._____	Software is installed on the school's network. The license will specify and the software will control a specific number of simultaneous users, such as 50, 100, 250, or 500. Cost varies based on number of computers.	Cost-effective method of allowing students and teachers throughout the school to have access to an application software program.
4._____	Frequently used with software distributed on CDs/DVDs. Any number of programs can be purchased for either Macintosh or PC platforms.	Very cost-effective method for school districts or states to purchase large quantities of software. Savings can be significant over individual CD or DVD pricing.

2. Matching

Instructions: Match each term from the column on the left with the best description from the column on the right.

_____ 1. filtering software
_____ 2. cyberbullying
_____ 3. Trojan horse
_____ 4. Web publishing
_____ 5. computer ethics

a. posting or sending detrimental or cruel text or images using the Internet or digital devices

b. moral guidelines that govern the use of computers, networks, and information systems

c. prevents browser from displaying materials from certain Web sites

d. a virus designed to look like a legitimate program

e. the development and maintenance of Web pages

3. Short Answer

Instructions: Write a brief answer to each of the following questions.

1. What are computer security risks? What different types of security risks threaten school computers? What are some safeguards that minimize security risks?

2. What is a virus? Describe three types of viruses. Why are viruses commonly found in schools? What can teachers do to minimize the impact of viruses both at home and at school?

3. What are computer ethics? List and briefly explain five important areas of computer ethics. Describe two recent government actions that protect children while using the Internet.

4. What is an overvoltage? What precautions should teachers take to protect their computers and other electronic equipment from overvoltages, both at home and at school?

5. What is an Acceptable Use Policy (AUP)? Why are AUPs so important for K-12 schools? Describe two other ways to limit student access to inappropriate Internet sites.

Teaching Today

INSTRUCTIONS: Teaching Today provides teachers with integration strategies and ideas for teaching and, more importantly, reaching today's digital generation. Each numbered segment contains one or more links that reinforce the information presented in the segment. To display this page from the Web, visit scsite.com/tdc5, click Chapter 8 at the top of the Web page, and then click Teaching Today on the left sidebar.

1. Teachers Helping Parents

Using the Internet in your classroom can be an important and easy way to integrate technology; there are so many resources, Web sites, and online tools available for teachers to use in every grade level. Did you ever wonder how parents feel about their children using the Internet? What kinds of concerns do you think they might have? According to the National School Board Association (NSBA), most parents support the use of the Internet in the classroom. Parents also believe that using the Internet is an excellent resource for learning and communications. The NSBA reports that most parents purchase computers to help their children with their education. Teachers need to help parents understand the benefits and pitfalls of their children's Internet and Web usage.

2. Acceptable Use Policy

You are an innovative teacher with three multimedia computers connected to the Internet in your classroom. You also have access to a wireless mobile lab and many other technologies. Your school has a schoolwide Acceptable Use Policy (AUP) for teachers, staff, students, and parents. You have been thinking, however, about having an additional AUP for your students and their parents, not only to protect the students, but also to have your students learn how to use different technologies responsibly and safely. What key components do you think your AUP should include? Do you think you should let your students help you create the AUP? Do you think this might be a good learning experience for the students? Why or why not? What are some consequences you think students should face for violating your classroom AUP? How will you enforce the AUP with students and parents?

3. Viruses

Recently, you have been hearing a lot about viruses. You have two computers in your classroom and they are connected to the Internet. In the past, you have not worried about viruses because your computers have never been infected. Other teachers, however, have been discussing a new virus affecting their computers. Where can you get reliable information about viruses? What kind of support is available on the Internet? Can you get a virus from the Internet? How can you protect your computers from getting a virus?

4. Fair Use

Based on Section 107 of the Copyright Act of 1976, also known as fair use, teachers are allowed to photocopy and use a limited amount of copyrighted materials in their classrooms under specific conditions for educational purposes. With the advent of digital media, the Internet, and the World Wide Web, legislators have had to reexamine fair use. Many teachers and students wrongly think they can copy anything from the Web and it becomes theirs. Is using materials found on the Web different from using materials found in a copyrighted book? How can you determine if your use of copyrighted materials is governed by fair-

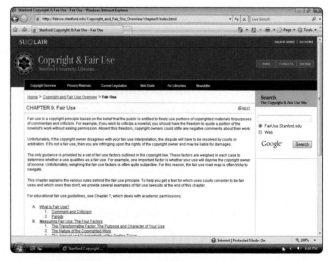

use rules? Because it has become so easy to copy materials from so many different sources, how will you teach your students about copyright laws and fair use?

Education Issues

Instructions: Education Issues provides several scenarios that allow you to explore controversial and current issues in education. Each numbered segment contains one or more links that reinforce the information presented in the segment. To display this page from the Web, visit scsite.com/tdc5, click Chapter 8 at the top of the Web page, and then click Education Issues on the left sidebar.

1. Research and Term Papers

For years, the only way to write a term paper was to visit the library, comb through card catalogs and resource books, and then walk through shelves of texts and journals to find what you needed — before you even started to write. Today, several Web sites provide a searchable database of term papers gathered from college and high school students. Students can download a research or term paper, make any necessary changes, print a copy, and then turn it in as their own. How can instructors keep students from claiming the work of others as their own? Explain how using the Web for research differs from using it to copy someone's work. What should be the consequences for plagiarizing content from a Web site?

2. Teacher and Student Monitoring

Your school district maintains a policy that states classroom computers and Internet access are to be used for instructional purposes only. The district instructs teachers not to send or receive personal e-mail messages or instant messages (IMs), surf the Internet for fun, or play games on classroom computers. The district uses monitoring software to observe Internet activities. Some teachers feel they should be allowed to use the Internet or work on their personal projects during their lunch periods and after school. What limits, if any, should be placed on teachers' use of classroom computers? How closely should the school district be able to monitor teacher and student use? Why? Network specialists can see anything and everything on your computer. Should administrative personnel be allowed to monitor your e-mail messages and files on your school computer? Why or why not? Should you be allowed to monitor your students' e-mail messages? Why or why not?

3. Software Ethics

You recently purchased a DK Multimedia CD using your own funds for use on one computer in your classroom. Another teacher borrows your CD so she can evaluate it for use in her classroom. A few weeks later, you find out that numerous other teachers in your school have a copy of the DK Multimedia CD. You ask the teacher about this and she says, "Oh, this is so cool. I have a CD-RW on my home computer and it is so easy to copy CDs. I am so proud of myself! I made one for everyone!" You know this breaks copyright laws, could get the school fined, and that it also is morally and ethically wrong. What to do? Should you tell the teacher, your principal, or technology facilitator? Could you be liable because you loaned her the original CD? How will you solve this dilemma?

4. Software Piracy

Software manufacturers are watching school districts closely for evidence of illegal use of software. Recently, a major school district was fined $300,000 for having multiple copies of nonlicensed software installed on classroom computers. Teachers often illegally install multiple copies of single-user programs on their classroom computers. What are some of the ethical issues regarding software piracy? Why is illegally installing software so prevalent in K-12 schools? How does the software industry deal with violators of software copyright law? Describe several ways in which school districts can prevent illegal software from being installed on school computers.

5. Students, School Buses and Lunches, and Biometrics

A Florida school district requires that students provide a biometric thumbprint both as they enter and as they leave their GPS-tracked school buses each day. The school system cites both safety and financial (the fact that more accurate counting and tracking of the bus usage will result in more state transportation funds) reasons for using GPS. An Ohio school system requires that students use a biometric thumbprint to pay for their school lunches. The school board cites the need to track the number of free and subsidized lunches that the schools provide better. Should children be required to provide biometric information to engage in common public school-related activities? Why or why not? What are the privacy issues involved and should parents be concerned?

Integration Corner

Instructions: Integration Corner provides extensive ideas and resources for integrating technology into your classroom-specific curriculum. To display this page from the Web and its links to approximately 100 educational Web sites, visit scsite.com/tdc5, click Chapter 8 at the top of the Web page, and then click Integration Corner on the left sidebar.

Integration Corner is designed for teachers and other educators who are looking for innovative ways to integrate technology into their content-specific curriculum. Integration Corner not only provides great Web sites with current information, but also shows what other educators are doing in the field of educational technology. These Corners are designed for all educators regardless of their area of interest. Be sure to review information and Web sites outside of your teaching area because many great integration ideas in one area can be modified easily for use in other curriculum areas.

Teachers and administrators will find other colleagues in their areas with whom to connect and share the successes and hurdles of integrating technology into the classroom or an entire school system. Consider Integration Corner your one stop for integration ideas and resources. Links to educational Web sites are organized in the following 12 Corners, and different Web resources are available for each chapter. Figure 8-45 shows examples of the Web resources provided in the Chapter 8 Research Corner.

Early Childhood Corner	*Math Corner*
Elementary Corner	*Science Corner*
Middle School Corner	*Special Education Corner*
Secondary Corner	*Post Secondary Corner*
Reading/Language Arts Corner	*Administrator Corner*
Social Studies/History Corner	*Research Corner*

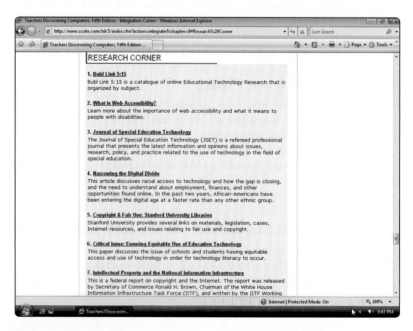

Figure 8-45 Examples of the Web resources provided in the Chapter 8 Research Corner.

Software Corner

1. Antivirus Programs

Computer viruses spread faster than the common cold! When you and your students download files from the Internet, open e-mail attachments, or transport files between computers, you are at risk of getting a virus. Norton AntiVirus or McAfee's VirusScan will detect viruses in e-mail attachments, in files, on USB flash drives, and in your computer's system files. Both companies allow users to update their virus protection files online. These antivirus programs can be set up to scan your computer automatically on a regular basis. Their Web sites provide information about the latest viruses as well as news releases and virus tips to help consumers better protect themselves.

2. Ad-Aware SE Personal Edition

When using the Internet, problems are sometimes just one click away. Students are often lured by the "You have won!" pop-up ads that display on numerous Web sites. Unfortunately, many Web sites, including those with pop-up ads, install hidden files on computers that visit these sites. These hidden files cannot be removed by antivirus programs and, unfortunately, slow computers down significantly, sometimes even shutting down routers. One software program that can "sniff" out these files and quarantine or remove them from your computer is called Ad-Aware SE Personal Edition. This program allows you to scan and clean your computer's internal and external storage devices for annoying adware and spyware programs, allowing you to maintain a higher degree of privacy while you surf the Web.

3. Monitoring Software

Having an AUP is not always enough! Due to all the types of illegal activities that can take place using computers, many businesses, the military, and schools are purchasing software to monitor all activities on their computers. Spector Pro is one of the top-selling software programs for monitoring and recording every detail or keystroke of PC and Internet activity. Spector Pro provides the equivalent of a digital surveillance tape so that you can see everything students, teachers, or employees are doing on their computers. Spector Pro contains seven integrated tools that record the following: chats, instant messages, e-mails sent and received, Web sites visited, search activities, keystrokes typed, programs launched, and peer-to-peer file searching and swapping. In addition to monitoring and recording, Spector Pro has an advanced warning system that informs the system administrator when a PC being monitored has been used in an inappropriate manner.

4. Windows Defender

Using the Internet can be wonderful because it opens your life to many different worlds. Unfortunately, it also opens your computer up to multiple security risks, making it important for you to protect it from invasion at all times. Windows Defender is a free program from Microsoft that protects your computer against multiple security risks. When used with other security programs, it adds to your computer's safety net. You can protect your computer from unwanted software attacks caused by spyware, pop-ups, viruses, and other security threats. A super feature of this software is the support for assistive technology for individuals who have physical or cognitive difficulties, impairments, and other disabilities.

Digital Media Corner

Instructions: Today's K-12 digital students need their learning to be meaningful and relevant to their lives. Digital Media Corner provides videos, ideas, and examples of how you can use digital media to enhance your teaching and your students' learning. To access the videos and links to additional information, visit scsite.com/tdc5, click Chapter 8 at the top of the Web page, and then click Digital Media on the left sidebar.

1. iTunes University

iTunes University (iTunes U) is a Web tool designed for higher education faculty, yet it has a global appeal by providing a centralized repository for storing courses, lectures, activities, presentations, video, audio, and more. Content is mostly tied to specific curricula and courses but it also contains other general information, which includes broad topics (such as geography, science, and technology) and specific topics (such as global warming and why baseballs have stitches). iTunes University is hosted on the iTunes Store and is devoted to education. Subscribers (enrolling free of charge) are given access to thousands of audio and video files. The popularity of iTunes U has grown exponentially and is a significant contributor to the schools without walls concept.

2. iWeb

Teachers are always looking for easy, user-friendly solutions to create Web pages for themselves and their students. Apple's iWeb, a template-based Web creation tool, is included with the iLife Suite. iWeb allows users to easily create and publish curriculum pages, Web sites, blogs, and wikis. It contains templates and themed design tools for those new to Web site creation, requiring very little upfront learning. Once the theme is chosen, users can drag and drop photos, movies, and other media onto the pages in the placeholders provided.

3. Viruses, Firewalls, and Spyware on Your Computer

You must protect your computer from many different security risks, such as viruses, unauthorized software attacks, and even spyware. Some programs install spyware when the program is installed, so you may be unaware your computer has spyware programs on it. Different types of spyware exist, such as keystroke recorder spyware and advertising spyware. There are videos on the Web that you can use to learn more about these threats; you also can use these video resources to teach your students about viruses and other programs that can harm computers.

4. Visual Communicator

Today, students are creating digital media elements, and sharing them with classmates in project-based learning environments. Software has become so user-friendly that even young learners can include digital media in their projects by using products such as Adobe's Visual Communicator. Visual Communicator is designed specifically for users who are novices at making videos. There are many ways educators can integrate the software into their discipline-specific curriculum through instruction, student projects, and assignments, such as multimedia video production projects, video booktalks, video science and math projects, video yearbooks, and more.

5. Video Yearbooks

Video yearbooks are not a new idea but some schools are trying a new idea this year. At the beginning of the school year, selected seniors are designated as journalists who are asked to record their daily lives and activities their senior year. Using smart phones or small handheld digital cameras, these journals are recorded and uploaded as video blogs or vlogs to a senior class Web site. These informal digital journals are then released to the students who can follow along. At the end of the year, the vlogs are consolidated using video postproduction editing techniques so they can be saved to a DVD for distribution as a video yearbook or combined with the traditional paper version of the yearbooks.

Assistive Technologies Corner

Instructions: Assistive Technologies Corner provides information on current hardware, software, and peripherals that will assist you in delivering instruction to students with physical, cognitive, or sensory challenges. To access extensive additional information, visit scsite.com/tdc5, click Chapter 8 at the top of the Web page, and then click Assistive Technologies on the left sidebar.

1. What Is the Federal Accessibility Initiative?

In 1998, Congress amended the Rehabilitation Act to require federal agencies to make their electronic and information technology accessible to people with disabilities. Under Section 508, agencies must give all persons with disabilities access to technology that is comparable to the access available to others. In addition, the World Wide Web Consortium (W3C) has developed accessibility guidelines encouraging Web authors worldwide to create accessible pages.

2. What Are Accessible Web Pages?

Accessible Web pages are constructed to be usable by anyone, even if the person is using assistive technology to access the Web page. Examples of assistive technologies are screen readers, screen magnifiers, voice recognition software, alternative keyboards, and Braille displays. We speak of accessible Web pages as being Section 508 compliant, or meeting Web accessibility guidelines.

3. Do I Have to Make My Web Pages Accessible?

The Individuals with Disabilities Education Act (IDEA) of 1997 guarantees access to curriculum for all users. Many school districts have accessibility policies in place and compliance with those policies is a professional responsibility. After a teacher-created Web page is posted, all should have access to it, including persons with disabilities.

4. So, How Can I Make My Pages Accessible?

An educator can consider the following issues when developing Web pages that meet accessibility guidelines.

1. **Use valid code.** WYSIWYG (What You See Is What You Get) programs for Web authoring, such as Dreamweaver, have means for checking that the HTML code in the pages is valid (correct). Use the option to check code validity in your program of choice.
2. **Use CSS (Cascading Style Sheets) in styling pages.** In the preferences of your WYSIWYG program, choose anything that says, Use CSS.
3. **Provide text alternatives to images.** When you add an image to a page, write a descriptive phrase for the image, which a screen reader will voice.
4. **Make meaning independent of color.** "Click the red triangle" can be a difficult task for a color-blind person, but making each choice a different shape instead of a different color makes the task independent of color.
5. **Include visible text links** on a page for images that have hyperlinked hot spots.
6. **Use column-and-row tables for data only.** Put column and row headers in those data tables.
7. If you choose to use frames, be sure to **title each frame** you use.
8. **Do not depend on scripts** to make your Web site work. Some users (not only disabled users) may not be able to run the scripts.
9. **Caption video** before putting it on your site.
10. Provide users with an option to **skip repetitive links,** such as site navigation links.

Follow the instructions at the top of this page to display additional information and this chapter's links on assistive technologies.

In the Lab

Instructions: In the Lab provides rubric development exercises that are divided into two areas, productivity and integration. To access the links to tutorials, productivity ideas, integration examples and ideas, and more, visit scsite.com/tdc5, click Chapter 8 at the top of the Web page, and then click In the Lab on the left sidebar.

PRODUCTIVITY IN THE CLASSROOM

Introduction: Effectively integrating technology in the curriculum allows students to demonstrate their learning using creative, motivating, and nontraditional means. Digital media projects and presentations, as well as other technology-oriented presentations provide students with authentic learning activities and require a different form of assessment. Rubrics can provide teachers with a more authentic assessment tool.

Chapter 7 introduced the use of rubrics as a means of alternative assessment. Rubrics assist students in understanding teacher expectations and provide a clear outline when creating projects. Students also can use rubrics as a self-assessment tool. This encourages students to be more involved and responsible for their learning.

Teachers easily can create rubrics using numerous software applications, such as word processing, spreadsheet, Web editors, or other commercial products. Free online resources also are available that walk teachers through the process of creating a variety of rubrics and performance checklists.

1. Creating and Formatting a Problem-Solving Math Rubric

Problem: To encourage students in your sixth-grade math class to use higher-order thinking skills, you are beginning a unit on problem solving. Students will be given problems and have to write out how they solve the problem and their reasoning for selecting the approach they use. You design a rubric to guide your students through this process. The rubric is shown in Figure 8-46. Open your word processing, spreadsheet, or Web editing software and create the rubric as described in the following steps. (*Hint:* Use any appropriate clip art image and font to personalize the rubric. Use Help to understand the steps better.)

Instructions: Perform the following tasks.

1. Insert clip art images.
2. Format the first heading line, Mrs. Georgiev's, in 20-point Times or Times New Roman bold font. Personalize the rubric by inserting your name instead of Mrs. Georgiev's.
3. Format the second heading line, 6th Grade Math Class, in 20-point Times or Times New Roman bold font.
4. Format the third heading line, Math Problem-Solving Rubric, in 18-point Times or Times New Roman font.
5. Insert a table with six rows and five columns, then enter the table text as shown in Figure 8-46.
6. Center the row headings and format them in 12-point Times New Roman bold font.
7. Format the remaining table text in 12-point Times New Roman font.
8. Personalize the school name and insert the current date. Format the school name and date in 12-point Times or Times New Roman bold font. Insert your e-mail address instead of Mrs. Georgiev's. Format the e-mail address in 12-point Times or Times New Roman, blue bold font.
9. Save the rubric to the location file of your choice using an appropriate filename. Print the rubric and then follow your instructor's directions for handing in the assignment.

In the Lab

Mrs. Georgiev's
6th Grade Math Class
Math Problem-Solving Rubric

Task	Beginning 1 - 2	Developing 3 - 4	Advancing 5	Score
Student uses math language to explain the problem.	Used a few math terms in the explanation of the solution and the explanation was brief.	Used some math terms in the explanation of the solution and the explanation was adequate.	Used math terms correctly throughout the explanation of the solution and the explanation was thorough and complete.	
Student explanation demonstrates understanding of the problem.	Misinterpreted parts of the problem.	Solved the problem with minor interpretation errors.	Answer demonstrates complete understanding of the problem.	
Student articulates plan for solving the problem.	The plan for solving the problem is partially correct.	The plan for solving the problem is correct but may lead to minor errors.	The plan for solving the problem is accurate and will lead to a correct solution.	
Student correctly solves the problem.	The answer is incorrect or not solved.	Part of the problem is solved correctly.	The answer is correct and the work supports the answer.	
			TOTAL POINTS	

Woodrow Wilson Middle School
April 12, 2009
b_georgiev@tricounty.k12.ia.us

Figure 8-46

In the Lab

Exercises

- Web Info
- Key Terms
- Checkpoint
- Teaching Today
- Education Issues
- Integration Corner
- Software Corner
- Digital Media Corner
- Assistive Technologies Corner
- In the Lab
- Learn It Online

Features

- Timeline
- Guide to WWW Sites
- Search Tools
- Buyer's Guide
- State/Federal Sites
- Professional Sites

2. Creating and Formatting a Multimedia Research Rubric

Problem: You want to introduce your high school students to a systematic approach to research. The students will access, evaluate, and use information from a variety of sources on an assigned topic. Then they will write a research paper and create a digital media presentation to present their findings to the class. At the beginning of the unit, you hand out the rubric shown in Figure 8-47. (*Hint:* Use any appropriate clip art images and fonts to personalize the page. Use Help to understand the steps better.)

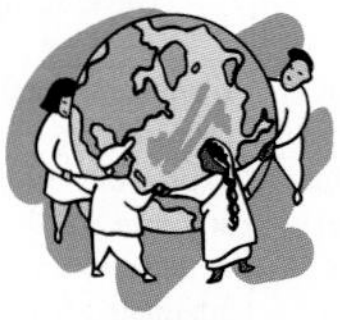

Mr. Hernandez
World History Class
Digital Media Research Project Rubric

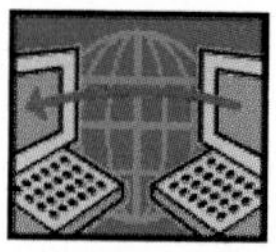

Student Name: ____________ Topic: ____________ Date: ____________

Research Process:	Level 1	Level 2	Level 3	Level 4	Self-Score	Teacher Score
Gathered information from journals, books, CD-ROMs, and the Internet	0 1 2	3 4 5	6 7 8	9 10		
Resources are current and reliable	0 1 2	3 4 5	6 7 8	9 10		
Extracted, synthesized, and applied appropriate information	0 1 2	3 4 5	6 7 8	9 10		

Writing Process:						
Organized information from resources to complete research paper	0 1 2	3 4 5	6 7 8	9 10		
Paper written following steps in writing process	0 1 2	3 4 5	6 7 8	9 10		
References documented using MLA citation style	0 1 2	3 4 5	6 7 8	9 10		

Multimedia Project:						
Presentation includes title slide, a minimum of seven content slides, and a bibliography slide	0 1 2	3 4 5	6 7 8	9 10		
Graphic images are used appropriately and gathered from a variety of resources	0 1 2	3 4 5	6 7 8	9 10		
Presentation is well organized, visually appealing, flows well	0 1 2	3 4 5	6 7 8	9 10		

Presentation:						
Demonstrates good speaking skills	0 1 2	3 4 5	6 7 8	9 10		

TOTAL POINTS:						

Figure 8-47

In the Lab

Instructions: Refer to Figure 8-47. Format the first and second heading lines in 16-point Lucinda Sans Unicode bold font. Insert your name in place of Mr. Hernandez. Format the third heading line in 14-point Lucinda Sans Unicode bold font. Insert clip art or graphic images. Format the Student Name, Topic, and Date headings in 10-point Lucinda Sans Unicode bold font. Format the section headings in 10-point Lucinda Sans Unicode bold underlined font. Format the the text in 10-point Lucinda Sans Unicode font.

After you have typed and formatted the rubric, save the rubric to the location of your choice using an appropriate filename. Print the rubric and then follow your instructor's directions for handing in the assignment.

3. Creating and Formatting a Subject-Specific Rubric

Problem: You want to create a rubric to evaluate student learning of a concept you are presenting. The rubric also will serve as a guide for students as they create their end-of-unit project that demonstrates their learning.

Instructions: Create a rubric similar to the rubrics illustrated in Figures 8-46 or 8-47. Use an appropriate layout; font types, styles, and sizes; and clip art images. Include your name and the subject area you teach. After you have created the rubric, save the rubric to the location of your choice using an appropriate filename. Print the rubric and then follow your instructor's directions for handing in the assignment.

INTEGRATION IN THE CLASSROOM

1. At the beginning of the school year, you want to establish classroom rules and criteria for positive behavior in your second-grade special education classroom. You decide to create a behavior rubric together with your students that will be used and sent home weekly to parents. You ask the students for their ideas about positive classroom behavior, and together, you and your students create a rubric on which you all agree. Create a sample behavior rubric for your students. Include your name, school name, and the current date on the rubric.

2. The students in your Earth Science class have been studying the environment and environmental hazards such as acid rain and oil spills. As a final project for the unit, students will work in groups and conduct a research activity. They will present their findings in either a PowerPoint presentation or a video. To encourage the students to take responsibility for their learning, you first assign each group to the task of developing a rubric that outlines the assessment criteria for their final project. You will assist the students as necessary; however, you believe they will have more ownership in their learning and be more motivated if they establish the majority of the criteria themselves. Create a sample rubric for your students to use as a guide. Include your name, subject area, project topic, and current date on the rubric.

3. To help your students understand rubrics, locate at least three different Web page evaluation rubrics. From your research, create a rubric to use as an example for your students. Include your name and class at the top of the rubric. Include your e-mail address and the current date at the bottom of the rubric. Then, ask your students to research Web page evaluation rubrics on the Internet. The students will work in groups to locate and print a minimum of five different Web page evaluation rubrics. They then will compare and contrast the different rubrics and determine what is important when creating a Web page. As a class, you will brainstorm, create a rubric, and then use this rubric to create Web pages. Include a column for self-evaluation. Share your rubric with the class and compare it with the class-generated one.

Learn It Online

Instructions: Use the Learn It Online exercises to reinforce your understanding of the chapter concepts and increase your computer, information, and integration literacy. To access dozens of interactive student labs, practice tests, learning games, and more, visit scsite.com/tdc5, click Chapter 8 at the top of the Web page, and then click Learn It Online on the left sidebar.

1. At the Movies

Click the At the Movies link to review a video about setting parental controls on your Macintosh computer.

2. At the Movies

Click the At the Movies link to review a video about computer viruses.

3. Using the Windows Vista Firewall

When you use the Internet, data is sent both from your computer to the Internet and from computers on the Internet to your computer. A firewall is a barrier that checks information coming from the Internet and either turns it away or allows it to pass through to your computer, based upon your firewall settings. It also checks data being sent from your computer to the Internet to ensure your computer is not sending unsolicited messages. Click the Windows Vista Firewall link to learn how to control the firewall usage on your computer.

4. Expanding Your Understanding

All states have content specific accountability standards. To learn more about your state's content standards, click the State Standards link.

5. Practice Test

Click the Practice Test link. Answer each question. When completed, enter your name and click the Grade Test button to submit the quiz for grading. Make a note of any missed questions. If required, submit your score to your instructor.

6. Who Wants to Be a Computer Genius?

Click the Computer Genius link to find out if you are a computer genius. Directions about how to play the game will be displayed. When you are ready to play, click the Play button. If required, submit your score to your instructor.

7. Wheel of Terms

Click the Wheel of Terms link to reinforce important terms you learned in this chapter by playing the Shelly Cashman Series version of this popular game. Directions about how to play the game will be displayed. When you are ready to play, click the Play button. If required, submit your score to your instructor.

8. Crossword Puzzle Challenge

Click the Crossword Puzzle link. Complete the puzzle to reinforce skills you learned in this chapter. Directions about how to play the game will be displayed. When you are ready to play, click the Play button. If required, submit the completed puzzle to your instructor.

Special Feature: Guide to Professional, State, and Federal Educational Web Sites

INSTRUCTIONS: To gain World Wide Web access to additional and up-to-date information and links to these sites, start your browser and enter the URL, *scsite.com/tdc5*. When the Teachers Discovering Computers home page appears, click the Professional Sites or the State/Federal Sites link on the lower-right side of the home page.

Guide to Professional Educational Organizations

Many public and private nonprofit professional organizations provide educators with a variety of Web resources, assistance with important issues that educators deal with on a daily basis, and much more. Professional educational organizations are dedicated to promoting and supporting improvement in student learning and educational practices, as well as to providing for professional growth in K-12 education and teacher education. These organizations also provide networking opportunities, information, and leadership in a variety of education areas, including information technology and other technologies integrated into the educational environment. A continually updated Guide to Professional Educational Organizations, which links the most current URLs for a representative cross section of professional organizations, can be found at the Teachers Discovering Computers Web site, *scsite.com/tdc5*.

Academy for Educational Development (AED)
www.aed.org

This independent nonprofit organization is committed to solving critical social problems in the United States through education, social marketing, research, training, policy analysis, and innovative program design and management.

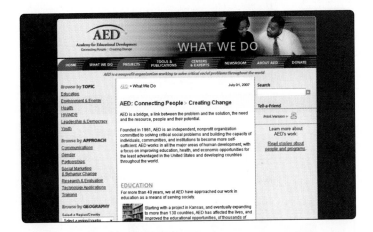

American Association of School Administrators (AASA)
www.aasa.org

The AASA, founded in 1865, is the professional organization for more than 13,000 educational leaders throughout the United States. The organization's focus is on supporting and developing effective school system leaders who are dedicated to the highest quality public education for all children.

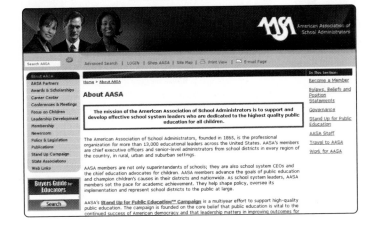

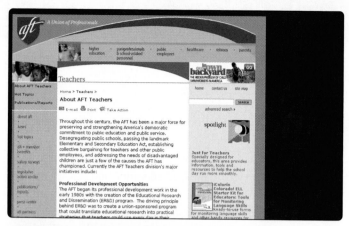

American Federation of Teachers (AFT)
www.aft.org

Founded in 1916, the American Federation of Teachers is a national organization committed to teachers' professional interests. The American Federation of Teachers was founded in 1916 to represent the economic, social, and professional interests of classroom teachers. The AFT has more than 3,000 local affiliates nationwide, 43 state affiliates, and more than 1.3 million members.

American School Counselor Association (ASCA)
www.schoolcounselor.org

ASCA is a professional organization for licensed school counselors. This organization provides information and resources that support school counselors' efforts to help students focus on academic, personal/social, and career development.

Association for Career and Technical Education (ACTE)
www.acteonline.org

The Association for Career and Technical Education is the largest national education association in the United States. It is dedicated to the advancement of career education for both youth and adults. ACTE offers a wide variety of valuable resources for teachers, counselors, and administrators.

Association for Educational Communications and Technology
www.aect.org

The mission of the Association for Educational Communications and Technology, founded in 1923, is to provide leadership in educational communications and technology by linking professionals, who hold a common interest in the use of educational technology and its application, to the learning process.

Association for Supervision and Curriculum Development (ASCD)

www.ascd.org

The ASCD, founded in 1943, is an international, nonprofit, nonpartisan association of professional educators of all grade levels and subject areas; it provides a forum for education issues and shares research, news, and information.

Association for the Advancement of Computing in Education (AACE)

www.aace.org

AACE, founded in 1981, is an international, educational, and professional not-for-profit organization dedicated to the advancement of the knowledge, the theory, and the improvement of the quality of learning and teaching at all levels with information technology.

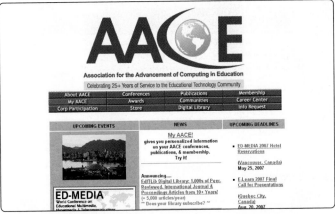

Computer-Using Educators (CUE)

www.cue.org

Computer-Using Educators, Inc. was founded in 1978 with the goal to promote and develop instructional uses of technology in all disciplines and at all educational levels from preschool through college. CUE is the largest organization of this type in the western U.S. and one of the largest in the United States.

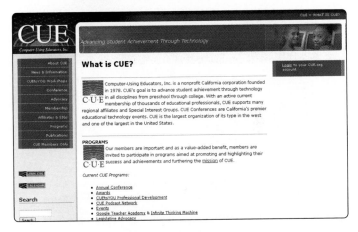

Consortium for School Networking (CoSN)

www.cosn.org

The Consortium for School Networking (CoSN) promotes the use of telecommunications to improve K-12 learning. Members represent state and local education agencies, nonprofits, companies, and individuals. CoSN is dedicated to promoting leadership development, advocacy, coalition building, and emerging technologies.

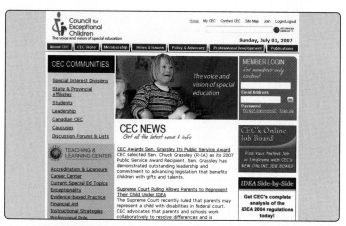

Council for Exceptional Children (CEC)
www.cec.sped.org

The Council for Exceptional Children (CEC) is the largest international professional organization dedicated to improving educational outcomes for individuals with exceptionalities, students with disabilities, and/or gifted students.

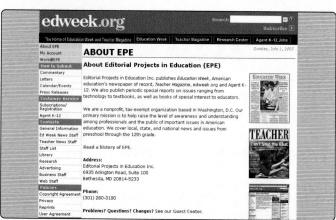

Education Week on the Web
www.edweek.org

Education Week is a non-profit organization based in Washington DC. Its primary mission is to raise awareness and understanding among professionals and the public about important issues in education.

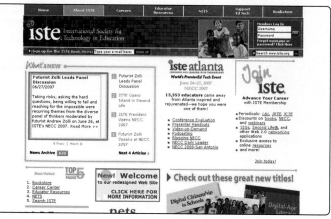

International Society for Technology in Education (ISTE)
www.iste.org

ISTE consists of international leaders in educational technology. The organization promotes appropriate uses of information technology to support and improve learning, teaching, and administration in K-12 and teacher education.

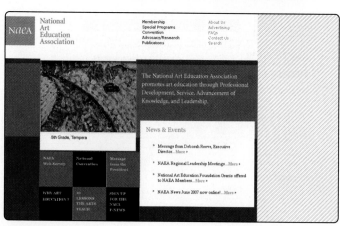

National Art Education Association (NAEA)
www.naea-reston.org

Founded in 1947, NAEA is a non-profit educational organization for early elementary educators to administrators that promotes art education through professional development, service, advancement of knowledge, and leadership.

National Association for Multicultural Education (NAME)

www.nameorg.org

NAME is an active, growing organization that is working to bring together individuals and groups with an interest in multicultural education at all levels of education, different academic disciplines, and from diverse educational institutions and occupations. Membership includes educators from preschool through higher education and representatives from businesses and communities throughout the United States.

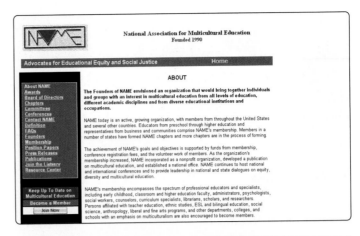

National Association for Music Education (MENC)

www.menc.org

MENC's mission is to advance music education as a profession and to ensure that every child in America has access to a balanced, sequential, high-quality education that includes music as a core subject of study.

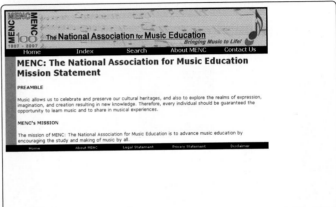

National Association for Sport and Physical Education (NASPE)

www.aahperd.org/naspe

The National Association for Sport and Physical Education is a non-profit membership association. Its mission is to enhance knowledge, improve professional practice, and increase support for high-quality physical education, sport, and physical activity programs through research, development of standards, and dissemination of information.

National Association for the Education of Young Children (NAEYC)

www.naeyc.org

Founded in 1926, NAEYC is the world's largest organization working on behalf of young children. It is dedicated to improving the well-being of young children, with focus on the quality of educational and developmental services for all children from birth to age 8.

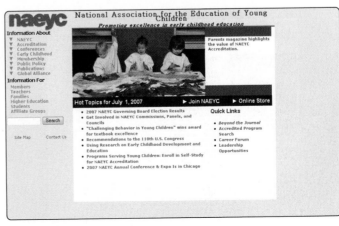

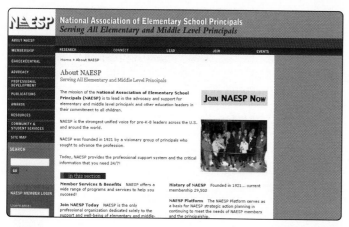

National Association of Elementary School Principals (NAESP)

www.naesp.org

NAESP was founded in 1921 by a visionary group of principals who sought to advance the profession. The mission of NAESP is to lead in the advocacy and support of elementary school principals, middle school principals, and other education leaders in their commitment to all children.

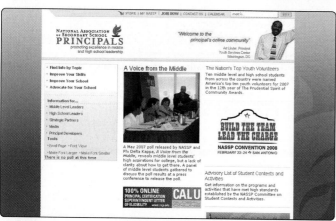

National Association of Secondary School Principals (NASSP)

www.principals.org

This professional organization, founded in 1916, includes tens of thousands of middle level and high school principals, assistant principals, and aspiring principals from the United States and other countries around the world. Its mission is to promote excellence in school leadership by offering a wide variety of programs and services.

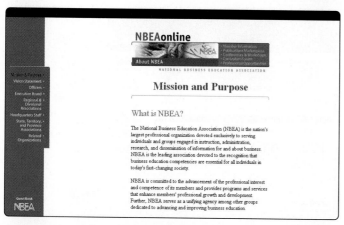

National Business Education Association (NBEA)

www.nbea.org

The National Business Education Association (NBEA) is the nation's largest professional organization devoted exclusively to serving individuals and groups engaged in instruction, administration, research, and dissemination of information for and about business.

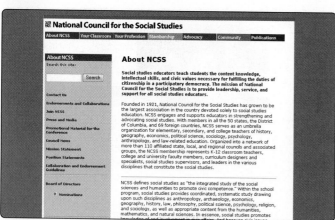

National Council for the Social Studies (NCSS)

www.ncss.org

Founded in 1921, NCSS's mission is to provide leadership, service, and support for all social studies educators. With members in all the 50 states, the District of Columbia, and 69 foreign countries, NCSS serves as an umbrella organization for elementary, secondary, and college teachers of history, geography, economics, political science, sociology, psychology, anthropology, and law-related education.

National Council of Teachers of English (NCTE)
www.ncte.org

NCTE's mission is to improve the teaching and learning of English and the language arts at all levels of education. Since 1911, NCTE has provided opportunities for teachers to continue growing professionally. In addition, they founded a forum to deal with issues that affect the teaching of English.

National Council of Teachers of Mathematics (NCTM)
www.nctm.org

For more than 75 years, NCTM has been a recognized leader in efforts to ensure excellent mathematics education for all students and an opportunity for every mathematics teacher to grow professionally. With about 100,000 members, NCTM is the largest association of mathematics educators in the world, providing professional development opportunities by holding annual regional leadership conferences, as well as publishing journals, books, videos, and software.

National Education Association (NEA)
www.nea.org

Founded in 1857, NEA is the nation's largest organization committed to advancing the cause of public education with more than 3.2 million members who work at every level of education, from preschool to university graduate programs. NEA has affiliates in every state and in more than 14,000 local communities across the United States dedicated to helping students.

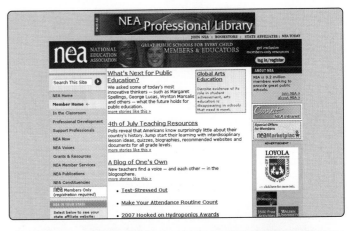

National High School Association (NHSA)
www.nhsa.net

The National High School Association is a nonprofit membership association dedicated to improving the professional knowledge of high school educators so that all high school students may experience academic success. Members include administrators, teachers, parents, policymakers, and others interested in student achievement.

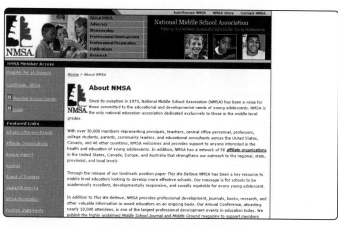

National Middle School Association (NMSA)
www.nmsa.org

The National Middle School Association is dedicated to improving the educational experiences of adolescents by providing vision, knowledge, and resources to all who serve them to develop healthy, productive, and ethical citizens. NMSA has over 30,000 members from across the United States, Canada, and 46 other countries.

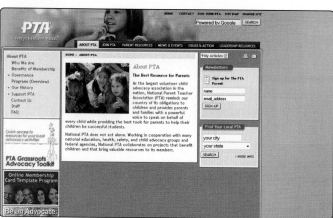

National PTA
www.pta.org

The National PTA is the largest volunteer child advocacy organization in the United States. It is an association of parents, educators, students, and other citizens who are active leaders in their schools and communities in facilitating parent education and involvement in schools.

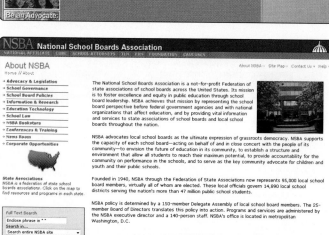

National School Boards Association (NSBA)
www.nsba.org

The mission of the NSBA is to foster excellence and equity in public education through school board leadership. The NSBA believes local school boards are the nation's preeminent expression of grass roots democracy and that this form of governance of the public schools is fundamental to the continued success of public education.

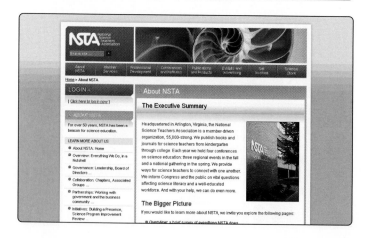

National Science Teachers Association (NSTA)
www.nsta.org

Founded in 1944, NSTA is the largest organization in the world committed to promoting excellence and innovation in science teaching and learning. NSTA's current membership of more than 55,000 includes science teachers, science supervisors, administrators, scientists, business and industry representatives, and others involved in science education.

National Staff Development Council (NSDC)

www.nsdc.org

The National Staff Development Council is a national non-profit association of about 12,000 educators. NSDC is the largest non-profit professional association committed to ensuring success for all students through staff development and school improvement.

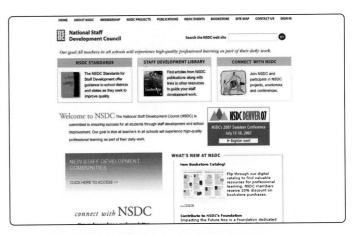

Phi Delta Kappa (PDK)

www.pdkintl.org

Phi Delta Kappa (PDK) is an international association of professional educators and was founded in 1906. Since its founding, this member-based association has served more than 500,000 members in communities across the United States and abroad. PDK's mission is to promote quality education, with particular emphasis on publicly supported education.

Rural School and Community Trust

www.ruraledu.org

The Rural School and Community Trust is a national nonprofit organization addressing the crucial relationship between good schools and thriving communities. This organization's mission is to help rural schools and communities get better together.

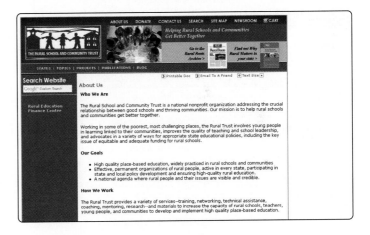

State and Federal Government Educational Web Sites

The federal government, state governments, and state institutions and organizations provide a multitude of Web resources for K-12 teachers and students. New and exciting education Web resources are continuously added to these sites. A continually updated Guide to State and Federal Government Educational Web Sites, which links to the most current URLs, can be found at the Teachers Discovering Computers Web site, *scsite.com/tdc5*.

State Departments of Education

Site Name	Location
Alabama	www.alsde.edu
Alaska	www.eed.state.ak.us
Arizona	ade.state.az.us
Arkansas	arkansased.org
California	www.cde.ca.gov
Colorado	www.cde.state.co.us
Connecticut	www.sde.ct.gov
Delaware	www.doe.state.de.us
District of Columbia	www.k12.dc.us
Florida	www.fldoe.org
Georgia	www.doe.k12.ga.us
Hawaii	doe.k12.hi.us
Idaho	www.sde.state.id.us
Illinois	www.isbe.state.il.us
Indiana	www.doe.state.in.us
Iowa	www.state.ia.us/educate
Kansas	www.ksbe.state.ks.us
Kentucky	www.education.ky.gov
Louisiana	www.doe.state.la.us
Maine	www.maine.gov/education
Maryland	www.marylandpublicschools.org/MSDE
Massachusetts	www.doe.mass.edu
Michigan	www.michigan.gov/mde
Minnesota	www.education.state.mn.us/mde/index.html
Mississippi	www.mde.k12.ms.us

Site Name	Location
Missouri	www.dese.mo.gov
Montana	www.opi.state.mt.us
Nebraska	www.nde.state.ne.us
Nevada	www.doe.nv.gov
New Hampshire	www.ed.state.nh.us
New Jersey	www.state.nj.us/education
New Mexico	sde.state.nm.us
New York	www.nysed.gov
North Carolina	www.dpi.state.nc.us
North Dakota	www.dpi.state.nd.us
Ohio	www.ode.state.oh.us
Oklahoma	sde.state.ok.us
Oregon	www.ode.state.or.us
Pennsylvania	www.pde.state.pa.us
Rhode Island	www.ridoe.net
South Carolina	www.ed.sc.gov
South Dakota	www.doe.sd.gov
Tennessee	www.state.tn.us/education
Texas	www.tea.state.tx.us
Utah	www.usoe.k12.ut.us
Vermont	www.education.vermont.gov
Virginia	www.pen.k12.va.us
Washington	www.k12.wa.us
West Virginia	wvde.state.wv.us
Wisconsin	www.dpi.state.wi.us
Wyoming	www.k12.wy.us

Federal Government

Site Name	Location	Comment
Ben's Guide to U.S. Government for Kids	bensguide.gpo.gov	Ben's Guide provides a comprehensive listing of government Web sites for kids.
Bureau of Land Management	www.blm.gov/education	This site, created by the U.S. Department of the Interior, presents learning opportunities associated with the 262 million acres of public lands that the Bureau of Land Management manages for all Americans; included is extensive information for students, teachers, and adult learners to use in the classroom, informal outdoor settings, or virtual classrooms.
Comprehensive Centers	http://www.ed.gov/about/contracts/gen/othersites/compcenters.html	ED was created in 1980 to promote student achievement and preparation for global competitiveness by fostering educational excellence and ensuring equal access. Links for students, parents, teachers, and administrators are included.
Department of Defense (DoD)	www.dodea.edu	This Web site provides general information about educational programs sponsored in whole or in part by the Department of Defense. This gateway to education effort is sponsored by the DoD.
Department of Energy's KidZone	http://www.energy.gov/forstudentsandkids.htm	This site, maintained by the Department of Energy Education, provides educational resources in science, technology, energy, math, and more. The site includes an Energy Glossary with more than 4000 energy definitions, as well as other energy-related terms for middle and secondary students.
EDSITEment	edsitement.neh.gov	This subject-based catalog from the National Endowment for the Humanities provides access to the top humanities sites on the Web. It includes online humanities resources from some of the world's great museums, libraries, cultural institutions, and universities for use directly in your classroom.
Educational Resources Information Center (ERIC)	www.eric.ed.gov	A nationwide information network funded by the U.S. Department of Education that acquires, catalogs, summarizes, and provides access to education information from many sources.
EPA — Kids, Students, and Teachers	www.epa.gov/epahome/students.htm	This U. S. Environmental Protection Agency (EPA) Web site provides fact sheets, interactive games, and more for kids, students, and teachers who want to learn about the environment or share what they know with others. The Web site can help you with all sorts of information about the EPA and the environment.
ERIC Clearinghouse for Science, Mathematics, and Environmental Education	www.ericse.org	This Web site, provided by ERIC, offers a variety of resources for teaching and learning about science, mathematics, and the environment.
Federal Bureau of Investigation	www.fbi.gov/fbikids.htm	This Web site is sponsored by the Department of Justice; it is designed for children and parents to learn more about the FBI.
Federal Communications Commission (FCC)	www.fcc.gov/learnnet	The FCC LearnNet Web site provides information about FCC programs that are working to bring every school in America into the information age.

(continued on next page)

Site Name	Location	Comment
Federal Resources for Educational Excellence (FREE)	www.ed.gov/free	FREE provides more than 1500 Internet-based education resources supported by federal agencies available at one great Web site.
FedWorld	www.fedworld.gov	FedWorld is a comprehensive central access point for searching, locating, ordering, and acquiring government information.
FirstGov for Kids	www.kids.gov	This U.S. government interagency Kids' Portal provides links to federal kids' sites along with some of the best kids' sites from other organizations all grouped by subject.
Food and Drug Administration (FDA)	www.fda.gov	Learn about the latest FDA developments that will help keep you and your students informed about important health issues.
healthfinder®	www.healthfinder.gov	This Web site is an important source for educators to find reliable consumer, health, and human services information.
Institute of Education Sciences	http://ies.ed.gov	The U. S. Department of Education provides educational research resources funded by Congress at this Web site.
Kidz Privacy	www.ftc.gov/bcp/conline/edcams/kidzprivacy/	This site from the Federal Trade Commission covers the very important issue of children's privacy and how it affects kids, their parents, and teachers.
Library of Congress	www.loc.gov	The Library of Congress is an incredible library resource for students and teachers.
National Aeronautics and Space Administration (NASA)	www.nasa.gov	This awesome Web site covers NASA's extensive education program.
National Archives and Records Administration (NARA)	www.archives.gov/education	The NARA site presents the Digital Classroom, which encourages teachers of students at all levels to use archival documents in the classroom.
National Endowment for the Humanities	www.neh.gov	Online projects at this Web site support learning in history, literature, philosophy, and other areas of the humanities.
National Gallery of Art	www.nga.gov	The National Gallery of Art (NGA) is home to the world's finest paintings and sculptures. This site offers a wealth of culture. It includes a link to NGA Kids for exciting animation and interactivity.
National Oceanic and Atmospheric Administration (NOAA)	www.noaa.gov	NOAA provides information about the weather, oceans, satellites, fisheries, climates, and more.
National Park Service (NPS)	www.nps.gov/learn/	LearnNPS is your one stop for finding education materials about America's national parks; includes zones for teachers and students, games, a gallery, and how to become a junior ranger.
National Register of Historic Places: Teaching with Historic Places (TwHP)	www.cr.nps.gov/nr/twhp/	TwHP offers great lesson plans and guidance on using historic places in teaching and learning.

(continued on next page)

Site Name	Location	Comment
National Science Foundation (NSF)	www.nsf.gov	The NSF Web site promotes the progress of science and health; it is a must stop for science teachers.
Peace Corps	www.peacecorps.gov/wws/	The Peace Corps World Wise Schools education program is designed to help students gain a greater understanding of other cultures and countries.
Recreation.gov	www.recreation.gov/	This is a fantastic Web site for anyone searching for information about recreational opportunities on federal lands.
Regional Educational Laboratories	http://ies.ed.gov/ncee/edlabs	This Web site provides information from research and practice to those involved in educational improvement at the local, state, and regional levels.
Regional Technology Consortia Program	http://wdcrobcolp01.ed.gov/Programs/EROD/org_list.cfm?category_cd=RTC	This Web site gives information about the programs that are funded by the U. S. Department of Education to help K-12 schools integrate technology.
Smithsonian Center for Education and Museum Studies	smithsonianeducation.org	This essential source includes lesson plans, resource guides, field trips, and more for all educators.
students.gov	www.students.gov/	This Web site contains great links to federal Web site resources for postsecondary students.
The Educator's Reference Desk	www.eduref.org	The Educator's Reference Desk provides high-quality resources and services to the education community; included are more than 2000 lesson plans, 3000 plus links to online education information, and more than 200 question archive responses.
The Kennedy Center ARTSEDGE	http://artsedge.kennedy-center.org/	The National Arts and Education Network links the arts and education through technology.
United States Department of Agriculture (USDA)	www.usda.gov/wps/portal/usdahome	The USDA provides extensive sources of research and education information about many important subjects for all ages.
United States Geological Survey (USGS)	education.usgs.gov/	The USGS Learning Web site is dedicated to K-12 education, exploration, and lifelong learning.
USA.gov	www.usa.gov	USA.gov is the U.S. Government's office Web site for information and services. You will find a wide variety of online information, services, and resources.
U.S. Census Bureau	www.census.gov	Through this Web site, expose your students to timely, relevant, and quality data about the people and economy of the United States.
U.S. Department of Education	www.ed.gov	All teachers should make this Web site a first stop as they embark on their teaching careers. The site provides information about student readiness, gives lesson ideas and materials, includes training and development sources, offers guidelines for applying for grants, and much more.
U.S. Department of Energy: Office of Science	www.science.doe.gov/	This Web site is dedicated to helping educate America's next generation of scientists.
U.S. Department of Health and Human Services (HHS)	www.os.dhhs.gov	The HHS offers a wealth of information related to public health, privacy issues, grant programs, and more at this Web site.
U.S. Department of the Interior (DOI)	www.doi.gov	The DOI is dedicated to the internal development of the United States and the welfare of its people.

(continued on next page)

Site Name	Location	Comment
U.S. Fish and Wildlife Service	*www.fws.gov*	Learn how to protect the homes and lives of fish and wildlife at this interesting Web site.
USDA Forest Service	*www.fs.fed.us*	This Web site is a great resource for information about public lands in the United States; it includes a special section just for kids.
USDA for Educators	*www.usda.gov*	This United States Department of Agriculture Web site includes a Browse by Subject section that educators and students can use to locate resources related to agriculture.
Welcome to the White House	*www.whitehouse.gov*	Welcome to the White House provides links to many collections, programs, and products of significant educational benefit; offers a wealth of information and news about the president, government, and history; and includes virtual tours and interactivity of value for all ages.

(continued from previous page)

Appendix A

References

This fifth Edition of *Teachers Discovering Computers* was created using information that was gathered, reviewed, and researched from various articles, books, Web sites, and other resources. You can review many of these resources by accessing the Teachers Discovering Computers, Fifth Edition Web site at *scsite.com/tdc5*. The textbook Web site contains links to hundreds of resources, including many research articles and Web sites dedicated to educational theory, education practice, instructional models, and research-based integration solutions. The following are additional references that were used in the preparation of this textbook.

Anderson, R. & Speck, B. (2001). *Using technology in k-8 literacy classrooms.* Columbus, OH: Prentice Hall.

Asgari, M. & Kaufman, D. (2004). Relationships among computer games, fantasy, and learning. *International Conferences on Imagination and Education 2004 2nd International Conference Proceedings on Imagination in Education.* Vancouver, BC. Retrieved June 30, 2007, from http://www.ierg.net/confs/2004/Proceedings/Asgari_Kaufman.pdf

Bandura, A. (1977). *Social learning theory.* New York: General Learning Press.

Bloom, B. S. (1956). *Taxonomy of educational objectives, Handbook I: The cognitive domain.* New York: David McKay Co, Inc.

Bradt, K. M. (1997). Story as a way of knowing. Kansas City, MO: Sheed & Ward.

Branigan, C. (2003). *Schools urged to teach '21st-century' skills.* Retrieved July 25, 2007, from http://www.eschoolnews.com/news/showStoryalert.cfm?ArticleID=4506

Cermak, L. & Craik, F. (1979). *Levels of processing in human memory.* Hillsdale, NJ: Erlbaum.

Clark, J. M. & Paivio, A. (1991). Dual coding theory and education. *Educational Psychology Review*, 3(3), 149–170.

Craik, F. & Lockhart, R. (1972). Levels of processing: A framework for memory research. *Journal of Verbal Learning & Verbal Behavior*, 11, 671–684.

D'Agostino, P. R., O'Neill, B. J., & Paivio, A. (1977). Memory for pictures and words as a function of level of processing: Depth or dual coding? *Memory & Cognition*, 5, 252–256.

Dean, K. (2002). *PDAs good for education*. Retrieved August 2, 2007, from http://www.wired.com/news/school/0,1383,56297,00.html

Dexter, S. & Anderson, R. (1999). Teachers' views of computers as catalysts for changes in their teaching practice. *Journal of Research on Computing in Education*, 31(3), 221–239.

Doman, J. R. (1984). Learning problems and attention deficits. J*ournal of the National Academy for Child Development*, 4(6).

eSchool News Editors Report. (2005). *Multimedia creation tools in the classroom*. Retrieved July 6, 2007 from http://www.eschoolnews.com/resources/reports/multimediacreation/index.cfm

eSchool News Online. (2007). Special report: converged wireless: new technologies allow convergence of voice, video, and data across wireless networks, Retrieved June 5, 2007, from http://www.eschoolnews.com/news/showStoryts.cfm?ArticleID=7155

eSchool News Online. (2007). *For some educators, gaming is serious business*. Retrieved March 15, 2007, from http://www.eschoolnews.com/news/showStory.cfm?ArticleID=6839&page=1

eSchool News Online. (2007). *21st-century school represent 'the will to change'*. Retrieved July 27, 2007, from http://www.eschoolnews.com/news/showStoryRSS.cfm?ArticleID=7032

eSchool News Online. (2007). *Augmented reality helps kids learn: project uses PDAs to teach math, literacy*. Retrieved May 15, 2007, from http://www.eschoolnews.com/news/showStory.cfm?ArticleID=6885

eSchool News Online. (2005). *Textbooks give way to digital curriculum*. Retrieved July 12, 2007, from http://www.eschoolnews.com/news/showStoryts.cfm?ArticleID=5781&page=1

eSchool News Staff Report. (2003). *Quick! Tell me how to buy classroom & curriculum planning software*. Bethesda, MD: eSchool News.

Flores, A. (2002). *Learning and teaching mathematics with technology*. Retrieved May 25, 2007 from http://www.citejournal.org/vol2/iss1/mathematics/article1.cfm

Forcier, R. & Descy, D. (2002). *The computer as an educational tool: productivity and problem solving* (4th ed.). Columbus, OH: Prentice Hall.

Friedman, T.L. (2006). *The world is flat: a brief history of the twenty-first century*. New York, NY: Farrar, Straus and Girous.

Garris, R., Ahlers, R., & Driskell, J. E. (2002). *Games, motivation, and learning: A research and practice model. Simulation & Gaming*, 33(4), 441–467.

Gee, J. P. (2005). What would a state of the art instructional video game look like? Innovate: *Journal of Online Education (1)*6, Retrieved August 2, 2007, http://www.innovateonline.info/index.php?view=article&id=80

Gee, J. P. (2003). *What video games have to teach us about learning and literacy*. New York: Palgrave MacMillan.

Grable, M. & Grable, C. (2007). *Integrating the Internet for meaningful learning* (5th ed.). Boston: Houghton Mifflin Company.

Gredler, M. (2005). *Learning and instruction: theory into practice* (5th ed.). Columbus, OH, Prentice Hall.

Gunter, G. (2001). Making a difference — using emerging technologies and teaching strategies to restructure an undergraduate technology course for preservice teachers. *Education Media International*, 38(1), 13–20.

Gunter, G. A. & Kenny, R. (2004). Video in the classroom: learning objects or objects of learning? *Association for Educational Communications and Technology International Conference (AECT) Annual*, Chicago, Illinois.

Gunter, G. A., Kenny, R. F., & Vick, E. H. (2006). A case for a formal design paradigm for serious games. *The Journal of the International Digital Media and Arts Association*, 3(1), 93–105.

Gunter, G. & Murphy, D. (1997). Technology integration: The importance of administrative support. *Education Media International*, 34(3), 136–139.

Intel Teach to the Future. (2003). *Intel innovation in education: Empowering 21st century teaching and learning.* Retrieved June 28, 2007, from http://www.intel.com/education/teach/

International Society for Technology in Education. (2007). *National educational technology standards (NETS) Refresh project.* Retrieved June 26, 2007, from http://cnets.iste.org

Kenny, R. F. (2004). *Teaching television in a digital world: Integrating media literacy* (2nd ed). Westport, CT: Libraries Unlimited.

Kenny, R. F. & Gunter, G. A. (2005). Literacy through the arts. *Association for Educational Communications and Technology Conference (AECT) Annual*, Orlando, Florida.

Kenny, R. F. & Gunter, G. A. (2004). Digital booktalk: pairing books with potential readers. *Association for Educational Communications and Technology International Conference (AECT) Annual*, Chicago, Illinois.

Lauritzen, C. & Jaeger, M. (1997). *Integrating learning through story: The narrative curriculum.* Albany, NY: Delmar.

Lever-Duffy, J., McDonald, J., & Mizell, A. (2004). *Teaching and learning with technology* (2nd ed.). Boston: Allyn & Bacon.

Mathematica Policy Research, Inc. (2001). *Analysis of the 1999–2000 annual performance reports for preparing tomorrow's teachers to use technology final report.* Retrieved July 15, 2007, from http://www.ed.gov/offices/OUS/PES/higher.html#pt3

Meyer, K. (2003). The Web's impact on student learning. *T.H.E. Journal*, 30(10), 14–24.

Microsoft. (2002). *Microsoft computer dictionary* (5th ed.). Redmond, WA: Microsoft Press.

Morrison, G. & Lowther, D. (2005). *Integrating computer technology into the classroom* (3rd ed.). Columbus, OH: Prentice Hall.

National Center for Educational Statistics. (1999). Teachers' tools for the 21st century: A report on teachers' use of technology. *Publication # NCES 2000102.* Retrieved June 23, 2007, from http://nces.ed.gov/surveys/frss/publications/2000102/

National Council for Accreditation of Teacher Education. (2005). *21st Century Learners: The Need for Tech-Savvy Teachers.* Retrieved July 7, 2007, from http://www.pt3.org/technologyineducation/21stcenturylearners/

New Measure. (2006). *Helping you design rubrics.* Retrieved May 17, 2007, from http://www.rubrics.com

Newby, T., Stepich, D., Lehman, J., & Russell, J. (2006). *Instructional technology for teaching And learning: Designing instruction, integrating computers, and using media* (3rd ed.). Columbus, OH: Prentice Hall.

O'Neil, H. F., Waines, R., & Baker, E. L. (2005, December). Classification of learning outcomes: Evidence from the computer games literature. *The Curriculum Journal*, 16(4), 455–474.

Ornstein, A. & Hunkins, F. (2007). *Curriculum foundations, principles, and theory* (4th ed.). Seattle, WA: Allyn & Bacon.

Paivio, A. (1986). *Mental Representations.* New York: Oxford University Press.

Paquin, M. (2002). Effects of a museum interactive CD-ROM on knowledge and attitude of secondary school students in Ontario. *International Journal of Instructional Media*, 29, 101–111.

Partnership for 21st Century Skills. Framework for 21st centruy skills. Retrieved July 28, 2007, from http://www.21stcenturyskills.org

Policy Information Center. (2000, October). *How teaching matters.* Princeton, NJ: Education Testing Service.

Prensky, M. (2001). *Digital games-based learning.* New York: McGraw-Hill.

Preparing Tomorrow's Teachers to Use Technology. (2006). Retrieved July 30, 2007, from http://www.pt3.org

President's Committee of Advisors on Science and Technology. (1997). *Report to the president on the use of technology to strengthen k-12 education in the United States.* Retrieved June 19, 2007, from http://www.agiweb.org/hearings/pcastedu.html

Restak, R. M. (2003). *The new brain: How the modern age is rewiring your mind.* New York: Rodale St. Martins Press.

Robyler, M. (2006). *Integrating educational technology into teaching* (4th ed.). Columbus, OH: Prentice Hall.

Schield, Milo. (2005). *Information Literacy, Statistical Literacy and Data Literacy.* Retrieved July 12, 2007 from http://www.augsburg.edu/statlit/pdf/2005SchieldIASSIST.pdf

Schunk, D. (2008). *Learning theories: An educational perspective* (5th ed.). Columbus, OH: Prentice Hall.

Shelly, G., Cashman, T., Gunter, G., & Gunter, R. (2006). *Teachers discovering computers: Integrating technology and digital media in the classroom* (4th ed.). Boston: Course Technology.

Shelly, G., Cashman, T., Gunter, R., & Gunter, G. (2005). *Teachers discovering and integrating Microsoft Office: Essential concepts and techniques* (2nd ed). Boston: Course Technology.

Shelly, G., Cashman, T., & Vermaat, M. (2008). *Microsoft Office 2007: Advanced Concepts and Techniques.* Boston: Course Technology.

Shelly, G., Cashman, T., & Vermaat, M. (2008). *Discovering computers 2008: A gateway to information.* Boston: Course Technology.

Smaldino, S. E., Lowther, D. L., & Russell, J. D. (2008). *Instructional media and technologies for learning* (9th ed.). Columbus, OH: Prentice Hall.

Squire, K. D. (2003) Video games in education. *International Journal of Intelligent Simulations and Gaming.* Retrieved June 29, 2007 from http://simschoolresources.edreform.net.

Tapscott, D. (1998). *Growing up digital - The rise of the net generation.* New York: McGraw Hill.

Tapscott, D. (1995). *The digital economy: Promise and peril in the age of networked intelligence.* New York: McGraw-Hill.

Taylor, R. & Gunter, G. A. (2006). *The k-12 literacy leadership fieldbook.* California: Corwin Press.

Thompson, A., Simonson, M. R., & Hargrave, C. (1996). *Educational technology: A review of the research* (2nd ed.). Ames, IO: Association for Educational Communications and Technology.

United States Department of Education. (2007). *No child left behind.* Retrieved August 3, 2007, from http://www.ed.gov/nclb/landing.jhtml

Universal Service Administrative Company. (2007). *E-rate.* Retrieved July 27, 2007, from http://www.sl.universalservice.org

Wikipedia. (2007). *Wikipedia: The free encyclopedia.* Retrieved June 30, 2007, http://en.wikipedia.org/wiki/Main_Page

Web-Based Education Commission. (2000). *The power of the Internet for learning. The president and the congress of the United States.* Retrieved July 4, 2007, from http://www.ed.gov/offices/AC/WBEC/FinalReport/index.html

Welliver, P. (1990). *Instructional transformation: a module for change.* A report of the Pennsylvania regional computer resource center. University Park, PA: Pennsylvania State University.

Willis, J., Thompson, A., & Sadera, W. (1999). Research on technology and teacher education: Current status and future directions. *Educational Technology Research and Development,* 47(4), 29–45.

Index

for recording, editing, and sharing high-quality videos on the Web, CDs, DVDs, and portable media players, including Apple's iPod and Microsoft's Zune. 161, 198–199, 306, 452, 466–467

Captivate (Adobe): a multimedia authoring software application that allows users to create engaging and interactive Flash videos. 161, 442

card readers/writers, purchasing, 256

careers, 14–15, 43, 124

Carmen Sandiego series, 386–387

carpal tunnel syndrome (CTS): inflammation of the nerve that connects the forearm to the palm of the wrist, which can be caused by repeated or forceful bending of the wrist, such as occurs during computer use. 497

carrying cases, 262

CAST (Center for Applied Special Technology), 361

catalogs, 394

CATV (cable television) networks, 64, 75, 76

CBI (computer-based instruction), 289

CBL (computer-based learning), 289

CBT (computer-based training): tool in which individuals learn by using and completing exercises using instructional software on computers. 277

CD-R (compact disc-recordable): compact disc that information can be recorded onto; part of the disc can be written on at one time and another part at a later time. Each part can be written on only one time and the disc's content cannot be erased. 235

CD-ROM (compact disc read-only memory): type of optical disc that uses the same laser technology as audio CDs for recording and can contain text, graphics, animation, video, and sound. A CD'ROM can hold from 650 MB to 1 GB of data. 234

CD-RW (compact disc-rewritable): erasable disc that can be written on multiple times. 235

CDs (compact discs), 232–237, 246, 256, 261, 322. *See also specific types*

CEC (Council for Exceptional Children), 520

cell: the intersection of a column and a row in a spreadsheet. 148–149

cell phone(s)
banning, 101
etiquette, 101

centers: area in a classroom that creates a learning environment, usually focused on specific curriculum content that allows students to complete projects or activities without leaving the classroom; often more than one center for students to rotate through. 351–352

challenge/confidence, 23–24

chart: graphical illustration of the relationship of numeric data. 149, 182

chat: real-time typed conversation that takes place on a computer. 92–93

chat client: program on computer that allows connection to a chat server. 93

chat room: communications medium, or channel, that permits users to chat with each other. 92–93

cheating, 36

checklist: predetermined list of performance criteria used in project-based and portfolio assessment. 405–407

Children's Encyclopedia, 279

chip: small piece of semiconducting material usually no bigger than one-half-inch square and is made up of many layers of circuits and microscopic components that carry electronic signals. 204, 487, 492

Cingular Wireless, 74

CIPA (Children's Internet Protection Act): Act passed by Congress in 2000 to protect children from obscene, pornographic, and other information on the Internet considered harmful to minors. 487

Citizendium, 193

Civil War, 303

class blogs, 458. *See also* blogs

classic conditioning, 368

ClassWorks, 305

ClearType technology, 265

Click Wheel: an input device that enables users to scroll through and play music, view pictures, watch videos or movies, adjust volume, and customize settings. 220

conferences, technology, 394–395

connector: the end portion of a cable that connects to a port on the system unit. 210–212

constructivism, 376–382

content: refers to information a Web page provides.
aggregators, 82
evaluating, 409
student-assisted/created, 453
teacher-created, 452–453

contests, 435

control unit: component of the CPU that directs and coordinates most of the operations in a computer. 206

converged media: the interaction of virtual reality with live performance. 5, 96

cooperative classroom activity: activity that is student-centered, with the teacher serving as a facilitator and the students as information seekers. 337

cooperative learning: method of instruction where students work collaboratively in groups to achieve learning objectives and goals. 337

COPPA (Children's Online Privacy Protection Act), 100, 487

copy: process of duplicating a portion of a document and electronically storing it in a temporary storage location called the Clipboard. 141

copyright: retention of ownership of a work by the original author or creator of the work and giving the creator exclusive rights to reproduce and distribute the creative work. 479, 486–491, 506

cordless keyboard: input device that is a battery-operated keyboard that transmits data using wireless technology. Also called wireless keyboard. 214

cordless mouse: mouse that is battery powered and transmits data using wireless technology. Also called wireless mouse. 215

CoSN (Consortium for School NEtworking), 519

country codes, 77–78

courseware: interactive CBT software usually available on CD, DVD, or the Web. 277

cover letters, 106–108

COW (computer lab on wheels): portable cart with wireless notebook computers that can be transported from one classroom to another. Also called wireless mobile lab. 341–342

CPUs (central processing unit): electronic device on the motherboard that interprets and carries out the instructions that operate a computer. Also called a processor or microprocessor.
described, 204–206
notebook computers and, 261
purchasing, 257
storage and, 229
system clock and, 207

cracker: individual who tries to access a computer or network illegally. 475

creating: process of developing a document by entering text or numbers, designing graphics, and performing other tasks using an input device such as a keyboard or mouse. 141

creativity: elements of originality, imaginative and innovative approaches, and artistic abilities in student projects. 17–18, 409

creativity application: educational software that often allows students to start with a blank canvas, allowing them to use imagination and ingenuity. 293

credit cards, 260

critical-thinking application: educational software that stimulates students to use critical-thinking skills in a variety of ways. 293

critical-thinking standards, 20–21

cross-discipline lesson: lesson that includes a combination of curriculum-specific areas, such as math or science, that are integrated with language arts. 431

CRT (cathode ray tube): large glass tube that is the core of some monitors. 222

CSS (Cascading Style Sheet): a simple mechanism for adding style (e.g. fonts, colors, spacing) to Web documents and defines style and formatting properties which are applied to HTML and/or XML-based Web pages. 80

CTGV (Cognition and Technology Group at Vanderbilt), 381

CTTE (Center for Technology Teacher Education), 104

CUE (Computer-Using Educations), 519

Curious Cat, 459

desktop: onscreen work area that uses common graphical elements such as icons, buttons, windows, menus, and dialog boxes, to make it easy and intuitive for users to interact with the computer. 139–140

desktop computers: name given to personal computers because they are designed so the system unit, input devices, output devices, and any other devices fit entirely on a desk. 8, 252–260

Dewey, John, 381–382

dial-up access: connection to the Internet using a computer and a modem to dial into an ISP or online service over regular telephone lines. 74–75, 255–256, 265

dialog box: special window displayed by a program to provide information, present available options, or request a response using command buttons, option buttons, text boxes, and check boxes. 139, 142

digital: representation of data using two discrete states: on and off. 202

Digital Booktalk, 360

digital camera: a type of camera that allows a user to take pictures and store the photographed images digitally (electronically) instead of on traditional film and uses a small reusable disk or internal memory to store the digital photographs. 209–210, 219, 246, 256, 312–322

digital citizenship, 21–22

digital divide, 101

digital equity, 74, 101

digital generation: the new generation. 15, 331, 342, 356, 367

digital kids: Kids who are (1) hyper-communicators who use multiple tools to communicate, (2) multitaskers who do several things at once with ease, and (3) goal oriented as they pursue multiple goals at the same time. 15–24

digital media: those technologies that allow users to create new forms of interaction, expression, communication, and entertainment in a digital format.
described, 6, 270–276
importance of, 298–299
revolution, 499–503
selecting, 345

digital media application: involves the use of digital media technology in education, business, and entertainment. 280–285

digital media journal: digital version of a journal distributed on CD, DVD, or via the World Wide Web. 280–281

digital media magazine: digital version of a magazine distributed on CD, DVD, or via the World Wide Web. 280–282

digital media presentation: a presentation that involves producing various digital media elements, defining the elements relationships to each other, and then sequencing them in an appropriate order. 151–154, 308–310, 459

digital media software: software used to create interactive digital media presentations that can include text, graphics, video, audio, and animation. 271–288

digital pen: slightly larger than a stylus, is available in two forms: some are pressure-sensitive, whereas others have a built-in digital camera. 218, 264

digital signal: individual electrical pulses that a computer uses to represent data. 62

digital students: Kids who are (1) hyper-communicators who use multiple tools to communicate, (2) multitaskers who do several things at once with ease, and (3) goal oriented as they pursue multiple goals at the same time. 15–24

digital video cameras, 256, 313, 318–322

DIMM (dual inline memory module): small circuit board that contains multiple RAM chips. 208

discipline-specific learning: learning how to apply teaching principles, knowledge, and ideas to authentic and practical classroom lessons and projects that can benefit students. 2–3

discovery learning: inquiry-based, nonlinear method of learning and teaching that involves branching off and investigating related topics as they are encountered. 79

discussions, blogs as tools for, 459

disk: commonly-used storage medium, which is a round, flat piece of plastic or metal on which data, instructions, and information can be encoded. 229

display device: output device that displays text, graphics, and video information. 222–224

distance learning: delivery of education from one location to another; the learning takes place at this other location. Also called distance education, Web-based education, and distributed learning. 285–286, 502

DLP (digital light processing) projectors, 226

document: piece of work created with an application program and saved on a storage medium with a unique file name. 140

documentation: any printed or online information that provides assistance in installing, using, maintaining, and updating the software. 399

domain name: text version of a computer address. 77–79

double quotes ("), 131

double-clicking: mouse operation that involves pressing and releasing a mouse button twice without moving the mouse. 215

download: process of copying files to your computer. 90, 157

dragging: mouse operation that involves moving data from one location to another. 215

Dragon Naturally Speaking, 179

Dreamweaver (Adobe): Web page authoring software. 80, 162, 445

drill-and-practice software: software that first supplies factual information and then through repetitive exercises allows students to continue to work on the specific materials to remember or memorize the information. Also called skills-reinforcement software. 290

DSL (digital subscriber line): high-speed alternative to a modem that uses broadband technology to transmit data on existing standard telephone lines. 50, 62, 64, 76, 255

DTP (desktop publishing) software: software used to design, produce, and deliver sophisticated documents that contain text, graphics, and brilliant colors. 159

dual coding theory, 371–372

dual-core processor: a single chip that contains two separate processors. 206

DVD drive: drive used to read a DVD-ROM. 211

DVD-ROM (digital video disc read-only memory): an extremely high-capacity CD capable of storing from 4.7 GB to 17 GB. 236–237

DVDs (digital video discs), 211, 232–237, 313, 322

dynamic Web page: visitors customize some or all of the viewed content, such as stock quotes, weather for a region, or ticket availability for flights; visitors see content unique to their settings. 78

earbuds: an audio output device that rests inside the ear canal. 228

earphones: an audio output device that rests inside the ear canal. 227–228

early learning application: educational software designed to provide students in grades K-3 with a developmental head start in reading, language arts, math, science, and other curricular areas. 294

ease of use: refers to anything that makes software easy to use. Also called user-friendliness. 399

e-book: small, book-sized computer that allows users to read, save, highlight, bookmark, and add notes to online text. 278–279

eCollege, 286

editing: process of making changes to a document's existing content. 141

EDMARK, 103

education: all the experiences, knowledge, and skills a learner gains from both school and society.
discussion lists, 395
magazines, 132, 520
organizations, guide to, 517–530
Web sites, 82

EDTECH: large, well-known discussion list that allows educators, administrators, technology coordinators, and media specialists to exchange information, comments, and ideas on educational issues. 395

Education Rate (E-Rate): Federal Communications Commission government initiative designed to provide discounts to schools and libraries on all communications services including network installation and Internet access. 25

Education Week on the Web, 520

Education World, 132

entertainment software: software that includes interactive games, videos, and other programs designed to support a hobby or just provide amusement and enjoyment. 168, 282–283

entertainment Web sites, 82, 111

ePALS: project designed to enable students to develop an understanding of different cultures through student e-mail exchanges. 95

ergonomics: an applied science devoted to incorporating comfort, efficiency, and safety into the design of items in the workplace. 268, 498

ESL (English as a Second Language) students, 294, 307, 457, 459

ESL and foreign language applications: educational software that provides K-12 students with assistance in learning English and other languages. 294

essential questioning technique: looking for the most important or fundamental part of a topic. 351

ethics, computer: moral guidelines that govern the use of computers, networks, and information systems. 484–496, 507

etiquette, Internet (netiquette): the code of acceptable behaviors users should follow while on the Internet. 94, 100

EULA (end-user license agreement): software license included with software packages purchased by individual users, which contain conditions about installation and distribution of the software. Also called single-user license agreement. 478–479

evaluate: process of determining an item's value or judging its worth. Evaluating educational technology involves determining if the technology is appropriate and enhances the teaching and learning process. 346

evaluation: method of appraising or determining the significance or worth of an item, action, or outcome. 404–411

evaluation process: process that includes assessing learner outcomes, reviewing, critiquing the learners' work or works based on specific standards, and evaluating reviews of the media and materials used. 346, 392–403

Excel (Microsoft), 171

exceptional education curriculum: curriculum that contains instruction in all areas with adaptations made for students with unique characteristics or special needs, including students who are gifted, learning disabled, physically disabled, emotionally disabled, or mentally disabled. 429–430

executing: control unit process of carrying out commands. 206

expansion card: circuit board inserted into a motherboard that adds new devices or capabilities to a computer. Also called adapter card or expansion board. 210

expansion slot: opening, or socket, where a circuit board can be inserted into the motherboard. 205, 210

exploratory learning, 451–454

ExpressCard module: adds memory, communications, multimedia, and security capabilities to computers and can be used as a removable flash memory device. 64, 210

ExpressCard slot: a special type of expansion slot that holds a ExpressCard module or PC Card. Also called a PC Card slot. 210

external hard disk: separate, portable hard disk that connects to a USB or FireWire port by a cable. 232, 256

eyestrain, 221

e-zine: digital publication available on the Web. Also called electronic magazine. 280–283

facebook: an online application that provides a way for college students to meet and chat. 81, 82

facilitator of learning: person who motivates students to want to learn, guides the student learning process, and promotes a learning atmosphere and an appreciation for the subject. 4, 331, 332, 337, 355, 412, 461

facsimile (fax) machine: output device that transmits and receives documents over telephone lines. 227

Fahlberg, Tim, 467

online course: a course that is taught mostly or completely on the Web, rather than in a traditional classroom. Often called Web-based course. 285–286

online courses, 285–286

online service providers (OSPs): organization that provides access to the Internet, as well as members-only features that offer a variety of special content and services. 74, 255, 258

online social network: a Web site that encourages members in its online community to share their interests, ideas, stories, photos, music, and videos with other registered users. Also called a social networking Web site. 82, 114

open learning system: integrated learning system that includes software titles from leading publishers. Also called advanced learning system. 292

open source software: software that has code available free to the public. 39, 174, 360

operating system: one of the more important programs on a computer that contains instructions that coordinate all of the activities of the hardware devices. *See also specific operating systems*
overview, 136–138
requirements, 254
role of, 136
using different, 136–137

optical disc: a type of storage medium that consists of a flat, round, portable disc made of metal, plastic, and lacquer that is written and read by a laser. 232–237

optical mouse: mouse that has no moving mechanical parts, instead it emits and senses light to detect the mouse's movement. 215

optical scanners, 217

OR operator, 131, 207

Oregon Trail, 245, 414

OSHA (Occupational Safety and Health Administration), 497

OSPs (online service providers): organization that provides access to the Internet, as well as members-only features that offer a variety of special content and services. 74, 255, 258

output: data that has been processed into a useful form called information. Four common types of output are text, graphics, audio, and video. 221

output device: hardware used to convey the information generated by a computer to a user; includes display devices, printers, data projectors, facsimile machines, multifunction devices, speakers, headphones, and earphones. 222–228

Overlay Maker (Intellitools), 361

overvoltage: situation that occurs when incoming electrical power increases significantly above the normal 120 volts. Also called power surge. 482

Owl & Mouse Educational Software, 359

packet: small piece of data sent over the Internet. 73–74

packet switching: technique of breaking a message into individual packets, sending the packets along the best route available, and reassembling the data. 74

page layout: process of arranging text and graphics in a document. 159, 422

PageMaker (Adobe), 361

Paint (Windows), 145

paint software: software used to draw pictures, shapes, and other graphics using various tools on the screen such as a pen, brush, eye dropper, and paint bucket. 145, 160

Paivio, Allan, 371–372, 389

Palm OS, 266, 268

Parallels Desktop for Mac, 39

parent(s)
newsletters, 361–362
podcasts and, 464
usage of computers by, 29

parental controls, 492–494

participatory Web: refers to Web sites that allow users to modify Web site content, provide a means for users to share personal information, and have application software built into the site for visitors to use. 78, 104

Partnership for 21st Century Skills, 14–15

passive learning, 451–454

password: part of a unique user identification that allows users to log on to the network to use e-mail, transfer files, and access other shared resources. 475, 476

paste: process of placing items stored on the Clipboard into a document. 141

Pavlov, Ivan, 368

Photo Credits

Chapter 1 Figures: 1-1, ©,Courtesy of EarthWalk Communications; 1-2a, ©, Michael Newman/Photo Edit; 1-2b, ©, Peter Beck/CORBIS; 1-2c, ©, Bob Daemmrich/The Image Works; 1-2d, ©, Hunter Freeman/Getty Images; 1-2e, ©, Thomas Schweizer/CORBIS; 1-3, © Bill Aron / PhotoEdit; 1-4a, Courtesy of Hewlett-Packard Company; 1-4b, Courtesy of D-Link Systems; 1-4c, Courtesy of Logitech, Inc.; 1-4d1, Courtesy of Seagate Technology 1-4d2, Courtesy of Hewlett-Packard Company; 1-4e, Courtesy of SanDisk Corporation; 1-4f, Courtesy of SanDisk Corporation; 1-4g, Courtesy of Motorola; 1-4h, Courtesy of Sony Electronics Inc.; 1-4i, Courtesy of Hewlett-Packard Company; 1-4j, © David Young-Wolff/Photo Edit; 1-5, Courtesy of IBM Corporation; 1-6, Courtesy of Apple; 1-7a, Courtesy of Hewlett-Packard Company; 1-7b, Courtesy of Apple; 1-8a, Courtesy of Apple; 1-8b, Courtesy of Acer America Corp.; 1-9, Motion Computing Inc.; 1-10, Courtesy of Hewlett-Packard Company; 1-11, Courtesy of Apple; 1-12, © Patti McConville/ Imagestate; 1-14a, © Sylvain Grandadam/Getty Images; 1-14b, ©, Ian Mckinnell/Getty Images; 1-14c, istockphoto.com; 1-14d, © Keith Goldstein/Getty Images; 1-14e, © Purestock/Getty Images; 1-14f, © Stephen Swintek/Getty Images; 1-15, Courtesy of the Partnership for 21st Century Skills, www.21stcenturyskills.org,; 1-16, © Getty Images; 1-21, © Ian Shaw/Alamy; 1-31, © David Young-Wolff/Photo Edit; 1-32, © Comstock Images; 1-33, © eStock Photo / Alamy; 1-34, © Reza Estakhrian/Getty Images; 1-36, © Tom McCarthy/Photo Edit; 1-37, Courtesy of Consolidated High School District 230/Handheld Computers; 1-38 ©, Jack Hollingsworth/Getty Images; 1-39, © Image Source/Imagestate; 1-40, © PM Images/Getty Images; 1-41, © Getty Images; Page 33, © Getty Images; Courtesy of EarthWalk Communications. **Special Feature 1:** Opener 1a, © 2002 Dynamic Graphics Inc.; Opener 1b, Courtesy of Apple; Opener 1c, Courtesy of Palm; Opener 1d, Courtesy of Nokia; Opener 1d, Courtesy of Fujitsu-Siemens Computers; Opener 1e, Courtesy of Fujitsu-Siemens Computers; Figure 1a, Courtesy of Sony Electronics Inc.; Figure 1b, Siemens press photo; Figure 1c, Courtesy of Sony Electronics Inc.; Figure 1d, Courtesy of Olympus; Figure 1e, Courtesy of Hewlett-Packard Company; Figure 1f, Courtesy of Epson America; Figure 4a, © Getty Images; Figure 4b, © Getty Images; Figure 4c, © Stockbyte; Figure 4d, Siemens press photo; Figure 5, © James Leynse/Corbis; Figure 5, © Justin Sullivan/Getty Images; Figure 5, Courtesy of D-Link Systems; Figure 5, Courtesy of 3Com Corporation; Figure 5, Courtesy of Intel Corporation; Figure 10, Courtesy of Fujitsu-Siemens Computers; Figure 11, Courtesy of Hewlett-Packard Company; Figure 11, Courtesy of Hewlett-Packard Company; Figure 11, Courtesy of D-Link Systems; Figure 11, Courtesy of Motorola; Figure 11, Courtesy of Palm, Inc;. Figure 12, Courtesy of Garmin Ltd; Figure 12, © George Simhoni/Masterfile; Figure 12, Courtesy of Wherify Wireless, Inc.; Figure 12, Courtesy of Wherify Wireless, Inc.; Figure 12, © Siemens AG Press Pictures; Figure 12, © Jasper James/Getty Images; Figure 12, Courtesy of Garmin Ltd; Figure 12, © Ron Chapple/Getty Images; Figure 12, © Dante Burn-Forti/Getty Images; Figure 13, Copyright © 2003 University of Central Florida Photos; Figure 17, Courtesy of Fujitsu-Siemens Computers; **Chapter 2 Figures:** 2-1a, Courtesy of IBM Corporation; 2-1b, Courtesy of IBM Corporation; 2-1c, Courtesy of Fujitsu-Siemens Computers; 2-1d, Courtesy of Hewlett-Packard Company; 2-1e, Engin Communications/istockphoto.com; 2-1f1, Courtesy of Nokia; 2-1f2, Courtesy of Nokia; 2-1g, Courtesy of Hewlett-Packard Company; 2-1h1, Courtesy of Toyota; 2-1h2, Courtesy of Garmin; 2-1, © Jason Reed/Getty Images; 2-1, © Digital Stock; 2-4a, Courtesy of Linksys, a Division of Cisco Systems Inc.; 2-4b, Courtesy of Belkin International, Inc.; 2-5, Courtesy of Hewlett-Packard Company; 2-5, Courtesy of Sony Electronics; 2-6a, Courtesy of Hewlett-Packard Company; 2-6b, Courtesy of Apple; 2-9, Courtesy of EarthWalk Communications; 2-10, Amy Etra/Photo Edit; 2-13, Courtesy of the National Science Foundation; 2-14,Courtesy of Linksys; 2-15, © Rob Lewine/CORBIS; 2-15, © Royalty-Free/Corbis; 2-15, © LWA-Dann Tardif/CORBIS; 2-15, © LWA-Dann Tardif/CORBIS; 2-15, © Paul C. Chauncey/CORBIS; 2-15, © Jiri Rezac / Alamy; 2-15, Courtesy of Motorola, Inc.; 2-16, Courtesy of Hewlett-Packard Company; 2-16, © Erik S. Lesser/Bloomberg News/Landov; 2-16, Courtesy of Motorola, Inc.; 2-16, Courtesy of Panasonic; 2-17 Step 2, Courtesy of Motorola, Inc.; 2-17 Step 3, Courtesy of Terayon Communication Systems, Inc.; 2-17 Step 4, © Stephen Chernin/Getty Images; 2-17 Step 5, Courtesy of National Science Foundation; 2-17 Step 6, Courtesy of Fujitsu Siemens Computers; 2-19a, Courtesy of Symbol Technologies, Inc.; 2-19b, Courtesy of Ashland High School Horticulture Department; 2-38, Courtesy of D-Link Systems; 2-38, Courtesy of Vonage; 2-38, Courtesy of Hewlett-Packard Company; 2-38, Courtesy of Siemens AG; **Special Feature 2:** Opener, © Masterfile Royalty-Free Division www.masterfile.com; page 126, © Image Source / SuperStock: **Chapter 3 Figures:** 3-1, © Digital Vision/Getty Images; 3-1, Courtesy of Xerox Corporation; 3-1, Courtesy of Intel Corporation; 3-5, Courtesy of Apple; 3-9, Courtesy of Agilix Labs Inc.; 3-17, © Scott Goodwin Photography; 3-21, Courtesy of Fujitsu-Siemens Computers; 3-25, Courtesy of Hewlett Packard Company; © Getty Images; 3-26, Courtesy of Sendo; 3-30, Courtesy of Microsoft Corporation; 3-31a, Courtesy of Microsoft Corporation; 3-31b, Courtesy of Apple; 3-42, © Spencer C. Grant/PhotoEdit; 3-43a, Courtesy of Intuit Inc.; 3-43b, © Digital Vision/Getty Images; 3-45,